THE

WILLARD J. GRAHAM SERIES

IN ACCOUNTING

BOOKS IN
THE WILLARD J. GRAHAM SERIES IN ACCOUNTING

CONSULTING EDITOR   ROBERT N. ANTHONY   *Harvard University*

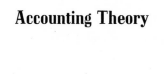

Accounting Theory

Accounting Theory

ELDON S. HENDRIKSEN
Professor of Business Administration
Washington State University

Revised Edition

1970 RICHARD D. IRWIN, INC.
HOMEWOOD, ILLINOIS
IRWIN-DORSEY LIMITED
GEORGETOWN, ONTARIO

To the memory of

PERRY MASON

*friend and professor and a major contribu-
tor to research in accounting theory, who
did much to create and stimulate my interest in accounting and accounting theory
by providing continual counsel and encouragement.*

Preface

The literature in the broad area of financial accounting theory continues to grow at a rapid pace; without a general frame of reference it becomes difficult, if not impossible, for a student of the subject to assimilate and evaluate the many articles and readings now available. While no single theory or set of theories relating to accounting has as yet been fully accepted as a general frame of reference for evaluating and developing accounting practice, several basic theories and concepts are implicit in many of the discussions of accounting theory. Therefore, one of the major objectives of this book is to provide an understanding of these implicit theories and concepts, thereby forming a general frame of reference that enables the student to better understand the vast number of books and articles on the many controversial topics in the area of accounting theory. An attempt has also been made to evaluate critically many of the divergent points of view. In many cases, the several viewpoints are criticized without attempting to suggest a solution or the best alternative. In other cases, the author has expressed his views and presented supporting evidence in order to stimulate thought and discussion; but in all cases, suggested solutions are tentative and subject to change as new evidence becomes available. Therefore, it should be emphasized that, at this level of study, the student should not rely entirely on a single text or book; there is no substitute for a critical analysis of the works and articles of many writers to obtain an understanding and balanced evaluation of the many diverse viewpoints in accounting.

This book is designed to provide a frame of reference for junior, senior, and graduate courses in financial accounting, accounting theory, and seminars in the theory of income, asset valuation, and history of accounting thought. It should also be useful for those who want a general survey of the field of financial accounting theory and for those who wish to study for the theory section of the Uniform CPA Examination. The book has been written on the assumption that the reader has a knowledge of the basic framework of accounting. However, experience has indicated that mature students can handle the subject matter with concurrent additional formal or independent study of this basic framework.

The approach to accounting theory is eclectic in nature, drawing upon several methodological frameworks and supported by empirical evidence wherever available. An attempt is made, wherever possible, to make explicit the logic used, starting with the basic objectives and postulates of financial reporting. Central in most of the discussions are theories relating to income determination and the measurement of cash and other resource flows. However, theories relating to the measurement of resources and commitments are also significant because of the relevance of stocks to the communication of financial information, and because of their relationships to the measurement of income and other flow concepts. And some of the objectives of financial reporting can be met by appropriate classifications in the financial statements and by other means of disclosure. Therefore, an attempt has been made to present a discussion of the several controversial areas of financial reporting.

This revision has as its basic objective the inclusion of the many new ideas in accounting theory proposed since the publication of the first edition. Critical discussions of official and unofficial pronouncements published by accounting societies as well as changes in accounting practice and in governmental requirements are also included. Foremost among the changes in this revision are: (1) a new full chapter on cash and funds flow concepts as well as a greater emphasis on these concepts throughout the book; (2) greater emphasis on measurement concepts in accounting; (3) greater emphasis on the role of the Securities and Exchange Commission in the formulation of accounting practice; (4) critical discussions of recent pronouncements published by the American Institute of Certified Public Accountants, the American Accounting Association, and several other accounting associations in the United States and in other countries; and (5) an attempt to indicate some of the differences in objectives and practices among several countries.

One of the best ways to explore the controversial areas in accounting theory is to start with the basic concepts and a review of their historical development. Therefore, the first four chapters present the general background for the development of accounting theory. These include a chapter on methodology; two chapters on the historical development of theory; and a chapter on the concepts, measurement, and structure of accounting theory. Following these are six chapters presenting the basic framework of accounting theory relating to income determination, cash and funds flows, and the basic problems of asset measurement and classification. A chapter on price changes emphasizes the effect on income determination but also discusses the problems of asset measurement under conditions of changing prices. The third section contains six chapters that discuss the applications of accounting theory to the reporting problems of specific asset and liability groups, particularly those problems relating to the measurement of assets and liabilities and the related problems of income determination. The final three chapters cover the basic problems regarding ownership equities and the disclosure of relevant information to investors, creditors, and other interested readers of financial statements.

At the end of each chapter is a list of suggested readings on specific topics. These articles and sections of books have been selected with care on the basis of their general quality and their ability to present the several sides of controversial questions. Where a difficult decision had to be made, the more recent article was selected on the ground that the author made use of the more recent discussions on the topic. No doubt some very excellent articles have been omitted, either because of the wealth of material on a specific topic or because of the failure on my part to find and recognize the best. Where this has occurred, I apologize for the omission. It is my hope that these lists will be useful to students and instructors in providing a starting point in researching and studying each topic. There is no substitute for wide reading in the area of accounting theory to obtain the many different points of view found in the literature.

At the end of the book is a group of questions classified by chapter topics selected from the theory section of the Uniform CPA Examinations of recent years. I wish to express my appreciation to the officers of the American Institute of Certified Public Accountants for their kind permission to reprint these questions.

The author also wishes to express appreciation to the many graduate students at Washington State University who have made helpful comments on the first edition of this book. For many of the ideas that have been carried forward from the first edition, I am deeply indebted to the late Willard J. Graham, formerly the consulting editor of the Irwin Series in Accounting. For assistance in this revision, I am particularly indebted to Roland F. Salmonson, who made detailed comments on the entire first edition; and to Russell A. Taussig, who made detailed comments on several chapters of the first edition. I also wish to express appreciation to my colleagues at Washington State University and to the many other friends and colleagues who have made helpful comments regarding the first edition. And, of course, this book could not have been written without the continual encouragement and full support of my wife, Kathleen.

Pullman, Washington   ELDON S. HENDRIKSEN
March, 1970

Contents

Equities. The Classification of Stockholder Equities: *Classification by Source of Capital. The Disclosure of Legal Capital. The Disclosure of Restrictions on the Disposition of Income. The Disclosure of Restrictions on Liquidation Distributions.* Consolidated Financial Statements: *The Purpose and Nature of Consolidated Financial Statements. The Classification of Consolidated Equities.*

Accounting Theory

chapter 1

The Methodology of
Accounting Theory

Probably the most relevant definition of "theory" as it applies to accounting is that theory represents ". . . the coherent set of hypothetical, conceptual, and pragmatic principles forming the general frame of reference for a field of inquiry."[1] Thus, accounting theory may be defined as logical reasoning in the form of a set of broad principles that (1) provide a general frame of reference by which accounting practice can be evaluated and (2) guide the development of new practices and procedures. Accounting theory may also be used to explain existing practices to obtain a better understanding of them. But the most important goal of accounting theory should be to provide a coherent set of logical principles that form the general frame of reference for the evaluation and development of sound accounting practices.

The *Dictionary for Accountants* defines theory as "A set of propositions, including axioms and theorems, which, together with definitions and formal or informal rules of inference, is oriented toward the explanation of a body of *facts* or treatment of a class of concrete or abstract operations."[2] However, two parts of this definition must be qualified with respect to accounting theory. First, theory does not explain all accounting practice. Theory is based on logic, and not all practice is logically conceived. But if the emphasis is placed on the explanation of concepts and results rather than on techniques, the definition is generally correct. Second, the body of facts being explained by accounting theory can be assumed to be either (1) financial facts as presented in accounting statements, (2) concepts implied in the presentation of accounting data, or (3) economic relationships of firms with other firms, individuals, and the economy as a whole as measured and summarized in accounting state-

---

[1] *Webster's Third New International Dictionary, Unabridged* (Springfield, Mass.: G. & C. Merriam Co., 1961), p. 2371.

[2] Eric L. Kohler, *A Dictionary for Accountants* (3d ed.; Englewood Cliffs, N.J.: Prentice-Hall, Inc., 1963), p. 493.

1

ments. Of these three, the first—the explanation of financial facts presented by accountants—is not the function of theory.

The "facts" being explained by accounting theory are not independently measurable and verifiable and, therefore, are not really facts. Rather, they are the economic relationships in the business world and concepts such as "value" and "income" that may appear differently to various observers. Thus, several theories may be developed from the same set of "facts" and concepts, each of which may appear logical within the framework of the observations of specific individuals. The choice of a most appropriate theory depends on how well it supports the development of procedures and techniques that best fulfill the objectives of accounting.

One of the first steps in the development of accounting theory, therefore, is a clear statement of the objectives of accounting. In descriptive statistics, a summarized description of a population cannot be made unless the statistician first understands the type of information that is wanted. A description of the height and weight of the individuals in a given country may be of little value to a person who is interested in their economic well-being. Similarly, the type of information useful to management in the making of decisions is not necessarily the same as the type of information needed by stockholders and prospective investors of the firm.

Managers need information that will tell them the effect of current decisions on future income and cash flows. Stockholders who have an effective control of management need information to be able to judge the relative efficiency of management. Stockholders, prospective investors, and creditors need information that will help them predict the future course of the firm and the probability of future financial success that will permit repayments and cash distributions. While these objectives may lead to a single set of accounting principles, different sets of principles may be required to meet the several objectives of accounting. The major emphasis in this book is on the development of financial accounting theory based on the objectives of reporting to stockholders, investors, creditors, and other outside interests, although the objectives of reporting to management are taken into consideration in specific instances where the objectives overlap. Consideration is also given to meeting the objectives of general social and economic interests of a nation or geographic area.

These objectives have changed over time as one or more of the several interested groups have dominated in their pressure for information from accountants. At various stages in the development of accounting, the owner-manager, the creditor, and the stockholder-invester have each dominated in determining the type of information reported in financial statements; and economists, politicians, and the legal profession have influenced reporting practices. Therefore, a good understanding of current objectives and accounting practices requires a study of the historical development of accounting theory. But objectives are also different among the many countries and areas of the world and these differences may lead to dissimilar theories and practices. A summary of the historical development is presented in the following two chapters and discussions of geographical differences are presented where relevant throughout the book.

THE SEVERAL APPROACHES TO ACCOUNTING THEORY

Once the objectives of accounting are determined, one or more of several approaches to accounting theory must be selected in order to derive logically conceived accounting principles. These objectives, however, may be modified with the development of theory; but a change in the basic objectives might require a reformulation of the entire theoretical structure. For example, one of the objectives of financial reporting might be to provide information to stockholders and other outsiders to permit them to make useful predictions regarding the future operations of the firm. This objective may lead to the development of an operating concept of income to the enterprise and to the stockholders and to information that will permit the prediction of cash flows. But if the objective should be the measurement of the social benefits of the firm, the measurement of these benefits should include the value added to the economy and all social benefits and costs not measured directly by the mechanism of the market.

Some of the approaches to the development of accounting theory that have been suggested and used include the following: (1) the deductive reasoning and the axiomatic approaches, (2) the inductive approaches, (3) the ethical approach, (4) the use of communication theory, (5) the application of behavioral relationships, (6) emphasis on sociological factors, (7) a macroeconomic approach, (8) the pragmatic approach, (9) nontheoretical approaches, and (10) a theory of accounts approach. These approaches, however, are not independent of each other. Generally more than one must be used either explicitly or implicitly in the development of accounting principles. The theories developed and discussed in the following chapters are eclectic in nature, drawing upon all of these several approaches at various points.

Deductive Reasoning

The deductive method of reasoning in accounting is the process of starting with objectives and postulates and, from these, deriving logical principles that provide the bases for concrete or practical applications. Thus, the practical applications and rules are derived from the logical reasoning; the postulates and logically derived principles should not merely support or attempt to explain accounting conventions or currently accepted practice.

The structure of the deductive process should include the following: (1) the formulation of general or specific objectives of financial reporting; (2) a statement of the postulates of accounting concerning the economic, political, and sociological environment in which accounting must operate; (3) a set of constraints to guide the reasoning process; (4) a structure, set of symbols, or framework in which ideas can be expressed and summarized; (5) the development of a set of definitions; (6) the formulation of principles or generalized statements of policy derived by the process of logic; and finally (7) the application of the principles to specific situations and the establishment of procedural methods and rules.

In the deductive process, the formulation of objectives is most important because different objectives might require entirely different structures and result in different principles. This is one of the main reasons why rules for determining taxable income are different in many respects from the generally accepted practice for the determination of financial income. While there may be many advantages in applying the same income concepts to both tax and financial accounting, the basic objectives are different and it is not likely that the same principles and procedures will meet the different objectives equally well. The frequent proposal for a single all-pervasive concept of income also has many advantages, but it does assume that such a concept could serve all accounting objectives equally well. While this is not true, it would not be desirable to set up an entirely different set of principles for every purpose served by accounting. Some compromises must be made, but there should also be some freedom to serve different objectives as well as possible. Thus, accounting theory should be flexible enough to provide the needs of different objectives but rigid enough to provide for some uniformity and consistency in financial reports to stockholders and the general public.

The objectives, postulates, constraints, and structural framework will be discussed at greater length in Chapter 4. However, they are all essential to the deductive process. The postulates are not necessarily numerous or complicated; they may even seem trivial or obvious. But it is desirable to make them explicit to provide a framework for subsequent logical reasoning. The constraints are restrictions to the development of principles derived from the objectives and postulates. These restrictions are necessary because of certain limitations of the environment, particularly those caused by uncertainty regarding the future and changes in the environment such as fluctuations in the value of the measuring unit—money.

Symbols and a general working framework are necessary to provide a means of communication of ideas. In accounting, the framework may be the accounting equation and the several derived financial statements. In this framework the statements should articulate with each other in order to provide internal consistency.

A more precise method of formulating the symbols, structure, and constraints is found in the axiomatic or mathematical approach to accounting theory. In this method, mathematical symbols are given to certain ideas and concepts. The framework is provided in the form of mathematical models utilizing matrix algebra or symbolic logic. Constraints can be applied in the form of mathematical expressions. Therefore, starting with basic postulates, axioms can be set up and, through mathematical operations, theorems can be formulated and tested for logic. Thus, the axiomatic method can provide a very useful framework for the deductive approach to accounting theory.

One of the main disadvantages of the deductive method is that if any of the postulates and premises are false, the conclusions may also be false. Also, it is thought to be too far removed from reality to be able to derive realistic and workable principles or to provide the basis for practical rules. But these criticisms generally stem from a misunderstanding of the purpose and meaning of theory. It is not necessary that theory be entirely practical in order to be useful in establishing workable procedures. The main purpose of theory is to provide a framework for the development of new ideas and new procedures and to help in the making of choices among alternative procedures. If these objectives are met, it is not necessary that theory be based completely on practical concepts or that it be restricted to the development of procedures that are completely workable and practical in terms of current known technology. In fact, many of the currently accepted principles and procedures are general guides to action rather than specific rules that can be followed precisely in every applicable case.[3]

The Inductive Approach

The process of induction consists of drawing generalized conclusions from detailed observations and measurements. After only a few observations, generalizations can be made regarding the entire universe or a group of similar situations. These generalizations, however, are subject to later confirmation or refutation after further experimentation and ob-

---

[3] For example, the capitalization of long-term leases that are, in substance, a purchase of property, as recommended by the AICPA Accounting Principles Board in *Opinion No. 5,* is a general guide that cannot necessarily be followed with precision in every case, particularly if the lease contract includes the purchase of services acquired jointly with the use of property. See Accounting Principles Board, "Reporting of Leases in Financial Statements of Lessee," *Opinion No. 5* (New York: AICPA, September, 1964). Reprinted in *Journal of Accountancy,* Vol. CXVIII (November, 1964), pp. 63–66.

servation. All principles inductively derived are, therefore, conceptually falsifiable. Thus, through the inductive process, Newton was able to observe the characteristics of motion and from these observations and measurements derive generalizations or laws of motion.

In accounting, the inductive process involves the making of observations of financial data regarding business enterprises. If recurring relationships can be found, generalizations and principles can be formulated. Thus new ideas and principles can be derived, particularly if the observer does not let himself be influenced by current principles and practices. For example, by observations of a number of firms, it may be found that a historical trend of past sales may be a better predictor of cash to be received from customers in the future than the actual record of cash received in the past because of leads and lags in the collection process. Although this may always be subject to later refutation, a generalized conclusion may be reached from this that revenue reported for several prior years is relevant in the reporting process.[4]

Just because the observer looks only at raw data does not mean, however, that he does not need some initial postulates and concepts. By the mere making of a choice regarding what to observe he is reflecting preconceived notions of what might be relevant. By restricting himself to the financial data of a firm, for example, he is drawing on certain postulates regarding the environment of accounting. Furthermore, if he restricts himself to observing only financial transactions, he may only confirm existing practice.

The advantage of the inductive approach is that it is not necessarily constrained by a preconceived model or structure. The researcher is free to make any observations he may deem relevant. But once generalizations or principles are formulated, they should be confirmed by the logical process of the deductive approach. However, the main disadvantage of the inductive process is that the observer is likely to be influenced by subconscious ideas of what the relevant relationships are and what data should be observed.

Another difficulty with the inductive approach is that, in accounting, the raw data are likely to be different for each firm. Relationships may also be different, making it difficult to draw generalizations and basic principles. For example, the relationship between total revenues and costs of goods sold may be a constant over time for some firms, but this does

---

[4] As a further example of the inductive process applied to accounting, the method of evaluating information adopted by the 1968 Committee on External Reporting of the American Accounting Association is suggested as a possible application. While the evaluation procedure used by the committee does not necessarily lead to generalizations, the suggested procedures found by applying the evaluation process can be assumed to be generalizations derived by the process of induction. See 1966–68 Committee on External Reporting, "An Evaluation of Current Reporting Practices," *Accounting Review,* Supplement to Vol. XLIV (1969), pp. 79–122.

not necessarily mean that the historical gross margin concept is necessarily a good measurement for the prediction of the future operations of a firm in all cases.

We should like to emphasize that it is difficult to divorce the inductive approach from other approaches to theory because other methods tend to provide a guide to the selection of the data to be studied. Such suggestions can come from the deductive approach, the pragmatic approach, the ethical approach, the communications or behavioral approaches, or even nontheoretical approaches to accounting. While all approaches are somewhat interdependent, the inductive approach must rely on at least one other approach to establish the goal or goals for making generalizations.

The Ethical Approach

As indicated above, the several approaches to accounting theory are not independent of each other. This is particularly true of the ethical approach; for defining it as a separate approach does not necessarily imply that other approaches do not have ethical content, nor does it imply that ethical theories necessarily ignore all other concepts. Pattillo, for example, stresses the ethical concept as primary but he states that in his approach

its basic standard is an ethical one, its method is logical and coherent, and the ultimate test of the formulations lies in its application to the real world.[5]

The ethical approach to accounting theory places emphasis on the concepts of justice, truth, and fairness. DR Scott suggested that the basis for the determination of accounting practice reaches back to the principles underlying social organizations. His basic concepts were: (1) accounting procedures must provide *equitable treatment* to all interested parties; (2) financial reports should present a *true* and *accurate* statement without misrepresentation; (3) accounting data should be *fair, unbiased,* and *impartial* without serving special interests. To these basic concepts he added the requirements that accounting principles should be subject to continual revision as necessary to allow for changing conditions and that accounting principles should be applied consistently whenever possible.[6]

Fairness, justice, and impartiality refer to judgments that accounting reports and statements are not subject to undue influence or bias. They should not be prepared with the objective of serving any particular individual or group to the detriment of others. The interests of all parties

---

[5] James W. Pattillo, *The Foundation of Financial Accounting* (Baton Rouge: Louisiana State University Press, 1965), p. 11.

[6] DR Scott, "The Basis for Accounting Principles," *Accounting Review,* Vol. XVI (December, 1941), pp. 341–49.

should be taken into consideration in proper balance, particularly without any preference for the rights of the management or owners of the firm who may have greater influence over the choice of accounting procedures. Justice frequently refers to a conformity to a standard established formally or informally as a guide to equitable treatment.

Truth, as it relates to accounting, is probably more difficult to define and apply. Many seem to use the term to mean "in accordance with the facts." However, not all who refer to truth in accounting have in mind the same definition of "facts." Some refer to accounting facts as data that are objective and verifiable. Thus, historical costs may represent accounting facts. On the other hand, the term "truth" is used to refer to the valuation of assets and expenses in current economic terms. For example, MacNeal stated that financial statements display the truth only when they disclose the current value of assets and the profits and losses accruing from changes in values, although the increases in values should be designated as realized or unrealized.[7]

Truth is also used to refer to propositions or statements that are generally considered to be established principles. For example, the recognition of a gain at the time of the sale of an asset is generally considered to be a reporting of true conditions, while the reporting of an appraisal increase in the value of an asset prior to sale as ordinary income is generally thought to lack truthfulness. Thus, the established rule regarding revenue realization is the guide. But the truthfulness of the financial reports depends on the fundamental validity of the accepted rules and principles on which the statements are based. Established rules and procedures provide an inadequate foundation for measuring truthfulness.

The concept of "fairness" has long been a basic objective in the presentation of audited financial statements. The generally accepted accountant's short-form report or certificate states, in part: "In our opinion, the accompanying statements present *fairly* the financial position of the company as of _____ and the results of its operations for the year then ended. . . ." Mautz and Sharaf indicate that this statement expresses the faithfulness in reporting the realities of the firm's operations and financial condition.[8] In discussing the concept of fairness, they include three subconcepts: accounting propriety, adequate disclosure, and audit obligation.

AICPA Statement on Auditing Procedure No. 33 implies a similar concept of "fairness." In a section entitled "Fairness of Presentation," the topics discussed include (1) conformity with generally accepted accounting principles, (2) disclosure, (3) consistency, and (4) compa-

---

[7] Kenneth MacNeal, *Truth in Accounting* (Philadelphia: University of Pennsylvania Press, 1939), p. 203.

[8] R. K. Mautz and Hussein A. Sharaf, *The Philosophy of Auditing*, American Accounting Association Monograph No. 6 (AAA, 1961), p. 158.

rability.[9] Thus, the concept of fairness is related closely to compliance with traditional and conventional practice. In this respect, it is similar to the second concept of "truthfulness" stated above. But Mautz and Sharaf imply that compliance is not enough. If compliance with generally accepted practices does not permit the presentation of statements that report the realities, the auditor must develop his own principles. These "realities," however, are similar to the "facts" referred to in the first definition of "truthfulness" above. The determination of realities, like the determination of facts, depends on the viewpoint of the observer.

A different concept of "fairness" is implicit in the comments by Leonard Spacek on AICPA *Accounting Research Study No. 3*. He states:

. . . a discussion of assets, liabilities, revenue and costs is premature and meaningless until the basic principles that will result in a *fair* presentation of the facts in the form of financial accounting and financial reporting are determined. This fairness of accounting and reporting must be for and to people, and these people represent the various segments of our society.[10]

Fairness, in this context means impartiality and justice to the individuals and groups having an interest in the statements as well as a fair presentation of the facts. The emphasis is on fairness *to* the readers of the statements rather than fairness *of* the data being presented. Reports that are prepared in a fair manner may also be impartial but, according to Spacek, both are necessary.

In the United Kingdom, the Companies Act of 1967 requires that the auditors shall state in their report whether or not a *true and fair* view is given in the balance sheet of the company's affairs as at the end of its financial year and in the statement of its profit or loss for its financial year. While the statement of the auditors implies an ethical judgment, the practical interpretation of it results in the acceptance of traditional accounting procedures in most cases.[11] However, accountants in the United Kingdom generally have greater freedom than do those in the United States in the choice of accounting methods in order to present a true and fair view.

Few accountants would deny that truth and fairness are good objectives in the presentation of financial statements. But as single objectives, they rely too heavily on subjective judgments. Because of this subjectivity, there is a tendency to rely on traditional rules and procedures to

---

[9] Committee on Auditing Procedure of the AICPA, *Auditing Standards and Procedures,* Statement on Auditing Procedure No. 33 (New York: AICPA, 1963), pp. 69–74.

[10] "Comments of Leonard Spacek," in Robert T. Sprouse and Maurice Moonitz, "A Tentative Set of Broad Accounting Principles for Business Enterprises," *Accounting Research Study No. 3* (New York: AICPA, 1962), p. 78.

[11] See F. J. O. Ryan, "A True and Fair View," *Abacus,* Vol. III, No. 2 (December, 1967), pp. 95–108, for an alternative interpretation of "true and fair view."

provide an objective measurement of truth. Unless these rules and pro-cedures are soundly based on logic, however, the resulting statements may turn out to be monstrosities of misrepresentation. In an attempt to present facts and realities, accountants may be likened to the three blind men reported by Confucius as describing an elephant as either like a wall, a tree, or a snake, depending on whether each was feeling the side, the leg, or the trunk of the elephant. The question may be not whether certain information is true or false or fair or unfair but whether or not it is relevant and logical in describing the financial operations and condition of an enterprise.

Probably the greatest disadvantage of a primary reliance on the ethical approach to accounting theory is that it fails to provide a sound basis for the development of accounting principles or for the evaluation of currently accepted principles. Principles must be evaluated on the basis of subjective judgments; or, as generally occurs, currently accepted practices become accepted without evaluation because it is expedient to do so.

An example of the application of the ethical approach is found in Pattillo's *The Foundation of Financial Accounting*. With respect to income, he concludes that the current operating concept produces results that are fair to all parties because with it there is full disclosure of extraordinary items so that distortion and confusion are avoided.[12] On the other hand, he finds that the use of historical cost is not fair to all parties because it does not provide a basis for determining the relative positions of all interested parties.[13]

Communication Theory Approach

Accounting can borrow profitably from other social sciences in estab-lishing a framework for the development of theory and in evaluating the proper objectives of accounting. One of the methodological techniques found useful in other areas is communication theory. While little has been done in applying communication theory to accounting, Bedford and Baladouni suggest an interesting relationship between communication theory and accounting.[14] They claim that accounting may be viewed as an integrated system of the communication process. This communication process involves a determination of what information regarding a firm should be gathered and how it should be interpreted, and the selection of the best method of communication. The process should be evaluated by observing the types of information needed by the users of accounting

---

[12] Pattillo, *op. cit.*, p. 117.

[13] *Ibid.*, p. 124.

[14] Norton M. Bedford and Vahe Baladouni, "A Communication Theory Approach to Accountancy," *Accounting Review*, Vol. XXXVII (October, 1962), pp. 650–59.

reports and by determining the ability of the users of the accounting statements to interpret the information properly.

An example of the application of the communication approach is found in "A Statement of Basic Accounting Theory," prepared by a committee of the American Accounting Association in 1966.[15] It defines accounting as

the process of identifying, measuring, and communicating economic information to permit informed judgments and decisions by users of the information.[16]

While the approach of the committee was eclectic in nature, applying deductive reasoning, pragmatism, and ethical concepts, as well as drawing from other approaches, one of the overriding goals is the establishment of a communication process.

Behavioral Approach

Accounting theory can also draw on a study of behavioral relationships as analyzed in the fields of psychology, sociology, and economics. Accounting is a means for providing information for proper decision making by firms, individuals, and governments. How these individuals and groups react to accounting data should be of direct concern to accountants. A procedure may be conceptually sound, but if it leads to erroneous decisions or to undesirable behavior it should be closely scrutinized for possible defects. On the other hand, if certain procedures are adopted only as expedients, they may be useful if their effect is to lead to good decisions and proper behavior. Thus, the emphasis is on how the accounting data are used rather than on the logical development of the reports. While this approach may be useful in research and evaluations, it is similar to the pragmatic approach and is subject to the same criticism that it relies heavily on subjective judgments regarding what behavior is good or appropriate and what is bad or inappropriate. While a behavioral approach is implicit in many discussions of accounting theory, it generally plays a minor role. Prince, however, suggests that motivational postulates should play a greater role in the development of accounting theory, although this theory may rely heavily on the pragmatic approach and deductive reasoning.[17] In the managerial accounting area, considerable behavioral research has already been done and several behavioral models have been proposed.[18]

---

[15] AAA, *A Statement of Basic Accounting Theory* (Evanston, Ill., 1966).

[16] *Ibid.*, p. 1.

[17] Thomas R. Prince, *Extension of the Boundaries of Accounting Theory* (Cincinnati: South-Western Publishing Co., 1963).

[18] See Jacob G. Birnberg and Raghu Nath, "Implications of Behavioral Science for Managerial Accounting," *Accounting Review*, Vol. XLII, No. 3 (July, 1967), pp. 468–79, for a review of behavioral research in accounting and a list of relevant references.

Sociological Approach

The sociological approach is similar to the behavioral approach in that accounting principles are judged by the resulting effects. But the goal is the broader sociological effect rather than the decisions of the immediate users of accounting data. It is more of a welfare approach than the behavioral approach. One of the objectives of accounting is, therefore, the reporting of the effects of business operations on all related groups in society whether or not they are direct users of accounting information. While accountants are not and should not be called upon to make judgments regarding welfare, it is occasionally suggested that accounting reports should provide the information necessary for broad welfare judgments. The main difficulty with this approach is that adequate principles and procedures cannot be established unless accountants have a basis for determining what welfare judgments are important and what information will aid in making these judgments.

Examples of a direct application of a sociological approach are difficult to find. In most cases, the sociological objective is only one of several concepts emphasized and in others the sociological objective can only be implied from the procedures proposed or in use. Ladd, for example, stated that his book rests upon two propositions, one of which is based on the assumption that "accounting has the vital social role of passing on to the public, information about the extent and uses of corporate powers."[19] Implied sociological objectives can be found in the reporting requirements of some countries. In the United Kingdom, for example, the requirement that all limited companies, regardless of size or ownership, file audited statements and returns annually with the Board of Trade was no doubt based in part on general welfare objectives. Likewise, the requirement that corporate contributions to political and charitable organizations be disclosed in annual returns is based on an assumed social obligation to disclose information about the uses of corporate powers.

Macroeconomic Approach

A macroeconomic approach is similar to the behavioral and sociological approaches in that one of the objectives of accounting is to direct the behavior of firms and individuals. However, the objective is directed toward the implementation of specific national economic policies. For example, national economic objectives might require accounting reports that will permit and even encourage higher dividends and larger capital expenditures during slack economic periods and discourage investments

---

[19] Dwight R. Ladd, *Contemporary Corporate Accounting and the Public* (Homewood, Ill.: Richard D. Irwin, Inc., 1963), p. ix.

during periods of inflation. While most countries implement such a policy through monetary and fiscal policies and direct controls, some countries, notably Sweden, do attempt to base accounting concepts and practices on macroeconomic goals.[20] One of the main aspects of this policy is the objective of reporting stable earnings from year to year. Thus, the use of reserves and flexible depreciation policies are examples of the legitimate smoothing of income.

In the United States, macroeconomic policy has had little influence on accounting. However, the influence of government administrators was partially responsible for the deferral of an opinion of the Accounting Principles Board of the AICPA in 1967 that would have made cost reduction and deferred recognition of the investment tax credit the preferred method as opposed to the flow-through method. The main reason for the governmental opposition was the fear that the opinion would have an adverse effect on government economic policy.

The Pragmatic Approach

Philosophical pragmatism is ". . . marked by the doctrines that the meaning of conceptions is to be sought in their practical bearings, that the function of thought is as a guide to action, and that the truth is preeminently to be tested by the practical consequences of belief."[21] Thus, the pragmatic approach involves the development of ideas that are in agreement with the real world and find usefulness in realistic situations. As applied to accounting theory, the pragmatic approach involves the selection of accounting concepts and techniques based on their utility. Principles and procedures are held to be useful if they accomplish the objectives of management or if they help stockholders or other readers interpret accounting statements and aid in meeting their specific objectives. Theory that does not have an immediate practical use is assumed to be poor theory.

While many authors have proposed utility as one of the main objectives of accounting,[22] Mueller has presented one of the best proposals for the application of the pragmatic approach to the development of accounting.[23] The main basis for his development of accounting procedures would be through induction from existing business practice. That is, accounting is thought to be an independent discipline which can be developed through the distillation of experience.

---

[20] See Gerhard G. Mueller, *International Accounting* (New York: Macmillan Co., 1967), pp. 27–30.

[21] *Webster's Third International Dictionary, Unabridged,* p. 1781.

[22] See for example James M. Fremgen, "Utility and Accounting Principles," *Accounting Review,* Vol. XVII, No. 2 (July, 1967), pp. 457–67.

[23] Mueller, *op. cit.,* pp. 60–63.

One of the advantages of the pragmatic approach is that accounting serves a function only if it is useful. But it must be assumed that accountants know what is most useful for their own firms or clients and for the users of external financial reports. No doubt, the lower-of-cost-or-market rule and conservatism had their origins in a pragmatic belief that creditors would rather see an understatement of current resources than an overstatement and that this presentation also resulted in better management decisions.

The pragmatic approach, however, has many serious disadvantages. The most serious criticism is probably that there are no basic criteria for determining what is meant by "useful." To whom should accounting data be useful, and for what purpose? Reports that fail to disclose certain losses or inefficiencies of management may be considered useful to management, but they would not necessarily be useful to stockholders or prospective investors. A clear statement of the objectives of financial accounting must precede an analysis of how specific procedures can help accounting fulfill its functions.

A second criticism of the pragmatic approach is that it has not been applied to accounting in a logical way and therefore cannot really be said to be a theoretical approach. However, the pragmatic objective has been combined with other approaches in the formulation of theoretical structures. Prince, for example, included a strong pragmatic objective in his behavioral approach to accounting.[24] The AAA Committee to Prepare a Statement of Basic Accounting Theory also applied pragmatic connotations.[25] Its standard of relevance and its guideline of appropriateness to expected use are pragmatic goals. On the whole, however, its approach is eclectic in nature. More formal applications of the standards were included in the reports of the 1968 Committee on External Reporting and the 1968 Committee on Managerial Decision Models.[26]

Nontheoretical Approaches

While an emphasis on a single one of the above approaches to accounting may lack a structure of logical reasoning and thus be nontheoretical, in most cases attempts have been made to weave the concepts into theoretical structures by combining them with other approaches. Most accounting practices, however, have been established without the benefit of a theoretical foundation. For example, the method used by the AICPA prior to 1959 (and to a large extent since) in the development of accounting principles was based primarily on practical nontheoretical arguments. Specific procedures or techniques were studied and certain procedures

---

[24] Prince, *op. cit.*, pp. 25–30.

[25] *A Statement of Basic Accounting Theory, op. cit.*, p. 9.

[26] American Accounting Association Committee Reports, 1969, *Accounting Review,* Supplement to Vol. XLIV (1969), pp. 79–122 and 43–76.

were recommended on the basis of their usefulness, without a reliance on a general overall framework of accounting theory and without the necessity for an interdependence of the several procedures recommended in different areas. The principles and procedures recommended, however, gained respectability as they subsequently became generally accepted. The final proof of the recommendations was, therefore, the general acceptance of the procedures in actual practice which was then thought to be proof of their utility.

By a reliance on general acceptance, this practical approach (frequently referred to as the pragmatic approach) leads to a form of "common law" in accounting. That is, principles, procedures, and techniques are considered to be good if there is a precedence for their general acceptance in a given area. Furthermore, acceptance may move into another area if the same type of utility can be found in the new area. For example, Lifo started as an accepted practice in only very restricted areas and only under specific conditions; but the usefulness of the method was applied to other areas until it has now become a generally accepted procedure in most areas of inventory valuation. As new problems arise, procedures are recommended on the basis of similarities to generally accepted practices. This is similar in many respects to the development of common law over time.

This approach to the discovery of useful accounting methods has occasionally erroneously been referred to as an inductive or empirical method. Research is directed toward the discovery of which accounting procedures are most commonly used and thought to be the most useful by accountants or users of financial statements. The research method utilizes questionnaires, interviews, and studies of accounting reports and statements. The results of the research method may point out those procedures most commonly thought to be useful, trends toward the general acceptance of newer procedures, or new procedures found useful in a few cases but which may be useful in many others if the advantages are made known.

A significant limitation of the practical approach is that generally accepted practice is not necessarily the most useful from the point of view of providing information relevant to good decision making. Many procedures are widely adopted because they are simple expedients or because they minimize the current payment of the corporate income tax. Just because procedures are widely used does not mean that they are necessarily useful, good, or logical.

While it may be helpful to know what methods are in common use, an investigation of practice is not likely to lead to new theories or ideas or even new procedures. In fact, the publishing of generally accepted procedures and the assumption that these are the best methods known may deter progress. Accountants may rely on the general acceptance of these procedures rather than attempt to experiment or develop better methods.

Theory of Accounts Approach

Attempts to set forth a theory to provide a logical explanation of the mechanism of double-entry bookkeeping and the nature of the relationships of accounts are probably the earliest formulations of accounting theory. Refinements of this approach are still found in the literature, particularly that of European writers.[27] The objective of such an approach is generally to provide a means by which all transactions can be booked easily and without fictitious constructions. It is also used to explain the double-entry system and the basic nature of assets, equities, revenues, expenses, and income. The main advantage of this approach is that it helps to permit an understanding of current accounting practices and their historical development. However, it has the disadvantage of being restricted by the formal structure of the mathematical identity of the accounting equation and concepts brought into this structure by nontheoretical means.

Eclectic Approaches to Accounting Theory

As indicated in the previous pages, practically all fully developed theories of accounting rely upon more than one basic approach to theory. Those that attempt to rely upon a single goal or approach are generally incomplete as a logical basis for the formulation of accounting procedures or for their evaluation. One reason for this is that the several approaches to theory are not independent of each other. The deductive and inductive approaches may be considered the most basic approaches, but these can be used equally well to supplement each other. Chambers, for example, claimed that his basic approach to accounting theory utilized both deductive and inductive methods.[28] Sprouse and Moonitz, on the other hand, in *Accounting Research Studies 1* and *3* relied heavily on the deductive approach but some of the other objectives are also implicit in their discussions.[29] Most of the other approaches listed place special emphasis on specific goals or specific aspects of accounting and generally cannot exist as full explanations of accounting theory.

---

[27] See, for example, Karl Kafer, *Theory of Accounts in Double-Entry Bookkeeping* (Urbana, Ill.: Center for International Education and Research in Accounting, 1966).

[28] Raymond J. Chambers, *Accounting, Evaluation and Economic Behavior* (Englewood Cliffs, N.J.: Prentice-Hall, Inc., 1966), pp. 28–31.

[29] Maurice Moonitz, "The Basic Postulates of Accounting," *Accounting Research Study No. 1* (New York: AICPA, 1961) and Robert T. Sprouse and Maurice Moonitz, "A Tentative Set of Broad Accounting Principles for Business Enterprises," *Accounting Research Study No. 3* (New York: AICPA, 1962).

THE USES OF ACCOUNTING THEORY

Most accounting theories can be classified as either normative or descriptive in nature. Normative theories attempt to prescribe what accounting ought to do and how it ought to do it; that is, they attempt to explain what should be rather than what is. Normative accounting theory may be used to evaluate current practice or it may be used to develop new procedures. The theories and recommendations of Sprouse and Moonitz in *Accounting Research Study No. 3*[30] and the theory and recommendations of Chambers[31] are largely normative in nature. Descriptive theories attempt to explain current practice or rationalize the use of certain procedures. They may also be used to find a common thread of logic or interrelationship among accepted accounting procedures in order to find a basis for accepting some procedures and rejecting others. But descriptive theories are probably most valuable for their attempt to understand the foundations and the effect of current practice. Littleton's development of theory is probably the most complete theory that applies the descriptive method.[32] More recently, Goldberg has presented a fairly complete theoretical development drawn from practice, although he claims that it is a framework for the evaluation of practice and in some respects it is normative in nature.[33]

Empirical Research in Accounting

Empirical research in accounting is the search for meaningful relationships in business enterprises; the testing of hypotheses; and the study of current or proposed accounting reporting practices and such things as (1) the prediction of future objects, activities, or variables; (2) motivation and other behavior; and (3) macroeconomic effects. While empirical studies are not likely to provide a complete basis for a theoretical approach, they may be very helpful in finding variables and relationships upon which accounting theory can be based and in testing hypotheses developed by accounting theory. In fact, in the view of some, theoretical hypotheses can be tested only through empirical research.[34] Regardless

---

[30] Sprouse and Moonitz, *ibid.*

[31] Chambers, *op. cit.*

[32] A. C. Littleton, *Structure of Accounting Theory* (American Accounting Association, 1953).

[33] Louis Goldberg, *An Inquiry into the Nature of Accounting*, Monograph No. 7 (AAA, 1964).

[34] See for example Carl L. Nelson, "Critical Synthesis of Conference Papers," *Empirical Research in Accounting, Selected Studies, 1967* (Chicago: Institute of Professional Accounting, Graduate School of Business, University of Chicago, 1968), p. 235.

of the validity of this statement, there is little question that empirical research can be a valuable aid in the formation and testing of accounting theories. In the opinion of the author, however, complete theories can be formulated and tested through the process of logical inquiry.

CONTROVERSY IN THE DEVELOPMENT OF ACCOUNTING PRINCIPLES AND PROCEDURES

The critical analysis of accounting principles and procedures presented in the following chapters is based on an eclectic concept of accounting theory. Each of the several approaches to accounting theory has some merit in helping to establish and evaluate accounting principles and procedures. The inductive approach permits a better understanding of data that provide the foundation for accounting. The pragmatic approach sets certain limitations on the application of abstract theory and helps in establishing the objectives of accounting; for accounting theory must be useful as well as logical. The ethical approach can also be applied in a general way as a basic objective in establishing logical accounting principles and procedures. No one has proposed that accounting statements should reflect information and relationships that are not true, just, or fair. The communication, behavioral, and sociological approaches can add to the controversies of theory development and application. While none of the several approaches to accounting theory is adequate by itself, any complete theory formulation must be accompanied by some deductive reasoning. Therefore, the accounting theory developed and applied throughout this book attempts to place all approaches to theory in proper perspective with special emphasis on the deductive process.

The following two chapters present the historical development of accounting theory. While accounting procedures have not always been logically conceived, it is relevant to study their development and change to understand why accounting is what it is today. The historical perspective also permits a better evaluation of the objectives and postulates of accounting theory.

One of the first steps in evaluating accounting theory is to examine the basic postulates, standards, and hypotheses on which it is based. A discussion of these postulates, standards, and hypotheses is presented in Chapter 4. Postulates, however, should include the objectives of accounting, the basic assumptions regarding the economic and political environment of accounting, and the constraints required because of the limitations of measurement, uncertainty, or other pragmatic reasons.

Once the postulates have been presented and discussed, the development of accounting theory requires an analysis of the accounting framework or structure. This discussion starts with the traditional framework of the accounting equation and the several financial statements stemming from this initial structure. While cohesiveness and greater logic are thought to follow if the statements are made to articulate with each other, the possibility of alternative structures is explored. Another basic part of a structure is the set of concepts that provides meaning to the statements and the data on which they are based. These concepts must be carefully defined to provide clear, logical reasoning in the evaluation of accounting controversy. A discussion of these concepts and definitions is left to later chapters.

Even with a logical development of postulates, accounting framework, and definitions, there may be alternative procedures that are logically developed. In these cases, the choice of a best method must be based on how well each satisfies the objectives established. But the effect of alternative postulates and concepts should also be studied. Thus, accounting theory could result in a single set of principles only if there were a single agreed set of postulates including the objectives and constraints and a full agreement on the structure and concepts to be applied. Much of the disagreement in accounting theory is based on a failure to agree on these postulates and concepts. Therefore, one of the functions of theory is to determine the basic nature of the disagreement so that an evaluation can be made at the proper level in the development of the logic.

In each of the following chapters, an attempt is made to develop the basic concepts necessary in the exposition of accounting theory and to evaluate alternative procedures on the basis of the concepts implied and the objectives. In many cases, the author has suggested certain procedures as being superior to others on the basis of specific criteria. The reason for making a choice is to provide an integrated theory throughout all aspects of financial accounting. Each or all of these suggested procedures are subject to further scrutiny and may be rejected even by the author on the basis of changes in the basic postulates, changes in definitions, or changes in objectives.

SELECTED ADDITIONAL READING ON CHAPTER TOPICS

General Methodology

BUCKLEY, JOHN W., PAUL KIRCHER, and RUSSELL L. MATHEWS. "Methodology in Accounting Theory," *Accounting Review* Vol. XLIII (April, 1968), pp. 274–83.

DEINZER, HARVEY T. "Conditions for Knowledge and the Activity of Knowing: A Reference Standard for Accounting," *Development of Accounting Thought*, chap. iv. New York: Holt, Rinehart & Winston, Inc., 1965.

DEVINE, CARL THOMAS. "Research Methodology and Accounting Theory Formation," *Accounting Review*, Vol. XXXV (July, 1960), pp. 387–99.

IMKE, FRANK J. "Relationships in Accounting Theory," *Accounting Review*, Vol. XLI (April, 1966), pp. 318–22.

Deductive Approach

CHAMBERS, R. J. "Blueprint for a Theory of Accounting," *Accounting Research,* Vol. VI (January, 1955), pp. 17–25. Reprinted in SIDNEY DAVIDSON, DAVID GREEN, JR., CHARLES T. HORNGREN, and GEORGE H. SORTER. *An Income Approach to Accounting Theory: Readings and Questions,* pp. 57–65. Englewood Cliffs, N.J.: Prentice-Hall, Inc., 1964.

——. "Detail for a Blueprint," *Accounting Review,* Vol. XXXII (April, 1957), pp. 206–15.

MATTESSICH, RICHARD. "Toward a General and Axiomatic Foundation of Accountancy with an Introduction to the Matrix Formulation of Accounting Systems," *Accounting Research,* October, 1957, pp. 328–56.

——. *Accounting and Analytical Methods, Measurement and Projection of Income and Wealth in the Micro- and Macro-Economy.* Homewood, Ill.: Richard D. Irwin, Inc., 1964.

SPENCER, MILTON H. "Axiomatic Method and Accounting Science," *Accounting Review,* Vol. XXXVII (April, 1963), pp. 310–16.

WILLIAMS, THOMAS H. and CHARLES H. GRIFFIN. "Mathematics and Logic: Deductive Analysis," *The Mathematical Dimension of Accountancy,* chap. ii. Cincinnati: South-Western Publishing Co., 1964.

Inductive Approach

SCHRADER, WILLIAM J. "An Inductive Approach to Accounting Theory," *Accounting Review,* Vol. XXXVII (October, 1962), pp. 645–49.

Ethical Approach

ARNETT, HAROLD E. "The Concept of Fairness," *Accounting Review,* Vol. XIII (April, 1967), pp. 291–97.

MACNEAL, KENNETH. *Truth in Accounting,* particularly chap. ix. Philadelphia: University of Pennsylvania Press, 1939.

PATTILLO, JAMES W. *The Foundations of Financial Accounting,* particularly chap. iii, "The Accounting Standard: Fairness to All Parties." Baton Rouge: Louisiana State University Press, 1965.

SCOTT, DR. "The Basis for Accounting Principles," *Accounting Review,* Vol. XVI (December, 1941), pp. 341–49.

SPACEK, LEONARD. "The Need for an Accounting Court," *Accounting Review,* Vol. XXXIII (July, 1958), pp. 368–79.

Communication Theory Approach

BEDFORD, NORTON M., and VAHE BALADOUNI. "A Communication Theory Approach to Accountancy," *Accounting Review,* Vol. XXXVII (October, 1962), pp. 650–59.

BEDFORD, NORTON M. "The Communication of Operational Income," *Income Determination Theory: An Accounting Framework,* chap. xii. Reading, Mass.: Addison-Wesley, 1965.

Behavioral Approach

BIRNBERG, JACOB G. and RAGHU NATH. "Implications of Behavioral Science for Managerial Accounting," *Accounting Review,* Vol. XLII (July, 1967), pp. 468–79.

PRINCE, THOMAS R. *Extension of the Boundaries of Accounting Theory.* Cincinnati: South-Western Publishing Co., 1963.

Sociological Approach

LADD, DWIGHT R. *Contemporary Corporate Accounting and the Public.* Homewood, Ill.: Richard D. Irwin, Inc., 1963.

Macroeconomic Approach

MUELLER, GERHARD G. "Accounting Within a Macroeconomic Framework," *International Accounting,* chap. i. New York: Macmillan Co., 1967.

Pragmatic Approach

COWAN, T. K. "A Pragmatic Approach to Accounting Theory," *Accounting Review,* Vol. XLIII (January, 1968), pp. 94–100.

DOPUCH, NICHOLAS. "Metaphysics of Pragmatism and Accountancy," *Accounting Review,* Vol. XXXVII (April, 1962), pp. 251–62.

FREMGREN, JAMES M. "Utility and Accounting Principles," *Accounting Review,* Vol. XLII (July, 1967), pp. 457–67.

MUELLER, GERHARD G. "Accounting and Conventional Business Practices," *International Accounting,* pp. 60–63. New York: Macmillan Co., 1967.

chapter 2

History and Development of Accounting Theory to 1930

Regardless of the approach selected, an understanding of the current position of accounting theory requires a study of the historical development of accounting thought and practice. Prior to 1930, accounting theory as a well-defined body of logical reasoning did not usually precede accounting practice, if indeed it can be said to do so today. Accounting developed historically as the needs arose, and changes occurred gradually in accounting techniques and concepts. But new accounting practices have been necessary to keep pace with changing economic institutions and relationships and the changing objectives of accounting. However, many techniques and concepts continue in use long after the conditions requiring them have ceased.

A need for a study of the history of accounting and accounting theory stems from this relationship with the past. Littleton and Zimmerman stated that

because of the wide availability of a growing technical literature, current accounting thought and actions may draw much more from the ideas accumulated through the past experience of many people than is consciously realized.[1]

In all disciplines, theories and concepts are developed in historical continuity. One thought leads to another. Where we are today depends in large part on where we were yesterday. In fact, many of the things we do are based on reasons no longer relevant; we have even lost sight of many of the reasons and continue in the same way because of a resistance to change. Change requires a reconsideration of where we are and where we are going. In the world of accounting practice, accountants usually do not have the time to stop to evaluate the reasons for their practices. The term "conventional wisdom" coined by Galbraith[2] is very appropriate in its

---

[1] A. C. Littleton and V. K. Zimmerman, *Accounting Theory: Continuity and Change* (Englewood Cliffs, N.J.: Prentice-Hall, Inc., 1962), p. 271.

[2] John Kenneth Galbraith, *The Affluent Society* (Boston: Houghton Mifflin Co., 1958).

application to accounting. Conventional wisdom is knowledge held because it is generally accepted; deviations from this conventional wisdom do not always find acceptance even when they are fully justified. An independent auditor may be required to withhold a clean certificate because the financial statements have not been prepared "in accordance with generally accepted accounting principles." While conventional wisdom need not necessarily provide the most useful foundation for current theory, we cannot deny that current accounting thought and practice are influenced by past developments. Therefore, to understand these generally accepted accounting principles, let us look back at the origins of accounting thought and at the changes that have led to the development of accounting theory.

THE ORIGINS OF ACCOUNTING THEORY

Record keeping dates back to about 3600 B.C., and some accounting concepts can be traced back to the early Greek and Roman periods. For example, a Roman architect of the early Christian era is quoted as stating that the valuation of a wall should be determined not by cost alone but only after deducting from the cost one eightieth for each year the wall has been standing.[3] While these very early records and concepts are of interest, mere record keeping adds little insight into the development of accounting theory to the present, and the concepts alone were not adequate to form a theory of accounting. Therefore, the origin of double-entry bookkeeping in about the 14th century is an appropriate starting point for a study of the development of accounting thought and accounting concepts.

The first record of a complete system of double-entry bookkeeping was found in the records of a medieval merchant of Genoa, Italy, originating about the year 1340. More recently, evidence has been found that double entry preceded this date and possibly originated simultaneously in several Italian trading centers gradually over a period of time.[4] Without going further into the recording techniques of this period, several concepts behind the method become apparent: (1) Double entry itself assumes a concept of the business entity and business relationships. (2) The fact that transactions were recorded in monetary terms implies that unlike items were compared in terms of a common monetary denominator. Thus, the assumption that economic events could be quantified in

---

[3] From Lyndon Lamarr, *Rate Making for Public Utilities* (New York: McGraw-Hill Book Co., Inc., 1923), p. 51, quoting from *Drexel Institute Monograph* by C. J. Tilden, February 16, 1916.

[4] Raymond de Roover, "The Development of Accounting Prior to Luca Pacioli according to the Account-books of Medieval Merchants," in A. C. Littleton and B. S. Yamey (eds.), *Studies in the History of Accounting* (Homewood, Ill.: Richard D. Irwin, Inc., 1956), p. 115.

terms of a monetary unit was implied from the beginning. (3) The use of expense and equity accounts implies at least a partial understanding of the distinction between capital and income. Before these concepts and techniques developed, however, certain specific antecedents in the development of knowledge were necessary.

The most important condition giving rise to the development of accounting was the rise of trade centering around the medieval Italian cities. The Crusades from the close of the 11th century to the latter part of the 13th century provided the impetus for the development of trade primarily among the Italian cities and with the East. The Crusaders needed ships and supplies and they brought back products from the East that served to stimulate the demand for such items. As trade continued to expand, wealth accumulated in the Italian cities and individual trading became largely replaced by trading through agencies and partnerships. The use of partnerships permitted the sharing of the risks of the long sea voyages and permitted the wealth of the capitalist to be combined with the daring of younger traders. In the silent partnership (*commenda*), the capital furnished by the silent partner was like a loan to the active partner, which arrangement avoided the payment of interest disapproved by the church at that time. The partnership was, therefore, important in the development of accounting because it led to the recognition of the firm as a separate entity distinct from the owners. The agency relationship was important because it required accountability.

A more basic antecedent of accounting is the ability of expression. This includes the art of writing, the development of arithmetic, and the widespread use of money as a common denominator. Although Roman numerals were used in formal accounts for several centuries after the advent of double-entry bookkeeping, the introduction of Arabic numerals greatly facilitated the growth of accounting. Imagine how cumbersome it would be to maintain ledger accounts and compute net income by the use of Roman numerals.

Some of the institutional antecedents include (1) the concept of private property, (2) the development of credit, and (3) the accumulation of capital. The existence of these antecedents, however, is not sufficient to explain the development of accounting theory. The institutions of private property and credit required records, but as a record of relationships between individuals, single entry was adequate. The joint venture and the partnership, as institutions to facilitate the accumulation and use of capital, were more influential in creating the need for the concept of the accounting entity and the necessity to compute profits.

The first published work describing the double-entry bookkeeping system and giving us insight into the reasoning behind the accounting records is the *Summa de Arithmetica, Geometria, Proportioni et Proportionalita* published by Luca Pacioli in 1494 in Venice. Pacioli was a

Franciscan friar who devoted most of his life as a teacher and scholar. His *Summa* was primarily a treatise on mathematics, but it included a section on double-entry bookkeeping. It is significant that this book was printed only some 25 years after the first printing press with movable metal type was set up in Venice. While Pacioli was not the originator of double-entry bookkeeping, his book did much to spread its use throughout all of Europe. Several books were published during the 16th century not only by Italian authors but also by German, Dutch, and English authors. The first book in Dutch was also translated into French. All of these books presented descriptions of bookkeeping similar to that presented by Pacioli and led to the spreading of the "Italian method" throughout Europe in the 16th and 17th centuries.

THE THEORY BEHIND THE ITALIAN METHOD

While we have already indicated that double entry developed logically with the growth of commerce, credit, and partnerships, there are several basic characteristics of the bookkeeping methods of the Italian cities that make interesting contrast with current methods and theory:

1. During the period prior to the 16th century, the major objective of accounting was to provide information for the owner. Pacioli stated that the purpose of bookkeeping was "to give the trader without delay information as to his assets and liabilities."[5] It also provided a means for reporting on stewardship and a basis for the granting of credit. As a result of this, the accounts were held in secrecy and there was no external pressure for accuracy or uniform standards of reporting.

2. A second characteristic related to the first was the reporting together of all of the personal and business affairs of a proprietor. Pacioli stated that the inventory should include cash, valuables, clothes, household goods, and other property possessed by the owner.[6] However, there is some evidence to support the theory that the business was recognized as a separate entity distinct from the personal affairs of the owner. Green stated that it was not infrequent to find a merchant keeping a set of books for his home and another for his shop.[7] Furthermore, Pacioli recommended that a partner's contribution of cash, property, or accounts receivable should be debited for the value of the contribution and the partner's capital account should be credited for the same amount.

3. The third characteristic was the lack of a concept of the accounting period or a continuing nature of the business enterprise. Most business

---

[5] Wilmer L. Green, *History and Survey of Accountancy* (New York: Standard Text Press, 1930), p. 91.

[6] *Ibid.,* p. 96.

[7] *Ibid.,* p. 101.

ventures were of short duration, or at least not continuous after a specific trading objective had been reached. As a result, profit was calculated only upon the completion of the venture. Without the concept of periodic profit, there was no need for accruals and deferrals. As fixed assets played only a small part in the affairs of businessmen, there was no need for the calculation of depreciation. For those businesses which were organized for longer periods of time, there was still little need for periodic computation of profit because the owners were in personal contact with the affairs of the business. Pacioli emphasized the importance of computing an inventory, but this inventory had its purpose in establishing a starting point for the business and the computation of final profit rather than as a cutoff valuation for the determination of periodic profit.

4. A fourth characteristic stems from the lack of a single stable monetary unit. Without some common denominator, double-entry bookkeeping is impossible; with many monetary units in existence during the medieval period, double entry was possible but awkward. As a result, entries in the Memorial or Day Book were quite descriptive and the inventories were explained in full detail. With respect to the Memorial, Pacioli stated that "not only was the name of the buyer or seller recorded, as well as the description of the goods with its weight, size or measurement, and price, but the terms of payment were also shown" and "wherever cash was received or disbursed, the record would show the kind of currency and its converted value. . . ."[8]

DEVELOPMENT IN THE 17TH AND 18TH CENTURIES

Starting with the close of the 15th century, the Italian cities began to decline politically and as the center of trade. With the discovery of the New World and the opening of new trade routes, the centers of commerce moved to Spain and Portugal and then to Antwerp and the Netherlands. It was natural, then, that the Italian system of double-entry bookkeeping should spread to these other countries. Little change was made in the bookkeeping techniques, however; but the writings began to show a change. According to Peragallo, during the period from 1458 to 1558,

writers were intent on setting forth the mechanics of bookkeeping as developed by business. No one attempted to develop a theory of double entry and no one went beyond the bookkeeping needs of the mercantile firm. In the second cycle, extending from 1559 to 1795, a new element appeared—the critique of bookkeeping. This was also the period when double entry extended its field of application to other types of organizations, such as monasteries and the state. With the critique and the widening sphere of bookkeeping, began theoretical research into the subject.[9]

---

[8] *Ibid.,* p. 97.

[9] Edward Peragallo, *Origin and Evolution of Double Entry Bookkeeping* (New York: American Institute Publishing Co., Inc., 1938), p. 54.

One of the significant developments early in this period was the practice of balancing the profit and loss at the end of each year rather than at the end of each venture. This led to a recommendation a half century later that balance sheets be drawn up at stated intervals. In 1673, the Code of Commerce in France required that a balance sheet be drawn up at least every two years by every businessman.[10] This development was largely a result of the fact that partnerships established for a single transaction or venture were becoming less frequent and many more businesses were organized with the purpose of establishing a continuity of manufacturing and trading over long periods of time.

The early description of double-entry bookkeeping dealt either with personal debtor and creditor relationships or with a statistical recording of impersonal items and transactions. The textbooks in the 17th and 18th centuries, however, began to personalize all accounts and transactions. This personification came about as a result of the attempt by authors to rationalize debit and credit rules when applied to impersonal and abstract accounts. Initially, all accounts represented personal relationships between merchants. With the development of double-entry bookkeeping, accounts were used for impersonal items such as "cash" and "inventory," and later the same techniques were used for abstract items such as expenses. The early terminology was clear without the use of personification, but when the term "debitor" or "debit" came to mean the left side and "creditor" or "credit" the right side, personification became necessary in order to establish general rules that would apply to all accounts.[11]

While personification, the practice of treating accounts as if they were independent, living entities, can be traced to the earliest writings on double-entry bookkeeping, it was most common in the writings of the 17th and 18th centuries; and it continued in different forms throughout most of the 19th century for setting forth the general rules of bookkeeping to be learned by rote. Because of the fictional characteristic of personification, little theory can be developed from it, and it is possible that personification hindered the development of accounting theory by the substitution of rationalization and detailed rules for logic.

Another development which originated independently from the double-entry bookkeeping methods but which was a possible source of the personification concepts is the "charge-and-discharge" method for estate accounting. The charge-and-discharge method probably originated in the early medieval period in England under the influence of the feudal system, and it was quite common in England in the 15th century. As property was held in trust, the accounting for the manors required the

---

[10] Witt Bowden, Michael Karpovich, and Abbott P. Usher, *An Economic History of Europe Since 1750* (New York: American Book Co., 1937), p. 36.

[11] A. C. Littleton, *Accounting Evolution to 1900* (New York: American Institute Publishing Co., Inc., 1933), p. 49.

concepts of agency and stewardship rather than ownership and proprietorship. The *charge* was that part of the estate entrusted to the agent.
The *discharge* was the satisfactory explanation of the disposition of the
property. This is probably the origin of the term "charge" as synonymous
with "debit."

Other important institutional and economic changes occurring during
the 17th and 18th centuries in western Europe and influencing the later
development of accounting theory include the start of the Industrial
Revolution and the growth of the joint-stock company and other forms of
organization. As the effect of these changes on accounting became mani-
fest in a later period, their entire development will be discussed below.

DEVELOPMENT IN THE 19TH AND EARLY 20TH CENTURIES

The 19th century saw a series of economic events which gave rise to a
tremendous expansion of accounting, providing the impetus for the development of a system of bookkeeping into a field of accountancy. Accounting expanded at an accelerated rate because of the rapid growth in
trade and industry, particularly in the United States and England. However, accounting theory was probably influenced to a greater extent by
the changes in the economic institutions and in the objectives and uses of
accounting data. In earlier periods, bookkeeping provided information
mainly for managerial uses; in the more complex economic society of the
19th century, financial information was also required by stockholders,
investors, creditors, and the government.

The period 1800 to 1930 is necessarily an arbitrary period and covers
many events not necessarily related to the development of accounting
theory. The year 1800 itself was not an important turning point, but the
general period was one of transformation. Although the Industrial Revolution was well on its way, many of the mechanical inventions of the 18th
century were not perfected or placed in widespread use until the 19th
century. Cartwright's power loom, for example, was patented in 1787, but
it was not entirely successful in its practical applications until some 30
years later. The turn of the century also marked a change in policy
regarding trade. The doctrines of Adam Smith's *Wealth of Nations,* published in 1776, and the influence of the physiocrats in France provided the
arguments for reducing the tariff barriers and establishing freer trade.
The first manifestation of this was the commercial treaty negotiated
between France and Great Britain in 1786. Economic changes were also
taking place in the United States, but these affected the development of
accounting less than did the economic changes taking place in Europe.

The year 1930 marks an appropriate ending for this period because in
this year the first discussions between the New York Stock Exchange and
the American Institute of Accountants (now the American Institute of

Certified Public Accountants) regarding the establishment of accounting principles began and the expanded reporting requirements of the British Companies Act of 1929 were initiated. The formal presentation of accounting theory by authoritative bodies emerged with the events that followed 1930.

The main influences on accounting theory during the period 1800 to 1930 can be classified as follows: (1) the textbook presentation of bookkeeping and the development of newer methods of teaching accounting; (2) the Industrial Revolution with its influence on cost accounting and the accounting for depreciation; (3) the growth and development of railroads; (4) government regulation of business; (5) the taxation of business; (6) the development of the corporation and the growth of industrial and financial giants through mergers; and (7) the influence of economic theory. Each of these will be discussed separately, but it must be kept in mind that accounting developed as a result of all influences simultaneously, and the discussion of the separate influencing factors is basically artificial.

The Textbook Theories of Bookkeeping and Accounting

The textbooks written prior to the 19th century were characterized in their exposition of bookkeeping by their emphasis on the journal as the most important record and the center of the system. As a result of this emphasis, the authors of these textbooks failed to obtain a broad perspective of the interrelationships of the accounts in the ledger and the financial statements. Therefore, they resorted to a long list of rules to be memorized by the student and to be followed in the preparation of journal entries. This method of teaching is exemplified in the following instructions:

First find the "case" or rule in the textbook which fits the transaction to be entered, look up the waste-book folio beside it, and trace the example through the journal and ledger.[12]

With this method of teaching came the rationalization of the rules through the personification of the accounts. This basic pattern continued throughout the 19th century in the majority of the textbooks on bookkeeping and accounting. The polemics in the field centered primarily in the type of personification which should be used to explain the accounts and the debit and credit rules. However, these writings did lead to a rejection of the journal as the center of bookkeeping and opened the way for a more complete analysis of the entire accounting structure.

The Ownership Theory of Accounts. The notion of proprietorship orig-

---

[12] J. G. C. Jackson, "The History of Methods of Exposition of Double-Entry Book-keeping in England," in Littleton and Yamey, *op. cit.*, p. 293.

inated with the attempt to place logic into the exposition of double-entry bookkeeping. Double entry itself required the concept "capital" to make the equation complete, but it did not require the central concept of ownership. The proprietorship or ownership theory places the proprietor in the central position of the equation. Assets represent things owned by the proprietor or benefits accruing to the owner; liabilities are debts of the owner. Expense and revenue accounts represent changes in proprietorship.[13] Another characteristic of the proprietorship theory is that the explanation of changes usually proceeds in terms of increases and decreases in the basic elements of the equation rather than in terms of debits and credits alone. The result is a structure based upon the accounting equation or the balance sheet rather than the journal. The journal is simply a facilitating procedure in the recording process, while the earlier personification theories explained the debits and credits in the journal and the ledger was only a final repository for these debits and credits. Therefore, the logic of the ownership theories could not gain headway as long as the ledger was subsidiary to the journal.

The widespread adoption of the ownership theory in the textbooks in the United States probably came about slowly during the last part of the 19th century and the early 20th century. However, it was presented in complete form by Sprague[14] in 1904 and 1907, by Hatfield[15] in 1909, and by Kester[16] in 1917. Baker suggested in 1935 that the ownership theory was the result of recent American teaching techniques.[17] Jackson, however, pointed out that the complete theory can be traced to earlier writings by European authors.

The Entity Theory. While the proprietorship theory was definitely a step forward in the development of a logical framework of accounting theory, it was not entirely satisfactory in its application to the corporation. The concept of the owner as the central figure for all accounting was descriptive enough of the individual proprietorship or the partnership, but the giant corporations emerging at the close of the 19th century

---

[13] The following is an example quoted from Hatfield's 1927 edition of *Accounting, Its Principles and Problems:*

"There is, in the first place, an exhibit in such detail as may seem appropriate, of the wealth owned and the debts for which the proprietor is liable; a showing of what one owns and what one owes. . . . The other aspect of business, which accounting attempts to exhibit, is the amount the proprietor is worth, and how his wealth increases or decreases from time to time." Henry Rand Hatfield, *Accounting, Its Principles and Problems* (New York: D. Appleton & Co., 1927), p. 1.

[14] Charles E. Sprague, *The Accountancy of Investment* (3d ed.; New York, 1906), pp. 5–11 (originally published in 1904), and *The Philosophy of Accounts* (New York, 1907).

[15] Henry Rand Hatfield, *Modern Accounting* (New York: D. Appleton & Co., 1909).

[16] Roy B. Kester, *Accounting Theory and Practice* (New York: Ronald Press Co., 1917), p. 67.

[17] J. W. Baker, *A History of Book-keeping Instruction in the United States* (1935), p. 19. Reference from Jackson, *op. cit.*

placed the owner or stockholder in a different position. The emergence of bondholders and several classes of stockholders and the separation of ownership from control meant that the owner could no longer be considered the direct owner of the firm's assets nor under direct obligation for the firm's liabilities.

The entity theory stresses the importance of the firm as a distinct organization separate from the activities of the owners. The fundamental equation becomes *Assets = Equities* rather than *Assets − Liabilities = Proprietorship*. The assets represent rights accruing to the firm or entity, and creditors stand in a position with stockholders as having rights in the firm or equities in the assets. The objective of accounting is to record and report the activities of the firm with respect to the utilization of the assets entrusted to it by all outsiders. Net income is usually defined as the excess of revenues over expenses incurred in the operation of the business rather than as a direct increase in proprietorship. Income remaining after the payment of dividends increases the stockholders' equity; in the proprietorship theory, revenue and expenses are defined directly as increases and decreases in proprietorship.

Littleton points out that the entity concept preceded the concept of the corporation and was implicit in the objective of some of the medieval bookkeeping.[18] Much of early bookkeeping was in the form of agency accounting for ventures and consignments. Many of the investors provided capital only, accepting the position of a partner and receiving a share of the profits only to avoid the charge of usury. The active partner was required to account for the capital entrusted to him, and the investing partner was treated as a creditor.

According to Littleton, elements of the entity theory were published as early as 1838 in Italy, 1869 in England, and 1873 in America.[19] He states, however, that

It can hardly be said that the entity theory had achieved its full stature as an organized exposition of the nature of double-entry bookkeeping prior to 1900. Much that was necessary to round out the early notions was added after the turn of the century.[20]

The major development of the entity theory is credited to German writers during the first part of the 20th century, while the American writers were still influenced primarily by the proprietorship theory. Paton is largely responsible for the expansion of the entity theory in the United States. In his 1922 edition of *Accounting Theory*, he wrote:

As commonly presented in current textbooks and other writings, the theory of accounting is saturated with the "proprietorship" concept. In fact, since the

18 Littleton, *op. cit.*, p. 193.

19 *Ibid.*, p. 194.

20 *Ibid.*, p. 200.

adoption of this expression by Sprague in his admirable "Philosophy of Accounts" most American writers have couched their explanations of the system of double entry largely in proprietary terms. . . .

In this book, accordingly, an attempt has been made to present a restatement of the theory of accounting consistent with the conditions and needs of the business enterprise *par excellence,* the large corporation, as well as applicable to the simpler, more primitive forms of organization. The conception of the business enterprise as in all cases a distinct entity or personality—an extension of the fiction of the corporate entity—is adopted, although not without important qualifications. . . .[21]

Sprague mentioned the entity theory in his 1907 edition of *The Philosophy of Accounts.*[22]

Most textbooks written since 1922 have been influenced by both the proprietary and entity concepts. The presentations, however, cannot generally be classified as purely either one or the other approach. The basic form of the entity theory is exemplified in the 1958 edition of Paton and Dixon.

The assets are the economic *resources* of the enterprise and the equities represent the *sources* of the funds—and the legal rights—reflected in the total assets. . . . Thus the basic relationship of accounting data is found in an equation of values, *assets equal equities.*[23]

Both the proprietorship theory and the entity theory were implied in accounting practice before they were stated in the literature as basic theories. When accountants took periodic inventories of all assets and liabilities of a firm in order to calculate the change in the proprietorship or net worth and thus obtain a measurement of profit, they were implying a proprietorship approach or theory. Later, when profit was measured by the matching of revenues with direct expenses and allocated costs, an entity theory was implied. The consolidation of the accounts of parent and subsidiary corporations during the late 19th and early 20th centuries also implied the concept of an entity rather than the proprietor as the central figure.

Recent developments in the basic approach to accounting theory can be found in the fund theory and in the enterprise theory, which is an extension of the entity theory. These will be discussed in Chapter 17 in connection with equities.

---

[21] William Andrew Paton, *Accounting Theory* (New York: Ronald Press Co., 1922), preface, pp. iii, iv.

[22] "The other theory adopts as its intermediary a supposed entity 'The Business.' All assets are regarded as 'owing' to The Business and The Business is regarded as owing all the 'liabilities' in which are included the proprietary claims." Charles E. Sprague, *The Philosophy of Accounts* (New York, 1907), p. 49.

[23] William A. Paton and Robert L. Dixon, *Essentials of Accounting* (New York: Macmillan Co., 1958), p. 35.

The Effect of Technological Changes

The tremendous changes in the technological methods of industry in the United States and England during the 19th and early 20th centuries had definite effects on the development of accounting thought. The direct effects were the development of the concept of depreciation and the development of cost accounting. Prior to the 19th century, depreciation was not an important concept, largely because fixed assets were not a significant aspect of commerce and industry. With the advent of the factory system and mass production, fixed assets became a sizable cost in the production and distribution process. There also arose a need for management information regarding the costs of production and the costs to be assigned to inventory valuations.

Indirect effects of technological changes include the increasing significance of the distinction between capital and income, the development of the going-concern concept, and the greater adherence to cost as the basis of asset valuation. Large requirements of capital necessitating the separation of the investor and the manager meant that one of the major objectives of accounting became the accounting to absentee owners. Thus, income as a return to investors had to be distinguished from a return of capital to the owners.

With the relative dominance of domestic production prior to 1800, heavy machinery was little used. Capital was primarily invested in inventories of raw materials, goods in the process of production, and completed products ready for marketing. Many mechanical inventions were made in the 18th century, but many of these techniques did not come into widespread use until late in the 19th century. One of the most important innovations was the development of power sources for the driving of machines. Prior to 1776, the waterwheel was the most important source of power, and it continued to be the most common source until about 1850 by which time steam power had largely supplanted it. Not until after 1914 did internal combustion and electric power make possible the dispersion of factories in areas removed from sources of coal and water power.

By the middle of the 19th century, the factory system was a common sight in England and in the United States but the industrial machines were relatively crude contraptions with still a large amount of handwork necessary. The development of the factory system expanded the use of accounting techniques to serve industrial activity; previously, accounting had served primarily commercial and financial activities. The period 1850 to 1914 marked a tremendous growth in the production of goods by mechanized and heavy equipment. As an example, the annual production of steel in the United States increased from about 20,000 tons in 1867 to about 24 million tons in 1914 and to about 56 million tons in 1929. This rapid expansion in the production of goods by mechanization and mass production represented huge investments in long-term assets.

The Development of Cost Accounting. The widespread growth of industrialization, particularly in England and the United States during the last half of the 19th century, gave rise to the development and expansion of cost accounting. The importance of this development for accounting theory is to be found in the changing concepts of inventory valuation, the allocation of overhead to products, and the adaptation of accounting records and statements to serve management as well as stockholders and creditors. In many ways the influence was slow, and cost accounting adapted itself within the framework of financial accounting rather than bringing about a rapid change in the structure and objectives of financial accounting. Particularly in the early period but continuing until the 1930's, the majority of cost accountants made their calculations based on statistical data obtained independently and not tied in with the general accounts.

While cost accounting is generally thought to have developed with industrialization and the factory system, the calculation of costs by products was found in the 14th and 15th centuries. For example, the early Florentine bookkeeping system adapted itself to the guild system with the keeping of separate records for the costs of each process. This was necessitated because the workmen belonging to different trade associations often performed the work in their own establishments. The costs, calculated, however, were only the prime costs.[24] Cost accounting is also found in the time of Henry VII of England (1485–1509), when a large number of woolen manufacturers moved from the cities to country villages and established industrial communities outside of the established guilds.[25] Without the strict restrictions of the guilds, the manufacturers found themselves competing with the guilds and among themselves, and cost records became a prerequisite for success.

Another example of the early use of cost accounting is the set of accounts belonging to the famous Antwerp printer and publisher of the 16th century, Christopher Plantin.[26] In his accounts, Plantin kept separate job accounts for each book printed, stock accounts in value and quantity for each kind of paper used, and a plant ledger. This presents an excellent example of the early development of a perpetual inventory system. Little progress in the development of cost accounting is evident

---

[24] Peragallo, *op. cit.,* p. 39.

[25] S. Paul Garner, "Historical Development of Cost Accounting," *Accounting Review,* October, 1948, p. 385; reprinted in Mary E. Murphy, *Selected Readings in Accounting and Auditing* (New York: Prentice-Hall, Inc., 1952), p. 204.

[26] Florence Edler de Roover, "Cost Accounting in the Sixteenth Century," *Accounting Review,* Vol. XII (September, 1937); reprinted in David Solomons (ed.), *Studies in Costing* (London: Sweet & Maxwell, Ltd., 1952), pp. 53–71.

during the next two centuries, although several cost systems have been found dating to the 18th century in England.[27]

It is natural to expect that a need for accurate cost information would be generated with the advent of the factory system. The domestic system emphasized the commercial aspects of the economy, while the factory system brought about a need for coordination and efficiency in production. The slow development of cost accounting during the 19th century is, then, surprising. Not until the last 20 years of the 19th century was there much literature on the subject of cost accounting in England, and even then very little was to be found in the United States. Most of the literature until this time emphasized the procedures for the calculation of prime costs only.

Several reasons for the late development of cost accounting are apparent: (1) In the early period of the factory system, costly machinery was uncommon and overhead was a small part of total cost. With the growth of heavy industry and mass production methods during the last part of the 19th century but particularly after 1914, costs other than labor and materials became a significant part of the total cost of production. (2) While many cost accountants were working on developments in their own firms, there was a tendency to keep their methods strictly secret. This deterred the spread of new ideas and is probably one of the reasons little mention is made of cost accounting in the textbooks prior to 1900. Along with the idea of secrecy there was the idea that cost problems were unique to each firm and to each industry and that publishing a firm's cost methods would be useful only to competitors. (3) Not until the late 19th and early 20th centuries did the manufacturing processes become quite complex, with one firm producing a wide variety of products. Prior to this time, management could mentally adjust the prime costs to include all other costs of producing the few products included in the firm's operations. (4) Probably most important in bringing about the development of cost accounting was the increasing use of heavy power equipment and the development of mass production techniques which made the recognition of overhead a necessity.

The most rapid development in cost accounting took place from about 1890 to about 1915. During this period, the basic structure of cost accounting was formulated and the mechanics for integrating the cost records with the general accounts were devised, although many firms did not integrate formally until after 1930. The procedures for distributing expenses to individual jobs had been well worked out.[28] Overhead allocation was common, although not necessarily integrated with the general

---

[27] Solomons, "The Historical Development of Costing," in his *Studies in Costing, op. cit.*, pp. 4–7.

[28] See for example A. Hamilton Church, *The Proper Distribution of Expense Burden* (New York: Engineering Magazine Co., 1921).

accounting records. The basic accepted concept was, however, that all actual expenses were allocable to the production process.

Of the more important influences on cost accounting during the first two decades of the 20th century were the work and writings of the so-called "scientific management" engineers. The best known of these was Frederick W. Taylor, who is sometimes considered the founder of the "scientific management" group in the United States. Other men influential in this field include Henry L. Gantt, Frank Gilbreth, Morris L. Cooke, Harrington Emerson, and the Frenchman Henri Fayol. Although most of the writings of these men appeared in the period 1900 to 1915,[29] the greatest impact on management and cost accounting did not come until after Taylor's death in 1915.

The principles of scientific management included primarily the methods and procedures for obtaining greater efficiency in production. As a means of measuring this efficiency, management and the engineers turned to the cost accountants or worked directly with them, leading to a change in emphasis from cost ascertainment to that of cost control. Cost accounting became a management tool for measuring efficiency, and accordingly required cost information before the event as well as a comparison afterwards. This led to the development of standard costs and the distinction between the "true" cost of production and the actual costs that included the costs of waste and inefficiency.

The early writers on standard costing included John Whitmore and Harrington Emerson, who were writing and lecturing in 1908 and 1909.[30] The main period of development is usually considered to be about 1916 to 1917, however, and the movement gained considerable momentum in the 1920's.

The rapid advance in cost accounting thought during the first three decades of the 20th century had a definite influence on the development of accounting theory. The integration of cost records into the financial accounts made possible an improved method for calculating income for industrial firms. Inventory valuations became more firmly rooted in the cost principle, and a better matching of revenues and expenses resulted. In the analysis of predetermined overhead rates and standard costs, a growing recognition of the difference between productive inventoriable costs and costs of inefficiency and idle capacity appeared. The emphasis on overhead costs was also partially responsible for the development of depreciation concepts.

Depreciation. The two most common early viewpoints regarding depreciation were: (1) depreciating property was accounted for as unsold merchandise—the value of the property was estimated and included in

---

[29] See for example the best known works of Frederick W. Taylor, *A Piece-Rate System* (1895), *Shop Management* (1903), *On the Art of Cutting Metals* (1906), and *The Principles of Scientific Management* (1911).

[30] Solomons, "The Historical Development of Costing," *op. cit.*, pp. 42–44.

the inventory of assets in the calculation of the proprietors' equity—and income was measured as the increase in proprietorship; and (2) depreciation was considered unnecessary so long as the property was maintained in proper working condition. Only the costs of maintenance were considered expenses of the current period. The first method was most common in manufacturing firms of the early 19th century, and the latter method was the accepted view of the railroads of the last half of the century.

Littleton points out that depreciation was not a clear concept in the writings before 1800, but in the 19th century the recognition of depreciation by the inventory method became unmistakable.[31] This treatment considered the fixed asset account as a merchandise account, debiting it at cost and crediting the account at the end of the period for the value of the property. This method was generally used by manufacturing firms throughout most of the 19th century. Depreciation as an annual deduction from cost was, however, mentioned in 1861 by W. Inglish as follows: "In such accounts (buildings and machinery), a yearly deduction of 5 and 10 per cent requires to be made from original cost, to allow for deterioration, or wear and tear."[32] This concept, however, probably represented the best practice of the time rather than the common method.

By the beginning of the 20th century, depreciation was widely accepted as a valuation concept. Mason quoted a writer in the *Accountant* of 1903 as stating:

So much has been said and written from time to time with regard to the subject of Depreciation that it would at first sight appear to be almost impossible that there existed any scope for further discussion on the matter.[33]

However, the concept was not completely understood. Even though a systematic write-off procedure had been established by many companies, depreciation was still thought of as a valuation procedure and a process of providing funds for replacement or funds for return to investors. Cole, for example, writing in 1908 stated:

Allowing for depreciation is usually called, in technical terms, "writing off." The expression means simply that the valuation formerly on the books is displaced by a new and smaller valuation.[34]

Cole then stated three policies with respect to depreciation:

. . . first, allowing the property to wear out or go to decay without replacement, on the theory that no use will ever again be had for its like; second, keeping

---

[31] Littleton, *op. cit.*, p. 225.

[32] W. Inglish, *Bookkeeping,* 1861; quoted from Littleton, *op. cit.*, p. 226.

[33] Quoted from Perry Mason, *Principles of Public-Utility Depreciation,* American Accounting Association Monograph No. 1 (Chicago: AAA, 1937), p. ix.

[34] William Morse Cole, *Accounts, Their Construction and Interpretation* (New York: Houghton Mifflin Co., 1908), p. 79.

the property up to the original standard by frequent repairs and replacements but without special provision for future replacements; third, allowing depreciation to continue to a certain point and accumulating, in the meantime, special funds to be available for replacement at whatever time it shall become necessary.[35]

The valuation concept is also present in the writings of Kester who wrote in 1917:

The difference between the present appraised value of the asset and its former value constitutes the loss through wear or other causes, and is termed depreciation.

Even though depreciation had not been widely accepted by industry as a systematic charge prior to World War I, several systematic depreciation methods had been devised and used, particularly in the public-utility field. Saliers, for example, writing in 1915 described in detail the following depreciation methods: straight-line, reducing balance method, sinking-fund and annuity methods, and unit cost method.[36]

From World War I until the early 1930's, depreciation was still a haphazard charge in the accounts of many industrial and commercial corporations. Hatfield wrote in 1927 that corporations were still apt to consider depreciation as an act of grace rather than of necessity and that the allowance was frequently less in poor years than in prosperous years. He saw considerable improvement since his first book in 1908, however. In 1908 it was uncommon for American corporations to record depreciation at all, and those who did became fainthearted when business was poor. During the 1920's, many more corporations were making charges for depreciation, even though such a charge might result in a net deficit.[37]

The Influence of Railroad Growth

The rapid development and growth of railroads in Europe and the United States during the 19th century created new problems in financing and accounting which had a definite influence on accounting thought. Railroads required a much larger investment and considerably longer lived equipment than most of the industrial activity of the mid-19th century. Both of these factors led to an increasing importance of the distinction between capital and income. During the early period of the railroad industry in the United States, it was not uncommon for promoters to pay huge dividends out of capital during the early life of the firm. Investors, believing this to be the true income of the firm, paid high

---

[35] *Ibid.*

[36] Earl A. Saliers, *Principles of Depreciation* (New York: Ronald Press Co., 1915), pp. 134–73.

[37] Hatfield, *Accounting, Its Principles and Problems, op. cit.*, p. 140.

prices for the stock only to find later that the huge dividends could not be continued without jeopardizing the future operations of the firm. When this became known, the market price of the stock would fall and the windfall gains made by the promoters and short-term speculating investors was offset by losses to the long-term investors (permanent stockholders). As a corollary to the distinction between capital and income came the concern for the maintenance of capital through depreciation or current maintenance charges.

In Great Britain the railway age began with the opening of the Liverpool and Manchester Railway line in 1830. The greatest promotion of railways came in the 1840's, and by 1870 about three fourths of the country's mileage had been completed.[38] In the United States, on the other hand, railroad construction, while important from 1830 to 1870, had its greatest growth during the period from 1878 to 1893. Growth continued at a lower rate until about 1916; after this year, little new construction was added and many small local and branch lines were abandoned. The last quarter of the 19th century saw a trend toward consolidations and the growth of great railroad systems.

Since almost the beginning of the railway age, considerable discussion centered about the allocation of expenditures between revenue and capital accounts. In England, the evidence submitted to the Select Committee on Audit of 1849 emphasized over and over again the necessity of keeping separate the two accounts of capital and revenue.[39] Some of this failure was a deliberate attempt to defraud, while most cases resulted from the absence of a clear distinction between capital and revenue expenditures. The Regulation of Railways Act of 1868 in England attempted for the first time to specify which items belonged to capital and which to revenue; however, there was still lack of uniformity after this date.

In the United States, the earliest prescribed instructions for keeping railroad accounts were issued in 1876 by the Railway Commissioners of Massachusetts.[40] An outline for a uniform system of accounts for railroads was prepared by a special committee of state commissioners and railroad accountants and adopted by all state railroad commissioners in 1879.[41] The first classification of accounts issued by the Interstate Commerce Commission appeared in 1894. However, it was not until after the Hepburn Act of 1906 that the ICC was authorized to prescribe the form

---

[38] Harold Pollins, "Aspects of Railway Accounting before 1868," in Littleton and Yamey, *op. cit.,* p. 332.

[39] *Ibid.,* p. 340.

[40] Percival F. Brundage, "Influence of Government Regulation on Development of Today's Accounting Practices," *Journal of Accountancy,* Vol. XC (November, 1950), p. 384.

[41] Edward H. Bunnell, *Railroad Accounting and Statistics* (Chicago: Watson Publications, Inc., 1955), p. 17.

and substance of uniform accounts for railways coming under its jurisdiction. Accordingly, a revised "Classification of Operating Expenses" was issued in 1907 and a complete "Accounting Classifications for Steam Railroads" became effective in 1914.

The early concern for a clear distinction between capital and revenue expenditures by the railroads caused considerable controversy over the recording of depreciation and other methods of providing for capital maintenance. Until the latter part of the 19th century a wide variety of methods intended to provide for the maintenance of capital was in use both in England and in the United States.[42] Toward the end of this period, the most commonly accepted method among railroad firms in the United States and England was the "replacement" or "renewal" method whereby all replacement expenditures were charged to expense at the date of the replacement or renewal; the original cost of the asset was not depreciated. The initial invested capital was assumed to be maintained permanently by regular expenditures for repairs and renewals. The property of a railroad company was considered so diverse that renewals were assumed to be made continuously and in amounts at least equal to what depreciation would have been if it had been accrued.

Prior to 1907, the prescribed account classifications provided for the charging of replacements and renewals to operating expenses without deductions for depreciation. Under the provisions of the 1907 classifications prescribed by the ICC, however, provisions for monthly charges to operating expenses for depreciation on various classes of equipment were included. But the Commission's regulations contained optional provisions that permitted the individual carriers to use their own discretion regarding the desirability or necessity for such accruals after taking into consideration such things as the financial condition of the carrier. In 1923, the Bureau of Accounts of the ICC proposed the mandatory setting up of depreciation accounts and reserves, which immediately met with opposition from the railroads. In hearings before the ICC, railroad executives stated:

. . . that it is not necessary to set up depreciation reserves for the purpose of equalizing retirements; that any such plan as the commission has tentatively proposed would result in such large reserves as to be uneconomical at this time; but, if the commission thinks the act is mandatory, which was not admitted, depreciation accounts should be confined to the larger and more costly structures. The executives argued that there is no appreciable depreciation in the fixed property in an operated railroad as a whole so long as it is properly maintained and kept in condition for efficient operation, and that where replacements of the individual units are timely and properly made there does not exist any ascertainable loss of service life in the composite property.

---

[42] See Pollins, *op. cit.*, p. 343; and Perry Mason, "Illustrations of the Early Treatment of Depreciation," *Accounting Review*, September, 1933, pp. 209–13.

As a practical matter, there is the perfectly obvious difficulty of determining correct or even approximately accurate rates for such theoretical depreciation. Structures, if kept in repair, by an intelligent program of current renewals of component parts, do not depreciate, but may be maintained indefinitely.[43]

This opposition was apparently sufficient to delay the mandatory use of accrual depreciation. Not until 1932 did the ICC order depreciation applied on a straight-line basis; but even then, the order was suspended because of the depression, and the railroads were permitted to omit depreciation and even exclude retirements and repairs from the operating expenses in the computation of net income.[44] The order, modified to some extent, was finally put into effect in 1943, but the practice of charging to expense the cost of new replacements of items retired as a substitute for depreciation is still used for rails, ties, and ballast.

The above brief summary of railroad accounting prior to 1930 is sufficient to see that the rapid growth of railroads during the 19th century had a definite effect in helping to clarify the concepts of capital and income and was influential in the development of the concept of depreciation. It is noteworthy, however, that railroads were late in accepting accrual depreciation. The system of accounts prescribed by the Interstate Commerce Commission in 1907 was in many respects superior to the current accounting practice at that time. Because of a resistance to change by both the Commission and the railroad executives, however, the uniform system of accounts soon became outdated. Through voluntary cooperation of the New York Stock Exchange, the Securities and Exchange Commission, and the American Institute of Certified Public Accountants with the ICC, most of the differences between railway accounting and "generally accepted accounting principles" have been corrected. In 1957, five of six remaining major variations between railroad accounting and accounting in other businesses were eliminated.[45] Subsequently, the ICC ruled that railroads need not follow ICC procedures in their outside reporting, so that independent accountants can insist that the railroads follow "generally accepted accounting principles" except in their reports to the ICC.

The Influence of Government Regulatory Bodies in the United States

The regulation of privately owned public service corporations, a unique process found only in the United States, has had its influence upon accounting thought, on the one hand, by forcing the regulated firms

---

[43] "Railroads Oppose Depreciation Rules," *Railway Age,* Vol. LXXV (November 24, 1923), pp. 976, 977.

[44] Brundage, *op. cit.,* p. 388.

[45] Editorial, *Journal of Accountancy,* May, 1957, pp. 25–26, and June, 1957, pp. 8, 10.

to adopt up-to-date accounting practices and uniform systems which lead to better interfirm comparisons. On the other hand, regulation and the demand for uniformity have brought about a stifling of independent research and experimentation by the independent companies. The usual historical development of regulatory commissions followed this pattern: first, they operated primarily as an information gathering body; later, they added the objective of controlling the accounting procedures through uniform systems of accounts; and finally, they became rate controlling bodies using accounting data as the main control mechanism.

The commissions that prescribe uniform systems of accounts include the several state regulatory commissions, the Interstate Commerce Commission, the Federal Power Commission, the Federal Communications Commission, and (in a less rigid form) the Securities and Exchange Commission. The control of railroads by the ICC has already been discussed, and the influence of the SEC will be treated in the following chapter, because its growth and influence have come in the period since 1930.[46] Accordingly, this section is restricted primarily to the regulation of public-utility firms furnishing electric, telephone, gas, or local transportation services. Other businesses affected with a public interest have been partially regulated by government bodies such as the Federal Trade Commission, but this type of regulation has not had as significant an influence on the development of accounting theory and practice.

Government regulation of public service corporations had its first impact on the railroad industry even though commercial gas distribution had started as early as 1816. The growth of railroads in the United States began during the 1830's, the telephone industry started about 1880, and the electric industry had its origin in 1882. Prior to the establishment of the ICC in 1887 and even until 1907, the primary function of the state commissions was to gather information for legislative action. Although extensive powers previously had been given to several state commissions, state commission regulation of public utilities began about 1907.[47] In this year, Wisconsin extended the jurisdiction of its railroad commission to include other public service corporations and New York established two commissions with jurisdiction over railroads, street railroads, common carriers, and gas and electric utilities.[48] State regulation by commissions soon spread to the other states. The National Association of Railroad and Utilities Commissioners formulated uniform classifications of accounts for electric and gas utilities in cooperation with the National Electric Light Association and the American Gas Association and recommended

---

[46] The FPC was also established after 1930, but the basic principles of regulation of public utilities had already been developed by state commissions.

[47] J. Rhoads Foster and Bernard S. Rodey, *Public Utility Accounting* (New York: Prentice-Hall, Inc., 1951), p. 26.

[48] *Ibid.*

these to the state commissions in 1922. Many commissions adopted these classifications without modification, and some adopted them with only slight modifications. In 1935, the Federal Power Commission was formed, with jurisdiction over companies owning facilities for transmitting or selling electricity in interstate commerce and over gas companies transporting or selling natural gas in interstate commerce. In 1936 a revised uniform system of accounts was recommended by the NARUC and adopted by the Federal Power Commission. The Federal Communications Commission, to which the jurisdiction over telephone companies had been transferred from the ICC in 1934, also adopted a revised uniform system of accounts in 1936.

The regulation of public utilities has not led particularly in the development of accounting thought. Rather, it has developed accounting along with the general development in unregulated firms, in some cases accelerating the development by requiring uniform procedures and in other cases retarding the development by holding to outmoded procedures. In general, discussions centering around accounting for regulation have been stimulating in the development of accounting theory. Many ideas regarding the distinction between capital and income expenditures and the various methods and concepts of depreciation have been brought out by the discussions of public utility accounting such as the "fair value" doctrine established by the *Smyth* v. *Ames* Supreme Court case in 1898. In this case the Court decided that investors should be permitted to earn a fair return on the fair value of the property invested rather than on its historical cost, thus introducing to accounting the concepts of replacement cost and reproduction costs. Considerable controversy followed regarding the meaning of *fair value* and *fair rate of return* until the decision was finally reversed in the *Federal Power Commission* v. *Hope Natural Gas Company* in 1944. Following this decision of the Supreme Court, the majority of the commissions expressed a preference for either original cost or prudent investment as the rate base.[49] Original cost, however, was required in the accounts by many commissions at a much earlier period. The concept sometimes referred to as *aboriginal cost* or cost at the time the property was first devoted to the public service was first adopted by the Wisconsin Commission in 1931.

Another concept important in the development of accounting theory is the concept of *utility operating income*, which is the return available to investors. This is sometimes referred to as the concept of *above and below the line*. All expenses chargeable against the consumers for services rendered are included "above the line." Deductions such as capital losses, interest, and donations are included "below the line." This is an example of the enterprise concept of income as opposed to the proprietary concept

---

[49] Foster and Rodey, *op. cit.,* p. 33.

expressed as "income to stockholders." Interest is included as a distribution of net income rather than a determination of it. A distinction is also made between utility income and nonutility income, but this distinction has greater relevance for public utility regulation than for nonregulated firms although it represents an early attempt to measure income for a specific class of business within a firm.

The Influence of Income Taxation

There is little question that the main objective of accounting for many small businesses is the preparation of the income tax return. Many firms did not keep records before they were necessary for tax purposes. Even for large corporations the taxation of income is a major problem for accountants. There is little wonder, then, that income tax regulations have been influential in establishing general procedures in accounting. And these procedures, in turn, have contributed to the formulation of accounting theory. On the other hand, many differences between the determination of income for tax purposes and the computation of income for financial purposes have resulted from differences in basic concepts and objectives.

Taxation of personal incomes was tried in Great Britain as early as 1799 and in the United States in 1862. Both of these, however, were short-lived. Current taxation of incomes in Great Britain dates from 1842, and in the German states from 1890. In the United States, however, taxation of corporate incomes began with the corporate excise tax law of 1909 and taxation of personal incomes became possible with the passage of the Sixteenth Amendment to the Constitution in 1913.

The 1909 Excise Act provided for a franchise tax on corporation net income, measured by cash receipts and cash disbursements. The act provided for a tax amounting to 1 percent of all net incomes received in excess of $5,000 after deducting expenses actually paid, losses actually sustained but not compensated by insurance, and a reasonable allowance for depreciation of property, if any. Reasonable compliance with the cash receipts and disbursements provision was not practicable because it was not in accordance with conventional accounting practice, and therefore it was never enforced. The Treasury Department soon issued regulations under which the corporations paid taxes on the basis of accrued income and expenses, which had been the accepted accounting procedure for many years before 1909.

The Revenue Act of 1913 also provided for the calculation of taxable net income on the basis of cash receipts and disbursements. But this too was met with considerable opposition and was interpreted by Treasury regulations to imply the acceptance of the accrual of income and expenses. The result was accomplished by the rulings that the words "paid" and "actually paid" did not necessarily contemplate actual disbursements and that deductions might be taken if the liability had been incurred and recognized in the taxpayers' books.[50] The act of 1916 was a step in the right direction by permitting that returns could be made on the basis on which the corporation kept its books if such method clearly reflected income. But together with the excess profits tax law of 1917, the procedures expressed were not completely workable.

The 1918 act was the first to recognize accepted accounting procedures in the determination of taxable income. Section 212(b) of this act stated in part:

The net income shall be computed upon the basis of the taxpayer's annual accounting period (fiscal year or calendar year, as the case may be) in accordance with the method of accounting regularly employed in keeping the books of such taxpayer; but if no such method of accounting has been so employed, or if the method employed does not clearly reflect the income, the computation shall be made upon such basis and in such manner as in the opinion of the Commissioner does clearly reflect the income.

While this policy has been reflected in each act since 1918, exceptions to the policy stated in the acts and the administration of the acts have created major differences between taxable income and financial income.

The intent of Congress in passing the act of 1918 was clearly to establish the closest possible harmony between tax accounting and general financial accounting.[51] The act stated that "approved standard methods of accounting will ordinarily be regarded as clearly reflecting income." The regulations also reflected this same philosophy and, in fact, included an outline of accepted accounting methods then recognized. With respect to inventories, the act provided that—

Whenever in the opinion of the Commissioner the use of inventories is necessary in order clearly to determine the income of any taxpayer, inventories shall be taken by such taxpayer upon such basis as the Commissioner, with the approval of the Secretary, may prescribe as conforming as nearly as may be to the best accounting practice in the trade or business and as most clearly reflecting income.

Since 1918 many differences between tax accounting and financial accounting have developed. Many of these differences have arisen as a result of a modification of the general concepts of income underlying the statutes and to close loopholes in the act, while other differences reflect the use of the tax laws to effect social reform or grant relief to specific

---

[50] George O. May, "Accounting and the Accountant in the Administration of Income Taxation," *Columbia Law Review,* Vol. XLVII (April, 1947), p. 379.

[51] Dan Throop Smith and J. Keith Butters, *Taxable and Business Income* (New York: National Bureau of Economic Research, Inc., 1949), "Historical Foreword" by George O. May, p. xix.

industries as a result of political pressures, or an attempt to attain equitable treatment.

The revenue acts and the Treasury regulations have not directly been responsible for much advance in accounting theory. The attempt in 1918 was to accept the best accounting practice of the time as the basis for determining taxable income, but there has been no attempt to improve upon the income theory implicit in the acts. Rather, the reluctance to change and the introduction of deviations and exceptions have led tax practice away from the best current accounting practice. Indirectly, however, the tax laws have been responsible for the development of accounting thought. *First,* the laws were important in bringing the average accounting practice up to the standards of the better practices of the times. This created an improvement in general accounting practices and in the maintenance of consistency. *Second,* the provision for depreciation included in the 1909 act and subsequent acts gave rise to the use of systematic depreciation methods, a search for better depreciation concepts, and more appropriate methods of calculating depreciation cost. *Third,* the requirement in the 1918 act making inventories mandatory where necessary in the determination of income brought about widespread discussion relating to the appropriate methods of inventory valuation. *Fourth,* the acceptance of cost or market, whichever is lower, in the valuation of inventories in the early regulations led to a general adoption of this procedure and to discussions regarding the propriety of the concept. *Fifth,* court cases regarding tax law have had considerable influence upon the development of accounting concepts. For example, in *Eisner* v. *Macomber,* the U.S. Supreme Court decided that a dividend in the corporation's common stock paid to common stockholders was not income.[52] This decision supported the view that profits exist only when the increment in wealth is realized.[53]

In more recent years, the income tax rules have had a considerable adverse effect on accounting theory and principles. The tendency to accept income tax provisions as accepted accounting principles and practices is unfortunate. The following are examples: (1) Any depreciation method acceptable for tax purposes is acceptable for accounting purposes also, regardless of whether or not it follows good accounting theory in the situation. (2) Lifo must be used for financial reporting purposes if it is used in the tax return. (3) Items (e.g., research and development expenditures) that should be capitalized in some cases are charged to expense to obtain the earliest possible tax deduction. (4) Since the tax law does not permit it, no provision is generally made for "accru-

---

[52] *Eisner* v. *Macomber,* 252 U.S. 189 (1920).

[53] See, for example, Henry Rand Hatfield, *Accounting, Its Principles and Problems, op. cit.,* p. 251.

ing" repair and maintenance expenses except indirectly and haphazardly through accelerated depreciation.

In summary, the effect on accounting theory of taxation of business incomes in the United States and in other countries has been considerable, but it has been primarily indirect in nature. The tax laws themselves have not pioneered in accounting thought. While the revenue acts did hasten the adoption of good accounting practices and thus brought about a more critical analysis of accepted accounting procedures and concepts, they have also been a deterrent to experimentation and the acceptance of good theory.

The Influence of the Corporation

Some of the influences of the corporate form of business organization on accounting theory have been direct. Other influences have been indirect and arose basically from the same factors that gave rise to the development of the corporation. Few basic ideas in accounting theory can be traced solely to the corporate form.

The concept of enterprise continuity preceded the corporation and was found in the partnership and joint-stock company forms of organization. However, the corporation provided a more effective instrument for the investment of capital over indefinite periods of time. The need for large amounts of capital was an outgrowth of the mechanization of industry and the development of the factory system and mass production. While the large requirements of capital necessitated a distinction between capital and income expenditures in order to permit an evaluation of current operations, the formation of the corporation made this even more important because of the ease of transferring ownership in the corporation, and thus the need to establish a price for the stock based on expectations regarding the future operations of the firm.

With the concept of enterprise continuity came the need for the maintenance of capital and the necessity for appropriate depreciation provisions in the determination of income. A corporation could not have an indefinite life and dissipate its capital by payments to stockholders in excess of income. The responsibility for measuring and reporting this income was assigned to the accountants. But with the advent of limited liability for corporate stockholders, the obligation to preserve the invested capital intact became a legal requirement as well as an accounting problem. Because stockholders have no liability for corporate debts, the creditor lost his right to claim the personal assets of the owners but he gained the right to the protection of his claim against corporate assets. This protection was provided in corporation laws by requiring a minimum of invested capital which could not be diminished by payments to stockholders.

The corporation also provided the advantages of greater specialization of the functions of the owner, creditor, and manager than could be obtained in the partnership or joint-stock company. This specialization led to the greater need for more information regarding the financial status and activities of the business. As long as the owner was also the manager, he had available considerable knowledge of the activities of the firm, particularly when the business was relatively small. With the growth in size of the firm and the divorce of ownership and management, the stockholders required more accurate and more complete accounting reports. Because of the limited liability granted to corporate stockholders, creditors also became more interested in the accounting reports of the corporation. In more recent years, the professionalization of management has created a need for accounting information which can be useful for management decisions.

The absence of stockholder liability and continuity of enterprise were the basic characteristics of the corporation which led to the entity theory of the firm. This concept stressed the separateness of the enterprise and the owners. Accounting under the entity concept is concerned with reporting to all interested parties who have contributed property to the operations of the business.

The historical development of the corporate concept has been traced to the problems of the church and the English borough. By the 15th century the corporate concept had developed in the church and later found its way into English and American legal doctrine.[54] The corporate characteristics common to the medieval church and borough were the idea of continuity separate from the lives of individual persons, the concept of each being a separate entity, the ownership of property by the entity, and the idea of no liability of individuals arising from activities of the entity.

Some of these characteristics, however, were found at an earlier date in the medieval partnership *en commendite* of the Italian cities in the 12th and 13th centuries. Under this form of organization, an investing partner could obtain a share of the profits of the venture without being liable beyond the amount of his contribution. This concept of limited partnership prevailed on the continent of Europe, but in England, all partners were jointly responsible to creditors.[55]

Starting with the 16th century, the common form of business organization for large enterprises in England was the joint-stock company. One of the earliest and most noted of these was the East India Company, chartered by Elizabeth I in 1600. The first continuous capital of the company was established in 1613, and the concept of permanently in-

---

[54] Norman S. Buchanan, *The Economics of Corporate Enterprise* (New York: Henry Holt & Co., Inc., 1940), pp. 65, 68.

[55] Littleton, *op. cit.*, p. 248.

vested capital was established by its charter of 1657. Throughout the
17th century, many joint-stock companies were formed by royal charter
or by special acts of Parliament. During the early part of the 18th
century, several of the large firms were linked with the public budget,
giving rise to the Bubble Act of 1720. This act declared illegal the raising
of funds or organizing without legal authority. More important, however,
was the fact that the act was used as an expression of policy to restrain
the formation of business corporations. The effect of the act was to
decrease the number of incorporations under royal charter and by acts of
Parliament and to arrest the development of joint-stock companies.
Businessmen, instead, took the risk of establishing unincorporated organizations. The Bubble Act was repealed in 1825.

General expansion of the corporate form of organization in England
was made possible by the Joint Stock Companies Act of 1844, which was
the first provision for incorporation by registration but with unlimited
liability. This act provided for the periodical balancing of the accounts
and the presentation of a "full and fair" balance sheet to stockholders.[56]
General registration with limited liability was first introduced in the act
of 1855 and in the more complete Companies Act of 1862. This latter act
was not materially changed until 1908. During this period, the general
principle with regard to accounting matters was basically one of non-
interference. In the acts of 1900 and 1908, a trend was started toward the
requirement of increasing amounts of specific and general financial disclosures in annual returns of corporations in the United Kingdom and in
other countries influenced by the British laws.

In Germany, speculation in corporation shares in the 1870's led to
early regulations regarding financial accounting. The German Companies
Act of 1884 required companies to declare their profits and present
balance sheets with assets valued at cost or the lower of cost or market.[57]

In the United States, the corporate form of organization was practically unused for business purposes prior to the beginning of the 19th
century. Prior to 1800, only 335 profit-seeking firms had been incorporated, all originating during the last decade of the 18th century.[58] These
firms were organized to carry out activities involving primarily a direct
public interest, including the construction of turnpikes, bridges, and
canals; the operation of banks and insurance companies; and the creation
of fire brigades.[59] The first important manufacturing firm to incorporate
in the United States was organized in Massachusetts in 1813. And until

---

[56] H. C. Edey and Prot Panitpakdi, "British Company Accounting and the Law,
1844–1900," in Littleton and Yamey, *op. cit.*, p. 356.

[57] Eugen Schmalenbach, *Dynamic Accounting* (London: Gee & Co., 1959), p. 17.

[58] Adolf A. Berle, Jr. and Gardiner C. Means, *The Modern Corporation and
Private Property* (New York: Macmillan Co., 1933), p. 10.

[59] *Ibid.*

1860, the corporate form was little used in manufacturing except among textile firms.

One of the more important uses of the corporation prior to 1860 was in the building of railroads. Following the Civil War, the corporate form soon became dominant among American railroads. By 1930, consolidation and competition among railroads had resulted in 86.6 percent of the first-class mileage being operated by 14 great railroad corporations.[60] From the close of the Civil War until the beginning of the 20th century, the corporate form spread rapidly among mining and quarrying and manufacturing firms. Mining and quarrying firms were 86 percent incorporated in 1902 and 94 percent incorporated in 1919. Manufacturing firms were 67 percent incorporated in 1899 and over 90 percent incorporated by 1930.[61]

During the early period of incorporation in the United States, a firm obtained its charter by direct negotiation with the state legislatures. The first incorporation act was passed in New York in 1811 with respect to manufacturing firms. However, the first modern statute permitting incorporation for any lawful business appeared in Connecticut in 1837. Between this date and 1900, most of the other states passed similar laws.

An interesting aspect of the early corporation laws was their requirement that dividends should not be paid out of capital. New York, for example, provided that the directors would be guilty of a misdemeanor if the dividends were not paid out of profits "arising from the operation of the business."[62] Only after the beginning of the 20th century did the concept of "paid-in surplus" come into existence. At this time, the corporation laws of most states were revised to permit only a portion of the contributed capital to be set up as capital and the balance to be designated "paid-in surplus." Thus paid-in surplus became generally available for the payment of dividends, as is the case today in many states. However, with the adoption of the 1962 Model Corporation Code by many states, the source of such dividends must be disclosed.

The historical development of the corporation during the latter part of the 19th century and early 20th century gave rise to new institutions and new relationships which in turn were to influence the development of accounting thought. Of these new developments, the more important include the development of the holding company as a common form of organization, the formation of the New York Stock Exchange, and the investment in American corporations by foreign investors and American investment abroad.

The growth and development of the holding company was partially an outgrowth of the Sherman Antitrust Act of 1890. Prior to this time, only

---

[60] *Ibid.,* p. 13.

[61] *Ibid.,* p. 14.

[62] *Ibid.,* p. 147.

a few corporations had the authority to own stock in other corporations, as this required individual special legislative action. The Sherman Act had the effect of outlawing the trustee device as a means of controlling several corporations, so other means of accomplishing the same objectives were attempted. In 1893 the New Jersey legislature amended its corporation laws permitting a corporation to own shares of other corporations. While this form was also permitted by other states, the holding company device was not successful in circumventing the Sherman Act, as evidenced by the decisions of the Supreme Court in the Northern Securities case of 1904 and the Standard Oil Company case in 1911. And the Clayton Act of 1914 made illegal the acquisition of stock in another corporation where such acquisition should tend to result in a lessening of competition.

Despite the failure to circumvent the Sherman and Clayton acts by means of the holding company, this form continued to grow in importance in the consolidation of enterprises which were largely noncompeting. While the first consolidated accounts were prepared as early as 1886,[63] they were not in common usage until the first decade of the 20th century. The rapid growth in the use of consolidated statements dates from the inception of the United States Steel Corporation in 1901. The first full report of the steel corporation in 1902 was not only an example of consolidation but it has also been hailed as the first really modern type of annual report which attempted to provide adequate financial information to stockholders.[64]

Some of the important ideas arising from the development of consolidated statements include the concept of the economic entity, problems of goodwill arising from consolidation, extension of the realization postulate to cover the economic unit rather than the firm, and discussions relating to the classification and presentation of stockholder equity.

While the New York Stock Exchange was organized as early as 1792 for the purpose of facilitating the exchange of corporate securities and governmental bonds, it did not attempt to obtain financial statements from listed companies until about 1866.[65] However, it met with little success until, in 1900, it requested that all companies applying for listing on the Exchange agree to publish annual reports of their financial condition and operating results. This agreement was expanded in 1926 to require all listed companies to publish and submit to stockholders an annual financial report prior to the annual meeting. From 1926 to 1933, the main emphasis of the Exchange was on the obtaining of adequate

---

[63] Maurice E. Peloubet, "The Historical Background of Accounting," from *Handbook of Modern Accounting Theory* edited by Morton Backer (New York: Prentice-Hall, Inc., 1955), fn. to p. 31.

[64] B. Bernard Greidinger, *Preparation and Certification of Financial Statements* (New York: Ronald Press Co., 1950), p. 4.

[65] *Ibid.*, p. 6.

disclosure of financial information for stockholders. The New York Stock Exchange was, therefore, influential in the development of accounting thought relating to the adequate disclosure of financial information through the presentation of financial statements.

The Influence of Economic Theory

The importance of economic theory as a general background for accounting and as a basis for the development of accounting theory was recognized in 1930, and before. An editorial in the *Journal of Accountancy* in that year stated ". . . it does not require any great stretch of imagination to regard economics as a vital part of the theory of accounts."[66] However, there is little evidence that accounting theory had been influenced to any considerable extent by economic theory prior to 1930. The influences that can be found are only indirect and not a result of any conscientious effort to borrow from economics.

The fields of accounting and economics developed during the 19th century and early 20th century independently of each other. The accountant was interested in obtaining information useful to owner-managers of enterprises and creditors and later to stockholders as a separate group. Economists were interested primarily in pricing and distribution problems and the effect of the firm on the economy. The problems of the two groups did not really cross until the second and third decades of the 20th century in the development of cost accounting methods.

However, many of the writers of accounting literature gave recognition to the relationship between accounting and economics and the similarity of some of the problems. For example, in 1917, Kester pointed out that the problem of the enterpriser is that of production and exchange and the distribution of the estimated returns to those who have contributed to its production:

And more and more as it has been necessary to make this distribution on the basis of estimated returns, has the need, the absolute necessity, for an accurate record of the costs of the activities and processes all along the line become apparent to him. The record, then, of the value of the rights of the various parties to this product, is the special field of work assigned to accountancy.[67]

The early discussions of cost accounting were influenced to some extent by the analysis of economists. Paton and Stevenson, for example, wrote in 1918:

. . . the manager might view the cost of production in the same light as does the economist who considers cost to mean the total *economic* cost, including

---

[66] Editorial, *Journal of Accountancy*, Vol. XLIX (June, 1930), p. 404.

[67] Kester, *op. cit.*, p. 13.

interest and profits at the margin, necessary for the production of a particular product. . . .

Several recent discussions of the subject clearly show the impropriety of charging to expense arbitrary sums which will naturally bear no very close relation to rates actually realized year by year by the specific concern (which charges are adjusted by concurrent fictitious credits to revenue). The doctrine seems to have been due to a confusion of commercial concepts and practice with certain ideas of economic theory, and appears to be losing adherents.[68]

Another area of accounting literature influenced by the writings of economists has been the problem of asset valuation and the determination of income by the comparison of asset valuations. For example, Paton stated in 1922:

A consideration of the relation of the class, "properties," to the economist's concept, "wealth," will serve to throw some light upon the fundamental nature of this accounting category. In general it may be said that anything which can constitute wealth may, under certain circumstances, become an asset to the accountant.[69]

Paton then continued by describing the similarities and differences between the accounting and economic concepts of wealth and capital. Hatfield drew considerably from the field of economics in his discussion of wealth and income. For example, he stated:

It is a common assumption that profits exist only when the increment in wealth is realized. In this opinion there is rather unusual agreement of many accountants, jurists, and economists.[70]

Several authors have been influential by discussing areas of interest to both accountants and economists. The most important of these works written prior to 1930 are a book on the economic problems of cost accounting by J. M. Clark[71] and an analysis of accounting theory and procedure from the point of view of the economist written by John B. Canning.[72]

Since 1930, there have been several attempts to borrow from the economists some of the aspects of marginal cost analysis, some of the valuation concepts, and some of the concepts of capital maintenance and income particularly in discussions relating to price-level adjustments.

---

[68] William Andrew Paton and Russell Alger Stevenson, *Principles of Accounting* (New York: Macmillan Co., 1918), pp. 614–15.

[69] Paton, *Accounting Theory, op. cit.*, p. 33.

[70] Hatfield, *Accounting, Its Principles and Problems, op. cit.*, p. 251. His major economic reference was to Irving Fisher's *Capital and Income.*

[71] J. M. Clark, *Studies in the Economics of Overhead Cost* (Chicago: University of Chicago Press, 1923).

[72] John B. Canning, *The Economics of Accountancy* (New York: Ronald Press Co., 1929).

SUMMARY

This chapter has presented the major historical developments that have been responsible for the development of current accounting theory. Accounting thought has evolved, like most disciplines, gradually over many years. Few new ideas are so revolutionary as to change completely any body of thought. This is particularly so in the field of accounting theory, where change is somewhat dependent upon the acceptance of ideas by a vast number of accounting practitioners. While some professional accountants have been leaders in the development of accounting thought, accountants as a group have been slow to accept new ideas unless there has been a definite tax advantage in so doing.

No attempt, however, has been made to discuss all of the possible influences and development which helped to bring about changes in accounting and accounting thought. The development of auditing in the United States and Great Britain no doubt was responsible for many advances in the field of theory. However, no attempt has been made in this chapter to explore the expansion of auditing and the accounting theory implicit in auditing principles developed prior to 1930. The demands of foreign investors in American enterprise were a great stimulus to the field of auditing, and in turn an impetus to the development of accounting thought.

Associations of accountants and particularly of public accountants have certainly also been influential in the development of accounting thought. In the United Kingdom, the first formal association of accountants was the Society of Accountants of Edinburgh incorporated by royal charter in 1854. In 1951, it merged with other Scottish bodies to form the Institute of Chartered Accountants of Scotland. The Scottish Institute and the Institute of Chartered Accountants in England and Wales, incorporated by royal charter in 1880, have been the two most influential bodies in the development of accounting thought in Great Britain and their influence has spread to many other countries. In the United States, the American Association of Public Accountants was organized in 1887 and was reorganized as the Institute of Accountants in the United States; the name was changed in 1917 to the American Institute of Accountants, and in 1957 to the American Institute of Certified Public Accountants. In 1917 the American Institute of Accountants cooperated with the Federal Reserve Board and the Federal Trade Commission in attempting to improve the form and content of financial reports of industrial and commercial corporations. The resulting bulletins on balance sheet audits and the preparation of financial statements had a considerable influence on the steps taken in the 1930's to develop "generally accepted accounting principles."

Current accounting theory is largely a result of institutional changes of the 19th and 20th centuries and accounting literature written almost entirely in the 20th century. The main institutional changes include changes in technology, growth of railroad transportation, the development of the corporation, regulation of quasi-public corporations, and the taxation of corporate and personal incomes. Among American writers, the development of accounting theory prior to 1930 is indebted to such people as Sprague, Cole, Hatfield, Paton, and Canning, not to mention a large number of other writers who contributed to accounting thought in textbooks and the journals.

Since 1930, accounting theory has made great strides. The American Institute of Certified Public Accountants and the American Accounting Association have fostered research and discussions that have been very fruitful. The Securities and Exchange Commission and the Regulatory Bodies have been influential. And a large number of books and articles have now formed a definite field of accounting theory. The effect of recent polemics, however, is difficult to evaluate, and it will be several years before many of the occurrences of this recent period can be placed in their proper perspective. The next chapter reviews primarily this period from 1930 to the present, but the polemics and discussions of specific developments in accounting theory are treated in the appropriate chapters following.

SELECTED ADDITIONAL READING ON CHAPTER TOPICS

Early Accounting History

Brown, R. Gene, and Kenneth S. Johnston. *Paciolo on Accounting.* New York: McGraw-Hill Book Co., Inc., 1963.

de Roover, Raymond. "New Perspectives on the History of Accounting," *Accounting Review,* Vol. XXX (July, 1955), pp. 405–20.

———. "The Development of Accounting Prior to Luca Pacioli according to the Account-books of Medieval Merchants," *Studies in the History of Accounting* (eds. A. C. Littleton and B. S. Yamey), pp. 114–74. Homewood, Ill.: Richard D. Irwin, Inc., 1956.

Edwards, James Don. "Early Bookkeeping and Its Development into Accounting," *Business History Review,* Vol. XXXIV (Winter, 1960), pp. 446–58.

Geijsbeek, John B. *Ancient Double Entry Bookkeeping,* pp. 8–16. Denver, Colo.: John B. Geijsbeek, 1914.

Green, Wilmer L. *History and Survey of Accountancy,* chap. iii. New York: Standard Text Press, 1930.

Littleton, A. C. *Accounting Evolution to 1900,* chap. ii. New York: American Institute Publishing Co., Inc., 1933.

―― and V. K. ZIMMERMAN. *Accounting Theory: Continuity and Change*, pp. 1–102. Englewood Cliffs, N.J.: Prentice-Hall, Inc., 1962.

PELOUBET, MAURICE E. "The Historical Background of Accounting," *Modern Accounting Theory* (ed. MORTON BACKER), pp. 5–27. Englewood Cliffs, N.J.: Prentice-Hall, Inc., 1966.

PERAGALLO, EDWARD. *Origin and Evolution of Double Entry Bookkeeping*, pp. 98–120. New York: American Institute Publishing Co., Inc., 1938.

Exposition and Concepts in the Nineteenth Century

JACKSON, J. G. C. "The History of Methods of Exposition of Double-Entry Book-keeping in England," *Studies in the History of Accounting* (eds. A. C. LITTLETON and B. S. YAMEY), pp. 288–312.

LITTLETON, A. C. *Accounting Evolution to 1900*, chaps. xi and xii.

Influence of the Corporate Form on Accounting

EDEY, H. C., and PROT PANITPAKDI. "British Company Accounting and the Law, 1844–1900," *Studies in the History of Accounting* (eds. A. C. LITTLETON and B. S. YAMEY), pp. 356–79.

LITTLETON, A. C. *Accounting Evolution to 1900*, chaps. xiii and xiv.

Development of Depreciation Accounting

Depreciation History and Concepts in the Bell System, chaps. 1–7. New York: American Telephone & Telegraph Co., 1957.

LITTLETON, A. C. *Accounting Evolution to 1900*, chap. xiv.

LUTHERLAND, D. A. "Fixed Asset Replacement a Half Century Ago," *Accounting Review*, Vol. XXVI (October, 1951), pp. 475–80.

MAY, GEORGE O. *Financial Accounting—A Distillation of Experience*, chaps. vii and viii. New York: Macmillan Co., 1946.

NASH, LUTHER R. *Anatomy of Depreciation*, chaps. i and ii. Washington, D.C.: Public Utilities Reports, Inc., 1947.

POLLINS, HAROLD. "Aspects of Railway Accounting before 1868," *Studies in the History of Accounting* (eds. A. C. LITTLETON and B. S. YAMEY), pp. 332–55.

Government Influences on Accounting

BRUNDAGE, PERCIVAL F. "Impact of Government Regulation on Development of Today's Accounting Practices," *Journal of Accountancy*, Vol. XC (November, 1950), pp. 384–91. Also in MARY E. MURPHY, *Selected Readings in Accounting and Auditing*, pp. 132–37. New York: Prentice-Hall, Inc., 1952.

SMITH, DAN THROOP, and J. KEITH BUTTERS. *Taxable and Business Income*, "Historical Foreword," by G. O. MAY. New York: National Bureau of Economic Research, Inc., 1949.

chapter 3

The Development of Accounting Theory Immediately Preceding and Since 1930

The development of accounting thought has been subjected to two major periods of turmoil in recent years—the early 1930's and the 1960's—although it is too early to evaluate clearly the effects of the controversies of the most recent decade. In both periods, considerable pressure came from individuals and groups outside the accounting profession accompanied by dissatisfaction by practicing accountants and academicians. As a result of the pressures building up, in 1930 the American Institute of Accountants[1] appointed a committee for the purpose of cooperating with the New York Stock Exchange in matters relating to the common interest of investors, exchanges, and accountants. Also in 1930 the Institute appointed its first standing committee to consider problems of accounting procedure and to make pronouncements that might carry weight in the profession. Earlier, questions of accounting procedure had been disposed of through the work of special committees created specifically to study the particular questions. Another important development in 1930 was the first ruling of the New York Stock Exchange relating specifically to accounting practice—that stock dividends of a subsidiary should not be taken into the income of the parent corporation in an amount greater than that charged against the earnings or earned surplus of the subsidiary.

In the United Kingdom, the Companies Act of 1929 had required sweeping reforms in the financial reporting of limited companies, including the requirement of a profit and loss account for the first time.

These events of the 1930's, however, were indicative of a desire to

---

[1] In 1957 the name was changed to the American Institute of Certified Public Accountants.

improve accounting practice rather than accounting theory as such. Furthermore, most of the accounting pronouncements and innovations of the 1930's were the result of developments in accounting thought of 10 to 20 years earlier. But it cannot be denied that the development of accounting theory was stimulated by the discussions that came out of these events of the early 1930's. In a round-table discussion of "Developments in Accounting Theory and Practice Since 1929" at the Fiftieth Anniversary Celebration of the American Institute of Accountants in 1937, the consensus was that there had been no developments in theory since 1929, only in practice. However, in these discussions, it was apparent that the disagreement on basic principles and the stimulation of accounting thought had done much to develop theory.

The most important shift in basic accounting thought coming out of the writings and discussions of the late 1920's and early 1930's was the change in the objective of accounting from that of presenting information to management and creditors to that of providing financial information for investors and stockholders. The pressure for this change in objective came from the financial sectors and stock exchanges rather than from accountants. The rapid growth in the widespread ownership of corporations, particularly during the several years following World War I, created new needs for accounting information. The average number of shares listed on the New York Stock Exchange in 1900 was about 60 million shares compared with 180 million in 1917 and 1,212 million in 1930 (unadjusted for stock splits).[2]

Two men, William Z. Ripley and J. M. B. Hoxsey, were particularly influential in stating the case for an improvement in accounting standards for reporting to stockholders and investors. Ripley, professor of economics at Harvard, made an attack on the accounting practices of the railroads in 1915[3] and criticized severely the paucity of information available to stockholders of industrial corporations in 1926.[4] Hoxsey, executive assistant to the Committee on Stock List of the New York Stock Exchange, in an address before the annual convention of the American Institute of Accountants in 1930, made a specific plea for the providing of adequate understandable information published in financial statements presented to stockholders. He argued that this information should avoid misleading the stockholders in any respect and should aid them in determining the true value of their investments.[5]

---

[2] *New York Stock Exchange Fact Book,* 1959, p. 38.

[3] William Z. Ripley, *Railroads, Finance and Organization* (New York: Longmans, Green & Co., 1915).

[4] William Z. Ripley, "Stop, Look, Listen!" *Atlantic Monthly,* September, 1926, included in *Main Street and Wall Street* (Boston: Little, Brown & Co., 1927).

[5] J. M. B. Hoxsey, "Accounting for Investors," *Journal of Accountancy,* Vol. L (October, 1930), pp. 251–84.

The change in the objective of financial statements led to the following changes in accounting thought: (1) a deemphasis of the balance sheet as a statement of values, by adhering more closely to the going-concern concept as opposed to liquidation, and by looking at the balance sheet as the link between two income statements rather than the reverse; (2) the increased emphasis on the income statement and a uniform concept of *income*; (3) the need for full disclosure of relevant financial information, by presenting more complete financial statements and increasing the use of footnotes; and (4) an emphasis on consistency in reporting, particularly with respect to the income statement. These changes are evident in the literature and in the pronouncements of several interested organizations before and after 1930. It is interesting to note that these changes in accounting thought were not the direct result of the stock market crash of 1929 nor the depression of the 1930's, but rather they were the result of institutional changes which had begun much earlier and to which accountants had not as yet adapted themselves. They were, of course, made more urgent by the events of the period.

One of the most significant of these changes was the shift in emphasis from the balance sheet to the income statement occurring in the United States and in Europe during the period from about World War I to the late 1930's. As early as 1908, Schmalenbach in Germany had pointed out that annual accounts should provide information about the operations of a business as well as about the state of its capital.[6] During the 1920's in the United States and in Great Britain, an increasing number of firms were providing information regarding their income accounts. The effect of this was, as we shall see from the writings and pronouncements of the 1920's and 1930's, to focus attention on the nature of allocations and accruals and their consequent effect on income. There is also evidence of an increasing arbitrary use during this period of deferrals of losses and income items to permit a smoothing of income from one year to the next. This led to the attempts in the 1930's to establish better standards for the presentation of the income statement.

THE DEVELOPMENT OF STANDARDS PRIOR TO 1930

As early as 1894, the American Association of Public Accountants (predecessor to the American Institute of Accountants and the AICPA) adopted a resolution recommending that the order of presentation in the balance sheet should be from the quickest realization to the least, indicating clearly an emphasis on providing information for creditors. A second step was taken in 1910 when a committee of the Association was appointed to formulate definitions of technical accounting terms in order

---

[6] Eugen Schmalenbach, *Dynamic Accounting* (London: Gee & Co., Ltd., 1959), p. 3.

to give uniformity to their meaning. Subsequent pronouncements were intended to standardize audit procedures and to facilitate the presentation of financial statements useful to bankers.

The Presentation of Financial Statements

In 1917, the Federal Reserve Board and the Federal Trade Commission recognized a need for standardization in the preparation of financial statements submitted to bankers for credit purposes. Accordingly, the Federal Trade Commission requested the American Institute of Accountants (AICPA) to prepare a memorandum on standardized procedures. After this memorandum was approved by the council of the Institute and the Federal Trade Commission, it was presented to the Federal Reserve Board for consideration. The Federal Reserve Board gave it tentative endorsement and submitted it to bankers and banking associations throughout the country for their consideration and criticism. The memorandum was published in the April, 1917 issue of the *Federal Reserve Bulletin* and reprinted (with minor changes) in 1917 in pamphlet form under the title *Uniform Accounting* and again in 1918 under the title *Approved Methods for the Preparation of Balance-Sheet Statements.*[7] A revised edition entitled *Verification of Financial Statements* was published by the Federal Reserve Board in 1929.

The 1929 edition, like the 1918 edition, set forth suggestions for the verification and preparation of statements specifically for credit purposes. It stated, however: "A more condensed form of balance sheet is usually prepared for general distribution, but in no case should any essential feature be omitted."[8] While the instructions contained in this bulletin were submitted for use by auditors, the reporting procedures as well as the auditing procedures were given, and these were believed to represent the best modern practice of the profession.

The following general observations on the content of the 1929 edition and the suggested procedures regarding the balance sheet reflect some of the accounting thought of the 1920's but stem largely from the credit objective of the statements: (1) Most of the instructions relate to the audit and presentation of balance sheet accounts, particularly current assets and current liabilities. (2) Inventories are to be stated at cost or market price whichever is lower. (3) In regard to the audit and presentation of fixed assets, emphasis was on the changes during the period and a

---

[7] "Uniform Accounting" also appeared in the June, 1919, issue of *Journal of Accountancy*, pp. 401–33 and in *Canadian Chartered Accountant*, July, 1917, pp. 5–33.

[8] *Verification of Financial Statements* (revised), A Method of Procedure submitted by the Federal Reserve Board for the Consideration of Bankers, Merchants, Manufacturers, Auditors, and Accountants (Washington, D.C.: U.S. Government Printing Office, 1929), Preface, p. v. See also *Journal of Accountancy*, May, 1929, pp. 321–54.

classification of the items included. Departures from the cost basis were permitted if disclosure was made regarding the basis of the appraisal.

The following observations relating to the profit and loss statement were suggested in the 1929 bulletin: (1) Depreciation is included under the caption "deductions from income" along with interest and taxes. (2) A distinction is made between "net income for the period" and "profit and loss for the period." The profit and loss for the period is the result of adding special credits to and deducting special charges from net income for the period. (3) Adjustments of prior periods are treated as additions to or subtractions from surplus. (4) The combined form of profit and loss and surplus statement is suggested.

The 1936 revision of the bulletin was prepared and published by the American Institute of Accountants and entitled *Examination of Financial Statements by Independent Public Accountants*. This bulletin serves as an interesting contrast to the 1929 edition. The preface to this edition states:

Developments of accounting practice during recent years have been in the direction of increased emphasis on accounting principles and consistency in their application, and of fuller disclosure of the basis on which the accounts are stated. . . . The suggestions contained in this bulletin are intended to apply to examinations by independent public accountants of financial statements prepared for credit purposes or for *annual reports to stockholders*.[9]

The following observations and quotations from the 1936 revision indicate some of the changes in accounting thought during the seven intervening years since the 1929 edition was published:

1. The first general observation is the change in the general objective of accounting statements:

Financial statements are prepared for the purpose of presenting a periodical review or report on progress by the management and deal with the status of the investment in the business and the results achieved during the period under review.

2. An increased emphasis on the cost basis and the going-concern concept is specifically stated:

One of the important accounting conventions is that the balance sheet of a going concern shall be prepared on the assumption that the concern will continue in business. Plant assets, permanent investments and intangibles are usually stated at cost or on some other historical basis without regard to present realizable or replacement value.[10]

---

[9] American Institute of Accountants, *Examination of Financial Statements by Independent Public Accountants* (New York, January, 1936), p. v. (Italics added for emphasis.)

[10] *Ibid.*, p. 2.

3. With the increased emphasis on the cost basis, the writers of the 1936 bulletin recognized the need for greater consistency in the application of procedures.

4. Reflecting the need for better information for investors, the need for an improvement in the reporting of income and the recognition of the earning power concept of income are stated in the bulletin:

From an investor's point of view, it is generally recognized today that earning capacity is of vital importance and that the income account is at least as important as the balance sheet.[11]

5. The emphasis on the income statement is then reflected in the general approach to the balance sheet, recognizing changes in the balance sheet from year to year rather than placing significance in a single statement.

6. The suggested profit and loss statement is more concise than that recommended in 1929. Nonoperating or extraordinary charges and credits are included in the "other income" and "other charges" captions. The item "net income for the period" is then eliminated, and the final figure is called "net profit (loss) for period carried to surplus."

One of the important characteristics of the 1936 bulletin was the elimination of all references to the balance sheet audit, the term "examination of financial statements" being substituted therefor. The balance sheet audit was first heard of about 1910 and achieved widespread popularity by 1917. The desire on the part of clients to save audit expenses and the fact that its special conservatism was acceptable to bankers appear to have been the main factors responsible for the popularity of the balance sheet audit. Its popularity was very important to the development of accounting theory because it temporarily counteracted those forces which normally would have shifted the emphasis from the balance sheet to the income statement much sooner. The development and growth of the large corporation, the rapid development of cost accounting methods, and the income tax laws all tended to emphasize the profit and loss viewpoint.[12]

Development of Standards in Regulated Industries

The development of uniform standards of reporting in the regulated industries started earlier than in the nonregulated, but in most cases the uniformity tended to stifle progress in the development of informative financial statements. Although the Interstate Commerce Act of 1887 did

---

[11] *Ibid.*, p. 4.

[12] Stephen Gilman, *Accounting Concepts of Profit* (New York: Ronald Press Co., 1939), pp. 35–37.

not specifically provide for a uniform system of accounts, the act was important in the development of accounting standards. In 1906, the Hepburn Act authorized the ICC to develop such a system with the cooperation of the Association of Railway Accountants, and the first uniform system for steam railroads became effective in 1907. The uniform classification was revised in 1914 and was followed by the promulgation of uniform classifications for certain classes of public utilities by the National Association of Railroad and Utilities Commissioners in 1922. Between 1905 and 1915, all of the states had enacted laws establishing public service commissions regulating public service corporations. Although accountants were frequently called to provide testimony in rate cases, the emphasis was almost always on the problem of property valuations. Therefore, improvement in accounting was not encouraged. One of the harshest criticisms of the NARUC classification of 1922 was that it did not adopt depreciation accounting. Instead, it approved the retirement reserve method. In presenting this method, it stated:

An account is provided in which to include charges made in order that corporations may, through the creation of adequate reserves, equalize from year to year, as nearly as is practicable, the losses incident to important retirements of buildings, dams, etc., or of large sections of continuous structures like electric line, or of definitely identifiable units of plant or equipment. "Losses" used above means in each case the excess of the original cost to the accounting company of the property retired plus the cost of dismantling or removing, over its salvage value at the time of its retirement.

It was not until 1936 that the NARUC advocated depreciation accounting.

ACCOUNTING PRACTICES OF THE 1920'S

Accounting practice reflects in many ways the accepted accounting theory with, of course, a lag of several years. The accounting practice of the 1920's, therefore, reflected the more advanced accounting thought of the early 1900's. But in 1930, the pressure to force rapid progress in accounting practice became considerable and harsh criticisms were made against the accounting profession. In his speech before the convention of the American Institute of Accountants in 1930, Hoxsey made the following specific criticisms of accounting practice:

1. *Depreciation.* A just appraisal of the asset valuations or the comparisons of earnings of different companies was not possible because of the many methods in use for the handling of depreciation. The financial statements, in general, did not provide adequate information for a good understanding of the depreciation policy pursued by the firm. In addi-

tion, many of the depreciation policies were clearly ultraconservative and others were unconservative.

2. *Consolidated Statements.* The introduction of consolidated financial statements was hailed as a definite pronounced step forward in the direction of adapting accounting to the needs of investors. But there was no standard regarding when consolidation should take place. In many cases, consolidation was not as inclusive as it should have been. In other cases, consolidation varied all the way from situations where the firm owned a bare majority of the voting stock to those where it owned more than 90 percent.

3. *Showing Volume of Sales or Gross Revenue.* In many cases, revenue had never been disclosed in the income statement, and in many other cases where it had been shown, the practice was abandoned. The main arguments against showing revenue were (*a*) that in certain instances it created sales resistance, particularly where the profit margin was wide, and (*b*) it gave advantage to competitors.

4. *Other Income.* There was a lack of consistency in the separation of operating income to the major activity of the business and other income with the itemization of material items. Hoxsey emphasized the duty of the accountant to insist upon such separation or to qualify his certificate in its absence.

5. *Surplus and Surplus Entries.* Earned surplus was not consistently segregated from all other surplus items or from capital accounts in the balance sheet.

6. *Stock Dividends Received.* It was not uncommon for firms to record stock dividends received at a larger figure than the proportionate amount charged against earned surplus by the firm declaring the dividend. The New York Stock Exchange would not knowingly list the securities of any corporation following this practice.

7. *Overconservatism in Accounting.* The emphasis upon providing information to creditors and to management-owners fully familiar with all of the details of the business provided some justification for making profits and ownership equities appear smaller than they really were. The techniques for doing this included excessive depreciation charges, the charging of new plant to operating expenses, the setting up of abnormal contingency reserves, and the undervaluation of inventories. When no outside investors relied upon this information, no one was actually deceived to his detriment, but the management-owners were deliberately fooling themselves.

In addition to the above criticisms, Daniels added the following: (1) The practice of showing "reserves" in a separate section of the balance sheet was misleading, and inadequate disclosure of the disposition of these reserves was made. (2) Treasury stock was often listed on the balance sheet as an asset. (3) Bond discount was usually treated as an asset. (4) Depreciation was commonly excluded from operating expenses in the income statement.[13]

The Income Statement

The inadequacy of depreciation in income statements is evident from the findings of the Federal Trade Commission in 1915–16, which showed that out of 60,000 successful corporations doing a business in excess of $100,000 a year, fully one half did not include depreciation at all.

The examination of annual reports in the 1920's by William Z. Ripley also revealed glaring inadequacies in reporting for stockholders. Ripley's main criticisms related to the inadequacy of income information for many large corporations with widely held stock. In some cases, income statements were omitted entirely, and in many other cases, the income statement was completely inadequate by failing to disclose revenue or by a failure to classify expenses. In some cases, the net income figure reported was even erroneous because of the direct charge to surplus of depreciation and other expenses.

The Balance Sheet

The treating of the balance sheet as a statement of valuations prior to the 1930's is evident from many of the corporate annual reports. During and following World War I, corporations began writing up assets as sound values were considered to be higher than recent costs. After 1929, however, many firms wrote down their assets to conform more closely to the current values of the 1930's and to provide for depreciation more in line with the then current revenues. Consolidated Oil Corporation stated in its annual report as of January 31, 1932, that—

It will be noted that the balance sheet valuations of the Consolidated properties have been written down to a very conservative level. . . . The only difference is that the stated values formerly assigned to these assets have been reduced to a figure more nearly conforming to present-day economic conditions.

The annual report for the Studebaker Corporation for 1931 stated:

If a write-down of plant facilities is made, substantial savings would result to the corporation in depreciation and other charges, thereby benefiting the profits of future years.

Ripley criticized the balance sheet as being inadequate or misleading in two principal respects:

---

[13] Mortimer B. Daniels, *Corporation Financial Statements* (Ann Arbor: University of Michigan, 1934), p. 1.

One is the downright omission of important items in the property accounts. Another is the failure to disclose the methods of valuation, whether it be of property or stock in trade.[14]

ACCOUNTING LITERATURE IN THE 1920'S AND 1930'S

The accounting thought expressed in some of the texts and journals published in the 1920's and 1930's was more advanced than accounting practice of that time. Hatfield, for example, discussed the current value concept in his 1909 and 1927 editions.[15] In his 1909 edition, however, he was more favorable to the valuation of inventories at the present value to the holders as a "going concern," while in his 1927 edition he favored the cost basis for fixed assets despite a subsequent decline in their value. For circulating assets, he considered current values as the most relevant, but questioned their acceptance when they exceeded the original cost. With respect to income, Hatfield discussed in his 1909 edition what were later to be called the all-inclusive and current operating concepts of income.

Canning made a valuable contribution to accounting theory in his *The Economics of Accountancy*,[16] published in 1929. The subtitle, "A Critical Analysis of Accounting Theory" helps explain this contribution. While Canning drew from the writings of Cole, Hatfield, McKinsey, Montgomery, Paton, Stevenson, and Sprague, he also compared the current accounting thought with economic theory, particularly with that set forth by Irving Fisher. The two most important areas discussed by Canning were the valuation problems and concepts and the measurement and concepts of net income.

Two significant publications of the mid-1930's treating specific areas of accounting theory are Perry Mason's *Principles of Public-Utility Depreciation*[17] and Henry Sweeney's *Stabilized Accounting*.[18] In addition to presenting a set of general principles for the treatment of depreciation by public utility commissions, Mason discussed the basic concepts of depreciation and provided a framework for a clearer understanding of the depreciation process. Sweeney's contribution was a presentation of the first complete discussion of the adjustment of financial statements for the effect of price-level changes. His major contribution to accounting theory was the criticism of the general acceptance of the

[14] Ripley, *Main Street and Wall Street, op. cit.*, p. 190.

[15] Henry Rand Hatfield, *Modern Accounting* (New York: D. Appleton & Co., 1909), and *Accounting, Its Principles and Problems* (New York: D. Appleton & Co., 1927).

[16] John B. Canning, *The Economics of Accountancy* (New York: Ronald Press Co., 1929).

[17] Perry Mason, *Principles of Public-Utility Depreciation*, American Accounting Association Monograph No. 1 (AAA, 1937).

[18] Henry W. Sweeney, *Stabilized Accounting* (New York: Harper & Bros., 1936).

monetary measurement as representing a stable purchasing power over time. His recommendations for the adjustment of financial statements by the use of a single conversion purchasing power index are discussed more fully in a later chapter.

Much of the writing of the early 1930's is summarized in a paper presented by Gilbert R. Byrne at the Fiftieth Anniversary Celebration of the American Institute of Accountants in 1937. His illustrative principles include the following:

(1) Accounting is essentially the allocation of historical costs and revenues to the current and succeeding fiscal periods.

(2) The investment in an industrial plant should be charged against the operations over the useful life of the plant.

(3) In computing the net income (available for dividends) for a period all forms of expense incurred in the production of such net income must be provided for.

(4) The income shall include only realized profits in the period during which realized; profit is deemed to be realized when a sale in the ordinary course of business is effected, unless the circumstances are such that collection of the sale price is not reasonably assured.

(5) Losses, if probable, even though not actually incurred, should be provided for in arriving at net income.

(6) Capital-stock and capital surplus accounts, taken together should represent the net contribution of the proprietors to the business enterprise.

(7) Earned surplus should represent the accumulated earnings of the business from transactions with the public, less distributions of such earnings to the stockholders.

(8) While it is not in many cases of great importance which of several alternative accounting rules is applied in a given situation, it is essential that, once having adopted a certain procedure, it be consistently adhered to in preparing the accounts over a period of time.[19]

Many of these principles may seem trite or axiomatic to the student who is accustomed to being concerned with the more complex problems of accounting. But in the early 1930's, these were the basic principles necessary for an improvement in accounting theory and practice. Item (1) emphasized the cost basis of accounting and with item (3) states the necessity for a proper matching of revenues and expenses. Item (2), in effect, states that depreciation should be taken; the method of depreciation was of less concern when many firms were still omitting depreciation entirely. Item (4) states the realization postulate, item (5) the doctrine of conservatism, and item (8) the necessity for consistency in accounting.

In 1938, at the request of the Haskins & Sells Foundation, Sanders,

[19] American Institute of Accountants, *Fiftieth Anniversary Celebration, 1937,* p. 249.

Hatfield, and Moore published *A Statement of Accounting Principles*.[20] In the "Letter of Transmittal" to the monograph, the authors stated:

In the preparation of its statement the committee has attempted to set forth the principles and rules of accounting which dictate what should appear in a balance-sheet and an income statement and in the accounts from which they are compiled.

However, the content of the monograph reveals that the authors were more concerned with accepted practice than with presenting the most advanced ideas of accounting theory. The "accounting principles" were obtained by personal interviews and correspondence with competent persons, by a review of accounting literature, by giving proper considera- tion to statutes and decisions referring to accounting, and by an examina- tion of current corporation reports. Thus, the monograph probably does represent the best accepted accounting practices of the 1930's.

In summary, the points of major emphasis in the monograph include the following: (1) a careful distinction between transactions relating to capital and those relating to revenue; (2) consistent application of accounting procedures; (3) the need for a conservative treatment of items to which judgment must be applied; (4) the application of the current operating concept of income; (5) the application of the cost or market rule with respect to current assets; and (6) in reporting deferred charges, particular care must be given to the distinction between charges inuring to the benefit of future periods and losses actually sustained.

In the second monograph published by the American Accounting Association in 1939, Daniels presented an evaluation of these accounting principles as they were reflected in financial statements.[21] He also com- pared the application of accounting principles with corporate published financial statements, noting considerable improvement since his review of published statements five years earlier.[22]

Also in 1939 Gilman published his *Accounting Concepts of Profit*.[23] This was the first comprehensive discussion of accounting theory since the shift in emphasis from the balance sheet to the income statement point of view. Gilman was particularly interested in the application of the entity theory, the effect of valuation on income determination, and the assignment of income to periods.

The most significant contribution to the development of accounting theory in this period was *An Introduction to Corporate Accounting*

---

[20] Thomas Henry Sanders, Henry Rand Hatfield, and Underhill Moore, *A State- ment of Accounting Principles* (New York: American Institute of Accountants, 1938).

[21] Mortimer B. Daniels, *Financial Statements,* American Accounting Association Monograph No. 2 (AAA, 1939).

[22] Daniels, *Corporation Financial Statements, op. cit.*

[23] Gilman, *op. cit.*

Standards by Paton and Littleton published in 1940 as Monograph No. 3 of the American Accounting Association.[24] The authors were members of the original Executive Committee of the American Accounting Association which prepared "A Tentative Statement of Accounting Principles Underlying Corporate Financial Statements," published in 1936. Monograph No. 3 was an attempt to present the basic theory underlying the "Tentative Statement." The intention was to present a framework of accounting theory conceived to be a coherent, coordinated, and consistent body of doctrine from which accounting standards could be formed. The theory presented was forward-looking and basic, being developed primarily deductively rather than directly from accounting practice.

DEVELOPMENT OF ACCOUNTING PRINCIPLES BY THE AMERICAN INSTITUTE OF CERTIFIED PUBLIC ACCOUNTANTS

What have become known in the United States as "generally accepted accounting principles" have been influenced considerably by the pronouncements of the AICPA. Particularly since the 1930's, this influence was the result of reports of special committees, *Accounting Research Bulletins* issued by the Committee on Accounting Procedure, *Accounting Terminology Bulletins* issued by the Committee on Terminology, *Research Studies* of the Accounting Research Division, and *Opinions* and *Statements* of the Accounting Principles Board. These pronouncements, not including the early *Accounting Research Bulletins,* have been brought together in a continuing reference service entitled *Accounting Principles* starting in 1968.[25]

The Special Committees

Prior to the formation of the continuing Committee on Accounting Procedure in 1938, special committees of the AIA (AICPA) had made material contributions toward the development of accounting standards. For example, a special committee worked from 1927 to 1930 on the development of the definition of earned surplus. Another special committee reported in 1929 on asset valuations in the balance sheet. Other committees studied topics such as terminology and accounting principles in foreign exchange.

In the early 1930's the New York Stock Exchange attempted to

---

[24] W. A. Paton and A. C. Littleton, *An Introduction to Corporate Accounting Standards,* American Accounting Association Monograph No. 3 (AAA, 1940).

[25] AICPA, *Accounting Principles,* Vols. I and II (Chicago: Commerce Clearing House, Inc., 1968).

improve the reporting of firms listed with it by seeking the assistance of corporate officials, the Controllers Institute (now the Financial Executives Institute) and the AIA. As a result, a Special Committee (of the AIA) on Cooperation with the Stock Exchanges was appointed to set forth some general objectives for the improvement of accounting standards. In a letter dated September 22, 1932, addressed to the Committee on Stock List of the New York Stock Exchange, the AIA committee made the observation that with the growing complexity of business units, the measurement of firm progress from year to year by annual valuations had become increasingly impracticable. As an alternative, the committee recommended the earning capacity of the enterprise as the real value of any large business. It also recommended the universal acceptance by listed corporations of certain broad principles of accounting that had won general acceptance, and that no attempt should be made to restrict the right of corporations to select their own accounting methods within these broad principles.[26]

The Institute's special committee recommended five rules to the New York Stock Exchange in 1933. These rules are summarized as follows: (1) Unrealized profit should not be credited to the income account either directly or indirectly. Profit is deemed to be realized when a sale in the ordinary course of business is effected except under special circumstances. (2) Capital surplus should not be used to relieve the income account of any year except upon reorganization or quasi-reorganization. (3) "Earned surplus of a subsidiary company created prior to acquisition does not form a part of the consolidated earned surplus of the parent company and subsidiaries; nor can any dividend declared out of such surplus properly be credited to the income account of the parent company." (4) Dividends on treasury stock should not be credited to income. (5) Notes or accounts receivable due from officers, employees, or affiliated companies must be shown separately. They also recommended the first standard form of auditors' report which included the term "accepted principles of accounting" later changed to "generally accepted accounting principles."

These five rules, plus a sixth rule regarding donated capital stock and asset valuation, were adopted by the Special Committee on Development of Accounting Principles and by the membership of the Institute in 1934. These six rules, together with the report of the Committee on Accounting Procedure to the Executive Committee in 1938, dealing with profits or losses on treasury stock, were published as *Accounting Research Bulletin No. 1* in September, 1939, and reprinted in Chapter 1 of *Accounting Research Bulletin No. 43.*

---

[26] AIA, *Audits of Corporate Accounts,* 1933. Reprinted in G. O. May, *Twenty-Five Years of Accounting Responsibility, 1911–1936* (New York: AIA, 1936), pp. 119–20.

The Committee on Accounting Procedure

From 1933 to 1936, a Special Committee on Development of Accounting Principles was comprised of seven members, each of whom was the chairman of a designated Institute committee. From 1936 to 1938 a similarly constituted committee had the title of Committee on Accounting Procedure. And from 1938 until 1959, the Committee on Accounting Procedure was comprised of 21 members. The decision of the Institute Council to expand the committee in 1938 and to authorize it to issue pronouncements on matters of accounting principle and procedure was based on the belief that this was necessary to establish practices that would become generally accepted by corporations.

As evidenced by the topics of the special committees and the *Accounting Research Bulletins* published by the Committee on Accounting Procedure prior to 1960, the AICPA devoted its attention almost entirely to resolving specific accounting problems and topics rather than developing general accounting principles. Because of the urgency of solving specific problems, it was necessary to use the limited resources of the Institute in putting out fires rather than in developing fire prevention.

The Accounting Research Bulletins. Prior to publication, the *Accounting Research Bulletins* were to be examined by the Technical Services Department and the Director of Research of the Institute and be approved by at least two thirds of the members of the Committee on Accounting Procedure. These bulletins, however, were not directives to the members of the Institute but received their authority only upon their general acceptance by the profession. In 1964, however, the Council of the Institute adopted recommendations that departures from effective *Bulletins* (as well as *Opinions* of the Accounting Principles Board) should be disclosed in financial statements or in audit reports of members of the Institute.

Of the first 42 bulletins, 8 were reports of the Committee on Terminology and were published separately in 1953 as *Accounting Terminology Bulletin No. 1*, "Review and Resumé." Of the remaining 34 bulletins, 31 were consolidated and rewritten as *Accounting Research Bulletin No. 43*. Three bulletins were omitted because they dealt specifically with wartime problems no longer relevant. Several others included in *Bulletin No. 43* have been superseded by Accounting Principles Board *Opinions*. Between 1953 and 1959, *Bulletins No. 44* through *51* were published, of which two have been superseded.

Evaluation of the specific recommendations of the bulletins is presented in later chapters where the specific topics are discussed. However, while the bulletins dealt with specific topics requiring greater uniformity of treatment or clarification of accepted standards, several general principles or standards are specifically stated or implied throughout. These are summarized as follows:

1. With respect to the determination of income, the current operating concept of income for material items is presented as the basic standard in Chapter 8 of *Accounting Research Bulletin No. 43*. Supporting this general recommendation, the combined statement of income and earned surplus is suggested in Chapter 2(B). These are superseded by APB *Opinion 9*.

2. The concept of revenue realization at the time of sale is implied in the recommendations regarding inventory pricing (Chapter 4). Exceptions are permitted in the case of precious metals (Chapter 4), cost-plus-fixed-fee contracts (Chapter 11A), and in the case of long-term construction-type contracts when estimates of costs to complete and the extent of progress are reasonably dependable *(Bulletin No. 45)*. Exceptions are also permitted in the cases where uncertainty is high, as in the case of foreign operations (Chapter 12).

3. The proper recognition of expenses when benefits are received and the distinction between expenses and losses are discussed under several topics. These include the amortization of intangible costs (Chapter 5); the handling of real and personal property taxes and income taxes (Chapter 10); the treatment of pension costs and employee stock options (Chapter 13 and *Bulletin No. 47*); the treatment of unamortized discount, issue cost, and redemption premium on bonds refunded (Chapter 15); and the acceptance of the declining-balance method of depreciation for accounting purposes and the adjustment of income taxes when the declining-balance method is used only for tax purposes *(Bulletin No. 44)*. Several of these have been superseded by APB *Opinions*.

4. The general acceptance of the cost basis of accounting is reflected in the discussions of inventory pricing (Chapter 4), accounting for depreciation during periods of high costs (Chapter 9A), and in the preparation of consolidated statements (Chapter 12 and *Bulletin No. 51*).

5. Proper disclosure and classification of balance sheet and income statement items are presented in several places. Disclosure is discussed in relationship to the presentation of comparative statements (Chapter 2A), the proper use of contingency reserves (Chapter 6 and *Bulletin No. 50*), the disclosure of long-term leases (Chapter 14), the dating of earned surplus *(Bulletin No. 46)*, and the presentation of earnings per share *(Bulletin No. 49)*. Proper classification is discussed in the presentation of current assets and current liabilities (Chapter 3) and in the proper distinction between capital and income accounts (Chapter 7 and *Bulletin No. 48*). Chapter 14 and *Bulletin No. 49* have been superseded.

The Terminology Bulletins.   While a Committee on Terminology had been constituted as early as 1920, the terminology bulletins summarized in *Accounting Terminology Bulletin No. 1* and the three bulletins published from 1955 to 1959 reflect the opinions of the Committees on Terminology from 1939 to 1959. As the members of this committee were chosen primarily from the membership of the Committee on Accounting Procedure, it is not surprising that general principles and standards implied in the stated definitions do not differ significantly from the general principles and standards implied in the *Accounting Research Bulletins.* These are summarized as follows: (1) The importance of the income statement is reflected in the definition of the balance sheet as a summary of balances carried forward—a step between two income statements (paragraphs 19 and 21 of *Bulletin No. 1*). (2) The emphasis on the cost basis is reflected in the definition of value (paragraph 36) and in the definition of depreciation (paragraph 56). (3) The general standard of revenue realization at the time of sale is implied in the definition of revenue in *Accounting Terminology Bulletin No. 2.*

The Accounting Research Division

Attempts to prepare a comprehensive statement of accounting principles that would be all-inclusive were made and abandoned by the Institute in 1939 and in 1949–50. But in 1959, acting on the recommendations of the Special Committee on Research Program, the Institute was reorganized to permit the advancement of "the written expression of what constitutes generally accepted accounting principles for the guidance of its members and of others."[27] One of the objectives of the reorganization was to be able to attack the broad problems of financial accounting at four levels: (1) the establishment of basic postulates; (2) the establishment of broad principles; (3) the setting up of rules or other guides for the application of principles in specific situations; and (4) research. Accordingly, a permanent accounting research staff was organized to carry out the research program.

Research studies are made by independent investigators or by members of the research staff under the advisement of the director of accounting research and a project advisory committee. Upon completion of a research project, the results of the investigation and the conclusions are published to stimulate interest and discussion before the Accounting Principles Board makes a pronouncement on the subject. The *Research Studies*, therefore, are not official pronouncements of the Institute but are published under the authority of the director of accounting research.

The major differences between the current approach to accounting research and the development of accounting principles and the earlier

---

[27] "Report to Council of the Special Committee on Research Program," *Journal of Accountancy,* Vol. CVI (December, 1958), p. 62.

approach of the Institute are as follows: (1) The approach of the Accounting Research Division was intended to be broader in scope and to rely more heavily on the deductive method in the development of accounting principles and their application to accounting practice. (2) The Research Division cooperates with the Accounting Principles Board, but it is a more independent division than was the Accounting Research Department in its relationships to the Committee on Accounting Principles prior to 1960. (3) The *Research Studies* are given wide publicity to stimulate discussion prior to being acted upon by the Accounting Principles Board. (4) The *Research Studies* are intended to provide a detailed discussion of the problems with a complete reasoning leading to the conclusions.

Accounting Research Study No. 1 entitled "The Basic Postulates of Accounting" and *ARS No. 3* entitled "A Tentative Set of Broad Accounting Principles for Business Enterprises" were the result of the directive in the Report of the Special Committee on Research Program and in the Charter Rules of the Accounting Principles Board which stated that

As soon as possible after its organization the Division shall undertake a study of the basic postulates underlying accounting principles generally . . . [and] undertake a study of the broad principles of accounting, and the preparation of a reasonably condensed statement thereof. The results of these, as adopted by the [Accounting Principles] Board, shall serve as the foundation for the entire body of subsequent pronouncements by the Institute on accounting matters, to which each new release shall be related.[28]

With the release of these two basic *Research Studies*, the Accounting Principles Board reacted promptly with a statement to the effect that they were too radically different from generally accepted practice for the Board to consider their acceptance at that time, while they recognized the contribution of the studies to accounting thought.

As a result of the rejection of *ARS Nos. 1* and *3*, on the grounds that they did not represent statements of what accounting principles were at that time, a new study was commissioned to review existing accounting principles. Thus, *ARS No. 7* was published under the title of "Inventory of Generally Accepted Accounting Principles for Business Enterprises." The purposes of this study were to discuss the basic concepts of accepted accounting principles, to summarize accepted principles and practices, and to summarize the pronouncements of the Accounting Principles Board and its predecessor committee. One major difference between this study and *ARS Nos. 1* and *3* is the emphasis on inductive and pragmatic methods and the practical applications of accounting instead of the deductive method. Accounting is thought to attain its validity through

---

[28] *Ibid.*

the test of experience, although a few alternative new methods are suggested as worthy of experimentation. Diversity in accounting is proposed as a basic concept, in recognition of diversity in business life. While this study has had greater acceptance by the accounting profession than did *ARS Nos. 1* and *3*, it has not led to a statement of broad principles of accounting. Accordingly, *Accounting Research Studies* continue to be ad hoc studies without a common foundation supporting them. Each study is based on the researcher's basic fundamental concepts and his findings in the specific area.

The Accounting Principles Board

As a result of the reorganization of 1959, the Accounting Principles Board was formed to supersede the Committee on Accounting Principles, with increased authority and responsibilities. The objectives of the Board were to advance the written expression of generally accepted accounting principles, narrow the areas of difference in appropriate practice, and lead in discussions of unsettled and controversial issues. Its official pronouncements were intended to be based primarily on the extensive studies of the Accounting Research Division; its conclusions were to be supported by reasoning; and the opinions were to include minority dissents by members of the Board. The composition of the Board has been made up of from 18 to 21 members, selected primarily from the accounting profession but also including members representing industry, the academic community, and government.

The *Opinions* of the Accounting Principles Board and effective *Accounting Research Bulletins* of the former Committee on Accounting Procedure are enforced primarily through the prestige of the Institute and the APB. In 1964, the Council of the Institute adopted recommendations that after 1965 all departures from APB *Opinions* and effective *Accounting Research Bulletins* should be disclosed in footnotes to financial statements or in audit reports of members. That is, all *Opinions* of the APB are considered to constitute substantial authoritative support for generally accepted accounting principles. And while the Institute recognizes that there might be other sources of authoritative support, the decision in these cases rests with the reporting member. If he decides that the principle or procedure does not have substantial authoritative support, he must handle the situation in accordance with the Code of Professional Ethics of the Institute. If he decides that it does have support outside the official pronouncements of the APB, he must disclose such departure if it is material. A failure to disclose is considered to be substandard reporting and is referred to the Practice Review Committee of the Institute. The activities of this committee are concerned with educating the reporting member and encouraging him to comply with the above recommendations. The committee also publishes bulletins periodically to encourage self-discipline among Institute members through education. While deviations from these recommendations are not covered by the Code of Professional Ethics of the Institute, the Council is reviewing the matter for the purpose of recommending a new statement regarding the status of *Opinions* of the APB.

While the Accounting Principles Board has issued some *Statements* which are primarily informative in nature, the official pronouncements are the *Opinions*. Lack of immediate enthusiasm for the two fundamental *Accounting Research Studies (Nos. 1* and *3)* was largely responsible for a shift in the efforts of the Board back to the ad hoc recommendations of principles and procedures regarding specific problems. To date, the Board has not established fundamental principles upon which other *Opinions* can be based.

Several of the APB *Opinions* relate to topics discussed in *Accounting Research Studies,* as was intended in the reorganization of the Institute in 1959. Other *Opinions* represent pronouncements on specific topics, amendments of prior *Opinions* or *Accounting Research Bulletins* and attempts to solve new or pressing problems. *Opinion No. 6* was an attempt to review the *Bulletins* before disclosure of departures from *Opinions* and *Bulletins* became mandatory. One of the results of this *Opinion* was the acceptance of a larger number of alternatives than previously recommended because of the inadequate time to study the problems and the resultant need to accept alternatives found in common practice at that time.

The recommendations of the *Research Studies* have not been followed in the *Opinions* for several reasons: (1) Independent reasoning and preconceived notions of Board members have led to different conclusions. (2) The research and argumentation of the *Studies* have not always been thorough or convincing. (3) Pressure has come from certain groups or bodies who have a vested interest in the specific procedures or results. (4) There is a natural resistance on the part of practitioners to rapid change because of the disturbance and confusion it causes. (5) Traditionally, new methods have been brought into practice as an addition to existing procedures, but the pressure to reduce the number of alternatives requires that a choice be made; therefore, the new ideas of the studies are deferred.

Before an *Opinion* is released, preliminary drafts are given wide distribution with a request for comments. In more than one case, the wording of recommendations has been changed or specific recommendations have been withdrawn at least temporarily pending further study. These outside pressures come from such groups as financial analysts, bankers, the Securities and Exchange Commission, and the Internal Revenue Service. One of the best known controversies is that regarding the investment tax credit. *Opinion No. 2* recommended that the investment credit be handled effectively as a deferral of the tax saving. Since this *Opinion* was issued with a considerable minority dissent, it is not surprising to find that it was not well received by professional accountants. Because of this difference of opinion, the SEC accepted both the deferral method and the flow-through method in reports filed with it. The confusion which resulted forced the APB to reconsider its position and release an amendment (*Opinion No. 4*) permitting several alternatives, including the immediate reduction of income tax expense. This failure of the APB to establish uniformity in this matter was one of the basic causes for the recommendation, mentioned above, that disclosures of departures from APB *Opinions* be made mandatory. A sequel to this conflict was an attempt to reinstate only one method for handling the investment credit in the *Opinion on Income Taxes (No. 11)*. General opposition, and specific opposition from the Internal Revenue Service in this case, caused the APB to withdraw this recommendation prior to the final draft in order to restudy the case. These situations serve to point out the difficulty in resolving conflict in accounting arising from diverse objectives and diverse origins of concepts accepted as valid accounting theory.

THE SECURITIES AND EXCHANGE COMMISSION

The Securities and Exchange Commission (SEC) was created by an act of Congress setting up an independent regulatory agency of the United States government to administer the Securities Act of 1933, the Securities Exchange Act of 1934, and several other acts. The Securities Act of 1933 (originally administered by the Federal Trade Commission) provides for the registration of securities with the SEC before they may be sold to the public (with certain exemptions). The act provides for the disclosure of specific financial and other information by means of a registration statement and a prospectus, both of which are available for inspection by the public. Among several other major provisions, the Securities Exchange Act of 1934 provides for the filing of an application for registration by any company which desires to have its securities registered and listed for trading on a national securities exchange. This filing requires the disclosure of information similar to that required under the Securities Act. In addition, however, the information available to the public must be kept up to date by periodic reports filed by the company.

Under the several acts administered by the SEC, the Commission has broad powers to prescribe accounting procedures and the form of accounting statements filed with it. During the years from 1936 to 1938, the Commission engaged in heated controversy regarding whether or not it should promulgate a set of accounting principles to be followed by all firms filing reports with it. Due in large part to the persuasiveness of the

Chief Accountant, the Commission decided in 1938 to permit the profession to lead the way in the formulation of accounting principles.[29] This policy was issued in the form of *Accounting Series Release No. 4,* which stated that the Commission would accept only financial statements prepared in accordance with accounting principles which have substantial authoritative support or in accordance with rules, regulations, or other official pronouncements of the Commission or the Chief Accountant. Thus was established the policy of relying on generally accepted principles and practices as developed in the accounting profession. However, since 1937, the SEC has put pressure on the AICPA to reduce the areas of differences in accounting practice with the threat that if the Institute did not do so, the SEC would.

While the SEC has influenced the development of accounting practice, its influence has been primarily indirect, through cooperation and discussions with the AICPA and comments on drafts of APB *Opinions.* In most cases, the SEC has approved drafts of *Opinions* before their final publication. However, it has also had a direct influence through the publication of Regulation S–X, *Accounting Series Releases* of the Commission or the Chief Accountant, and official decisions. In a few cases, the SEC has in effect overruled the APB *Opinion* or acted when the APB refused to do so. For example, in *Accounting Series Release No. 96,* the SEC gave acceptance to several methods of handling the investment credit, while the APB in *Opinion No. 2* had previously recommended only those methods resulting in deferral of the effect on income. In another case, the APB had considered expressing an opinion regarding the classification of deferred income taxes relating to installment receivables, but decided not to require uniform classification in this case. Upon the petition of a national public accounting firm, the Commission issued *Accounting Series Release No. 102* specifying that the deferred income taxes should be classified consistent with the classification of the related accounts receivable.

Thus, while the SEC has exercised its authority to determine accounting practices for firms filing statements with it in only a few cases, its influence upon the development of generally accepted principles and practices through indirect means has been quite effective in several cases. The SEC's early stand in opposition to the write-up of asset values has been one of the reasons for the strong support for the cost basis of accounting in the United States. In the presentation of income, the SEC took an early stand in favor of the all-inclusive concept, but after exposing drafts of a proposed revision of Regulation S–X, several changes were made to reflect a compromise worked out with the Executive Committee of the AIA. This position and the final form specified in Regulation S–X

---

[29] Carman G. Blough, "Development of Accounting Principles in the United States," *Berkeley Symposium on the Foundations of Financial Accounting* (Berkeley: Schools of Business Administration, University of California, 1967), p. 5.

were no doubt influential in the formulation of APB *Opinion No. 9* "Reporting the Results of Operations." One of the important factors regarding the influence of the SEC has been its willingness to work closely with the accounting profession and permit some experimentation. Fortunately, government regulation in the United States has not placed rigid controls on the presentation of general financial statements or on the variety of accounting procedures in use. Rigid controls would have stifled the development of accounting theory and the progress in accounting practice stemming from new ideas in theory.

THE DEVELOPMENT OF ACCOUNTING STANDARDS BY THE AMERICAN ACCOUNTING ASSOCIATION

The American Association of University Instructors in Accounting, established in 1916, changed its name to the American Accounting Association in 1935 and expanded its activities to include the following official purposes: (1) to encourage and sponsor research, and (2) to develop accounting principles and standards and seek their endorsement in practice. Accordingly, the Executive Committee of the Association published in 1936 "A Tentative Statement of Accounting Principles Underlying Corporate Financial Statements."

The general approach of the Executive Committee was that of establishing broad basic principles upon which corporate financial statements could be based and made sufficiently uniform and understandable to justify opinions regarding the financial condition and progress of the firm. This first attempt was not intended to cover the entire field of accounting theory, but was considered an experimental formulation of principles relating to the most important aspects of reporting. Major emphasis was placed upon those areas where current practice was generally thought to be in error. Some of the "principles" stated, therefore, were really specific rules rather than basic principles. In contrast to the specific approach of the American Institute, this broad approach was adopted by the American Accounting Association primarily because of the limited resources of the Association and because of the theoretical orientation of its members.

In 1941, the Executive Committee revised the 1936 statement and dropped from the title the phrase "A Tentative Statement." The format and content of the 1941 statement were similar to the 1936 statement except that the 1941 statement was divided into four sections—cost, revenue, income, and capital—rather than the three in the 1936 statement—costs and values, measurement of income, and capital and surplus.

In 1946, the president of the AAA appointed a Committee on Revision of the Statement of Principles of the American Accounting Association. The revision presented by the committee in 1948 was entitled "Accounting Concepts and Standards Underlying Corporate Financial Statements." The term "principles" was omitted from the title, apparently because of the general criticism that the term implied a greater force and a more universal validity than intended by the statement. The term "standards" was added because of the inclusion of a special section on standards of financial statement presentation. In general, few basic changes were made from the 1941 statement.

In 1949, a Committee on Accounting Concepts and Standards was appointed to institute a continuous program of study and research by the Association. From 1950 to 1954, the committee prepared eight supplementary statements to clarify or expand on the 1948 statement as an aid in the development of accounting principles.

In 1955, the Committee on Concepts and Standards Underlying Corporate Financial Statements began preparation for a revision of the 1948 statement. This resulted in the "Accounting and Reporting Standards for Corporate Financial Statements—1957 Revision." A major change in this statement from the earlier statements is an emphasis on basic concepts that may serve as a foundation for accounting theory rather than an emphasis on specific rules and standards.

Five supplementary statements to the 1957 revision were prepared and published by separate special committees. Supplementary Statement No. 1 on "Accounting for Land, Buildings, and Equipment"[30] and Supplementary Statement No. 2 on "Inventory Measurement"[31] are extensions of the 1957 statement and are concerned primarily with the use of current or replacement costs and the accounting for holding gains and losses. Three unnumbered supplements published in 1965 represented the results of three separate committees on the realization concept, the entity concept, and the matching concept.[32]

In 1964, a committee was appointed with the charge to develop an integrated statement of basic accounting theory not necessarily bound to the format or content of previous statements. In meeting its charge, the committee published in 1966 *A Statement of Basic Accounting Theory*, which opened up some new directions in accounting thought by redefining accounting and setting forth some basic standards and guidelines for communicating accounting information. Four committees were subsequently appointed to evaluate current practice and suggest improvements

---

[30] Committee on Concepts and Standards—Long-Lived Assets, American Accounting Association, "Accounting for Land, Buildings, and Equipment," Supplementary Statement No. 1, *Accounting Review*, Vol. XXXIX (July, 1964), pp. 693–99.

[31] Committee on Concepts and Standards—Inventory Measurement, American Accounting Association, "A Discussion of Various Approaches to Inventory Measurement," Supplementary Statement No. 2, *Accounting Review*, Vol. XXXIX (July, 1964), pp. 700–714.

[32] AAA 1964 Concepts and Standards Research Committees Reports, *Accounting Review*, April, 1965: "The Realization Concept," pp. 312–22; "The Entity Concept," pp. 358–67; "The Matching Concept," pp. 368–72.

in light of the standards set forth in the 1966 statement in the areas of external reporting, managerial decision models, not-for-profit organizations, and international accounting. Because of a lack of clarity in how these standards should be made operational, it is not surprising that the four committees applied the standards in different ways.

A Comparison of the AAA Statements

The several basic statements and the supplementary statements and committee reports of the American Accounting Association reflect the thinking and conditions at the time of writing of each, and a comparison of them reflects the development of accounting theory from the 1930's to the present. The 1936 and 1941 statements and, in part, the 1948 statement and its eight supplements were attempts to correct malpractices in the accounting profession. Certain corporate accounting practices were thought to involve such uncertainties as to render the financial statements valueless for purposes of comparison. These first three statements also reflect a definite distrust on the part of the writers of the use of subjective judgments by accountants in the preparation of reports. A review of the accounting practices of the 1920's and early 1930's certainly provided a good basis for this distrust. But, unfortunately, this distrust did not lead to the development of good accounting theory. These and other influences are apparent in the following comparison of the basic ideas expressed in the several statements. Specific comments and discussion are reserved for later chapters.

Objectives of Financial Statements. While all of the statements direct their attention to the presentation of general-purpose statements, there is a slight change in emphasis. The 1936 statement implied an emphasis on the preparation of financial statements for creditors and investors. The 1941 statement expanded this objective to include stockholders, creditors, and the general public. In the 1948 statement, focus was directed toward the use of financial statements by persons having an interest in the firm or in the broader problems of the economy. Specific groups having an interest in financial statements are stated to be investors, management, labor, and government. The 1957 statement states that its basic purpose is the presentation of concepts and standards to be used as a guide in the preparation of general-purpose reports to stockholders and others interested in the enterprise. However, the distinction between *enterprise* net income and *net income to shareholders* implies a recognition of different concepts for different groups of readers.

The 1966 statement emphasized the need for the presentation of information relevant to the needs of users of external reports. However, the committee suggested improvements in reporting which it felt could lead to a greater reliance on general-purpose reports for a wide range of users. But in attempting to evaluate current practice, the 1968 Committee on External Reporting found it necessary to identify the user and his needs. Accordingly, it emphasized the objective of reporting to creditors and equity investors.

Asset Valuation. The authors of the 1936 statement sought to eliminate the confusion arising from the revaluation of assets up or down according to changes in price levels and expected business conditions. Accordingly, their main emphasis was on the use of the cost basis of accounting and the writing off of that part of cost not applicable to future operations. The implication is that values other than unamortized costs should not be used, but if they are, they should be shown as collateral notations only. While the 1941 statement also strongly emphasized cost, the wording does not imply such opposition to the use of values other than cost as supplementary data when supported by substantial evidence. In 1948, an attempt was made to define assets but emphasis was again placed on cost because it is thought to be based on objective evidence. In 1957, both the definition and measurement of assets were stated without being tied directly to cost. Cost is referred to as a typical method for the valuation of nonmonetary assets and indicated as acceptable when it can be presumed to be a satisfactory measurement of expected future service value at the time of acquisition. However, in the supplementary statements published in 1964 and 1965, current cost and replacement cost are recommended as superior to historical cost. The 1966 statement recommended the presentation of both historical and current costs.

The Measurement of Income. Distrust of the individual judgments of the accountants and managements of corporations is apparent in the first three basic AAA statements of 1936, 1941, and 1948 in their consistent recommendation of the all-inclusive concept of income. The authors of the statements sought to eliminate the current confusion and inconsistencies regarding the treatment of the unusual cost or revenue items. The objective of the all-inclusive concept as stated in the 1936 statement (paragraph 8) was to present in the assembled income statements all gains and losses of the enterprise for any period of years. While the 1941 statement recommended the recognition in the income statement of all revenues realized and all costs and losses written off during the year (section C), the 1948 statement went further and specified that all costs should be written off and included in the income statement if they had not been previously deducted from revenue and if they did not apply to future periods. The strongest position is expressed in paragraph 5 of the 1958 statement, which states that "an assignment of all or a portion of the cost of an asset to expense, made in good faith after considered judgment and after competent review, in accordance with the accepted accounting concepts and standards of the time, is not subject to reversal in a later period." Supplementary Statement No. 5, however, modified this statement to permit the correction of judgment errors in special cases.

Although the 1957 statement does not present a clear statement regarding the acceptance or nonacceptance of the all-inclusive concept, it is clear that a retreat from the strong position of the previous statements was intended. Realized net income is defined as including gains and losses from sales, exchanges, and conversions, but should not be affected by transactions recognized in the current period but related primarily to prior activities. The 1957 statement also recognized that the determination of income requires the use of estimates and the exercise of judgment.

In the proposal of the all-inclusive concept of income, the first three basic statements emphasize the need to classify the items in the income statements as those affecting current operations or as nonoperating charges and credits. While the 1957 statement does not make this classification, it does state that the net income of the enterprise measures its effectiveness as an operating unit; noncurrent items are thus assumed to be omitted from the income statement. Supplementary Statements Nos. 1 and 2 to the 1957 revision and the committee reports on realization and matching recommend a separate disclosure of holding gains and losses. The 1966 statement recommended an income statement based on historical costs, with separate columns showing the presentation of the statement in terms of current costs. In the latter presentation, the recommended statement shows net gains separately from current cost valuations and purchasing power gains on net debt, before arriving at "net income" but after "net income after federal income taxes on transaction basis." Thus, the discussions by AAA committees in the 1960's have been concerned with the presentation of current cost or current value data much more than in previous years.

Accounting Research. One of the significant reforms of the 1935 reorganization of the Association was the establishment of a program to sponsor the publication of the results of research. Out of this came the monograph series and the publication of the results of special research studies such as the one on price-level adjustments. In 1965, research was given greater emphasis by the approval of a plan to centralize the resources and authority for research under the research director, who was given authority to solicit projects as well as approve Association sponsorship. The first of the American Accounting Association *Studies in Accounting Research* was published in 1969.

THE DEVELOPMENT OF ACCOUNTING STANDARDS BY OTHER SOCIETIES AND AGENCIES INTERESTED IN ACCOUNTING

Several other accounting societies in the United States and in other countries have also made valuable contributions to the development of accounting theory. These include the National Association of Accountants and the Financial Executives Institute in the United States, The Institute of Chartered Accountants in England and Wales, and The Canadian Institute of Chartered Accountants. The work of these associations and agencies is summarized only briefly in the following paragraphs.

The National Association of Accountants

The National Association of Accountants (formerly the National Association of Cost Accountants) has been interested in research in cost accounting and in managerial and financial accounting problems since its origin in 1919. From 1920 to 1933, the NAA published several research studies related to cost accounting and topics of general interest to management. In 1936, the NAA started a series of research studies to report the current practices of the firms of certain members of the Association. In 1945, a committee on research was appointed to suggest and review the studies of the research staff. Shortly after its formation, this committee announced that it would publish statements of good practice that would assume an authoritative position in the area of managerial accounting, but it subsequently abandoned this plan.

In 1968, the NAA Long-Range Objectives Committee recommended that the research program of the Association be continued and broadened. Specifically, it recommended that the research "encompass the entire range of socioeconomic information needed by those who manage a business and by those who provide its capital."[33] The objectives of this program are to develop new concepts and reporting procedures oriented to the needs of specific users as well as toward current practice. Accordingly, it was recommended that a Committee on Accounting and Reporting Concepts be formed to develop and promulgate pronouncements regarding accounting and reporting concepts relating to specific uses of information, including the use of economic information by external groups such as stockholders, creditors, and governments. This committee will also recommend research projects, review the findings of all NAA research projects, and respond to position papers of other bodies. Thus, the NAA has taken a step toward becoming more influential in the development of accounting concepts and principles through the weight of its stature and authority.

The Financial Executives Institute

Contributions to the development of accounting thought have been made by the Financial Executives Institute (formerly the Controllers Institute of America), founded in 1931, and its subsidiary, the Financial

---

[33] "Report and Recommendations of the Long-Range Objectives Committee of the NAA," *Management Accounting*, August, 1968, Section 3.

Executives Research Foundation (formerly the Controllers Institute Research Foundation). Several interesting and provocative studies have been published by the Foundation, such as studies on mergers and acquisitions and reporting by conglomerate corporations. These studies have helped significantly in the development of accounting theory. Also, a major contribution of the FEI has been its cooperation with the AICPA through the FEI's Panel on Accounting Principles. The panel's major responsibilities are to review the research studies of the AICPA and the prepublication drafts of proposed pronouncements of the AICPA Accounting Principles Board, circulate the panel's recommendations, and report its views and recommendations to the AICPA.

The Institute of Chartered Accountants in England and Wales

In 1942, the Institute of Chartered Accountants in England and Wales inaugurated a series of statements similar to the *Research Bulletins* of the American Institute of Certified Public Accountants. These are called "Recommendations on Accounting Principles" and have been intended to be statements of the best practice—rules to be adopted as a guide to action. No attempt has been made by the Institute to develop general basic principles of accounting. The importance of these recommendations is apparent, however, from the fact that they have been adopted and reissued almost verbatim by the leading accounting societies in Australia and New Zealand, and some of the recommendations have been incorporated in the British Companies Acts of 1948 and 1967 and the New Zealand Companies Act of 1955.

As of 1968, 24 recommendations had been published by the English Institute. However, several of these have become obsolete or have been replaced by later bulletins. *Recommendation No. 18*, "Presentation of Balance Sheet and Profit and Loss Account," is rather broad in its scope and is basically a supplement to the statement presentation requirements in the Companies Act of 1948, and some of the recommendations were incorporated in the 1967 Companies Act. Many of the other statements relate to specific topics. *Recommendation on Accounting Principles No. 22*, entitled "Treatment of Stock-in-Trade and Work in Progress in Financial Accounts," for example, is a detailed discussion of the computations of cost and the application of the cost or market rule. A monograph entitled "Terms Used in Published Accounts of Limited Companies" was published by the Institute in 1962. In addition, several separate research studies have been published and several research projects are in process, sponsored by the Research Committee and authored either by the Research Committee or individual chartered accountants or academicians.

The British Companies Acts of 1948 and 1967 require disclosures in accounting statements or in the auditor's report and in the director's report, but, in general, they do not prescribe accounting procedures. Accountants, in general, are free to choose from a wide range of procedures in order to make the statements present a "true and fair view." The recommendations of the Council of the Institute are widely accepted, although they are not required procedures. Some of these basic recommendations are as follows: Emphasis is placed on accounting for costs although revaluations are permitted. The balance sheet is considered to be a historical document that is not intended to show the realizable value of assets. With respect to the income statement (the profit and loss account), it is permissible to use either the current operating concept or take into account all profits and losses relating to the current year with proper disclosure of material items.

The Canadian Institute of Chartered Accountants

In Canada, the Committee on Accounting and Auditing Research of the Canadian Institute of Chartered Accountants issued its first bulletin in 1946. This bulletin (superseded by *Bulletin No. 14* in 1957) had as its basic purpose the presentation of the best accepted accounting practices developed since the presentation of accounting standards of disclosure in the Canadian Companies Act of 1934. *Bulletin No. 14*, "Standards of Disclosure in Financial Statements," is fairly broad in presenting minimum standards of disclosure, but no attempt is made to present basic accounting principles. The other bulletins deal with specific topics, as do the bulletins of the AICPA and the recommendations of the English Institute. In 1957, the Canadian Institute also published a monograph entitled *Accounting Terminology*.

The main objective of the Accounting and Auditing Research Committee of the Canadian Institute has been to attempt, through the publication of bulletin recommendations, to eliminate alternative bases of reporting in situations where there is thought to be no basis for differences. However, in 1967 the research program of the Canadian Institute was expanded into the area of basic or fundamental research. A study group recommended that the Research Committee engage more extensively in initiating and overseeing basic research rather than merely making recommendations regarding the best current practice.

Other Associations and Agencies

In Australia, two professional bodies, the Institute of Chartered Accountants in Australia and the Australian Society of Accountants, are engaged in accounting research and the publication of bulletins and studies with the objective of improving financial reporting. The Central

Accounting Research Committee of the Australian Society also sponsors research by individuals on topics approved by the Committee under the guidance of small advisory panels. In the United States, considerable developmental work is undertaken by several of the large accounting firms. While most of their position papers are intended as guides for their own staffs and clients, a few have been made available to interested parties.

The development of accounting theory has also been influenced by the several federal and state regulatory agencies, such as the Interstate Commerce Commission, the Federal Power Commission, and the state public utility commissions. While the rigid requirements of the commissions have retarded accounting progress in some areas by requiring uniformity in the accounts, they have permitted considerable freedom in the preparation of financial reports to stockholders and others. Their influence on accounting theory has been indirect, through the discussions of specific accounting problems as related to regulation.

THE FRONTIERS OF RESEARCH IN ACCOUNTING THEORY

In addition to the research sponsored by the major organizations interested in furthering the basic foundations of accounting, many less formal groups and individuals are engaged in such research. While no basic trend can be discerned at the present time, some of the major areas of research conducted in the 1960's are summarized briefly as follows: (1) attempts to construct fully integrated structures of accounting theory based on a given set of postulates or premises, (2) research into measurement theory as it relates to accounting, (3) the extension of empirical research in accounting theory, (4) research into the decision-making processes both within the firm and by external users, (5) the impact of changes in the sociological and economic environment upon accounting theory and practice, and (6) explorations into the international aspects of accounting and accounting theory.

While these developments are apparent from the many articles, monographs, and books published during the decade, a few examples are cited below. Discussions of many of these publications will be presented in the relevant chapters of this book. Among the attempts to present fully integrated structures of accounting are *Accounting and Analytical Methods, Measurement and Projection of Income and Wealth in the Micro- and Macro-Economy* by Richard Mattessich[34] and *Accounting Evaluation and Economic Behavior* by Raymond J. Chambers.[35] Another broad

---

[34] Homewood, Ill.: Richard D. Irwin, Inc., 1964.
[35] Englewood Cliffs, N.J.: Prentice-Hall, Inc., 1966.

study is *An Inquiry into the Nature of Accounting*, by Louis Goldberg, published as Monograph No. 7 of the American Accounting Association in 1965.

Measurement has been an important aspect of accounting for a long time. However, only recently have accountants and researchers become interested in studying the measurement process itself, not only to permit a better evaluation of current accounting measurement practices but also to provide a basis for the development of better measurement processes. Among the publications in this area which should be mentioned are *The Foundations of Accounting Measurement* by Yuji Ijiri[36] and *Research in Accounting Measurement*, a collection of papers published by the American Accounting Association.[37]

Empirical research in accounting theory involves primarily the testing of meaningful hypotheses. Hypotheses can be stated and tested for the logic and acceptance of their premises, but the real test comes in the application of the hypothesis to the real world. Thus, many statistical or behavioral studies have been made to find if assumed relationships and behavior patterns actually exist. That is, are assumed measurements and relationships good predictors of future activities and events, and do the presentation and analysis of accounting information permit adequate decisions by those relying on accounting reports? Partial answers to these questions may be found by studying past and current behavior, or by the simulation of the real world by the use of statistical techniques and by the use of computers to speed the simulation process. While many such studies have been published in articles, monographs, and books, a major interest in empirical research in accounting has been aroused by the annual Conference on Empirical Research in Accounting conducted at the University of Chicago and published as a supplement to the *Journal of Accounting Research*.

Accounting is a process of communication of economic information for decision-making purposes by both management and those who must rely upon external financial reports. Managerial decision models have been the subject of considerable research in recent years and some of these models are presented and evaluated by the 1968 Committee on Managerial Decision Models of the American Accounting Association.[38] Less has been done in the development of decision models for investors, creditors, financial analysts, and other external users of financial information. However, several attempts have been made to develop descriptively the

---

[36] Englewood Cliffs, N.J.: Prentice-Hall, Inc., 1967.

[37] Robert K. Jaedicke, Yuji Ijiri, and Oswald Nielsen (eds.), *Research in Accounting Measurement*, AAA Collected Papers, 1966.

[38] "Report of the Committee on Managerial Decision Models," *Accounting Review*, Supplement to Vol. XLIV (1969), pp. 43–76.

needs of investors and financial analysts.[39] Only a few attempts have been made to develop a normative model for the decision process of investors and creditors.[40] There is, therefore, a considerable need for the investigation and development as well as testing of descriptive and normative models for use by investors, creditors, and other external users of accounting information.

There is increasing evidence that sociological and economic changes have a considerable impact on accounting practice and accounting thought. The decades of the 1950's and 1960's have seen many environmental changes that have affected directly and indirectly the work of accountants and, in many cases, these changes have forced upon the accounting profession the adoption of new methods and new thought about the accounting process. In the technological field, the computer is probably one of the most important developments. However, the sociological and economic changes have been just as significant. In meeting new situations, the business community has developed techniques for the sale and lease-back of plant and equipment, the merger of large firms into new conglomerate corporations, the development of elaborate pension plans for employees, the use of stock options as partial compensation for executives, and the extensive use of convertible securities in obtaining new finance capital. In many of these cases, new accounting techniques had to be developed to report the new situations and in other cases, old procedures were changed or adapted to meet the new conditions. In many of these cases, the accounting procedures generally accepted or available for use have been very influential in determining the behavior of managements in entering into certain transactions. In other cases, of course, tax advantages are the most important consideration. However, an area of considerable interest and potential research is the extent to which accounting procedures influence managerial behavior.

While accounting thought has developed over time in response to many changes in the economic and sociological environment and because of continued research, it has also developed along geographical lines to meet the different needs of the many national cultures and economic and political systems. Many nations have followed the lead of the more advanced countries of the world, but there is increasing evidence that no single nation or group of nations has a monopoly on the development of accounting thought and accounting research. This places a greater emphasis than previously on an international exchange of ideas and an understanding of the basic reasons for differences in accounting thought and practice throughout the world.

---

[39] See for example Corliss D. Anderson, "The Financial Analyst's Needs," *Berkeley Symposium on the Foundations of Financial Accounting, op. cit.*, pp. 98–109.

[40] 1966–68 Committee on External Reporting, "An Evaluation of External Reporting Practices," *Accounting Review,* Supplement to Vol. XLIV (1969), pp. 79–122.

In summary, recent developments in accounting theory are proceeding in several directions at the same time. Many of these developments are necessary to keep up with the changing economic institutions and to meet the new economic and sociological situations. But many of the changes challenge the fundamental basis of accounting theory. While a wholesale rejection of "received" accounting theory will not occur rapidly, accountants should be receptive to new ideas and recognize that accounting theory is not and probably never will be in a completely stable state.

SELECTED ADDITIONAL READING ON CHAPTER TOPICS

Development of Accounting Theory Prior to Mid-1930's

DANIELS, MORTIMER B. *Corporation Financial Statements.* Ann Arbor: University of Michigan, 1934.

MAY, GEORGE O. *Financial Accounting—A Distillation of Experience,* chap. iv, pp. 51–71, and Appendix to chap. iv. New York: Macmillan Co., 1946.

Development of Principles by the AICPA

BLOUGH, CARMAN G. "Accounting Principles and Their Application," *CPA Handbook* (ed. ROBERT L. KANE, JR.), Vol. II, chap. xvii. New York: American Institute of Accountants, 1953.

POWELL, WELDON. "Inventory of Generally Accepted Accounting Principles," *Journal of Accountancy,* March, 1965, pp. 29–35.

SPROUSE, ROBERT T., and DETLEV F. VAGTS. "The Accounting Principles Board and Differences and Inconsistencies in Accounting Practice: An Interim Appraisal," *Law and Contemporary Problems,* "Uniformity in Financial Accounting," Autumn, 1965, pp. 706–26.

STOREY, REED K. *The Search for Accounting Principles—Today's Problems in Perspective.* New York: American Institute of Certified Public Accountants, Inc., 1964.

"History of the Accounting Procedure Committee—from the Final Report," *Journal of Accountancy,* Vol. CVIII (November, 1959), pp. 70–71.

"Report to Council of the Special Committee on Research Program," *Journal of Accountancy,* Vol. CVI (December, 1958), pp. 62–68.

The Securities and Exchange Commission

BLOUGH, CARMAN. "Development of Accounting Principles in the United States," *Berkeley Symposium on the Foundations of Financial Accounting,* pp. 1–14. Berkeley: Schools of Business Administration, University of California, 1967.

PINES, J. ARNOLD. "The Securities and Exchange Commission and Accounting Principles," *Law and Contemporary Problems*, "Uniformity in Financial Accounting," Autumn, 1965, pp. 727–51.

RAPPAPORT, LOUIS H. *SEC Accounting Practice and Procedure*, chaps. ii and iii. 2d ed. New York: Ronald Press Co., 1963.

The American Accounting Association

Committee for the Collection of Historical Materials, *American Accounting Association, Fiftieth Anniversary 1916–1966*. AAA, 1966.

DEINZER, HARVEY T. "The American Accounting Association–Sponsored Statements of Standards for Corporate Financial Reports—A Perspective." Gainesville: College of Business Administration, University of Florida, 1964.

VATTER, WILLIAM J. "Another Look at the 1957 Statement," *Accounting Review*, Vol. XXXVII (October, 1962), pp. 660–69.

chapter 4

Concepts, Measurement, and Structure of Accounting Theory

Historically, little was done until recently to develop integrated formal structures for the formulation of accounting principles and theory. Prior to 1930, accounting was based more on rules than on basic principles, and these rules were based primarily on implicit assumptions and objectives. However, in 1922, William Paton stated and examined some of the basic premises and postulates implicit in accounting thought of that time.[1]

In the search for accounting principles during the 1930's and in an attempt to improve financial reporting, neither the American Institute of Accountants (AICPA) nor the American Accounting Association made specific attempts to develop complete logical structures, either to develop new accounting practices or to evaluate or justify current practice. In directing its efforts to the solution of specific problems, the Institute presented and discussed specific rules and recommendations as isolated problems in the context of an implicit structure of postulates and basic principles. The American Accounting Association in its statements of 1936, 1941, and 1948 attempted to set forth some of the bases upon which financial statements rest, but it did not attempt to present basic postulates of accounting nor a formal structure of accounting thought. Only in the 1957 revision of the AAA statements was an attempt made to discuss basic concepts underlying the conventions of accounting.

The need to develop a framework of accounting theory to encourage the logical development of accounting principles and practices and to assess current practices has long been felt. The current interest in this area was sparked by the recommendations in 1958 of the AICPA Special Committee on Research Program, which suggested that research studies should be undertaken by the AICPA to set forth the basic postulates and

---

[1] William Andrew Paton, *Accounting Theory* (New York: Ronald Press Co., 1922), chap. xx, pp. 471–99.

principles of accounting.[2] As a result of this recommendation, *AICPA Accounting Research Study No. 1*[3] was prepared by Maurice Moonitz and *Accounting Research Study No. 3* was prepared by Robert T. Sprouse and Maurice Moonitz.[4] Subsequent studies have been published by a Study Group at the University of Illinois, Richard Mattessich, Raymond J. Chambers, Louis Goldberg, and others.[5]

THE STRUCTURE OF ACCOUNTING THEORY

The type of structure used to house the theory of accounting may be quite formal, as in the axiomatic approach to theory; or it may be informal or implicit, as in the pragmatic and ethical approaches. Using the inductive approach, Littleton suggested a structure whereby rules of action can be converted into accounting principles.[6] Starting with accounting conventions and rules that are thought to be relevant to assumed accounting objectives, accounting principles can be derived as justifying reasons. While postulates appear to be omitted from this structure, they are implicit in the formulation of the conventions and rules. That is, the conventions and rules are inductively derived from accounting and its environment. However, the implicit postulates need to be examined to determine the soundness of the system.

In the deductive approach to accounting theory, the structure for logical reasoning should be fairly formal in order to obtain general agreement on the argumentative method and to discover the point or points in the reasoning where disagreement may exist. The structure is also necessary to point out the generally agreed assumptions behind the propositions, and to indicate which propositions are more basic than others; that is, a distinction should be made between the major and the minor premises. If the premises are relevant and generally assumed to be

---

[2] "Report to Council of Special Committee on Research Program," *Journal of Accountancy,* Vol. CVI (December, 1958), pp. 62–68.

[3] Maurice Moonitz, "The Basic Postulates of Accounting," *Accounting Research Study No. 1* (New York: AICPA, 1961).

[4] Robert T. Sprouse and Maurice Moonitz, "A Tentative Set of Broad Accounting Principles for Business Enterprises," *Accounting Research Study No. 3* (New York: AICPA, 1962).

[5] Study Group at the University of Illinois, "A Statement of Basic Accounting Postulates and Principles" (Urbana: Center for International Education and Research in Accounting, University of Illinois, 1964).

Richard Mattessich, *Accounting and Analytical Methods* (Homewood, Ill.: Richard D. Irwin, Inc., 1964).

Raymond J. Chambers, *Accounting Evaluation and Economic Behavior* (Englewood Cliffs, N.J.: Prentice-Hall, Inc., 1966).

Louis Goldberg, *An Inquiry into the Nature of Accounting,* American Accounting Association Monograph No. 7 (AAA, 1965).

[6] A. C. Littleton, *Structure of Accounting Theory,* American Accounting Association Monograph No. 5 (AAA, 1953), particularly pp. 186–87.

true or can be derived logically from other premises that may be assumed to be true, the derived principles should be sound. However, it is possible that certain practical difficulties in carrying out these principles may act as constraints to the basic principles. Therefore, the accounting principles and the rules derived from them may have to be modified to make them operational. Finally, accounting theory can be made operational only in a structure that can meet the objectives of accounting. This requires a set of definitions, methods of classification and measurement, and methods of presentation of financial data in summarized forms.

A theoretical structure for accounting can start either with the selection of what should be reported, on the basis of a given set of postulates, or it can start with assumptions regarding the needs of the users of accounting information. In either case, a logically derived theoretical structure for the development of sound accounting practices should include the following considerations:

1. An agreement on postulates regarding the nature of the accounting entity and its environment.
2. An evaluation of the user's needs and his constraints regarding his ability to understand, interpret, and analyze the information presented to him.
3. The selection of what should be reported. This should include a selection of the objects and activities of the entity or its environment and the specific attributes that are relevant to the objectives of accounting.
4. An evaluation of the possible measurement and descriptive processes for communicating information regarding the firm and its environment.
5. An evaluation of constraints regarding the measurement and description of the entity and its environment.
6. The development of principles or general propositions that can be used as guidelines in the formulation of procedures and rules.
7. The formulation of a structure and format for the gathering and processing of data and for summarizing and reporting the relevant information.

Regardless of the starting point in the development or evaluation of sound accounting practices, all of the above factors should be given adequate consideration. If we wish to evaluate current reporting practices, it may be necessary to start with the format, procedures, and rules and attempt to establish from these presuppositions or assumed objectives and postulates. The soundness of the reporting practices rests, then, upon the validity of the objectives and postulates and an evaluation of the measurement processes. If the presuppositions regarding the objectives and postulates are not acceptable, or if the measurement procedures are invalid, the current practices can be assumed to be inadequate or misleading, at least until and unless other presuppositions can be found to support the validity of the accepted practices. In the development of new practices, the theory structure should follow the above steps; however, upon completion, all assumptions should be reexamined for their validity and the logic should be reexamined for its internal consistency.

THE NATURE OF ACCOUNTING POSTULATES

According to *Webster's Third New International Dictionary*, the most relevant definitions of postulates appear to be (1) "a proposition advanced with the claim that it be taken for granted or as axiomatic," and (2) "an underlying hypothesis or assumption."[7] The first of these definitions refers to statements which are assumed to be generally accepted but the validity of which is necessary for the acceptance of other postulates or general principles, standards, or procedures. Even though such a postulate is generally accepted, however, it may be falsifiable upon further investigation or found to be irrelevant to further development of accounting thought. The second definition of a "postulate" refers to a hypothesis that is as yet unproven and may, in fact, not require proof if it leads to relevant ideas and a logical development of thought and useful conclusions.

In general, propositions that are advanced with the claim that they be taken for granted relate to observations or experiences that are not likely to be refuted or to propositions which can be verified or are likely to be validated by research. These are usually descriptive statements; that is, statements regarding the nature of things or what is as opposed to what ought to be. Examples of descriptive statements would include one proposed by Moonitz which states, "Most of the goods and services that are produced are distributed through exchange, and are not directly consumed by the producers."[8] A postulate proposed by Chambers states that, "In respect of all properties attributed to persons, individuals differ."[9] Both of these statements are descriptive of the nature of things and are not likely to be challenged. For this reason and because their relationship to accounting propositions is quite remote, many critics have called them trivial and unnecessary. To the extent that they are not controversial and because they do not necessarily serve as a basis for other controversial propositions, it is not important that they be stated. Furthermore, since there may be such a large number of propositions descriptive of the environment of accounting, it is uneconomical to make an encyclopedic listing, and incomplete to list only a few. Therefore, it is

---

[7] *Webster's Third New International Dictionary, Unabridged* (Springfield, Mass.: G. & C. Merriam Co., 1961), p. 1773.

[8] Moonitz, *ARS No. 1, op. cit.*

[9] Chambers, *op. cit.,* p. 75.

the opinion of the author that descriptive statements regarding the environment of accounting may be omitted if they are not directly supportive of propositions which are necessary to the logic or if other statements provide more basic support for the propositions.

A second type of descriptive proposition which may be true but which may not lead to a logical development of accounting theory is one which tries to explain what accountants do. For example, Moonitz stated that, "The results of the accounting process are expressed in a set of fundamentally related financial statements which articulate with each other and rest upon the same underlying data."[10] This is a true statement, but the danger of stating it as a postulate is that it will be interpreted as a normative statement; that is, that it *should* be true. As a normative statement, it is subject to research and debate. This does not mean, however, that such descriptive statements should not be made. On the contrary, any evaluation of current accounting practice should set forth propositions regarding what accountants do as well as the presuppositions regarding why it is done. Only by such a process can an evaluation of current practice be made sufficiently convincing to gain general acceptance.

Postulates which are normative in formulation, that is, those which prescribe what accounting should do or how it should be done, should be stated explicitly rather than assumed by general consent or agreement. Furthermore, they require the greatest amount of support to establish their validity. Their explicit statement in any proposed logical development stems from the fact that if they are not adequately supported, the conclusions derived from them can only be tentative. It is also important that they be stated so that areas of disagreement can be located and argued at the proper level. Examples of normative propositions would include the imperative postulates set forth by Moonitz in *Accounting Research Study No. 1*. One of these "imperatives" states that "the procedures used in accounting for a given entity . . . should be followed consistently from period to period."[11] This may be a desirable goal but, nevertheless, it may be subject to debate and rejection. Such statements, however, are more in the nature of hypotheses to be tested than postulates that can be assumed to require no proof for their validity.

In summary, therefore, postulates are basic assumptions or fundamental propositions concerning the economic, political, and sociological environment in which accounting must operate. The basic criteria are that (1) they must be relevant to the development of accounting logic; that is, they must serve as a foundation for the logical derivation of further propositions; and (2) they must be accepted as valid by the

---

[10] Moonitz, *ARS No. 1, op. cit.*
[11] *Ibid.*

participants in the discussion as either being true or providing a useful starting point as an assumption in the development of accounting logic. It is not necessary that the postulates be true or even realistic. For example, the assumption in economics of a perfectly competitive society has never been true, but it has provided useful insights into the working of the economic system. On the other hand, an assumption of a monopolistic society leads to different conclusions that may also be useful in an evaluation of the economy. The assumptions that provide the greatest degree of prediction may be more useful than those that are most realistic.

One of the major criticisms of the postulation approach is that if postulates are stated broadly enough to secure general agreement, they can likely serve as a basis for many further propositions and thus they do not necessarily support a single set of logical propositions. On the other hand, if they are stated specifically, so as to lead to specific propositions, they are likely to fail in gaining general agreement. And since most postulates of this type cannot be tested, there is no way of testing alternative sets of propositions by testing the validity of the postulates. Furthermore, it can be argued that postulates are frequently formulated with the objective of supporting preconceived propositions rather than using the postulates to derive the further propositions. However, the order in deriving postulates and principles is not important so long as the final argumentative structure is based on internally consistent logic and provides a basis for prediction. To this extent, we may find that several different logical structures support each other, rather than reach the conclusion that one structure is right and the others wrong.

Many of the postulates and assumptions set forth by Moonitz, Chambers, Mattessich, and others include propositions regarding the objectives of accounting and measurement in accounting. Since these are special areas requiring specific investigation, they are discussed separately below.

As indicated in the introduction to this chapter, an agreement on postulates is the first step in the logical development of accounting theory. However, this does not mean that postulates should be developed without consideration of the other steps in the logic. On the contrary, the selection of postulates may be interrelated with the objectives of accounting and the measurement and descriptive processes.

ENVIRONMENTAL POSTULATES

The environment of accounting has a direct bearing on the objectives of accounting and on the logical derivation of principles and rules. But not all aspects of society are relevant to accounting. Some are clearly irrelevant, others are only indirectly relevant, and many economic, social, and political aspects are directly relevant. What may be relevant at one period of time may be irrelevant at another and vice versa. For example, the development of the railroads and the proximity of a plant to a railroad may have been much more important to some firms before the construction of high-speed highways. On the other hand, international trade and the international balance of payments may be more significant for many firms today than in an earlier period. However, the relevance of environmental conditions may also be different geographically, that is, among the various nations of the world. For example, governmental economic policy is more important in some countries than in others. Even in those areas where certain aspects of society are relevant to accounting, there may be conflicting situations or a variety of institutions that may affect accounting differently. The objective of stating environmental postulates is to point out what aspects of society are relevant to accounting and to decide which of conflicting situations or of several institutions are more significant for providing a framework for broad generalizations.

Most statements of environmental postulates include an assumption that exchanges in the economy take place in markets and that market prices have significance for accounting. However, there is not agreement regarding which prices are relevant. Moonitz, for example, states that "accounting data are based on prices generated by past, present or future exchanges which have actually taken place or are expected to."[12] Chambers, on the other hand, states as a postulate that "the domain of accounting is the range of retrospective and contemporary measurements and calculations."[13] Thus, Chambers rejects expected prices while Moonitz would include them. This difference arises from the different objectives of the two authors and their assumptions regarding measurement concepts. However, if it were not for certain measurement constraints, Chambers' postulates and objectives could lead to the presentation of expectations in financial reports because of the importance he places on expectations in informed action.

Other environmental postulates relate to assumptions regarding the behavior of the users of accounting information. Chambers, for example, states a number of postulates relating to the behavior and beliefs of individuals.[14] In other works, Prince states several motivational postulates regarding the firm.[15] Pattillo postulates certain broad social responsibilities of the business enterprise.[16]

Other frequently stated postulates relate to the accounting entity, the

[12] *Ibid.*, p. 37.

[13] Chambers, *op. cit.*, p. 102.

[14] *Ibid.*, pp. 35–39.

[15] Thomas R. Prince, *Extension of the Boundaries of Accounting Theory* (Cincinnati: South-Western Publishing Co., 1963), p. 175.

[16] James W. Pattillo, *The Foundation of Financial Accounting* (Baton Rouge: Louisiana State University, 1965), chap. II.

measurement process, or objectives of accounting. The postulates regarding the accounting entity are discussed in the following section. The objectives of accounting and the measurement process are discussed separately, because of their basic nature and because they cannot be classified as postulates in the same way as the environmental postulates.

The Accounting Entity

Most sets of postulates and concepts include assumptions regarding the nature of the accounting entity. The main reason for the significance of this concept is that it defines the area of interest and thus narrows the possible objects and activities and their attributes that may be selected for inclusion in financial reports. Furthermore, postulates regarding the *nature* of the entity may also further narrow the selection of what to include in reports and aid in determining how best to present information regarding the entity so that relevant features are disclosed and so that irrelevant features do not cloud the basic information.

One approach to the definition of the accounting entity is to determine the economic unit which has control over resources, accepts responsibilities for making and carrying out commitments, and conducts economic activity. Such an accounting entity may be either an individual, a partnership, or a legal corporation or consolidated group engaged in carrying out either profit-seeking or not-for-profit activity. This is the basic view of Moonitz in *Accounting Research Study No. 1* and of the Study Group at the University of Illinois.[17] For example, postulate A–2 of *ARS No. 1* states that "economic activity is carried on through specific units or entities."[18]

An alternative approach is to define the entity in terms of the area of economic interest of particular individuals, groups, or institutions. This definition is that selected by the AAA 1964 Concepts and Standards Research Study Committee on The Business Entity Concept.[19] It states, for example, that "the boundaries of such an economic entity are identifiable (1) by determining the interested individual or group, and (2) by determining the nature of that individual's or that group's interest."[20] Thus, this approach is oriented to the interests of the users of financial reports.

Both approaches may lead to the same conclusions, but the user-oriented approach may lead to a selection of different information than

---

[17] Study Group at the University of Illinois, *op. cit.*, p. 8.

[18] Moonitz, *op. cit.*, p. 22.

[19] "The Entity Concept," *Accounting Review,* April, 1965, pp. 358–67.

[20] *Ibid.,* p. 358.

the economic activity approach; and it may extend the boundaries of the entity to include some environmental activity, such as attempts to improve sociological relations within the enterprise or the community and information regarding the social responsibilities of the enterprise.

The concept of the accounting entity may include the legal enterprise, a division of the enterprise, or a superenterprise such as a consolidation of several interrelated firms. The choice of the appropriate entity and the determination of its boundaries depends upon the objectives of the reports and the interests of the users of the reported information. The nature of the entity and the interests in the entity may be classified according to proprietary, entity, funds, enterprise, or commandership theories. These theories are discussed in Chapter 17.

Continuity. A further observation generally made regarding the nature of the relevant accounting entity is that most economic units are organized for operation over an indefinite period of time. Therefore, it is frequently argued that it is a logical step to recognize that the entity should be viewed as remaining in operation indefinitely under normal circumstances (the traditional going-concern postulate). Moonitz included this postulate among the classification of "imperatives," apparently because accounting practice does not generally recognize this assumption throughout the entire accounting process. But if continuity is a generally accepted proposition and if it is necessary to support subsequent propositions, it should be considered an environmental postulate.

As generally applied, the continuity postulate assumes that the accounting entity will continue in operation long enough to carry out its existing commitments. Sterling argues, however, that since commitments are of varying time periods, new commitments will have to be made continually into the future to carry out all commitments, thus in effect making the continuity assumption one of indefinite life.[21] If there is evidence that it will not continue in existence long enough (for example, where there are large and persistent losses or where it appears unlikely that the firm can continue at a profitable level), general accounting principles would not apply and the accountant has the responsibility of informing the reader accordingly. The reason for including the continuity postulate is generally to support the benefit theory of valuation, or in some cases to support the use of historical costs as opposed to liquidation values.

Not all theorists agree, however, with this interpretation of the continuity postulate and several do not include it among the relevant postulates. Chambers, for example, states that a going concern is a firm that adapts itself by the sale of its assets in the ordinary course of its

---

[21] Robert R. Sterling, "The Going Concern: An Examination," *Accounting Review,* July, 1968, pp. 481–502.

business, that is, in orderly liquidation as opposed to forced liquidation.[22] This assumption, then, supports his proposition regarding the relevancy of current cash equivalents. On the other hand, Mattessich assumes a set of hypotheses regarding the expected life of the entity without necessarily assuming that it will be indefinite.[23] This would include an expected life of zero. Ijiri[24] and Sterling[25] do not include a postulate regarding continuity, either because they feel it is not necessary or because it is not desirable to do so, or both. Vatter, however, states that "the continuity concept is not an assumption, but a condition—one that is at least to a large extent, a verifiable attribute of the business system."[26] He contends that it is a status quo assumption that is really an extension of the measurement process.

In opposing the necessity and desirability of including continuity as a postulate, Sterling contends that as a status quo assumption it is falsifiable and misleading.[27] Rather than making continuity an assumption, it should be a prediction. Furthermore, the mere fact that we assume that a firm will not be forced into liquidation does not justify valuations based on historical cost; other valuations may be more relevant. As indicated earlier, postulates should be accepted on the basis of their ability to permit predictions. Information regarding a specific firm should be presented in such a way that users of financial reports can make their own assessments regarding the future of the enterprise. Therefore, in this author's opinion, the continuity postulate should not be interpreted to be a status quo assumption nor a justification for historical cost, or even the benefit concept, in the valuation of assets; but it is a relevant postulate, leading to the presentation of information regarding resources and commitments and operational activity (such as the sales of goods and services over several years, or even for one year), on the ground that such information may aid in the prediction of future operational activity. Continuity assumes some connection between the past and the future, although not necessarily that the future will be a repetition of the past. In the case of a discontinuity, such as a forced liquidation, the usual accounting procedures would not apply and the accountant should disclose the nature of the discontinuity.

---

22 Chambers, *op. cit.*, p. 218.

23 Mattessich, *op. cit.*, pp. 44–45.

24 Yuji Ijiri, "Axioms and Structures of Conventional Accounting Measurement," *Accounting Review,* January, 1965, pp. 36–53.

25 Robert R. Sterling, "Elements of Pure Accounting Theory," *Accounting Review,* January, 1967, pp. 62–73.

26 William J. Vatter, "Postulates and Principles," *Journal of Accounting Research.* Vol. I (Autumn, 1963), p. 189.

27 Sterling, "The Going Concern," *op. cit.*

THE OBJECTIVES OF ACCOUNTING

The starting point for any field of study is to set forth its boundaries and determine its objectives. In the field of accounting, the objectives can be considered part of the postulates in the formal structure or they can be viewed as a set of propositions above or at the same level as the postulates. But it cannot be denied that some agreement on objectives is necessary to determine what postulates are relevant to accounting and to evaluate the principles and rules based on the postulates in order to determine whether or not they fulfill the requirements of the system. That is, the principles and rules should be logically derived from the postulates and meet the test of squaring with the basic objectives of accounting.

In setting forth the objectives of accounting as a part of the logical process of developing principles and procedures, there are two major approaches.

One approach is to assume that financial statements are prepared for a set of unknown users with multiple objectives. The objective then focuses on providing relevant information necessary for the making of economic decisions by many persons or organizations outside the reporting enterprise or entity. These interested parties include primarily stockholders, other investors, and creditors; secondarily, they include employees, customers, and the public. The government is also an interested party, but generally it does not rely only on the published financial statements; it requires that the usual statements be supplemented by special reports for specific purposes.

A second approach is to set as an objective the providing of information relevant to specific user decision models. This involves defining the user and his needs fairly specifically and determining either what information he wants or, by the use of normative models, what information he should have to make the predictions necessary for his decision making. This involves either the preparation of separate financial statements for different classes of users or the preparation of statements that include information that is irrelevant to some users but relevant to others.

The first approach to the objectives of accounting has been widely held for many years, partly because of the need to focus on a single set of financial statements for external uses and partly because of a lack of knowledge regarding users and their specific needs. This general objective is found in the 1957 Statement of the American Accounting Association, which said:

The primary function of accounting is to accumulate and communicate information essential to an understanding of the activities of an enterprise. . . .[28]

---

[28] Committee on Accounting Concepts and Standards, "Accounting and Reporting Standards for Corporate Financial Statements—1957 Revision," p. 1.

Moonitz, in *Accounting Research Study No. 1* of the AICPA, restricted the accounting description of the enterprise and its activities to information regarding wealth, changes in wealth, and claims to wealth. In his definition of accounting, he stated that:

The function of accounting is (1) to measure the resources held by specific entities; (2) to reflect the claims against and the interests in those entities; (3) to measure the changes in those resources, claims, and interests; (4) to assign the changes to specifiable periods of time; and (5) to express the foregoing in terms of money as a common denominator.[29]

This definition serves as a basis for the emphasis in *Accounting Research Study No. 3* on the balance sheet and the income statement as measurements of wealth and changes in wealth.[30]

Pattillo also emphasizes all-purpose reporting by stating the objective of accounting as follows:

The objective of financial accounting is to provide an external information-communication system by gathering, compacting, interpreting, and disseminating economic data, which give a financial representation of the relative economic rights and interest of the economy segments, in order to facilitate judgment formulation or action-taking by those economy segments.[31]

This view is similar to that taken by Arthur Andersen & Company, as follows:

. . . the one basic accounting postulate underlying accounting principles may be stated as that of fairness—fairness to all segments of the business community (management, labor, stockholders, creditors, customers and the public), determined and measured in the light of the economic and political environment and the modes of thought and customs of all such segments—to the end that the accounting principles based upon this postulate shall produce financial accounting for the lawfully established economic rights and interests that is fair to all segments.[32]

Note that the objectives specified by Moonitz and by Pattillo and Arthur Andersen & Company are not basically different. However, the postulates, principles, and procedures applied to these objectives can be quite different. This is one of the difficulties with this approach of attempting to define the enterprise and its activities for all external users. The objectives are not defined clearly enough to permit agreement on an appropriate selection of the items to be included in financial reports nor on their measurement. The solution has been to include as much information as

29 Moonitz, *op. cit.*, p. 23.

30 Robert T. Sprouse and Maurice Moonitz, *op. cit.*, p. 53.

31 Pattillo, *op. cit.*, p. 45.

32 Arthur Andersen & Co., *The Postulate of Accounting—What It Is, How It Is Determined, How It Should Be Used* (Chicago, 1960), p. 31.

possible that accountants can justify on the basis of verification and measurement standards. The selection criterion adopted by the AICPA, as indicated in *Accounting Research Study No. 7*, has been to limit the selection of reported information to financial transactions and events.

The second approach is the presentation of information in financial reports selected on the basis of the needs of specific users of accounting statements. This approach is in accord with the definition of accounting specified by the Committee to Prepare a Statement of Basic Accounting Theory of the American Accounting Association, which stated that accounting is "the process of identifying, measuring, and communicating economic information to permit informed judgments and decisions by users of the information."[33] This definition leads to the identification of users of external financial reports and the selection of the information needed for the predictions required in their decisions and judgments regarding the firm. Note that the selection of reported information is based on known or presumed decision models, but the reported information is intended only to aid the users in making predictions; no attempt should be made to make the predictions except where the errors of measurement and prediction can be estimated and reported.

An attempt to apply this specific selection approach was made by the 1966–68 Committee on External Reporting of the American Accounting Association.[34] In its study, specific normative investors' and creditors' decision models were formulated and a dividend prediction model of the firm was assumed in order to establish the variables and relationships relevant to the decision processes of the investors and creditors. Other decisions toward which accounting information might be directed would include (*a*) decisions requiring an evaluation of the efficiency of management by the stockholders and others; (*b*) financial decisions requiring an estimate of the ability of the enterprise to pay current or future debts as they mature; and (*c*) decisions regarding the fairness of resource allocations.

One difficulty in applying this second approach is in the selection of the information relevant to the various prediction and decision models of the users. However, initially, these models can be established on a normative basis and improved by empirical research. While it may be possible to establish the decision models by finding out how the users actually make the decisions and what information they want, this procedure may not lead to the best results, because users are limited by the accounting information now available or because they may not be

---

[33] Committee to Prepare a Statement of Basic Accounting Theory, *A Statement of Basic Accounting Theory* (Evanston, Ill.: AAA, 1966), p. 1.

[34] Committee on External Reporting, "An Evaluation of External Reporting Practices," *Accounting Review,* Supplement to Vol. XLIV (1969), pp. 79–122.

using the best models based on information that might be made available to them. The accounting process should be educational as well as informative with respect to user needs.

A second difficulty is that this selection procedure leads to different reports for different users or it will require the presentation of a considerable amount of information, much of which will be irrelevant to any specific user. Thus, if a single set of reports is prepared, the process of selection and summarization will be left to the user, making the financial reports less useful to any single set of users.

Relevance

The approach to accounting objectives that assumes a set of unknown users of financial reports has also assumed that information regarding wealth and/or economic transactions of an enterprise is relevant for the many data needs of the users. That is, if information regarding income and financial position is adequately described and presented in financial statements, it is assumed that this information will be useful without attempting to explain what information is intended to be used for which purposes. A well-informed reader of financial statements is assumed to be able to select the information he needs and make adequate decisions from the information presented.

Recently, this general assumption of usefulness has been challenged on the grounds that accountants need to know more about what information is needed by specific users of financial statements, as well as more about who these users are and what their objectives are in using the accounting information. This changing emphasis toward the communication of information intended for specific users and for specific purposes has led to a greater refinement of the concept of relevance. The Committee to Prepare a Statement of Basic Accounting Theory defined accounting in such a way that relevance became their primary standard. They stated that

Relevance . . . requires that the information must bear upon or be usefully associated with actions it is designed to facilitate or results desired to be produced.[35]

In order to make the concept of relevance operational, it is necessary to set forth the specific type of information required in the decision-making processes of users of financial reports. As indicated above, this specific type of information can be derived from either normative or descriptive decision models. Accounting information could be considered relevant to these decision processes if it could aid the users in making predictions of the several elements of the decision model. For example, if

---

[35] Committee to Prepare a Statement of Basic Accounting Theory, *op. cit.*, p. 7.

an investor wishes to make a decision regarding the purchase of common stock in one of several firms to hold as a long-term investment, he must make some predictions regarding the future dividends that will be paid by these firms. Therefore, any information such as past dividends, trends in the sales of goods and services, and restrictions regarding the future payments of dividends would all be relevant in aiding the investor to make his predictions.

Some data may be more relevant than others for making specific predictions, but it is not always possible to obtain nor desirable to present all relevant information because of measurement problems and user constraints. Some of these measurement problems and constraints are discussed in the following paragraphs.

USER CONSTRAINTS

The environmental postulates and the objectives of financial reporting provide a general framework for the development of accounting principles. However, limitations of the users of external financial reports place restrictions on the logical derivation of principles from these postulates and objectives alone. Principles could be derived logically from these postulates and objectives; but without specific qualifications, the principles might not find ready acceptance and therefore they might not fulfill the needs of the users of the reports. These restrictions or constraints should, therefore, be made explicit and taken into consideration in the development of principles. But the constraints should not determine the principles; they only require modifications of basic principles.

The major constraints arise because the accountants have very little control over the ability of the users to handle large masses of data or to interpret summarized data in making their predictions, regardless of the refinement of the accounting statements and the presentation of all necessary information to permit the predictions necessary for decisions based on them. Although the "standard" reader can be assumed to be one who has an adequate acquaintance with accounting reports, the statements should be prepared only after taking into consideration the amount of detail that the reader can assimilate (the relative materiality of detailed information), the consistency of the reports of a firm from one year to the next to permit intertemporal comparisons and predictions based on trends, and the uniformity or comparability of information presented for different firms.

Materiality

The concept of materiality in accounting is very similar to the concept of relevance in many respects. As indicated above, the concept of relevance implies that all information should be presented which may aid in the prediction of the types of information required in the decision processes or which may aid directly in the making of decisions. But materiality has also been used in a positive sense to determine what should be disclosed for general undefined uses. That is, information may be considered to be material, and thus disclosure is necessary, if the knowledge of this information may be significant to the users of accounting reports. According to the 1957 statement of the American Accounting Association, "an item should be regarded as material if there is reason to believe that knowledge of it would influence the decisions of an informed investor."[36]

On the other hand, materiality may be looked upon as a constraint determined by the inability of the specific users to handle large masses of detail. Financial information that may be relevant for investment and other decisions can generally be made available in considerable detail, particularly with the widespread use of computers and other communication devices. One of the responsibilities of the accountant in financial reporting is to summarize this mass of data in such a way that it will be meaningful to the users of the reports. Too much data can be just as misleading as too little. If too much information is presented, the relevant items are buried and the reader must base his decisions on inadequate data, in which case the decisions are not likely to be sound. Just as too little information does not promote good predictions and decisions, information that is replete with insignificant details may also detract from good prediction and decision making. Thus materiality places a restriction on what should be disclosed.

Materiality may relate to the significance of value changes, to corrections of errors in prior reports, or to the several means of disclosure of quantified data and relevant descriptions or qualifications of this data. These changes, corrections, and descriptions should be considered to be material if they are large enough or significant enough to influence the decisions of the users of financial reports.

The types of items where materiality may be involved in the decision to disclose or not include the following: (1) quantitative data such as items affecting net income and asset valuation; (2) the extent of aggregation or itemization of quantitative data in the formal statements; (3) quantitative data that cannot be estimated accurately enough to be included in the statements; (4) qualitative features that must be disclosed by descriptive phrases or sentences; (5) special relationships between the firm and particular individuals or groups affecting the rights and interests of other individuals or groups; and (6) relevant plans and expectations of management. Materiality regarding the measurement of

---

[36] AAA Committee on Accounting Concepts and Standards, *Accounting and Reporting Standards for Corporate Financial Statements and Preceding Statements and Supplements* (Columbus, Ohio: AAA, 1957), p. 8.

accounting data is implied throughout most of the remainder of this book.

Consistency

The doctrine of consistency has been a basic tenet in accounting for many years. It has been used to refer to the use of the same accounting procedures by a single firm or accounting entity from period to period, the use of similar measurement concepts and procedures for related items within the statements of a firm for a single period, and the use of the same procedures by different firms. This latter meaning of the term is discussed below in the discussion of "uniformity" and the term "consistency" will be applied only to the first two meanings.

Consistency in the use of accounting procedures over time is a user constraint because of the difficulty in making predictions based on time series data that are not measured and classified in the same way over time. If different measurement procedures are used, it is difficult to project trends or discern the effects on the firm from period to period caused by external factors such as changes in economic conditions or actions of competitors. If different methods are used from period to period, the user will have difficulty in separating the fluctuations in the data caused by the changes in procedures from the fluctuations caused by internal and external economic factors. If assets are valued at cost in some periods and at replacement cost in others, both the fluctuations from period to period and the trend may be distorted if price changes are significant over time.

The consistency constraint is valid, however, only when there is a choice among two or more equally relevant and valid procedures. The general argument that consistency within a single firm over time overcomes the practice of diversity in the use of procedures among different firms cannot be supported on theoretical grounds because these comparisons are of a different nature.[37] The argument for consistency also loses its force on the ground that if all relevant information is presented each period, with adequate disclosures of measurement concepts and procedures being used, consistency will be implicit to the extent that it is necessary or relevant for the making of predictions for user decisions regarding the firm. Also, the constraint does not hold when a change can be made to a method that provides more accurate or more useful information for predictions or decision making. When a change is made, however, the objective of disclosure would require that the effect of the change be stated clearly so that the users of the data can take the change into

---

[37] However, for an empirical support for consistency, see Andrew M. McCosh, "Accounting Consistency—Key to Stockholder Information," *Accounting Review,* Vol. XLII (October, 1967), pp. 693–700.

account in their decisions. Of course, disclosure is not necessary if the change would not affect any of the decisions likely to be based on the accounting data.

Consistency within a given set of statements of a firm at a specific date and for a specific time period also is not necessary as a specific constraint if emphasis is placed on the presentation of all relevant information necessary for the making of the predictions by the users. Examples of inconsistency within the statements would be the presentation of plant and equipment at cost and the related depreciation on the basis of replacement cost; or the aggregation of several inventory amounts, some based on Fifo and some on Lifo. If the aggregated amounts and the relationships are relevant, consistency in the use of measurement concepts and procedures might be necessary for the presentation of the appropriate data.

Uniformity and Comparability

Uniformity among firms in their financial reporting is frequently thought to represent a desirable goal for its own sake. That is, the goal of uniformity frequently implies the presentation of financial statements by different firms using the same accounting procedures, measurement concepts, classifications, and methods of disclosure, as well as a similar basic format in the statements. As used in this context, the concept is rightfully criticized. The objective should be comparability, not strict uniformity. The primary objective of comparability should be to facilitate the making of predictions and financial decisions by creditors, investors, and others. It may be defined as the quality or state of having enough like characteristics to make comparison appropriate.

Uniformity is one of the basic guidelines of *A Statement of Basic Accounting Theory*, but diversity is described as a basic concept in *Accounting Research Study No. 7* of the AICPA. This apparent conflict regarding uniformity and diversity, however, is modified somewhat by qualifications on both sides. The Committee to Prepare a Statement of Basic Accounting Theory recognized that departures from uniformity may be justified in the choice of the best method because of the importance of the standard of relevance and the guideline of appropriateness to intended use. Grady, on the other hand, recognized that diversity should not imperil the attempt to narrow the areas of difference in accounting and to promote comparability in financial statements. The basic questions, therefore, are how much uniformity should be required and how much diversity should be permitted?

The main opposition to uniformity is based on the claim that (1) it would infringe on the basic rights and freedoms of management; (2) it would place accounting in a straitjacket of rules and procedures that would make financial statements less comparable; and (3) it would stifle progress and prevent desirable changes. On the other hand, the arguments for some degree of uniformity are that (1) the wide variety of acceptable practices makes comparability among different firms impossible or at least difficult; (2) the freedom of managements to choose their own methods may introduce the possibility of bias, through manipulation of reported information to suit the purposes of those who control the reports; and (3) if the accounting profession does not take steps to achieve greater uniformity, it may be imposed by the Securities and Exchange Commission or some other governmental agency.

In determining how much uniformity is desirable, the basic needs of the users of financial reports should be considered. Comparability may be an important concept if it is assumed that users rely upon comparisons of detailed aspects of the firms rather than evaluating the firms as a whole. For example, specific ratios such as the current ratio or the debt-equity ratio may be used as surrogates for an evaluation of the risk inherent in being a creditor of each of several firms; or the rates of return on stockholders' investment may be used as a substitute for present values of the expected dividends of several firms. In these cases, it is desirable that these ratios be as comparable as possible, and that they be based upon information computed by uniform procedures in those cases where there is no evidence that one procedure is better than another. Differences in procedures used by the various firms within an industry would be permissible only if conditions in the several firms were not alike. Therefore, in each case, the procedure providing the most accurate or most reliable data would be in use, and where there is little difference in the various procedures, a uniform procedure would be adopted.

On the other hand, it may be argued that all relevant information for each firm should be presented to permit the investors and creditors to make predictions regarding each specific firm. The investors and creditors should then use these predictions to make subjective estimates of the present value of the firm and to evaluate the risk inherent in each firm. Comparisons should then be made for decision making only at the aggregated level. That is, the estimated subjective present values and subjective evaluations of risk should be used in making the final comparisons, rather than relying on comparisons of detailed information regarding the firms. Therefore, accountants should be concerned with presenting relevant information for each firm rather than being concerned with presenting comparable detailed data. However, it is still important that predictions regarding several firms be made based on equally reliable data. In the absence of specific guidelines for determining what information is relevant for specific firms, some general standards are necessary regarding the choice of information to be presented, the degree of detail to be presented, and the selection of measurement concepts and procedures relevant for specific users in their making of predictions and decisions.

Timeliness

It is not only necessary that users have financial information that is relevant to their predictions and decisions; the information should also be current in nature rather than relating only to prior periods. That is, the information used by investors and creditors should be current at the time of making the predictions and decisions. This, of course, is included in the concept of relevance, but it should be stressed as an important constraint on the publication of financial statements. The accumulation and summarization of accounting information and its publication should be as rapid as possible to assure the availability of current information in the hands of the users. This also implies that financial statements should be presented at frequent intervals, to reveal changes in the firm's situation which may in turn affect the user's predictions and decisions.

MEASUREMENT IN ACCOUNTING

The first step in the presentation of information to external users of financial statements is to select objects and activities or events and their attributes relating to the firm that are relevant to the needs of specific or general users. Examples of objects would include receivables, plant and equipment, and long-term debt; examples of activities would include sales of goods and services and dividend payments. Before measurement can take place, however, the specific attribute to be measured must be selected. In the case of receivables, the selected attributes might include the number of dollars to be received and the expected date of collection. Attributes of plant and equipment might include physical capacity to produce, resource outlay at the time of acquisition, or resources necessary to replace the assets currently. The selected attributes may be considered relevant to users' needs if they aid the user in his predictions and decision making. It should be recognized that most attributes are relevant only because they can be used to represent something else; that is, they represent a surrogate of the real attribute desired. For example, historical cost under certain circumstances may be relevant as a surrogate for the current value of an asset, which in turn may aid in the prediction of future values.

Measurement in accounting has traditionally meant the assignment of numerical values to objects or events related to an enterprise and obtained in such a way that they are suitable for aggregation (such as the total valuation of assets) or disaggregation as required for specific situations. However, measurement also involves a process of classification and identification, and accountants have recognized the need for many years for the presentation of information that is nonquantifiable in nature, such as disclosures frequently placed in footnotes or elsewhere in the statements. An emphasis on quantitative measurement is found in the postulates of Moonitz in *Accounting Research Study No. 1* and as one of the basic standards of *A Statement of Basic Accounting Theory,* as well as in the assumptions of Chambers[38] and Mattessich.[39]

These attempts to set forth a general framework for accounting theory also emphasize the importance of a market system in an exchange economy as a valuable source of quantitative data. Since goods and services are generally exchanged in terms of money, a monetary measurement of economic data can be assumed to be useful in decision making, particularly for those decisions relating to wealth and changes in wealth and the production of goods and services. Following from the assumption of an exchange economy, it is logical that exchange prices (market prices) would be relevant to external reporting. And it also follows that since economic decisions can affect only current and future outcomes, current and future exchange prices are more relevant than past exchange prices. However, certain constraints discussed below, particularly the existence of uncertainty and the need for objectivity and verifiability, may make current market prices more reliable than future prices and, in many cases, past exchange prices more reliable than current prices.

Traditionally, accounting has looked to the transactions or exchanges directly affecting the accounting entity itself for its monetary measurements. However, many recent proposals have suggested that market prices determined by exchanges between other entities may be relevant for the measurement of goods and services for a specific accounting entity. For example, current costs and appraisal values may be relevant in certain circumstances, as indicated in *ARS No. 3;* and Chambers emphasizes the measurement of current cash equivalents primarily determined from prices existing in organized markets.

While it cannot be denied that many types of monetary data may be relevant in external reporting, it is also possible that nonmonetary data, such as productive capacity in tons or number of employees, may be found relevant for certain predictions and decision making. Accountants should also search for improved alternative methods of measuring and presenting both monetary and nonmonetary data. For example, it might be possible to present data showing probability intervals and ranges (in probabilistic form) as well as single-valued data (in deterministic form). Also, it may be desirable to present multiple values representing different attributes of objects and activities if they are all found to be relevant. In

---

[38] Chambers, *op. cit.,* pp. 101–102.
[39] Mattessich, *op. cit.,* p. 52.

addition, consideration should be given to the presentation of budget data as evidence of managements' plans and expectations.

MEASUREMENT CONSTRAINTS

As indicated above, measurement in accounting should be directed toward providing information relevant for specified uses. However, limitations of available data and certain characteristics of the environment place restrictions on the accuracy and reliability of measurements. These restrictions or constraints should, therefore, be made explicit and be taken into consideration in the development of accounting principles and procedures. But the constraints should not determine the principles; they only require modifications of basic principles. Nevertheless, since the constraints cannot be removed by accountants, either because they are caused by the nature of the environment or because of a lack of adequate measurement tools, they should enter directly into the selection of measurement concepts and procedures. Insofar as they can be removed, the restrictions are not basic constraints of accounting measurement.

The major measurement constraints arise because economic data are presented on the assumption that they have some relevance for a prediction of the future. Since the relationship between the present and the future is generally highly uncertain, it is generally difficult to determine the relevant measurements for this purpose. But the inability to make reliable measurements of specific attributes that are thought to be relevant is due to the lack of reliable measurement techniques and the inability to find measurement procedures that adequately describe the attributes being measured. Thus constraints are caused by uncertainty, the lack of objectivity and verifiability in measurements, and the lack of a stable monetary unit. While conservatism acts as a constraint on accounting measurement because it is so highly ingrained in the minds of managements and accountants, it should be removed as a constraint by appropriate educational methods.

Uncertainty

Uncertainty in accounting arises from two main sources: (1) Accounting data generally relate to entities that are expected to have continuity of existence into the future; since allocations are frequently made between past and future periods, assumptions must be made regarding the logic of these allocations and on the basis of expectations regarding the future. Although some of these assumptions and expectations regarding allocations may be validated in later periods, many allocations can never be verified completely. (2) Accounting measurements are frequently assumed to represent monetary expressions of wealth which require estimates of uncertain future amounts. While the reliability of these estimates may vary considerably, no monetary quantification of wealth can be known with certainty.

If the future were known with certainty, the assumptions regarding the relevance of reporting for specific periods of time would be adequate for principles relating to measurements based on future conditions. For example, the assignment of depreciation to several periods requires an estimate of the life of an asset and the scrap value at the end of the life. If these two factors are uncertain, any measurement based on estimates can only be tentative. However, this does not mean that estimates and predictions should not be made as accurately as possible if they are relevant. But it does imply that measurements based on past estimates should be scrutinized closely and adjusted as new and more reliable estimates become possible.

Objectivity and Verifiability

In order that accounting measurements can be as reliable as possible in presenting information relevant for predictions and decision making of investors and other users of financial reports, accountants must decide what attribute is being measured and then select a measurement procedure that is likely to describe accurately the attribute. In this attempt to produce reliability, accountants have turned to the concept of objectivity to either justify current practice or to claim superiority of certain principles and procedures over others. However, objectivity has meant different things to different writers. Several of these meanings are: (1) measurements that are impersonal or existing outside the mind of the person making the measurement, (2) measurements based on a consensus of qualified experts, (3) measurements based on verifiable evidence, and (4) the narrowness of the statistical dispersion of the measurements of an attribute when made by different measurers.

The first meaning of objectivity implies that the measurement has a separate existence from the person making the measurement. Thus, there is assumed to be an absence of subjective valuation and personal bias. For example, the reporting of revenue at the time of sale is said to be objective because it can be measured from the results of an external transaction. However, particularly in accounting, there is considerable question whether there can exist a measurement independent of the measurer. Even though the accountant may look at specific external evidence, it is impossible for him to obtain this measurement without going through the mental process of determining what it is. Even though an external transaction may exist, the accountant must determine the value of what is given up and the value of what is received.

In the second definition (a measurement based on verifiable evidence) the emphasis is on the evidence rather than on the measurement itself. For example, Paton and Littleton place considerable emphasis on verifiable, objective *evidence* as a test of the accuracy of a statement.[40] The evidence provides the means whereby the measurement itself can be verified. For example, revenue is accepted as realized on the basis of the sale as the evidence. As another example, cost has traditionally been accepted as objective evidence of the value of an asset. The difficulty with this approach is that while the evidence may be verifiable, the selection of the evidence as a basis for the measurement desired may be subject to personal bias. If historical cost has been selected as evidence of the current value of an asset, the evidence (cost) may be objective but its selection as the current value of the asset may reflect personal bias. Accountants traditionally reflect this type of bias when they report historical costs in financial statements but move to a current market price when this is lower than cost.

The third meaning of objectivity has greater significance for measurement theory in accounting. Measurements can be said to be objective if they can be verified by intersubjective consensus of qualified experts. Moonitz, for example, states that "objective . . . means . . . unbiased; subject to verification by another competent investigator."[41] This meaning is similar to the standard of verifiability proposed by the Committee to Prepare a Statement of Basic Accounting Theory. The committee defined verifiability as

that attribute of information which allows qualified individuals working independently of one another to develop essentially similar measures or conclusions from an examination of the same evidence.[42]

If several investigators use the same or similar methods of measurement of an attribute based on similar evidence, the several resulting measurements will most likely provide a range of values. If the measurements are free from personal bias, it is probable although not necessary that a frequency distribution of these measurements will produce a symmetrical curve. For any given number of observations or measurements, the degree of objectivity or verifiability depends upon the dispersion of the measurement values around a mean or average figure. This is

[40] W. A. Paton and A. C. Littleton, *An Introduction to Corporate Accounting Standards,* American Accounting Association, 1955, pp. 18–21.

[41] Moonitz, *ARS No. 1, op. cit.,* p. 42.

[42] Committee to Prepare a Statement of Basic Accounting Theory, *op. cit.,* p. 10.

demonstrated by the following two measurement procedures which result in the same average value:

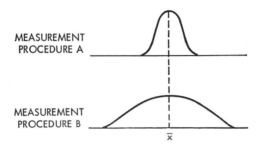

Measurement procedure A is more verifiable than procedure B since any measurement value x_i has a greater probability of being close to the mean value $\bar{x}$ by using procedure A than by using procedure B. Thus, verifiability is a relative concept. Very few procedures will result in values upon which many accountants would have complete agreement. Although objectivity or verifiability cannot be obtained unless the measurements are relatively free from personal bias, measurement errors and differences in interpretation may also result in the loss of verifiability. Note, however, that the relative degree of objectivity or verifiability alone does not determine the reliability of the measurement procedure to describe accurately the attribute under consideration. Even the mean value $\bar{x}$ may fail to measure accurately the attribute.

Freedom from Bias

The Committee to Prepare a Statement of Basic Accounting Theory included "freedom from bias" as one of its basic standards. It used this term to mean that "the facts have been impartially determined and reported" and that they are free from built-in bias.[43] The Committee on External Reporting, in applying these standards to an evaluation of accounting information, subsequently included personal bias in the application of the standard of verifiability and interpreted "freedom from bias" to represent the ability of the measurement procedure to provide an accurate description of the attribute under consideration.[44]

Bias inherent in the measurement procedure can be demonstrated by the following diagrams:

---

[43] *Ibid.*, p. 7.

[44] Committee on External Reporting, *op. cit.*, pp. 94–95.

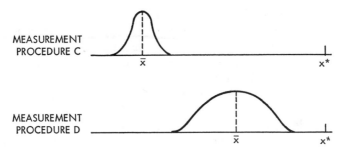

Bias is determined by the relative deviation of the mean value $\bar{x}$ determined by the measurement procedure and the alleged or "true" value x^* of the attribute. Therefore, while measurement procedure C is more verifiable than D, procedure D is less biased than C because the mean value produced lies closer to the alleged value x^*. Since a "true" value for an attribute cannot be determined, the difference between the mean value $\bar{x}$ and the alleged value x^* must be based upon expert judgment, taking into consideration the logical relationship between the measurement procedure and the attribute being measured. For example, historical cost is not likely to be free from bias in measuring the current market value of an asset if prices have changed radically since the date of acquisition. On the other hand, a procedure which adjusts historical cost for changes in the specific prices of that class of asset may be less verifiable but result in less bias.

Reliability is defined by Ijiri and Jaedicke as the degree of objectivity or verifiability plus the bias factor. For a statistical measure of reliability, they suggest the use of the mean-square-error.[45] However, such a computation would be difficult because of the unknown nature of the "true" or alleged value x^*. It might be better to judge verifiability and bias separately and then evaluate the trade-offs, taking into consideration the nature of the information and its relevance for prediction of the several elements required in the decision models of users.

Limitations of the Monetary Unit

While accounting data are not limited to measurement in terms of a monetary unit, accounting reports have traditionally included primarily financial information. And in many cases, the monetary unit provides the best measurement unit, particularly where aggregation is necessary or

---

[45] Yuji Ijiri and Robert K. Jaedicke, "Reliability and Objectivity of Accounting Measurements," *Accounting Review,* Vol. XLI (July, 1966), pp. 480–83. Also included in Yuji Ijiri, *The Foundations of Accounting Measurement* (Englewood Cliffs, N.J.: Prentice-Hall, Inc., 1967), pp. 142–45.

desirable. However, the monetary unit has its limitations as a method of communicating information. The most serious limitation or constraint is due to the fact that the value of the monetary unit is not stable over time. Since many predictions and decisions must rely on valid comparisons of accounting data over time, the lack of a stable monetary unit means that accounting data based on past exchange prices must be adjusted to be comparable with current and future exchange prices in order to be relevant and reliable for the making of appropriate predictions and decisions. In other words, the measurement constraint of instability of the measuring unit requires some modification in the use of exchange prices of different time periods expressed in terms of money. The problems resulting from this instability and the effect on the derivation of accounting principles are discussed at greater length in Chapter 7.

Conservatism

The general constraint of uncertainty has served as a basis for the traditional accounting concept of conservatism. As it is generally stated, the concept of conservatism is not a postulate of accounting nor should it be one of the constraints. But in its operational form, it serves as a constraint to the presentation of data that may otherwise be reliable and relevant. To understand conservatism in accounting, we should try to understand the conditions that give rise to it and point out the element of truth in the constraint, if indeed there is any.

The term "conservatism" is generally used to mean that accountants should report the lowest of several possible values for assets and revenues and the highest of several possible values for liabilities and expenses. It also implies that expenses should be recognized sooner rather than later and that revenues should be recognized later rather than sooner. Therefore, net assets are more likely to be understated than overstated, and income is more likely to be understated. Thus, pessimism is assumed to be better than optimism in financial reporting.

One of the arguments for conservatism is that the tendency toward pessimism is assumed to be necessary to offset the overoptimism of managers and owners. The entrepreneur is naturally optimistic about his enterprise and it is assumed that this optimism tends to be reflected in both the selection and emphasis in accounting reports. Through the pressure of creditors and other users of financial reports, the accountants of the 19th century were continually under pressure to refrain from reflecting this optimism in their reports. Thus, many of the traditional tenets in accounting were supported by conservatism and many of these concepts permeate accounting practice today. In this context, conservatism has no place in accounting theory. Deliberate understatements may lead to poor decisions just as frequently as do overstatements.

A second argument for conservatism is that overstatement of profit and valuations is more dangerous for the business and its owners than understatement. That is, it is assumed that the consequences of loss or bankruptcy are much more serious than the consequences of a gain. Therefore, it is argued that there is no reason why the measurement and recognition rules for losses should be the same as for gains when the consequences are different.[46] The objection to this argument is that the accountant is in a better position to evaluate risk than is the investor or creditor. However, the evaluation of risk and the preference or aversion for risk are subjective judgments which cannot be assumed by the accountant. Instead of applying conservatism, the objective of financial reports should be to provide adequate information to permit the users to make their own evaluations of risk.

A third argument for conservatism is based upon the assumption that the accountant has much more information available to him than can be communicated to investors and creditors and that the accountant is faced with two types of risk. On the one hand, there is the risk that what is reported may turn out subsequently to be untrue. On the other hand, there is the risk that what is not reported may subsequently turn out to be true. This is similar to the *alpha and beta* risks of statistics. The *alpha* risk involves the acceptance of a hypothesis that is in fact unacceptable and the *beta* risk involves the rejection of a hypothesis that is in fact acceptable. With respect to favorable items, the support for the rejection of that which might be true is greater than the support for the acceptance of that which might be untrue, and vice versa for unfavorable items.[47] The objection to this practice is that there is no basic evidence that the consequence of the one risk is so much greater than the consequence of the other to justify this bias in accounting reports. The accountant should attempt to balance these risks as much as possible and provide information for a proper evaluation of the risk whenever possible.

Conservatism is, at best, a very poor method of treating the existence of uncertainty in valuation and income. At its worst, it results in a complete distortion of accounting data. Its main danger is that, because it is a very crude method, its effects are capricious. Therefore, conservatively reported data are not subject to proper interpretation even by the most informed readers. It should be noted also that conservatism conflicts with the objective to disclose all relevant information, and with consistency to the extent to which that is a relevant constraint; and it can

---

[46] See Eugen Schmalenbach, *Dynamic Accounting* (English translation, London: Gee & Company Ltd., 1959), pp. 81–82.

[47] See Arthur L. Thomas, *Revenue Recognition* (Ann Arbor: University of Michigan Press, 1966), pp. 53–54; and Carl Thomas Devine, "The Rule of Conservatism Reexamined," *Journal of Accounting Research*, Vol. I (Autumn, 1963), pp. 137–38.

lead to a lack of comparability, because there can be no uniform standards for its implementation.

THE ACCOUNTING FRAMEWORK

The general structure of accounting theory requires for its implementation a set of symbols and a framework in which ideas and data can be expressed and summarized. The traditional framework that has served accounting well for many years includes double entry, with the concepts of accounts, ledgers, and trial balances, and the presentation of accounting data in the form of financial statements that articulate with each other. *Accounting Research Study No. 1* confirms the utility of this structure by stating that "the results of the accounting process are expressed in a set of fundamentally related financial statements which articulate with each other and rest upon the same underlying data."[48] While some type of framework is necessary, the selection of any particular set of symbols and reports should not be included among the postulates. *ARS No. 1* does not necessarily limit the structure to conventional types of financial statements, but it does state that they should articulate with each other and rest on the same underlying data. While these restrictions may be desirable, they should be evaluated on the basis of their usefulness as a structure rather than as a postulate.

The characteristics of a desirable framework, however, can be derived from the objectives of accounting, the environmental postulates, the measurement concepts, and the constraints. Articulation has been thought to be desirable in order to make the information more understandable and more useful for decision making, because of the availability of consistent and comparable summaries. It has been thought that if the statements are related and based on the same underlying data, the entire structure can be made more formal, resulting in greater logic, better consistency, and a greater degree of uniformity. However, articulation and the rigid application of double entry have resulted in the presentation of meaningless or misleading information in one statement as a result of an attempt to improve reported information in another. The application of the Lifo procedure for inventory valuation is an example. There is also little evidence that retained earnings or total stockholders' equity is meaningful for predictions or decision making or that the articulation of the income statement with the funds statement provides relevant information. Nevertheless, articulation is likely to continue so long as accountants and users of financial reports believe that it provides some assurance that some relevant information is not omitted or some as-

---

[48] Moonitz, *op. cit.*, p. 52.

surance that management is not manipulating the information released for its own benefit. In fact, articulation provides no assurance that either of these is true.

The types of financial statements presented in formal reports should meet the objectives of potential users of the reports in accordance with the measurement standards and in light of realistic constraints. Prior to the 1930's, the balance sheet was thought to be the most useful, primarily because it provided information to creditors. Subsequently, the income statement came to be considered the most relevant statement, on the ground that it provided better information for investors and stockholders. More recently, the funds statement and experiments in the development of statements that adjust for changes in the level of prices have been added to the reports considered relevant for external users. Future developments in the accounting framework and the reporting structure are imperative to permit the optimum amount of relevant information to be presented in external reports. The external reports should probably include at least information regarding resources and commitments and also regarding funds and resource flows, both historically and as plans for the future. In the interests of economy, a single data base should probably be devised upon which reports for both internal and external uses can be built.

SELECTED ADDITIONAL READING ON CHAPTER TOPICS

Postulates

CHAMBERS, R. J. "Why Bother with Postulates?" *Journal of Accounting Research,* Vol. I (Spring, 1963), pp. 3–15.

DEINZER, HARVEY T. *Development of Accounting Thought,* chaps. 8 and 9. New York: Holt, Rinehart & Winston, Inc., 1965.

GORDON, MYRON. "Postulates, Principles, and Research in Accounting," *Accounting Review,* Vol. XXXIX (April, 1964), pp. 251–63.

MAUTZ, R. K. "The Place of Postulates in Accounting," *Journal of Accountancy,* January, 1965, pp. 46–49.

METCALF, RICHARD W. "The Basic Postulates in Perspective," *Accounting Review,* Vol. XXXIX (January, 1964), pp. 16–21.

MOONITZ, MAURICE. "The Basic Postulates of Accounting," *Accounting Research Study No. 1.* New York: American Institute of Certified Public Accountants, 1961.

——. "Why Do We Need 'Postulates' and 'Principles'?" *Journal of Accountancy,* Vol. CXVI (December, 1963), pp. 42–46.

VATTER, WILLIAM J. "Postulates and Principles," *Journal of Accounting Research,* Vol. I (Autumn, 1963), pp. 179–97.

Continuity

FREMGREN, JAMES M. "The Going Concern Assumption: A Critical Appraisal," *Accounting Review*, Vol. XLIII (October, 1968), pp. 649–56.

STERLING, ROBERT R. "The Going Concern: An Examination," *Accounting Review*, July, 1968, pp. 481–502.

Objectives

BEAVER, WILLIAM H., JOHN W. KENNELLY, and WILLIAM M. VOSS. "Predictive Ability as a Criterion for the Evaluation of Accounting," *Accounting Review*, Vol. XLIII (October, 1968), pp. 675–83.

RAPPAPORT, ALFRED. "Establishing Objectives for Published Corporate Accounting Reports," *Accounting Review*, Vol. XXXIX (October, 1964), pp. 951–62.

Materiality and Relevance

BERNSTEIN, LEOPOLD A. "The Concept of Materiality," *Accounting Review*, Vol. XLII (January, 1967), pp. 86–95.

HICKS, ERNEST L. "Materiality," *Journal of Accounting Research*, Vol. II (Autumn, 1964), pp. 158–71.

RAPPAPORT, DONALD. "Materiality," *Journal of Accountancy*, April, 1964, pp. 42–48.

SHWAYDER, KEITH. "Relevance," *Journal of Accounting Research*, Vol. VI (Spring, 1968), pp. 86–97.

Consistency

BEDFORD, NORTON, and TOSHIO, IINO. "Consistency Reexamined," *Accounting Review*, Vol. XLIII (July, 1968), pp. 453–58.

McCOSH, ANDREW M. "Accounting Consistency—Key to Stockholder Information," *Accounting Review*, Vol. XLII (October, 1967), pp. 693–700.

Uniformity and Comparability

HENDRIKSEN, ELDON S. "Toward Greater Comparability Through Uniformity of Accounting Principles," *New York Certified Public Accountant*, Vol. XXXVII (February, 1967), pp. 105–15.

SIMMONS, JOHN K. "A Concept of Comparability in Financial Reporting," *Accounting Review*, Vol. XLII (October, 1967), pp. 680–92.

"Uniformity in Financial Accounting," *Law and Contemporary Problems*, Vol. XXX (Autumn, 1965).

Accounting Measurement

IJIRI, YUJI. *The Foundations of Accounting Measurement.* Englewood Cliffs, N.J.: Prentice-Hall, Inc., 1967.

JAEDICKE, ROBERT K., YUJI IJIRI, and OSWALD NIELSEN (eds.). *Research in Accounting Measurement.* American Accounting Association, 1966.

Objectivity

CHAMBERS, R. J. "Measurement and Objectivity in Accounting," *Accounting Review,* Vol. XXXIX (April, 1964), pp. 264–74.

IJIRI, YUJI, and ROBERT K. JAEDICKE. "Reliability and Objectivity of Accounting Measurements," *Accounting Review,* Vol. XLI (July, 1966), pp. 474–83.

McDONALD, DANIEL L. "Feasibility Criteria for Accounting Measures," *Accounting Review,* Vol. XLII (October, 1967), pp. 662–79.

STANLEY, CURTIS HOLT. *Objectivity in Accounting.* Ann Arbor: Bureau of Business Research, Graduate School of Business Administration, University of Michigan, 1965.

Conservatism

DEVINE, CARL T. "The Rule of Conservatism Reexamined," *Journal of Accounting Research,* Vol. I (Autumn, 1963), pp. 127–38.

STERLING, ROBERT R. "Conservatism: The Fundamental Principle of Valuation in Traditional Accounting," *Abacus,* Vol. III (December, 1967), pp. 109–32.

chapter 5

Income Concepts for
Financial Reporting

As indicated in Chapter 3, the computation and reporting of enterprise net income gained considerably in importance during the early 1930's. While supplementary statements, such as the funds flow statement, are becoming more common in financial reports to stockholders and others outside the firm, emphasis on net income reporting continues to be strong in the United States and it appears to be increasing in some other countries. However, already there are rumblings that the income statement will see its demise in the near future unless drastic changes are made to improve the story it tells. Some of the reasons for this potential demise are: (1) the concept of accounting income has not yet been clearly formulated; (2) generally accepted accounting practices permit inconsistencies in the measurement of periodic income of different firms and even between different years for the same firm; (3) price-level changes have modified the meaning of income measured in terms of historical dollars; and (4) other information may prove more useful to investors and stockholders for the making of investment decisions.

Recognizing that the measurement of income has considerable conceptual and practical problems, several suggestions have been made to provide theoretical and practical solutions. While it is difficult to classify the many positions taken regarding the measurement of income, the following five major positions probably represent most of the suggestions regarding the problem of income measurement: (1) One belief is that future progress in accounting theory depends upon agreement on a single concept of income which will conform more closely to what is referred to as "economic income." (2) Others support a single operational concept of income. (3) Some writers subscribe to the idea that several concepts of income should be measured and reported for different purposes. (4) Much of the discussion today centers on an attempt to improve the reporting of what may be called "accounting income" by focusing on transaction data and the accrual process. (5) More recently, several suggestions have been made to the effect that all measurements of income are deficient and that they should be superseded by other measures of economic activity. The concepts of "economic income," "operational income," and "accounting income" are discussed in this chapter following a discussion of the objectives of income reporting. The theory and measurement of the several elements making up accounting income are discussed in the following chapter, and suggestions for the substitution of alternative measures of economic activity are discussed in Chapters 8 and 19.

THE OBJECTIVES OF NET INCOME REPORTING

While a knowledge of different measurements of a firm's net income may be useful for different purposes, there is a definite advantage in the general acceptance of one all-pervasive concept of net income for external reporting purposes. However, a close analysis of the various concepts and objectives of net income indicates clearly that a single concept cannot serve all purposes equally well. At least two choices are possible—a single concept that meets most of the objectives fairly well or several net income figures clearly labeled to serve the several objectives. Disadvantages and difficulties in both of these choices are discernible in the following discussion.

The primary objective of income reporting, of course, is to provide useful information to those who are most interested in financial reports. But more specific objectives must be spelled out in order to obtain a clearer understanding of income reporting. One of the basic objectives assumed to be most important for all users of financial reports is the need to distinguish between invested capital and income—between the stocks and flows—as a part of the descriptive process of accounting. More specific objectives include the use of income as a measurement of the efficiency of management, the use of historical income figures to aid in predicting the future course of the business, and the use of income as a measurement of accomplishment and as a guide to future managerial decisions. Each of these objectives is discussed at greater length in the following paragraphs. Other objectives not discussed at this point include the use of income as a base for taxation, the use of income as a means of regulating firms vested with a public interest, and the use of income figures by economists in evaluating the allocation of resources.

Capital versus Income

In the terms of the economist Irving Fisher,[1] capital is a *stock* of wealth at an instant of time. Income is a *flow* of services through time.

---

[1] Irving Fisher, *The Nature of Capital and Income* (New York: Macmillan Co., 1906), p. 51.

Capital is the embodiment of future services, and income is the enjoyment of these services over a specific period of time. With these definitions, it does not seem possible to confuse the two terms. The one relates to the amount in the reservoir at any one time, and the other refers to the amount flowing out of the reservoir during a period of time.

When these terms are related to a business enterprise, however, they take on slightly different meanings. While, in the above definition, income is the enjoyment from the use of capital, a business enterprise does not exist for the purpose of enjoyment. Its purpose is to provide a flow of wealth for the benefit of its owners or beneficiaries—the equity holders. While capital is still the *stock* of wealth that can provide future services, income is thought of as the *flow* of wealth or services in excess of that necessary to maintain a constant capital. Although a firm may be thought of as relatively permanent in nature, it is not the responsibility of the accountant to see that the invested capital is preserved. This is the responsibility of management or possibly the decision of the owners or equity holders. The accountants' responsibility is to report the amounts that have been made available to the beneficiaries for their enjoyment or reinvestment and the change in the capital of the enterprise. Thus, there is an important distinction between the flows to beneficiaries that represent amounts that can be enjoyed without impairing the future cash flows and those flows that represent reductions in wealth. In accounting terms, this is the distinction between income and a return of capital.

Why is it important to distinguish between enterprise income and a return of captial? The answer is twofold. First, changes in the capital of the enterprise may affect the amount of future flows to residual equity holders (the holders of common stock) and thus the value of their equity at any point in time. Second, changes in enterprise capital may affect the relationships among the various equity holders, including the holders of debt and preferred stock.

The residual equity holders are interested not only in how much they can expect to receive from the enterprise during the following period, but also in the net changes in the power of the enterprise to provide future flows. Current investor interest is focused not only on the ability of the firm to maintain dividends, but in many cases on its growth potential. The knowledge of these changes is even more important when the ownership rights to these future flows are transferred frequently during the life of the enterprise. During the early period of the railroad industry in the United States, it was not uncommon for promoters to pay huge dividends out of capital during the early life of the firm. Investors, believing this to be the true income of the firm, paid high prices for the stock only to find later that the ability to pay dividends in the future was being eroded because of these huge early dividends. Equity requires that both buyers and sellers of common stock should have adequate information to make expectations regarding the current and future dividends of the firm.

With the separation of ownership and control in most large corporations, accounting also has the responsibility to report on the stewardship of the management group entrusted with the proper use of the invested capital. A proper distinction between income and changes in capital is one of the means of determining the extent to which management has carried out the function of operating the enterprise for the benefit of the owners.

The concept of capital maintenance is also important to bondholders, preferred stockholders, and the providers of short-term credit. All of these equity holders are interested in the probability of repayment at some future date. The prospect of repayment is greater if the total invested capital of the enterprise is maintained at a constant level or permitted to increase. The prospect of repayment is less if the capital is diminished either through losses or by the payment of dividends in excess of earnings. The creditors cannot always be protected against losses but, if they are properly notified, they may be able to protect their position before it is too late. To a certain extent, creditors are protected legally and often contractually from the impairment of invested capital by the payment of dividends in excess of earnings.

The various classes of equity holders are also interested in the return on their investment, whether it be contractual, as interest on debt, or dependent on earnings, as dividends on preferred and common stock. Since invested capital reflects, in part, the ability of the firm to continue the payment of a return to equity holders in the future, changes in the amount of invested capital are vital in decisions regarding the future flow of this return to any class of equity holders.

The concepts of capital and income, however, are not clearly formulated. Capital can be defined in terms of the current monetary unit or a monetary unit of constant value; in physical terms; in terms of capacity to produce goods and services; or in terms of the future expectations regarding future flows to stockholders. The measurement difficulties in separating capital and income are even greater. These conceptual and measurement difficulties are discussed at greater length later in this chapter and in Chapter 6.

Income as a Measurement of Efficiency

The efficient operation of an enterprise affects both the current dividend stream and the use of the invested capital for providing a future dividend stream. Therefore, all equity holders, but particularly the common stockholders, are interested in the efficiency of management. The present equity holders can take the necessary steps to obtain a new management if the present management is not operating efficiently, or they may provide for incentives or bonuses to efficient managements. Prospective stockholders will attempt to evaluate the efficiency of management before investing or placing a value on the stock of the firm. In either case, a measurement of the efficiency of the firm provides a basis for decisions.

How can a measurement of past income provide a basis for determining the efficiency of a firm? Efficiency is a relative term and has meaning only when compared with an ideal or some other base. It also depends on whether the goal of the firm is to maximize income or to provide a fair or reasonable return on investment. If the capital employed by the firm is constant from year to year, the income figure itself may be used as a measure of the efficiency of the firm. The income of the current year can then be compared with prior years, and some judgment would have to be made whether or not the income of any year has reached the proper goal. However, if the capital invested changes from year to year, the income must be compared with some changing magnitude, such as invested capital or total revenue.

When net income is divided by invested capital, the result is called the rate of return on investment. This can be computed by dividing the net income to stockholders by the stockholders' equity—the rate of return on stockholders' investment; or by dividing the net income plus interest (net of taxes) by the total capitalization of the firm, including long-term debt and stockholder equity—the rate of return on total equity. In either case, a measurement of the efficient utilization of the capital employed in the enterprise is thought to be obtained. But, again, the criterion of efficiency depends upon the standard used. The rate of return for prior years, the rate of return earned by other firms, an arbitrary rate, or a market-determined rate can be used as the standard. One important aspect of the rate of return as a measure of efficiency should be noted. Its validity depends on not only the proper measurement of income but also the proper measurement of capital employed in the business.

Another base for comparing income is the total revenue of the period. While the total revenue of the period can be measured more accurately than the capital invested, it has some definite disadvantages. A comparison of the net income to sales for several years is valid only if capacity utilization is the same each year or if the failure to utilize capacity is considered a part of the inefficiency of management. Comparisons with other firms are even more difficult to make. Only if the capital turnover (sales divided by capital) is the same for several firms, would the ratio of income to sales be comparable. As this is not likely, this ratio is not valid for interfirm comparisons.

Income as a Predictive Device

The management of a business enterprise must study historical data in order to plan for the future, either to increase the level of income in the future or to maintain a reasonable level. However, most of the decisions of creditors and investors, including the stockholders of large corporations, require a prediction of the future distributions by the firm. Historical distributions represent water over the dam; the important decisions regarding the purchase or sale of stock or bonds of the firm or the making of a loan to the firm require expectations regarding the future.

The current value of a firm and the value of a share of stock in the firm are dependent upon the expected future stream of distributions to stockholders. Based on these expectations, a current stockholder may decide either to sell his shares or continue to hold them. An investor who is not currently a stockholder may decide either to purchase shares in the firm or to invest his capital elsewhere. Thus, expectations regarding future distributions are paramount in these investment decisions. If there is a relationship between reported income and dividend distributions, investors may focus their attention on their expectations regarding future incomes of the firm. For many firms, income predictions are assumed to be more relevant in predicting the future market price of stock than are predictions of short-term dividend distributions; and long-term distributions are assumed to be dependent upon retained income and growth factors. Therefore, expectations of future incomes are used by many investors as a main factor in predicting future dividend distributions and expected dividends are an important factor in placing a current value on shares of stock or on the entire firm.

Bondholders and short-term creditors are also interested in the future income. The greater the expectation of income for the firm, the greater the expectation that the creditors will receive their annual return and also the greater the expectation that they will receive repayment of the principal when the debt matures.

How can a knowledge of past incomes aid in the prediction of future incomes and thus in the current value of the firm? It is certainly not a substitute for a crystal ball. But there is some validity in the observation that all economic changes, and most physical changes, for that matter, are dependent in large part upon past conditions and events. It is safer to predict what the weather will be like this afternoon by observing the weather conditions in the morning than it is to ignore the preceding conditions. A firm that has suffered losses for several years is not as likely to yield high incomes in the future as a firm that already has a record of high incomes.

But just as the weatherman observes recurring and nonrecurring patterns and looks for signs of change, so the investor must analyze the recurring nature of the favorable and unfavorable aspects of operations and observe other factors which are likely to cause changes in incomes. While historical net incomes are valuable in making predictions regarding future incomes, the prognosticator should analyze the favorable and unfavorable aspects, including only those items that are recurring by nature. The more difficult task is to predict what nonrecurring events will occur in the future. Thus, while the starting point may be the historical net income figures, other information must be considered in order to obtain the maximum predictive ability.

Managerial Decision Making

While the formal financial statements are directed primarily to the external users of accounting data, accountants must also furnish management with the tools and raw material required for rendering good decisions. Just as the investor is interested primarily in future dividend flows, so also is management interested primarily in what will happen in the future. Decisions can affect only future events. But management is not so interested in predicting future income as it is in making proper decisions to meet its goals regarding current and future incomes.

How can a knowledge of past incomes help in making good decisions? The answer is basically in the learning process. *Experientia docet.* However, experience can teach only if the methods used and the outcomes can be analyzed to determine the factors which gave rise to the experienced result.

Income is the net result of many past decisions. A good manager will continually evaluate these past decisions to improve his process for arriving at expectations necessary in making future decisions. In each case, the original expectations and plans should be compared with the actual outcome. An explanation should be attempted for any deviations of the final outcome from the expectations. Income, therefore, should measure those economic events which should have been anticipated. Extraneous and exogenous events should be reported separately.

THE SEVERAL CONCEPTS OF INCOME

At the beginning of this chapter it was stated that the income statement has been losing some of its prestige because the concept of accounting income has not yet been clearly formulated. Some of the reasons for the inability to formulate a clear concept of income are: (1) the lack of a good measuring device for determining the value of the future stream of services and changes in this value; (2) the inability to agree on what should be included in the computation of net income; and (3) the disagreement with respect to the persons or groups who are the beneficiaries of net income.

The lack of a good measuring device stems in part from an inability of accountants to state clearly just what they are trying to measure, in large part from the uncertainties in the measurement of future values, and in part from changing prices and price levels. Even if the entire life of the firm is used as the measuring period, many of the difficulties of income measurement are still present. The effect of price-level changes and the selection of the appropriate beneficiaries of net income are still problems of major proportions. But the more difficult problems arise in the measurement of income for periods shorter than the life of the enterprise. In the following concepts of income we are primarily interested in the measurement of income by periods in order to provide information relevant to the making of decisions regarding the firm.

Two major approaches to the measurement of periodic income are the capital maintenance and operational approaches. The capital maintenance approach is sometimes referred to as the balance sheet approach, and the operational approach is sometimes referred to as the transactions-based approach or the income statement approach, although the operational and transactions-based approaches are treated separately below because of differences in emphasis. In the capital maintenance approach, income for a specific period is determined by comparing the net assets at the end of the period with those at the beginning and adjusting for dividends and capital transactions. In the operational and transactions-based approaches, income is measured by the matching of expenses with revenues reported during the period. The conventional approach to income measurement is a combination of the operational and transactions-based approaches and the capital maintenance approach. Most revenues, expenses, gains, and losses are measured by the results of specific transactions; however, accruals, deferrals, inventory valuations and other year-end adjustments are also included in the measurement of income in practice. Thus, it is possible to place the main emphasis on either operations or capital maintenance while recording most changes on the basis of transactions.

Two other basic problems in income measurement are: (1) What types of transactions and what types of changes in capital values should be included in income and which should be excluded? (2) Who are the beneficiaries of income? While both of these questions involve a choice of what should be included in income, the type of choice is entirely different. The former choice is related to the measurement of operations, while the latter is a classification by income recipients.

The Capital Maintenance Concepts of Income

Among the economists, Adam Smith was the first to define income as that amount that can be consumed without encroaching upon capital, including both fixed and circulating capital. Hicks elaborated upon this by saying that income is the amount that a person can consume during a period of time and be as well off at the end of that time as he was at the beginning.[2] However, there is no clear understanding or agreement as to the precise meaning of "well-offness." Several approaches to this concept are discussed in the following paragraphs, but the measurement of "well-offness" during periods of price-level changes is discussed in Chapter 7. In the following discussion, we assume for argument's sake that the general value of money remains constant over time and that meaningful measurements of wealth can be obtained and expressed in money terms.

The concept of capital maintenance implies an overall view of the capital invested in the firm. Once the concepts are developed, we shall see that they can be applied to the analysis of specific transactions; but, in the following discussion, income is computed by placing a valuation on the net assets of the firm at the end of the period and comparing this with the valuation at the beginning of the period. For example, if the net assets of the firm were $80,000 at the end of the period and $76,000 at the beginning, the net income would be $4,000 in the absence of capital transactions and the payment of dividends. If additional capital stock in the amount of $11,000 had been sold and if dividends in the amount of $8,000 had been paid during the period, the net income would have been $1,000.

The greatest difficulty with this approach is in the measurement of the net assets at the beginning and end of the period. Several methods of valuation include (1) capitalization of the expected future net stream of cash or services to be received over the life of the firm; (2) the aggregation of the selling prices of the several assets of the firm less the summation of the liabilities; (3) valuation of the firm on the basis of the current stock market prices applied to the total stock outstanding; and (4) valuation of the firm by using input values (either historical or current cost) for nonmonetary assets and adding the present cash value of monetary assets and subtracting liabilities.

Capitalization. One of the suggested concepts for measuring the net assets at the beginning and end of the year is the capitalization of all expected future cash distributions by the firm to stockholders. This capitalized value can be defined as the present discounted value of the expected cash distributions to stockholders by the firm during the remaining life of the enterprise, including the final amount expected to be paid at liquidation. In computing this capitalized value, three factors must be estimated—the amount of the net cash distributions expected to be paid each year, the number of years of remaining life, and the appropriate discount factor. This relationship can be expressed by the following formula:

$$P_0 = R_1(1 + i)^{-1} + R_2(1 + i)^{-2} + R_3(1 + i)^{-3} \ldots + R_n(1 + i)^{-n}$$

$$(1)$$

---

[2] J. R. Hicks, *Value and Capital* (Oxford: Clarendon Press, 1946), p. 172.

or as:

$$P_0 = \sum_{t=1}^{n} \frac{R_t}{(1+i)^t} \tag{2}$$

where:

P_0 = The present value or capitalized value at time 0.
R_t = The net cash distribution expected in period t.
i = The appropriate discount factor.
n = The number of years of expected life.

Income can be computed for the first year by the following formula:

$$I_1 = P_1 - P_0 + R_1 \tag{3}$$

where the value of P_1 is as follows:

$$P_1 = \sum_{t=2}^{n} \frac{R_t}{(1+i)^{t-1}} \tag{4}$$

As an example, let us assume certainty and the following cash distributions during a life of five years for a firm:

Year	1	2	3	4	5
Cash flow (net)	$100	$300	$200	$400	$500

In the case of certainty, the appropriate discount rate would be the opportunity cost to the owners (assumed to be 5 percent in this case) and the present value of the firm would be $1,261.[3] At the end of the first year the capitalized value of the remaining cash distributions would be $1,224[3] and the net income for the first year would be computed as follows:

------

[3] These present values are computed as follows:

Beginning of First Year	End of First Year
$100 \times 0.9524 \left[\left(\dfrac{1}{1.05}\right)\right] = \$\ \ 95$	$300 \times 0.9524 \left[\left(\dfrac{1}{1.05}\right)\right] = \$\ 286$
$300 \times 0.9070 \left[\left(\dfrac{1}{1.05}\right)^2\right] = \ \ 272$	$200 \times 0.9070 \left[\left(\dfrac{1}{1.05}\right)^2\right] = \ \ 181$
$200 \times 0.8638 \left[\left(\dfrac{1}{1.05}\right)^3\right] = \ \ 173$	$400 \times 0.8638 \left[\left(\dfrac{1}{1.05}\right)^3\right] = \ \ 346$
$400 \times 0.8227 \left[\left(\dfrac{1}{1.05}\right)^4\right] = \ \ 329$	$500 \times 0.8227 \left[\left(\dfrac{1}{1.05}\right)^4\right] = \ \ \underline{411}$
$500 \times 0.7835 \left[\left(\dfrac{1}{1.05}\right)^5\right] = \ \ \underline{392}$	$\$1,224$
$\$1,261$	

Cash distributed at the end of the first year ...... $ 100
Capitalized value at the end of the first year of the
   cash flows for the remaining years 1,224

Total value of the firm at the end of the first year
   assuming no distributions to stockholders $1,324
   Less: Capitalized value at the beginning of
     the year 1,261

Income for Year .... $ 63

Since this income of $63 represents the increase in the total value of the firm during the year, it also represents 5 percent of the initial capitalized value of $1,261. It represents, in effect, interest on the capital invested. If the cash distribution each year is greater than the income (interest), the income would decline each year. In the case cited, the incomes for each of the five years would be $63, $61, $49, $42, and $24. Note that this has no direct relationship to the cash distributions in each year. However, if the initial income of $63 were distributed to stockholders and the remaining amount of available cash were reinvested by the firm in projects which will yield 5 percent, both the income and the capitalized value of the firm would remain constant into the future.

In the absence of certainty, the future cash payments represent expected values of probability distributions. For example, if the subjective estimates of the cash dividend for the first year are either $120 with a probability of 0.6 or $70 with a probability of 0.4, the expected value would be $100.[4] The number of probable values could be few or many, including all possible values of the monetary unit. Each value would be assigned a probability value such that the sum of all probabilities is one. Note that the expected value is subjective because of the necessity of estimating the possible values and because of the assignment of subjective probability values to these.

The appropriate discount rate in the case of certainty is the opportunity rate that could be earned on a riskless security. In the case of uncertainty, most authors define the appropriate rate as the subjective required rate for investments of equal risk or the target rate of return. While there are some theoretical difficulties in including the adjustment for risk in the interest factor, this will be discussed in Chapter 9 and a subjective rate will be assumed at this point in order to focus on the income concepts. Therefore, in the absence of changes in expectations and if the actual cash distribution the first year is equal to the expected cash payment, income as computed in the above example is equal to the

---

[4] The expected value of the cash flow would be computed as follows:

$$\$120 \times 0.6 = \$\ 72$$
$$70 \times 0.4 = \underline{\ \ 28}$$
$$\$100$$

subjective rate of return multiplied by the beginning (or average) capitalized value. Edwards and Bell call this the subjective profit, because it is defined as the interest at the target rate on the subjective value of the firm's assets at the beginning of the period.[5]

But if the anticipations at the end of the period have changed since the beginning of the period, the actual subjective profit for this period will differ from the anticipated subjective profit. While the anticipated subjective profit is based on the subjective value of the firm's assets at the beginning of the period, the actual or *ex post* subjective profit includes changes in the subjective value of the assets at the end of the period. For example, if the cash flow during the first period is $100 as anticipated, but at the end of the period the cash flows for the following four periods are now expected to be $400 a year instead of $300, $200, $400, and $500, the income for the first year would be computed as follows:

Cash distributed at the end of the first year	$ 100
Capitalized value at the end of the year of remaining expected cash flows of $400 a year for four years	1,418
Total value of the firm at the end of the year	$1,518
Less: Capitalized value at the beginning of the year	1,261
Income for Year	$ 257

This income of $257 is made up of the following:

Anticipated subjective profit	$ 63
Increase in subjective value of the firm	194
Total Income	$257

There is some question as to whether the increase in subjective value of the firm of $194 is really income. One contention is that this change in expectations is really an adjustment of the original value of the firm, which was in error at the beginning of the year. In fact, one argument is that with the current expectations at the end of the year, the value at the beginning of the year should have been $1,446 instead of $1,261. Therefore, the net change in capitalized value can be analyzed as follows:

Subjective profit or interest (5% × $1,446)	$ 72
Adjustment of original subjective value ($1,446 less $1,261)	185
Total Increase in Capitalized Value	$257

If, on the other hand, the expectations regarding future cash flows do not change, but the cash receipt for the first year is $130 instead of $100 as anticipated, the income for the period would be as follows:

---

[5] Edgar O. Edwards and Philip W. Bell, *The Theory and Measurement of Business Income* (Berkeley and Los Angeles: University of California Press, 1961), pp. 38–44.

Cash distributed at the end of the first year	$ 130
Capitalized value at the end of the year of remaining expected cash flows (unchanged)	1,224
Total value of the firm at the end of the year (before dividend payment)	$1,354
Less: Capitalized value at the beginning of the year	1,261
Income for Year	$ 93

This income of $93 is made up of the following:

Anticipated subjective profit (interest)	$63
Increase in the cash distributed over that expected	30
Total income	$93

What does this concept of income include and what does it mean? (1) The main part of the income is the subjective interest on the capitalized value of the firm. Note that this is a function of only time, the interest rate, and the expected cash flows in the future. The expected cash flows, however, may be due to either current or future production and sales efforts. (2) The changes in expectations regarding future cash flows arise because of changes either in the appraisal of management's efficiencies or deficiencies, or in expectations regarding economic conditions (such as changes in tastes). They may also be due to general optimism or pessimism. (3) The difference between the actual cash available for distribution and that expected may be due to windfall gains and losses from external causes or miscalculations in original expectations.

Conventional accounting practice recognizes some of these concepts, but rejects them most of the time. In a few cases, such as the recognition of interest on investments, the accrual concept requires the reporting of income on the basis of time alone. Actual cash receipts in excess of the expected amount are traditionally included in ordinary income or classified as extraordinary gains or losses. However, accounting practice does not require the actual receipt of the cash for this recognition; changes in anticipated cash flows may be recorded when they become fairly certain and the amount is verifiable, such as when an asset is sold under a contract requiring payment at a later date. Other changes in expectations, however, are generally denied recognition.

While the capitalization concept has merit as an economic concept of income, it has some specific conceptual and practical disadvantages for accounting purposes. The practical disadvantages arise primarily from the subjective nature of the expectations. Even though the accountant may be independent in his judgments, he is likely to be overly optimistic or overly pessimistic in the eyes of management, stockholders, or other users of the financial reports. The ideal would be to provide adequate information to permit each user of accounting statements to apply his own judgment regarding expectations of future cash flows and the selection of an appropriate discount factor.

But the capitalization concept is also deficient conceptually for the following reasons: (1) Expectations regarding future cash flows cannot be converted into single values or certainty equivalents without knowing the risk preferences of the users of the information; the adjustment for risk by including it in the subjective discount rate is conceptually inappropriate. (2) Emphasis is placed upon the time factor and expected cash flows; all other economic events and activities are ignored. (3) The income measurement does not disclose whether it is due to commendable actions of management or only to fortuitous circumstances; that is, it does not provide information useful for measuring management efficiency. (4) The value of the firm is determined by discounting all expected cash flows indefinitely into the future, many of which have no relationship to current or past activity. (5) One of the main deficiencies is that it places the cart before the horse. Net cash flows of future periods must be predicted accurately in order to compute current income. In a world of certainty, there would be no reason to compute periodic income, as this would be known in advance; and under conditions of uncertainty, expected cash flows are used to determine current income. However, one of the objectives of measuring current income is thought to be to permit the users of financial reports to make reliable predictions of future cash flows. Since predictions must be based at least in part on current and past economic activity, the users of financial data should be given some measurements of past activity in order to make their own predictions or evaluate the predictions of others. (6) Finally, in a world of uncertainty, expectations are dependent at least in part on the state of optimism or pessimism existing at the time. A consistent treatment of uncertainty from one period to another would be difficult to accomplish.[6]

Market Valuation of the Firm.   As an alternative to the capitalization of future cash flows, it may be possible to determine what investors may be willing to pay for the entire firm. Thus, the expectations of others are substituted for the expectations of the accountant. However, even if such valuations were obtainable, it would be difficult to separate the income based on the subjective rate of return from the change in value arising from changes in expectations. The burden of subjective determination is passed to persons other than the accountants; otherwise, it has all of the difficulties of the capitalization method.

An alternative is to measure the value of the firm by multiplying the number of shares outstanding by the market price of the stock as determined by exchange markets. The advantage of this procedure is that a verifiable valuation can be obtained that is based on the market's evaluation of future cash flows to stockholders. This is different from the capitalization method because the opportunity rate of return and the adjustment for risk in the market may be different than the accountant's

---

[6] For a further discussion of valuation on the basis of discounted expected cash flows, see pp. 261–64 in Chapter 9.

subjective discount rate. Another major difference is that the quoted market price represents the price of a few shares but does not imply that all shares could be purchased at that price. Thus, this method has many of the disadvantages associated with the capitalization process except for its verifiability. But verifiability may be offset by a lack of freedom from bias, particularly since stock prices are affected by external and capricious factors.

Current Cash Equivalent. As an alternate to the capitalization of a firm, the firm's capital can be defined as the sum of the money or cash equivalent of all assets less the sum of the money equivalent of the liabilities. The current cash equivalent can be defined as the market selling price or realizable price of the assets held by the firm.[7] By computing the net assets of the firm at the end of the period and subtracting the net assets computed in a similar fashion at the beginning of the period, and adjusting for capital transactions, the net income for the period can be determined.[8]

The value of the firm determined by the summation of market prices is assumed to be more objective or verifiable than the capitalized value of the firm, because these prices depend upon the expectations of others outside the firm. Note that these are opportunity cost values. They represent values for which the existing assets could be exchanged in the market. The capitalized value of the firm would normally be greater than the sum of the market prices of the specific assets, because if it were not, the firm would be better off by selling its assets in the market. This difference is due, in part, to the exclusion of goodwill and other intangibles that do not have separate market prices from the summation of asset prices. However, it may also be due to the evaluations of expectations, the selections of discount factors, and the adjustments for risk as well as costs involved in the sale and transfer of specific assets.

In addition to the increased verifiability by the use of cash equivalents, the computation of income by comparing changes in the market prices of assets and liabilities has the advantage of providing a better basis for judging the alternatives open to management. But it provides a limited basis for the prediction of future changes because it does not disclose the nature of the changes arising in prior periods.

A major disadvantage of using market valuations is the lack of a ready market for many of the assets owned by a firm. For many items of plant and equipment, the only market prices available would probably represent liquidation or forced-sale values rather than the price that could be obtained in organized markets. As a result, the net income would be similar to that which would be obtained if the firm were liquidated at

---

[7] See Raymond J. Chambers, *Accounting Evaluation and Economic Behavior* (Englewood Cliffs, N.J.: Prentice-Hall, Inc., 1966), p. 92.

[8] *Ibid.,* pp. 112–14.

the end of each period and then started over with the liquidation valuations for the next period.

In some cases, however, market values can be obtained by using product sales prices (output prices). These prices must be discounted to account for the time for production and sale, and they must be adjusted for additional costs of production and transfer. This procedure can be useful particularly in the case of inventories and other assets that can be identified directly with specific products or service outputs of the firm. In some respects this valuation is similar to the process of capitalization. Product prices and cash flows related to the product must be estimated and discounted to the present. The main difference is that each asset is valued separately, while the capitalization of the firm requires the discounting of the net cash flows of the entire enterprise.

Input Prices. A concept of capital maintenance similar to that accepted in practice is the use of input prices either in terms of historical costs or current costs (less depreciation where necessary). In the absence of price changes, real invested capital is maintained if the assets at the end of the period, expressed in terms of input prices (costs), are equal to the total input prices of the assets at the beginning of the period. Income is reflected in an increase in these values adjusted for capital transactions and dividend payments. This income results from the conversion of input prices into market values by the process of sale and exchange. Cash and receivables are received in exchange for the assets valued at cost. Therefore, some of the asset values at the end of the period as well as some at the beginning (the monetary assets) are expressed in terms of market values (output prices).

The computation of net income by the comparison of net asset values at the end of the period with those at the beginning of the period results in a concept of income which is all-inclusive. No classification of income by source can be made. Some of the net income will be the result of normal operations, and a part will arise from abnormal transactions and from capital gains resulting from unexpected value changes. If assets are expressed in terms of historical costs, however, only so-called "realized" capital gains and losses will be included.

When the inputs are expressed in terms of current values, the computation of net income is the same as with historical costs, but the net income resulting includes capital gains and losses arising from price changes— whether or not these capital gains and losses have been realized through sale or exchange. That is, the net income will include gains and losses from the holding of assets as well as the normal operating profit. By expressing the asset values at the beginning of the period in terms of end-of-period input costs, some of these gains and losses can be eliminated; but unless adjustments are made for changes in input values of costs incurred during the period, capital gains and losses will still be included.

Maintenance of Constant Purchasing Power. One of the arguments of economists is that income should be measured in real terms rather than in terms of maintaining monetary values. When changes in the general level of prices occur, the measurement of income by comparing capital values at different times in terms of the monetary unit at each time results in measurements that do not represent changes in real capital. Therefore, many suggestions have been made for the adjustment of capital values so that income can be measured in terms of a constant purchasing power or in terms of a constant value of the monetary unit. These suggestions and the problems involved in making adjustments for changes in the purchasing power of money are discussed at greater length in Chapter 7.

Summary of Capital Maintenance Concepts of Income. The following tabulation summarizes the several concepts of capital that could be used

Concept	Basic Characteristics	Type of Income Included
Capitalization of firm.	Subjective, depends upon expectations of future cash flows.	Subjective interest on capitalized value; windfall gains and losses; changes in expectations, either internal or external.
Market value of total equity.	Based on expectations of investors.	Similar to capitalization, but may also include speculative gains and losses.
Market values of specific assets and liabilities:		
Current cash equivalent.	Based on expectations of others. Does not assume permanence of the firm.	Reflects losses because of the inability of the firm to buy and sell in the same market. Income represents the excess of market values over opportunity costs as a result of changes in liquidation prices or the sale of assets.
Output values.	Based on discounted product sales prices adjusted for additional costs.	Similar to capitalization but each asset is valued separately.
Input values:		
Historical costs.	Maintenance of monetary capital. Verifiable.	Includes only realized income and realized gains and losses.
Current costs.	Maintenance of invested costs in terms of current prices.	Excludes monetary gains and losses from holding initial assets during period of price changes, but includes such gains and losses from holding assets acquired during the period whether realized or not.

in the measurement of business income. All of the capital maintenance concepts of income require an evaluation of total or specific assets and liabilities at the beginning and end of each period. The measurement of capital is based on expectations regarding future cash flows or on market prices as substitutes for subjective expectations. A part of current accounting practice is devised and defended on the basis of the capital maintenance concepts. However, aside from some of the theoretical difficulties with the capital maintenance concepts, a practical disadvantage is their inability to provide adequate information regarding the specific operational activities of the firm.

The Operational Approach to Income Measurement

The operational approach to income differs from the capital maintenance approach in that it focuses on a description of the activities of a firm rather than on the change in its value over time. That is, income is assumed to arise when certain activities or events take place rather than only from the passage of time or from changes in expectations regarding future cash flows. For example, operational income would be recorded during the planning, production, and sale processes as well as possibly during the collection process. Income is reported as a result of accomplishments rather than as an expectation of accomplishments.

One of the advantages of operational income is that it permits the measurement of several different concepts of income which can be used for different purposes. Income arising from the production and sale of merchandise involves different types of evaluations and predictions than does the income arising from buying and selling securities or from holding assets for expected capital gains. The efficiency of management can be measured better if income is classified according to the different types of operations or activities which are subject to more or less control by management. Furthermore, the classification of income by types of operations permits better predictions because of the different behavioral patterns of the different types of activities.

Operational income is also supported, however, because it is assumed to provide a better measure of a single concept of income. Many of those who argue that a single concept of income should be presented for all purposes also support the operational concept, on the grounds that it presents a measurement of actual overall activities of the firm during the period and that this is more useful for general purposes than income based on the capital maintenance concept. This greater utility is assumed because a description of current activity and accomplishments may provide a better basis for prediction of the future and evaluation of the past and present than would a report based only on value changes or changes in expectations of management or accountants.

The Transactions Approach to Income Measurement

The transactions approach to income measurement is the more conventional approach used by accountants. It involves the recording of changes in asset and liability valuations only as these are the result of transactions. The term "transactions" is used in the broad sense to include both internal and external transactions. External transactions arise from dealing with outsiders and the transfer of assets or liabilities to or from the firm. Internal transactions arise from the use or conversion of assets within the firm. Changes in values are excluded if they arise from changes in market valuations or changes in expectations alone. To the extent that asset valuations are adjusted at the end of the period to take these changes into consideration, there is a deviation from the pure transactions approach; this adjustment represents an application of the annual inventory method implicit in the capital maintenance approach.

To the extent that new market valuations replace the input (cost) valuations when an external transaction takes place, income is recognized when the external transaction occurs. While internal transactions could lead to valuation changes, only those that result from the use or conversion of assets are usually recorded. When conversions take place, the value of the old asset is usually transferred to the new asset. Therefore, the transactions approach lends itself readily to the concept of realization at the time of sale or exchange and to the cost convention in accounting.

The main advantages of the transactions approach are: (1) The components of net income can be classified in several ways, such as by product or class of customer, in order to obtain more useful information for management. (2) The incomes arising from the various sources such as from operations and from external causes can be reported separately. (3) It provides a basis for the determination of the types and quantities of assets and liabilities existing at the end of the period. Other valuation methods can then be applied more easily to this inventory. (4) Business efficiency requires the recording of external transactions for other reasons. (5) The various statements can be made to articulate with each other to permit greater understanding of the underlying data.

The general procedure is to record revenues and expenses as they arise from external transactions. The problems of timing and valuation are present in the recording of each transaction, but the main problem is focused upon the proper matching of expenses with the related revenue reported during the specific period. These problems are discussed in the next chapter. As we shall see in our later discussion, the several concepts of net income computed by the several methods of determining capital maintenance can be incorporated into the transactions approach by making adjustments to revenues and expenses at the time of recording each transaction and by making adjustments to asset valuations at the end of each period. Thus, current accounting practice is a combination of capital maintenance concepts of income, operational concepts, and the transactions-based approach to income measurement.

What Should Be Included in Income?

The computation of income by an annual valuation of net assets raises important questions regarding the proper valuation methods that provide the most meaningful measurement of net income. A more important limitation of the annual valuation procedure is the inability to reveal the nature and composition of income necessary in meeting most of the objectives for computing net income discussed at the beginning of this chapter. The transactions approach, on the other hand, makes it possible to record changes when specific events occur and to summarize these changes in financial statements according to the operational activities of the firm.

One of the major objectives of business enterprise is the maximization of the dividend flow to stockholders over the entire life of the enterprise, or the maximization of the liquidation value or market value of the enterprise at the end of its life, or at intermediate points, or some combination of these. All economic changes are relevant for an evaluation of the overall success or failure of the enterprise over its lifetime. But the more common objectives of income measurement require a measurement of income for shorter periods of time in order to provide a means of control and a basis for decisions of stockholders, creditors, and management on a continuing or periodic basis. The overall measurement of income for the entire life of the enterprise does not provide the information when it is most useful, nor does it describe the causes of success or failure. Success may be the result of good fortune or efficient management. The sources or causes of net income are thus important in a proper evaluation of the progress of the firm. But some accountants have held that the figure called "net income for the period" should include all recorded economic events and that income arising from specific sources should be labeled properly. This controversy has led to two basic concepts of income—the current operating concept and the all-inclusive concept of income—and an intermediate position recommended in Accounting Principles Board *Opinion No. 9*.

The Current Operating Concept of Income. The current operating concept of income focuses on the measurement of the efficiency of the business enterprise. The term *efficiency* relates to the effective utilization of the firm's resources in operating the business and earning a profit. In the broad economic sense, it relates to the proper combination of the factors of production—land, labor, capital, and management. An evaluation of relative efficiency, however, requires a comparison with a given standard or ideal. This necessarily requires some subjective evaluation, but as a starting point, comparisons can be made with the results of previous periods and with the incomes of other firms or industries.

In the computation of income, particular emphasis is placed on the terms *current* and *operating*. Only those value changes and events that are controllable by management and that result from decisions of the *current* period should be included. However, this statement must be qualified to include the use of factors acquired in a prior period but used in the current period. Each period is not a separate economic experience. Most of the capital equipment and even the services of most of the workers will have been obtained or contracted for in prior periods. The decisions of the current period involve the proper use and combination of these factors. The changes that should be excluded are those which actually arose in prior periods but were not recognized or recorded previously. For example, equipment that is discovered to be obsolete in the current period may have become obsolete in prior periods. The decision to abandon its use in the current period may be the result of efficient management and, therefore, this is not an expense of the current period. Likewise, recognition of an error in the computation of a prior period's income is no reflection on the efficiency of management in the current period. But one note of caution—errors in the computation of income for prior periods do affect the evaluation of the efficiency of management in those prior periods.

The second aspect of this concept is that the relevant changes arise only from *normal* operations. A better comparison can be made with other years and with other firms if the net income relates only to the regular operations. Also, it is here that the relative efficiency of management shows up best. While nonoperating activities may also be affected by managerial efficiency, it is more difficult to obtain a standard with which to measure the period results. At least, a different standard must be used, and this requires a separation of the results of the operating and nonoperating activities. It is also frequently suggested that nonoperating activities should be reported separately because they are nonrecurring. This is really a different reason for separate classification, and it is discussed more fully below. If nonrecurring items arise from normal operations, the current operating performance concept of income should include them to provide a good measure of the firm's earning power and a means of projecting and evaluating income trends.

Proponents of the current operating concept suggest that the resulting reported net income is more meaningful for interperiod and interfirm comparisons and for making predictions. They also suggest that while classification of operating and nonoperating items may be difficult, the trained accountant is in a better position to make this classification than outsiders or nonaccountants. While there should be full disclosure of noncurrent and nonoperating items, financial analysts and other users of accounting data frequently emphasize one figure for the net income for the year. Thus, it is proposed that if only one figure is quoted, the current operating net income is more useful as a measure of current operating performance.

The All-Inclusive Concept of Income. The all-inclusive concept of income, sometimes referred to as the clean-surplus concept, is defined as the total change in proprietorship recognized by the recording of transactions or the revaluation of assets and liabilities during a specific period, except for dividend distributions and capital transactions. All changes in the retained earnings section of the stockholders' equity should arise from either net income, dividend distributions, appropriations of net income, or the return of appropriations to "free" retained earnings. If a classification of operating and nonoperating or recurring and nonrecurring items is desirable, it should be made in the income statement before arriving at the figure labeled "net income for the period." This concept is clearly reflected in the 1936 statement of the American Accounting Association:

The income statement for any given period should reflect all revenues properly given accounting recognition and all costs written off during the period, regardless of whether or not they are the results of operations in that period. . . .[9]

Similar statements or implications appeared in the 1941 and 1948 statements of the American Accounting Association.[10]

Sprouse and Moonitz (in AICPA *Accounting Research Study No. 3*) also imply the all-inclusive concept of income in the following definition:

The net profit (earnings, income) of a business enterprise during any given period of time is the amount of the increase in the owners' equity, assuming no changes in the amount of invested capital during the period either from price-level changes or from additional investments and no distributions of any sort to the owners.[11]

But they also recognize the need for other concepts of income to serve different purposes as indicated by the following:

In general, the accounting process must provide more than a measurement of the net amount earned during a period of time. Information about the components of profit is needed as a basis for evaluating the past and forecasting the future.[12]

---

[9] Executive Committee of the AAA, "A Tentative Statement of Accounting Principles Underlying Corporate Financial Statements," *Accounting Review,* Vol. XI (June, 1936), sec. 8.

[10] See Chapter 3 for a more complete description of the position of the AAA.

[11] Robert T. Sprouse and Maurice Moonitz, "A Tentative Set of Broad Accounting Principles for Business Enterprises," *Accounting Research Study No. 3* (New York: AICPA, 1962), p. 45.

[12] *Ibid.*

Proponents of the all-inclusive concept of income claim the following reasons for this measurement of income:

1. The annual reported net incomes, when added together for the life of the enterprise, should be equal to the total net income of the enterprise. It is claimed that the charges resulting from extraordinary events and from corrections of prior periods tend to exceed the credits, resulting in an overstatement of the net income for a series of years if these are omitted.

2. The omission of certain charges and credits from the computation of net income lends itself to possible manipulation or smoothing of the annual earnings figures. As noted in Chapter 3, this fear in the 1930's was well founded.

3. An income statement that includes all income charges and credits recognized during the year is said to be easier to prepare and more easily understood by the readers. It is not subject to the personal judgments of management or the accountants preparing the statement. This is based on the assumption that accounting statements should be as verifiable as possible; several accountants working independently on the same figures should be able to arrive at similar results.

4. With full disclosure of the nature of income changes during the year, the reader of the statements is assumed to be more capable of making appropriate classifications to arrive at an appropriate measurement of income than are the accountants and management, who cannot anticipate the specific needs of the users.

5. The distinction between operating and nonoperating charges and credits is not clear-cut. Transactions classified as "operating" by one firm may be classified as "nonoperating" by another firm. Furthermore, items classified as nonoperating in one year may be classified as operating by the same firm in a subsequent year. This, in itself, leads to inconsistencies in making comparisons among different firms or over several periods for the same firm. But the definition of operating income becomes even more clouded when we look beyond the trees and see that some extraordinary events are really ordinary and expected over a longer period of time and that the frequent occurrence of "nonoperating" events may be normal to business operations. The head of a household can budget his entire income for the normal requirements of the family, such as food, housing, clothing, and entertainment; special items such as medical bills, car repairs, and semiannual payments for property taxes are not normal expenditure items in any one single month. If the head of the household, however, does not make some plans for these extraordinary items, he may soon find himself in financial difficulties. Each item may be extraordinary for any single month, but as a group, the extraordinary items become normal.

A major difference between the current operating and the all-inclusive concepts of income is in the assumed objective for reporting net income. While the current operating net income emphasizes the current operating performance or efficiency of the firm and the possible use of this figure for predicting the future performance and earning power, the proponents of the all-inclusive net income claim that both the operating efficiency and the prediction of future performance can be improved if they are based on the entire historical experience of the firm over a series of years. Because the useful lives of assets usually extend over many periods and because income-producing transactions are not at uniform stages of completion at the end of each period, the net income of a single period is, at best, an estimate based on good judgment. Because of this necessarily subjective nature of accounting, the net income of a single period is tentative and always subject to verification at later dates.

The main differences of opinion between proponents of the all-inclusive and the current operating concepts of income stem from disagreement regarding the emphasis to be placed upon a single figure labeled "net income for the year" and upon the extent to which objectivity in accounting can be enforced or is even desirable. Should the demands of the consumers of accounting information be met by providing them with a single net income figure, or should accountants force them to make their own computations? Regarding objectivity, accountants and managements have certainly become more reliable and consistent in their modes of behavior since the irresponsible days of the 1920's. But are they yet ready to serve all of the needs of the many users of accounting data? The answers, of course, are neither black nor white.

Recurring and Nonrecurring Income. The proponents of the current operating performance concept of income frequently claim that operating items are generally defined as recurrent features of business operations and that nonoperating items are generally considered to be irregular and unpredictable.[13] However, this is not necessarily true. Many items may be operating in nature but not necessarily recurring. The necessity to pay overtime labor rates during a rush period and the acquisition of raw materials under extremely fortunate circumstances are both operating events, but are possibly nonrecurring. On the other hand, some nonoperating events are recurring in nature. Annual floods in unavoidably hazardous areas may result in nonoperating charges, but they are recurring in nature.

A net income figure based on recurring events is generally more useful to investors in predicting possible future income and dividend flows. Recurring nonoperating events are just as important as those recurring

---

[13] AICPA, *Accounting Principles* (Chicago: Commerce Clearing House, Inc., 1968), Vol. II, p. 6559.

events which are the result of normal operations. The distinction between operating and nonoperating, however, is more useful for measuring management efficiency. The assumption upon which this statement is based is that operating events tend to be more controllable than nonoperating events. This, of course, may also be disputed in many instances.

The advantage of classifying income charges and credits as recurring or nonrecurring is based upon the improved usefulness of the resulting net income figure in the making of predictions by investors. It is probably more difficult for outsiders to distinguish between recurring and nonrecurring events than it is for them to distinguish between operating and nonoperating items.

The disadvantages of the classification and reporting of recurring income are similar to the disadvantages of the current operating concept of income. These disadvantages can be readily recognized in the above discussion of the all-inclusive concept of income.

Extraordinary Gains and Losses. The Committee on Accounting Procedure of the American Institute of Certified Public Accountants in 1947 recognized the justification for omitting certain extraordinary items from the income statement. The specific extraordinary items recommended to be excluded from net income included the following, if they are material and if their inclusion would impair the significance of net income by misleading readers of the reports: (1) items related specifically to prior years, (2) gains and losses resulting from the sale of assets not acquired for resale and not of a type ordinarily acquired for resale, (3) losses of a type not generally covered by insurance, (4) the write-off of intangibles, and (5) the write-off of unamortized bond discount or premium and expense at the time of retirement or refunding.[14] The effect of these exclusions is the presentation of a net income similar to the current operating concept with emphasis on the concept of materiality.

In 1966, the Accounting Principles Board of the AICPA published *Opinion No. 9,* which changes the basic nature of the final figure of net income. In this *Opinion,* the Board concluded that all changes recognized during the period should be reflected in the income statement with the sole exception of adjustments of the incomes of prior years. However, extraordinary items of a nonrecurring nature should be shown separately following the results of ordinary operations. That is, a separate computation entitled "income before extraordinary items" is followed by the addition or subtraction of "extraordinary items" to arrive at "net income."

The apparent intent of the Board was that the final net income figure

---

[14] *Accounting Research Bulletin No. 32,* "Income and Earned Surplus," restated in Chapter 8 of *Accounting Research Bulletin No. 43,* included in AICPA, *Accounting Principles, op. cit.,* pp. 6027–31.

would generally represent an all-inclusive concept, as they state that prior period adjustments will be rare items. In order to accomplish this result, prior period adjustments are limited to those items which

(a) can be specifically identified with and directly related to the business activities of particular prior periods, and (b) are not attributable to economic events occurring subsequent to the date of the financial statements for the prior period, and (c) depend primarily on determinations by persons other than management and (d) were not susceptible of reasonable estimation prior to such determination.[15]

Therefore, according to these limitations, prior period adjustments are not to be made because of changes in expectations or because economic events turn out to be different than expected, where expectations were considered measurable. Prior period adjustments are thus limited to those cases where economic events have occurred in the past but where the uncertainties regarding the situation were so great that any meaningful measurement could not be approximated at that time. Examples given by the Board include nonrecurring adjustments of income taxes, the results of renegotiation proceedings or rate cases, and the results of litigation.

As in most committee decisions, this is apparently a compromise position of the Board, as it reflects neither a current operating concept nor an all-inclusive concept of income. And the definition of prior period adjustments does not provide any assurance that the reported net income will represent *current* income that will be meaningful for the measurement of efficiency or for predictions. There may be little difference between an approximated measurement which turns out later to be wide of the mark and the inability to measure the effect of an event which turns out later to be material in amount. In both cases, the adjustment relates to a prior period, but only in the latter case would an adjustment of retained earnings be clearly in accordance with the recommendations of APB *Opinion No. 9.* As a second criticism, it is difficult to imagine any situation where the adjustment would not be a result of economic events subsequent to the prior period being adjusted. The payment of cash as a result of a law suit or tax settlement is an economic event. The Board apparently had a different definition of "economic event" in mind, but this leaves an ambiguity in the ability to comply with the recommendations on a consistent basis.

Extraordinary items are defined specifically as those that are material and nonrecurring. While it is assumed that they will usually not be related to normal operations, this distinction is not clearly made. Therefore, the caption "net income before extraordinary items" cannot be assumed to represent current operating income. Furthermore, there is no

---

[15] APB *Opinion No. 9,* p. 115, published in AICPA *Accounting Principles, op. cit.,* pp. 6557–72.

assurance that nonrecurring items are not included in the computation of "net income before extraordinary items"; for example, a significant nonrecurring increase in an operating item would be included in the results of normal operations. Therefore, the separation of extraordinary items from other income statement items does not result in a separation of recurring and nonrecurring items, nor a separation of operating from nonoperating activities. While the attempt to clarify these concepts is to be commended, APB *Opinion No. 9* needs considerable clarification before it can reach the desired goals. However, presentation of these extraordinary items in the body of the income statement may at least make readers more aware of their existence, and an emphasis on behavioral characteristics of at least some items is a step in the right direction.

The SEC has required the all-inclusive concept of income, with exceptions permitted on a case-by-case basis. However, as contrasted with the recommendation of APB *Opinion No. 9*, special items may be reported in the income statement below the figure caption "net income or loss," followed by a caption "net income or loss and special items."[16] These regulations, however, are difficult to evaluate because of their lack of objective and clarity.

In the United Kingdom, the English Institute has not stated a preference for any specific concept of income. As it places emphasis on consistent reporting rather than uniformity among firms, it permits the application of either the all-inclusive concept of income or the current operating concept, provided that one or the other is selected and applied consistently or, if a change is made, that the nature of the change and its consequences are disclosed.

Net Income to Whom?

Stemming from the proprietary approach to accounting, net income has usually been assumed to mean net earnings or net profits accruing to current stockholders or owners of the business. However, there may be valid reasons for the presentation of a net income figure which represents net earnings to a narrower or broader group of recipients.

The Value-Added Concept of Income. Broadly speaking, it is possible to view the enterprise as having a large group of claimants or interested parties, including not only owners and other investors, but also employees, and landlords of rented property. This is the value-added approach.[17] In economic terms, value added is the value of the output of an enter-

---

[16] United States Securities and Exchange Commission, Regulation S–X, Rule 5–03.

[17] For a fuller discussion of this concept, see Waino W. Suojanen, "Accounting Theory and the Large Corporation," *Accounting Review*, Vol. XXIX (July, 1954), pp. 391–98.

prise less the value of the goods and services acquired by transfer from other firms. Thus, all employees, owners, creditors, and governments (through taxation) are recipients of the enterprise income. This is the total pie that can be divided among the various contributors of factor inputs to the enterprise in the production of goods and services. How this pie is divided is usually subject to contractual agreements and bargaining.

This concept becomes most meaningful when it is applied to the very large corporations that affect the lives of thousands of individuals and have a general social and economic significance beyond the narrow interests of the owners or stockholders. The value-added income would include wages, rent, interest, taxes, dividends paid to stockholders, and undistributed earnings of the corporation. A question arises regarding the nature of retained earnings in this concept. It does not necessarily accrue to the owners alone but also to all of the other recipients or claimants of corporate value added. Only in the case of liquidation do common stockholders have the residual claims. In the long run, the retention of earnings provides for a growth in the firm's capital which, through increased productivity, may provide increased flows of income to all recipients. If the corporation is assumed to have perpetual or indefinite life, the stockholders may never receive the direct and sole benefit from the retention of earnings in the business.

Enterprise Net Income. According to the 1957 statement of the American Accounting Association, ". . . interest charges, income taxes, and true profit-sharing distributions are not determinants of enterprise net income."[18] The conclusion follows, then, that these items are distributions of net income rather than deductions before arriving at net income. It also follows that stockholders, holders of long-term debt, and governments are beneficiaries of the corporation.

This concept of net income has an advantage from the point of view of separating the financial aspects of the corporation from the operating. The net income to the enterprise is an operating concept of net income. Interest to debt holders and earnings to stockholders are financial in nature. Income taxes are neither financial nor strictly operating; and their exclusion from the computation of enterprise net income has some merit, because they do not represent controllable input costs. But the treatment of governments as beneficiaries of the corporation when employees and other groups are excluded is of dubious merit from a logical point of view.

Net Income to Investors. In accordance with the entity concept of the business enterprise, both stockholders and holders of long-term debt

---

[18] Committee on Accounting Concepts and Standards, *Accounting and Reporting Standards for Corporate Financial Statements and Preceding Statements and Supplements* (Columbus, Ohio: AAA, 1957), p. 5.

are considered equally as investors of permanent capital. With the separation of ownership and control in the large corporation, the differences between stockholders and debt holders are no longer as important as they once were. The main differences arise in the priorities of claims against income and against assets in liquidation. With the emphasis on the observed indefinite life of most large corporations, the claims in liquidation become less important. When we observe the claims against income more closely, we find that the differences between many bond issues and some preferred stock issues are quite fuzzy. Holders of income bonds, for example, may have less security in their claim against income than some holders of cumulative preferred stock and holders of convertible bonds may obtain rights in undistributed earnings by converting their interests to common stockholder claims.

In the entity concept, income to investors includes the interest on debt, dividends to preferred and common stockholders, and the undivided remainder. This concept of income has considerable merit for several purposes: (1) The decisions regarding the sources of long-term capital are financial rather than operating matters. Therefore, the net income to investors reflects more clearly the results of operations. (2) Because of differing financial structures, comparisons among firms can be made more readily by using this concept of income. (3) The rate of return on total investment computed from this concept of income portrays the relative efficiency of invested capital better than does the rate of return to stockholders.

In the computation of net income to investors, income taxes are treated as expenses. This is the treatment recommended by the Committee on Accounting Procedure of the AICPA.[19] It is the author's opinion that this is the realistic position.[20] The government is not a beneficiary of the corporation in the same way that investors are. The corporation does receive direct benefit from the government, although not in direct proportion to the amount of the tax. The right to operate in a viable economy and to obtain the protection of the courts and obtain protection from external force and violence are only a few of these benefits. Furthermore, corporate income *after* taxes is much more stable—by industries—than income before taxes; income taxes seem to be "passed on" much as other expenses.[21] Also, both investors and managers seem to make most of their decisions on the basis of income after taxes.

---

[19] *Accounting Research Bulletin No. 43,* chap. x, p. 88.

[20] See Eldon S. Hendriksen, "The Treatment of Income Taxes by the AAA 1957 Statement," *Accounting Review,* Vol. XXXIII (April, 1958), pp. 216–21.

[21] See Marian Krzyzaniak and Richard A. Musgrave, *The Shifting of the Corporation Income Tax* (Baltimore: Johns Hopkins Press, 1963), pp. 65–66.

Net Income to Stockholders. The most traditional and accepted viewpoint of net income is that it represents the return to the owners of the business. While this concept has its firm foundation in the proprietary approach, many authors apply it to the entity approach and consider the accounting profit of the entity to be a liability to the owners.[22] The 1957 statement of the American Accounting Association stated specifically that net income to shareholders shall be computed by deducting interest charges, income taxes, and profit-sharing distributions. The AICPA also clearly indicates throughout the accounting research bulletins and Accounting Principles Board *Opinion No. 9* that net income means net income to all stockholders. And this position was also maintained by Sprouse and Moonitz in AICPA *Accounting Research Study No. 3*.[23]

The concept of net income to shareholders also has its support in the field of economics. Although the definition of economic profits is different from the meaning of accounting profits, economists usually treat accounting profits statistically as the total return to the entrepreneurs in their various roles as managers, investors of capital, risk takers, and rentiers. While it may or may not be desirable, it is a realistic fact that the users of accounting statements usually interpret net income to mean the return to shareholders.

Net Income to Residual Equity Holders. In financial statements presented primarily for stockholders and investors, the net income available for distribution to common stockholders is usually thought to be the most important single figure in the statements. Net income per share of common stock and dividends per share are the most commonly quoted figures in financial news, along with the market price per share. Therefore, there is pragmatic support for presenting statements from which the net income to residual equity holders can readily be obtained.

In a profitable enterprise with indefinite life, the residual equity holder would be the common stockholder or an investor who can become a common stockholder through conversion or exercise of other rights. But there is always the possibility that through reorganization, or because of default in the payment of preferred claims, one of the other groups of investors—preferred stockholders or bondholders—might become the residual equity holders. Therefore, the priorities in the claims to income are important to all groups. The residual net income indicates the degree of security of the priority claims as well as the amount available for distribution to the residual claimants.

The holders of common stock and the prospective buyers of common stock are interested primarily in the future flow of dividends. Normally,

---

[22] See for example Stephen Gilman, *Accounting Concepts of Profit* (New York: Ronald Press Co., 1939), p. 598.

[23] Sprouse and Moonitz, *op. cit.*, p. 45.

only a part of the residual net income is distributed as dividends, but the knowledge of the net income available and the financial policy of the corporation may provide useful information to common stockholders in their evaluation of the firm and in their prediction of the total amount of annual dividend distributions in the future. However, in order to predict the amount of dividends he may receive in the future, an investor must also predict the number of shares that will be outstanding in each period. To the extent that there are outstanding senior stock or debt securities convertible into common shares or stock options, warrants, or agreements for the sale of common stock at less than market prices, a potential dilution of earnings per share and dividends per share exists. APB *Opinions No. 9* and *No. 15* recognized this potential dilution and recommended that supplementary pro forma computations of earnings per share should be presented, showing what the earnings per share would have been if the conversions or options had been executed. The computation of earnings per share when potential dilution is present is discussed at greater length in Chapter 18.

Thus, while it is possible to view current net income as the return to current outstanding stockholders, potential residual equity holders must be taken into consideration in predictions regarding future earnings and dividends per share. Furthermore, if current net income is not distributed to current stockholders, the amount added to retained earnings may be shared by these potential holders of common stock. In discussing this potential dilutive effect, APB *Opinion No. 15* uses the term "common stock equivalent," which is defined as

a security which is not, in form, a common stock but which usually contains provisions to enable its holder to become a common stockholder and which . . . is in substance equivalent to a common stock.[24]

Summary of Net Income Classification by Income Recipients. The following tabulation summarizes the several concepts of corporate income classified by the income recipients. Note that the value-added concept requires the recognition of income during production, as all product values are expressed in terms of selling prices. The other concepts are more liberal in their acceptance of the several methods of income recognition.

SUMMARY OF CONCEPTS OF ENTERPRISE INCOME

The concept of income most appropriate for reporting financial operations of business enterprises is determined largely by the objectives of the

---

[24] APB *Opinion No. 15* (New York: AICPA, 1969), p. 225. Also in AICPA *Accounting Principles, op. cit.,* p. 6614.

Income Concept	Income Included	Income Recipients
Value added.	Selling price of firm's product less cost of goods and services acquired by transfer.	All employees, owners, creditors, and governments.
Enterprise net income.	Excess of revenues over expenses; all gains and losses. Expenses do not include interest charges, income taxes, and true profit-sharing distributions.	Stockholders, bondholders, and governments.
Net income to investors.	Same as enterprise net income, but after deducting income taxes.	Stockholders and holders of long-term debt.
Net income to shareholders.	Net income to investors less interest charges and profit-sharing distributions.	Stockholders (preferred and common.)
Net income to residual equity holders.	Net income to shareholders less preferred dividends.	Current and potential common stockholders unless priority payments cannot be met.

intended recipients of the summarized accounting data. A concept useful for one group of individuals or for one purpose may not be the best choice for another. The main questions regarding the choice of an appropriate concept of income are: (1) What are the major objectives of income reporting? (2) What are the basic elements of each of the several income concepts and how well do they meet the objectives? (3) What types of changes should be included in or excluded from the computation of net income? (4) Who are the major income recipients? This last question is, of course, related to the objectives of income reporting.

The major objectives of income reporting can be summarized as follows: (1) Information should be presented in such a way that stockholders can evaluate changes in their invested capital. This requires a careful distinction between capital and income. A return *of* capital has a different significance to stockholders than a return *on* capital. (2) An evaluation of capital, and the distinction between capital and income, are also relevant to judgments regarding the stewardship of management. (3) Net income and its components are frequently used as measures of the efficiency of management. (4) The net incomes of several periods may be useful in the making of predictions regarding the future operations of a firm if proper care is taken to include other relevant factors. While investors are most interested in income prediction, other groups may also wish to make predictions in order to make appropriate decisions regarding their relationships with the firm. (5) An analysis of net income may also be useful for evaluating past decisions by management and aiding in future planning.

The several concepts of income used as bases for accounting theory and practice include the following: (1) The capital maintenance concepts are assumed by many to be most basic because they derive their support from economic theory. Changes in the capitalized value of expected cash receipts serve as the foundation of this concept; however, accruals, amortization procedures, and current market valuations, as well as suggested alternatives to practice, are frequently justified on the basis that they represent surrogates (reasonably acceptable substitutes) for current value. (2) A commonly accepted concept of income is that it should reflect the major activities of the firm. This concept is given as justification for the reporting of revenue at the time of sale and for the matching of expenses with revenues. (3) A third alternative is that income should be more closely tied to cash or funds flows. Cash flow activity is considered more relevant than any attempts to measure value changes. This concept will be discussed at greater length in Chapter 8. (4) A final argument is that all concepts of income are both theoretically and practically unsound in the presentation of relevant information to investors and others. Alternative information systems are suggested that may permit the readers of the statements to select the relevant data and make their own predictions regarding the value of the firm and other evaluations necessary in their decision making.

What should be included in the computation of net income is dependent upon which of the several objectives are considered to be the most relevant. Income based on the maintenance of capital requires the inclusion of all changes during the period. A report on stewardship should emphasize those changes that are controllable by management. For predictive purposes, changes that are recurring and changes with distinct behavioral characteristics should be disclosed along with these characteristics. The separation of extraordinary items and the exclusion of certain corrections of prior periods suggested in APB *Opinion No. 9* is a step in this direction, but it is inadequate to fulfill this objective. Management is interested primarily in those operating changes that are variable or controllable and are thus relevant for managerial planning and decisions. Because of these several uses for reported income and income components and the different types of information needed for each use, suggestions have been made that several concepts of income should be reported. A single concept of income may serve several purposes at least partially, but it is not likely to serve all objectives equally well.

From a broad social and economic point of view, all income generated by the firm should be reported as income. But the division of this income among the income recipients should be reported as well as the total generated. More complete information can probably be presented if the residual net income is restricted to a few income recipients. In any case, the report of net income should state to whom the income accrues. If a broad classification such as net income to the enterprise is used, the division of this income should also be presented. Furthermore, when a dilution of income per share is likely because of outstanding convertible securities, warrants, or grants, the probable effect of such a dilution should also be presented.

Conventional accounting practice has tended to emphasize a single net income to stockholders or to the entity. But the computation of this net income has been based on an eclectic approach. One of the major difficulties with discussions regarding alternative accounting procedures is that the writers do not usually indicate the basic concepts of income that they have in mind; therefore, many arguments are fruitless, since the opposing statements are based on different premises without a clear indication of these premises nor a clear discussion of the basic concepts upon which the arguments rest. A critical analysis of conventional accounting practices regarding valuation procedures and in terms of the various concepts of income will be found in the following chapters.

SELECTED ADDITIONAL READING ON CHAPTER TOPICS

Capital Maintenance Concepts of Income

ALEXANDER, SIDNEY S. "Income Measurement in a Dynamic Economy," revised by David Solomons and reprinted in W. T. BAXTER and SIDNEY DAVIDSON, *Studies in Accounting Theory,* pp. 126–200. Homewood, Ill.: Richard D. Irwin, Inc., 1962.

CHANG, EMILY CHEN. "Business Income in Accounting and Economics," *Accounting Review,* Vol. XXXVII (October, 1962), pp. 636–44.

HANSEN, PALLE. *The Accounting Concept of Profit: An Analysis and Evaluation in the Light of the Economic Theory of Income and Capital.* Amsterdam, Holland: North-Holland Publishing Co., 1962.

PHILIPS, G. EDWARD. "The Accretion Concept of Income," *Accounting Review,* Vol. XXXVIII (January, 1963), pp. 14–25.

SHWAYDER, KEITH. "A Critique of Economic Income as an Accounting Concept," *Abacus,* Vol. III (August, 1967), pp. 23–35.

——. "The Capital Maintenance Rule and the Net Asset Valuation Rule," *Accounting Review,* Vol. XLIV (April, 1969), pp. 304–16.

Accounting Concepts of Income

BALL, RAY and PHILIP BROWN. "An Empirical Evaluation of Accounting Income Numbers," *Journal of Accounting Research,* Vol. VI (Autumn, 1968), pp. 159–78.

BEDFORD, NORTON M. *Income Determination Theory: An Accounting Framework.* Reading, Mass.: Addison-Wesley, 1965.

CARSON, A. B. "Cash Movement: The Heart of Income Measurement," *Accounting Review,* Vol. XL (April, 1965), pp. 334–37.

LEMKE, KENNETH W. "Asset Valuation and Income Theory," *Accounting Review,* Vol. XLI (January, 1966), pp. 32–41.

MOONITZ, MAURICE. "Should We Discard the Income Concept?" *Accounting Review,* Vol. XXXVII (April, 1962), pp. 173–80.

PETERSON, WILLIAM A. "Significance of Prospective Income Data," *Accounting Review,* Vol. XLI (April, 1966), pp. 275–82.

SOLOMONS, DAVID. "Economic and Accounting Concepts of Income," *Accounting Review,* Vol. XXXVI (July, 1961), pp. 374–83.

VATTER, WILLIAM J. "Income Models, Book Yield, and the Rate of Return," *Accounting Review,* Vol. XLI (October, 1966), pp. 681–98.

What Should Be Included in Income?

ARNETT, HAROLD E. "The Distinction Between Ordinary and Non-ordinary Gains and Losses," *New York Certified Public Accountant,* Vol. XXXVII (April, 1967), pp. 267–78.

BERNSTEIN, LEOPOLD. "An Analysis of APB Opinion No. 9, 'Reporting the Results of Operations'," *New York Certified Public Accountant,* Vol. XXXVII (March, 1967), pp. 196–202.

——. *Accounting for Extraordinary Gains and Losses,* particularly chaps. 1, 2, and 3, and appendix B. New York: Ronald Press Co., 1967.

POWELL, WELDON. "Extraordinary Items," *Journal of Accountancy,* Vol. CXXI (January, 1966), pp. 31–37.

Income Reporting Objectives

BIERMAN, HAROLD, JR. and SIDNEY DAVIDSON. "The Income Concept—Value Increment or Earnings Predictor," *Accounting Review,* Vol. XLIV (April, 1969), pp. 239–46.

chapter 6

Revenues and Expenses, Gains and Losses

As indicated in the previous chapters, the several objectives of accounting require the reporting of information and measurements that will permit evaluations and predictions of the activities and future cash distributions of the firm. While the reporting of net income on a periodic basis may aid in these evaluations and predictions, a more thorough analysis requires, among other items, information regarding specific operational activities of the firm. While an annual valuation of assets and liabilities is useful in exploring concepts of income and may be useful in making evaluations and predictions regarding the firm, the transactions approach provides a more direct route to the reporting of some of the basic activities of the firm. The problem of valuation is not avoided, however. It is merely shifted to the measurement of assets and liabilities entering or leaving the firm and to the classification of changes in the measurement of assets held by the firm.

The main emphasis in the transactions approach is the recognition and classification of favorable and unfavorable changes during the accounting period. Favorable changes are classified as revenues or gains, and unfavorable changes as either expenses or losses. The main problems of recording these changes during an accounting period include problems of classification, timing, and valuation. Each of the several favorable and unfavorable changes will be discussed separately in relationship to these problems.

REVENUES

The concept of revenue is difficult to define because it is generally associated with specific accounting procedures, certain types of value changes, and assumed or implicit rules for determining when revenue should be reported. The measurement and timing of revenue are interesting problems of accounting theory, but they should be approached with an open mind; they should not be restricted by a narrow definition of revenue. Conversely, revenue should be defined separately from the valuation and timing problems. Therefore, revenue is discussed here from the following specific points of view: (1) the nature of revenue, (2) what should be included in revenue, (3) the measurement of revenue, and (4) the timing of revenue (the period in which revenue is recorded).

The Nature of Revenue

The concept of revenue has not generally been clearly defined in accounting literature, primarily because it has usually been discussed in relationship to its measurement and timing and usually in the context of the double-entry system. However, the basic nature of revenue activity and its relevant attributes should be explored before we tackle the measurement and timing problems. Two approaches to the concept of revenue can be found in the literature, one focusing on the inflow of assets resulting from the operational activities of the firm and the other focusing on the creation of goods and services by the enterprise and the transfer of these to consumers or other producers. That is, revenue is considered to be either an inflow of net assets or an outflow of goods and services.[1]

The more traditional definition of revenue is that it represents an inflow of assets or net assets into the firm as a result of sales of goods or services. This was the approach of the 1948 American Accounting Association statement.[2] It was also the approach of Sprouse and Moonitz in their definition of revenue as "the increase in the net assets of an enterprise as a result of the production or delivery of goods and the rendering of services."[3] However, this confuses the *measurement* and *timing* of the revenue with the revenue *process*. Assets are generally increased or liabilities liquidated at the time of sale or delivery of goods or services, and the amount of the revenue is traditionally determined by the monetary measurement of the assets received. This definition is, therefore, in accord with traditional practice, but it does not permit a broader perspective of the measuring and timing processes. The inflow approach also requires a careful statement of which inflows should be

---

[1] See George J. Staubus, "Revenue and Revenue Accounts," *Accounting Research,* Vol. VII (July, 1956), pp. 284–94. Reprinted in Sidney Davidson, David Green, Jr., Charles T. Horngren, and George H. Sorter, *An Income Approach to Accounting Theory: Readings and Questions* (Englewood Cliffs, N.J.: Prentice-Hall, Inc., 1964), pp. 78–88.

[2] AAA Committee on Accounting Concepts and Standards, *Accounting and Reporting Standards for Corporate Financial Statements and Preceding Statements and Supplements* (Columbus, Ohio: AAA, 1957), p. 15.

[3] Robert T. Sprouse and Maurice Moonitz, "A Tentative Set of Broad Accounting Principles for Business Enterprises," *Accounting Research Study No. 3* (New York: AICPA, 1962), p. 46.

considered revenues and which should not. Assets may increase and liabilities decrease for many reasons, of which revenue is only one. Also, if revenue is defined in this way, the exceptions must be clearly stated. For example, in a few cases revenue is reported prior to sale and before there is an actual inflow of assets.

Revenue is also frequently defined in terms of its effect on stockholders' equity. The revenue account has a credit balance and is closed at the end of the accounting period to retained earnings through the revenue and expense summary account. Therefore, it has the effect of increasing the stockholders' equity. But many offsets (expenses) are directly associated with the revenue before there can be a net change in stockholders' equity. Also, there are several reasons for increases in stockholders' equity not associated with revenue. This definition also has the disadvantage of relating revenue to the double-entry system rather than to its basic nature.

The basic concept of revenue is that it is a flow process—the creation of goods or services by an enterprise during a specific interval of time. Paton and Littleton called it the product of the enterprise.[4] Note that this definition does not dictate either the amount or the timing of the revenue but is neutral with respect to these aspects. Generally, revenue is expressed in monetary terms, although the measurement of revenue under this concept is open for discussion without changing the nature of the item being measured.

Several similar definitions also state that the revenue is the product of the enterprise, but they imply that the product must leave the firm (an outflow concept). For example, the Committee on Accounting Concepts and Standards of the American Accounting Association defined revenue in the 1957 statement as follows:

Revenue . . . is the monetary expression of the aggregate of products or services transferred by an enterprise to its customers during a period of time.[5]

Bedford also defined revenue as an outflow of goods and services rendered to customers.[6] While Sprouse and Moonitz defined revenue initially as an inflow of assets, they stated later on the same page that

. . . revenue of an enterprise during a period of time represents a measurement of the exchange value of the products (goods or services) of that enterprise during that period.[7]

---

[4] W. A. Paton and A. C. Littleton, *An Introduction to Corporate Accounting Standards,* American Accounting Association Monograph No. 3 (AAA, 1940), p. 46.

[5] AAA Committee on Accounting Concepts and Standards, *op. cit.,* p. 5.

[6] Norton M. Bedford, *Income Determination Theory: An Accounting Framework* (Reading, Mass.: Addison-Wesley, 1965), p. 92.

[7] Sprouse and Moonitz, *op. cit.*

In the opinion of the author, the definition of revenue as the product of the enterprise is superior to the outflow concept and the outflow concept is superior to the inflow concept. The product concept is neutral with respect to both timing and measurement, and the inflow concept as it is generally proposed avoids neither.

What Should Be Included in Revenue?

The definition of revenue as the product of the enterprise seems clear enough, but the several attempts to describe revenue or the nature and content of income do not agree on what should be included in the revenue concept. On the one hand, it is suggested that all changes in the net assets of a firm other than capital transactions reported during a period should be considered revenue. On the other hand, other proposals suggest that a distinction should be made between the revenue-producing activities of a firm and other gains or losses. Most discussions of income, however, are not clear with respect to a classification of revenue as distinct from gains. While such a classification may, at times, appear artificial, the view expressed in this book is that a better understanding of accounting may be obtained by making a distinction between the wealth-producing activities of the firm and unexpected transfers of wealth arising from gifts or windfalls.

Among those who propose a comprehensive view of revenue are committees from both the American Institute of Certified Public Accountants and the American Accounting Association. The AICPA *Terminology Bulletin No. 2* included in revenue

. . . gains from the sale or exchange of assets (other than stock in trade), interest and dividends earned on investments, and other increases in the owners' equity except those arising from capital contributions and capital adjustments.[8]

The *Terminology Bulletin* also stated that

revenue for a period less the cost of goods sold, other expenses, and losses will give the net results of business operations for the period.[9]

This implies that all revenue, including gains and other increases in the owners' equity, should appear in the income statement before arriving at net income for the year. The 1948 revision of the American Accounting Association statement defined revenue similarly to include gains from the sale or exchange of assets other than stock in trade and gains from the advantageous settlement of liabilities. Since this statement recommended

---

[8] AICPA, *Accounting Research and Terminology Bulletins, Final Edition* (New York, 1961), p. 34 of "Accounting Terminology Bulletins."
[9] *Ibid.*

the use of the all-inclusive income concept, all revenue, defined in the broad sense, would be included in the income statement.

In more recent statements, the AICPA has been less clear regarding what should be included in the revenue concept. *Accounting Research Bulletin No. 43* recommended, in effect, the current operating concept of income for material items, thus suggesting that the term "operating revenue" might be used to represent the product of the enterprise leaving the firm. The recommendation of Accounting Principles Board *Opinion No. 9* that extraordinary items should be segregated in the income statement implies that normal recurring items should be included in revenue while extraordinary nonrecurring items should not. However, the definition of "extraordinary items" places emphasis on their being different from the customary activities of the firm and on their nonrecurring nature. Revenue is neither defined explicitly nor mentioned in the *Opinion.*

The more narrow definition of revenue as the products or services of the enterprise was expressed in the 1957 statement of the American Accounting Association. *Net income* was defined as

. . . (1) the excess or deficiency of revenue compared with related expired cost and (2) other gains or losses to the enterprise from sales, exchanges, or other conversions of assets.[10]

Thus, *revenue* does not include gains in this definition. Paton and Littleton also expressed this view by recognizing the flow of accomplishment as the primary source of revenue.[11] But they were careful to include in revenue the entire range of goods and services furnished by the enterprise regardless of the relative amount of a particular item. Sprouse and Moonitz also made a distinction between revenues and gains in *Accounting Research Study No. 3.*[12]

In the following discussion, the term "revenue" will be used in the latter narrower sense. Gains will be treated separately. Note, however, that the product of the enterprise refers to all types of services, including rentals and interest-bearing loans. Thus, revenue may be operating or nonoperating, recurring or nonrecurring.

The Measurement of Revenue

Revenue is best measured by the exchange value of the product or service of the enterprise. This exchange value represents the cash equivalent or the present discounted value of the money claims to be received

---

[10] AAA Committee on Accounting Concepts and Standards, *op. cit.,* p. 5.

[11] Paton and Littleton, *op. cit.,* p. 47.

[12] Sprouse and Moonitz, *op. cit.,* p. 46.

eventually from the revenue transaction. In many cases, this may be equivalent to the price established in the transaction with the customer. But appropriate allowance must be made for the necessity to wait for final collection. A cash sale for $100 produces $100 of revenue, but a similar sale permitting the same payment a year later produces less than $100 of revenue because of the necessity to discount the latter amount. When the waiting period is short, the discount may be ignored for three pragmatic reasons: (1) At reasonable rates of discount the amount of the discount is small and does not materially affect the total revenue valuation. For example, if the claim is to be paid in 60 days, the amount of the discount at a rate of 6 percent per year would be less than 1 percent of the revenue. (2) Because interest is classified as a part of total revenue, the main effect is that of timing. Interest should be recorded subsequent to the recording of the revenue from the initial transaction. But if the interest is not material in amount, including it in the sales revenue would have little effect on periodic net income. (3) The classification of revenue arising from waiting (interest) would be lost and included in the classification of revenue arising from the sale of the product or service. Again, if the implicit interest is not material in amount, little useful information is lost by the failure to classify it separately.

The above criterion for the measurement of revenue refers to the present value of the money or money equivalent finally to be received as a result of the production process or the revenue transaction. From this criterion it is clear that all returns, trade discounts, and other reductions of the billed prices should be deducted from the revenue resulting from the specific transactions. The treatment of cash discounts and losses resulting from uncollectible accounts may not be quite so clear. However, these are also reductions from billed prices, even though unintentional, as in the case of the bad debt losses.

Cash discounts are granted, in part, to equate the value of the money received within the discount period with the present discounted value of the money which would be received under the granted credit terms. But one of the main purposes of the cash discounts is to reduce the bad debt losses. If the cash discount rates were set rationally, the seller would be indifferent whether he received the net discounted price or the gross price less a normal expectation of bad debt losses. In many cases, the seller may be able to obtain the same results with a lower cash discount rate than the maximum he would be willing to grant. Cash discounts and expected bad debt losses are, therefore, similar in nature.

In a world of certainty, the actual amount to be received finally in cash, discounted appropriately for the necessity of waiting, should be recorded as the revenue from the transaction. With uncertainty, the principle remains the same, but the cash discounts expected to be taken and the expected bad debt losses must be estimated. These items are, therefore, true deductions from revenue. Their traditional treatment as expenses does not result in a distortion of period net income, but it should be recognized that they do not have the basic characteristics of expenses as discussed later in this chapter.[13]

The Timing of Revenue Reporting

In our definition of revenue as the product of the enterprise as measured by an exchange value or cash equivalent, we still have the problem of deciding the point or points in time when we should measure and report the revenue. From an economic point of view, the value added by productive activity is a continuous process. The product of the enterprise appears gradually as raw materials are assembled and changed in form or processed by the application of labor and capital equipment. The transportation of raw materials to the plant and the finished product to the market are also part of the production process in an economic sense. Likewise, storage, either as a part of the production process or as a necessary requirement of meeting market demand, is also a part of the service provided by a firm. As indicated in the previous chapter, value added by the firm is the excess of the exchange value of the firm's products over the value added by other firms or individuals. Product exchange price, therefore, represents the distributions to all factors of production, including the contribution (a positive or negative residual) by the firm itself—the return to the several equity holders.

Revenue reporting entails not only the acknowledgment that the firm has produced economic value in the form of goods or services but also the measurement of that value. As indicated in the previous section, the product or service can be measured best by the money or money equivalent expected to be received for the product at some time in the future. It is the uncertainty of this expected receipt and the search for verifiable measurements that have led accountants to the adoption of specific rules for the timing of revenue.

Sprouse and Moonitz stated that

revenues should be identified with the period during which the major economic activities necessary to the creation and disposition of goods and services have been accomplished, provided objective measurements of the results of those activities are available. These two conditions, i.e., accomplishment of major eco-

---

[13] Those who claim that cash discounts and bad debt losses are true expenses argue that they represent alternatives to other expenses, such as collection expense and interest expense. While there is an element of truth in this approach, it is the opinion of the author that the concepts of revenue and expense are made clearer if these items are treated as revenue deductions. Also, it does not seem logical to classify any item on the basis of an alternative action. There are many cases where revenues are reduced as an alternative to increasing expenses.

nomic activity and objectivity of measurement, are fulfilled at different stages of activity in different cases, sometimes as late as time of delivery of product or the performance of a service, in other cases, at an earlier point of time.[14]

The author is in general agreement with this view that revenue should be acknowledged and reported at the time of the accomplishment of the major economic activity if its measurement is verifiable and free from bias.

An alternative to the reporting of revenue at the time of accomplishing the major economic activity is the *critical event* (or crucial event) concept of revenue reporting.[15] In most cases, the value added by the firm (reported as the net income) is jointly associated with the entire process of planning, producing, providing the goods or services for customers, and the final collection of cash and, in some cases, the providing of services (such as repairs under warranties) beyond the collection process. Because of the jointness of this value added over time, it is impossible to make a logical allocation to the several processes. Therefore, an expedient alternative is to report the value added by the firm at a single point in time. The critical event concept suggests that the most appropriate moment of time is when the most critical decision is made or when the most difficult task is performed. This could be at the point when the contract is signed, the time when the services are performed, when the cash is collected, or at some other time.

The 1964 AAA committee which reported on *The Realization Concept* proposed the crucial event concept, but it suggested that some of the revenue should be recognized later if additional economic functions or activities are to take place subsequently. While the committee rejected the reporting of income on the basis of costs incurred, it implied that the value added by the firm should be allocated to more than one point in time. Even if the value added by the firm is reported at a single point in time, the amount of revenue represented by the value added by other economic factors should be reported at a later time if, in fact, the services provided by these factors follow the main point of recognition. This is the net realizable value concept—the final cash sales price less additional costs to produce and sell.

The term *revenue realization* is used in a technical sense by accountants to establish specific rules for the timing of revenue reporting under circumstances where no single solution is necessarily superior to others in the above context of revenue. The realization concept has, therefore, be-

---

[14] Sprouse and Moonitz, *op. cit.*, p. 47.

[15] See John H. Myers, "The Critical Event and Recognition of Net Profit," *Accounting Review*, Vol. XXXIV (October, 1959), pp. 528–32; and the 1964 Concepts and Standards Research Study Committee, "The Realization Concept," *Accounting Review*, Vol. XL (April, 1965), p. 316.

come a pragmatic test for the timing of revenue. While many attempts have been made to give it theoretical content, it continues to lack analytical precision, as suggested by Sprouse and Moonitz.[16] However, many writers in the area suggest that the realization concept enriches accounting terminology and reporting.[17]

One of the main difficulties with the realization concept is that it means different things to different people. In a broad sense, the term has been used to mean simply the recognition (reporting) of revenue.[18] While many writers who use the term in this sense have in mind specific rules applying to the reporting of transactions, others would include all value increases, regardless of their type or source. The general view, however, is that realization represents the reporting of revenue when an exchange or severance has occurred. That is, goods or services must have been transferred to a customer or client, giving rise to either the receipt of cash or a claim to cash or other assets. In this view, realization cannot take place by the holding of assets or as a result of the production process alone. Thus, the term "realization" has come generally to mean the reporting of revenue when it has been validated by sale.[19] The reporting of revenue prior to or subsequent to the point of sale is generally considered an exception to the realization rule.

The 1957 American Accounting Association statement defined realization broadly as follows:

The essential meaning of realization is that a change in an asset or liability has become sufficiently definite and objective to warrant recognition in the accounts. This recognition may rest on an exchange transaction between independent parties, or on established trade practices, or on the terms of a contract performance of which is considered to be virtually certain.[20]

This definition has the advantage of being broadly stated, with emphasis on the necessity for objectivity. It also seems to apply equally well to expenses, gains, and losses and to other changes in assets and liabilities.[21]

---

[16] Sprouse and Moonitz, *op. cit.*, p. 15.

[17] For example, see Charles T. Horngren, "How Should We Interpret the Realization Concept?" *Accounting Review*, Vol. XL (April, 1965), p. 325.

[18] See for example Eric L. Kohler, *A Dictionary for Accountants* (2d ed.; Englewood Cliffs, N.J.: Prentice-Hall, Inc., 1957), p. 422.

[19] Paton and Littleton, however, stated that the dominant view was that realization includes the test of " . . . validation through the acquisition of liquid assets." Paton and Littleton, *op. cit.*, p. 49.

[20] AAA Committee on Accounting Concepts and Standards, *op. cit.*, p. 3.

[21] For a discussion of the application of this definition to the various types of changes, see Floyd W. Windal, "The Accounting Concept of Realization," *Accounting Review*, Vol. XXXVI (April, 1961), pp. 249–58; and Floyd W. Windal, *The Accounting Concept of Realization*, Occasional Paper No. 5 (East Lansing: Bureau of Business and Economic Research, Michigan State University, 1961).

The 1964 AAA committee on the realization concept recommended that the term "realization" would be improved if the following criteria were applied in use of the term: (1) Revenue must be capable of measurement, even though this measurement may of necessity be an estimation. (2) The measurement must be verifiable on the basis of a market transaction, to which the accounting entity must be a party. (3) The crucial event in the revenue process must have occurred.[22] A substitute for this last criterion, however, is that economic value must have been added by the firm to its product. Horngren stated that goods or services must have been rendered, thus removing the restrictions against the assets.[23] An additional criterion suggested by the author is that because the computation of net income may be considered more relevant than the computation of revenue alone, revenue should be recognized only if the related expenses can be estimated with a fair degree of accuracy.

In view of the confusion, emotionalism, and even mysticism that have surrounded the realization concept, this author suggests that accountants abandon the term. In its place, emphasis should be placed on the reporting of valuation changes of all types, although the nature of the change and the reliability of the measurement should also be disclosed. Furthermore, accountants may be able to provide more relevant information to users of external reports if less emphasis is placed on the relationship of revenue to net income and more emphasis on the informational content of the several measurements of revenue. For example, it is likely that several attributes of revenue—such as sales price of goods produced, goods and services sold, and the final amount of cash received for goods and services rendered—may be relevant to external users. Acceptance of one attribute should not necessarily exclude disclosure of other attributes.

The Reporting of Revenue during Production. The traditional accrual basis of accounting recognizes revenue as earned if there is a simultaneous increase in the claim against the customer or client. This is the general practice with respect to services. The product of the enterprise emerges as the services are provided. The amount of the claim is usually determined by prior agreement or contract, or often by established trade prices, even though the client or tenant may not be required to make payment until a later date or at least until a determinable amount of service has been provided.

Examples of the accrual basis of revenue recognition are rent, interest, commissions, and personal services performed on a time basis. In each of these examples the basic criteria for revenue reporting are met. The services are usually performed on a time basis and the performing of ser-

---

[22] 1964 Concepts and Standards Research Study Committee—The Realization Concept, *op. cit.,* p. 318.

[23] Horngren, *op. cit.,* p. 325.

vices may be assumed to be crucial. The amount of the revenue has been established by prior contract or agreement. Related expenses are usually determinable simultaneously with the revenue. In addition, a valid claim arises against the customer, client, or tenant even though the amount is not billed and payment is not required until a later date.

Long-Term Contracts. A second accepted application of the reporting of revenue during production is the recognition of revenue on long-term contracts. The general acceptance in this case is based on pragmatic grounds and supported by theory. An individual or firm would usually object to publication of financial statements showing no income for a year during which the firm spent considerable effort in obtaining partial completion of a contract that will permit a reasonable profit with a fair degree of certainty. If contracts are completed at irregular intervals, the reporting of income only when the contracts are completed could result in a hardship or injustice to stockholders who wish to sell their interests prior to the completion of major contracts because of a lack of relevant information. The annual income statement might have less meaning also from either a managerial or a financial point of view.

What conditions support the recognition of revenue during production in this case? The most important consideration is that the total price of the contract is determined in advance or is determinable. Uncertainty regarding the selling price is minimized and uncertainty regarding collection is usually not very great, particularly if the buyer is a governmental unit or a large established corporation. Two areas of uncertainty remain, however: (1) At any particular point, it may be difficult to determine the sale price of the product produced to date. (2) The total costs of the project may be difficult to estimate with accuracy. If the actual costs of completion differ from the estimated costs, the net income of each period will have been affected.

The percentage of completion is usually computed by comparing the costs incurred in a specific accounting period with the total estimated costs for the project. The expected profit on the contract is then allocated to each period on the basis of these costs. This procedure has two main difficulties: (1) It assumes that the firm's profit is earned as costs are incurred. But an important part of the firm's contribution may come from the planning stage, before large costs are incurred. Furthermore, many of the costs involve work performed by subcontractors and are not the result of the firm's contribution. An alternative might be to include only those costs included in the concept of value added. But the assumption that each dollar of cost produces the same amount of revenue implies that the value added by the firm is related to the use of other economic factors, an assumption that is conceptually unacceptable. (2) A second difficulty arises because the percentage is computed by using total costs as the denominator. As noted above, total costs also may be uncertain, particularly where excavation and weather conditions may present unknown hazards.

The second area of general uncertainty is the estimation of expected net income. While the total contract price may be fixed, the costs are uncertain, so it becomes difficult to allocate this uncertain income to periods. In the case of cost-plus-fixed-fee contracts, the total income is determined in advance and only the percentage of completion may be uncertain. Uncertainty, however, should not be a cause for the failure to report revenue when the value increase can be measured. Reasonable estimates based on contract prices and expert judgment regarding costs may provide better information regarding the progress of the firm than can the holding to the narrow realization concept.

The AICPA has accepted in principle the percentage-of-completion method of revenue recognition. *Accounting Research Bulletin No. 43* states as follows:

It is . . . a generally accepted accounting procedure to accrue revenues under certain types of contracts and thereby recognize profits, on the basis of partial performance, where the circumstances are such that total profit can be estimated with reasonable accuracy and ultimate realization is reasonably assured. Particularly where the performance of a contract requires a substantial period of time from inception to completion, there is ample precedent for prorata recognition of profit as the work progresses, if the total profit and the ratio of the performance to date to the complete performance can be computed reasonably and collection is reasonably assured. Depending upon the circumstances, such partial performance may be established by deliveries, expenditures, or percentage of completion otherwise determined. This rule is frequently applied to long-term construction and other similar contracts; it is also applied in the case of contracts involving deliveries in instalments or the performance of services. However, the rule should be dealt with cautiously and not applied in the case of partial deliveries and uncompleted contracts where the information available does not clearly indicate that a partial profit has been realized after making provision for possible losses and contingencies.[24]

Accretion. Related to the reporting of revenue during production is the recognition of increased values arising from natural growth or an aging process. This natural growth or aging over time is just as much a part of the production process from an economic point of view as the process of changing the form of commodities. In an economic sense, then, accretion gives rise to revenue. Examples include growing timber, nursery stock, and livestock, and the aging of certain liquors and wines.

The revenues or income from accretion can only be recognized through the process of making comparative inventory valuations. This recognition

[24] AICPA, *Accounting Principles* (Chicago: Commerce Clearing House, Inc., 1968), Vol. II, p. 6042.

is not the result of transactions. Therefore, it does differ from the cases of revenue reporting during production discussed so far. But this does not affect the logic of reporting the increases in asset measurement. The limitations are primarily from a practical standpoint. The present discounted value is difficult to determine because it depends upon expectations regarding future market prices and expectations regarding future costs of providing for growth and future costs of harvesting and getting the product ready for market. In some cases, such as nursery stock and livestock, the product has a market price at the various stages of growth and the valuation process is simplified. But these measurements, even though verifiable, are also only approximations of the discounted net future values. If the product is held for future sale, it may be presumed that the owner feels, at least subjectively, that the present value is greater than the current market price; otherwise he would sell the product in the current market. So the current market price less costs of harvesting is probably a conservative estimate of the present discounted value.

The argument that accretion is not income because it cannot be available for dividends is the wrong criterion for the recognition of revenue. Current accounting practice recognizes many situations where income results in liquid assets, but for several reasons, prudent financial management may preclude the payment of dividends. The important criterion is the certainty regarding the final sales price of the product and the additional costs required to permit optimum growth and preparation for sale. If a reasonable market is not assured, or if additional costs are highly uncertain, the reporting of revenue from accretion may be highly improper. The wide range of probable outcomes may prohibit objective verification or even the valid estimation of a single-valued amount of revenue or income.

The Reporting of Revenue at the Completion of Production.   When a product is completed, one of the former uncertainties—the cost of production—can now be computed with a fair degree of accuracy. The selling price and the additional costs of selling and delivering may still remain uncertain. But when these can be estimated reliably, there is good justification for reporting the revenue at this time. In many industries, the production process may be a crucial part of the firm's operations. From an economic point of view, value is added in all of the necessary economic activities of the firm, including production.

The reporting of the revenue at the completion of production, however, is dependent upon the degree of certainty with which the selling price and the additional costs can be estimated. When there is a firm contract for the production and delivery of a given product, the selling price is known and the costs of selling have already been incurred. The remaining uncertainties include the possibility of failure to collect the selling price and the additional expenses of delivery. These, however, can usually be estimated fairly accurately, and accountants have generally expressed approval of reporting revenue on this basis.

In a few cases, the reporting of revenue at the completion of production is permitted even though the products are not manufactured under contract. The main criteria are (a) the existence of a determinable selling price or stable market price, (b) no substantial cost of marketing, and (c) interchangeability of units. Some question can be raised as to whether (c), interchangeability, is really necessary if criterion (a) is met. Prices in a ready market are relevant only if they apply to the specific commodity in question, which implies some interchangeability. Gold and silver are the most common examples that meet these criteria, particularly where there is an effective government-controlled market at fixed prices. Other commodities, such as precious metals and agricultural commodities, may also meet the above criteria if there is a ready market for the commodity with a determinable market price. In these cases, technical production rather than selling activity is the major activity of the firm. In many cases, however, market prices fluctuate widely and considerable uncertainty exists regarding the price at which the product will be sold.

The American Institute of Certified Public Accountants has recommended the recognition of revenue at the completion of production under the above criteria only for "precious metals having a fixed monetary value with no substantial cost of marketing. . . ."[25] Similar treatment is acceptable for agricultural and other mineral products only if the firm is unable to determine appropriate approximate costs. In all cases, however, the sales prices should be reduced by the estimated costs of disposal. Note, however, that the lack of cost measurement is not a basic standard for using market prices; rather it is an extenuating circumstance under which market prices are permitted, according to the AICPA.

Sprouse and Moonitz recommend that all types of commodities should be included if they meet the tests of having a ready market at known prices and have little or no marketing activity required to dispose of them, so that the costs of disposal are negligible or readily predictable. They would also apply this procedure where a marketable commodity is used in the production of other products.[26]

The inability to determine costs is not a logical reason for recognizing revenue at the completion of production. The main consideration should be the ability to obtain verifiable measurements of revenue and additional costs which are reliable. For most commodities, the lack of a stable

---

[25] *Ibid.,* p. 6017.

[26] Sprouse and Moonitz, *op. cit.,* p. 47.

market price is a major stumbling block for the general acceptance of the recognition of revenue at the completion of production.

The Reporting of Revenue at the Time of Sale. For many years the time of sale has been the general rule for the reporting of revenue. This rule is supported on several grounds: (1) The price of the product is now established rather definitely. (2) The product has left the firm and a new asset has taken its place—an exchange has occurred. (3) For most concerns, the sale is assumed to be the most significant financial event in the economic activity of the firm. (4) Most of the costs relating to the manufacture or acquisition of the product and the costs of disposal have now been incurred or are now readily determinable.

The uncertainties regarding the final measurement of revenue are minimal at the time of sale, but they are not eliminated. Accepted business practice may permit the return of all or a part of the merchandise, thus canceling the sales contract. Failure to collect the sale price is often a possibility, the likelihood of which may depend upon the credit rating of the customer. Also, additional expenses may arise, many of which are unexpected. These would include abnormal collection charges and expenses of meeting express or implied customer warranties. However, usually the uncollectible accounts and the additional expenses may be estimated from past experience.

When does a sale take place? From a legal point of view, the sale occurs when title passes and a claim for payment arises. Because of the technicality of the passing of title, accountants generally recognize the sale as occurring when delivery of the merchandise is made to the customer or to a common carrier. But the sale is also assumed to occur when merchandise is physically segregated or marked for the customer after he has indicated a desire to purchase. As with all rules, however, exceptions are not uncommon. In many cases, the fact of delivery or segregation is not sufficient. The intent on the part of both parties to consummate a sale must also be present. For example, the delivery of merchandise on consignment does not generally carry with it the intent to bring about an exchange between the consignor and the consignee. A delivery on approval may carry a similar intent, as the customer has not indicated his direct intention to buy. Evidence of a completed transaction is lacking. To say that the sale should be recorded when an invoice is presented to the customer is a weak criterion for the timing of revenue, but nevertheless it has some merits. The burden of deciding when the evidence is strong enough to record a sale is transferred to the sales department, and the accountant accepts this decision. This is merely another way of saying that revenue should be reported at the time of sale; no basic criterion is established.

A more precise set of criteria for the recognition of a sale would include (1) the appearance of definite evidence that the buyer intends to buy and that the seller intends to sell, (2) the identification of the specific completed merchandise in question, and (3) an agreement between the buyer and seller regarding the price or a formula for establishing the price.

The Reporting of Revenue Subsequent to Sale. Cash receipts or anticipated cash receipts are significant in the measurement of revenue, but they are not generally crucial in the operational process giving rise to the increase in net assets of the firm. Thus, while the expected cash receipts to be received subsequent to sale provide a verifiable measurement of revenue, there is little theoretical justification for delaying the reporting of revenue beyond the time when a valid claim against customers arises and the basic activity regarding such sale of products or services has been accomplished. However, delaying the reporting of revenue beyond the time of sale may be justified if one of the two following criteria is met: (1) if it is impossible to measure the assets received in the exchange with a fair degree of accuracy, or (2) if additional material expenses are likely and if these cannot be estimated with a fair degree of accuracy.

With respect to the valuation of the assets received in the exchange, two types of situations may lead to the deferral of revenue reporting. *First*, a tangible asset or other nonmonetary asset may be received. If the asset does not have a recognized market value and if appraisal is difficult or impossible, the reporting of revenue may have little meaning. Only when the valuation of the asset can be measured by sale or by other verifiable means will the measurement of the revenue be meaningful. These cases, however, should be the exception. Such transactions are not common in business practice, and when they do occur a valuation can usually be placed on the assets received. In those rare cases where a valuation cannot be placed on the assets received, there is justification for transferring the input price of the goods sold to the new asset received so that revenue is not recorded and net income would not result. *Second*, the claim against the customer may be of dubious collection. In general this can be handled by estimating the probable amount of uncollectible accounts. Only rarely is this impossible, and therefore only very few situations justify the deferral of revenue recognition on the ground that collection is too doubtful to establish a reasonable current valuation of the receivables.

If additional material expenses cannot be estimated with a fair degree of accuracy, there may be some justification for the deferral of revenue reporting in order to permit a better matching of revenue and expenses. However, here again, such situations are unlikely. The most common cases where deferral is suggested are those cases involving material billing and collection expenses and material repair and replacement expenses required under customer warranties. In general, however, income reporting can be improved by estimating these expenses in advance.

The most often quoted example of justifiable deferral of revenue reporting is the case of installment sales. Collection is said to be doubtful because the customers who enter into these installment contracts often overextend themselves and therefore are poor risks. Billing and collection expenses subsequent to the time of sale are usually large, and warranty expenses may also enter into the picture. These arguments are usually quite weak, however. Even though uncollectible accounts may be large, they can usually be estimated on the basis of past experience of the specific firm or of other firms in the industry. Furthermore, the accounts are usually protected by the fact that title to the goods does not usually pass to the customer until the claim is fully paid. Billing and collection expenses can also be estimated fairly accurately, and warranty expenses should be very little different from those cases following open account or cash sales.

In a few cases where a venture is highly speculative there may be justification for the deferral of revenue reporting. The final net income from a project may depend on the sale of a minimum quantity of the product, or the existence of joint costs may result in period income determination which is highly tentative. In these unusual circumstances, an alternative may be to consider the life of the venture the relevant period for income determination. A resort to the cash basis does not necessarily render the reporting of period net income more accurate; the result may often be the reverse with uniform time periods.

A modification of the installment basis has often been suggested for highly speculative ventures where cash collections are received in installments and where the collection of the final installments may be doubtful. Under these circumstances, the final net income or loss cannot be determined until all collections have been received. Accordingly, the first installments are considered to be a return of invested costs, and income is recorded only after all costs have been recovered. After all costs have been recovered, all additional installments are treated as income. A good example is where a bond is in default and payments of principal and interest are made as cash becomes available through liquidation of the mortgaged property or through other means. Because of the uncertainty regarding future payments under the bond contract, all collections, whether considered payments of principal or interest by the trustee, are treated as a return of the bond investment until such investment has been fully recovered.

The position of the AICPA Accounting Principles Board in *Opinion No. 10* was that ". . . revenues should ordinarily be accounted for at the time a transaction is completed, with appropriate provision for uncollectible accounts"; and in the absence of circumstances where the sale price is not reasonably assured, it concluded that the installment method of recognizing revenue is not acceptable. A footnote, however, weakened this position by recognizing exceptional cases where there may be no reasonable basis for estimating the degree of collectibility. In the author's opinion, this exception is not warranted because installment sales would not normally be made under such conditions.

Summary of Revenue Reporting. The recording of revenue in accounting statements should be based on the following criteria: (1) Economic value must have been added by the firm to its product. (2) The amount of the revenue must be capable of measurement. (3) The measurement must be verifiable and relatively free from bias. (4) Related expenses must be capable of being estimated with a fair degree of accuracy.

In general, accounting statements are improved if revenue is reported at the earliest possible point after the value increase can be measured. The following tabulation summarizes the several periods and the conditions under which reporting may be appropriate:

Time of Reporting	*Criteria*	*Examples*
During production.	Establishment of a firm price based on contract or general business terms or existence of market prices at various stages of production.	Accruals; long-term contracts; accretion.
At completion of production.	Existence of a determinable selling price or stable market price. No substantial cost of marketing.	Precious metals; agricultural products; services.
At time of sale.	Established price for the product. Reasonable method for estimating amount collectible. Estimation of all material related expenses.	Most merchandise sales.
At time of cash collection.	Impossible to value assets received with fair degree of accuracy. Additional material expenses are likely, and these cannot be estimated with a fair degree of accuracy at the time of sale.	Installment sales; exchange for fixed asset without verifiably determined value.

EXPENSES

Like the term *revenue*, the term *expense* is also a flow concept, representing the unfavorable changes in the resources of the firm. But not all unfavorable changes are expenses. More precisely defined, expenses are the using or consuming of goods and services in the process of obtaining revenues. They are the expirations of factor services related either directly or indirectly to the producing and selling of the product of the enterprise. The values of these factor services expire when they leave the enterprise by final consumption or by the transfer of the product to customers; they acquire new measurements of value by the reporting of revenue prior to sale. When service expirations result in a product still held by the enterprise, but on which revenue has not been reported, the measurement of the goods and services used is assumed to become embodied in the measurement of the product (a transformation of the service value) and there is no final expiration or transfer out of the firm.

The unfavorable aspect of revenue operations (expenses) has a tendency to reduce the stockholders' equity in the firm. Expenses are often defined in this context. But it is not meaningful to emphasize the unfavorable aspects without also referring to the favorable (revenues). Both determine net operating income, which results in a net change in the owners' equity. Because of this close relationship to revenues and because expenses do not include all of the unfavorable changes in equities, expenses should not be defined solely in terms of their effect on stockholders' equity.

Frequently expenses are defined in terms of cost expirations or cost allocations. For example, the 1957 statement of the American Accounting Association defined expense as follows:

Expense is the expired cost, directly or indirectly related to a given fiscal period, of the flow of goods or services into the market and of related operations.[27]

However, the valuation of expenses is a problem distinct from the definition of the term *expenses*. Expenses are measured by the valuation of the goods or services used or consumed, but this measurement does not define the expense. The reader should be careful to distinguish between the measurement of an expense based on cost and the definition of an expense as an activity or process. Emphasis on the latter has the advantage of leaving the measurement of expense open for further discussion.

Sprouse and Moonitz define expense as

the decrease in net assets as a result of the use of economic services in the creation of revenues or of the imposition of taxes by governmental units.[28]

Rather than emphasizing the process of using economic services, this definition is expressed in terms of the result of the process—the decrease in net assets. While this approach is not in error, the author prefers an emphasis on the process itself rather than on the result. The specific reference to taxes has an advantage of clarity, but it can be subsumed under the classification of services used.

The questions arising with respect to the term "expense" are similar to the questions asked regarding revenue. They are: (1) What should be included in the term "expense"? (2) How should expenses be measured? (3) When are expenses incurred and when should they be reported for accounting purposes?

---

[27] AAA Committee on Accounting Concepts and Standards, *op. cit.*, p. 6.

[28] Sprouse and Moonitz, *op. cit.*, p. 49.

What Should Be Included in Expense?

In the above definition of expenses, only those unfavorable changes incurred in the process of obtaining revenue are included. The converse of this is that asset expirations or asset reductions not required in the process of providing goods or services to customers or clients should be classified as losses rather than as expenses. This does not deny their rightful place in the income statement under certain circumstances. Losses and expenses may both be relevant changes in the computation of net income to stockholders or to the enterprise; but only expenses can be matched with revenues of the period in the computation of "net operating income."

Several authorities, however, define expenses broadly to include the expiration of both operating and nonoperating costs. For example, the 1948 statement of the American Accounting Association defined expenses as consisting of both operating costs and losses.[29] On the other hand, the 1957 AAA statement clearly distinguished between expenses and losses. While both were defined as expired costs, only expenses relate to current operations; losses were defined as those cost expirations not benefiting the revenue-producing activities of the enterprise.[30] This distinction will be carried into the following discussions in order to maintain clarity of exposition.

The controversy between the all-inclusive and the current operating concepts of income discussed in the previous chapter is relevant in the necessity to classify unfavorable changes as either expenses or losses; but it does not alter the nature of these changes. The all-inclusive concept of income includes all expenses and losses recognized during the current period; there is no need to differentiate between the two in the computation of net income. On the other hand, the current operating concept excludes from the computation of net income those expenses actually incurred in a prior period but not recognized until the current period, and all losses. This is a problem, however, of choosing a meaningful concept of net income rather than a problem of defining expenses. Extraordinary items (deductions) are not the same as losses, as will be discussed later.

In the proper delineation of expenses, care should be taken to distinguish between those unfavorable changes that are expenses and those that are offsets to revenue or valuations of revenue. Sales returns and allowances are normally treated as revenue offsets, and rightly so. On the other hand, sales discounts and bad debt losses have been treated con-

---

[29] AAA Committee on Accounting Concepts and Standards, *op. cit.*, p. 15.
[30] *Ibid.*, p. 5.

ventionally as expenses. In the opinion of the author, however, it is more logical to classify them as offsets to revenue than as expenses.[31] Sales discounts do not represent the use of goods or services. A small part of such discounts may represent the monetary discount or interest equal to the cost of waiting in the absence of uncertainty. But if the discount is taken, the net price represents the price of the goods; the discount is a reduction of the revenue and not a cost of borrowing funds. Likewise, bad debt losses do not represent expirations of goods or services but rather reductions of the amount to be received in exchange for the product.

A careful distinction should also be made between expenses and offsets to capital or stockholders' equity. Asset expirations and obligations incurred in relation to capital transactions should not be classified as expenses but shown as reductions of capital or one of its components. Costs incurred in the sale of capital stock, for example, are not expenses but reductions of the amount of capital received by the corporation. Likewise, the write-off of capital stock discount has no place in the income statement. Thus we see that the use of goods and services is not a sufficient definition of expenses. The objective of obtaining revenue must also be present, although the relationship to revenue might be quite indirect, as in the case of expenditures necessary to service debt.

The classification of expenses as "selling," "administrative," or "cost of goods sold" may be useful for analytical purposes within the firm, such as establishing functional responsibilities. However, for external reporting purposes, it serves no particular useful function. The reader of financial reports is not better able to make predictions by using this classification nor is he able to evaluate the contributions of the several functions. While each classification may represent the use of goods or services at different times in the enterprise operating process, they are all expenses. The "cost of goods sold" is an expense just as much as salesmen's salaries, although AICPA *Terminology Bulletin No. 4* makes a distinction between the term *cost* as used in the former and *expense* as related to the latter. Care should be taken to avoid the assignment of priorities to expenses; all are equal in the determination of income. Expenses are not recovered in preferential order. There can be no meaningful income measurement until all expenses have been subtracted from the total revenues.

A classification of expenses that might be useful to investors and others in making predictions and in evaluating current management decisions would be one that describes the behavioral nature of the expenses. That is, expenses should be classified and described according to whether they are variable or fixed in nature with respect to production or sales

---

[31] See note 13 above.

volume, or whether they vary with respect to some other factor. There may also be an advantage in describing their relationship to cash flows. Items that result from cash expenditures of a prior period have a different effect upon the firm than expenses resulting from current or future cash outflows.

How Should Expenses Be Measured?

Measurement of the goods and services used in the operations of the enterprise does not have a simple solution. This is so because the objectives for such measurement are not clearly defined and the measurement found acceptable is determined in large part by the income concept applied. Many of the controversial discussions regarding the appropriate measurement do not lead to solutions, primarily because the proponents of the different viewpoints have in mind different objectives or different income concepts, which are not generally clearly stated.

According to those who define expenses as decreases in the net assets of the firm, a logical measurement is the value of the goods and services at the time they are used in the operations of the enterprise. These are the unfavorable aspects of revenue operations and represent the economic sacrifice required to obtain the revenue. While the term "value" has many meanings, it is usually used in this context to represent the exchange price of the goods or services or their opportunity cost. On the other hand, those who emphasize the reporting of cash flows of the enterprise usually suggest that expenses should be measured in terms of transactions to which the firm is a party and measured by the past, current, or future cash expenditures. In either view of income, the purpose is to measure the amounts assignable to the current period and to defer to future periods those amounts that represent transformations of goods or services to be used in future periods. The most common measurements of expense are (a) historical cost, (b) current measurements such as replacement cost, and (c) opportunity costs or current cash equivalents.

Historical Cost. The conventional method of measuring expenses is in terms of the historical cost to the enterprise. The main reason for adhering to historical costs is that they are assumed to be verifiable, since they represent cash outlays by the firm. But it is also claimed that they represent the exchange value of the goods and services at the time they were acquired by the enterprise. An essential feature of this argument is that management considered the value of the goods and services to be at least as great as the cost at the time of acquisition or they would not have been acquired. Also, there is no real evidence that the firm would have acquired the goods and services if it had had to pay a higher price for them. Thus, the best evidence available indicates that they were worth just what they cost the firm, no more or less.[32] If the goods and services turn out to be worth more than the historical cost, the excess represents a gain to the firm which will be included in aggregate income at the time revenue is reported if the expense is then reported at historical cost. The opposite is the case if the goods and services are subsequently worth less than cost. The main disadvantages of historical cost are that it frequently does not represent a relevant measurement of the goods and services used in attempting to meet the objectives of the external users of financial reports, and that it does not permit a separation of operating activity from gains and losses arising from fortuitous purchases or unpredictable price changes. The measurement and timing of these gains and losses are discussed later in this chapter.

What is meant by cost and what should be included in the term? Basically, cost is measured by the current value of the economic resources given up or to be given up in obtaining the goods and services to be used in operations; this is the value in exchange. When cash is paid or agreed to be paid for merchandise, supplies, and personal services, the measurement of cost is fairly definite. The cash paid or agreed to be paid represents the exchange value determined by the market price or by agreement between the buyer and seller. The cash represents the monetary value of claims to economic resources given up by the buyer.

When economic resources other than cash or claims to cash are given up in the exchange, however, the problem of valuation still remains. A possible solution can be found in the market price of the goods and services acquired, or in the market price of the goods given up in the exchange. If the goods or services given up were acquired previously for cash or its equivalent, this original cost may now be assumed to be the cost of the newly acquired goods and services. Because this latter cost is considered more verifiable than the current market price of either the goods received or the goods given up, it would usually be preferred by accountants, but its relevance is suspect. Suppose, for example, that a plot of land is exchanged for a piece of equipment to be used in the business. The original cost of the land would be considered the basis for valuing the expense of using the equipment, but such cost may have little relevance to current conditions or objectives.

The complexities of cost determination will be discussed more fully in the following chapters. But the following situations suggest some of the problems that are relevant in the measurement of expenses in terms of cost: (1) The total agreed price may be payable at a deferred date, in which case the discounted price may be the appropriate measurement of the expense. (2) The appearance of joint costs may permit no adequate

---

[32] For an additional discussion of cost, see Chapter 9, pp. 266–68.

solution to the measurement of the several types of expenses. (3) Cost prices that are not the result of arm's-length transactions may be less valid than other methods of measurement. (4) The aggregate cost price should include all of the costs necessary to acquire the goods or services, not only the invoice or quoted price.

Current Prices. As revenue is usually measured in terms of the current prices received for the product, the expenses matched against this revenue should also be measured in terms of the current prices of the goods or services used or consumed. Income resulting from the sale transaction is the excess of the cash or claims received over the amount of the resources used. Thus, the measurement of expenses in terms of current prices has the advantage of distinguishing between (a) the income arising from the transaction, and (b) the gains or losses arising from the holding of assets prior to use. The holding of assets for a period prior to use (or allocation to expense) may result from a deliberate decision to speculate or from the necessity to acquire goods and services prior to use. The gains and losses occurring prior to use may arise from price changes, from deterioration, or from obsolescence or other factors. When the acquisition of goods or services prior to use is necessary and the loss or deterioration is also necessary and can be anticipated, this reduction in value should be included in the measurement of the expense; it is a necessary part of the revenue operations of the firm.

Current prices can be obtained to represent either a current liquidation (sale) price or a replacement cost. A current liquidation price or current cash equivalent may be relevant in the measurement of expense because it represents the opportunity cost to the firm in using the specific asset. Furthermore, this measurement of the expense does not require speculation regarding the future possibility of replacement. If there is a good market in which the item can be purchased and sold with little loss, the liquidation price may be particularly relevant. On the other hand, the current replacement cost represents the acquisition price at the time of use, and therefore it may permit a better prediction of the results of future firm activity if there is likely to be continuity of the past into the future. One of the difficulties with the use of a replacement cost is that there may not be a current price available for the same type of goods or services previously acquired or there may be no verifiable measurement of such a price.

Many expenses are contracted for or obtained currently, so that cost is not far removed from the current price. Those cases where the costs may be materially different from the current prices comprise primarily the valuation of inventories and fixed assets. These problems are discussed more fully in Chapter 7 and in the later chapters on inventories and fixed assets. In the following discussion of the timing of expenses, reference will be made primarily to costs, but it should be recognized that the term "current prices" could be substituted for "costs" at any point.

The Timing of Expenses

By definition, an expense is incurred when goods or services are consumed or used in the process of obtaining revenue. The timing or reporting of expense is brought about by recording this activity in the accounts or including it in financial reports. The reporting of the expense may coincide with the activity of using the goods or services, or it may follow it, or, in unusual circumstances, it may precede it.

When expenses should be reported is, in part, determined by the approach to income being proposed either explicitly or implicitly. The definition of income as changes in values generally suggests that expenses should be reported whenever there is a decrease in value, or when there is no apparent benefit or value to be received in the future arising from the use of goods or services. The concept of income that emphasizes cash flows leads to the conclusion that expenses should be reported as close to the actual cash expenditure as is reasonable. Traditional accrual accounting is somewhat between these two extremes, but it leans toward the value concepts somewhat in that it suggests that input (cost) prices should be retained until an increase in value is reported by the substitution of the exit (sales) prices. That is, expense should be recognized in the period in which the associated revenue is recognized. This is the matching process—the timing of revenue reporting comes first, followed by the reporting of related expenses in the same period. Only in unusual cases are revenues deferred until expenses can be measured or identified.

The Matching Concept. If revenues were reported gradually over the entire operating process of the firm, the measurement of the product of the firm would be increased as value was added by the firm and other factors of production. In this case, there would be no necessity for a matching concept. But because revenue and expense transactions are reported separately, and because the acquisition and payment for goods and services do not usually coincide with the sales and collection processes related to the same product of the enterprise, matching has come to be considered a necessity or at least desirable. The leads and lags in the acquisition and use of, and payment for, goods and services are assumed to be the reason for accruals or deferrals in order to match the expenses with associated revenue.

As defined by the 1964 AAA committee on the matching concept, matching is the process of reporting expenses on the basis of a cause-and-effect relationship with reported revenues. The committee advocated that costs (defined as product and service factors given up) should be related to revenues realized within a specific period on the basis of some discernible positive correlation of such costs with the recognized revenues.[33]

That is, the measurement of net income is assumed to represent the excess of revenues reported during a period over the expenses associated and reported during that same period. A proper matching is assumed to occur only when a reasonable association is found between the revenues and expenses. The timing of expenses, therefore, requires (1) association with revenue, and (2) reporting in the same period as the related revenue is reported.

The matching of expenses with revenues thus requires the finding of a proper association between the two. All expenses, by definition, are incurred as a necessary part of the revenue operation. This does not mean, however, that revenue will always result; expenses may be incurred without revenue resulting. Several calls by a salesman may be necessary before a sale is made; but all calls should be included in the expenses, as they are necessary in the revenue operations. In fact, even if no sales were made the calls would nevertheless be included in the operating expenses. As another example, normal breakage of merchandise should be classified as an expense even though no revenue can be associated with it. The display of merchandise that permits this breakage is necessary in the revenue process, and it is this fact that requires the classification as an expense.

The association of expenses with revenue is, therefore, a difficult step. In fact, in some cases, no association may be possible. This difficulty has led accountants to establish specific rules and procedures or to establish basic criteria for the timing of expenses. These basic criteria are established by drawing a distinction between direct expenses (product costs) and indirect or period expenses. Direct expenses are reported in the same period as the related revenue. Indirect expenses are reported in the period in which the goods or services are used; or they are reported when a decline in economic value can be measured, or is assumed to occur because of an inability to relate the expenses to any future benefit.

Direct or Product Matching. By associating costs or other measurements of goods or services used with products, and by charging these as product costs to expenses at the time of reporting the associated revenue, a matching of expenses with revenues is obtained. That is, a transformation is assumed to take place; the measurement of the factor costs is assumed to be a proper measurement of the product prior to reporting any value added by the firm. The use of goods and services is associated with a specific product, and the product is then associated with the

---

[33] AAA 1964 Concepts and Standards Research Study Committee—The Matching Concept, *op. cit.*, p. 369.

revenue at the time it is reported. If the revenue is reported at the time of sale, the product leaves the firm and the reporting of its cost or recorded value as an expense is logical since a new asset (cash or a receivable) has taken its place. On the other hand, until the product leaves the firm, all associated costs can be assumed to represent a measurement of future benefits to the firm which can logically be carried forward as assets. But even under ideal conditions, the matching of product costs with revenues gives rise to several knotty problems. Among these will be discussed the following: (1) How can the use of goods and services be identified with the product of the firm? (2) When expenses can be associated directly with future revenue but do not increase the value of any specific product or products, how should they be reported while awaiting the reporting of these associated revenues? (3) When associated expenses are expected to be incurred subsequent to the reporting of the related revenues, how should they be recorded?

1. The Identification of Product Costs.   The various methods for valuing inventories and for charging these values to expenses will be discussed in Chapter 11. But the problem of identification of product costs is relevant at this point. According to the general view of the matching concept, all reasonable and necessary costs of production should be assigned to the product and reported as expenses at the time of reporting the associated revenue. Costs relating to the product on hand, either as unsold finished goods or as uncompleted goods, should be inventoried and carried forward as assets until the time of sale or revenue reporting. Some of these production costs can be associated directly with the production of specific products. Others can be associated only with production in general and must be allocated to products by the best means available if product matching is to be attained.

Direct product costs include the costs of raw materials and labor incurred in the production of the specific product and the costs of other goods and services for which a direct association can be found with the product. It is also considered appropriate to include normal waste material and labor time required in setting up for production. Whenever labor and material costs are insignificant in relation to aggregate costs, they may be omitted from direct product costs for practical reasons. Thus, we see that even in the accounting for direct product costs, several methods of classification may be considered appropriate. And in some cases, no simple answer can be found. For example, when raw materials are used jointly in the production of two or more products, no meaningful allocation procedure may be possible. Allocations should not be attempted unless they result in meaningful measurements to the users of accounting reports.

Indirect product costs represent goods and services used in the process of production which cannot be identified with specific products. However, they are usually assigned to products on an assumed reasonable basis or by an expedient method. Accountants are not agreed, however, that all indirect production costs should be assigned to products. This disagreement rests on two separate controversies: (a) Costs that do not result in a salable product, such as idle capacity costs and abnormal spoilage costs, are claimed by some to represent losses or period expenses rather than product costs. (b) Under the concept of "direct costing," only variable production costs are said to be meaningful as inventoriable costs. Nonvariable production costs are then charged off as period expenses.[34]

2. *Expenses Associated Directly with Future Revenues but Not Included in Product Costs.* In a few cases, costs that can be associated with future revenue cannot be assigned directly to the product of the enterprise because they do not represent value added to any specific products. In most cases, these are selling and administrative costs that can be associated clearly with future revenues. A common example is the carrying forward of organization costs that cannot be associated with a product, usually because there is no product at the time they are incurred. However, since they can be associated with the revenues of some future periods, they are usually capitalized and carried as intangible assets on the basis that they represent the value of the organization to the firm in its future operations.

Accountants are generally reluctant to carry forward other selling and administrative costs because of the uncertainty regarding their association with future revenues. But a case can be made for delaying expense recognition in a few instances. If an extensive market research program is carried out before placing a new product on the market, these costs may be associated directly with the revenues expected to be obtained from the new product. The classification and amortization of these costs will be discussed more fully in later chapters.

Other costs that may be carried forward are basically in the nature of prepaid expenses. Sales commissions, for example, may be paid at the time that a customer signs a contract for future delivery; but the revenue may not be recognized until the goods are delivered or, in some cases, until the goods are finally paid for. In these cases, it may be assumed that the services are not fully received until the transaction is completed, in which case the commission represents a prepayment for a service not yet received. However the commission cost should be carried forward, either because it is a prepaid expense or because of a deferral of revenue recognition and the necessity to match costs with related revenue.

One note of caution should be made at this point. Selling and administrative costs should not be carried forward to be matched with future revenue unless there is a reasonable assurance of future revenue with

---

[34] See Chapter 9, pp. 272–78, for a more complete discussion of direct costing.

which it may be associated. The lack of current revenue or the possibility of recording an operating loss in the current period is not adequate reason for deferral. If no associated revenue is foreseeable, or if such revenue is highly uncertain, the expenses should be recognized in the current period even if they result in an operating loss.

The relevance of deferring the reporting of the use of goods and services as expenses when there is no direct association with any specific future product or service of the firm is questionable. The argument is that if the use of goods and services does not benefit the current period and does not represent a loss, it must benefit future periods; and therefore it should be allocated to future periods in order to match the expenses with the associated revenue. But, since there is no specific revenue associated with the expense, the matching process does not apply. The result is merely the smoothing of income by spreading the expense over several years. The information provided to users of financial statements is not improved by such allocations. An example would be the deferral and allocation of basic research and development expenditures which cannot be associated directly with any specific revenues. Even though these expenditures may benefit many periods, there may be no method of applying the matching concept in a meaningful and relevant way.

3. Direct Expenses Incurred Subsequent to the Reporting of Related Revenue. Occasionally, direct expenses will occur subsequent to the reporting of related revenue. For example, if a warranty is given at the time of sale of merchandise, a future related expense is quite probable. Proper matching requires that the expense be recorded at the time of sale (or other point of revenue reporting) and that a liability be recorded for the estimated cost of future repairs or replacements. Just the fact that this cost is uncertain is not an appropriate reason for delaying its recognition. If any reasonable estimation of the probable costs of future warranties can be found, they should be recorded at the time of revenue recognition. For a single sale transaction, an estimation may be impossible, but for a large number of sales during the year, a reasonable approximation can usually be found. If costs under express or implied warranties do occur in excess of all reasonable expectations, they should be recorded as losses rather than operating expenses. The proper criterion is the reasonableness or probability of their occurrence. This same reasoning can be applied to collection costs and other related administrative costs.

When revenue is reported prior to final delivery of merchandise, additional costs of completion and delivery are probable. In these cases it may be appropriate to record the revenue at the selling price less expected additional costs to complete and sell. The related receivable or inventory is then usually valued in the same way. This concept of net realizable value is discussed more fully later in Chapter 11.

In the case of installment sales, revenue may not be recognized until the cash is finally collected. The receivable is usually recorded at the full sales price, and a special account is set up for "deferred gross profit on installment sales." The recognition of both the revenue and the product costs are delayed by carrying forward the net amount. While this account is often called a deferred credit, it really represents an offsetting account to the receivable in order to be consistent with the reporting of revenue when cash is received. It is a valuation of the asset "installments receivable" rather than a liability.

Occasionally, it is recommended that a portion of revenue be deferred until the final activity regarding the servicing of a product subsequent to sale has been accomplished, the amount of the revenue to include an amount sufficient to equal the probable "after costs" and a portion of the income or value added by the firm.[35] However, the value added by the firm cannot be measured by separate activities. As indicated earlier, there is no logic in assigning an equal amount of revenue to each dollar of expenditure.

Indirect or Period Matching. The reporting of expenses in the periods in which the goods and services are used is a process of matching the measurement of goods and services with the period in which they are used rather than reporting them in the period of acquisition or payment. Therefore, this is not matching in the sense of associating the expenses with the related revenues. However, it is frequently justified as either an approximation of the matching of expenses with revenues or as an exception to it; the following are frequently presented as justifications for indirect matching: (1) Many period expenses are associated indirectly with the revenue of the current period, so there is no material deviation from the matching principle if the expenses are reported when the goods or services are used. For example, rent of a retail store can be associated with the sales during the period the store is rented. (2) In many cases there is an inability to find any direct association with revenue, but if the expenses are necessary for overall operations, they should be charged to the current period. For example, in the expense of maintaining a parking lot for employees in all activities of the firm, there is no direct association with any specific revenue. (3) A corollary to (2) is that if there is no measurable association with future revenue or no measurable benefit to future periods, there is no justification for carrying the expense forward to later periods. While the parking lot example might be appropriate in this case also, another example might be the expense of maintaining recreational facilities for employees of all departments. (4) If the expenses are regular and recurring, there may be no material effect on the net income of any period other than the first and last periods of the

---

[35] See for example Norton M. Bedford, *Income Determination Theory: An Accounting Framework* (Reading, Mass.: Addison-Wesley, 1965), pp. 103–104.

business life, even if perfect matching is not obtained. For example, reporting research and development expenses currently may not result in a serious distortion of income if such expenses are recurring and fairly constant in amount; an allocation might result in similar expenses for most periods. (5) Many costs are joint costs, necessitating somewhat arbitrary allocations to different activities. An arbitrary allocation to different periods may be more misleading than no allocation because allocation implies a preciseness that may not be present. An example is property taxes on land and buildings which cannot be allocated to areas of activity within the plant except on an arbitrary basis.

The first step in the process of assigning expenses to periods is the determination of when the expiration of the goods or services occurs. The second step is the classification of the expenses by major activity. If the activity is the selling function of the enterprise, it may be assumed that the related revenue is recognized currently. Much of the sales activity relates to providing goods and services during the current period. To some extent, however, there is a lag in the reporting of sales revenue following the selling activity. But if the selling expenses are regular and recurring, there will be little effect on the amount of net income of most periods. Arbitrary allocations of selling expenses to future periods may result in less meaningful statements than those in which the selling expenses are classfied as period charges.

The joint-cost problem also presents a problem of allocation not only to different periods but also to different classifications. In reality, all enterprise activity can be classified as either relating to production or to the selling function of business. That activity that aids jointly both production and selling is classified as administrative. The top executives of the firm must direct their energies to the direction of all functions of the enterprise. Likewise, many service and staff departments, such as accounting and personnel, incur costs that are difficult to allocate to the selling and producing functions. Because this difficulty is often insurmountable, these expenses are usually classified as period charges.

Other costs of general operations and selling operations obviously relate in part to the production of future revenues. But if there is no reasonable means of associating these costs with future revenue, or if the benefit to future operations is highly uncertain, the only practical solution is to charge them to current operations. Advertising is a good example. Most advertising has a carry-over or cumulative effect with respect to revenue. Repeated advertising of a product, firm name, or trade name is more effective than a single advertisement. But the effect is always uncertain, and there is no possible method of determining, even in retrospect, which advertisement caused which revenue. Thus, period matching is most appropriate under normal circumstances.

Frequently it is suggested that in special circumstances it may be appropriate to carry forward all costs of operations to be matched against the revenues of future periods. For example, it is considered appropriate to capitalize the costs of organizing a firm in order to charge these costs against the revenues of future periods. Other production and selling costs are carried forward to future periods during this period of organization if they are necessary in the preparation for future production and sales. Thus, if one year is required to organize and prepare for the production and sale of a product, all normal costs are capitalized and carried forward to be allocated to future periods. But if, in the second year, production bottlenecks prevent the manufacture of the expected quantity, or if the demand for the product fails to materialize, the costs of the second year should not be carried forward except to the extent that reasonable costs can be included in the inventories. Costs should not be carried forward merely because a loss would result by charging them to the current period. However, costs are frequently carried forward to be matched with future revenues on the ground that they are assumed to benefit some future periods. This type of matching appears to the author to be of little relevance to users of financial statements, because the allocation process is not based on any direct association with revenues reported in any period or periods. The result is merely a spreading of the effect of the expense so that no single period discloses the true effect of the activity. The allocation procedure is discussed at greater length later in Chapter 14.

EXTRAORDINARY GAINS AND LOSSES

Gains and losses represent favorable and unfavorable events not related to the normal operations of the enterprise. What is normal and what is not normal is a difficult decision to make in many cases, and consistent treatment among firms and for different periods may be almost impossible. But the distinction is valid and useful in a proper interpretation of the several concepts of income.

The term *normal operations* refers to the intent of the enterprise regarding its major and related activities. These activities are usually regular and recurring. Nonoperating activities are usually sporadic. However, nonoperating activities may also include ancillary activities of a recurring nature not related to the continuing objectives of the enterprise. The purpose of separate classification should be to disclose to the reader of the financial statements the results of the current activities of the firm that may be comparable with past and future activities and permit a basis for prediction of future results. Paton and Littleton state that

to justify segregation as nonoperating items . . . gains (or losses) should be clearly extraordinary and connected with the avowed purpose of the business in only an incidental way.[36]

---

[36] Paton and Littleton, *op. cit.*, p. 60.

The following statement of the Committee on Accounting Procedure of the AICPA emphasizes the definition of gains and losses as nonoperating:

It must also be recognized that the ultimate distinction between *operating* income and charges and *non-operating* gains and losses, terms having considerable currency in the accounting profession, has not been established. The former are generally defined as recurrent features of business operation, more or less normal and dependable in their incidence from year to year; the latter are generally considered to be irregular and unpredictable, more or less fortuitous and incidental. . . .[37]

While Chapter 8 of *Accounting Research Bulletin No. 43* recommended criteria for excluding abnormal items from the computation of net income, Accounting Principles Board *Opinion No. 9* subsequently altered this recommendation by stating that all extraordinary items related to the current period should be included in the income statement but disclosed separately after "income before extraordinary items." The Board's definition of extraordinary items appears to be similar to that of the Committee on Accounting Procedure quoted above. APB *Opinion No. 9* states that

they will be of a character significantly different from the typical or customary business activities of the entity . . . which would not be expected to recur frequently.[38]

Examples of extraordinary items suggested by the Board include (*a*) gains or losses arising from the sale or abandonment of plant or a significant segment of the business, (*b*) gains or losses arising from the sale of investments not acquired for resale as a normal activity, (*c*) the write-off of goodwill due to current events, (*d*) losses from the condemnation or expropriation of properties, and (*e*) losses from a major devaluation of a foreign currency.

As with previous definitions of extraordinary items, the definition given in APB *Opinion No. 9* is not clear and the examples are ambiguous. Gains and losses from the sale of operating plant assets are usually determined by the measurement procedures applied to the assets. If the costs of the assets have been depreciated, the amount of the reported gain or loss at the time of sale is in part a correction of the allocations of prior periods, and in part a result of price changes since the acquision of the asset. Gains and losses arising from the sale of operating property may reflect incorrect allocations to prior periods, as well as windfall gains and losses. A premature sale or abandonment of equipment at a loss, for example, may result from an unexpected and abnormal obsolescence of the equipment or its products. A gain on the sale of plant may result from

---

[37] AICPA, *Accounting Principles, op. cit.*, p. 6027.
[38] APB *Opinion No. 9* (New York: AICPA, 1967), p. 114.

excessive depreciation charges in the past or from an increase in the sale price of the asset (assuming no change in the value of money).

While the disclosure of extraordinary items in the income statement has some merit in permitting predictions of future firm activities, the criteria for classifying items as extraordinary are not clear enough to permit uniform treatment of similar items. The distinction between customary business actvities and nonoperating activities is far from clear, particularly in view of the diversification of the activities of many large business corporations. The sale of plant and equipment, for example, may be a normal activity for many firms. If the emphasis is placed on the recurring nature of the items, the significance of the disclosure for permitting predictions may be improved, but many difficulties remain. The Board does not indicate the time period to determine whether or not a type of activity or event is recurring. If it occurs once every two or three years, is it nonrecurring, or must it occur not more frequently than every 10 years to be nonrecurring? Is once a year frequent enough to classify an item as recurring? If the emphasis is placed on the recurring nature of activities, operating activities should also be classified as recurring or nonrecurring. Furthermore, items which vary widely in amount from year to year should also be disclosed separately because they may be just as important in making predictions as the so-called nonrecurring items.

Gains

Gains and losses in many respects are opposites and thus may be treated similarly. However, the differences are sufficient to warrant separate discussion. One common feature is that both gains and losses are reflected as net amounts. The favorable and unfavorable aspects of the transaction are combined, and only the net result is shown as either a gain or a loss. Therefore, the terms "gains" and "losses" are not comparable with the terms "revenues" and "expenses."

In accordance with the definition given previously, gains represent the net favorable result arising from transactions or events not related to the normal operations of the business. Gains may arise from a net increase in asset valuations or from a favorable settlement of debts. But this definition is not sufficient in delineating the types of transactions or events that could result in gains to the enterprise. Favorable events that increase the monetary measurement of capital (stockholders' equity not intended to be available for dividends) of the firm through transactions with stockholders should not be treated as gains. Conversely, favorable events resulting in an increase in the amount available for distribution as dividends should be included in the classification "gains" if they do not relate to normal operations.

Gifts to the enterprise may be classified as either capital or income, depending on the intent of the donor and the circumstances surrounding the gift. The American Accounting Association, in the 1948 statement, only went as far as saying that revenue does not arise from a gift. Paton and Littleton state that in the broadest sense of the term, a gift may be considered a gain, but that it should be excluded from both current income and retained earnings.[39] However, in a few cases the intent of a gratuity may be to increase the income of the firm, as in the case of "conscience payments" or extra payments to show gratitude for special services received. But in the case of contributions in aid of construction required before service can be supplied to some public utility customers, and in the case of special donations to attract a firm into a community, the intent is to provide permanent capital.

Gifts should be measured like revenues—by the current value of the assets received. Most other gains result from an exchange, so that a matching of the favorable and unfavorable aspects is required. The measurement of the favorable aspect is similar to the measurement of revenue—by the current value of the assets received or recognized or by the current value of debt reduction.[40] The unfavorable aspects should be measured similarly to expenses—by the value of the goods and services used or exchanged in the transaction. Only those items directly associated with the transaction, however, are matched against the favorable aspects in computing the gain. In the sale of assets not usually traded by the firm, these unfavorable aspects would include the value of the assets sold plus the direct costs of sale. The allocation of income taxes to the transaction will be discussed in Chapter 16.

Cost, book value, or other recorded value is usually used in computing the gain, for several reasons. Probably the most significant of these reasons is that it is not important to make a distinction between a true windfall gain and a correction of prior periods arising from an incorrect allocation of cost to the expenses of those periods. Other reasons are that costs are verifiable and are assumed to represent the exchange value of the assets at the time they were acquired by the enterprise. But if the increase in value is due in part to the changing value of the monetary unit, cost is not appropriate; a part of the increase in value represents an increase in the monetary capital of the firm rather than an increase in retained earnings. This is discussed further in Chapter 7.

The timing of the recognition of gains is similar to the recognition of revenues except that accountants generally have held more closely to the realization concept. That is, gains are not generally recognized until an exchange or sale has taken place. The 1957 statement of the American

---

[39] Paton and Littleton, *op. cit.,* p. 61.
[40] See above, pp. 163–65.

Accounting Association, for example, states that income includes ". . . other gains and losses to the enterprise from sales, exchanges, or other conversions of assets."[41] The "other conversions," however, relate to losses rather than to gains. But the 1957 statement also defines realization as occurring when a change in the value of an asset or liability has become sufficiently objective and definite to warrant recognition. This suggests that a gain could be recognized if an increase in value is sufficiently objective and definite that it is not likely to be reversed. Therefore, an increase in the market value of securities may, under some circumstances, be sufficient evidence to recognize a gain. But most accountants require that the increase in value be almost impossible of reversal before making recognition.[42] From a theory point of view, this is an extreme position. The most probable outcome in uncertain situations should be recorded, rather than limiting recognition to only those cases that are certain. Also, there is an inconsistency in using a double standard for the recognition of gains and losses; both should be recognized on the same basis of probability.

Paton and Littleton stated that the recognition of appreciation in value is not justified for the following reasons: (1) Appreciation does not represent effective income; it does not measure the progress of operating activity. (2) Appreciation is not the result of any transaction or conversion; as an estimate of an appraiser, it is of doubtful validity. (3) Appreciation does not make available additional liquid resources. (4) It has little or no legal standing as income.[43]

Basically, the reluctance of accountants to record appreciation stems from two sources: (a) the uncertain and possibly ephemeral nature of the increase in value, and (b) the fact that an increase in value does not give rise to liquid resources that can be used for the payment of dividends. This emphasis on liquid resources or cash flows may be relevant for some types of decisions, but not for the measurement of most concepts of income. For income determination, relative certainty and verifiable measurements are more relevant criteria. If a long-term investment in bonds is made at a cost less than the face value of the bonds, accountants usually consider it appropriate to write up the value of the investment to the face value at maturity. The total increase is definite, according to a contract, and verifiable, even though the amount of increase each year may be indeterminate. For investments in marketable securities, the recording of gains and losses arising from material changes in market prices is becoming more acceptable in accounting practice because both veri-

---

[41] AAA Committee on Accounting Concepts and Standards, *op. cit.*, p. 5.

[42] See for example Windal, "The Accounting Concept of Realization," *op. cit.*, p. 256.

[43] Paton and Littleton, *op. cit.*, p. 62.

fiability and liquidity are present, even though the change has not been validated by a sale or exchange in which the firm is a party. But if land increases in value, it is generally thought inappropriate to increase the recorded valuation above cost. However, to the extent that verifiable measurements can be obtained regarding the changes in the market price of land, changes in its price may be just as relevant in the determination of income as are changes in the value of bonds or investments in marketable securities. The economic gain or loss is not more real just because the securities or land are sold and the proceeds used to reacquire securities or land of the same type. The opportunity to do so, however, may be relevant information regarding the firm, even though the intent is not to sell.

Losses

The term "loss" is used by accountants to designate the excess of expenses over the revenues of a period—the opposite of net income. But the term is used here as the opposite of gains, relating to the net unfavorable events not arising from normal business activities. The Committee on Terminology of the AICPA defined the term *loss* in this usage as ". . . the excess of all or the appropriate portion of the cost of assets over related proceeds, if any, when the items are sold, abandoned, or either wholly or partially destroyed by casualty or otherwise written off."[44] Paton and Littleton defined a loss as ". . . an expiration of cost incurred without compensation or return, in contrast to charges which are absorbed as costs of revenue."[45] The American Accounting Association has defined a loss similarly as ". . . expired cost not beneficial to the revenue producing activities of the enterprise."[46]

A basic part of the definition of losses is that they represent expirations of value not related to the normal operations of any period. That is, they result from extraneous and exogenous events that are not recurring or anticipated as necessary in the process of producing revenues. If they were anticipated, they possibly could have been avoided; if they were necessary in the production of revenues, they should be included among the expenses. To the extent that value expirations represent corrections of the expenses of prior periods, they should not be included among the losses but separately classified as prior period corrections. But this distinction is usually very difficult to make. Unforeseen declines in value represent losses; but if they had been foreseen, would they have been

---

[44] AICPA, *Terminology Bulletin No. 4*, July, 1957, p. 2.

[45] Paton and Littleton, *op. cit.*, p. 93.

[46] AAA Committee on Accounting Concepts and Standards, *op. cit.*, p. 6.

included in the allocations to expenses? The answer to this question is not always clear. In some cases, if the decline in value had been foreseen, the asset would not have been acquired; in this case the recognition of the decline is clearly a loss.

The measurement of losses is similar to the measurement of expenses except that any proceeds are offset directly to reflect a net amount. As with expenses, it seems preferable to define losses as value expirations rather than as cost allocations. With this definition, the question of measurement is left open for further discussion. As with expenses, cost represents a verifiable measurement and the exchange value of the assets at the time they were acquired. But in many cases current value may be more appropriate in the measurement of the loss. For example, a building destroyed by fire before the end of its useful life represents a loss to the firm (to the extent that it is uninsured), even though it may be fully depreciated in the accounts. Technically speaking, depreciation for prior periods should be adjusted and a loss recorded. However, since these are offsetting items in their effect on total stockholders' equity, accountants may prefer to refrain from attempting a measurement of the loss in favor of disclosure in some other way.

The criteria for the recognition of losses are similar to the criteria for the recognition of period expenses. Losses cannot be matched with revenue, so they should be recorded in the period in which it becomes fairly definite that a given asset will provide less benefit to the firm than indicated by the recorded valuation.

In the case of a sale of assets not traded normally, and in the case of a loss by fire or other catastrophe, the timing of the event is fairly definite. But, when the decline in value is gradual over several periods, it is difficult to determine exactly when the loss occurs. The asset may eventually be sold or abandoned; but if the asset has lost its usefulness, it is unreasonable to withhold the recognition of the loss until the final disposition. Reporting should occur as soon as it appears quite probable that the asset has lost its usefulness and that this loss of usefulness is not likely to be reversed in the future.

In no case should a loss be deliberately carried forward to later periods. If it is fairly definite and if the amount of the loss can be measured reasonably well, it should be recorded as soon as it is ascertainable. For example, when equipment is replaced, the undepreciated cost should not be added arbitrarily to the cost of the new asset. Also, when bonds are refunded, the unamortized discount and call premium represent a change in the value of the bonds and should be written off rather than carried forward and allocated over the life of the new bonds.[47]

---

[47] For an extended discussion of the treatment of unamortized bond discount at the time of refunding, see Chapter 15, pp. 453–55.

Corrections of Prior Periods

According to the all-inclusive concept of income, all changes in the measurement of assets and liabilities, except those arising from capital transactions and dividend distributions, are included in the income statement in the period in which they are discovered or determined to be measurable and in which they meet the criteria for reporting revenues, expenses, gains, and losses. To the extent to which such changes would have been reported in a prior period if they had been known to exist at that time and had met the criteria of measurability and verifiability, they do not represent measurements of the firm's activity of the current period. Under the current operating concept of income, such items would be excluded from the income statement because they cannot be matched with current revenues nor do they represent gains or losses of the current period.

As discussed in Chapter 5,[48] according to the recommendations of the Accounting Principles Board in *Opinion No. 9,* only a few corrections of prior periods are permitted to be included in the retained earnings statement instead of in the income statement of the period during which the item is reported. Among the items to be reported in the statement of retained earnings are corrections of the revenues or expenses of prior periods, or certain gains or losses, but only to the extent that they are not the result of a change in the evaluation made previously by management or the accountants. This position is similar to that made by the American Accounting Association 1948 statement, which was subsequently reversed but which stated that errors made in good faith should not be corrected subsequently.[49] While APB *Opinion No. 9* is not clear regarding the proper treatment of errors previously made in good faith, there is an implication that corrections of depreciation for prior periods and similar corrections should be classified as extraordinary items in the income statement or adjusted by altering the allocations to future periods.

The corrections of prior periods permitted by APB *Opinion No. 9* as adjustments of retained earnings, therefore, are similar to extraordinary items, and there appears to be no logical reason to exclude them from the income statement. As indicated earlier, the net income reported in any period is the result of activities and events of several periods. The exclusion of corrections of prior periods from the income statement implies, erroneously, that the income reported in the current period reflects only activities and events of that period. There is merit, however, in classify-

---

[48] See pp. 148–49.

[49] AAA Committee on Accounting Concepts and Standards, *op. cit.,* p. 16.

ing items in the income statement according to the type of activity or event giving rise to the item and according to the period when the major activity occurred. There is no merit in allocating such corrections or extraordinary items over future periods.

SELECTED ADDITIONAL READING ON CHAPTER TOPICS

The Nature of Revenue

STAUBUS, GEORGE J. "Revenue and Revenue Accounts," *Accounting Research,* Vol. VII (July, 1956), pp. 284–94. Reprinted in SIDNEY DAVIDSON, DAVID GREEN, JR., CHARLES T. HORNGREN, and GEORGE H. SORTER. *An Income Approach to Accounting Theory: Readings and Questions,* pp. 78–88. Englewood Cliffs, N.J.: Prentice-Hall, Inc., 1964.

The Timing of Revenue Reporting

American Accounting Association 1964 Concepts and Standards Research Committee—The Realization Concept. "The Realization Concept," *Accounting Review,* Vol. XL (April, 1965), pp. 312–22.

ARNETT, HAROLD E. "Recognition as a Function of Measurement in the Realization Concept," *Accounting Review,* Vol. XXXVIII (October, 1963), pp. 733–41.

BLACKMAN, WILLIAM W., JR. "Accounting Principles for Long-Term Construction Contracts," *New York Certified Public Accountant,* Vol. XXX (November, 1960), pp. 759–67.

HORNGREN, CHARLES T. "How Should We Interpret the Realization Concept?" *Accounting Review,* Vol. XL (April, 1965), pp. 323–33.

MYERS, JOHN H. "Critical Event and Recognition of Net Profit," *Accounting Review,* Vol. XXXIV (October, 1954), pp. 528–32.

SPILLER, EARL A., JR. "The Revenue Postulate—Realization or Recognition," *NAA Bulletin,* Vol. XLIII (February, 1962), pp. 41–47.

STOREY, REED K. "Revenue Realization, Going Concern and Measurement of Income," *Accounting Review,* Vol. XXXIV (April, 1959), pp. 232–38.

THOMAS, ARTHUR L. *Revenue Recognition.* Michigan Business Reports No. 49. Ann Arbor: Bureau of Business Research, Graduate School of Business Administration, University of Michigan, 1966.

WINDAL, FLOYD. *The Accounting Concept of Realization.* Occasional Paper No. 5. East Lansing: Bureau of Business and Economic Research, Michigan State University, 1961.

——. "The Accounting Concept of Realization," *Accounting Review,* Vol. XXXVI (April, 1961), pp. 249–58.

The Matching of Expenses and Revenues

American Accounting Association 1964 Concepts and Standards Research Study Committee—The Matching Concept. "The Matching Concept," *Accounting Review*, Vol. XL (April, 1965), pp. 368–72.

BEDFORD, NORTON M. *Income Determination Theory: An Accounting Framework*, pp. 101–110. Reading, Mass.: Addison-Wesley, 1965.

HYLTON, DELMER P. "On Matching Revenue with Expense," *Accounting Review*, Vol. XL (October, 1965), pp. 824–28.

Gains and Losses

ARNETT, HAROLD E. "The Distinction Between Ordinary and Non-Ordinary Gains and Losses," *New York Certified Public Accountant*, Vol. XXXVII (April, 1967), pp. 267–78.

BERNSTEIN, LEOPOLD. *Accounting for Extraordinary Gains and Losses*. New York: Ronald Press Co., 1967.

DEVINE, C. T. "Loss Recognition," *Accounting Research*, Vol. VI (October, 1955), pp. 310–20. Reprinted in SIDNEY DAVIDSON, DAVID GREEN, JR., CHARLES T. HORNGREN, and GEORGE H. SORTER. *An Income Approach to Accounting Theory: Readings and Questions*, pp. 162–72. Englewood Cliffs, N.J.: Prentice-Hall, Inc., 1964.

chapter 7

Business Income and
Price Changes

An unstable monetary unit is a measurement constraint in the formulation of accounting theory, particularly when measurements are based on historical prices or when comparisons of price aggregations among different years are made. Either modifications must be made to the accounting system which utilizes prices of different years, or a new structure of accounting must be derived which will avoid comparisons or aggregations of prices of different periods. Generally, the former approach is suggested as preferable to the latter, being more acceptable to the accounting profession and permitting greater continuity with traditional accounting practices.

The fact of a changing dollar value is now well recognized among accountants, but the theoretical and practical means of adjusting for it have not been fully developed. During the period since 1900, the long-run trend in prices has been upward in the United States, although the major increases in prices have occurred during and immediately following the two major wars. Significant price declines occurred in the early 1920's and from 1929 to 1933. From 1915 to 1919, the Wholesale Commodity Price Index rose from a level of 45.2 to 100.4, with prices in 1947–49 representing 100. The low point reached in 1932 was 42.1. From 1940 to 1946, the index rose from 51.1 to 78.7, and reached 119.5 by 1959; from 1959 to 1964, it fluctuated very little, and from 1964 to 1968 it increased by about 10 percent. Other price indexes show a similar pattern of fluctuations, but the Consumers Price Index fluctuated less widely than the Wholesale Price Index in earlier years, and it has increased more rapidly in recent years.

While prices have increased only moderately during the past decade in the United States, this is not so in several other countries of the free world. Not only have rapid price changes affected the financial reports of firms within these countries, but they have also affected firms in other countries having subsidiaries or investments in these countries. The magnitude of some of these changes is demonstrated in Figure 1.

Most economists would probably agree that there is now little likeli-

FIGURE 1

**Relative Rates of Change for Consumer Price Indexes
for Selected Countries
(vertical scale logarithmic)
1958 = 100**

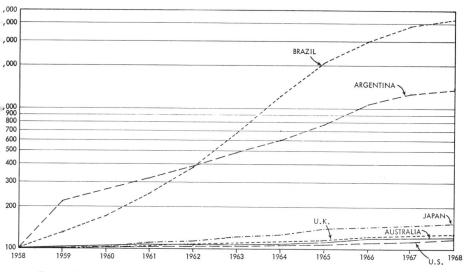

Source: *United Nations Monthly Bulletin of Statistics, Vol. XXIII* (January, 1969), pp. 166–79.

hood of rapid and severe price declines, as occurred in the early 1920's and in the period from 1929 to 1933. Since these dates, the monetary and banking structure of the United States has been strengthened, and monetary policy and fiscal policy have come to be recognized as important controls on price changes and business conditions. Strengthening these forces toward stability in the economy is the Full Employment Act of 1946. This act did not provide for specific actions to control the economic conditions, however, and its policies were broadly stated. For example, the act states:

The Congress hereby declares that it is the continuing policy and responsibility of the Federal Government to use all practicable means . . . to promote maximum employment, production, and purchasing power. (Section 2.)

More important than the statement of broad policy in the act was the setting up of the Council of Economic Advisors under the Executive and the Congressional Joint Committee on the Economic Report. These two bodies have been very influential in keeping governmental officials informed on economic conditions and in making proposals for action by the government in its attempt to maintain the economic health of the country.

Federal economic policy in recent years has placed major emphasis on permitting continued prosperity and economic growth with some attempt to control inflation. While stable prices have been a stated policy of government officials, there are many indications that other economic goals have had priority. Whereas the prevention of price-level changes is a desirable economic goal, accountants should not ignore the possibility of major changes in the future. The development of an accounting theory that is able to cope with changing prices should be an important objective.

THE NATURE OF PRICE CHANGES

Prices reflect the exchange value of goods and services in the economy. These goods and services include the several factors of production and items at intermediate stages of production, items held for speculative purposes, and goods and services acquired for consumption purposes. In general, these prices can be classified as either input prices (prices of factors of production or of goods and services at intermediate stages, acquired for further production or resale) or output prices (prices of goods and services sold as the product of the enterprise).

Price changes occur only when the prices of goods or services are different from what they were previously in the same market. The fact that a firm buys a commodity in its input market at one price and sells it to its customers at a higher price does not mean that the price of the commodity has changed. A price change occurs only if a price increases or decreases either in an input market or in an output market or in both.

Price changes can be classified as one of three types, although these classifications are interdependent and not mutually exclusive. These are (1) general, (2) specific, and (3) relative price changes. General price changes reflect increases or decreases in the value of the monetary unit. They may be caused by changes in the supply or velocity of money that are greater or less than the changes in the total supply of goods and services in the economy, or by an imbalance in the total supply and demand of goods and services in general. Specific price changes occur for several reasons, including changes in tastes of consumers, technological improvements, speculation, and natural or artificial changes in the supply of particular products or as a result of changes in the value of money. Relative price changes reflect the change in the structure of prices or the change in the price of one commodity relative to the prices of all goods and services. General and relative price changes are both reflected in changes in the prices of specific goods. Although it is difficult, if not impossible, to separate the two effects on specific prices, they are different economic phenomena conceptually.

General Price-Level Changes

A general price-level change occurs as a result of a change in the value of the monetary unit during periods of inflation and deflation. In the absence of structural or relative price movements, all prices would move together by the same percentage. However, if prices are moving at different rates, a measure of general price changes can be obtained only by computing an average or index of prices to express the general level of current prices compared with some base period. The ratio of the current index of prices to the base-period index expresses the relative change in all prices included in the index. The reciprocal of this ratio expresses the change in the value of the dollar or the change in *purchasing power*. For example, if the price index should increase from 100 to 200, prices would have doubled but the purchasing power of the dollar would have decreased to one half of its previous level.

The term *purchasing power* refers to the ability to buy goods and services with a given quantity of money (e.g., one dollar) compared to what the same quantity of money could have purchased at an earlier date. To obtain a good comparison of the purchasing power of money at two different dates, the goods and services available at the two dates must be the same or similar. Since the types and qualities of goods and services available change considerably over time, good comparisons of purchasing power cannot be obtained over several decades.

General purchasing power refers to the ability to buy all types of goods and services available in the economy, and it is measured by changes in the general price level. Specific purchasing power refers to the ability to buy specific goods and services at different dates. Thus, specific purchasing power can be measured by changes in specific prices. In between the concepts of general purchasing power and specific purchasing power are many concepts relating to the ability to buy certain goods and services that may be purchased by specific groups of individuals or that may be used for certain purposes. For example, the Consumers Price Index of the U.S. Bureau of Labor Statistics measures the average change in prices of a specific "market basket" of goods and services bought by families of wage earners and clerical workers living in cities. Therefore, this index can be used to measure the ability of these individuals to maintain their level of living by purchasing the "basket" of goods and services usually acquired by them. In a like manner, it is also possible to measure the purchasing power of business enterprises to buy the goods and services usually acquired by them. These concepts of specific purchasing power (purchasing power for certain groups) are discussed at greater length below in the discussion of the choice of a proper index.

Specific Price Changes

In the absence of general price movements or changes in the value of the monetary unit, a change in the price of a specific commodity represents a change in its exchange value. Changes in prices in an input market result in increases or decreases in costs or expenses of the firm, while changes of prices in the output market result in a shift in revenues (assuming that the price change does not affect the quantity sold). In the traditional transactions approach to accounting, the original transaction price of goods or services acquired is matched with the revenue associated with the period or the goods sold. Changes in the specific input prices of goods sold are, therefore, included in the computation of the reported net income for the period. A more relevant matching is thought to be obtained by reporting as expenses the current prices of the goods used in the process of obtaining revenue. This matching of the current input prices with the current output (revenue) prices is thought to be more relevant as a measure of operating efficiency and as a better basis for the prediction of the results of future transactions.

Although there is no general agreement regarding the nature of the changes in specific prices of goods held by a firm, one view is that an increase in prices results in a "holding gain," and a decrease results in a "holding loss." According to this view, these should be included in the computation of the income of the firm, because they represent changes in the value of the stockholders' equity (the net assets of the firm. However, most authors would not include these holding gains and losses in the computation of operating income because it is thought that they do not result from the normal recurring activities of the firm. That is, profit from normal operations is assumed to be the excess of selling price (or other determined revenue) over the current input price (current cost) of the product of the enterprise less other operating expenses.

The cost convention in accounting reports no change in value of assets until revenue is reported, usually at the time of sale. If current costs are used, holding gains and losses may be reported as prices change, although these gains and losses may be classified as either realized or unrealized.[1] For example, if a commodity has been purchased for $100 and sold for $150 at a time when its current input price (replacement cost) is $120, the operating gross profit is $30 and the holding gain is $20. If the increase in the input price had occurred in a prior period, Edwards and Bell would consider the $20 to be realizable cost savings (unrealized) in the earlier period, but realized in the current period when the item is sold.[2]

Current costs represent current exchange prices, and thus their use

---

[1] Edgar O. Edwards and Philip W. Bell, *The Theory and Measurement of Business Income* (Berkeley and Los Angeles: University of California Press, 1961), particularly pp. 111–15.

[2] *Ibid.*

results in a deviation from the historical cost basis. An objection is frequently made regarding the use of current costs, on the ground that a subjective value is substituted for a verifiable exchange price (historical cost). However, verifiability may still be present in those cases where the current exchanges prices are obtained from well-organized markets. Furthermore, while some verifiability may be lost in the use of current costs rather than historical costs, the former are likely to be more relevant in meeting the objectives of the users of financial reports. However, current input prices can be assumed to represent current costs to the firm only if the firm generally purchases the same types of assets and is continuing to do so. If the firm is not purchasing the same type of asset, there is no evidence that it would acquire the asset in use at the current price, and therefore the current price of an asset acquired earlier at a lower price may not represent the relevant price, either in evaluating the firm's activities or in making predictions regarding the future.

In *ARS No. 3*, Sprouse and Moonitz recommended the use of current costs in the accounts in order to show a clean-cut distinction between profit from holding an item and profit from "operating margins." However, they did not draw a distinction between realized and unrealized holding gains and losses: ". . . no useful purpose is served by delaying recognition of the changes."[3] The author is in agreement with this position insofar as it relates to items that are not likely to be replaced. When continuous replacement of like items is expected, the difference between historical costs and current costs may be considered a purchasing power change instead of income, as discussed later in this chapter.

The 1957 statement of the American Accounting Association said that ideally (1) the cost of goods sold should be expressed in terms of current costs, (2) inventories at the end of the period should be expressed in current terms, and (3) gains and losses resulting from the price changes should be identified.[4] Supplementary Statements Nos. 1 and 2 to the 1957 statement included much stronger recommendations of the use of current costs in financial statements.[5] The Committee to Prepare a Statement of Basic Accounting Theory[6] and the 1966–68 Committee on External

---

[3] Robert T. Sprouse and Maurice Moonitz, "A Tentative Set of Broad Accounting Principles for Business Enterprises," *Accounting Research Study No. 3* (New York: American Institute of Certified Public Accountants, 1962), p. 30.

[4] AAA Committee on Accounting Concepts and Standards, *Accounting and Reporting Standards for Corporate Financial Statements and Preceding Statements and Supplements* (Columbus, Ohio: AAA, 1957), p. 6.

[5] Committee on Concepts and Standards—Long-Lived Assets, AAA, "Accounting for Land, Buildings, and Equipment," Supplementary Statement No. 1, *Accounting Review*, Vol. XXXIX (July, 1964), pp. 693–99; and Committee on Concepts and Standards—Inventory Measurement, AAA, "A Discussion of Various Approaches to Inventory Measurement," Supplementary Statement No. 2, *Accounting Review*, Vol. XXXIX (July, 1964), pp. 700–714.

[6] AAA Committee to Prepare a Statement of Basic Accounting Theory, *A Statement of Basic Accounting Theory*, 1966, pp. 30–31.

Reporting[7] also recommended the reporting of current prices and/or historical costs in those cases where they might be relevant in the making of evaluations or predictions regarding the firm. The several studies of the American Accounting Association and the use of current costs will be discussed at greater length in the following chapters.

Relative Price Changes

In the usual situation, prices of goods and services are moving at different rates, and some even in different directions. The extent to which specific prices move at a different rate or in a different direction from an index of all prices represents a relative price change. That is, if all prices increase by 20 percent and the price of product A increases by 32 percent, the relative price increase of product A is 10 percent (132/120 − 1.00).

In traditional accounting, with the use of historical costs, no price changes are isolated for separate reporting; all price changes are included in income as a result of transactions. The accounts and statements can be adjusted for general price-level changes without making adjustments for specific price changes, in which case costs and expenses would be adjusted for changes in the value of money and the price-level effect of these restatements would be excluded from the income calculation. But holding gains and losses resulting from relative price changes would not be measured or separated from reported net income.

If current prices are used instead of historical costs, net operating income can be computed without including any of the effects of price changes. But holding gains and losses cannot be measured unless the accounts are adjusted for both specific price changes and changes in the general price level. That is, the full effect of relative price changes cannot be measured and disclosed unless the accounts are adjusted for changes in the value of money and for changes in specific prices.

THE MONETARY AND NONMONETARY CLASSIFICATIONS

Monetary assets are claims to a fixed quantity of the monetary unit (e.g., dollars) representing general purchasing power. Although prices of goods and services may change, claims expressed in a given number of dollars remain unchanged, but the purchasing power, or ability to convert these claims into goods and services, is altered. Monetary assets include cash; contractual claims to a specific amount of money in the future, such as accounts and notes receivable; and investments that pay a fixed amount of interest or dividends and will be repaid at a fixed amount in the future, although the date of repayment need not be specified—as in

---

[7] AAA Committee on External Reporting, "An Evaluation of External Reporting Practices," *Accounting Review* (Supplement to Vol. XLIV, 1969), pp. 113–19.

the case of preferred stock. *ARS No. 6* suggests that some prepaid expenses may also be classified as monetary because they represent fixed dollar amounts of receivables collectible in goods or services.[8] However, these items do not fit the definition of monetary assets presented above, because the prices in terms of dollars of the goods or services to be received may change before they are received.

Monetary liabilities represent obligations to pay a fixed amount of dollars at some time in the future, regardless of what happens to the value of the monetary unit. They also include obligations to pay a fixed number of dollars, even though the exact amount is not known for certain. The important criterion is that the amount to be paid does not depend upon changes in the value of the monetary unit. These would include accounts and notes payable, accruals such as wages and interest payable, and long-term obligations payable in a fixed sum. *ARS No. 6* suggests that some "deferred credits," such as rents and royalties received in advance, may be considered monetary in nature because the price has been agreed upon in advance. However, they do not fit a proper definition of monetary liabilities, because the market price of the goods and services to be provided under the agreement may change. They may meet the criterion of monetary liabilities only if the firm has a reasonable alternative and intent to refund the number of dollars received from the customers. Convertible debt is a hybrid form which may be monetary in nature if there is serious deflation (if prices in general decline significantly) and if the growth in the value of the common stock does not offset this general price decline. In most cases, where there is a possibility of future conversion, convertible debt should not be treated as a monetary obligation because it is not likely to be retired by the payment of a fixed number of dollars.

APB *Statement No. 3* classified assets and liabilities as monetary if ". . . their amounts are fixed by contract or otherwise in terms of numbers of dollars regardless of changes in specific prices or in the general price level."[9] However, this definition is inadequate because the "amounts" of most assets and liabilities are fixed by contracts and the definition does not indicate how the "amounts" are to be measured. The additional specification that the classification should be based on the fact that holders gain or lose purchasing power is also inadequate, because it bases the classification on an assumed effect rather than determining the effect from the classification and a change in the price level.[10]

---

[8] American Institute of Certified Public Accountants, "Reporting the Financial Effect of Price-Level Changes," *Accounting Research Study No. 6* (New York: AICPA, 1963), p. 139.

[9] Accounting Principles Board, "Financial Statements Restated for General Price-Level Changes," *Statement No. 3* (New York: AICPA, June, 1969), p. 8.

[10] *Ibid.,* note 4 on p. 8.

Nonmonetary assets, on the other hand, include those items whose prices in terms of the monetary unit may change over time, or claims to a variable amount of the monetary unit representing a predetermined amount of purchasing power. These would include all rights to goods and services and all other rights to future benefits other than claims or rights expressed in terms of a fixed dollar value at some future time. Nonmonetary liabilities would include the obligation to provide given amounts of goods and services or an equivalent amount of purchasing power, even though the payment might be in the form of cash. For example, an obligation to pay cash equal to the price of a given quantity of goods or services would be nonmonetary in nature.

Gains and Losses on Monetary Items

Inflation is known to be beneficial to debtors and detrimental to creditors. Increased price levels usually mean increased dollar incomes, making repayment of debt easier in terms of the economic sacrifice involved. If A should borrow $1,000 from B and repay it after a period during which the price level has increased by 60 percent, A has an economic gain and B has an economic loss. While A repays $1,000, this represents only five eighths (62.5 percent) of the purchasing power it had when he borrowed it. From the point of view of capital maintenance, if A has held the value of what he borrowed in the form of assets that have increased in monetary value with the price level, he will have realized a gain of $600 by selling the asset and repaying the loan. The creditor will have sustained a loss of $600 in purchasing power.

The gain or loss from the holding of net monetary assets by a firm is not so easily evaluated. Normally a firm will have cash and receivables in excess of monetary current liabilities. With a positive net monetary current position, an economic loss occurs as price levels increase and an economic gain occurs as price levels fall. During periods of inflation, the purchasing power of this working capital is not maintained. In fact, if the volume of business remains constant in real terms, working capital must usually be increased, requiring additional investments in monetary assets.

A gain or loss also occurs because of the holding of long-term monetary assets, such as long-term receivables and investments in government bonds and preferred stocks, and because of outstanding long-term debt. If the long-term debt exceeds the long-term monetary assets, an economic gain will occur when the price level rises, and vice versa when the price level falls.

The computation of the purchasing power gains or losses on monetary items involves two distinct steps: (1) The amount of the claim is first restated for the change in the purchasing power of the dollar during the accounting period, or during the period it was held or outstanding if for less than a year. (2) This restated amount is then compared with the current value of the asset or liability at the end of the period or at the time the item was reduced. The difference is the gain or loss in purchasing power. This computation is similar to the restatement of nonmonetary items for changes in the value of money and a subsequent revaluation for changes in specific prices. However, monetary items are already expressed in current terms, so the computation is necessary only to measure the gain or loss arising from changes in their value expressed in terms of purchasing power.

Writers on this subject are not in agreement on the nature of this gain or loss or on the method of disclosing it in financial reports. Because it is similar to the holding gain or loss on nonmonetary items, it should be included in the computation of net income but not in income from operations. This is the opinion of the staff of the AICPA research division as stated in *Accounting Research Study No. 6:*

Because it is a new category in accounting, with no counterpart in conventional (unadjusted) statements, we feel that it should not be "buried" in owners' equity, but instead should be shown either as the last element in or immediately following the calculation of net income. It should be distinctly labeled and separately set forth.[11]

In APB *Statement No. 3*, the Board concluded that these gains and losses should be included in the income of the current period.[12]

The fact that these gains and losses have no counterpart in conventional accounting has been responsible for much of the disagreement on the subject. Traditional accounting concepts and principles emphasize the allocation of costs to expenses and the recognition of gains through realization only at the time of external transactions. The discussions regarding the use of current costs and the recognition of holding gains and losses are not entirely comparable to the gains and losses on monetary items, because the former refer primarily to nonmonetary assets and the latter do not even appear unless adjustments are first made for changes in the value of money.

An alternative view suggested by Deupree is that the purchasing power gain from the holding of liabilities (during periods of general price-level increase) represents a reduction in the cost of the assets acquired with the debt financing.[13] As an adjustment of the cost of assets, these

---

[11] Staff of the Accounting Research Division, "Reporting the Financial Effects of Price-Level Changes," *Accounting Research Study No. 6* (New York: AICPA, 1963), p. 13.

[12] APB *Statement No. 3, op. cit.,* p. 17.

[13] *Ibid.,* pp. 153–65. See also Arthur Andersen & Co., *Accounting and Reporting Problems of the Accounting Profession* (2d ed.; Chicago, 1962), pp. 16–17. Russell Morrison holds a similar view, except he offsets current liabilities against the current monetary assets and considers only the gains and losses from the holding of long-term debt as adjustments of the cost of assets. See AICPA *Accounting Research Study No. 6, op. cit.,* pp. 250–51.

credits (or debits in the case of deflation) should be taken into income as the assets are allocated to expenses, by depreciation or otherwise, or when they are sold. This view holds that the cost of an asset should be measured by the amount of cash finally paid for the asset rather than the amount intended to be paid at the time of acquisition. It also holds strictly to the realization rule that the difference between this cost and the revenue against which it is matched should not be recognized until the asset is allocated to expense or sold.

This view, therefore, holds to the narrow concept of realization but applies a different concept of historical cost. Cost is generally thought of as representing the amount paid or agreed to be paid for an asset. If an obligation incurred in the acquisition of the asset is subsequently canceled, the cancellation would be treated as a gift rather than as a reduction of the cost of the asset. By applying the narrow concept of realization, any change in the value or current cost of the asset or any evidence of this value would be denied if it differs from the amount eventually paid. In this case, the amount originally agreed to be paid for the asset is good evidence of its value at that time, and this should be expressed in terms of the purchasing power of the dollar in the current period, regardless of the amount of long-term debt outstanding.

The concept of realization was applied initially by Sweeney to all purchasing power gains and losses from the holding of monetary items.[14] He attempted to distinguish between realized gains and losses and those not realized on the basis of whether or not the items had been used, paid, or had otherwise left the firm. For example, the loss from the holding of cash during an inflationary period would be realized only when the cash was used. He did not recognize that the measurement of monetary items is generally verifiable and that severance is not necessary.

Another interpretation is that because of the rapid turnover of monetary working capital items, the purchasing power gains and losses on these items can be considered to be realized as they occur, but that the purchasing power gains and losses from the holding of long-term debt should not appear in the current operating statement until they are realized through the payment of the bonds.[15]

Another view is that from the point of view of the enterprise, the gains and losses on long-term debt are not a determinant of income but rather an adjustment of the total equity of the firm—a shift from the bondholders' equity to the stockholders' equity. During periods of price-level increases, stockholders gain and bondholders lose, but the enterprise as a

---

[14] Henry W. Sweeney, *Stabilized Accounting* (New York: Harper & Bros., 1936), pp. 21–23.

[15] See Perry Mason, *Price-Level Changes and Financial Statements—Basic Concept and Methods* (Columbus, Ohio: American Accounting Association, 1956), fn., pp. 23–24.

whole is not affected by the existence of the long-term debt. Therefore, if the income statement shows the income to the enterprise before interest on long-term debt, the purchasing power loss on the long-term debt should not be included. But in showing net income to stockholders, the gain or loss should be included. Since most income statements are prepared with the latter objective, the gain or loss on the long-term debt should be included. However, since the equity of the *enterprise* is relevant for some comparisons, a distinction should be made between the gains and losses on monetary working capital and the gains and losses on the long-term debt.

Some of the objections to the reporting of purchasing power gains and losses on monetary items are: (1) the problems of measurement are assumed to be too great to provide reliable results; (2) such gains and losses are based on changes in subjective values, expressed in terms of personal utilities, which can be applied to an individual but not to a business enterprise; and (3) purchasing power gains and losses do not assist the user of financial statements in evaluating the firm nor in making predictions regarding future cash flows, although this assumption needs to be tested.

If there are significant changes in the value of the monetary unit, the measurement of the purchasing power gains or losses depends to a large extent upon the timing of the increases or decreases of monetary assets or liabilities. For example, if the sum of $100,000 is borrowed at the beginning of a year during which the general price level increased from an index of 100 to 110, and if the amount were owed during the entire period while the cash is invested in nonmonetary assets, a purchasing power gain of $10,000 would be reported in end-of-year dollars. On the other hand, if the amount is borrowed at midyear, the gain would be only $4,762, assuming that the price-level index is 105 at midyear. In the usual adjustment proposals, all current assets and liabilities are usually shown as net monetary assets and arbitrary assumptions are made regarding when net increases or decreases occur. If different assumptions are made regarding timing, the amount of the reported purchasing power gain or loss would vary, and thus it may be subject to considerable bias. That is, a considerable difference in the amount of the reported purchasing power gain or loss may result from shifting the dates at which the changes in the monetary items are assumed to occur.[16]

As indicated in Chapter 5, the presentation of income as representing changes in the value of the firm to stockholders is subject to many theoretical and practical difficulties. Since the value of a firm is dependent upon expectations regarding future cash flows and the individual utility

---

[16] See R. J. Chambers, "A Study of a Price Level Study," *Abacus,* Vol. II (December, 1966), p. 99.

preferences of stockholders, accounting reports can only provide the bases for the making of predictions and the evaluation of risk. Furthermore, changes in the value of the firm as a whole cannot be measured by summing the changes in exchange prices or purchasing power of specific assets and liabilities. Furthermore, since purchasing power gains and losses are measured by the use of general purchasing power indexes, this measurement may be relevant to neither the firm nor the stockholder, as both may be interested in the ability to purchase specific goods and services; although this possibility has not been verified by adequate research. This concept is discussed later, on pages 224–28.

The third objection to reporting purchasing power gains and losses in income is the assumption that they are not relevant to most decisions of investors and other users of external reports. For example, if prices were rising, a firm could borrow money in order to pay a cash dividend or purchase treasury stock and thus report a purchasing power gain. But such a gain may not be relevant to a description of the assumed basic activities of the firm nor to predictions by investors of the firm's future. Likewise, the holding of cash acquired by the sale of preferred stock may permit the firm to acquire operational assets that may significantly improve the income of the firm in the future; the presentation of a purchasing power loss on the holding of this cash while awaiting the proper opportunity may be deceptive with respect to the advisability of such a transaction and the future expectations regarding the firm. Therefore, it is likely that a separate reporting of purchasing power gains and losses does not provide relevant information, because of their interrelationship with all other activities of the firm.

The Restatement of Nonmonetary Items

Nonmonetary assets acquired in one period and held for use or sale in a later period should be measured in terms of the exchange prices existing at the time of reporting as assets or expenses, rather than in terms of the historical cost. The current exchange prices are more relevant because they permit a better comparison with other prices expressed in terms of the current value of money, because they permit more meaningful aggregations or disaggregations of monetary measurements, and because they permit a better matching of current measurements of goods and services used with current revenues.

These nonmonetary assets may be measured by historical prices, restated for either general or specific price changes, or by substituting current prices for the historical prices. A frequent argument for the use of general price-level indexes has been that they retain the objectivity of historical costs while the use of current costs substitutes a less objective measurement base—a current value. However, this difference is not necessarily significant so long as input prices are used in both cases. For example, if land was purchased in period t_2 at a cost of $120,000, when the index of general prices was 60, and if the index in the current period t_9 is 124, the restated cost in current dollars would be $120,000 times 124/60 or $248,000. On the other hand, if the current market price of the land happens to be $248,000, the adjustment is really $120,000 times 248/120, or $248,000, which is the same as substituting the current price for the historical price. In evaluating the two measurement systems—historical cost adjusted by a price index and the substitution of a current input price—consideration should be given to the relevance and verifiability of the resulting amounts.

Another major controversy regarding the adjustment of nonmonetary items is the effect of the adjustment on reported income. According to *ARS No. 6* and APB *Statement No. 3*, adjustments of historical cost for changes in the general price level represent restatements of nonmonetary asset measurements and also a restatement of stockholders' equity; no gain or loss should be recorded as a result of the adjustment. According to the Edwards and Bell approach, if the general price level is constant but specific input prices increase, a holding gain results.[17] If specific prices are changing at a different rate or in a different direction from general prices, the relative price changes result in holding gains or losses. On the other hand, a position held by Gynther, for example, is that these holding gains and losses should be treated as capital items rather than as items affecting income.[18]

THE OBJECTIVES OF ADJUSTING FOR PRICE-LEVEL CHANGES

Historical dollar reporting serves a useful purpose in providing accountability for stewardship of cash funds, for cash flow analysis, and in tracing dollars through the business processes. For most other purposes, neglecting price-level changes may result in serious errors in reporting. Under the concepts of income based on either the maintenance of capital or the matching of expenses with revenues, adjustments should be made for price-level changes in order to provide better information for measuring efficiency, to provide a basis for prediction of future income, and for managerial decision making—the objectives discussed in Chapter 5. But adjustments are also necessary to restore the balance sheet to a respectable and useful position among financial statements. Balance sheets that express all items in like terms are more meaningful in the evaluation of business enterprises than those based on unadjusted historical costs.

---

[17] Edwards and Bell, *op. cit.*, p. 73.

[18] R. S. Gynther, *Accounting for Price-Level Changes: Theory and Procedures* (Oxford, England: Pergamon Press, 1966), p. 79.

Net Income Reporting

As a measure of the operating efficiency of the firm, the reported net income should not include the increase in the monetary measurement of the firm due to decreases in the value of money. While buying at the right time and at the right price is a part of being efficient, gains from speculating on future price-level changes are not the objective of most business firms. Only by measuring the income of the firm in terms of dollars of the same purchasing power, and excluding the difference between historical cost and the restated cost, can the income figure be made meaningful as a measure of efficiency. And as efficiency is a relative term, this adjustment of net income will make it more comparable with that of other firms and with the net income of prior periods.

When income is to be used as a predictive device, the reported net income of a firm should be adjusted for price-level changes for three reasons: (1) Prediction requires an emphasis on recurring events and an attempt to obtain signs of material nonrecurring changes in the future. Although price-level changes may be recurring, they do not recur in a way that can be predicted reasonably. (2) Past income figures may be useful for predicting future income only if all income statement figures are expressed in the same terms. If the purchasing power of the dollar changes, income computed on the basis of historical dollars loses comparability with incomes of other periods. (3) From the investors' point of view, it is much less meaningful to predict changes in the aggregate of historical monetary measurements than to predict the value of the firm from measurements expressed in terms of a constant purchasing power and from changes in this total purchasing power. The stockholders may be better off if the total purchasing power of the firm increases, but an increase in the money value of the firm does not mean that they will necessarily be better off if the price level has increased at a more rapid rate.

For managerial decisions, net income data should provide the basis for a comparison of financial results with plans and anticipations. This also requires the use of comparable data—planned data must be compared with the actual results. Both should be expressed in dollars of the same purchasing power.

Matching Expenses with Revenues. In the transactions approach to income, revenues should be reported as soon as a crucial event has occurred and a verifiable measurement can be obtained. Expenses should be matched against these revenues, either directly or indirectly, as closely as possible. In traditional accounting procedures, revenues are expressed in terms of the transactions of the current period (and therefore in terms of the dollars of current purchasing power), while expenses may represent expirations or allocations of historical cost resulting from transactions of the current or prior periods. Thus, expenses expressed in dollars of an earlier purchasing power should be adjusted for the change in purchasing power from the date of acquisition of the goods or services until the date of reporting the related revenues. Note that matching is attained by expressing the expenses in terms of the current specific input prices as well as by adjusting for general price-level changes.

If the income statement is to be stated in terms of the average price level for the year, the major items that require adjustment generally are inventories and depreciation. The two items—cost of goods sold and depreciation—generally cause the greatest amount of distortion in the unadjusted statements, because they are generally computed on the basis of costs incurred in previous periods at different price levels.

The Maintenance-of-Capital Concept of Income. One of the capital maintenance concepts of income discussed in Chapter 5 was a comparison of values at the beginning and end of the period, in terms of historical input costs for nonmonetary items and in terms of current net realizable values or other output values for monetary assets. This concept provides an all-inclusive concept of income because all changes in dollar values are included. However, during and following periods of price-level changes, the net income computed on this basis would include a fictitious gain or loss due to the fact that the values at the beginning and end of the period are not expressed in terms of the same purchasing power. When the nonmonetary items at the beginning and end of the period are restated in terms of the same purchasing power, adjusted net income can be computed. But this income is all-inclusive in the sense that it includes the purchasing power gains and losses from holding monetary assets and monetary liabilities as well as the current operating income.

The Balance Sheet

As indicated in Chapter 3, the balance sheet is currently considered to be a step between two income statements; many of the items included in the balance sheet are merely unallocated debits and credits. This is due, in part, to an attempt to match current expenses with current revenues by using procedures such as last-in, first-out. Thus, many items in the balance sheet do not even reflect historical cost. Accordingly, the balance sheet has lost its meaning as a financial statement because of these allocation procedures, as well as because of the difference between historical costs and costs adjusted for changes in the purchasing power of money.

The main objectives for restating the items in the balance sheet are: (1) to restore or elevate the usefulness of the balance sheet to provide meaningful financial information; (2) to provide for a more adequate basis for the computation of periodic net income; and (3) to disclose the effect of inflation or deflation on the various classes of equity holders.

An adjusted balance sheet can provide useful financial information in several ways. If all items are restated in terms of dollars of the same purchasing power, the summation of various asset or liability valuations has more meaning than the summation of unlike items. A comparison of total asset or equity valuations over time will provide a useful measurement of the real growth of a firm. Financial ratios computed from unadjusted balance sheet items may provide misleading information; these same ratios may be improved by stating both the numerator and the denominator of the ratios in similar terms. The rate of return on investment is one of the best examples of a ratio that can be greatly improved by using figures restated in terms of a common dollar.

AN EVALUATION OF PRICE-LEVEL RESTATEMENTS

Some of the main controversies regarding price-level restatements center around the following questions: (1) Are price-level restatements relevant to financial reporting? (2) Should the reported price measurements be adjusted by a single price-level index, or for the price changes of specific items, or both? (3) What is the nature of the purchasing power gains and losses on monetary items? (4) What is the nature of the general price-level adjustment of nonmonetary items? (5) How should changes in specific prices of nonmonetary items be treated? (6) What is the effect of relative price changes? The answers to these questions depend in large part on the assumptions regarding the objectives of the firm and on assumptions regarding the objectives of the measurements and the concept of income proposed. The controversies in the literature regarding price-level adjustments cannot be settled unless agreement can be found regarding these basic issues.

The following examples are drawn from the discussions initiated by Chambers.[19] The models assume a basic classification of assets and liabilities as monetary and nonmonetary, a transactionless interval, and either a general price-level change or changes in the prices of specific items or both.

General Price-Level Adjustments

Let us assume a firm with net monetary assets M, total nonmonetary assets N,[20] and residual equity R, all expressed in dollars at time t_0:

---

[19] R. J. Chambers, *Towards a General Theory of Accounting* (University of Adelaide, 1961) and *Accounting, Evaluation and Economic Behavior* (Englewood Cliffs, N.J.: Prentice-Hall, Inc., 1965), pp. 223–27.

[20] Nonmonetary liabilities are assumed to be negligible.

$$M_0 + N_0 = R_0 \tag{1}$$

Assume also that adjustments are to be made by the use of an index of changes in the general level of prices p, representing the change in the general price level such that $p = \dfrac{P_1}{P_0} - 1$, where $P_1 =$ the price index at t_1, and $P_0 =$ the price index at t_0. Then the restatement of the financial condition of the firm in terms of prices at t_1 is as follows:[21]

$$M_0(1 + p) + N_0(1 + p) = R_0(1 + p) \tag{2}$$

By multiplication we have:

$$M_0 + M_0 p + N_0 + N_0 p = R_0 + R_0 p \tag{3}$$

and because the amount of net monetary assets (M) remains constant from t_0 to t_1, we subtract $M_0 p$ from both sides and change M_0 to M_1:

$$M_1 + (N_0 + N_0 p) = (R_0 + R_0 p) - M_0 p \tag{4}$$

According to ARS No. 6, $(N_0 + N_0 p)$ represents the original price of the nonmonetary assets expressed in terms of a common dollar at t_1; $(R_0 + R_0 p)$ represents the stockholders' equity at t_0 restated in terms of the purchasing power of the dollar at t_1. By emphasizing the concept of firm value and the concept of capital maintenance, we can assume that stockholders would be as well off at t_1 as at t_0 if $R_1 = R_0 + R_0 p$. Since the dollar amount of monetary assets (M) cannot increase merely because of the increase in the general price level, R_1 is less than $R_0 + R_0 p$ by the amount of $M_0 p$; thus $M_0 p$ represents the purchasing power loss from the holding of net monetary assets while prices in general are rising. ($M_0 p$ would represent a gain if $M < 0$ or if $p < 0$).

We can expand upon the above example by separating the net monetary assets (M) into two parts, net monetary current assets C and net monetary long-term debt L, such that $M = C - L$. By substitution in equation (1), we have at t_0:

$$C_0 - L_0 + N_0 = R_0 \tag{5}$$

and by multiplying all expressions by $(1 + p)$, we have at time t_1:

$$C_0(1 + p) + N_0(1 + p) - L_0(1 + p) = R_0(1 + p) \tag{6}$$

or:

$$C_0 + C_0 p + N_0 + N_0 p - L_0 - L_0 p = R_0 + R_0 p \tag{7}$$

---

[21] Note that for simplification, it is assumed that there are no changes in the net monetary assets (M) or in the nonmonetary assets (N) and that no depreciable assets are included.

Because both C and L remain constant from time t_0 to t_1 (that is, $C_0 = C_1$ and $L_0 = L_1$), we must subtract C_0p from both sides and add L_0p to both sides of the equation:

$$C_1 + (N_0 + N_0p) - L_1 = (R_0 + R_0p) + L_0p - C_0p \qquad (8)$$

If income is measured by the net change in the purchasing power of the residual equity, L_0p represents a gain from the outstanding debt during the period and C_0p represents the loss from holding monetary current assets from time t_0 to t_1. The argument that L_0p and C_0p are not gains and losses can be supported only on the basis of a different concept of income. For example, under the transactions concept of income these are not part of income because they do not represent the results of activity on the part of the firm.

Another argument that the gain on long-term debt (L_0p) is not a part of the income for the period is based on the assumption that capital invested in the firm includes both debt and residual equity capital, $R + L$. Therefore, capital is maintained if $R_1 + L_1$ at time t_1 is equal to $(R_0 + R_0p) + (L_0 + L_0p)$. Any loss to bondholders is equal to the purchasing power gain to stockholders, but the effect on the firm as a whole is neutral.[22]

Restatements for Specific Price Changes

If assets are restated for the price changes of individual assets rather than for changes in general purchasing power, each nonmonetary asset must be adjusted by the rate of change in its specific price, s_i; net monetary assets are not adjusted because their specific prices in dollars do not change. Since each nonmonetary asset or group of similar assets N_i must be adjusted separately, equation (1) should be restated as follows:

$$M + \sum_{i=1}^{k} N_i = R \qquad (9)$$

where

$$\sum_{i=1}^{k} N_i = N_1 + N_2 \dots + N_k$$

By adjusting the nonmonetary assets for the rate of specific price changes (s_i), we obtain the following equation:

$$\sum_{i=1}^{k} N_i(1 + s_i) = \sum_{i=1}^{k} N_i + \sum_{i=1}^{k} N_is_i \qquad (10)$$

where

$$\sum_{i=1}^{k} N_i(1 + s_i) = N_1(1 + s_1) + N_2(1 + s_2) \dots + N_k(1 + s_k)$$

---

[22] See for example Gynther, *op. cit.*, p. 140.

so that the exchange price at time t_0 of each nonmonetary asset in the total set owned by the firm from asset N_1 to asset N_k is adjusted by the specific price change (s_i) relating to each asset.

Therefore, by adding $\sum\limits_{i=1}^{k} N_i s_i$ to each side of equation (9) and combining as indicated in equation (10), we obtain the following equation:

$$M_0 + \sum_{i=1}^{k} N_{0i}(1 + s_i) = R_0 + \sum_{i=1}^{k} N_{0i}s_i \qquad (11)$$

The effect of equation (11) is to show on the left-hand side all net assets at their current prices; and on the right hand side the total residual equity at the time period t_0, plus the increase in the prices of specific nonmonetary assets. Mathews argues that this adjustment results in no gain or loss to the firm, because the specific purchasing power of the net assets is the same as it was at the beginning of the period.[23] This is so because he assumes that the firm will continually reinvest its funds in assets which are related to the particular activity of the firm and thus similar to the assets currently held. Thus, he assumes a fairly static economy.

Gynther proposes similar adjustments for changes in the prices of specific nonmonetary assets, but he suggests that the purchasing power loss from the holding of net monetary current assets should be reported.[24] However, he recommends that the gains or losses on monetary current items should be computed by using the price indexes of the goods generally acquired by these monetary assets. That is, the firm can maintain its capital only if it maintains its purchasing power in terms of the specific goods it generally purchases. This position has some merit, as discussed below on pages 226–28.

Relative Price Changes

If there is no change in the general purchasing power of the dollar, the increase in residual equity indicated in equation (11) represents a holding gain, according to some proponents of general price-level adjustments. That is, the firm is assumed to be as well off at the end of the period as at the beginning if $R_1 = R_0 + R_0 p$, but if $p = 0$, $R_0 p = 0$; thus, the increase in the prices of specific nonmonetary assets permits the firm to be better off at the end of the period in terms of its ability to use its resources to purchase goods and services in general. The entire specific price changes in this case are assumed to be relative price changes.

If the prices of the specific goods held by the firm change at a different

---

[23] R. L. Mathews, "Price-Level Changes and Useless Information," *Journal of Accounting Research,* Vol. III (Spring, 1965), p. 143.

[24] Gynther, *op. cit.,* p. 156.

rate from the rate of change of general prices, the differences between the two rates represents the relative price change. For example, if the specific price of asset N_i has increased by the rate s_i and if this rate is greater than p, the increase in the general level of prices such that $(s_i > p)$, the holding gain due to the relative price increase would be $N_i(s_i - p)$. This result is obtained by subtracting the price of the specific asset N_i at t_0 adjusted for changes in the general price level from the current price of the asset at t_1. Thus:

$$N_i(1 + s_i) - N_i(1 + p) = N_i + N_i s_i - N_i - N_i p = N_i s_i - N_i p = N_i(s_i - p)$$

The current price of the specific asset can then be approximated as the sum of the price of the asset N_i at time t_0 adjusted for the change in the general level of prices and the relative price change of this asset. Thus:

$$N_i(1 + p) + N_i(s_i - p) = N_i + N_i p + N_i s_i - N_i p = N_i + N_i s_i = N_i(1 + s_i) \tag{12}$$

Therefore, for the entire firm, the nonmonetary assets can be expressed in terms of the current specific prices by adjusting first for changes in the general level of prices and then adding the relative price changes to both sides of the equation. This can be computed as follows, starting with equation (9):

$$M_0 + \sum_{i=1}^{k} N_{0i} = R_0 \tag{9}$$

and adjusting both sides by the change in the level of general prices, we obtain:

$$M_0(1 + p) + \sum_{i=1}^{k} N_{0i}(1 + p) = R_0(1 + p) \tag{13}$$

By multiplication, and subtracting $M_0 p$ from both sides, we have:

$$M_0 + \sum_{i=1}^{k} N_{0i}(1 + p) = R_0 + R_0 p - M_0 p \tag{14}$$

Then by adding the relative price changes to both sides, we reach the following equation:

$$M_0 + \sum_{i=1}^{k} N_{0i}(1 + p) + \sum_{i=1}^{k} N_{0i}(s_i - p) =$$

$$(R_0 + R_0 p) - M_0 p + \sum_{i=1}^{k} N_{0i}(s_i - p) \tag{15}$$

Since $(R_0 + R_0 p)$ is necessary at time t_1 to maintain the residual equity in terms of a constant general purchasing power, $M_0 p$ represents the loss in purchasing power from the holding of a constant amount of monetary items and $\sum_{i=1}^{k} N_{0i}(s_i - p)$ represents the gains arising from the increase in relative prices of nonmonetary assets.

Since the practical application of equation (15) leaves much to be desired, a simpler application suggested by Chambers[25] has considerable merit, although it does not permit the separation of purchasing power gains and losses on monetary items and the gains and losses from the holding of nonmonetary assets. Chambers' suggestion can be interpreted as follows:

By combining the general and relative price adjustments of nonmonetary assets on the left side of equation (15) and expanding the right hand side, we obtain:

$$M_0 + \sum_{i=1}^{k} N_{0i}(1 + s_i) = (R_0 + R_0 p) - M_0 p + \sum_{i=1}^{k} N_{0i}s_i - \sum_{i=1}^{k} N_{0i}p \quad (16)$$

and since $M_0 p + \sum_{i=1}^{k} N_{0i}p = R_0 p$, we can substitute $R_0 p$ in equation (16) and obtain the following:

$$M_0 + \sum_{i=1}^{k} N_{0i}(1 + s_i) = (R_0 + R_0 p) + \left[\sum_{i=1}^{k} N_{0i}s_i - R_0 p \right] \quad (17)$$

Therefore, according to equation (17), nonmonetary assets need be adjusted only for specific price changes, and the income effect of the general and specific price changes is measured by adding the sum of the increases in the specific price changes of nonmonetary assets and subtracting a capital adjustment $(R_0 p)$ so that the total adjustment is $\left[\sum_{i=1}^{k} N_{0i}s_i - R_0 p \right]$.

This net adjustment to income could, of course, be positive or negative, depending upon the relative rates of change of s_i and p.

Equation (17) is significant because it points out the major difference between those who propose adjustments for only specific price changes and those who propose adjustments for general and relative price changes. If the $+ R_0 p$ and the $- R_0 p$ on the right-hand side of equation (17) are canceled, we then have equation (11), which represents the adjustments necessary according to those who propose the adjustment only for specific price changes. However, the interpretation is different, because the adjustment for specific price changes in equation (11) is assumed to represent an adjustment of capital, whereas in equation (17) it is a part of the adjustment of income. Therefore, the differences between the proponents of specific price adjustments only and the proponents of adjustments for

---

[25] Chambers, *Accounting, Evaluation and Economic Behavior, op. cit.*, p. 246.

general and relative price changes is primarily based on the assumptions regarding the nature of the firm and the objectives of financial reporting. If the objective is to approximate the value of the firm and report changes in this value as income, the central question is one of a choice of a proper index of purchasing power, discussed in the next section. However, as discussed in Chapter 5 and in Chapter 9, an attempt to measure the value of the firm has considerable limitations, both with respect to the problems of measurement and with respect to its relevance to the needs of investors. Since one of the objectives of external financial reporting should be to present information relevant to the prediction of future cash flows to equity holders, reporting the effect of price changes should aid in this prediction. However, the relationship between changes in purchasing power, or changes in relative prices and future cash distributions, rests on unsubstantiated premises and thus the validity of adjustments for general and specific price changes needs to be tested. But this does not mean that the adjustment of nonmonetary assets for changes in specific prices is not relevant as a current measure of assets employed, and possibly as an aid in the prediction of cash flows when supplemented with other information.

THE CHOICE OF A RELEVANT PRICE INDEX

Most of the proposals and studies for the adjustment of financial statements by the use of a single price index have stated or assumed that the index should measure the changes in prices in general, reflecting changes in general purchasing power or changes in the general value of the dollar. For example, *Accounting Research Study No. 6* states that

. . all elements of the financial statements should be restated by means of a single index of the *general price level* as of the balance-sheet date so that all the financial data will be expressed in terms of dollars of the same purchasing power . . . (as measured by an index of the movement in *all prices*).[26]

This is also the position of APB *Statement No. 3*. Jones also had this concept of generalized purchasing power in mind when he stated the basic objectives of his study as

to develop and test techniques and methods for the preparation of supplementary financial statements expressed in constant-value units, that is, in dollars of uniform purchasing power measured by a general index of prices.[27]

However, not all writers on the subject have had the same interpretation of general purchasing power. Sweeney, for example, referred to

---

[26] AICPA *Accounting Research Study No. 6, op. cit.*, pp. xi–xii. First italics added.

[27] Ralph Coughenour Jones, *Price Level Changes and Financial Statements, Case Studies of Four Companies* (American Accounting Association, 1955), p. 2.

replacement cost computed on the basis of specific indexes as being a measure of general purchasing power.[28] And Terborgh emphasized that we must rely on some measure of *generalized* purchasing power, but that we must still ". . . ask whether it is purchasing power over capital goods or consumers' goods."[29]

The purchasing power concept attains its validity from the objective of maintaining capital and distinguishing between invested capital and income. Capital must be maintained in terms of its purchasing power for a firm to be as well off at the end of the period as it was at the beginning. There are several concepts of purchasing power, however, that may be relevant in the measurement of the capital maintenance. Generalized purchasing power has already been mentioned, but we should also consider the relevancy of purchasing power of stockholders, the investment purchasing power of the firm, and specific replacement purchasing power.

General Purchasing Power

General purchasing power, as measured by a general index of prices, shows the general tendency of all prices of goods and services in the economy to rise or fall or remain constant on the average as appropriately weighted, and reflects changes in the value of money. No index of all prices in the economy has ever been computed, and none is likely to be computed, but several available indexes may be used as close approximations. Sweeney considered a cost-of-living index the best and most appropriate measure of general purchasing power, but he used Snyder's General Index because of its availability at that time. Jones used the Consumers Price Index of the Bureau of Labor Statistics for the following reasons: (1) It is widely used and generally accepted as an index of the general price level. (2) It agrees rather closely with the Gross National Product Implicit Price Deflator. (3) Technological changes affect it less than they do some of the more specialized index numbers. (4) It fluctuates less than other currently available general indexes.[30]

The Gross National Product Implicit Price Deflators produced by the U.S. Department of Commerce are probably the best currently compiled indexes of the general level of prices in the United States. They are computed by dividing the current-dollar series of gross national product by the corresponding constant-dollar series, and therefore reflect all

---

[28] Sweeney, *op. cit.*, p. 51.

[29] George Terborgh, *Depreciation Policy and the Price Level* (Chicago: Machinery and Allied Products Institute, 1947), reprinted in W. T. Baxter and Sidney Davidson (eds.), *Studies in Accounting Theory* (Homewood, Ill.: Richard D. Irwin, Inc., 1962), p. 328.

[30] Jones, *op. cit.*, p. 3.

exchange prices in the economy. Annual estimates are available from 1919, and quarterly estimates are available since 1947.[31] However, because the index does not generally reflect secular quality improvements and the emergence of superior products, the index does not provide a good comparison for years not close to each other.

But even if an index can be found to measure changes in the general price level (reflecting changes in the value of money), there is some question whether or not this is the relevant concept. With a general purchasing power concept, it is assumed that the investor had a free choice to spend his money in the economy any way that he wished at the time of his investment, and that when the capital is recovered through the sale of product or services the investor will again have the freedom to spend his money any way that he wishes. That is, the operating cycle of the business is assumed to flow from cash to nonmonetary assets and back to cash, and the cash is then available to the investor for general spending. This is a single-venture concept that is not relevant to large corporate enterprises. An alternative way of looking at it is to assume that the firm is continually making choices to invest and reinvest its capital in the economy for all types of goods and services.

Purchasing Power of Stockholders

One of the earliest concepts of purchasing power is that capital is maintained only if the ability of the stockholders to purchase a given quantity and quality of consumers' goods and services is held constant. For example, Sweeney held the view that the cost-of-living index was the ideal, and this concept has been implied by many other writers. It is generally claimed that investors buy production goods only because they hope to obtain, eventually, more consumption goods than they could have had by consuming rather than investing. However, this is unrealistic for two reasons: (1) Large corporations usually intend to continue in business indefinitely rather than liquidate so that stockholders can consume their investments. (2) Stockholders do not usually liquidate their holdings in order to consume the amount of the investment. Although investors are constantly liquidating their holdings, it is more common for stockholders to reinvest their savings and consume only the income from the investments than it is for them to consume the amounts invested in corporate stocks.

The Consumers Price Index measures the average change in the prices of a specific "market basket" of goods and services bought by families of

---

[31] For annual estimates since 1919 and five-year averages for the period 1889 to 1921, see U.S. Department of Commerce, Bureau of the Census, *Historical Statistics of the United States, Colonial Times to 1957*, A Statistical Abstract Supplement (Washington, D.C.: U.S. Government Printing Office, 1960), p. 139.

wage earners and clerical workers living in several of the large cities in the United States. Even as a measure of the purchasing power of the families in this group it has some severe limitations. And when it is applied to other areas and to other groups, it is appropriate only in a very general way. Price changes are never uniform throughout the country or among the various commodities and services; purchasing power, therefore, is dependent upon the specific items usually purchased by an individual. This does not mean that averages are not useful; however, we must recognize their limitations and apply them carefully. The price changes of consumer goods and services purchased by stockholders can hardly be described by this average. Stockholders of United States corporations fall into all income classifications, but by far the largest dollar value of stock is owned by the upper-income groups. However, as an index of the goods and services purchased by the upper-income groups is not available, the CPI may not be entirely inappropriate as an approximation of the purchasing power of stockholders. What is more important is the fact that the purchasing power of stockholders is not a relevant concept in the adjustment of corporate financial statements.

Investment Purchasing Power of the Firm

The postulate of continuity assumes that the firm will continually reinvest its assets in order to maintain its *invested capital*. Thus, the operating cycle of the business is from nonmonetary assets to cash to nonmonetary assets. However, continuity of life does not imply that the firm must replace specific assets. But it does mean that the firm should maintain its purchasing power to acquire investment goods.

Investment purchasing power can be looked at from at least three different views: (1) the ability of the firm to reinvest in an equal quantity of investment goods in general; (2) the ability of the firm to reinvest in capital goods generally purchased by all firms in the industry; and (3) the ability to reinvest in investment goods similar to those it has acquired in the past. Each of these views is a relevant description of some parts of the economy. Some firms diversify their investments over time, and actually move from one industry to another or branch out into different industries. Other firms remain in the same industry but change the composition of their investment to keep up with technological innovations and to produce new products. And many firms do reinvest in capital goods and inventories similar to those they have had in the past.

The first view—general investment purchasing power—is probably the most relevant to a dynamic economy such as in the United States. While there are some institutional frictions to movement, many firms do branch out into different industries, and accounting data should indicate when this is desirable. Adjustments for price-level changes in this case would require the use of an overall investment price index. While no such comprehensive index is now available, an approximation could be obtained by combining the implicit price deflators for the "other new construction" and "producers' durable equipment" segments of GNP and adjusting for changes in the prices of inventories. A single investment index for the economy has the advantage of uniformity among firms and ease of application once the index is determined.

The second view—industry investment purchasing power—is inappropriate because firms are generally free to diversify and reinvest in several industries, and many firms do so. It would require a different investment index for each industry. A major practical difficulty in applying this approach is the fact that many firms produce a wide variety of products, so it is impossible to determine exactly in which industry they operate.

The third view—purchasing power relating to the past behavior of a specific firm—is probably the least relevant, because past investment behavior is not necessarily a good indication of what the firm will do in the future. Also, technological changes in methods of production and in products require firms to alter their investment mix continually. Furthermore, it would be difficult and costly to compute a price-level index for each specific firm.

Specific Replacement Purchasing Power

Most of the firms that have made adjustments in their financial statements for price-level changes in the United States and in other countries have used either current or reproduction costs rather than a single index representing general price-level changes.[32] However, most of these firms consider this procedure to be an adjustment for price-level changes and an adjustment for the purchasing power of capital.[33] In accordance with this view, these firms consider the adjustment of equity to be a restatement of capital or "revaluation surplus" rather than holding gains and losses. Under common dollar accounting, both an adjustment of permanent capital and holding gains and losses should be shown if the effect of relative price changes is also to be reported.

There is an element of truth, however, in the argument that specific replacement costs can be used to measure the specific replacement purchasing power of the firm. When specific or group price indexes are used to adjust historical costs to a current replacement cost basis, the result

[32] See Appendix D to AICPA *Accounting Research Study No. 6, op. cit.,* pp. 169–218.

[33] See for example A. Goudeket, "An Application of Replacement Value Theory," *Journal of Accountancy,* Vol. CX (July, 1960), p. 38. See also the comment on this procedure by Willard Graham in "Letters," *Journal of Accountancy,* Vol. CX (August, 1960), pp. 28–31.

may be a close approximation of costs restated in terms of dollars with the same specific purchasing power. The result may be similar to using a single investment index for the firm to measure firm purchasing power if the firm does, in fact, reinvest in the same types of investment goods. Note that specific indexes are used in this case to measure specific purchasing power rather than to obtain current values; therefore, no holding gains and losses would result from the adjustment.

Several writers use a similar concept of income, except that they would use current cost or assessed valuations as a measure of current value of specific assets that must be recovered before income is earned. For example, Kerr stated that

under the current-cost concept of income the emphasis is placed on things, physical assets, rather than money or purchasing-power-units, as a result of which the capital at the beginning of the period is considered as comprising a group of physical assets which is eventually converted into funds, a portion of the funds being used to replace the physical assets and the balance being the income for the period.[34]

This is based on a concept of capital maintenance in terms of productive capacity instead of the maintenance of specific or general purchasing power. But this is just another way of saying that dollars recovered must be adequate to provide for the purchase of the specific assets or for the equivalent productive capacity—a specific purchasing power concept.

This differs from the more general purchasing power concepts in that it assumes that the firms will continually replace their assets with assets of the same type. For example, Gynther stated that

firms do tend to remain in their particular industries. . . . Companies in a particular industry use certain kinds of assets and stocks, and the tendency is for these to be replaced by similar kinds of assets and stocks. To picture the case of a company changing from one industry to another is to forgo the going concern concept, for here we have the virtual liquidation of one company and the setting up of another.[35]

While this assumption may be true for a large part of the economies of England and Australia, it is not a general observation of the way large corporations operate in the United States.

In those cases where replacement costs are recommended for a complete adjustment of financial statements for changes in the price level, the gains and losses on monetary items must be computed by using some general index or several specific relevant indexes. The Philips Incandescent Lamp Works Company (N. V. Philips Gloielampenfabrieken),

---

[34] Jean St. G. Kerr, "Three Concepts of Business Income," *Australian Accountant*, Vol. XXVI (April, 1956), p. 141.

[35] R. S. Gynther, "Accounting for Price Level Changes—One *General* Index or Several *Specific* Indexes?" *Accountancy*, Vol. LXXIII (July, 1962), p. 562.

for example, uses a general cost-of-living index to compute the gains and losses on all monetary items.[36] Gynther, however, recommends that gains and losses on monetary items be computed by using specific indexes representing the price changes of the goods for which the monetary items are held. For example, gains and losses on accounts receivable might be computed by using an index of the prices of merchandise generally purchased by the firm. For cash items, an index representing changes in the prices of supplies, wages, and operating expenses might be used.[37] This approach is consistent with the replacement cost approach, but a broader index would probably be more appropriate because monetary assets are not generally held for specific purchases and monetary liabilities do not generally finance specific items.

PARTIAL METHODS OF ADJUSTING FOR PRICE-LEVEL CHANGES

Proposals for adjusting financial statements for changes in the general purchasing power of the dollar have not found general acceptance among the members of the accounting profession, for several reasons. Those who oppose complete adjustments for price-level changes do so either for theoretical or for pragmatic reasons. Among the theoretical arguments are: (1) the objective of accounting should be to determine monetary income rather than economic income; (2) replacement costs and price-level adjusted costs are not relevant to the accounting process; and (3) statements adjusted for changes in the price level by the use of indexes overstate the case because of technological innovations and obsolescence. The practical objections are that (1) the purposes for the adjustments are not well formulated; (2) the adjustment procedures are too complex and would not be understood by most users of financial statements; (3) current partial adjustment procedures serve well to take care of the situation; (4) appropriate indexes are not available; (5) the cost of making the adjustments would be too great; and (6) the continual growth of firms and the relatively slow rate of price increases for most developed countries make the adjustment process unnecessary at the present time.

The objection to complete price-level adjustments because they are unduly complicated and confusing is stated by Tyson in his comments to *Accounting Research Study No. 6*.[38] He believes that the only items that are not already in current terms are inventories, investments, and properties, and that it is better to concentrate on making adjustments for these items than to introduce needless confusion into accounting. Others

---

[36] Goudeket, *op. cit.*, p. 41.

[37] R. S. Gynther, *Accounting for Price-Level Changes: Theory and Procedures, op. cit.*, pp. 155–58.

[38] AICPA *Accounting Research Study No. 6, op. cit.*, pp. 252–53.

have suggested that an adjustment of income statement items is all that is necessary, since the main objective of accounting is to present a meaningful concept of income. It is frequently claimed that the use of the last-in, first-out method of accounting for inventories, combined with a replacement cost method of depreciation, would adjust for almost all of the error in the operating income as presented in conventional statements. Note, however, that purchasing power gains and losses from the holding of monetary items do not result from these partial adjustments. Also, the balance sheet is generally left in terms of historical costs or with meaningless amounts because of the effect of Lifo.

Last-In, First-Out

The impelling force for the use of Lifo in the United States has been its acceptance for income tax purposes. Thus, Lifo did not originate as an approach to the problem of inflation but rather as an approach to the problem of specific price fluctuations. The concept is one of matching replacement cost, rather than historical cost adjusted for changes in purchasing power, against revenues.

Lifo is a step toward the elimination from current net income of the holding gains and losses from specific price changes and the change in price due to general shifts in the price level. However, only the costs of the goods sold or used are adjusted; the costs of goods not sold or used remain unadjusted. But the matching of current costs with current revenues is not accurate unless replacement purchases are coincident with sales. Under the periodic inventory method, however, the items sold during the period may be replaced at the end of the period so that the end-of-the-period costs may be charged to cost of goods sold. In this case, Lifo becomes a form of Nifo (next-in, first-out) and the profits may be distorted, intentionally or involuntarily, by the management of production or purchases, particularly toward the end of the period.

How well does this method adjust for price-level changes? *First*, Lifo adjusts only for specific price changes; it is not an adjustment for changes in the value of money. *Second*, it must be recognized that the Lifo method attempts to adjust income only. It does not purport to adjust asset valuations in the balance sheet; in fact, the result is a distortion of balance sheet valuations. *Third*, the adjustment is limited to only a part of the costs recorded in the determination of income. It is at best a partial adjustment of income. Only if merchandise costs are a significant part of total costs will the adjustment provide a material adjustment of net income. Some claim, however, that any adjustment is better than none. Others argue that a partial adjustment slows down the progress toward an acceptance of a more satisfactory complete adjustment. *Fourth,* Lifo does not adjust for price changes since the last purchase. Only if turnover is very high is there a close approximation of a good matching of current revenues and costs expressed in current terms. If turnover is slow or if price movements are rapid, this deficiency may prove significant. *Fifth,* with a periodic inventory method, a concentration of purchases at the end of the period may result in the matching of end-of-period costs with revenues arising during the entire period. *Sixth,* when sales exceed current purchases, the gap between historical costs and current selling prices becomes very broad. The result is that the price increases for a number of years are included in the normal income for a single year, defeating the purpose of the Lifo method. Thus, as a method of adjusting for price-level changes, Lifo is inferior and does not even provide a temporary method of reporting relevant measurements when prices are changing.

Replacement Cost Depreciation

The term "replacement cost" has been used in accounting discussions to mean one of three distinct concepts: (1) the current input value of nonmonetary assets; (2) historical cost restated in terms of the current specific purchasing power of the dollar; and (3) the physical invested capital. In each of these concepts, depreciation based on the replacement cost is matched with current revenues to obtain the current net income from operations. Operating profit is obtained in each case only if the economic value of the resources received exceeds the economic value of the resources given up. The main difference between these concepts is that in the first meaning, holding gains and losses arise from the difference between replacement cost and historical cost, or historical cost adjusted for changes in the general price level; while in the latter two concepts, the entire difference between replacement cost and historical cost is assumed to represent an adjustment of capital not distinguishable from an adjustment for a change in the general purchasing power of money.

The procedure usually suggested for adjusting depreciation charges for changes in replacement costs is the application of relevant replacement cost indexes, depending on the types of assets being depreciated. The objective is to charge to expense an amount equal to the depreciation of a similar asset assumed to be constructed under current conditions. The plant and equipment items in the balance sheet may be restated in terms of current costs or they may be left in terms of historical costs. If the assets are restated, a capital adjustment account would appear in the stockholders' equity section of the balance sheet, representing the difference between the current cost of the assets and their historical cost. This is the procedure used by the Indiana Telephone Corporation. However, the capital adjustment account is separated into two parts—that which has been charged to income in the past and that which will be charged to income in future periods.[39] If the assets are not restated, the capital adjustment account is credited each period for the excess of the depreciation expressed in terms of replacement cost over the historical cost depreciation.

From the point of view of the financial statements as a whole, replacement cost depreciation is objectionable because it is incomplete. If it is used together with Lifo for inventories, it is generally thought that most of the errors in income arising from price-level changes will be corrected. However, replacement cost depreciation does not permit the computation of holding gains and losses on nonmonetary items, and generally does not include a presentation of the purchasing power gains and losses on monetary items.

Another objection to replacement cost depreciation is that the adjustment does not reflect changes in the purchasing power of money, and therefore the results are not comparable among firms or among industries. However, this objection could be overcome by using broader indexes of industry or general investment goods prices or a general index of all prices.

Appropriation Reserves

The appropriation of retained earnings cannot correctly be called a partial adjustment for price-level changes, but it has been suggested as a method of disclosure of the amount by which income has been overstated because of price-level increases. The appropriation also serves as a notice to stockholders that this is the amount that management feels that it needs to withhold from dividend payments in order to maintain its level of operations.

The same objective of disclosure can be obtained by presenting the information in a footnote to the financial statements or in the president's letter to stockholders in the annual report. At best, any attempt at simple disclosure is a stopgap measure until the income and balance sheet accounts can be adjusted directly. The greatest danger with simple disclosure is that the amount appropriated is most likely to be a very rough estimate of the effect of price-level changes. Management is not likely to request a systematic calculation of the amount. Accordingly, the basic assumptions and techniques used in making the estimate are not usually disclosed, giving little real meaning to the final figures.

---

[39] See Indiana Telephone Corporation annual reports or AICPA *Accounting Research Study No. 6, op. cit.*, pp. 194–99.

CURRENCY DEVALUATIONS AND PRICE CHANGES

In those cases where it is desirable to aggregate assets or liabilities or transactions expressed in different currencies, a translation of the amounts expressed in the different currencies should be made in terms of the currency of the country in which most of the readers of the financial statements reside. The need for translation generally occurs when the statements of a branch or subsidiary are consolidated with a domestic parent corporation, or when the statements of an independent foreign corporation are translated for use in a different country.

The traditional view expressed in Chapter 12 of *Accounting Research Bulletin No. 43* was based primarily on AICPA *Accounting Research Bulletin No. 4,* published in 1939, and special statements of the Institute published in 1931 and 1933. According to these statements, fixed assets and permanent investments should be translated into the domestic currency at exchange rates prevailing when the assets were originally acquired. Cash, accounts receivable, and other current assets—including inventories and current liabilities—are translated in most cases at the rate of exchange prevailing on the date of the statements. *ARB No. 43* also recommends that capital stock, long-term debt, and long-term receivables should likewise be translated in terms of the exchange rates prevailing at the date of the balance sheet. However, APB *Opinion No. 6* approved the use of either the historical rate or the current rate for long-term receivables and long-term liabilities.

The translation of foreign currency measurements is not the same problem as the making of adjustments for changes in the price level; because an actual exchange rate does exist at a specific point in time, while it is not possible to exchange purchasing power at one point in time with purchasing power at another time. However, some of the concepts relating to adjustments for price changes are also relevant in the translation of foreign currencies. For example, the monetary and nonmonetary classifications are relevant in the selection of an exchange rate and in the measurement of devaluation gains and losses.

Nonmonetary assets should be translated at the exchange rates prevalent at the dates of acquisition if emphasis is to be placed upon the historical cost concept. That is, the traditional assumption has been that the historical cost in dollars or other domestic currency of the parent firm is the equivalent number of dollars that would have been needed to purchase the foreign currency which, in turn, was used to acquire the asset. A devaluation of the foreign currency subsequent to the date of acquisition does not result in a loss, because the historical cost in equivalent dollars has not changed. But the use of a current exchange rate for the translation of inventories measured at the lower of cost or market, as recommended by *ARB No. 43*, is inconsistent unless the measurement in the foreign currency represents a current exchange price.

All monetary assets and monetary liabilities in a foreign currency reflect current purchasing power in the foreign country and, therefore, should be translated at the exchange rate existing at the date of the balance sheet. A devaluation of the foreign currency, therefore, may result in a gain or loss upon translation if it is intended to convert the cash back into the domestic currency of the parent firm. However, if the monetary assets and monetary liabilities of the foreign subsidiary are to be used or paid in terms of the local foreign currency, no gain or loss results, from an operational point of view. The difference upon translation results in an adjustment of the stockholders' equity. APB *Opinion No. 9*, however, suggests that a major devaluation should be reported as an extraordinary gain or loss.

Accounting Research Bulletin No. 43 stated that long-term receivables and long-term liabilities should be translated at historical exchange rates, but APB *Opinion No. 6* stated that current exchange rates may be appropriate in many circumstances. This represented a shift from emphasis on the current or noncurrent nature of items as the criterion for using a current exchange rate or a historical one to the classification as monetary or nonmonetary as the basic criterion, with the exception of inventories. However, the translation of nonmonetary assets at predevaluation rates while all monetary assets and liabilities are translated at post devaluation rates would result in a net gain which some accountants are reluctant to report in the earnings of the current year. The reason for this reluctance arises because the amortization of nonmonetary assets expressed at predevaluation rates may result in lower reported earnings in the future, because of a matching of expenses translated at predevaluation rates with revenues translated at postdevaluation rates. The solution to this problem would seem to be to express all nonmonetary assets at the current exchange prices in the local foreign currency and translate all items into the domestic currency of the parent at the current exchange rate.

Adjustments for specific price changes and for price-level changes in a foreign country are relevant in the reporting of foreign operations particularly in those cases where there is an intent to continue such foreign operations. That is, the purchasing power in the specific or general goods and services in the foreign country is relevant to external financial reporting if operations are expected to continue in that country. Changes in the prices of the specific or general goods and services of the country of the parent company are relevant only when cash is remitted to the parent company.

APB *Statement No. 3*, however, recommends that when the financial statements of a foreign branch or subsidiary are combined or consolidated with the statements of the parent domestic company, the amounts expressed in the foreign currency should first be translated into U.S. dollars and then restated for changes in the general purchasing power of the U.S. dollar.[40] But this procedure is based upon historical cost concepts that are themselves suspect and upon an implicit assumption that transactions in a foreign currency are the equivalent of transactions in the domestic currency. Since these assumptions appear to be of doubtful validity, additional research is necessary before conclusions can be reached in this area.

SELECTED ADDITIONAL READING ON CHAPTER TOPICS

Price-Level Adjustment Concepts

PATON, W. A. "Observations on Inflation from an Accounting Stance," *Journal of Accounting Research*, Vol. VI (Spring, 1968), pp. 72–85.

PEIRSON, GRAHAM. "Three Kinds of Adjustments for Price Changes," *Accounting Review*, Vol. XLI (October, 1966), pp. 729–36.

General Price-Level Adjustments

Accounting Principles Board. "Financial Statements for General Price-Level Changes," *Statement No. 3.* New York: American Institute of Certified Public Accountants, June, 1969.

American Institute of Certified Public Accountants, Staff of the Accounting Research Division. "Reporting the Financial Effects of Price-Level Changes," *Accounting Research Study No. 6.* New York: AICPA, 1963.

CHAMBERS, R. J. "A Study of a Price Level Study," *Abacus,* Vol. II (December, 1966), pp. 97–118.

PARKER, W. E. "Changes in the Purchasing Power of Money," *Accountancy,* Vol. LXXIV (January, 1963), pp. 8–14, and (February, 1963), pp. 121–26. Also in *Accountant,* Vol. CXLVII (November 3, 1962), pp. 568–74, and (November 10, 1962), pp. 604–8.

TIERNEY, CECILIA. "Price-Level Adjustments—Problem in Perspective," *Journal of Accountancy,* Vol. CXVI (November, 1963), pp. 56–60.

General versus Specific Price Changes

CHAMBERS, R. J. "The Price Level Problem and Some Intellectual Grooves," *Journal of Accounting Research,* Vol. III (Autumn, 1965), pp. 242–52.

——. "Price Variation Accounting—An Improved Representation," *Journal of Accounting Research,* Vol. VI (Autumn, 1967), pp. 215–220.

---

[40] APB *Statement No. 3, op. cit.,* pp. 18–19.

GYNTHER, R. S. "Accounting for Price Level Changes—One *General* Index or Several *Specific* Indexes?" *Accountancy,* Vol. LXXIII (July, 1962), pp. 560–64.

HENDRIKSEN, ELDON S. "Purchasing Power and Replacement Cost Concepts—Are They Related?" *Accounting Review,* Vol. XXXVIII (July, 1963), pp. 483–91.

MA, RONALD. "A Comparative Review of Some Price Level Accounting Systems," *Abacus,* Vol. I (December, 1965), pp. 107–30.

MATHEWS, R. L. "Price-Level Changes and Useless Information," *Journal of Accounting Research,* Vol. III (Spring, 1965), pp. 133–55.

——. "The Price-Level Controversy: A Reply," *Journal of Accounting Research,* Vol. V (Spring, 1967), pp. 113–18.

——. "Price Variation Accounting—A Rejoinder," *Journal of Accounting Research,* Vol. VI (Autumn, 1968), pp. 284–85.

WINBORNE, M. G. "A Wrinkle on an Intellectual Groove," *Journal of Accounting Research,* Vol. IV (Autumn, 1966), pp. 245–52.

MOONITZ, MAURICE. "General v. Specific Price Changes: A Note," *Journal of Accounting Research,* Vol. III (Autumn, 1965), pp. 253–54.

Specific Price Changes

CHAMBERS, R. J. "Edwards and Bell on Business Income," *Accounting Review,* Vol. XL (October, 1965), pp. 731–41.

GYNTHER, R. S. *Accounting for Price-Level Changes: Theory and Procedures.* Oxford, England: Pergamon Press, 1966.

STEPHENS, MATTHEW J. "Opening Pandora's Box of Current Cost," *Financial Executive,* Vol. XXXV (May, 1967), pp. 56–65.

ZEFF, STEPHEN A. and W. DAVID MAXWELL. "Holding Gains on Fixed Assets —A Demurrer," *Accounting Review,* Vol. XL (January, 1965), pp. 65–75.

Relative Price Changes

MATHEWS, R. L. "Income, Price Changes and the Valuation Controversy in Accounting," *Accounting Review,* Vol. XLIII (July, 1968), pp. 509–16.

Monetary Items

American Institute of Certified Public Accountants, Staff of the Accounting Research Division. "Reporting the Financial Effects of Price-Level Changes," *Accounting Research Study No. 6,* Appendix C, "Gains and Losses Attributable to the Holding of Monetary Items When the Price Level Changes," pp. 137–52. New York, 1963.

JOHNSON, GLENN L. "The Monetary and Nonmonetary Distinction," *Accounting Review,* Vol. XL (October, 1965), pp. 821–23.

The Choice of an Appropriate Price Index

HANNUM, WILLIAM H. and W. WASSERMAN. "General Adjustments and Price Level Measurement," *Accounting Review,* Vol. XLIII (April, 1968), pp. 295–302.

HENDRIKSEN, ELDON S. *Price-Level Adjustments of Financial Statements— An Evaluation and Case Study of Two Public Utility Firms,* chap. iii. Pullman: Washington State University Press, 1961.

TIERNEY, CECILIA. "The Index Number Problem," in *Accounting Research Study No. 6,* pp. 61–115.

TRACY, JOHN A. "A Dissent to the General Price-Level Adjustment Proposal," *Accounting Review,* Vol. XL (January, 1965), pp. 163–75.

Empirical Studies

DICKERSON, PETER J. *Business Income—A Critical Analysis.* Berkeley: Institute of Business and Economic Research, University of California, 1965.

HENDRIKSEN, ELDON S. *Price-Level Adjustments of Financial Statements—An Evaluation and Case Study of Two Public Utility Firms,* particularly chap. iv. Pullman: Washington State University Press, 1961.

LIVINGSTONE, JOHN LESLIE. "Electric Utility Plant Replacement Costs," *Accounting Review,* Vol. XLII (April, 1967), pp. 233–40.

ROSENFIELD, PAUL. "Accounting for Inflation," *Journal of Accountancy,* Vol. CXXVII (June, 1969), pp. 45–50.

SPENCER, CHARLES H., and THOMAS S. BARNHISEL. "A Decade of Price-Level Changes—The Effect on the Financial Statements of Cummins Engine Company," *Accounting Review,* Vol. XL (January, 1965), pp. 144–53.

chapter 8

Cash and Funds Flows

In the final analysis, cash flows into and out of a business enterprise are the most fundamental events upon which accounting measurements are based and upon which investors and creditors base their decisions. Cash attains its significance because it represents generalized purchasing power which can be transferred readily in an exchange economy to any individuals or organizations for their own specific needs in acquiring goods and services desired by them and available in the economy. By far the most significant method of transferring cash (claims for generalized purchasing power) is the bank check or other means of instructing a bank to transfer bank credit from one individual or organization to another. Currency and coins represent only a small fraction of the total means of transferring cash to and from a business firm.

With only a very few exceptions, business firms acquire asset rights and goods and services in order to produce other goods and services for sale to customers, with the intent of distributing interest and dividends to long-term investors. Very seldom do stockholders receive benefits from the firm in a form other than cash.

Most accounting measurements are based upon past, present, or expected flows of cash. Revenues are generally measured in terms of the net cash expected to be received from the sale of goods or services. Expenses are generally measured in terms of the cash paid or expected to be paid for goods and services used by the firm. Accruals represent the allocation to the current period of expected future receipts or disbursements for services. Deferrals represent the allocation to current and future periods of past receipts and disbursements for goods and services.

The theoretical measurements of assets, liabilities, and income are also based heavily on actual and expected cash flows. As will be discussed in Chapter 9, the present value of an asset is frequently defined as the discounted expected net receipts to be derived from the asset. Liabilities can be measured in terms of the discounted amount to be paid in the future. One of the definitions of income discussed in Chapter 5 was that it represents the excess of the discounted expected net cash distributions to stockholders as measured at the end of the period over the same expectations at the beginning of the period plus actual dividend payments.

Income and balance sheet items measured on the accrual basis are usually proposed and accepted on the basis that they provide useful measurements of firm efficiency and relevant information for the prediction of future firm activity and dividend payments. Because of the deliberate and inherent biases created by the use of allocation procedures and historical transaction prices, there is some doubt that traditional accounting methods are adequate to report the complex economic activities of today. One way of avoiding some of these biases is to emphasize the reporting of cash flows, supplemented by other information and appropriate classifications, to permit the users of financial statements to make their own predictions regarding the future.

While very few writers advocate a complete elimination of income statement and balance sheet reporting, many suggest a preference for certain procedures on the basis of their approximation of cash flows and their avoidance of allocations to several periods that appear to be arbitrary in nature. For example, the use of direct costing of inventories, the flow-through method of treating interperiod tax differences (nonallocation), and the tax reduction method of handling the investment credit are all advocated at least in part because they are more closely related to the actual cash flows.

Historical cash flow information as well as budgeted cash flows may provide relevant information, either alone or as supplements to conventional financial reports for investors and creditors in their evaluation of the firm and in their predictions of expected dividend payments. A step in this direction is the use of funds flow statements, although the relevance of the information and the type of information communicated by these reports is dependent somewhat upon the concept of "funds" employed and the extent of the information presented.

Since not all cash flows are necessarily relevant for external reporting, and since many financial events and relationships do not result from cash flows, statements presenting different concepts of funds flows are frequently suggested or used for financial reporting. The several concepts and objectives of funds flows are discussed following the discussion of cash flow information.

THE OBJECTIVE OF CASH FLOW INFORMATION

One of the main objectives of cash flow statements is to provide information which will (1) permit the investor or creditor to predict the amount of cash likely to be distributed to him in the future in the form of dividends or interest, and in the form of liquidation distributions or repayment of principal; and (2) permit him to evaluate the probable risk. The evaluation of these future distributions and risk is relevant to investors and creditors because it is the basic information required in the determination of the present value of securities.

The investment model is basically a choice among available alternatives which can be reduced to a common denominator by computing the utility-adjusted present value of the expected gain or loss from acquiring and holding a security for a given period of time. This basic model states that the net subjective gain or loss to be obtained from a specific investment in stock or bonds is the sum of the present values of the expected cash distributions to the investor less the current price of the security. Since the cash distributions (particularly for dividends) in any one year can be represented by a probability distribution, an expected value for each year must be selected and adjusted by a certainty equivalent factor determined by the investor's personal utility preference for risk. Both the expected cash flow for each year and the expected opportunity discount factor should also be adjusted for marginal tax effect.[1]

Cash Flows and the Prediction of Dividends

Net income is frequently claimed to be an indication of the ability of the firm to pay dividends. However, the dividend decision must take into consideration many other factors, such as the availability of cash; the opportunities and objectives of the firm with respect to capital growth and expansion; and the policies of the firm regarding external financing, as well as ability of the firm to obtain outside funds. But one of the greater deficiencies of reported net income as a predictor of future dividends is that it may be considerably biased, because of the inability in many cases to obtain a proper matching of expenses with revenues, and because of the inability to find appropriate allocation procedures for past and future cash outlays which may benefit many periods. The use of cash

---

[1] This basic investment valuation model as suggested by the American Accounting Association Committee on External Reporting can be expressed as follows:

$$P_{ok} = \sum_{i=1}^{n_k} \left(\frac{(\alpha_{ik}) \ (D_{ik}) \ (1 - T_{ik})}{[1 - r(1 - T_{ik})]^i} \right) - I_0$$

P_{ok} = The subjective present value of the gain or loss to be obtained by an investor (k) for a specific investment at time period (0).
n_k = The time horizon used by the investor (k).
D_{ik} = The expected value of each cash distribution to the investor in year (i).
α_{ik} = The adjustment for the investor's utility preference for risk.
T_{ik} = The expected marginal tax rate for each cash flow.
r = The before tax opportunity rate for a riskless investment.
I_0 = The investment price at the time of decision.

From: Committee on External Reporting, "An Evaluation of External Reporting Practices," *Accounting Review*, Supplement to Vol. XLIV (1969), pp. 80–83.

See also Alexander A. Robicheck and Stewart C. Myers, *Optimal Financing Decisions* (Englewood Cliffs, N.J.: Prentice-Hall, Inc., 1965), chaps. v and vi.

flows as a predictor of future dividends, therefore, avoids the biases of reported net income, except to the extent that the timing of certain cash receipts and disbursements can be altered by management.

One of the difficulties in using historical cash flows as a predictor of future cash dividends is that many cash flows including dividends are interdependent. For example, available cash or expected cash receipts may be used for capital expenditures or for the repayment of debt as well as for the payment of dividends. Therefore, plans and expectations of management, as well as other information such as a statement of the resources and commitments of the firm, should supplement the cash flow information.

While the dividend decision of the firm each period is based on many complex factors, the investor may be able to obtain some assistance in the prediction of future dividends if he has information regarding the following types of flows: (a) cash flows relating to the basic current operations of the enterprise, (b) recurring or occasional cash flows unrelated to current operations but arising from either unexpected events or the desire to maintain a good environment for the firm in the future, (c) cash flows required to increase operating facilities and inventories or obtained from their sale when not needed for future operations, (d) cash obtained from or repaid to bondholders and stockholders as a part of firm financing, and (e) payments of interest and dividends to investors with priority claims. Dividends to common stockholders can be looked on as that amount available after the above expected flows are predicted. However, as indicated above, many of these flows are interrelated, and consideration should also be given to the needs of the firm for holding cash or increasing its cash holdings. In addition to the knowledge of past cash flows, the investor should have information regarding the philosophy or attitudes of the firm regarding the payment of dividends and regarding the investment or reinvestment of cash available or obtainable by additional financing.

In making predictions regarding future cash flows from operations, it is important to start with historical information classified according to the behavioral characteristics of the cash flow requirements. For example, the various types of cash flows relating to operations should be classified according to major product groups or product categories, so that predictions can be made regarding future demand for the products and regarding special cost relationships related to specific product groups. Geographic distribution of source and sales of products may also be significant, particularly where foreign countries are involved. Furthermore, classifications of cash flows should permit a prediction of changes in future flows which are related to other known or predictable variables. For example, cash flows that are committed should be classified separately from cash flows that are variably related to the quantity of sales or production.

One of the most difficult of cash requirements to predict is that needed for capital expenditures. Depreciation as generally computed for measuring income is not relevant for this purpose because replacements are not necessarily related to either the cost of items acquired in the past nor to period allocations of this cost. While capital expenditure patterns in the past may provide some guide to the future, expectations of management regarding its plans and opportunities would greatly assist this prediction.

The use of historical cash flow information in the making of predictions regarding future dividends is, therefore, a complex process. However, the reliability of the predictions which take cash flow information into account may be considerably greater than predictions made from historical income data alone. If this is true, and some empirical studies have already provided evidence that it is, the presentation of historical cash flow information in external financial reports should be encouraged. Furthermore, the disclosure of budgeted cash receipts and expenditures for the following period and plans for long-run capital outlays and long-run financing should be of aid to investors and investment analysts, particularly if past plans can be compared with the actual results of the same planning period.

THE PRESENTATION OF CASH FLOW INFORMATION

The presentation of historical cash flows should not be considered a part of the presentation or computation of net income. That is, revenues and expenses should not be computed according to specific procedures on the ground that these procedures result in amounts that are more closely related to the actual cash flows. For example, the flow-through method of presenting interperiod tax differences and the direct costing of manufactured goods are occasionally proposed as valid because they reflect more closely the actual cash flows. While these methods may be relevant for other reasons, as discussed elsewhere in this book, they should not be included in the income statement merely because they reflect cash flows. Although the income statement and cash flow statement are related to the same information over time, they represent different information and different concepts.

Because of the leads and lags between cash receipts and disbursements on the one hand, and the operational activities giving rise to these cash flows on the other, a cash flow statement for a single period has little significance. A comparison of cash flows over several periods is necessary to begin to observe the behavior of recurring flows and to predict the likelihood and frequency of nonrecurring flows. Receipts and disbursements relating to the recurring activities of the enterprise should be classified by product groups and according to whether they are committed or discretionary. Capital expenditures should be classified in such a way that the effect on future cash flows can be predicted. That is, major expenditures that are nonrecurring or discretionary should be classified in such a way that the reader can predict whether the effect will be a replacement or continuation of existing operations, an improvement in efficiency that will reduce future annual expenditures, or an addition to capacity that will permit an expansion of future receipts.

One of the major difficulties with a reliance on cash flow information is that occasionally, significant transactions are carried out without a transfer of cash. For example, common or preferred stock may be exchanged for additional capacity or for new businesses, as in the acquisition of an operating firm to continue as a subsidiary. In these cases, supplementary information should be provided to indicate the extent to which the cash flows in the future are likely to be different from the cash flows in the past. Furthermore, supplementary information should be presented whenever new contracts or changes in contracts, such as pension commitments or long-term leases, will affect future cash flows.

FUNDS FLOW CONCEPTS

One of the main difficulties with the presentation of cash flow information for evaluative and predictive purposes is that many cash receipts and disbursements over short periods of time, or even over a year, do not behave in a predictive way or even in a way that describes the basic cash flows over time. For example, the receipt or payment of cash may frequently be advanced or deferred for short periods of time at the request of suppliers or customers, or to permit a better control of the firm's cash position. Furthermore, the firm may engage in many types of cash transactions, such as borrowing from the bank on short-term loans and transfers of cash to short-term securities and back again into cash, all of which are incidental to the basic operations of the enterprise. An additional problem arises in the definition of cash itself. Currency and bank deposits are the most common types of money claims considered to be cash; but many near-cash items, such as savings accounts and U.S. Treasury notes or short-term certificates, may be the equivalent of cash.

An alternative to the presentation of cash receipts and disbursements is the use of a concept of funds which may be interpreted narrowly or broadly. In the narrow sense, the term "funds" may be used to represent the short-term monetary assets, a concept which has the advantage of eliminating from the reports transactions which represent the conversion of monetary assets into cash, or transfers of cash into near-cash items. A second alternative is to define "funds" as net monetary assets, which has the advantage of eliminating the short-term borrowing and repayment of cash without affecting the basic availability of cash for other uses. A more traditional view of the concept of funds is that it represents the net current resources of the firm conventionally defined as net working capital. A much broader concept is to treat funds as representing all of the economic resources of the firm. While this broad view has the advantage of disclosing changes in the structure of the firm's resources, it has the disadvantage of not disclosing the extent to which cash may be available for distribution to stockholders or for commitment to other uses.

Short-Term Monetary Asset Flows

Monetary assets that represent resources readily convertible into cash can be treated for practicable purposes as cash or near-cash items. In situations where the firm has excess cash for immediate needs, it may transfer these funds to interest-bearing notes or deposits or invest them in marketable securities. On the other hand, if additional cash is needed at the present, these marketable securities may be sold and receivables may generally be converted into cash upon short notice by factoring or discounting, with little cost to the firm, even though the amount is not collectible from the customers at the present time. Therefore, transfers into noncash monetary items or from these items into cash may be a part of cash management but provide little information regarding the longer run sources and needs for cash.

A second advantage of the monetary asset concept is that it is consistent with the concept of constructive receipt. An increase in a monetary asset represents a constructive receipt of cash if such asset is readily convertible into cash. A rigid adherence to the cash concept results in the making of arbitrary distinctions between cash and near-cash items. Particularly from the point of view of making predictions and decisions based on cash and funds flow information, the presentation of inflows and outflows of monetary current assets may be more relevant than a presentation of cash flows only. However, while monetary asset flows may be more relevant than cash receipts and disbursements, care must be taken in both the definition and the classification of the specific items included in the concept. Securities that are marketable should be included only if they are held as temporary depositaries of funds. That is, if they are held as cash resources, their sale and subsequent use in the acquisition of plant and equipment or the repayment of long-term debt is essentially only one transaction. Thus, with a proper classification, a short-term monetary asset flow concept may be more meaningful than a strict cash flow concept.

Net Monetary Asset Flows

A further refinement of the funds concept is obtained by subtracting short-term obligations requiring cash from the current monetary assets. The advantage of this definition is that many of the cash transactions relating to short-term borrowing or the repayment of short-term debt are irrelevant to the basic decisions of investors and creditors regarding the firm. That is, by netting many of these short-term cash movements, the more basic cash flows can be highlighted. This is close to what is frequently referred to as net quick assets or net monetary current assets. However, the inclusion of the current portion of long-term debt among the current liabilities leads to a distortion of current net monetary asset flows. The reclassification of long-term debt is not the equivalent of a cash or monetary asset outflow.

A further advantage of this concept is that short-term monetary obligations represent constructive outflows of cash. The timing of these payments can frequently be altered by agreements with creditors or by short-term bank financing. Therefore, the more basic cash movements can be disclosed by eliminating the transactions resulting from the management of net current monetary assets.

The effect of increases and decreases of short-term obligations on the availability of cash for different purposes is not apparent without further analysis. For example, how long is a "short term"? In answering this question, consideration should be given to the relevance of the information. The traditional concept of one year is not necessarily a relevant criterion. In many cases, obligations due after about six months are not neutral with respect to the availability of funds for other purposes. Cash obtained under a six- or nine-month loan should probably be reported as a funds inflow and the repayment of the loan as a funds outflow, since this may be relevant information for the predictions and decisions of investors. An arbitrary cut-off point is difficult to make without considerably more information regarding the relevance of the information. However, a disclosure of the terms of loans outstanding would be of assistance in predicting future cash outflows. Although intent is frequently difficult to determine, it may be relevant in making cash flow projections. For example, short-term loans that are intended to be repaid from the proceeds of the sale of bonds or stock should be considered to be long term from the start, as they are not neutral with respect to the availability or disposition of cash.

In summary, the definition of funds as net current monetary assets (excluding the current portion of long-term debt and other obligations that are intended to be converted into long-term obligations) has many advantages over a strict cash flow concept. Increases in receivables arising from the sale of goods and services can be considered a constructive receipt of cash, although some minor adjustments for cash discounts and uncollectible accounts may be necessary. Increases in accounts payable may be considered to represent the constructive payment for goods and services received. The collection of receivables and the actual payment of accounts payable, on the other hand, represent conversions from one monetary form into another rather than actual funds flows. Short-term borrowings and their repayment represent cash flows, but their elimination from the reporting of funds flows can be supported on the ground that they do not represent relevant transactions that will affect the ability of the firm to pay dividends and interest and repay long-term obligations over the relevant time horizon.

Working Capital Concept of Funds

The most traditional concept of funds is its definition as net working capital. In this definition "funds" represent the net current resources available to the firm or expected to become available for distribution or recommitment. Funds are increased whenever current assets are increased or current liabilities are decreased, when these changes are not offset by changes in other working capital items. Funds are decreased, on the other hand, when current assets are decreased or current liabilities are increased without affecting other current accounts.

Several advantages of the working capital concept of funds have been suggested from time to time by well-known writers on accounting principles and procedures.[2] These include the following: (1) A funds statement constructed on the basis of the working capital concept is readily articulated with the income statement and the balance sheet. (2) It follows closely the traditional definitions used in financial reporting, and therefore it is more understandable to the users of financial statements who are acquainted with conventional accounting procedures. (3) It tends to concentrate the information presented on the infrequent inter-firm transactions rather than the day-to-day transactions resulting from regular operations. (4) It has been proposed as a means of presenting the general liquidity of the firm.

The above propositions are only partially true, depending on the objectives of the funds statement. While a funds statement based on the working capital concept is usually a brief presentation, many significant interfirm transactions are not disclosed. For example, significant additions to inventories financed by short-term notes would not be shown because the two items are offset in the computation of the net change in working capital. Furthermore, transactions not affecting working capital, such as the acquisition of plant and equipment by the issuance of common stock, would not be included in the statement. Therefore, the funds statement in this presentation would not disclose structural changes in the financial relationships in the firm nor major changes in policy regarding investments in current assets and short-term financing.

---

[2] See L. S. Rosen and Don T. DeCoster, " 'Funds' Statements: A Historical Perspective," *Accounting Review,* Vol. XLIV (January, 1969), particularly pp. 129–30.

One of the major disadvantages of the working capital concept of funds is that nonmonetary assets, such as inventories and prepaid expenses, and a few nonmonetary liabilities, such as advance receipts for services to be performed by the firm in the future (frequently referred to as "unearned income" or "deferred credits to income"), are included.[3] The inclusion of inventories and prepaid expenses in the concept of "funds" is particularly disturbing if the information is to be relevant to investors and creditors in their predictions of future funds and cash flows. The main reason for this is that the dollars assigned to inventories and prepaid expenses are the result of allocations of cost or other measurement over several periods. An increase in the reported amount of these items, for example, could not be interpreted as an increase in general purchasing power available for other uses. An exception to this might be made in the case of inventories such as refined gold and other precious metals, and work performed under cost-plus-fixed-fee contracts, in which cases the reported measurement may be expressed in terms of the cash expected to be received in the near future, thus making them similar to receivables.[4]

The All Financial Resources Concept of Funds

One of the basic objections to the working capital concept of funds is that many interfirm transactions are omitted from the funds statement merely because they do not directly affect working capital. Thus, important information regarding changes in the resources of the firm and in the financial structure of the firm are omitted. A suggested alternative to alleviate this omission is an all resources concept of funds that would permit the inclusion of such transactions as the acquisition of property in exchange for stock or bonds, the receipt of property as a gift, and the exchange of noncurrent assets for other noncurrent items.

An advantage of the all financial resources concept is that some of the most significant transactions would otherwise be omitted from the funds statement, or acquisitions would be grossly understated by presenting only the cash exchanged in the transaction rather than the entire transaction. While writers differ regarding the amount of detail that should be shown in the funds statement, working capital is frequently presented as a net item. Therefore, a decrease in working capital would be a source of funds and an increase in working capital would be an application or use of funds. Since all resources are taken into consideration, sources of

---

[3] Advance receipts for services are classified as nonmonetary because the obligation is expected to be discharged by providing a given quantity of specified services rather than a specified quantity of cash representing general purchasing power.

[4] See Maurice Moonitz, "Reporting the Flow of Funds," *Accounting Review,* Vol. XXXI (July, 1956), pp. 375–85.

funds must by definition equal the applications of funds, rather than a single concept of funds such as cash or working capital representing the net increase or decrease in funds.

A major disadvantage of the all financial resources concept of funds is that the concept of financial resources is vague and ill defined. The separate items included in the classifications of sources and applications of funds do not necessarily represent increases and decreases of resources. Therefore, there is no direct disclosure of the extent to which the total resources of the firm have changed during the period. A second disadvantage is that acquisitions of property in exchange for stock cannot be measured with the same degree of reliability as assets acquired for cash. Therefore, the summation of gross additions to plant and equipment, for example, may result in misleading interpretations of the amount of resources acquired.

The All Significant Financial Events Approach

One of the interpretations of the all resources concept is that the funds statement should disclose the effects of all significant interfirm transactions.[5] In effect, the funds statement is prepared so that it reflects all material changes in balance sheet accounts from the end of one period to the end of the next, with the exception that all intrafirm transactions are omitted. This has the effect of treating current assets and current liabilities as separate items. Therefore, significant changes in the working capital section of the balance sheet would be disclosed, rather than treating working capital as a net item. For example, increases in receivables and inventories would be reported as separate changes even though they are offset by increases in short-term liabilities.

By presenting the material changes in specific assets and liabilities, the major shifts in the resources of the firm and their financing can be highlighted. Many of these changes can be observed from a comparative balance sheet, but the balance sheet figures show only the net change in specific classifications. For example, expenditures for new plant and equipment may be difficult to compute from balance sheet figures if several types of transactions—such as sale, abandonment, trade-in, and acquisition by merger in addition to acquisition by purchase—all occur during the same period. Likewise, increases and decreases in capital stock accounts may be a result of a combination of transactions, including the purchase of treasury shares, the sale of new shares, and bond conversions. All of these types of transactions should be disclosed in a funds statement. Generally, however, current practice does not disclose in the funds

---

[5] See for example Donald A. Corbin and Russell Taussig, "The AICPA Funds Statement Study," *Journal of Accountancy*, Vol. CXIV (July, 1962), pp. 57–62.

statement the reclassifications of major items of long-term debt or stockholders' equity, such as the conversions of bonds and preferred stock into common stock. If the funds statement is to reflect structural changes in the financial relationships in the firm, these types of transactions should probably be included even though they might be disclosed elsewhere in the financial statements or in notes thereto.

Accounting Principles Board *Opinion No. 3*

APB *Opinion No. 3* was significant in its pronouncement in 1963 in that the frequency of appearance of funds statements in annual reports increased considerably after this date. But in recommending that the statement be presented as supplementary information, and recommending that it be optional whether or not it is covered in the report of the independent accountant, the Board was less forceful than it could have been.

The concept of funds recommended in APB *Opinion No. 3* for external reporting is the all significant events concept described above. That is, it recommends the all resources concept in order to include in the statement interfirm transactions not affecting working capital, such as the acquisition of property through the issuance of securities. But it also recommends that individual current asset and liability changes should be shown separately when they are material and not otherwise disclosed in the financial statements. Therefore, the objective is to show the more significant financial events of the period.

While it is not explicitly stated, the *Opinion* implies that depreciation should not be added back to net income to give the impression that it is in any sense a source of funds. There is also an aversion to the presentation separately of the funds flow from operations frequently referred to as "cash flow." Since this "cash flow" is generally derived by adding depreciation to the net income, it represents only one source of funds and may give the impression that by itself it is a good predictor of future dividends, since it is presented as "cash flow per share," and may be given more prominence than the earnings per share figure.

AN EVALUATION OF CASH AND FUNDS FLOW CONCEPTS

The concept of funds most meaningful for external reporting is the one most relevant for the predictions and decisions of investors, creditors, and other outside users of financial statements. However, different types of information can be obtained with the different concepts, so that the choice of a single funds concept depends upon the objectives to be achieved. One of these objectives is the presentation of information that will permit the investor to make predictions regarding future cash distributions. In meeting this objective, the presentation of historical and possibly projected cash flows should be of assistance to the investor if the flows are classified according to their behavioral or predictive characteristics.

A substitution of the current monetary asset concept for cash has considerable merit in meeting the above objective because of the interchangeability of several of the monetary items. For the same reason, the net current monetary asset concept may be useful for this purpose. However, in none of these cases should the cash or funds flow from operations be shown as a net figure or be presented by adding nonfund changes to the reported net income. The more significant predictions should be made from the basic operating inflows and outflows, such as cash or receivables obtained in exchange for goods and services sold and several classifications of cash or monetary asset outflows required to conduct the business on a continuing basis. This does not deny the importance of discretionary cash outflows for capital expenditures and corporate acquisitions, but it would at least recognize the fact that major inflows and outflows should be reported separately rather than being presented as net figures.

The working capital concept of funds is inferior to the cash or net current monetary asset concepts, not only because statements presented on this basis generally include a net figure for funds from operations but also because the working capital amount includes nonmonetary assets and occasionally nonmonetary liablities. These nonmonetary items are generally measured in terms of amounts resulting from historical transactions allocated to several periods; therefore they do not represent homogeneous items, and the net working capital figure is far from homogeneous since it includes both the nonmonetary and monetary items. As a result, the reported changes in working capital do not reflect changes in a fund that can be interpreted conceptually in a uniform manner. Since nonmonetary assets, particularly inventories and prepaid expenses, are included in working capital, the net change in working capital and the source of funds from operations are likely to be subject to bias because of the many acceptable methods of computing these items.

A second major objective of the funds statement is to present major changes in the types of resources held by the firm and significant changes in the financial structure of the firm. While some of this information can be obtained from comparative balance sheets, the funds statement can highlight these changes, particularly if the all resources concept and the presentation of all significant events is included. This objective, however, is not met by the traditional funds statement, even if it is modified to reflect a net monetary current asset concept of funds.

In conclusion, it appears that a single funds statement cannot meet all of the objectives required of it. It may be necessary to present two statements, one to provide the information to permit the prediction of future cash and monetary asset flows, and another to permit the prediction of the basic changes in the resources of the firm and its financial structure. The very brief summary of changes in funds traditionally presented in annual reports, however, should probably be supplanted by one or more statements of cash and resource flows that will meet the needs of investors and others in the evaluations and predictions necessary for the making of decisions. Considerable research and experimentation is necessary, however, before definitive conclusions can be reached regarding the basic objectives and the best means of meeting these objectives in financial statements.

SELECTED ADDITIONAL READING ON CHAPTER TOPICS

Cash Flow Concepts and Reporting

American Accounting Association, Committee on External Reporting. "An Evaluation of External Reporting Practices," *Accounting Review* (Supplement to Vol. XLIV, 1969), pp. 79–122.

BODENHORN, DIRAN. "A Cash-Flow Concept of Profit," *Journal of Finance*, Vol. XIX (March, 1964), pp. 16–31. Reprinted in STEPHEN H. ARCHER and CHARLES A. D'AMBROSIO, *The Theory of Business Finance: A Book of Readings*, pp. 6–21. New York: Macmillan Co., 1967.

MASON, PERRY. "Cash Flow Analysis and the Funds Statement," AICPA *Accounting Research Study No. 2*, part i. AICPA, 1961.

Historical Development of the Funds Statement

ROSEN, L. S. and DON T. DECOSTER. " 'Funds' Statements: A Historical Perspective," *Accounting Review*, Vol. XLIV (January, 1969), pp. 124–36.

Funds Concepts

ANTON, HECTOR R. *Accounting for the Flow of Funds*, chap. iv. Boston: Houghton Mifflin Co., 1962.

CORBIN, DONALD A. and RUSSELL TAUSSIG. "The AICPA Funds Statement Study," *Journal of Accountancy*, Vol. CXIV (July, 1962), pp. 57–62.

FESS, PHILIP E. and JERRY WEYGANDT. "The Funds Statements: Trends and Recommendations," *New York Certified Public Accountant*, Vol. XXXIX (February, 1969), pp. 120–24.

JAEDICKE, ROBERT K. and ROBERT T. SPROUSE. *Accounting Flows: Income, Funds, and Cash*, chaps. v and vi. Englewood Cliffs, N.J.: Prentice-Hall, Inc., 1965.

STAUBUS, GEORGE, JR. "Alternative Asset Flow Concepts," *Accounting Review*, Vol. XLI (July, 1966), pp. 397–412.

chapter 9

Assets and Their Measurement

As indicated in Chapter 3, asset valuation has been placed in a position subordinate to income determination. The balance sheet has become a step between two income statements, and asset valuation has become a process of computing how much to carry forward to future periods. But the balance sheet is still often called "a statement of financial position," and there is strong support for the development of a statement that will present clearly some relevant measurement or measurements of the resources and commitments of a firm at a specific point in time.

As discussed in the previous chapter, one of the objectives of financial reporting should be the presentation of information that will permit investors and creditors to make their own predictions regarding future cash flows from the firm. Information regarding the resources and commitments of the firm are relevant to these predictions. But the computation of period net income continues to be a significant reporting device interrelated with the concepts of resource valuation. Under the capital maintenance concepts of income discussed in Chapter 5, valuation is central to the problem of income determination. That is, income may be determined by analyzing the changes in net asset valuations between two points in time. But even under the transactions approach to income measurement, the income statement and the balance sheet are usually considered interdependent. This articulation of accounting statements and accounts is thought to be desirable because of the interrelationship of the information and the necessity for the systematic accumulation and presentation of accounting data. However, we should not lose sight of the several objectives of asset measurement. All objectives should be given equal treatment if this is possible. The purpose of this chapter is to appraise the various measurement concepts in light of the several objectives. Emphasis will be placed on assets and their valuation. Liabilities will be discussed in a later chapter.

THE NATURE OF ASSETS

If accounting theory is to provide the proper guidelines for the development of accounting thought and accounting principles, there is considerable merit in an explicit definition of assets and an analysis of the basic nature of all assets. A discussion of the classification and valuation of assets may be of help in this analysis, but the initial emphasis should be on the characteristics that are common to all assets. Several attempts have been made to tackle the problem in this way. One of the first to attempt a fairly comprehensive definition was Canning, who defined assets as follows:

> An asset is any future service in money or any future service convertible into money (except those services arising from contracts the two sides of which are proportionately unperformed) the beneficial interest in which is legally or equitably secured to some person or set of persons. Such a service is an asset only to that person or set of persons to whom it runs.[1]

While Canning felt that this expressed what accountants meant by the term "assets," he did feel that the definition would be improved if the parenthetical material were removed.

Because of the emphasis on the determination of income, many of the formal discussions of assets have stressed, either directly or indirectly, their nature as unallocated costs or as amounts to be carried forward to future periods. The Committee on Terminology of the American Institute of Accountants, for example, defined assets in 1941 and restated this definition in 1953 in AICPA *Accounting Terminology Bulletin No. 1* as follows:

> Something represented by a debit balance that is or would be properly carried forward upon a closing of books of account according to the rules or principles of accounting (provided such debit balance is not in effect a negative balance applicable to a liability), on the basis that it represents either a property right or value acquired, or an expenditure made which has created a property right or is properly applicable to the future. Thus, plant, accounts receivable, inventory, and a deferred charge are all assets in balance-sheet classification.[2]

The emphasis in this definition is clearly on the amount carried forward in a trial balance, with the main objective being the computation of periodic income. However, the qualification that it should represent a property right or value does limit the term somewhat by at least denying the inclusion of a loss.

More recently, official pronouncements and other writings have emphasized the definition of assets as service potentials or rights to prospective

---

[1] John B. Canning. *The Economics of Accountancy* (New York: Ronald Press Co., 1929), p. 22.

[2] Committee on Terminology, American Institute of Certified Public Accountants, "Review and Résumé," *Accounting Terminology Bulletin No. 1* (New York, 1953), p. 13.

benefits accruing to the business enterprise.[3] The Committee on Concepts and Standards of the American Accounting Association stated in 1957 that "assets are economic resources devoted to business purposes within a specific accounting entity; they are aggregates of service-potentials available for or beneficial to expected operations."[4] Sprouse and Moonitz defined assets similarly in *Accounting Research Study No. 3*, as follows: "Assets represent expected future economic benefits, rights to which have been acquired by the enterprise as a result of some current or past transaction."[5]

The emphasis on defining assets as rights to service potentials or as rights to future economic benefits is correct, because it provides for an all-inclusive definition and because it permits the problem of measurement to be treated separately. With this basic definition, the following characteristics are essential:

1. There must exist some specific right to future benefits or service potentials. Rights and services that have expired cannot be included. Also, the rights must have a positive benefit; rights with zero or negative potential benefits are not assets. If a building has lost its service value and if the cost of removal is exactly equal to the salvage value of the materials, the building is not an asset. In fact, if the cost of removal is greater than the salvage value, the valuation of the land would be reduced, but the building is not an asset or even a negative asset. However, the fact that the future value of a right or service potential may be uncertain does not remove it from the definition of assets. The uncertainty affects the valuation, but it changes the nature of the item only if the uncertainty is so great that the expected future benefit is zero or negative.

2. The rights must accrue to a specific individual or firm. The right to benefit from driving on public highways does not result in an asset. The right must permit the exclusion of others, although in some cases the right may be shared with specific firms or individuals. Ijiri placed considerable emphasis on *control* criteria in his definition of assets.[6] That is, assets are

---

[3] See for example, William J. Vatter, *The Fund Theory of Accounting and Its Implications for Financial Reports* (Chicago: University of Chicago Press, 1947), pp. 17–19; and Maurice Moonitz and Louis H. Jordan, *Accounting, an Analysis of Its Problems* (rev. ed.; New York: Holt, Rinehart & Winston, Inc., 1963), Vol. I, p. 163.

[4] AAA Committee on Accounting Concepts and Standards, *Accounting and Reporting Standards for Corporate Financial Statements and Preceding Statements and Supplements* (Columbus, Ohio: AAA, 1957), p. 3.

[5] Robert T. Sprouse and Maurice Moonitz, "A Tentative Set of Broad Accounting Principles for Business Enterprises," *Accounting Research Study No. 3* (New York: American Institute of Certified Public Accountants, 1962).

[6] Yuji Ijiri, *The Foundations of Accounting Measurement* (Englewood Cliffs, N.J.: Prentice-Hall, Inc., 1967), p. 70.

resources under the control of the entity. However, control can be interpreted broadly enough to include the ability of the firm to exercise its rights. Chambers also defined assets as means under the control of an entity, but he stressed the severable nature of the assets.[7] However, the severance characteristic is necessary only in Chambers' model to fit his measurement scheme. However, eventually the asset rights must be able to be transformed or utilized in such a way that other assets are severable.

3. There must be a legally enforceable claim to the rights or services. Services that can be withdrawn at will by some other firm or individual or by the government without compensation should not be included as assets. This does not mean, of course, that the firm must have a formal legal title or even a formal contract. In most cases, the accountant must rely upon the apparent intent of those who may have an interest in the asset rather than on the strict legality of the right.

In addition to the above characteristics, it should be noted that all assets are fundamentally identical regardless of the conventional classification. Cash and intangibles both provide rights to future benefits. The classification does not change the nature of the items as assets.

It should also be noted that the method of acquisition of the right is not relevant to the definition of an asset. Sanders, Hatfield, and Moore stated that a general condition applying to the listing of assets is "that the business has acquired them at a cost."[8] But most accountants would recognize as assets items arising from a gift or by discovery. The qualification expressed in the definition of assets quoted above from Sprouse and Moonitz that the rights must have been acquired as a result of some current or past transaction is also possibly irrelevant. The important characteristic is that the rights do exist at a specific date. Rights that have not as yet been obtained cannot, of course, be included among the assets. But the means by which the rights were obtained does not change the nature of the rights as assets.

THE OBJECTIVES OF ASSET MEASUREMENT

Accounting places emphasis on the quantification of economic relationships and economic changes in terms of a monetary unit. The quantification of assets in terms of a monetary unit is the valuation process, although other measures, such as physical units, may be relevant in

---

[7] Raymond J. Chambers, *Accounting, Evaluation and Economic Behavior* (Englewood Cliffs, N.J.: Prentice-Hall, Inc., 1966), p. 103.

[8] Thomas Henry Sanders, Henry Rand Hatfield, and Underhill Moore, *A Statement of Accounting Principles* (New York: American Institute of Accountants, 1938). Reprinted by the American Accounting Association in 1959, p. 58.

specific circumstances. And since some form of valuation is necessary in the accounting process, the objectives of valuation are in part the same as the objectives of accounting. The following will, therefore, summarize only briefly the objectives of valuation, with specific emphasis on the valuation of assets.

As with the income concept, we find that there is a definite advantage in the general acceptance of one all-pervasive concept. But a close analysis of valuation indicates that a single concept cannot serve all purposes equally well. The appropriate concept in each case requires the knowledge of who will use the information and for what purpose it will be used. While we are primarily interested in the development of valuation concepts useful to investors and included in external financial reports, creditors and management may require different concepts.

Valuation as a Method of Measuring Income

According to traditional accounting thought, at least since about 1930, the most important object of valuation has been to provide a measure for the determination of income. As discussed in Chapters 5 and 6, accounting income results from two basic concepts—the maintenance of capital and the matching of expenses with revenues. The capital maintenance concepts require the valuation of assets in terms of input costs or in terms of output values, and income arises from the increase in these values over time. In the transactions approach to income, the matching process requires an appropriate valuation of the inputs and outputs and a computation of the difference between input and output valuations as related to current transactions.

Valuation as a Measure of Accretion. According to the accretion concept, income accrues to a firm as asset valuations increase (or as liability valuations decrease) in the absence of capital transactions. Thus, income results from increasing valuations from input values to output values or from increasing discounted net realizable values to cash values. For example, inventory valuations, initially recorded at cost, may be increased to discounted net realizable values when the revenues have been earned, at the completion of production or at the time of sale. The discounted net realizable values may then be increased to cash values when the receivables are collectible or converted into cash. Other types of assets are increased in value by the accrual of interest receivable, rent receivable, and other claims to cash.

Note that the objective of valuation in this concept is to approach the output values and cash values as soon as the basic services have been performed by the firm and as soon as verifiable measurements can be obtained. By so doing, income is recorded on an accretion basis. The income may be separated into realized and unrealized elements, but this is not necessary to meet the objectives of this approach. The accretion approach results in an all-inclusive concept of income, but the extraordinary gains and losses can be separately reported by combining this with the transactions approach.

The importance of this approach to valuation is that the emphasis is on recognizing and recording all changes in value based on the best evidence of the final output value or the amount of cash finally to be received. Thus, net realizable value should take precedence over input values; current replacement cost may be closer to net value to the firm than historical cost; and historical cost may be relevant if it represents the current value to the firm. The type of valuation selected depends on whether or not the basic services have been performed by the firm, the verifiability and relative freedom from bias of the valuation procedure, the relative certainty of the expected conversion to cash, and the ability to measure related expenses. The objective of the valuation, however, remains: to measure the increment in specific asset valuations, rather than to present the value of the firm as a whole to the investors or to any other group.

Valuation as a Step in the Matching Process. The conventional approach to valuation is to record monetary assets on an accretion basis and record nonmonetary assets in terms of input values until they are allocated to expenses and either matched with product revenues or charged to a specific period. Therefore, the objective of valuation for nonmonetary assets is to obtain a basis for the computation of the gross operating margin and the income from all transactions. This computation is the difference between total revenues and the input value of all expenses associated with these revenues or with the period.

Total operating income results from the assumed matching of valuations in terms of historical costs with the related revenues. With changes in the value of the monetary unit, a better measure of income may be obtained by restating the historical costs in terms of dollars representing the same purchasing power as the current revenue. A separation of current operating income from holding gains and losses may also be obtained by valuing the inputs in terms of current replacement costs.

Two basic approaches to valuation for income determination purposes are: (1) The emphasis may be placed on the valuation of the inputs as they expire. For example, the cost of goods sold may be valued on a current basis, by the use of Lifo or current replacement costs, while the ending inventories are left in terms of residuals. (2) The nonmonetary assets may be restated at the balance sheet date or periodically during the year, permitting an appropriate matching as these assets expire. The application of these procedures, particularly to inventories and plant and equipment, will be discussed at greater length in the following chapters.

The main difficulty with using the matching process as a basis for determining asset valuations is that most enterprise activities do not lend themselves to accurate matching. As a result, many, if not most, of the allocations of asset valuations to products or expenses are arbitrary in nature. Therefore, the valuations carried forward have no particular relationship to any specific future benefits. This has led to the adoption of many procedures that cannot be supported on logical grounds. The use of the deferred charge classification and the allocation of the cost of intangibles are examples which cast considerable doubt on the usefulness of the matching concept to provide relevant information to investors and other interested parties.

The Presentation of Financial Position to Investors

The summarization of information regarding the resources, commitments, and equities of a firm is generally presented to stockholders and other investors at periodic intervals as one of the objectives of accounting. But accountants are not agreed on the valuation concepts that should be used. The term "financial position" is often used to mean the balance sheet as it is drawn from accounting ledgers and based on current accounting conventions and accounting practice. As a result, the statement of financial position is a residual statement—a step between two income statements. As such, it provides little information useful to investors in the evaluation of the future prospects of the firm. An alternative view is that the statement of financial position presented to investors should be restored to a more useful status by including valuation concepts and other information that would be more meaningful for investment decisions.

The Balance Sheet as a Step between Two Income Statements. With the emphasis on the income statement, the balance sheet has become a statement of residual amounts to be carried forward to future periods. It is said to be a point of arrival and departure in the accounting process, but it is related more closely to the past than to the future. Monetary accounts such as cash and receivables may represent current purchasing power or expectations of future funds flows, but the nonmonetary accounts reflect only past costs and residuals resulting from past amortization and expensing procedures.

In spite of these deficiencies, there are several positive claims for the residual type of balance sheet. *First,* it is claimed that the conventional balance sheet provides for the accountability of the dollars invested by the owners. Actual dollars invested can be traced either through enterprise operations or to residual valuations at the end of the period. Thus, fraud and embezzlement can be detected more readily than if other valuation concepts were substituted. *Second,* one of the functions of the position statement is to summarize the nature of the operations of the enterprise and the nature of the monetary assets and unused services of the firm. It is claimed that the process of determining value is too subjective and that the best that can be accomplished is a fairly complete disclosure of the economic relationships by the use of adequate terminology and descriptions. It is also claimed that the nature of operations of the firm can be disclosed by the use of supplementary statements such as the funds statement. *Third*, it is claimed that history has shown that when subjective valuations are permitted in the balance sheet not only does the balance sheet become less informative but the income statement also becomes distorted. Thus, it is better to have one statement—the income statement—objectively determined and understandable than to have both statements misleading and failing in comparability. In the view of the author, these claims are completely inadequate in supporting the residual type of balance sheet.

The Position Statement as a Means of Prediction.   As discussed in the previous chapter and in Chapter 5, investors are clearly interested in predicting the future flows to stockholders in the form of dividends and other distributions, in order to make decisions regarding the purchase or sale of shares of the enterprise. While a series of income statements and cash and funds flow statements are relevant for this purpose, a position statement should also provide relevant information for the making of these predictions. In discussing the ideal meaning of "financial position," Canning stated:

Beyond doubt the accountants would like to mean by "financial position" a position declared by direct positive measures of funds to be provided by enterprise operations.[9]

In order for a statement of financial position to provide information relevant to a prediction of future cash flows, it should include quantitative measurements of resources and commitments for comparisons with other periods or with other firms. The quantities of resources available to the firm, however, are relevant to predictions only if they are related to the cash flows likely to be generated by the firm. That is, valuations of assets held by the firm can provide relevant information only if the investor can detect some relationship between such measurements and expected cash flows. In some cases, the relevant attribute of available resources may be measured in terms of current replacement costs. In other cases, the best measure may be the current output values or some other available measurement.

The Presentation of the Claims of the Several Equity Holders.   According to traditional accounting concepts, the invested capital of a firm is equal to the valuation of the net assets of the enterprise. While this figure

---

[9] Canning, *op. cit.*, p. 191.

cannot represent the value of the firm as a whole to the equity holders, it is possible that the accounting statements may be able to give the equity holders some information regarding their relative rights and risks. Commonly, several classes of equity holders are represented in the capital structure of a firm, including some whose rights may change through the conversion of bonds into stock, or of one class into another, or by the exercise of warrants. Many of these relationships cannot be described by single measurements or even in quantitative terms, but certain valuation procedures may provide at least partial information, such as the relative amount of buffer that may exist for the protection of equity holders with priority rights.

Valuation for Use by Creditors

In the early part of the 20th century and before, one of the major objectives of the balance sheet was the presentation of financial information to creditors. Because of the lack of reliable information, creditors had to rely heavily on any indication of the security of the loan. Liquidation values were thus considered more important than other valuation concepts, and the doctrine of conservatism gained a strong influence in reporting. But if the probability of enterprise continuity is good, current output values are probably more important than liquidation values for an evaluation of the enterprise by creditors. Current debt will generally be paid from funds becoming available to the firm in the future rather than from the forced sale of assets now held. However, if it should become apparent that a firm will not have continuity of existence, the expected conversion values may be at or close to forced liquidation levels.

Valuation for Use by Management

For managerial purposes, the valuation process should provide information relevant to the making of operating decisions. But the information required by management is not necessarily the same as that required by investors and creditors. While investors and creditors are interested primarily in predicting the future course of the business, from an evaluation of the past and from other information, management must continually make decisions that determine the future course of action. Therefore, management has greater need for information regarding valuations arising from different courses of action. For example, managements must continually compare the benefits of using assets in the firm with their liquidation values. Also, opportunity costs, marginal or differential costs, and present values from expected differential cash flows are relevant for many types of management decisions. But just because they are relevant to managerial decisions does not necessarily mean that they are also relevant to the decisions of investors and creditors. Therefore, these valuations do not have to be reported in the position statement; they can be made readily available to management in supplementary reports. These uses for valuation concepts will be treated only briefly in the following discussion.

VALUATION CONCEPTS

Valuation in accounting is the process of assigning meaningful quantitative monetary amounts to assets. Since the business enterprise is not a consuming unit, economic values based on subjective utility are not relevant in accounting. Therefore, the relevant valuation concepts should be based on exchange or conversion values. There are, however, two markets in which the firm operates, and therefore two types of exchange values—output values and input values. Output values reflect the expected funds to be received by the firm in the future, based particularly on the exchange price for the firm's product or output. This term is used broadly, however, in order to include fund items and receivables. Input values reflect some measure of the consideration given up in obtaining the assets used by the firm in its operations—the inputs.

Canning drew a distinction between direct and indirect valuation that is similar in some respects to the distinction between the concepts of output and input values.[10] Direct valuation applies to those assets for which the conversion to future cash flows is capable of being measured with some reliability. Indirect valuation must be applied when there is no means of estimating directly the funds to be provided. Canning stated that it would be desirable, ideally, to have direct measures of all assets.[11]

A direct measure of the valuation of all assets is, however, impossible, because most of the resources of a firm contribute jointly to the net cash flows of the firm. However, in a few cases the best concept of valuation is one that is related to the expected future net receipt of funds directly associated with the asset. In those cases where there is no direct association with future cash flows, one or more alternative valuation concepts may provide better information regarding the quantity of resources available to the firm. Output values (exit prices) measured in current markets may be substituted for expectations of future net receipts in many cases, and it may be argued that they are more relevant or more verifiable than valuations based on expectations. On the other hand, many assets are held by a firm for use without any direct relationship to future cash receipts. In such cases, input values or entry prices are more relevant for describing the resources of the firm and for providing

---

10 *Ibid.*, pp. 182–83.

11 *Ibid.*, p. 184.

information which may permit rational decisions by investors and creditors.

Exchange Output Values

Output values are based on the amount of cash or the value of other consideration to be received when an asset or its service finally leaves the firm by an exchange or conversion. Those assets that represent money or claims to money should be expressed in terms of their current values. What can or will be done with the money is not relevant at this point. Nonmonetary assets that have fairly certain exchange prices likely to be received at specific future periods can be treated similarly to receivables. When the future exchange price is less certain, a current exchange output price may be substituted. And in those cases where the normal exchange market has disappeared or where circumstances require disposition in a different market, forced liquidation values may be relevant.

Discounted Future Cash Receipts or Service Potentials.   When expected cash receipts require a waiting period, the present value of these receipts is less than the actual amount expected to be received. And the longer the waiting period, the smaller is the present value. Conceptually, the present value is determined by the process of discounting. But discounting involves not only an estimate of the true interest, which is the opportunity cost of the money, but also an estimate of the probability of receiving the expected amount. The longer the waiting period, the greater is the uncertainty that the amount will be received.

This valuation concept was considered a useful abstraction by the Committee on Accounting Concepts and Standards of the American Accounting Association in its 1957 statement, as indicated by the following:

The value of an asset is the money-equivalent of its service potentials. Conceptually, this is the sum of the future market prices of all streams of service to be derived, discounted by probability and interest factors to their present worths.[12]

Sprouse and Moonitz also recognized the discount factor in *Accounting Research Study No. 3.* In their discussion of the measurement of assets, they state:

As a general rule, the valuation of these assets (money or claims to money) should be based on the amount of cash into which they will be converted, that is, their discounted future exchange prices.[13]

---

[12] Committee on Accounting Concepts and Standards, *op. cit.*, p. 4.

[13] Sprouse and Moonitz, *op. cit.*, p. 24.

This valuation concept requires the knowledge or estimation of three basic factors—the amount or amounts to be received, the discount factor, and the time period or periods involved. The following examples demonstrate the technical process of valuation when these factors can be quantified. In the first example, assume that $1,000 is to be received at the end of three years. If the appropriate discount factor is 6 percent, the present value of the asset is $839.62. Using v for the present value of the asset, a for the monetary value to be received, i for the discount factor, and n for the number of years of waiting, the formula for the computation of the present value is

$$v = a(1 + i)^{-n}, \text{ or } v = \frac{a}{(1 + i)^n}$$

This can be expressed graphically as follows:

Present Value	Amount to Be Received and Period		
$839.62			$1,000
	1	2	3

If the amounts to be received are at different time periods, each amount must be discounted at the appropriate discount rate for the specific waiting period. For example, suppose that $500 is to be received at the end of the first period, $400 at the end of the second, and $300 at the end of the third.[14] The present value of this series can be expressed graphically as follows:

Present Value	Years and Amounts to Be Received		
	1	2	3
$ 471.70	$500		
356.00		$400	
251.89			$300
Total $1,079.59	$500	$400	$300

This type of computation can be expressed by the following formula, where P_0 is the present discounted value of the expected cash flow at the time t_0, R_j represents the expected cash to be received at the end of year j (representing each of the years from t_1 through t_n), and i is the opportunity rate of interest.

$$P_0 = \sum_{j=1}^{n} \frac{R_j}{(1 + i)^j}$$

[14] It should be recognized that these receipts are net amounts. For example, the gross receipts at the end of the first year might be $1,100 and additional outlays might be $600. If the additional outlays are required at time periods different from the gross receipts, each must be discounted separately; the present value of the asset would then be the excess of the discounted gross receipts over the discounted additional outlays.

While the interest rate in the above formula is assumed to be a constant, the formula can easily be changed to include the case where different opportunity rates are expected for each of the periods.

The above formula is similar to the one presented in the previous chapter[15] which expressed the present value of a firm to an investor as the discounted value of expected future distributions to stockholders. However, two basic differences are that in the above formula, the individual income tax adjustment and the utility preference for risk factors are omitted. The omission of the risk factor makes the formula less complete, although we can assume that the expected cash flows are certainty equivalents—that is, single-valued amounts treated as the equivalent of cash flows that are certain.

While the discounted cash flow concept has validity in the valuation by an investor of an entire firm, or in the valuation by owners of single ventures, it is of doubtful validity when applied to separate assets of a firm, for the following reasons: (1) The expected cash receipts generally depend upon subjective probability distributions that are not verifiable by their nature. (2) Even though opportunity discount rates might be obtainable, the adjustment for risk preference must be evaluated by management or the accountants, and it would be difficult to convey the meaning of the resultant valuation to the readers of financial statements. (3) When two or more factors, including human resources as well as physical assets, contribute to the product or service of the firm and the subsequent cash flows, a logical allocation to the separate service factors is generally impossible. While it has been suggested that the marginal net receipts associated with the asset can be used, Arthur Thomas has correctly pointed out that the sum of the individual marginal net receipts is not likely to add to the total net receipts from the product or services.[16] (4) The discounted value of the differential cash flows of all of the separate assets of the firm cannot be added together to obtain the value of the firm. This is partly due to the jointness of the contributions of the separate assets, but it is also due to the fact that some assets, such as intangibles, cannot be separately identified.

In spite of the above difficulties, the discounted cash flow concept has some merit as a valuation concept for single ventures where there are no joint factors requiring separate accounting or where the aggregation of assets can be carried far enough to include all of the joint factors. But it is also relevant for monetary assets where waiting is the primary factor determining the net benefit to be received in cash by the firm. For

---

[15] See Chapter 8, p. 239, fn. 1.

[16] Arthur L. Thomas, "Discounted Services Again: The Homogeneity Problem," *Accounting Review,* Vol. XXXIX (January, 1964), pp. 1–11. See also Arthur L. Thomas, "The Allocation Problem in Financial Accounting Theory," *Studies in Accounting Research No. 3* (Evanston, Ill.: American Accounting Association, 1969).

example, if a note receivable is fairly certain of being collected and if the timing of the payments is specified by contract, the discounted value of the note represents the amount of cash that the firm would be indifferent to holding as compared to holding the note. The minimum amount, however, would be the amount of cash that could be obtained by discounting or selling the note to a bank or other financial institution. The longer the waiting period, however, the greater the uncertainties will usually be, making the discounted cash receipts concept less applicable. On the other hand, when the waiting period is short, the discounting process can usually be ignored for monetary assets, because the amount of the discount is usually not material. For example, if a receivable of $1,000 is due in 30 days, the discounted present value of this at 6 percent would be $995.02. Since the discount of $4.98 is probably not material, it can usually be ignored, and the receivable is not significantly overstated if it is valued at $1,000.

Current Output Prices. When the product of the enterprise is generally sold in an organized market, the current market price may be a reasonable estimate of the actual selling price in the near future. Therefore, the current output price may be a close substitute for the discounted expected cash receipt value of merchandise inventories, and products or by-products at or close to the completed stage. If, however, the product is not expected to be sold within a short period, the current market price (used as a substitute for the expected sales price) should be appropriately discounted. If additional costs of production or expenses of selling are anticipated, these costs as a minimum should be subtracted from the current sales price to obtain an approximation of the current valuation. This current valuation is referred to as the *net realizable value.*

A current output (exit) price has some serious limitations as a generalized valuation concept. First, it applies only to assets that are held for sale, such as merchandise, special manufactured products, investments, and plant and equipment or land no longer of use to the firm in its operations. Second, since it is a surrogate for a future sales price, the relevance of the transformation is open to question. The current sales price represents the amount that is being paid by the marginal buyer and does not necessarily represent the amount that will be paid in the future except under conditions of *ceteris paribus.* Third, because all assets of the firm cannot be valued on the basis of a current sales price, different valuation concepts must be applied, and the aggregation of assets measured by different valuation concepts has little meaning. Therefore, alternative measurement concepts would include *current cash equivalents* and liquidation values.

The use of a current output price results in the reporting of income or loss prior to the final exchange of the product or service. In Chapter 6, it was pointed out that this valuation results in the reporting of revenue during production or at the completion of production, and that this reporting is appropriate when the current output price is a good estimate of the future sales price and when there is good evidence that the product will be sold at this price in the near future. If the expected future sales price is discounted for a possible waiting period, only the operating income is reported currently and the income representing interest will be reported at the completion of the exchange.

Current Cash Equivalents. The term current cash *equivalent* has been proposed by Chambers as a single measurement concept for all assets, representing their present realizable prices.[17] It represents the amount of cash or generalized purchasing power that could be obtained by selling each asset under conditions of orderly liquidation, which may be measured by quoted market prices for goods of a similar kind and condition. This current cash equivalent is assumed to be relevant because it represents the position of the firm in relation to its adaptive behavior to the environment. That is, it is assumed by Chambers to be the contemporary property of all assets which is relevant for all actions in markets and thus uniformly relevant at a point in time. Past prices are irrelevant to future actions and future prices can be nothing more than speculation. Therefore, the current cash equivalent concept avoids the necessity to aggregate past, present, and future prices.

One of the major difficulties with the current cash equivalent concept is that it provides justification for excluding from the position statement all items that do not have a contemporary market price. For example, nonvendible specialized equipment, as well as most intangible assets, would be written off at the time of acquisition because of an inability to obtain a current market price. However, Chambers would modify the procedures somewhat to provide approximations of the current cash equivalents by the use of specific price indexes and by making subjective depreciation computations. From the author's point of view, the main deficiency in using the current cash equivalent concept for all assets is that it does not take into consideration the relevancy of the information to the prediction and decision needs of the users of financial statements. Larson and Schattke criticize the concept on the basis that it has a nonadditive property, because the summation of the current cash equivalents of the individual assets is not equal to the cash equivalent of the assets as a group; and the sale of assets in combination or the sale of the firm as a whole may be just as relevant or more relevant than the sale of individual assets in the adaptive behavior of the firm.[18] These criticisms, however, do not deny the current cash equivalent concept as being meaningful in accounting measurement.

---

[17] Chambers, *op. cit.*, p. 92.

[18] Kermit Larson and R. W. Schattke, "Current Cash Equivalent, Additivity, and Financial Action," *Accounting Review*, Vol. XLI (October, 1966), pp. 634–41.

Liquidation Values. Liquidation values are similar to current output prices and to current cash equivalents, except that they are obtained from different market conditions. Current output prices assume normal selling operations and usually a normal profit, and current cash equivalents assume at least orderly liquidation. But liquidation values assume a forced sale, either to regular customers at greatly reduced prices or to other firms or dealers usually at prices considerably below cost. The application of liquidation values usually results in the writing down of asset valuations and the recognition of losses. Because they are not realistic under normal circumstances, liquidation values should be used only under two main situations; (1) when merchandise or other assets have lost their normal usefulness, have become obsolete, or have otherwise lost their normal market; and (2) when the firm expects to discontinue business in the near future, so that it will not be able to sell in its normal market.

Exchange Input Values

Input values are often assumed to be more appropriate than output values, because they are possibly more verifiable or because they do not permit the reporting of revenue before it is "realized." Actually, however, accounting is eclectic in nature, choosing output values in some cases and input values in others. While output values may be better conceptually for the presentation of the financial statements, as discussed above, there are many situations where input values are more appropriate, because they may represent the maximum value to the firm or because an output market does not exist, so that it is impossible to obtain exchange output values. Input values may be expressed in terms of actual historical costs, current costs, future costs, or costs imputed from expected output values.

Historical Costs. Cost has been the most common valuation concept in accounting and, in fact, it has often been assumed to be the same as value or synonymous with accounting valuation. For example, the Committee on Terminology of the American Institute of Accountants (AICPA) stated that

since accounting is predominantly based on cost, the proper uses of the word *value* in accounting are largely restricted to the statement of items at cost, or at modifications of cost.[19]

The American Accounting Association has also given emphasis to valuation based on cost particularly in the 1936, 1941, and 1948 statements. The 1948 statement, for example, said:

---

[19] Committee on Terminology, *op. cit.,* p. 16.

The most commonly useful financial statements report the origin and disposition of the assets of an enterprise in terms of costs established and recorded at the time the assets are acquired.[20]

But the 1957 statement also asserted:

Non-monetary assets—inventories, plant, long-term investments, and deferred items generally—are not as amenable to accurate money measurement. Such assets are typically stated at acquisition cost or some derivative thereof. Assuming a free market, acquisition cost expressed in the bargained price of an asset is presumed to be a satisfactory quantification of future service expectations at the time of acquisition.[21]

Cost is the exchange price of goods and services at the time they are acquired. When the consideration given in the exchange consists of nonmonetary assets, the exchange price is determined by the current value of the assets given up in the exchange. Cost is thus the economic sacrifice expressed in monetary terms required to obtain a specific asset or a group of assets. Very often, cost is not represented by a single exchange price, but it includes many sacrifices of economic resources necessary to obtain the asset in the form, location, and time in which it can be useful to the operations of the firm. Thus, all of these sacrifices should be included in the concept of cost valuation. But it should be recognized that the term "cost" is used in many senses and for various purposes. In many cases, it includes only a part of the total sacrifices, and in other cases, it includes too much. This problem is discussed later in this chapter and throughout much of the discussion of the following chapters.

Cost as a valuation concept for nonmonetary assets has its main advantage in the fact that it is verifiable. Cost represents the exchange price agreed upon by the buyer and seller in a relatively free economy. While it is possible that the firm may occasionally pay more than it should for an asset, it is usually assumed that prudent judgment was used and that the firm could not have obtained the same asset or service elsewhere for a lower total cost. It is also assumed that cost represents the value of the asset to the firm at the time of acquisition, but this cannot be proved, since all factors of the enterprise are used jointly in providing the cash available for distribution to investors. One of the strongest reasons for adhering to historical cost, however, has been its close relationship to the realization concept in the measurement of income.

One of the main disadvantages of historical cost valuation is that the value of the asset to the firm may change over time; after long periods of time it may have no significance whatever as a measure of the quantity of

---

[20] Executive Committee, AAA, "Accounting Concepts and Standards Underlying Corporate Financial Statements, 1948 Revision," in Committee on Accounting Concepts and Standards, *op. cit.*, p. 14.

[21] *Ibid.*, p. 4.

resources available to the enterprise. Historical cost valuation is also disadvantageous because it fails to permit the recognition of gains and losses in the periods in which they may actually occur. Also, because of changes over time, costs of assets acquired in different time periods cannot be added together in the balance sheet to provide meaningful sums. The historical cost valuation concept has the added practical disadvantage of blocking out other possibly more useful valuation concepts; accountants often become so imbued with cost methods and concepts that they are unable to consider anything else.

Current Input Costs. Current costs and historical costs are the same only on the date of acquisition of an asset. After that date the same asset or its equivalent may be obtainable for a larger or smaller exchange price. Thus current costs represent the exchange price that would be required today to obtain the same asset or its equivalent. If a good market exists in which similar assets are bought and sold, an exchange price can be obtained and associated with the asset owned; this price represents the maximum value to the firm, except for very short periods, until a replacement can be obtained. It should be noted, however, that this current exchange price is a cost price only if it is obtained from quotations in a market in which the firm would acquire its assets or services; it cannot be obtained from quotations in the market in which the firm usually sells its assets or services in the normal course of its operations, unless the two markets are coincident.

Current costs have several advantages over the historical cost concept. Among these are the following: (1) The current cost represents the amount the firm would have to pay today to obtain the asset or its services; therefore, it represents the best measure of the value of the inputs being matched against current revenues for predictive purposes. (2) This matching of current costs against current revenues permits the separation of gains and losses from the holding of assets and the recognition of profit and loss from operations. (3) The current cost represents the value of the asset to the firm if the firm is continuing to acquire such assets and if value has not been added by the enterprise to the asset. (4) The summation of assets expressed in current terms is more meaningful than the addition of historical costs incurred at different time periods.

One of the disadvantages of the current cost concept is that some objectivity has been lost; unless the assets currently sold in the market are identical in all respects, some subjectivity must be applied in transferring current exchange prices to assets held. Also, current costs might not represent the current value to the enterprise. If the firm were required to pay the current costs, it might be economically advantageous to acquire other asset forms instead. The present value of the benefits to be provided by the asset may not be equal to the current or replacement cost of the asset. This is particularly true when technological changes have occurred in the production process or when significant changes have occurred in the demand for the product. For example, if the demand for a product has declined significantly, the specialized equipment required for its production has declined in service value to the firm; the depreciated cost of acquiring similar equipment is not a good measure of the value of the asset to the enterprise.

Discounted Future Costs. Most nonmonetary assets represent flows of future goods or services acquired in advance. These goods or services are usually acquired in advance because (1) it is less costly to acquire them in large quantities; (2) some assets (e.g., a building or equipment) by their nature represent a stream of future services that cannot be acquired separately; (3) it is often desirable to purchase future services (e.g., leasehold) in order to be sure that they will be available when they are needed; and (4) it is often desirable to obtain rights to property to protect other investments such as leasehold improvements. In these cases, the equivalent cost of the service at the time of *use* may be the most relevant valuation concept. In this context, the present value of these services (the asset) is the discounted value of the future costs.

In those cases where the services will be available in the near future, the process of discounting will not have a material effect on the valuation of the asset. For example, many prepaid expenses would cost the same if they were acquired when needed rather than in advance; thus the recording of these assets at acquisition cost may be very close to the valuation based on the future expected costs or the discounted future costs.

In other cases, however, the cost price may be less than the amount that would have been required if the services had been acquired when needed. For example, a leasehold purchased in advance for 10 years would probably be less than the sum of 10 payments paid annually during the same period. In part, this difference is due to the interest factor, and in part to other causes. In either case, the present valuation of the leasehold should not exceed the discounted value of the 10 rents if the other terms of the contract are the same. This same concept can be applied to the valuation of plant and equipment and other assets, but usually on a less precise basis. Nevertheless, the concept is useful in valuation problems. The present value of an asset is assumed to be equal to the discounted value of the future expected service costs. It should be noted that this is a cost concept; the discounted amounts are input exchange prices, not output service values.

While the discounted future cost concept may be relevant in the acquisition decision in those cases where the firm has the alternative of purchasing the services as required rather than in a lump sum, after the asset has been acquired the discounted future cost concept has serious limitations. Even if the current input price of the services acquired separately can be obtained, the firm no longer has the alternative of purchasing the services separately once the advance commitment has been made. Also, even if the total cost could be assumed to be equal to the value of the asset at the date of acquisition, this identity of discounted future expected costs of equivalent services and the current value of the asset to the firm is not likely to persist in subsequent periods. Therefore, the discounted future cost concept has all of the disadvantages of historical cost plus the limitations applicable to the discounted service potential concept.

Standard Costs.   Although standard costs have their primary significance as a managerial tool of cost control, they also provide a useful concept of valuation for produced assets. Standard costs can be defined as a valuation on the basis of what costs should be under certain assumptions regarding the desired level of productive efficiency and capacity utilization. Valuation on the basis of standard costs is an input valuation concept based on the appropriate exchange prices of the proper quantities of goods and services necessary for the production of the product.

A major advantage of the standard cost concept is that the costs of inefficiencies are omitted. A product is not worth more because it is produced under inefficient conditions. Nor is it worth more because of the existence of idle capacity. The costs of inefficiency and idle capacity are losses incurred by the firm in the current or past periods. They should not be carried forward to future periods to be matched against future revenues, and they cannot be converted into future funds flows.

From a valuation point of view, however, standard costs are not necessarily superior to actual costs. An efficiently produced product is not necessarily worth less than one that is produced under less efficient methods. The value of a product to the firm depends more on its future service potential or expected sales price than upon either what it did cost or what it should cost. Thus, since the standard cost concept is an input exchange value, it has many of the disadvantages of other input valuations.

The appropriateness of the standard cost concept as a good measure of input exchange values depends in large part on the type of standard cost chosen and the way it is applied. Ideal standards may be useful for managerial purposes but they tend to understate asset valuations because they tend to exclude some of the normal costs of inefficiency and idle capacity. Current standards that take these normal inefficiencies into account may be more appropriate; but there is always a difficulty in keeping them current by incorporating changes in prices and production methods.

Absorption Costing and Direct Costing.   One of the major problems in determining the valuation of manufactured assets is the decision regarding which costs are relevant to future periods and thus should be included in asset valuations and which should be charged against current income. We have already seen that costs of inefficiency and idle capacity do not provide service potentials, and therefore they should not be included in asset valuations. And because they are not related to future revenues, they cannot be carried forward to provide a proper matching of revenues and expenses. But the question of including fixed costs in asset valuations is controversial. It should be noted, however, that both absorption and direct costing are input cost concepts and they can be applied to either historical costs or current costs.

Absorption Costing. Under the total input cost concept, all costs necessary in the production of an asset or service potential should be included in the appropriate valuation. Input costs should be included in product costs if they could not have been eliminated or omitted in the production process. This concept of full costing is claimed to be appropriate from both the service-potential and the matching points of view. From a service-potential viewpoint, the costs are assumed to represent benefits to the firm that can be converted into money through the normal operations of sale and collection. In the matching of costs with revenues, full costing provides the mechanism for carrying forward the costs necessary in obtaining the related operating revenue. Remember that revenue is not recognized during or at the end of production when input values are used, so that the proper measurement of income requires the carrying forward of all costs, fixed and variable, direct or allocated. The only exception occurs when it becomes apparent that the costs have lost their service value; in this case, they should not be carried forward, because they will not benefit the firm in the future and there is no expected revenue against which they can be matched.

As a measure of the service potential of an asset, absorption costing has some serious deficiencies, not only because it is based on input prices rather than future cash flows or net realizable values but also because of the procedures for allocating fixed and joint costs to products. In the computation of full costs, two transformations must be made. First, the fixed costs must be allocated to the periods, either on the basis of use or on the basis of time, both of which lack conceptual validity. Second, the costs assigned to the period must be allocated to products, again on the basis of some assumed relationship to the total, such as the associated direct labor costs or time in production. As a result, two transformations are made in associating the fixed costs incurred with specific products, so that the representation of the net result as the service potential of the asset is suspect. For these same reasons, the use of absorption costing as a process of matching costs with associated revenues is of doubtful validity. The association is very indirect and reaches the point of being completely arbitrary.

Direct Costing. Under direct costing, more appropriately called variable or marginal costing, only the variable costs of production are included in the asset valuation; all fixed costs are classified as period costs and charged off in the current period. The main advantage of direct or variable costing is in providing management with information for the making of decisions and for the managerial control of costs. Decisions for which variable costing is appropriate include those relating to the marketing of new products, the evaluation of expansion or contraction plans for old products, the introduction of technological improvements, and decisions regarding pricing. But many of the proponents of variable costing claim that it is also the most appropriate concept for the valuation of assets for external reporting purposes. The advantages for managerial purposes cannot be denied, but there is some question of its validity in the valuation of assets and in the determination of periodic income. The following discussion is directed to this question.

By definition, variable costs are those costs that vary directly with the quantity of production or sales; they would not be incurred at zero output or sales. They are incurred with the anticipation of obtaining current and future benefits, in the form of either increased revenues or decreased costs in a later period. Only if they result from inefficiencies or from errors in estimating the possible future benefits should they be charged against current income immediately when they accrue, rather than being associated with specific products or revenues. The variable costs normally include all direct labor and direct material costs and that part of overhead costs that can be classified as variable—for example, power costs.

One claim for variable costing is that if inventories are constant from year to year, net income would be the same under either variable or absorption costing except in the first and last years of enterprise life. And since variable costing provides valuable information to management, it can just as well be used for external purposes also. However, this view is not valid for two main reasons: (1) The assumption of constant inventories is not realistic for most firms, and very seldom is a policy of holding constant inventories desirable in a dynamic economy. (2) Balance sheet valuation, in this view, is held to be only a step between two income statements; as a concept of asset valuation to be included in a meaningful statement of financial condition, it is wholly inappropriate.

Three reasons why variable costing for external reporting purposes is claimed to be superior are that (1) enterprise net income is presumed to be more meaningful when inventories are computed on a variable cost basis if production is not equal to the amount sold in each period; (2) direct costing eliminates management's ability to influence—perhaps distort—periodic reported profits by its production policy; and (3) under certain circumstances, particularly when there is idle plant capacity, fixed costs do not benefit future periods by either increasing future revenues or decreasing future costs. Each of these claims will be evaluated more fully below.

The first claim that net income based on direct costing is more meaningful can be demonstrated by the following example:

Operating Statistics

	January	February
Production (units)	20,000	5,000
Sales (units)	10,000	15,000
Variable costs per unit	$0.50	$0.50
Fixed costs (total)	$6,000	$6,000
Fixed costs per unit assuming a normal capacity of 20,000 units	$0.30	$0.30
Inventory, beginning (units)	–0–	10,000
Inventory, end of period (units)	10,000	–0–

Income Statements Based on Absorption Costing

	January	February
Sales (at $1 per unit)	$10,000	$15,000
Less cost of sales:		
Inventory, beginning	$ –0–	$ 8,000
Variable costs of production	10,000	2,500
Normal fixed costs of production	6,000	1,500
Total	$16,000	$12,000
Less inventory, end of period	8,000	–0–
Cost of sales	$ 8,000	$12,000
Operating margin	$ 2,000	$ 3,000
Less unabsorbed overhead		(4,500)
Less selling and administrative expenses	(1,500)	(1,500)
Net Operating Profit (Loss)	$ 500	($ 3,000)

Income Statements Based on Variable Costing

	January	February
Sales (at $1 per unit)	$10,000	$15,000
Less cost of sales:		
Inventory, beginning	$ –0–	$ 5,000
Variable costs of production	10,000	2,500
Total	$10,000	$ 7,500
Less inventory, end of period	5,000	–0–
Cost of sales	$ 5,000	$ 7,500
Operating margin	$ 5,000	$ 7,500
Less fixed expenses:		
Fixed manufacturing expenses	(6,000)	(6,000)
Selling expenses	(1,500)	(1,500)
Net Operating Profit (Loss)	($ 2,500)	$ –0–

In the first claim for variable costing for external purposes, the emphasis is on the meaning of net income. With absorption costing, the January operations show a profit of $500 and the February operations show a net loss of $3,000. Since the sales of February were 50 percent greater than those of January, this result is deemed inappropriate. Logic should dictate that the results of operations are really better in February than in January because of the increase in total sales revenue. And this is the result when variable costing is used. The operations of January show a net loss of $2,500, and the firm just broke even in February.

In support of the second claim, that direct costing eliminates management's ability to influence reported income by its production policy, management, by using absorption costing, could have reduced or eliminated the February loss by increasing its production in that month. For example, if the February production had been 20,000 units (with sales still 15,000 units), full costing would have shown a reported income of $1,500; the unabsorbed overhead of $4,500 would have been carried forward as a part of the cost of the inventory. With variable costing, the inventory at the end of the month would include only the variable costs of $0.30 a unit, so that the reported net income would still be zero.

The above reasoning, however, is based on the conventional accounting practice of associating net income with sales operations only. The variable costing statement does not reflect the fact that 20,000 units were produced in January and only 5,000 in February. Even in the absorption costing statement, no profit is recorded on the production of the 10,000 units remaining unsold until February.

On the basis of the matching of costs with related revenues, absorption costing results in the carrying forward of $3,000 of January fixed overhead to be matched against February revenue. The proponents of variable costing claim that this results in overmatching, since in February the total charges against revenues include not only the $3,000 of January overhead but also the total $6,000 of February overhead. However, if the sales in February had been $30,000 ($10,000 greater than the maximum production capacity of that month), variable costing would have understated, by $3,000, the overhead to be matched against the revenue of that period.

There are at least two alternatives to direct costing whereby more accurate income information can be presented with absorption costing: (1) The $4,500 of unabsorbed overhead could be shown in February as a loss due to idle capacity rather than as an expense in the computation of net operating income. All or part of this idle capacity loss could be included as a loss in an earlier period only if it could have been anticipated. (2) If the variations in either production or sales operations are due to seasonal factors, the fixed overhead should be spread over the year's production on the basis of the expected level of production, or the cost of idle capacity could be charged as a loss for the year rather than being allocated to specific months.

The third claim for variable costing as a meaningful valuation concept for external reporting purposes is based on the principle that an asset valuation exists only if there is benefit to the firm in the form of either greater expected future revenues or less future expected costs.[22] It is apparent in the above example that the 10,000 units produced for inventory in January could have been produced just as easily in February without any additional cost. On January 31, therefore, the inventory should be valued (on the basis of input costs) at $5,000, the variable cost of production; the $3,000 of fixed costs do not benefit the firm because they will be incurred in February regardless of when the 10,000 units are produced. Therefore, if there is a possibility of undercapacity utilization, the incurring of fixed costs in one period will not benefit a future period because it does not result in a reduction of future costs.

The above arguments, however, are based on the assumption that there is likely to be idle capacity in a future period or that the production for inventory will not increase future revenues. There are many cases where these assumptions are true, but there are also situations where they are not true. For example, suppose that potential sales in February were $30,000. Since only 20,000 units can be produced in February, sales of 10,000 units would have been lost if they had not been produced in January. In this case, the full cost of producing the 10,000 units of inventory in January (including the $3,000 fixed costs) is beneficial to the future operations of the firm. As a second example, assume that 20,000 units are produced and sold in February and that it is desirable to carry 10,000 units of inventory in order to meet the maximum potential sales in each period. In this case, the production of the 10,000 units for stock in January is clearly beneficial to the future operations of the firm, and the asset valuation should include the fixed costs as well as the variable costs. If these units had not been produced, additional manufacturing capacity would be necessary or some of the future revenue would be lost. In either case, the use of the productive facilities in January provides future service potential to the firm.

Relevant Costing. Relevant costing can be defined as the carrying forward of any cost as an asset if "it has a favorable economic effect on expected future costs or future revenues."[23] The main distinction between relevant costing and direct costing is that the former emphasizes

---

[22] See Charles T. Horngren and George H. Sorter, "Direct Costing for External Reporting," *Accounting Review,* Vol. XXXVI (January, 1961), pp. 84–93; and George H. Sorter and Charles T. Horngren, "Asset Recognition and Economic Attributes— The Relevant Costing Approach," *Accounting Review,* Vol. XXXVII (July, 1962), pp. 391–99.

[23] *Ibid.,* p. 393.

the expectation of future benefits while the latter emphasizes the relationship of cost behavior to the quantity of goods produced or sold. Therefore, relevant costing could include fixed costs, as in the case cited above where goods are produced for inventory in anticipation of full capacity utilization in future periods. Therefore, relevant costing includes the time utility of goods, and it may approximate absorption costing under assumptions of a prudent management that produces inventory only as needed for future sales that could not be met from future production, and with an absorption costing procedure that includes only normal production costs.

The Evaluation of Direct Costing and Absorption Costing. The controversy between direct costing and absorption costing for external reporting purposes has been discussed by many writers—mainly on emotional grounds, but rationalized on the basis of which method results in the more relevant income figure based on the matching concept, or on the basis of which measures better the value of the future benefits of the asset to the firm. In general, it has been assumed that the choice is between these two concepts, and the proponents of direct costing generally assume that absorption costing must include the allocation of all costs of the period to the production of that period. However, neither is necessarily relevant for external reporting as a basis for valuation or as a basis for matching. In the author's opinion, variable costing is appropriate for the matching of associated variable costs with revenues, but it is too restrictive in its assumptions to serve as a basis for valuation in all situations. In most cases, where there is prudent management, it can be assumed that the benefit to the firm is greater than the variable costs of production or else the inventory would not have been produced. But full costing is not necessarily correct in all cases either. Full (absorption) costing provides a poor basis for matching because of the dual allocation process of assigning fixed costs first to periods and then to products, which results in a very indirect and possibly arbitrary matching of costs with associated revenues. Although full costing may result in valuations that are closer to realizable values in many cases, it is at best a very poor substitute for a net realizable value, even if it is based on current replacement costs. But there is considerable merit in reporting both fixed and variable costs separately because of their different behavioral characteristics. Such reporting would permit better predictions of future cash flows.

The Formal Acceptance of Direct Costing. Direct costing for external reporting purposes has not been formally accepted by the Accounting Principles Board in the United States, although it has been used as a generally accepted practice by some firms and many accountants propose that it should be formally accepted. The formal statements and research studies of some of the accounting societies in the United States indicate this difference of opinion. The Committee on Accounting Concepts and

Standards, in the 1957 revision of the American Accounting Association statement, said, for example:

> . . . the cost of a manufactured product is the sum of the acquisition costs reasonably traceable to that product and should include both direct and indirect factors. The omission of any element of manufacturing cost is not acceptable.[24]

Two of the seven members of the committee dissented from this opinion, however.

The American Institute of Certified Public Accountants is less definite in its statement, but, while there is an implication that direct costing would not be acceptable, the proponents of direct costing claim that it is not precluded. *Accounting Research Bulletin No. 43* states:

> The primary basis of accounting for inventories is cost, which has been defined generally as the price paid or consideration given to acquire an asset. As applied to inventories, cost means in principle the sum of the applicable expenditures and charges directly or indirectly incurred in bringing an article to its existing condition and location.[25]

and

> It should . . . be recognized that the exclusion of all overheads from inventory costs does not constitute an accepted accounting procedure.[26]

Sprouse and Moonitz, in AICPA *Accounting Research Study No. 3*, do not discuss specifically the direct costing problem. They imply, however, that full costing is appropriate unless there is evidence that this amount exceeds the future benefits to the firm. They state, for example:

> The measurement of these other assets is frequently made by the process of aggregating the costs of acquiring them and of bringing them to their existing condition and location. This procedure has two important attributes. One, each acquisition cost represents the evaluation of the market at that time and therefore represents *prima facie* evidence of an objective (i.e., unbiased, impersonal) appraisal of the economic value of the assets. And two, that appraisal is supported by one or more overt transactions and is therefore capable of independent verification.[27]

In emphasizing the importance of current costs, they say:

> The relevance of current (replacement) cost to a going concern is underlined whenever the enterprise continues to manufacture or purchase the items contained in its inventory. This behavior creates a forceful presumption that cur-

---

[24] Committee on Accounting Concepts and Standards, *op. cit.*, p. 4.

[25] Committee on Accounting Procedure, AICPA, "Restatement and Revision of Accounting Research Bulletins," *Accounting Research Bulletin No. 43* (New York, 1953), p. 28.

[26] *Ibid.*, p. 29.

[27] Sprouse and Moonitz, *op. cit.*, pp. 25–26.

rent (replacement) costs represent at least the minimum economic value of those items to the enterprise.[28]

The National Association of Accountants represents the other view, that direct costing is relevant for use in external reports. It says:

> Since expiration of benefits provided by period costs is more closely related to time than to production, it seems realistic to match period costs against revenues of the same period. The preceding chapter . . . presented evidence from the field study showing that users of direct costing believe that direct costing gives periodic net income figures that are more useful to management. There seems to be no reason why the same figures are not also more useful to stockholders.[29]

In the United Kingdom, the Institute of Chartered Accountants in England and Wales recommended that the cost of inventories (stock-in-trade) should include "such part, if any, of the overhead expenditure as is properly carried forward in the circumstances of the business."[30]

The Lower of Cost or Market

The "lower-of-cost-or-market" valuation procedure is neither an output nor an input valuation concept but a mixture of the two concepts. The term "market" may refer to either an output or an input price. When the concept is applied to inventories, the term "market" usually refers to replacement cost (an input concept), but it may refer to selling price or net realizable value (output concepts) under certain conditions. When it is applied to the valuation of investments in securities, "market" usually refers to the selling price, although in this case, the costs and selling prices are obtained from the same market; the difference between the two is represented primarily by the costs of buying and selling. However, since securities are not usually purchased with the purpose of selling in a different market at a higher price, both the cost and selling price of securities can be considered output prices. The application of the lower-of-cost-or-market rule to securities and inventories will be discussed in later chapters. The following discussion emphasizes the evaluation of the basic concept itself.

The lower-of-cost-or-market concept has a long history in accounting, going back to the 19th century and before. One of the reasons for its early prominence is the early emphasis on the balance sheet as a report to creditors. Without a reliable report on which to base expectations regarding future operations, creditors emphasized the lowest probable conver-

---

[28] *Ibid.,* p. 29.

[29] National Association of Accountants, *Current Application of Direct Costing,* NAA Research Report 37 (New York, 1961), p. 87.

[30] The Institute of Chartered Accountants in England and Wales, Recommendation No. 22, "Treatment of stock-in-trade and work in progress in financial accounts," 1960. Reprinted in "Recommendations on Accounting Principles," 1967.

sion value of assets. Thus, a policy of conservatism was adopted with regard to balance sheet valuations. The valuations presented in the statements could be assumed to be worth at least as much as stated.

With the change in emphasis to the income statement, the cost or market rule took on new meaning. It was now the income that would be conservatively stated. By reducing asset valuations at the end of a period because of a fall in prices, the net income for the period would be smaller. All possible losses would be included in the current income determination, but all probable gains would be deferred until the usual recognition at the time of sale or later. The recognition of gains is based on different criteria than the recognition of losses. Gains are not recognized until there is little or no possibility of their being reversed, but losses are recognized whenever there is some available evidence that they might occur.

There is some question whether the cost or market rule is a basic accounting concept or merely an accepted accounting procedure. It does not use any valuation concept different from the concepts discussed above, but because it does not apply any one of the valuation concepts consistently, it can be considered a different concept at least in its application or it can be considered an eclectic application of various valuations concepts. Regardless of the level of dignity ascribed to the method, it has been vigorously criticized for many years in discussions of accounting theory. Its most amazing attribute is that it has found so many followers for so many years. It has even maintained formal recognition by the American Institute of Certified Public Accountants, The American Accounting Association, the Securities and Exchange Commission, The Institute of Chartered Accountants in England and Wales, and other associations and agencies.

The acceptance of the cost or market concept by the AICPA is stated in *Accounting Research Bulletin No. 43* as follows:

A departure from the cost basis of pricing the inventory is required when the utility of the goods is no longer as great as its cost. Where there is evidence that the utility of goods, in their disposal in the ordinary course of business, will be less than cost, whether due to physical deterioration, obsolescence, changes in price levels, or other causes, the difference should be recognized as a loss of the current period. This is generally accomplished by stating such goods at a lower level commonly designated as *market*.[31]

In this context, the term "market" is used to mean replacement cost, with net realizable value as an upper limit and net realizable value less a normal profit margin as a lower limit.

The formal statements of the AAA have been less precise in their recognition of the cost or market concept, but it is implied, with the qualification that "market" should represent net realizable value (an

---

[31] *Accounting Research Bulletin No. 43, op. cit.*, p. 30.

output price) rather than replacement cost (an input price). The 1936 statement recommended that—

Every business enterprise should eliminate from its accounts those costs which are applicable to assets no longer useful or salable, and should reduce the carrying values of assets in use or ultimately to be marketed to such amounts as may reasonably be expected to be recoverable in the course of future operations.[32]

The 1957 revised statement confirms this viewpoint as follows:

Assuming a free market, acquisition cost expressed in a bargained price of an asset is presumed to be a satisfactory quantification of future service expectations at the time of acquisition. . . . The aim of all measurements of assets is to state the amount of available service potential in the most objective and realistic terms.[33]

Sprouse and Moonitz, in *Accounting Research Study No. 3,* oppose the cost-or-market concept; instead they propose the use of current (replacement) cost for inventories in all cases, whether it is above or below acquisition cost. This recommendation is supported by the following:

If current replacement cost is objective, definite, verifiable and more useful when it is lower than acquisition cost, it also possesses those attributes when it is greater. By the use of current replacement cost, a change in "utility" is recognized in the period when the change takes place. And inventory items would still be measured at amounts which are below current selling prices by the amount of the operating margin (gross profit).[34]

The author is in full agreement with the above recommendation by Sprouse and Moonitz for those assets for which the present value of the future utility or net realizable value cannot be measured with a fair degree of certainty and objectivity. The lower-of-cost-or-market concept is unacceptable in accounting theory for the following reasons:

1. As a method of conservatism, it tends to understate total asset valuations. Individual asset valuations may also be understated, but because valuations are not increased above acquisition cost in those cases where future service or sales values have increased, the total valuations would tend to be understated whenever the cost or market concept is applied. While this understatement may not harm creditors, it is deceiving to stockholders and potential investors, and management is kidding itself if it believes its own statements.

2. The conservatism in asset valuations is offset by an unconservative statement of net income in a future period. A lower asset valuation in the

[32] Executive Committee, AAA, "A Tentative Statement of Accounting Principles Underlying Corporate Financial Statements," *Accounting Review,* Vol. XI (June, 1936), p. 189.

[33] Committee on Accounting Concepts and Standards, *op. cit.,* pp. 4–5.

[34] Sprouse and Moonitz, *op. cit.,* p. 31.

current period will result in a larger reported profit or smaller loss in some future period when the asset valuation is charged off as an expense. Because gains are not reported currently, the resulting net income will be less useful as a predictive device or as a measure of efficiency.

3. While the cost or market concept can be applied consistently from year to year, it is internally inconsistent. No single valuation concept is used consistently; one valuation concept may be applied one year and another concept the next year. Also, there is no consistent application of valuation concepts to a single asset classification in the same year.

4. A less convincing argument is that the cost or market rule applies to decreases in costs as well as to diminished utility due to deterioration, obsolescence, or decreased earning capacity. There may not be any changes in net realizable value just because costs have changed. While there is some merit in this argument when the net realizable value can be estimated, for many cases a change in current costs is a good indication of a change in output value.

5. One of the least convincing arguments is that costs should always be carried forward and matched with related revenues in the period of sale. It is claimed that no gain or loss is realized until an exchange has taken place. While the matching of costs and revenues is a desirable goal in income determination, there is no logical reason to hold strictly to acquisition cost as the measure of input value if other reliable and objective valuation methods are available.

SUMMARY OF VALUATION CONCEPTS

In the valuation of assets, there is no single concept or procedure that is ideal in the presentation of the statement of financial position, in the determination of income, or in the presentation of other information relevant to the decisions of investors, creditors and other users of financial statements. The objectives of asset valuation are basically twofold: (1) to provide a relative measurement of the resources available to the firm in the generation of future cash receipts, and (2) to provide information which will permit the prediction of future cash outflows required to acquire similar resources in the future in the continuation of business operations. In the prediction of future cash receipts, output concepts are generally superior to input valuation concepts. Thus, net realizable values and current cash equivalents may be relevant for many predictions. But when the expected future benefits are highly uncertain, the use of input valuations may offer a good substitute. And as a prediction of future cash outflows, current input costs and expected future input prices are more significant than past input valuations. A separation of fixed and variable costs may also permit a better prediction of future cash flows. The following tabulation summarizes these various asset valuation concepts and the general conditions under which they are applicable:

Valuation Concept	Conditions Where Applicable
Exchange output values:	*When reliable evidence of output values is available:*
1. Discounted future expected cash receipts or service potentials.	1. When expected cash receipts or the equivalent are known or can be estimated with a high degree of certainty and when the waiting period is relatively long.
2. Current output values.	2. When current sales prices represent the future output price.
3. Current cash equivalents.	3. When the best alternative is orderly liquidation.
4. Liquidation values.	4. When the firm is not likely to be able to sell its product in the usual marketing channels or it is not likely to be able to utilize normal expected service values.
Exchange input values:	*When reliable evidence of output values is not available or as an indication of future cash requirements:*
5. Historical cost.	5. As a measure of current input value when acquired recently.
6. Current input costs.	6. When verifiable evidence of current input values can be obtained.
7. Discounted future costs.	7. When future services of known or estimated cost are purchased in advance instead of being acquired when needed.
8. Standard costs.	8. When they represent current costs under normal conditions of efficiency and capacity utilization.
9. Direct costing.	9. When the asset could be produced in a future period without causing any increment in total fixed costs of the future period, or when the use of current fixed facilities will not increase future revenues.
10. Relevant costing.	10. When the cost represents the favorable effect on future costs or future revenues.
Eclectic concepts:	
11. The lower of cost or market.	11. Inferior to all of the above concepts.

VALUATION METHODS

Each valuation method should attempt to approach as closely as possible one of the above valuation concepts. An appraisal of how closely the various valuation methods do approximate the best valuation concept applicable in each case will be made in the following chapters relating to specific classifications of assets. The following is a brief summary of the methods generally used to quantify assets for the purposes of balance sheet presentation and income determination:

1. Expected Cash Receipts. Future cash flows can be estimated from the terms of written contracts, general claims, or normal expectations regarding the conversion of monetary assets. These expected cash receipts can be discounted for the expected waiting period or valued in terms of their current or near-future conversion values.

2. Market Exchange Prices. Objective evidence of current valuation can be obtained from prices quoted or paid in organized markets. In some cases the relevant market is that in which the firm ordinarily sells its product or other assets, and in other cases the relevant market is that in which the firm usually purchases its assets. When the output or selling market is used, transportation and other costs of selling should be subtracted to obtain the net valuation to the firm; when the buying market for the firm is used, transportation and other costs should be added.

3. Acquisition Costs. For most cases where there is not an organized market from which a given price can be obtained, the exchange price at the time of acquisition can be assumed to be equal to the value of the consideration given in exchange for the asset. When many items or factors of production are used in obtaining an asset in a usable or salable form, the total acquisition cost is the sum of the amounts paid or other valuation of the goods and services used in the production process.

4. Depreciation and Amortization. For assets that provide services in more than one accounting period, the allocation of cost or other valuation basis to current or past periods does not alter the proper basis for valuation of the remainder. The undepreciated or unamortized portion should represent the proper valuation (quantification) of the remaining services of the asset, or the presentation should provide information regarding the total quantity of services available each period and the life expectancy.

5. Appraisal. The appraisal process is a valuation procedure and not a valuation concept. Kohler, for example, defines "appraise" as follows: "To establish cost or value by systematic procedures that include physical examination, pricing, and often engineering estimates."[35] Bonbright also emphasized this point in discussing the nature of appraisal:

---

[35] Eric L. Kohler, *A Dictionary for Accountants* (Englewood Cliffs, N.J.: Prentice-Hall, Inc., 1957), p. 33.

What is called the "theory of appraisal" is a systematic treatment of two problems that arise in every valuation of property. The first problem is to secure a definition of "value" acceptable for the purpose of the particular inquiry. The second problem is to determine the method by which the quantum of this value shall be estimated.[36]

Accountants have generally considered the appraisal process a method of obtaining by independent appraisers the reproduction cost less depreciation for fixed assets. However, many other valuation concepts have been used and are relevant in different circumstances.

Note that the proper choice of a valuation method is independent of the possible necessity for a restatement of cost or other value in terms of dollars of constant purchasing power, as measured by an index or indexes of general price-level changes.

SELECTED ADDITIONAL READING ON CHAPTER TOPICS

Nature of Assets

LALL, R. M. "An Enquiry into the Nature of Assets," *New York Certified Public Accountant*, Vol. XXXVIII (November, 1968), pp. 793–97.

SPROUSE, ROBERT T., and MAURICE MOONITZ. "A Tentative Set of Broad Accounting Principles for Business Enterprises," *Accounting Research Study No. 3*, chap. iii, pp. 19–22. New York: American Institute of Certified Public Accountants, 1962.

VATTER, WILLIAM J. *The Fund Theory of Accounting and Its Implications for Financial Reports*, pp. 17–19. Chicago: University of Chicago Press, 1947.

Discounted Service Potentials

KOLLARITSCH, FELIX. "Future Service Potential Value," *Journal of Accountancy*, Vol. CXIX (February, 1965), pp. 57–62.

LEMKE, KENNETH W. "Asset Valuation and Income Theory," *Accounting Review*, Vol. XLI (January, 1966), pp. 32–41.

STAUBUS, GEORGE J. "Comment on Felix P. Kollaritsch's Article 'Future Service Potential Value'," Letter to the Journal, *Journal of Accountancy*, Vol. CXX (July, 1965), pp. 17–18.

THOMAS, ARTHUR L. "Discounted Services Again: The Homogeneity Problem," *Accounting Review*, Vol. XXXIX (January, 1964), pp. 1–11.

Current Cash Equivalents

CHAMBERS, RAYMOND J. "Measurement in Accounting," *Journal of Accounting Research*, Vol. III (Spring, 1965), pp. 32–62.

---

[36] James C. Bonbright, *The Valuation of Property* (New York: McGraw-Hill Book Co., Inc., 1937), Vol. I, p. 10.

——. *Accounting, Evaluation and Economic Behavior*, particularly pp. 91–93. Englewood Cliffs, N.J.: Prentice-Hall, Inc., 1966.

——. "Continuously Contemporary Accounting—Additivity and Action," *Accounting Review*, Vol. XLII (October, 1967), pp. 751–57.

——. "Measures and Values, A Reply to Professor Staubus," *Accounting Review*, Vol. XLIII (April, 1968), pp. 239–47.

LARSON, KERMIT and R. W. SCHATTKE. "Current Cash Equivalent, Additivity, and Financial Action," *Accounting Review*, Vol. XLI (October, 1966), pp. 634–41.

STAUBUS, GEORGE J. "Current Cash Equivalent for Assets: A Dissent," *Accounting Review*, Vol. XLII (October, 1967), pp. 650–61.

Historical Costs

BEDFORD, NORTON M. *Income Determination Theory: An Accounting Framework*, chap. vii, "The Determination of Acquisition Cost," pp. 111–27. Reading, Mass.: Addison-Wesley, 1965.

IJIRI, YUJI. *The Foundation of Accounting Measurement*, particularly pp. 64–67, "The Significance of Historical Cost Valuation." Englewood Cliffs, N.J.: Prentice-Hall, Inc., 1967.

KOHLER, ERIC L. "Why Not Retain Historical Cost?" *Journal of Accountancy*, Vol. CXVI (October, 1963), pp. 35–41.

SOLOMONS, DAVID. "Economic and Accounting Concepts of Cost and Value," chap. vi of *Modern Accounting Theory*, edited by Morton Backer. Englewood Cliffs, N.J.: Prentice-Hall, Inc., 1966.

SPROUSE, ROBERT T. "Historical Costs and Current Assets—Traditional and Treacherous," *Accounting Review*, Vol. XXXVIII (October, 1963), pp. 687–95.

STANLEY, CURTIS H. "Cost-Basis Valuations in Transactions between Entities," *Accounting Review*, Vol. XXXIX (July, 1964), pp. 639–47.

Current Costs

EDWARDS, EDGAR O., and PHILIP W. BELL. *The Theory and Measurement of Business Income*, particularly chap. ix. Berkeley and Los Angeles: University of California Press, 1961.

THOMAS, ARTHUR L. " 'Value-itis'—An Impractical Theorist's Reply," *Accounting Review*, Vol. XXXIX (July, 1964), pp. 574–81.

Direct Costing

FESS, PHILIP E. "The Relevant Costing Concept for Income Measurement—Can It Be Defended?" *Accounting Review*, Vol. XXXVIII (October, 1963), pp. 723–32.

FREMGREN, JAMES M. "The Direct Costing Controversy—An Identification of Issues," *Accounting Review*, Vol. XXXIX (January, 1964), pp. 43–51.

HORNGREN, CHARLES T., and GEORGE H. SORTER. "Direct Costing for External Reporting," *Accounting Review*, Vol. XXXVI (January, 1961), pp. 84–93.

LEMKE, KENNETH. "Biased Matching Concepts of Direct Costing," *Management Accounting*, Vol. XLVIII (April, 1967), pp. 51–54.

SORTER, GEORGE H., and CHARLES T. HORNGREN. "Asset Recognition and Economic Attributes—The Relevant Costing Approach," *Accounting Review*, Vol. XXXVII (July, 1962), pp. 391–99.

STAUBUS, GEORGE J. "Direct, Relevant or Absorption Costing," *Accounting Review*, Vol. XXXVIII (January, 1963), pp. 64–71. Also "Postscript," pp. 71–73, and GEORGE H. SORTER and CHARLES T. HORNGREN, "A Reply to a Postscript," pp. 73–74.

Other Valuation Concepts

DEINZER, HARVEY T. *Methodological Presuppositions in Financial Accounting Models.* Gainesville: Accounting Department, College of Business Administration, University of Florida (no date).

MOBLEY, SYBIL C., "Revenue Experience as a Guide to Asset Valuation," *Accounting Review*, Vol. XLII (January, 1967), pp. 114–23.

Lower of Cost or Market

See suggested additional reading at the end of Chapter 11.

chapter 10

Current Assets and Current Liabilities

Classification is necessary for the study and communication of relevant information in all of the physical and social sciences. Accounting is no exception. The classification of the resources and commitments of a firm into appropriate categories is needed in order to present relevant summaries of accounting information which can be understood and analyzed by investors and other users of financial statements in their decision processes. Historically, the main categories and subclassifications of assets and liabilities have been carried forward into the present on the basis of traditional practices, devised originally to meet specific assumed needs which in many cases are no longer relevant. For example, assets and liabilities are usually presented in published financial statements in some order of solvency or liquidity, to meet the assumed special needs of creditors. In the first part of this chapter, the objectives of the current asset and current liability classifications are evaluated. Alternative methods of classification and their objectives are also discussed and related to various aspects of accounting theory.

Following this discussion of the objectives and definitions, attention is given to an examination of the valuation concepts and procedures relevant to specific categories of current assets and current liabilities. However, the subject of inventories is deferred to the following chapter.

In this and the following chapters, the reader should keep in mind the fundamental relationships between the problems of valuation, income determination, and cash flows; but we should not be bound by the limits of the double-entry accounting system when we discuss the development of theoretical accounting concepts and their application to the communication of relevant accounting information. In practice, some of the concepts discussed in Chapter 6 relating to the reporting of revenues and gains and losses may dictate the valuation concept applied. At other times, however, the guidelines for valuation applied in practice seem to dictate the timing and classification of revenues, gains, and losses. The following discussion attempts to evaluate the objectives and keep the process of valuation, income determination, and the presentation of cash flows in proper balance.

THE OBJECTIVES OF ASSET AND LIABILITY CLASSIFICATIONS

The main purpose of asset and liability classifications is to provide meaningful summaries of financial data. The grouping of like items is necessary to permit the readers of financial statements to obtain a reasonable understanding of the financial position and operations of a firm, make meaningful comparisons with past periods and with other firms, and make predictions regarding future cash flows. If unclassified data were presented to those interested in the firm, the reader would be forced to make his own summarization; the mind can cope with only a reasonable amount of data at one time. But if the summarization and classification are performed for the reader, a choice is made for him regarding what information is important and what is not important and what items should be emphasized more than others. When the readers of external reports have different objectives or different backgrounds regarding their knowledge of the firm, this summarization and classification necessarily omits some information and relationships that may be of value to specific readers or groups of readers. Thus, the principal guidelines for summarization and classification are an important part of accounting theory. But an evaluation of these guidelines depends upon who the intended readers are and what information they need.

The Presentation of Solvency to Creditors

The earliest objective of the current asset and current liability classifications was the presentation to creditors of information showing the relative security of their debts. The primary test of this security was the liquidity of specific assets and their availability for the payment of debts, particularly those debts falling due within the following year. This emphasis on the liquidity of assets and on the order in which debts would become payable stemmed from the lack of other reliable operating data and from the fact that creditors (particularly short-term creditors) represented the major group demanding financial information.

Today, the objectives of financial reporting have broadened considerably, and the balance sheet has become only one of several financial reports. But current accounting practice and thought still carry many of the earlier ideas and practices. Assets and liabilities are still generally classified according to their relative liquidity; the lower-of-cost-or-market rule still finds many ardent supporters; and the time period of a year is still the general rule in the classification of many assets and liabilities as current.

The objective of presenting the solvency of the firm by the classification of assets and liabilities as current and noncurrent is less important today than earlier for several reasons: (1) Other statements, particularly the income statement and the funds statement, may provide better information regarding expectations of solvency. (2) External financial reports are used more by investors and other groups than by creditors. (3) Corporations are generally considered to be more permanent in nature and more stable than were most of the 19th-century firms. (4) The widespread use of some valuation procedures, such as Lifo, has made the working capital ratio less meaningful than it once was. (5) The demand by creditors and others for a "favorable" working capital ratio forces managements to take certain actions such as the payment of current liabilities immediately preceding the balance sheet date, and places pressure on accountants to permit reclassifications to make the working capital appear favorable, even though in so doing the operations and solvency of the firm are not affected. (6) Business enterprises are becoming highly complex, so that no predetermined working capital ratio can be deemed to be necessary for adequate solvency. (7) The increased entry of many firms into the service industries has made the solvency of firms less dependent upon resources classified as current.

The Description of Enterprise Operations

One of the objectives of financial statements is to describe the operations of the enterprise. This can be achieved partially by an appropriate classification of items in the statements according to (1) the frequency of opportunity to decide about the continued commitment or recommitment of enterprise resources to specific forms of investment and (2) the frequency of the necessity to obtain commitment for specific forms of capital sources. Thus, if the current assets and current liabilities are classified according to the operations of the specific firm, the reader of the statements will be able to obtain a better picture of the firm than if the classification were based on some other objective.

As we shall see in the following discussion, the description of the operations of the firm is currently one of the objectives of balance sheet classification. The AICPA definitions of current assets and current liabilities are expressed in terms of the operating cycle of the business, and many published balance sheets show working capital (current assets less current liabilities) as a separate item. Thus the groupings are in terms of their function in the operations of the enterprise rather than in terms of the timing of their conversion into cash. Working capital thus provides an operational concept.

In proposing this operational objective of classification, it is generally assumed that working capital items are closely related to current operations and that long-term assets and liabilities are related to the long-term planning functions of the organization. This distinction is also reflected in the classifications in the income statement; expenses related to the use of current resources are often classified separately from the amortization and depreciation of long-term assets. And it is also clearly reflected in the funds statement; the sources of funds (often defined as working capital) from operations are usually classified separately from the funds obtained from other sources.

One of the main difficulties in applying the operational objective of classification is that in most firms, there is little relationship between working capital and current operations. Cash flows becoming available for the payment of liabilities may be as closely related to the use of long-term resources as to the sale of inventories. This is particularly true in the service industries, where inventories may be relatively small or nonexistent and current obligations will be paid from the revenues derived from the use or leasing of depreciable assets.

The Prediction of Cash Flows

As indicated in Chapter 8, the presentation of information which will permit the prediction of the future cash flows of the firm should be one of the objectives of financial reporting. While no classification of resources and commitments alone can permit predictions of future cash flows, a classification may be relevant when it is associated with historical and budgeted cash flow information. Such a classification should provide information regarding the likely timing of conversions of resources into cash, or their availability for conversion and the timing of the payment of obligations.

Classification According to the Accounting Process

Accounting classifications have often been established because of their convenience in the bookkeeping process. The deferred charge classification, for example, has often been used as a resting place for unallocated debits. As a result, items such as unamortized discount on bonds payable, discount on preferred stock, and losses carried forward have found a place among the assets of published balance sheets.

Classification according to the accounting process, however, is not necessarily irrelevant to the readers of published financial statements. It may be meaningful to draw a distinction between those items that will be disposed of through charges and credits to income and those items that will result directly or indirectly in cash flows. Gilman called the former items "deferred charges and credits to revenue" and the latter items "deferred charges and credits to cash."[1] Deferred charges to cash would include receivables, marketable securities, and long-term investments, while deferred charges to revenue would include prepaid expenses, plant and equipment, and inventories. Most liabilities are deferred credits to cash, but obligations to provide specific goods or services are considered deferred credits to revenue.

The main difficulty with this objective is that it is an attempt to explain the results of technical accounting procedures and it is, therefore, nontheoretical in nature. Because of its lack of logical orientation, the use of deferred charges and deferred credits permits the application of procedures that have no logical basis, or at least do not permit an explanation of the meaning of the deferral. Therefore, the classifications of deferred charges to revenue and deferred credits to revenue are highly objectionable.[2]

Classification According to Valuation Methods

Most of the valuation concepts discussed in the previous chapter are used in published financial statements, and very often many of the concepts are used in the same balance sheet. From a theory point of view, an eclectic procedure is not necessarily objectionable, as the valuation concept chosen should depend upon the available evidence and the degree of uncertainty in each case and an attempt to approach the relevant concept of income. But groupings of assets and liabilities that include different valuation concepts may be misleading to even informed readers of published statements.

A grouping of assets according to valuation concepts would include the following classifications: (1) cash and expected cash receipts (properly discounted when appropriate); (2) assets valued in terms of current or expected sales prices (output prices); (3) assets valued in terms of current costs (input prices); and (4) assets valued in terms of historical costs or costs restated to adjust for changes in the general level of prices. Other classifications may be used when appropriate. The main advantage of classification according to valuation concepts would be to provide better interpretation of the balance sheet and its relationship to the income statement and funds flow statement. In the author's opinion, however, adequate disclosure of valuation procedures can be obtained by parenthetical notations and in other ways, rather than through the grouping of assets.

---

[1] Stephen Gilman, "Accounting Principles and the Current Classification," *Accounting Review*, Vol. XIX (April, 1944), p. 114.

[2] See below, pp. 459-60 for a discussion of the meaning of the term "deferred credits to revenue," and p. 442 for a discussion of "deferred charges" and the objections to this terminology and classification.

WORKING CAPITAL

The concept of working capital refers to the net investment required in a business enterprise to maintain the day-to-day operations, as opposed to that investment that is committed for a longer period. This has sometimes been called "circulating capital." The investment in assets committed for long periods includes land, plant, and equipment that provide the facilities for enterprise operations; generally, these assets provide services and wear out gradually, but some assets represent indefinite commitments. The investment in working capital, on the other hand, is in a continual process of change through daily transactions. Because the short-term liabilities are not generally thought of as providing permanent invested capital but are closely related to the financing of the working assets, the term "working capital" is used to mean the excess of current assets over current liabilities.

The conventional classification of assets and liabilities as current and noncurrent is not based on either the accounting process or similarities in valuation. But the classification may serve at least partially the objectives of presenting information to short-term creditors regarding the solvency of the firm, and of presenting a partial description of enterprise operations.

The objective of presenting information regarding solvency was probably the most important objective in early balance sheet presentations, although many of the early writers did not state specifically their objectives. Sprague, for example, emphasized the importance of liquidity and debt-paying ability, but he also implied the importance of the description of enterprise operations. He stated:

> The arrangement of the items in the balance sheet is of some importance especially if the list is voluminous. . . . In our example the order of availability has been followed, or, as it might be termed, the order of liquidation. . . . In an industrial enterprise where it was thought that productivity or earning power was more important than readiness in debt-paying, it might be that the fixed plant was entitled to the first place among the assets and that the cash on hand would be placed at the end as the least productive of assets. But, at any rate, *some* principle of arrangement is better than haphazard.[3]

The presentation of working capital does provide some valid information to the grantors of short-term credit, because it indicates the degree of protection or the amount of buffer carried by long-term creditors and stockholders. But neither the amount of working capital nor the working capital ratio is necessarily a good indication of the ability of the firm to pay current liabilities as they come due. This is because working capital

---

[3] Charles E. Sprague, *The Philosophy of Accounts* (New York, 1908), p. 32.

is a static concept and debt-paying ability is dynamic. Cash becoming available for the paying of debt arises primarily from operations, not from the liquidation of particular assets. Cash and other liquid assets available at a particular balance sheet date are likely to be used in operations for the payment of liabilities not yet incurred at balance sheet date (e.g., current payroll), rather than being held for the payment of the balance sheet liabilities as they mature.

The current classification as a description of operations has long been established in governmental fund accounting. The current assets and current liabilities are often set up as a separate fund, either in the accounts or in the statements or in both. The term "fund" is used in this situation to refer to a segregation of assets and liabilities for a given purpose as a specific unit of operations or as a center of interest. Vatter has suggested that the current classification is also very appropriate in the application of fund theory to general financial accounting. In his 1947 monograph, he stated:

> One of the most direct and simple ways in which the fund theory may find expression in the balance sheet is in connection with the distinctions that conventionally are maintained between the "current" and "fixed" captions. . . . Typical American practice [in commercial and industrial reporting] has been to make this classification only in the form of groups and subtotals in the balance sheet. In England, however, certain kinds of enterprises are legally required to employ the "double-account form" of balance sheet. . . . The point to be made here is that the double-account form of balance sheet amounts to "funding" the current and fixed balance-sheet accounts, so as to report separately the effects of operations upon the current and capital "funds."[4]

The use of the concept of working capital as a partial description of enterprise operations is reflected in the practice of subtracting current liabilities from current assets in the balance sheet, a practice that gained considerable popularity in the 1940's and is commonly employed in the United States today. This objective is also implied in the AICPA accounting research bulletin on "Current Assets and Current Liabilities— Working Capital" originally issued in 1947 and later included in *Accounting Research Bulletin No. 43*. The implication comes from the change from the one-year rule for classification to the criterion of the operating cycle of the business. But this change did not reflect entirely a change in objective, as it was thought that it would also provide better information for creditors.

A major criticism of the working capital concept is that it is merely a net figure obtained by subtracting some of the liabilities from some of the

---

[4] William J. Vatter, *The Fund Theory of Accounting and Its Implications for Financial Reports* (Chicago: University of Chicago Press, 1947), p. 60. Copyright 1947 by the University of Chicago.

assets, without a necessary relationship between the two classifications or their components. Furthermore, the net figure has little meaning as either a homogeneous grouping of net resources or as a margin or buffer available for the protection of creditors. The current classification includes both monetary and nonmonetary items, which should be measured with different objectives in mind or with different degrees of reliability, even if an attempt is made to make them homogeneous. The description of working capital as a buffer assumes that current liabilities will be paid from resources classified as current, and that the current assets will not be required for other purposes having priority over the payment of the current liabilities; since neither of these assumptions is realistic, the presentation of working capital as a net figure is of doubtful relevance in financial reporting.

The Definition of Current Assets

According to *Accounting Research Bulletin No. 43,* current assets are defined as "cash and other assets or resources commonly identified as those which are reasonably expected to be realized in cash or sold or consumed during the normal operating cycle of the business." This compares with the earlier, much narrower, definition presented by Sanders, Hatfield, and Moore: "those assets which in the regular course of business will be converted into cash and those assets acquired with a view to their availability for conversion into cash."[5] The one-year rule was common in the application of this earlier definition.

Three main changes can be noted in the more recent definition as compared with earlier ones: (1) a greater emphasis on the *intent* regarding conversion, (2) a broadening of the scope of current assets in order to include prepaid expenses (items to be consumed), and (3) an emphasis on the normal operating cycle of the business rather than on the one-year rule. Each of these changes improves the term for use by creditors as well as for describing the operations of the business.

But the above definition from *Accounting Research Bulletin No. 43* does not place the main emphasis on the nature of the operations of a going concern. The emphasis should be on the frequency of the opportunity to decide whether or not to recommit the funds for use in current operations. Current assets in the aggregate may be just as permanent as the investment in noncurrent assets, but the opportunity for reinvestment in current operations occurs within the current operating cycle of the business. However, once assets are committed by management for investment in specific long-term forms, they should not be classified as current

---

[5] Thomas Henry Sanders, Henry Rand Hatfield, and Underhill Moore, *A Statement of Accounting Principles* (New York: American Institute of Accountants, 1938), p. 70.

assets. For example, cash, securities, or other assets committed by management for the later acquisition of plant and equipment or for other noncurrent uses should not be included among the current assets. The commitment need not be legally binding on management, but it should be explicit. The investment is not intended to become available for the current operations of the business nor for investment opportunities other than that for which it is allocated. It is necessary but not sufficient that the current assets be capable of being converted readily into cash or other monetary assets; they must also be free of commitment for long-term uses. The earlier reference to availability for conversion emphasized the liquidity of the assets, while the criteria of intent and commitment emphasize the operating aspects of the business.

A major criticism of the emphasis on intent, however, is that it is frequently difficult to determine and may be subject to change. As a result, investments are frequently classified as current because of the intent to convert them when and if needed for current operations, even though there may be very little expectation that they will ever be needed. Furthermore, there is also an inclination to classify investments as current because of the desire to make the working capital position appear more favorable.

Prepaid expenses were included in the definition because if they had not been acquired, they would require the use of current assets in the normal operations of the business. But, in this regard, they are the same as inventories; both would require the use of current funds if they had not been acquired previously. The main reason for their inclusion is that they represent resources committed for only a short period—the current operating cycle. Like inventories, they result in current funds becoming available for recommitment through the sale of the product or services and the collection of the proceeds. A question might be raised, however, as to why the current portion of the cost (next year's depreciation and amortization) of plant and equipment and intangible assets should not also be included. Since they do enter into the operations of the current period and, in a profitable enterprise, provide an opportunity for the recommitment of funds, there is some merit in including them. But since, in a going concern, they are normally recommitted for long-term uses, there is some justification in excluding them from the current asset classification. And, what may be more important, the basic nature of plant and equipment items as long-term commitments is not altered from an operational point of view in the period of use or sale.

The operating cycle is defined as the time it takes to convert cash into the product of the enterprise and then to convert the product back into cash again. This concept permits an operational demarcation between short-term commitments and long-term commitments. Plant and equipment items are omitted from the current asset classification because their turnover period covers many product turnover periods. While the operating cycle concept is superior to the arbitrary period of one year from an operational point of view, it should not be applied rigidly either. For example, while some insurance policies may cover more than one operating cycle, little advantage would be gained by classifying these separately as long-term commitments.

One of the difficulties in the way the operating cycle concept is applied in practice is that if it is less than one year, the one-year rule still applies; the result is that the current asset classification does not disclose consistently the frequency of the circulation of assets. But even if the operating cycle criterion were applied consistently, there would still be some major difficulties because of the complexity of many business enterprises and the resultant inability to determine the length of the operating cycle. However, the frequency of circulation of assets is relevant to the prediction of cash flows, but the ability to tie this information to the income and cash flow information is difficult when all current assets are classified as if they had the same frequency of circulation. Classification on the basis of the operating cycle is also opposed on the grounds that it might obscure more significant relationships.[6] Because of these difficulties regarding the concept of the operating cycle and because of the lack of evidence regarding the relevance of the current asset classification to any specific user's needs, other methods of classifying assets should be investigated.

The Definition of Current Liabilities

Accounting Research Bulletin No. 43 defines current liabilities from both a solvency and an operational point of view. The former is reflected in the statement that

the term *current liabilities* is used principally to designate obligations whose liquidation is reasonably expected to require the use of existing resources properly classifiable as current assets, or the creation of other current liabilities.[7]

The operational point of view is reflected in the following statement:

As a balance-sheet category, the classification is intended to include obligations for items which entered into the operating cycle, such as payables incurred in the acquisition of materials and supplies to be used in the production of goods or in providing services to be offered for sale. . . .[8]

---

[6] See William Huizingh, *Working Capital Classification* (Ann Arbor: Bureau of Business Research, Graduate School of Business Administration, University of Michigan, 1967), p. 109.

[7] AICPA, *Accounting Principles* (Chicago: Commerce Clearing House, Inc., 1968), Vol. I, paragraph 2031.07, and Vol. II, p. 6011.

[8] *Ibid.*

Frequently, current assets are defined in terms of their availability for the payment of current liabilities. But generally, the relationship between current assets and current liabilities is not as direct as this. Current liabilities are more directly related to operating cash flows than to the assets existing at a specific date. They generally arise from the short-term financing of current operations, and they are usually paid from cash generated by current operations.

While current liabilities tend to be fairly permanent in the aggregate, they differ from long-term liabilities in several ways. The main distinctive features are: (1) they require frequent attention regarding the refinancing of specific liabilities; (2) they provide frequent opportunities to shift from one source of funds to another; and (3) they permit management to vary continually the total funds from short-term sources.

One of the major differences between the definition of current assets and the definition of current liabilities is that the current portion of long-term debt is reclassified each year as a current liability while the current portion of fixed assets is not. The reason for this difference is found in the conventional emphasis on liquidity and the effect on cash and cash flows; the current portion of long-term debt will require current cash or cash becoming available, but the current depreciation is only indirectly related to any obligations or cash flows during the current period. From an operational point of view, however, the current portion of long-term debt is not a part of the short-term financing operations of the firm. Although the payment of the current portion of long-term debt does require the use of current funds, so do payments of dividends declared after the date of the balance sheet and requirements for capital expenditures. If the current portion of long-term debt were not reclassified as current, however, the cash or other current resources intended or committed to be used for the payment of this debt should be classified as noncurrent, just as cash and other resources committed for other nonoperating purposes.

Disadvantages of the Current Asset and Current Liability Classifications

While the conventional definitions of current assets and current liabilities do provide some information to users of financial statements, they are far from perfect in meeting the desired objectives. These disadvantages can be summarized as follows:

1. While one of the main objectives of the classification is to present information useful to creditors, it is far from adequate in serving this purpose. Creditors are primarily interested in the ability of the firm to meet its debts as they mature. This ability depends primarily on the outcome of projected operations; the pairing of current liabilities with current assets assumes that the latter will be available for the payment of the former.

2. Creditors are also interested in the solvency of the firm—the probability of obtaining repayment in case the firm is liquidated. Vatter suggests that special statements should be prepared for this purpose.[9] Such a statement should show the expected sources of cash in liquidation and the special restrictions regarding the use of particular assets or sources of cash. In the conventional balance sheet, the pairing of current assets with current liabilities leads to the false assumption that, in liquidation, the short-term creditors have necessarily some priority over the current assets and that only the excess is available to long-term creditors. A solvency statement should show the specific priorities that do exist and the rights of all general creditors, regardless of whether they are short term or long term in nature.

3. As a device for describing the operations of the firm, the classification is also defective. Certain assets such as interest receivable do not arise from the same type of operations as accounts receivable and inventories, but they are all grouped together as current assets. Among the current liabilities, dividends payable does not arise from the same type of operations as accounts payable, and from an operational point of view, the current portion of long-term debt is not dissimilar to the remainder of the long-term debt.

4. From the point of view of invested capital, it is sometimes argued that the distinction between working capital and the investment in noncurrent assets is superficial. The investment of the long-term equity holders is tied up in receivables and inventories just as much as in plant and equipment. For a going concern, they all represent permanent investments; there is no greater intent to liquidate receivables and inventories as a whole than there is to liquidate the plant and equipment. This argument is usually directed at the liquidation objective, however; it is not valid as a criticism of the objective to describe operations.

5. The current asset and current liability classifications do not help in the description of the accounting process or in the description of valuation procedures. In the opinion of the author, the first is not necessary and the latter objective can be met by other means.

While the current asset and current liability concepts are deficient in meeting the main objectives of financial statements, the reason seems to be that conventional statements attempt to do too much. It would be better to concentrate on a classification that would permit a valid description of operations and then present specific information of interest to creditors in a separate statement. It may be better to restrict the objectives and present special statements for special purposes than to present a general-purpose statement without specific stated objectives.

---

[9] Vatter, *op. cit.*, p. 58.

MONETARY CURRENT ASSETS

Monetary current assets are claims to a fixed number of dollars of general purchasing power becoming available and intended to be used in current operations within the operating cycle of the business or one year, whichever is the longer. These include money in its various forms and claims to money. The claims generally are represented by formal or informal contracts specifying that a second party pay the firm a given sum of money at a specified date or within a specific time period (possibly implied from general business practice).

Money

Cash and the various other forms of money are expressed in terms of their current value, which is definite. Therefore, any gains or losses resulting from the exchange of other assets for the given amount of cash or money forms should have been recognized; no gain or loss should be recognized from the holding of cash and money forms except in consideration of purchasing power gains and losses during periods of price-level change, as discussed in Chapter 7. Holdings of convertible foreign currency or moneys should be expressed in terms of the domestic equivalent at the balance sheet date.

Receivables

Receivables and monetary securities should be valued in terms of the discounted value of the cash to be received in the future. Since the cash is not available until after a waiting period, the receivable is not worth its maturity value (the amount finally due under the contract). Unless it is specifically stated, the rate of interest or discount that should be used is the market rate for credit of equal risk. However, there is some merit in using the firm's cost of capital rate or its internal rate of return, because these represent an approximation of the opportunity cost of the money to the firm. But, the actual differential cost of granting credit to customers may be very low or even negative because of the possible loss of product revenue if credit were not granted. Although the timing of income is still a factor, it was suggested in Chapter 9 that for most short-term receivables, the amount of interest (discount) is usually small and therefore not material in the computation of the firm's net income for the year. However, as recommended in APB *Opinion No. 6*, material amounts representing specific finance charges and interest should be deducted from the related receivables.

Another factor in the proper valuation of receivables is the treatment of the uncertainty of collection. As indicated in Chapter 6, revenue should be measured by the expected amount to be collected. The receivables should be valued at this same amount, usually by deducting an allowance based on a large number of receivables. The amounts actually collected are likely to be closer to the expected values when a large number of receivables are involved in the estimate than when there are few receivables.

The estimate of the allowance for doubtful accounts is most accurate when it is based on the age and characteristics of the outstanding accounts at the balance sheet date. On the other hand, the "bad debt loss" (reduction of revenue) associated with the revenue of the current period is more accurate when it is based on an estimated percentage of the revenue of the period. In the former procedure, the bad debt loss is residually determined, and in the latter procedure, the allowance for bad debts is the residual. Theory dictates that both should be placed in proper perspective. For income statement purposes, the percentage of revenue based on statistical analysis of past experience adjusted for current conditions should be used. The valuation of the receivables in the balance sheet, however, should be based on expectations regarding the specific composite of accounts existing at the balance sheet date. Any differences between the two methods would represent corrections of prior periods and would be reported as extraordinary gains or losses if material. The commonly accepted procedure of adjusting the current year's charge to bad debt losses for any errors of estimation in prior years is unacceptable under the current operating concept of income, unless the amounts involved are clearly immaterial.

As discussed in Chapter 6, revenue should be reported whenever there is verifiable evidence of the value of the asset received in exchange for the product. Since a receivable is generally expressed in money terms, there is a verifiable measure of valuation, and the revenue should have been reported at the time of sale or before; after the period of sale, any effect on net income should arise only from interest (implicit or actual) during the waiting period or from corrections for errors in estimation of uncollectible amounts.

The Installment Basis. The Accounting Principles Board, in *Opinion No. 10*, stated that the installment method of reporting revenue is not acceptable except when the collection of the sales price is not reasonably assured. As indicated in Chapter 6 (p. 174), this exception is not generally justified. Collection statistics are available for most types of loans if a firm has not obtained its own experience data. But if the installment basis is at all justified for other reasons, the deferred gross profit account should be treated as a valuation account to the receivables rather than as deferred income. The nature of installment sales is to defer the reporting of income until the cash has been received. Thus, at the time of the sale, the receivable takes the place of the product inventory and the receivable should be valued in terms of the product cost (the input value) rather than in terms of the present value of the receivable (the output value). Consistency requires that if the revenue is not recorded until after the time of sale, the receivables should be valued in terms of the product costs. Treating the deferred gross profit as a liability does not affect the computation of net income on the installment basis, but it does distort the asset and liability relationships.

When the revenue from installment sales is reported at the time of sale for accounting purposes but at the time of collection for income tax purposes, a deferred tax credit arises.[10] SEC *Accounting Series Release No. 102* requires, and APB *Opinion No. 11* recommends, that the deferred tax credit relating to installment sales be classified as a current liability when the related installment receivable is classified as current, and as noncurrent when the related receivable is classified as noncurrent. This paired classification is based on the assumption that the collection of the receivable will result in a tax liability payable in the same year that the receivable is collected. While there is a time lag for the payment of the tax after the collection of the receivable, the assumption that both relate to the same operating cycle is basically correct. However, there is theoretical support in this case for presenting the installment receivable at a valuation net of the expected tax, as the specific obligation to pay the tax arises only when the receivable is converted into cash.

Monetary Investments

Monetary securities with known maturity dates and values should be treated similarly to receivables, with proper adjustment for the discount factor and for uncertainties of collection. The interest is usually included in the contract, however, and the uncertainties of collection are usually negligible. But the current values (market exchange values) of these securities often change because of changing market rates of interest. Under conventional accounting procedures, securities (when held for current working capital purposes) are generally recorded on the basis of the lower of cost or market. The argument for this method has been that cost is generally the most relevant basis for measuring the gains or losses realized when the securities are sold. If market price rises above cost, the increase in value is not generally recorded, because it is thought that this gain is unrealized in the technical sense of the word and because it is possibly ephemeral in nature and may disappear before the asset is sold. If the market value of the securities is less than cost, however, it is thought that the loss should be recorded and the securities should not be shown in the balance sheet in excess of their current realizable value.[11]

---

[10] See below, pp. 463–70, for a more complete discussion of income tax allocation.

[11] See Chapter 9, pp. 278–81, for a more complete discussion of the lower-of-cost-or-market rule.

The use of current market price for the valuation of securities classified as current assets, or the disclosure of such valuation parenthetically, has increased in recent years in the United States. In Great Britain, the Companies Act of 1967 requires that the market value of quoted investments be disclosed in financial statements. Thus, some of the financial statements in the United States and many published in other countries are reporting marketable investments in accordance with the recommendations of Sprouse and Moonitz, who stated:

Where securities of this class will be converted into cash by resale rather than by redemption at maturity, as in the case of shares of stock, they should be measured by their current market price.[12]

The author is in full agreement with the authors of *Accounting Research Study No. 3* that investments in marketable monetary securities held as current assets should be valued at current market prices. The reasons for adhering to current market values are summarized as follows: (1) Market values are as verifiable as cost in most cases (except where the market is "thin"), and they provide more useful information to investors. (2) They provide better information regarding the effects of holding securities. The gains and losses from holding securities are just as important as the gains and losses from selling them. (3) When identical securities are acquired at different prices, it seems reasonable that they should be given identical values. (4) Current assets are more homogeneous when all items are expressed in terms of current values. Thus, the investment classification presents a better description of these resources and it is more likely to be meaningful in aiding the prediction of cash flows.

When long-term marketable corporate bonds are acquired at a premium or discount and held as temporary investments, the maturity value does not reflect the amount that will be received when the bonds are sold. Therefore, the amortization of the premium or discount is not appropriate[13]; current market quotations are better not only because the bonds are expected to be sold in the near future but also because the current market price reflects changes in the market rate of interest, while amortization assumes a constant rate.

When corporate bonds are held as long-term investments, the accepted procedure is to amortize the discount or premium over the remaining life of the bonds. The current market price or the lower of cost or market is not generally considered applicable in this case because there is no intent

---

[12] Robert T. Sprouse and Maurice Moonitz, "A Tentative Set of Broad Accounting Principles for Business Enterprises," *Accounting Research Study No. 3* (New York: AICPA, 1962), p. 25.

[13] However, premiums may be amortized because of the favorable tax effect of so doing.

to convert the bonds into cash until the maturity date. Gains and losses arising from temporary fluctuations in bond prices would tend to offset each other because of the fixed-dollar maturity value. But, since the amortization procedures assume a constant rate of interest, current values would, even in this case, provide a better base for the computation of current income under current market interest rate conditions. However, since the difference between the computed interest income and the income based on current market rates is not usually material, the amortization procedure may be appropriate for long-term investments in corporate bonds.

NONMONETARY CURRENT ASSETS

Nonmonetary current assets are rights or claims that cannot be converted into a currently known quantity of dollars at a specific future date. The most common examples are investments in common stock of other corporations, product inventories, and prepaid expenses. These items have a common characteristic different from monetary assets in that their current value cannot be estimated by discounting a future maturity value and adjusting for the uncertainties of collection. But they do not have homogeneous characteristics among themselves. Marketable investments in common stocks are similar to monetary investments in that they may be converted directly into cash when such funds are needed for current operations. The conversion of inventories into cash requires the sale through the marketing operations of the business and through the final collection of receivables. Prepaid expenses are not converted directly into cash; the benefits are received by the firm through their use in current operations. From a procedural point of view, however, inventories and prepaid expenses are usually treated alike as amounts to be allocated to expense in the future. Nonmonetary securities and prepaid expenses will be discussed more fully in the following paragraphs; inventories will be discussed at length in the following chapter.

Nonmonetary Investments

Temporary investments in common stocks of other corporations are usually treated similarly to monetary current investments. Balance sheet valuations are conventionally expressed in terms of either cost or the lower of cost or market. Since a final sale price is not known, they cannot be treated as receivables, and thus other valuation methods must be used. Cost is generally considered the most verifiable, but the lower of cost or market is generally accepted because of the desire to record anticipated losses. Marketable common stocks fluctuate widely in price and, as a result, the current price is a better indication of a possible loss when the security is sold in the near future than some past cost. But the lower-of-cost-or-market rule is objectionable for the same reasons as indicated earlier. In its place should be substituted the current market price in all cases. However, it should be recognized that the current market price is less valid as a measure of the expected sales price of the securities than in the case of monetary investments. Since the current market prices of nonmonetary investments reflect changes in expectations of corporate income and dividends rather than primarily changes in the market rate of interest, they usually fluctuate more widely than the prices of monetary securities.

Temporary investments are generally held as secondary cash reserves. Therefore, dividend and interest income on these investments and gains and losses from holding and selling them are incidental to the main operations of the business. While interest income is accrued and recorded in the period in which it is earned, dividend income is not. Dividend income is generally recognized when it is declared, because the stockholder has no legal claim prior to that time and because of the uncertainty of the amount that will be declared, if any. However, if expectations regarding the payment of dividends are good, there is no theoretical reason why dividends could not be estimated and accrued. The validity of recording the accrued dividend asset and the resulting income depends more on the validity of the estimate than on the legal right to receive the dividend.

Gains and losses arising from the holding of securities while the market prices change also occur gradually. Current generally accepted procedures recognize these gains and losses only at the time of sale or on the basis of the lower-of-cost-or-market rule. However, the reporting of gains or losses from changes in market price may provide more useful information to investors, creditors, and management. Investors may be able to obtain a better picture of the current worth of the enterprise and an evaluation of managerial decisions regarding investments; creditors may be able to obtain a better view of the solvency of the firm; and managers can obtain a better evaluation of the effect of holding securities as well as the effect of selling them.

When the cost basis is used for several identical lots of marketable securities acquired at different prices, a question arises regarding the measurement of the gains or losses when some of the securities are sold. The gains and losses are computed by taking the difference between original cost and the current net selling price. But how should we select the relevant costs? Is it the specific cost of the certificates sold, or should the cost be computed on the basis of a Fifo or Lifo flow concept or on the basis of an average cost? Since this problem is similar to that faced in the valuation and expensing of inventories, it will be deferred until the next chapter, where it will be discussed at length. It should be noted at this point, however, that if the securities are all valued at current market prices, the problem does not exist; all lots are then valued in terms of the same prices.

While the above discussion has related specifically to temporary nonmonetary investments, much of the discussion is also relevant for long-term investments in common stocks. Such investments may be held for a variety of reasons, such as providing permanent financing to suppliers or customers, maintaining partial or complete control of subsidiaries, or obtaining diversification of the firm's investment. Because these investments are not classified as current assets and because the eventual sales price at some distant date is impossible of estimation, the conventional practice is to record these at cost and reduce them to a lower value only if a reduction in market price appears to be drastic and permanent. The lower-of-cost-or-market rule is not generally applied, because changes in market price are considered temporary and unrelated to the eventual conversion price. However, where there is a valid market price, there are still good reasons for using this as a basis for presenting the current value in the balance sheet. Even in this case, current values provide better information to equity holders. The advantages of showing the holding gains and losses, however, are not as great as for short-term investments because management is committed to a long-term investment and does not have the option of selling to maximize gains or minimize losses. Where long-term investments do not have valid market prices, cost may be the only objective valuation available. Under current methods of reporting, the firm's equity in the book value of the subsidiary would not provide much greater information than cost; but it could be helpful and possibly be a useful substitute if the subsidiary in turn valued its assets in current terms.[14]

Prepaid Expenses

Prepaid expenses are benefits to be received by the firm in the future in the form of services. They include such items as office and factory supplies, prepaid rent, unexpired insurance, prepaid interest, and prepaid taxes.

While the various prepaid expenses have some common characteristics for classification purposes, they also have some major differences. Some represent specific tangible assets (e.g., supplies), others represent the right to use assets owned by others (e.g., prepaid rent), and still others are related quite closely to other assets or liabilities. Canning, for example, asserted that prepaid taxes and prepaid insurance are really valuation accounts relating to the specific assets for which they are

---

[14] For a more complete discussion of long-term investments, see Chapter 14, pp. 440–42.

incurred.[15] A building for which taxes and insurance have been prepaid is worth more than a building for which no taxes or insurance have been prepaid. While there is some merit in this argument, the presentation of these items as additions to plant and equipment would not necessarily provide better information to investors. From an operating point of view, they are more closely related to current than to noncurrent assets. Taxes and insurance must be paid at current intervals unrelated to the life-span of the plant and equipment.

The procedures for allocating the prepaid expenses to periods depend primarily on the type of asset to be amortized. Tangible assets, such as supplies, are normally transferred to expenses as they are consumed or used. Prepayments that relate to a specific time period—such as prepaid rent, unexpired insurance, and prepaid taxes—are normally charged off to costs or expenses on the basis of the passing of time, similar to the straight-line method of depreciation. In both cases, the objective is to allocate the cost or other basis of valuation to the periods in which the goods or services are used or when the benefits are received by the firm.

As indicated in Chapter 6, expenses should be recorded in the period in which the related revenue is reported. If possible, there should be a proper matching of expenses with associated revenue. Thus, when prepaid expenses are associated with the production process, the amounts are transferred to product costs. In most other cases, however, prepaid expenses cannot be associated directly with revenue. Therefore, indirect or period matching must be used; they must be charged to expenses in the period in which they are used or in which the services are received by the firm.

In the case of supplies, costs are usually identified with specific items, and these are then charged to expense when the items are used. The methods for cost identification are similar to the problem of inventories treated in the following chapter. While current values may provide useful information for some purposes, costs are generally adequate as a measurement of supplies used because (1) the costs are generally recent exchange prices and therefore they will usually represent close approximations of current values, and (2) the differences between costs and current values are usually not material in relationship to net income. When price levels are changing rapidly, however, restatements should be made, as suggested in Chapter 7.

As indicated above, for prepayments of services to be received on a time basis, the straight-line method of amortization is the method most commonly found in practice. The assumption is that the services are to be received continually over a specific time period and that the final benefits

[15] John B. Canning, *The Economics of Accountancy* (New York: Ronald Press Co., 1929), p. 37.

are received in these same periods. While this assumption may not necessarily be true, the short period over which the prepayments are to be allocated and the immaterial effect of different allocation methods are convincing pragmatic reasons for the use of a simple allocation procedure. The theory involved in evaluating amortization procedures is similar to the theory for the evaluation of depreciation procedures, to be discussed in Chapter 13. One observation should be made at this point. The argument for straight-line depreciation on the basis of a similarity of plant and equipment to prepaid expenses is not valid. Straight-line amortization may not be appropriate for either, but its use in the amortization of prepaid expenses is of less concern in meeting the basic objectives of financial reporting.

THE MEASUREMENT OF CURRENT LIABILITIES

The problem of defining liabilities and many of the problems connected with measuring and recording them will be deferred to Chapter 15. The objective at this point is to focus on the measurement of current liabilities and its effect on the presentation of working capital and on the computation of net income.

Monetary Current Liabilities

Most current liabilities are monetary in nature; they require the payment of a fixed sum of money at some time in the near future. The amount of the liability is therefore generally thought to be a definite amount fixed by the terms of a formal or informal contract. If the contract requires the payment of a specific amount at a later date without interest, the present value of the liability is the discounted amount. When the liability is an open account to be paid after a short period of time, the discount can be ignored because it is not material. But when the amount of discount or interest is material, the present value of the liability should be recorded. Accountants are not generally consistent in this regard; interest-bearing notes are usually recorded at their present (face) value, while noninterest-bearing notes are recorded at their maturity value (also referred to as face value). Both should be recorded at the present discounted value. What is frequently referred to as "prepaid interest" should be deducted from the face value of the note to present the current discounted value. For practically all current liabilities, there is little or no uncertainty regarding the amount of dollars to be paid under the contract. Uncertainties and contingencies will be discussed in a later chapter.

The point at which a liability should be recognized is generally thought to be quite definite; the obligation arises as a result of a transaction. But the point in time when the transaction takes place is not always clear. As indicated in Chapter 6, an expense should be recognized when the goods or services are consumed or used in the process of obtaining revenue. If the obligation to pay for these goods and services has not already been recorded, it must be done no later than the time the expenses are recognized. In many cases, however, the goods or services are received prior to the time they are used. In these cases the asset and the liability should be recorded, unless, of course, payment is made immediately. The obligation arises when the right to use the goods and services is obtained.

Accrued liabilities are not basically different from other payables. The liability arises from the use of services by the firm and the obligation to pay for them under the terms of a formal or informal contract. Because the services are usually received continuously, the recording of the expense and the accrual is usually made at the end of the accounting period. Failure to record the accrual would misstate current income and the amount of current liabilities in the balance sheet.

In the above cases, the recognition of the current liability is dependent upon the simultaneous recognition of an asset or expense. In fact, the necessity to recognize the asset or expense is often the impelling reason for the recognition of the liability. But in the case of a loss arising from a claim against the firm without current or future benefit to the firm, the focus of recognition must come from the liability itself. The amount of the obligation and the timing of its recognition determine the amount and timing of the loss recognition. As soon as the obligation becomes definite and capable of being estimated, it should, therefore, be recognized and the loss recorded.

Accountants have usually been careful to avoid the offsetting of current assets against current liabilities in balance sheet presentations. Even though specific funds are available for the payment of specific liabilities, both should be shown on the balance sheet as separate items. The intent to use specific resources does not justify the offsetting. But in a few cases, the offsetting may be justified. The conditions for justification may be summarized as follows: (1) There must exist a legal right of offset or an agreed unconditional setoff. A receivable and a payable to the same firm would be a good example. But a negotiable note payable to Firm A cannot be offset against a receivable from Firm A without an unconditional agreement to that effect, because otherwise the right of offset would not be legally binding on a holder in due course. (2) There must be an intent to apply the right of offset. If the items will be treated as other assets and liabilities, the offsetting would not be descriptive of the circumstances. (3) The amount offset against a liability cannot be greater than the amount of the liability and vice versa.

The Accounting Principles Board, in *Opinion No. 10*, stated as a general principle that assets and liabilities should not be offset except where a specific right of setoff exists. Cash and other assets, for example, should not be offset against taxes payable. The only exception is when the purchase of certain securities is in substance an advance payment of taxes and the securities are specifically designated by the relevant governments as being acceptable for the payment of taxes owing to them.

Nonmonetary Current Liabilities

Nonmonetary current liabilities are those obligations to provide goods or services of specified quantity and quality. They usually arise from the advance payment for services by customers. Subscriptions to periodicals and season tickets are good examples. Other obligations arise from advances by customers for special merchandise. It should be noted, however, that not all advances are nonmonetary in nature. Some advances represent a given number of dollars that may be applied against a future purchase or purchases at the prices existing when the advance is liquidated. These are monetary advances because they represent the obligation to repay a given number of dollars or the equivalent in goods or services at a future date. The nonmonetary obligations are expressed in terms of predetermined or agreed prices for specific goods or services. Thus, the monetary value of the goods and services may change but the quantity and quality would not.

These nonmonetary obligations have frequently been classified as "deferred income" or "deferred credits." Technically, deferred income represents income items received by the firm but not yet reported as income. However, it is also used to refer to revenue that would normally have been included in income but where the recognition is deferred until later expenses can be matched with it—frequently referred to as deferred revenue. The term "deferred credit" is frequently used synonymously with deferred income and deferred revenue, but it is also used in a broader sense including monetary advances by customers.

These terms do not have clear meanings because they include a heterogeneous group of items and they are not consistently classified in the balance sheet. Some of the deferred income and deferred credit items found in published annual reports are classified as current liabilities, others are classified as noncurrent liabilities, a few are reported as "unearned revenue" in the stockholders' equity section, and a majority are found listed as an unclassified item between the liabilities and the stockholders' equity section of the balance sheet.[16] The latter presentation is partly a carry-over from a former classification in a "reserve" category. However, it is frequently rationalized on the ground that it represents amounts that will be added to income in a subsequent period

---

[16] AICPA, *Accounting Trends and Techniques* (New York: AICPA, 1967), pp. 110–11.

but excluded in the current period, for one of several reasons. The deferred income concept apparently arose from the idea that the "realization" of income is closely related to the receipt of cash, but that when the services have not yet been performed or when the amount is likely to be reduced because of subsequent related expenses or losses, the income reporting should be deferred. However, the separate classification of "deferred income" does not indicate the nature of the items included in the classification and it is subject to abuse, just as was the former "reserve" classification.

Frequently, the advance payments for goods or services by customers have been considered to represent a mixture of liabilities and profit. If cost is the predominant element, the entire amount could be considered a liability; but if cost is only a small part of the total, it is argued that the whole may be considered a deferred credit to income (gross income) rather than a current liability, presumably classified as unearned income in the stockholders' equity section of the balance sheet. If the advance payment represents both costs and income, it is argued that it may be divided between the amount of prospective cost which should be included among the current liabilities and the amount representing prospective income, which should be classified as "unearned income."[17]

This separation of the advance payment into the cost element and the part representing prospective profit stems from the traditional reliance upon the cost concept and the reporting of revenue only after all services have been performed and when all expenses can be measured and matched with the associated revenues. However, it may be more relevant to report the obligation to perform services or provide goods in terms of the output (sales price) of such goods or services. The important consideration is that unless the funds are returned to the customer, the advance payment does not represent an outflow of cash in the future. Regardless of how it is measured, it cannot be identified with specific goods or services to be acquired in the future and used in operations. Some of the services will have been acquired in the past in the form of plant and equipment and thus will be classified as noncurrent assets; others will represent inventories and prepaid expenses classified as current assets; and many of the associated expenses will represent goods and services not yet acquired at the time of the receipt of the advance. Therefore, the advance cannot be associated with costs incurred or to be incurred.

Accounting Research Bulletin No. 43 (page 22) specifically includes among the current liabilities advances for the delivery of goods or the performance of services in the normal course of operations. However,

---

[17] Eric L. Kohler, *A Dictionary for Accountants* (2d ed.; Englewood Cliffs, N.J.: Prentice-Hall, Inc., 1957), p. 160.

such obligations extending over long periods in the future are specifically excluded from the current liability classification, although *Bulletin No. 43* does not state how these long-term obligations should be classified. This treatment of the advance as a current liability is correct for two reasons: (1) The advance is a current financing transaction rather than a revenue-producing one.[18] While other reasons may give rise to the advance, such as an attempt to avoid bad debt losses, the result is an aid in the financing of the operations of the enterprise. (2) The obligation to provide goods or services is generally a part of current operations. Only in the case of incidental transactions would the advance generally represent an obligation extending beyond the normal operating cycle of the business.

While value is added to the firm during the entire process of production, selling, and collection, revenue is generally reported at a single point in time, as discussed in Chapter 6 above. If the critical event in the operations is the providing of the goods or services rather than the collection of the cash, no profit, deferred or current, should be reported at the time of the receipt of the advance. The entire amount is a liability, regardless of whether it is to be repaid in cash or in goods or services. Accounting terminology would therefore be improved if the term "advances from customers" were substituted for the term "deferred income."

There are a few cases, however, where the reporting of "deferred income" arises for reasons other than an advance from a customer. In these cases, the services have been provided and the revenue-producing operations have been completed, but the reporting of the income is deferred because of uncertainties in the collection of the receivables or because of uncertainties regarding additional expenses. These so-called "deferred credits" are not liabilities, as there is no obligation to the customers. They should be included in the income of the current period, less the estimated additional expenses and uncollectible receivables. But, as indicated above in the discussion of installment sales (page 300), if the deferral of income is at all justified, the deferral can be accomplished by carrying the receivables at the input (cost) values. That is, the "deferred gross profit" can be used as a valuation or offset account deducted from the receivables in the balance sheet. However, in almost all cases, the uncertainties are not so great that estimates are impossible. Therefore, the income should be reported on the basis of the best estimates, and the expected future related costs should be reported as current liabilities. In all too many cases, the existence of uncertainties is used as an excuse for

---

[18] See William A. Paton, " 'Deferred Income'—A Misnomer," *Journal of Accountancy,* Vol. CXII (September, 1961), p. 38; and for a criticism, see Robert W. Hirschman, "A Look at 'Current' Classifications," *Journal of Accountancy,* Vol. CXXIV (November, 1967), p. 55.

the deferral of income reporting, with the goal or result being the smoothing of income artificially. For these many reasons, the "deferred income" concept should be ousted from the kit of tools for financial reporting.

SELECTED ADDITIONAL READING ON CHAPTER TOPICS

Working Capital

Fess, Philip. "The Working Capital Concept," *Accounting Review*, Vol. XLI (April, 1966), pp. 266–70.

Mauriello, Joseph A. "The Working Capital Concept—A Restatement," *Accounting Review*, Vol. XXXVII (January, 1962), pp. 39–43.

Winborne, Marilynn G. "The Operating Cycle Concept—Accepted?" *Accounting Review*, Vol. XXXIX (July, 1964), pp. 622–26.

Current Assets and Current Liabilities

American Institute of Certified Public Accountants, Committee on Accounting Procedure. "Restatement and Revision of Accounting Research Bulletins," *Accounting Research Bulletin No. 43*, chap. iiia, "Current Assets and Current Liabilities," pp. 19–23. New York, 1953.

Fess, Philip E. "Improving Working Capital Analysis," *New York Certified Public Accountant*, Vol. XXXVII (July, 1967), pp. 506–12.

Glickman, Richard, and Richard Stahl. "The Case of the Misleading Balance Sheet," *Journal of Accountancy*, Vol. CXXVI (December, 1968), pp. 66–72.

Goldberg, L. "A Note on Current Assets," *Abacus*, Vol. I (September, 1965), pp. 31–45.

Huizingh, William. *Working Capital Classification.* Ann Arbor: Bureau of Business Research, Graduate School of Business Administration, University of Michigan, 1967.

Stamp, Edward. " 'A Note on Current Assets': A Comment," *Abacus*, Vol. I (December, 1965), pp. 188–89.

Deferred Credits

Hirschman, Robert W. "A Look at 'Current' Classifications," *Journal of Accountancy*, Vol. CXXIV (November, 1967), pp. 54–58.

Paton, William A. " 'Deferred Income'—A Misnomer," *Journal of Accountancy*, Vol. CXII (September, 1961), pp. 38–40.

chapter 11

Inventories

The separate classification and measurement of inventories are necessary because of their significance as a basic resource of many firms and because the basis of valuation of inventories has a direct effect on the reported income and the funds flow presentations. An evaluation of current and suggested measurement procedures should take into consideration the basic nature of inventories in relationship to the firm's operations, and the objectives and basic concepts of accounting as discussed in the earlier sections of this book. In recent years, emphasis has been placed on the computation of the cost or other input value to be matched against revenues at the time of revenue reporting (usually the point of sale). While an emphasis on net income is not necessarily misdirected, it has led to inventory valuation practices that distort the inventory amounts in the balance sheet. One of the objectives of accounting theory should be to provide useful guides in the search for valuation procedures that will provide better measurements of the inventory resources and better information regarding the potential cash flows of the firm. The objective of this chapter is to evaluate the several bases for measurement of inventories and the several procedures for matching input values against related revenues.

THE NATURE OF INVENTORIES

AICPA *Bulletin No. 43*[1] defines the term "inventory" as follows:

The term *inventory* is used herein to designate the aggregate of those items of tangible personal property which (1) are held for sale in the ordinary course of business, (2) are in process of production for such sale, or (3) are to be currently consumed in the production of goods or services to be available for sale.

As used in this context, the term includes merchandise destined for sale in the normal course of business and materials and supplies to be used in the

---

[1] American Institute of Certified Public Accountants, *Accounting Principles* (Chicago: Commerce Clearing House, Inc., 1968), Vol. I, paragraph 5121.02, and Vol. II, p. 6014.

process of production for sale. Excluded from this category are supplies that will be consumed in nonproducing operations, securities held for resale but incidental to the operations of the firm, and plant and equipment in use or awaiting final disposition upon termination of use. By definition, inventories are current assets, because they will normally be converted into cash or other assets within the operating cycle of the business. Obsolete and unsalable merchandise, however, if material in amount, should be classified as noncurrent unless it can be disposed of in available markets within normal selling periods.

Inventories are usually thought of as *stocks* of merchandise, although the accounting for the *flow* of the merchandise is usually considered more important. The stocks at the end of one period are interrelated with the flows of that period even though they may be residually determined. The valuation of the stocks, therefore, is affected by the matching of the input values with revenues for the period preceding the balance sheet date, and it may also be affected by the matching process of prior periods.

In the valuation process, inventories are different from both monetary assets and prepaid expenses. Monetary assets represent amounts of purchasing power available or to become available at some time in the future. The current value of monetary assets can, therefore, be computed by discounting the expected cash receipts or conversions. Prepaid expenses, on the other hand, represent services to be received by the firm in the process of obtaining its revenue. Generally, there is no possible way of determining the value of these services in terms of the additional revenue to be generated by them. They can be valued only in terms of their acquisition value—a current or past cost. Inventories, however, are between the two extremes. They are not monetary assets, because the amount of cash or other liquid resources to be generated by their sale is usually dependent upon expectations regarding future price changes; but even when prices can be predicted accurately, the timing of the future cash receipts may also be uncertain, making estimates of present values difficult. The validity of output prices for inventories also depends on the amount of additional direct expenses and the use of joint resources and joint activities of the firm required in selling the goods and collecting the proceeds. In this regard, they are similar to prepaid expenses. But generally speaking, the present value of merchandise can be estimated more readily from expected future cash flows than can prepaid expenses.

THE OBJECTIVES OF INVENTORY MEASUREMENT

One of the objectives of inventory measurement is to indicate the amount of funds that is expected to be generated from the sale of merchandise. Canning, for example, stated that "an inventory valuation, as such, can have no significance except as an index of funds to be produced. . . ."[2] Chambers recommended valuation on the basis of the current cash equivalent or resale price of finished goods inventories, on the ground that it represents the amount that the firm can receive in the liquidation of its inventories in the ordinary course of business.[3] However, he suggests that the resale price should be reduced by the expected margin, which changes the objective to that of presenting the amount of cash the firm would have to hold if it did not possess the goods but had to acquire them.

A related objective is to present information regarding the inventories that will help permit investors and other users to predict the future cash flows of the firm. This can be accomplished from two points of view. First, the amount of inventory resources available will support the inflow of cash through their sale in the ordinary course of business. Second, the amount of inventory resources available will, under normal circumstances, have an effect on the amount of cash required during the subsequent period to acquire the merchandise that will be sold during the period. The inventory should be measured in ways that will aid in the prediction of both the inflows of cash from sales and the outflows required for the acquisition of the merchandise.

A third objective of the measurement of inventories is frequently stated to be the presentation of the value of the goods to the firm.[4] This value is generally assumed to be the net difference in the value of the firm with a specific asset compared to the value of the firm without it. For assets that are readily replaced, the value of the asset is close to the replacement cost; but the loss of some inventory items would result in a reduction of production or sales, so their value may be greater than their replacement cost. For other items of inventory, their value may be less than replacement cost. However, this objective of measuring the value of the inventories to the firm does not meet any specific objective of the users of financial statements. As discussed in Chapter 8, the subjective value of the firm cannot be measured by the summation of the assumed values of the individual assets of the firm.

The most common objective of inventory measurement is the attempt to match costs with related revenues in order to compute net income. This emphasis on the computation of income based on the reporting of revenues at the time of sale requires an allocation of cost or other basis to the periods of sale of merchandise. Thus, the relationship of inventories to

---

[2] John B. Canning. *The Economics of Accountancy* (New York: Ronald Press Co., 1929), p. 227.

[3] Raymond J. Chambers, *Accounting, Evaluation and Economic Behavior* (Englewood Cliffs, N.J.: Prentice-Hall, Inc., 1966), p. 232.

[4] See for example F. K. Wright, "A Theory of Inventory Measurement," *Abacus*, Vol. I (December, 1965), pp. 152–53.

the process of income measurement is similar to the common character-istics of prepaid expenses and plant and equipment. This requires the valuation of inventories on the basis of an input price, and the assign-ment of this valuation to cost of goods sold on some explicit or implicit pricing and flow assumptions. However, the use of output values (sales prices) may also meet the objective of income measurement under certain conditions.

THE DETERMINATION OF INVENTORY QUANTITIES

The computation of inventory valuation and the calculation of the cost or other value to be matched with current revenues require both a determination of physical quantities and an assignment of a price to each item. A large number of homogeneous articles and the continual flow to customers or into production is a common characteristic of inventories. Thus, the quantity determinations are just as important as the assign-ment of unit values. The most common methods of determining quantity are: (1) the use of a periodic count of inventory on hand, (2) a perpetual record of each item, (3) a combination of periodic and perpetual meth-ods, and (4) methods of determining total value amounts by aggregative relationships.

A count of merchandise on hand is usually considered a necessary prerequisite to the audit and presentation of unqualified published finan-cial statements. If beginning and ending inventory quantities are accu-rate, it is generally assumed that net income is properly determined. But it should be kept in mind that the quantity sold is a residual computed by subtracting the amount remaining at the end of the period from the total available during the period. This residual may include quantities lost by theft, evaporation, spoilage, or other causes. With the all-inclusive concept of income, the separation of the quantity sold from the quantity lost is not important; but if the loss is to be reported separately as an expense or as an extraordinary item, the periodic inventory method alone is not sufficient.

A perpetual inventory procedure has the opposite effect. The quantities sold or used are determined from the records, and all items not sold are assumed to be on hand at the end of the period. Thus, any losses are included in the ending inventory. The result is that if there are losses, the inventory valuation in the balance sheet is overvalued and the all-inclusive net income is overstated. Thus, the best procedure is obtained when a perpetual system is maintained but verified by a count at the end of each accounting period. Although this procedure may not disclose the cause of losses, at least the quantities sold and the quantities lost would be known separately.

The aggregative methods, particularly the gross profit method and the retail inventory method, will be discussed under the topic of pricing. It should be noted at this point, however, that these procedures have some of the same difficulties as the perpetual inventory methods unless they are supplemented by periodic inventory counts.

THE BASES FOR VALUATION OF INVENTORIES

As indicated in Chapter 9, the best concept of valuation is one that is related to the expected future net receipt of funds. This also ties in with the concept that revenue should be reported whenever the amount is verifiable and can be estimated with a reasonable degree of certainty. Thus, output values should be used whenever possible. But when selling prices or other conversion values are highly uncertain, some measure of cost or other input value may be the best method of valuation for balance sheet presentation and income determination.

Output Values

Inventories appear at various stages in the operating process of a business. In some cases they appear at the beginning of the process, as raw material or as a semifinished product with considerable economic activity still required before they can be transferred to customers. In other cases, very little additional economic activity is required. While in the former case input values may be appropriate, in the latter case the crucial events have occurred, so that inventories should be valued in terms of their current or expected output values in order to meet the income reporting objectives and to present a description of resources related to the expected future receipt of cash. The types of output values appropriate in this case would include (1) discounted money receipts, (2) current selling prices, and (3) net realizable values.

Discounted Money Receipts. Two important facts must be known before inventories can be valued in terms of the discounted future money flows. First, the amount to be received by the future sale or exchange of the merchandise must be definite or determinable with a reasonable degree of certainty. Second, the timing of the expected cash receipts must be fixed or fairly definite. Very seldom are these facts known with reasonable certainty, except when merchandise is produced and sold under specific contracts. But if merchandise is held for future delivery under a contract with specific terms regarding price and payment, the inventory should be treated as a receivable and valued accordingly.

Current Selling Prices. AICPA *Bulletin No. 43*[5] states that an exception to the usual realization rule is permissible in the valuation of gold

---

[5] AICPA, *op. cit.,* Vol. II, p. 6017.

and silver at selling prices when there is an effective government-controlled market at a fixed price. The two necessary characteristics are: (1) the existence of a controlled market with a fixed price applicable to all quantities brought to the market; and (2) no material costs of selling. A further requirement would be that there is little expected delay in receiving the sale price in cash, so that any interest (discount) is not a material factor in the measurement of income.

A similar situation may exist where there is a delivery contract with little delay in collection. In these cases, the firm's product is completed and any additional effort is negligible. The revenue should be reported, and the selling price is the best measure not only of the revenue but also of the funds to be received in exchange for the goods.

Net Realizable Values. One of the most important aspects of income determination is the proper matching of revenues with costs or other input values. Therefore, whenever output values are used in the measurement of inventories, additional costs of completion or sale and collection should be estimated and recorded in the period in which the revenue is reported. An alternative is to deduct these estimated future costs and expenses directly from the output value in arriving at a *net realizable value* of the inventory. Net realizable value is, therefore, defined as the expected net proceeds from sale less all additional anticipated incremental costs and expenses (exclusive of tax effects) relating to the completion, sale, and delivery of the merchandise. Additional expenses of collection should also be deducted if material .

Sprouse and Moonitz state that ". . . inventories which are readily salable at known prices with negligible costs of disposal, or with known or readily predictable costs of disposal, should be measured at net realizable value."[6] They suggest further that this should not be an exception to usual acceptable valuation procedures, but rather, it should be considered ". . . in keeping with the major objectives of accounting."[7] *Bulletin No. 43*, on the other hand, states that "only in exceptional cases may inventories properly be stated above cost."[8] According to this source, cost is the primary basis for inventory valuation.

Because of this difference in approach to the concept of net realizable value, the two above sources present different conditions required for its use. As to be expected, the conditions prescribed by *Bulletin No. 43* are more restrictive than those prescribed by Sprouse and Moonitz. In *Accounting Research Study No. 3*, Sprouse and Moonitz state two basic conditions both of which are necessary: (1) inventories must be "readily salable at known prices," and (2) additional costs must be known or

---

[6] Robert T. Sprouse and Maurice Moonitz, "A Tentative Set of Broad Accounting Principles for Business Enterprises," *Accounting Research Study No. 3* (New York: AICPA, 1962), p. 27.

[7] *Ibid.*, p. 28.

[8] AICPA, *op. cit.*, Vol. II, p. 6017.

readily predictable. These conditions are consistent with the objective of recognizing revenue whenever it has been earned as a result of the firm's activities and whenever it can be measured objectively. The term "known prices," however, should not be interpreted as known with certainty. Even government-controlled prices may be subject to change. But the amount of the anticipated revenue (the sales price) should be readily determinable with a reasonable degree of certainty. If minor fluctuations in price are anticipated, for example, the expected value could be selected.

The conditions required by *Bulletin No. 43* for stating inventories above cost are as follows: (1) immediate marketability at quoted prices; (2) interchangeability of units; (3) deduction of additional expenditures to be incurred in disposal; and (4) difficulty or inability to estimate appropriate costs. This last condition is not required for "precious metals having a fixed monetary value and no substantial cost of marketing." The first condition, immediate marketability, implies that the product must be completed so that substantially all of the value has been added; external quoted prices are required because of the desirability of objective evidence. The condition of interchangeability of units is stated in order to assure that the quoted market prices are applicable to the merchandise in question. But actually, if the first condition holds, the second condition is either true by definition or it is unnecessary. That is, marketability implies that the specific goods can be sold at the quoted prices, regardless of whether the quoted prices refer to the specific goods only or to interchangeable goods.

The condition that exceptions to cost must be justified by an inability to measure costs stems from a rigid adherence to the cost basis in *Bulletin No. 43*. Except in the case of precious metals, it is assumed that revenue should not be reported until "realization" at the time of sale, but it is permitted earlier as a necessary expedient. Thus, the main reason why selling prices are used in practice for some products is the inability to measure costs. However, the author's opinion, consistent with that of Sprouse and Moonitz, is that the inability to compute costs is not a logical basis for using net realizable value. If the net realizable value can be measured objectively, it should be used regardless of whether costs can or cannot be computed.

One of the major difficulties with the net realizable value concept is that it is usually quite difficult to estimate the additional out-of-pocket costs necessary to complete, sell, and deliver the product. As an alternative, a normal *gross* margin is frequently deducted from selling price to be sure that all possible additional costs are taken into account; but this may approximate an input value if the additional expected costs are not large.[9]

Another difficulty with the net realizable value concept is that the net

---

[9] See below, p. 325.

income from the transaction is reported before all of the activities of the firm relating to the sale have been accomplished. If it can be assumed that value is added by the firm throughout the entire period during which activities relating to the sale are performed by the firm, some of the income will have been reported before it has been "earned." An alternative is to deduct from net realizable value the normal profit on activities yet to be performed. Thus, income would be accrued as the several activities are performed by the firm for the production, storing, selling, shipping, and possibly servicing of the merchandise. The main difficulty with this alternative is in making the allocation of the normal operating income to the various activities. Ideally this could be accomplished by making the allocation on the basis of the value added by the firm in the several activities, but an allocation on the basis of total costs incurred and expected might be a reasonable alternative in many cases. Because of these difficulties of measurement and the little advantage of the extra refinement, this approach should probably remain a theoretical ideal rather than a practical goal.

Input Values

Input values may be defined as the value of resources required to obtain the inventory in its present condition and location. However, usually only those resources used in production or other resources assignable to the product should be included as input values. Resources used in general administration and selling should not generally be included, because of the difficulty of defining cause and effect and thus the difficulty of assigning them to specific products. The difference between the input values and output values, generally called the gross profit or gross margin, should, therefore, represent the nonproduct input values of the firm plus the profit or minus the net loss to the firm. The effect of all input valuation methods is to defer the recognition of revenue and net income until a later period. This delay in the recognition of revenue is justified whenever considerable services are yet to be performed by the firm or whenever verifiable output values cannot be obtained.

While input values are generally expressed in terms of historical costs, they can also be expressed in terms of current costs or standard costs. Current costs can often be estimated by starting with net realizable value and subtracting a normal gross margin (normal markup). While the lower-of-cost-or-market rule has its own peculiarities, it is classified here as an input valuation method because the term "market" as used in this context is basically an input concept.

Historical Cost. The validity of historical costs rests on the assumption that they represent the input value of the resources obtained at the time of acquisition or use in the process of production. They are measured by the net monetary payment made in the past or to be made in the future in the acquisition of the goods or services. If payment is to be made in the distant future, the amount should be discounted to obtain the present cost. When nonmonetary assets are exchanged for current goods or services, the current value of the nonmonetary assets represents the cost of the goods or services acquired; but accountants generally go back to the original monetary payment for the asset given up in the exchange. Thus, historical cost generally means the monetary consideration paid or to be paid in the acquisition or production of merchandise, including all of those services necessary in obtaining the merchandise in a salable state.

Care must be taken, however, to exclude from historical cost payments not intended or anticipated by the buyer at the time of the purchase decision. Costs should include only that amount which the purchaser considered the item to be worth to him at the time of purchase. The mere fact that a cost is incurred does not justify including it in the initial asset value.

Historical costs of production should include the normal direct costs of material and labor and the normal indirect costs that can be allocated to the product on the basis of logical association. Normal wasted material and normal idle labor time are logical costs of production, but excessive material waste and abnormal amounts of idle time are not costs of production but losses to the firm. What are normal and what are abnormal uses of resources depends, of course, on the production standards of the firm. But, within given limits, necessary production costs can be determined from existing engineering and institutional standards of performance.

Similar concepts of cost can be applied to the acquisition of retail merchandise. Normal costs of transportation, storage, and handling should be included as a part of total inventoriable costs. But excessive costs of shipping because of the acquisition of inefficient lot sizes, or excessive costs due to reshipping or rehandling, should be excluded from inventory valuations.

The advantages of historical cost for the valuation of inventories can be summarized as follows: (1) For inventories of raw material and newly acquired merchandise, little value has been added by the firm's activities, so that cost represents the best measure of the quantity of resources available. (2) When selling prices are highly uncertain or when additional costs cannot be predicted with reasonable accuracy, a net output value cannot be estimated. Cost thus serves as a reasonable alternative to net realizable value. (3) Cost is based on a past exchange transaction; therefore, it is considered verifiable and not subject to the biases of management or the accountants. (4) Because cost is measured by the value of the consideration given at the time of acquisition of the merchandise, there should be evidence that the purchaser considered the cost to represent the value to the firm at that time; with prudent management, it can generally be assumed that the willingness or intent to pay the specific amount is evidence of what management considered to be its value. (5) Valuation in terms of cost permits the matching of costs with revenues and the reporting of all income from related transactions at the same time. This is also a disadvantage, however, because it does not permit a separation of the causes of this income. This will be discussed further in the following section on current costs.

Some of the major disadvantages of historical cost are as follows: (1) While cost may represent value to the firm at the time of acquisition, it soon becomes outdated; not only do input prices change over time but also the value to the firm changes as value is added by the firm. (2) When two or more items in the inventory are acquired at different times, the costs are not comparable because they do not necessarily relate to the same value of money; their addition may not result in a meaningful sum. (3) Many cost computations require the allocation of joint costs, and even the best allocation methods are inadequate in reflecting causal relationships. (4) Because costs are historical, the matching of costs with revenues does not provide a meaningful measure of the results of current operations.

The authority for cost as the basis for inventory valuation is deep-rooted in current accounting principles. In fact, for many years, it has been considered the only acceptable basis for most inventories, except when the lower-of-cost-or-market rule is applicable. For example, the American Accounting Association Committee on Concepts and Standards stated in 1953 that "ideally, the measurement of accounting profit involves the matching precisely of the identified costs of specific units of product with the sales revenues derived therefrom."[10] The AICPA, in *Bulletin No. 43*, also recognized cost as the primary basis applicable to inventories.[11] The Institute of Chartered Accountants in England and Wales stated that the normal basis for valuation of inventories is cost less any amounts that need to be written off.[12]

Current Replacement Costs. In an attempt to avoid many of the disadvantages of historical costs, current replacement costs have been suggested by several writers, including particularly Edwards and Bell,[13]

---

[10] AAA Committee on Accounting Concepts and Standards, *Accounting and Reporting Standards for Corporate Financial Statements and Preceding Statements and Supplements* (Columbus, Ohio: AAA, 1957), Supplementary Statement No. 6, "Inventory Pricing and Changes in Price Levels," p. 36.

[11] AICPA, *op. cit.*, Vol. II, p. 6014.

[12] Institute of Chartered Accountants in England and Wales, *Recommendations on Accounting Principles* (London: 1967 reprint), Recommendation N 22, p. 1.

[13] Edgar O. Edwards and Philip W. Bell, *The Theory and Measurement of Business Income* (Berkeley and Los Angeles: University of California Press, 1961).

Sprouse and Moonitz,[14] and the 1963 Committee on Concepts and Standards—Inventory Measurement, American Accounting Association.[15] The 1966 AAA Committee to Prepare a Statement of Basic Accounting Theory also recommended the use of current costs, but as an addition to the reporting of historical costs rather than a substitute for them.[16] The use of current costs has been recommended for inventory valuation by these writers for the following three main reasons: (1) It permits a matching of current input values with current revenues to measure the result of current operations. (2) It permits the identification of holding gains and losses, thus reflecting the results of inventory management decisions and the impact of the environment on the firm not reflected in transactions. (3) It represents the current value of the inventories at the end of the period if the firm is still acquiring such merchandise and if net realizable values are not applicable.

Three major objectives of replacement cost appear in the literature, although they are not always clearly stated and at times they appear to merge. (1) Replacement cost is frequently recommended as a means of meeting the price-level problem. The replacement cost represents the amount necessary to maintain the physical capital of the enterprise and the amount that should be recovered before income emerges. If replacement costs are computed by restating historical costs on the basis of specific price indexes, this represents an adjustment for specific purchasing power. As indicated in Chapter 7, no holding gains or losses arise in this interpretation of replacement costs. (2) Replacement cost is recommended by some primarily to permit the segregation of the usual gross margin measure into holding gains and losses and gains and losses from trading transactions.[17] Thus, the primary objective is to permit a matching of current costs with current revenues. (3) Replacement cost is recommended as a substitute for net realizable value where the possible revenues, length of time before sales can be accomplished, and additional costs cannot be estimated with a reasonable degree of accuracy.[18]

Replacement cost as a means of meeting the price-level problem is not relevant to this discussion, even though the effect on inventory valuation may be the same as in the other objectives. In the second objective, the emphasis is on the distinction between trading and price facets of business operations to provide better information for management decisions

[14] Sprouse and Moonitz, *op. cit.*, p. 29.

[15] Committee on Concepts and Standards—Inventory Measurement, AAA, "A Discussion of Various Approaches to Inventory Measurement," Supplementary Statement No. 2, *Accounting Review*, Vol. XXXIX (July, 1964), pp. 700–714.

[16] Committee to Prepare a Statement of Basic Accounting Theory, *A Statement of Basic Accounting Theory* (AAA, 1966), p. 30.

[17] See particularly Edwards and Bell, *op. cit.;* and Committee on Concepts and Standards—Inventory Measurement, *op. cit.*, p. 705.

[18] See Sprouse and Moonitz, *op. cit.*, pp. 28–29.

and to provide a better measure of managerial efficiency. According to the recommendations of the Committee on Concepts and Standards—Inventory Measurement, the majority of the committee ". . . believes that replacement cost is a superior conceptual measurement device; historical cost is a practical substitute where price losses or gains are insignificant."[19] The committee does not recommend net realizable value or any variant of it, except in very limited situations, because it believes that too many subjective measurements are required.[20]

The third objective of replacement costs assumes that net realizable value is the best measure of inventory valuation because it looks to the future. However, current replacement costs are assumed to be better than historical costs because they reflect current exchange prices rather than historical transactions. In other words, replacement costs are better than historical costs, but they should replace net realizable values only when a future exchange value and other measurement factors cannot be estimated with a fair degree of certainty.

The advantages of current replacement costs can be summarized as follows: (1) They overcome the defect of historical costs, which become outdated. (2) Since all items in the inventory are valued in terms of current conditions, their addition provides meaningful sums. (3) A matching of current costs with current revenues permits a better measure of current operating profit and a separate disclosure of holding gains and losses. (4) If the prices are obtained from current acquisition exchange quotations, the costs are verifiable and relatively free from subjective bias. (5) The application of current values eliminates the need for any assumption regarding the actual or arbitrary flow of merchandise or costs. Thus, the application of Fifo, Lifo, or weighted average methods is unnecessary.[21] (6) It avoids the inconsistencies of the lower-or-cost-or-market rule.

Some of the disadvantages of current replacement costs are as follows: (1) Current costs or quotations are not available for seasonal and style items and for goods produced by obsolete methods. Estimates of the current input values of these items may, therefore, be subjective in nature. (2) Changes in current costs do not always reflect changes in current selling prices. Values do not necessarily change because of changes in costs. (3) Increases in costs would result in gains recorded in the current period (through the holding of inventories) even though they have not been realized through sale. For example, an increase in labor

---

[19] Committee on Concepts and Standards—Inventory Measurement, *op. cit.,* p. 706.

[20] *Ibid.,* p. 708.

[21] This is not necessarily true if holding gains and losses are to be classified as "realized" or "unrealized," as some writers propose.

costs would appear to be profitable in the current period even though sales prices have remained stable. (4) Gains and losses caused from changes in specific cost prices would be included in the net income from operations unless the cost of sales, as well as the ending inventory, is valued in terms of costs current at the time of sale.

A major qualification with respect to the usefulness of current replacement costs is that they may be irrelevant in those cases where the firm would not have acquired the items if it had had to pay the current costs. For example, if merchandise is acquired at a low price because of a liquidation of a supplier's stock or for other special reasons, the current replacement cost in the regular markets may be irrelevant. The net realizable value of the merchandise, in this case, is dependent on the expected sales prices, and this is more relevant than the current cost when the firm would not acquire the goods at this price. Also, the trading margin representing the difference between the expected sales price and the current cost has no significance either to the firm or to readers of financial statements.

Net Realizable Value Less a Normal Markup. When replacement costs are not available, they can sometimes be estimated by subtracting a normal gross profit margin from the net realizable value (estimated selling price less additional expected incremental costs). Before this procedure can result in a good approximation of current cost, however, there must be a direct relationship between costs and selling prices. If these do not move together, the result will not be an approximation of current costs. The normal markup assumed, of course, must also apply to the specific items in question as well as to the original items from which they were derived.

Net realizable value less a normal markup is also occasionally suggested as a measure of the net value of the inventory to the firm when this value is below historical cost and current cost. The assumption is that a loss should be recorded currently and the normal profit should be permitted when the goods are sold. However, this is an incorrect usage of the concept. While this method is often used in the valuation of used equipment received by an equipment dealer as trade-ins on new equipment, it must be recognized that the trade-in allowance does not necessarily represent cost. In most cases, valuation at net realizable value alone would be more appropriate.

In the application of the lower-of-cost-or-market rule, replacement cost does not represent the current utility to the firm when it is below net realizable value less a normal markup. The application of the concept in this context is discussed further below.

The Lower of Cost or Market. As discussed in Chapter 9,[22] the lower-

---

[22] Above, pp. 278–81.

of-cost-or-market rule is internally inconsistent and is not a logical basis for the valuation of inventories. But since it has received such widespread support over the years, it is important to understand the logic or rationalization of the rule. The following discussion pertains primarily to the concepts applied in AICPA *Bulletin No. 43* in the valuation of inventories. Because "market" is initially defined as replacement cost, we have chosen to classify it here as an input valuation method, although in some cases it is an eclectic method, reflecting output values at some times and input values at others.

While federal income tax regulations have consistently defined "market" as the current bid price for the specific item as generally purchased by the taxpayer, accountants have looked more at the utility value of the merchandise. Sanders, Hatfield, and Moore, for example, defined "market" as "the cost of reproduction or replacement, unless the realization prices are lower, in which case they would govern."[23]

AICPA *Bulletin No. 43* extended the concept of utility by stating that ". . . in accounting for inventories, a loss should be recognized whenever the utility of goods is impaired by damage, deterioration, obsolescence, changes in price levels, or other causes."[24] In measuring utility, however, it defines market as replacement cost, but with both an upper and a lower limit. The upper limit (ceiling) is net realizable value; utility to the firm cannot exceed the expected sales price less additional costs of completion and disposal. The lower limit (floor) is net realizable value less a normal profit margin. No loss should be recognized if the fall in replacement cost does not reflect a similar fall in expected sales price. That is, a loss should not be recognized in the current period if it will result in the recognition of an abnormal profit in a later period. The existence of the potential abnormal profit is evidence that the loss was overstated. Note, however, that any write-down below net realizable value results in the creation of profit in the following period equal to the amount of the reported loss in the current period.

The following example describes this procedure:

		Market		
Case	*Cost*	*Replacement Cost*	*Net Realizable Value (Ceiling)*	*Net Realizable Value Less Normal Profit Margin (20%) (Floor)*
A.	*$1.00*	$1.04	$1.20	$0.96
B.	1.00	*0.96*	1.10	0.88
C.	1.00	0.80	1.05	*0.84*
D.	1.00	0.92	*0.90*	0.72

---

[23] Thomas Henry Sanders, Henry Rand Hatfield, and Underhill Moore, *A Statement of Accounting Principles* (American Institute of Accountants, 1938). Reprinted in 1959 by American Accounting Association, p. 73.

[24] AICPA, *op. cit.*, Vol. II, p. 6016.

In Case A, cost is below replacement cost and net realizable value, so there would be no adjustment of cost. Note that the gross profit to be recognized in the period of sale (assuming no additional changes in prices) will be less than normal. But it would be incorrect to show a loss in one period just so that a normal profit could be reported in a later period. As Moonitz and Jordan so aptly phrased it, "to write down assets in order to be able to book a subsequent 'profit' appears to be dangerously close to manipulation of the accounts."[25]

In Case B, replacement cost would be chosen because it is below cost and between the upper and lower limits of "market." There is some question whether the net utility to the firm has really fallen when net realizable value is still above cost, however. But if net realizable value is quite uncertain, replacement cost may be the best measure of utility to the firm.

In Case C, replacement cost is below historical cost, but if it is used in the valuation of the inventory, the resulting expected profit in the subsequent period would be greater than normal. Therefore, the net utility to the firm is assumed to be not less than the net realizable value less a normal markup. This, however, results in a normal reported profit in the subsequent period as a result of the current write-down.

In Case D, replacement cost is below cost but above net realizable value. Since the utility to the firm cannot exceed net realizable value, this should be used as the "market" valuation. However, the valuation should not be reduced below net realizable value just so that a profit can be recorded in the period of sale.

Bulletin No. 43 recognizes that these concepts cannot generally be precisely determined but that they should be used as a basis for judgment. However, if all of the valuation concepts can be measured with equal certainty, the rule is internally inconsistent. The best measure of utility to the firm is net realizable value in all cases where this can be measured with a reasonable degree of certainty. Cost is relevant when no value has been added by the firm or when the sales price is highly uncertain. As a measure of current input value, however, replacement cost is more significant, both as a measure of current utility valuation and as a means of matching current costs with current revenues. This leaves "net realizable value less a normal profit margin" with very little support. Its reliability is based on the certainty of net realizable value; but as indicated above, if net realizable value can be measured with reasonable certainty, it should be used as the inventory valuation. The only possible case for "net realizable value less a normal profit margin" is where the sales price is fixed by contract or a stable market but most of the services

---

[25] Maurice Moonitz and Louis H. Jordan, *Accounting, an Analysis of Its Problems* (rev. ed.; New York: Holt, Rinehart & Winston, Inc., 1963), Vol. I, p. 250.

relating to the item are still to be performed by the firm. However, the concept and measurement of "normal profit margin" are generally nebulous and imprecise, with the result that replacement cost is probably more accurate in these cases.

The English Institute recommends that the lower-of-cost-or-market rule should be applied by taking the lower of cost or net realizable value, so that the amount of the write-down represents the portion of cost that is expected to be irrecoverable. However, it also accepts the use of replacement cost when it is lower than either cost or net realizable value under any of the following circumstances: (1) when the net realizable value is uncertain, the replacement cost may be the best guide; (2) when selling prices are based on current replacement costs; and (3) when a write-down to replacement cost represents inefficiency in buying or production.[26]

The cost or market concept when applied to inventories is tied closely to the concept of realization of revenue at the time of sale, but with the recognition of loss as soon as evidence of the loss appears. But even in this context, it has been criticized severely by many writers. The major objections can be summarized as follows: (1) It violates the concept of consistency because it permits a change in valuation base from one period to another and even within the inventory itself. (2) It has been said to be a major cause of distortion of profit and loss.[27] (3) While it may be considered conservative with respect to the current period, it is unconservative with respect to the income of future periods. (4) The current period may be charged with the results of inefficient purchasing and management, which should be included in the measurement of operating performance at the time of sale.[28] However, it may also be argued that these should be recorded in the current period rather than in the period of sale. (5) An increase in the "market" price in a subsequent period may result in an unrealized gain if the original cost is always used as the basis for comparison with the current market price (assuming, of course, that "market" in both periods is below the original cost). This would not be the case if the inventory valuation at the beginning of the period is considered "cost" for subsequent accounting purposes regardless of the computation in arriving at this valuation, as recommended by AICPA *Bulletin No. 43.*[29] (6) The cost or market rule is said to permit excessive subjectivity in the accounts. This is based on the assumption that "market" is always more subjective than cost.

---

[26] Institute of Chartered Accountants in England and Wales, *op. cit.,* pp. 6–7.

[27] Stephen Gilman, *Accounting Concepts of Profit* (New York: Ronald Press Co., 1939), pp. 459–460.

[28] Carl Thomas Devine, *Inventory Valuation and Periodic Income* (New York: Ronald Press Co., 1942), p. 79.

[29] AICPA, *op. cit.,* Vol. II, p. 6014, note 2.

Standard Costs.   Current standards reflect what a product should cost to produce under current conditions of prices and technology and with a desired standard of efficiency. Current standard costs, therefore, resemble replacement costs, with the exception that costs of inefficiency and idle capacity are excluded. However, replacement costs may also exclude some of these costs that are unnecessary in the production process. The main difference is that standard costs are determined independently of past production techniques, on a scientific basis, while current replacement costs may be computed by applying current factor prices to past production techniques.

There is always a danger that when standard costs are used for inventory valuation purposes they may not reflect current conditions unless they are revised frequently. Thus, they are often considered undesirable for inventory valuation purposes because they tend to represent neither current costs nor historical costs. While they are admittedly useful for control purposes and for other managerial uses, they are considered undesirable for valuation purposes because they are thought to be more subjective than either historical costs or replacement costs. An additional objection is that if actual costs are less than standard costs, the valuation at standard results in the recognition of increases in value before the point of sale.[30]

AICPA *Bulletin No. 43* states that "standard costs are acceptable if adjusted at reasonable intervals to reflect current conditions so that at the balance-sheet date standard costs reasonably approximate costs computed under one of the recognized bases." Such recognized bases would include average cost and first-in, first-out. The implication is, however, that standard cost should not be used to reflect current replacement cost. It is the author's opinion that one of the major advantages of standard costs in the valuation of inventories may be that they can be used to reflect current production costs under efficient and normal conditions.

Normal-Stock Valuation.   The base-stock and last-in, first-out inventory methods are frequently classified as normal-stock methods. The main common attribute of these methods is that the inventory valuation represents an arbitrary amount or a residual of previously incurred costs. There is no pretense that they represent either the utility of the inventory to the firm or costs that should be matched against some future revenue. As a result, they cannot be said to represent true input *valuation* methods.

The main objectives of the normal-stock methods are to match current costs with current revenues and to remove "paper" profits and losses arising from the changes in inventory prices. The original base-stock

---

[30] Devine, *op. cit.*, p. 59.

method was founded on the assumption that a normal quantity of inventory was necessary as a part of the permanent investment of the firm, and therefore it should be treated as a fixed asset. As a fixed asset, no profit or loss arising from changes in prices should be recognized until the base stock is finally sold, presumably when the firm is liquidated. Current operating profit is assumed to arise from purchases and sales in excess of the normal base inventory.

In the original base-stock method, the base inventory was to be written down at the time of acquisition to an amount below that to which any future replacement cost could be expected to fall.[31] The amount of the write-down was considered to be a capital adjustment charged to retained earnings. Modifications of the base-stock method place a valuation on the normal inventory in terms of the historical cost when it was first acquired. Amounts held in excess of the "normal" are recorded on the basis of an average cost, first-in, first-out, or last-in, first-out. When the last-in, first-out method is used, it becomes very similar to the current application of Lifo.

The inventory valuation is, therefore, a residual amount set at some arbitrary low level or determined by the costs occurring at the time the method happened to have been started. The result is that net assets are understated[32] and the recognition of gains from price increases relating to the normal inventory or the Lifo base is deferred almost indefinitely. Since the normal inventory quantities are not intended to be sold, it was thought that gains from price increases were not "realized." This reasoning is related to two other objectives: (1) Under the replacement theory, income is assumed to arise only if the revenues from sale exceed the replacement cost of the goods sold. The replacement goods are assumed to carry the same valuation as the goods they replace. (2) The relevant income is assumed to be the "disposable income" arising from the excess of revenues over replacement costs. Cash is available for dividends only after inventories have been replaced. Unrealized gains and losses arising from the holding of a normal-stock inventory do not affect the amount of cash available for the payment of dividends. Note that the objective is to report net income based on the replacement cost concept of capital maintenance rather than a money investment concept.

As a basic concept of inventory valuation, the normal-stock methods are objectionable for the following reasons: (1) The inventory valuation does not begin to approximate the utility value to the firm. (2) Inventories acquired at different times and inventories of different firms are not expressed in comparable terms. (3) Because the inventory amounts repre-

---

[31] *Ibid.*, p. 92.

[32] Unless the Lifo method was started during a period of higher costs than currently prevailing.

Summary of Valuation Bases

Base	Extent of Revenue and Income Reported	When Applicable
I. Output values:		
A. Discounted money receipts.	All revenue reported except interest.	1. Sale price known. 2. Timing of cash receipts known.
B. Current selling prices.	All revenue and gains and losses included.	1. Sale price known. 2. Collection period short.
C. Net realizable value.	All net revenue reported.	1. Same as B. 2. Costs of disposal are known or predictable.
II. Input values:		
A. Historical cost.	No recognition of operating revenue or gains and losses from changes in specific prices until time of sale.	1. When revenue has not been earned by the firm, or 2. When selling prices are highly uncertain.
B. Current replacement costs.	Gains and losses from changes in specific prices included in income. Operating revenue not included.	Same as II.A, but when current costs can be measured objectively.
C. Net realizable value less a normal profit margin.	All value changes included in income but with deferral of normal gross profit.	As an approximation of replacement cost or as a minimum valuation when it is above replacement cost. Not recommended as a standard.
D. Lower of cost or market.	Income includes losses but not gains from specific price changes. Operating revenue reported only at time of sale.	Although currently acceptable, it has little justification in current accounting theory.
E. Standard cost.	Income includes abnormal gains and losses arising from inefficiency or idle capacity. Operating revenue reported only at time of sale.	To reflect current production cost under efficient and normal conditions.
F. Normal-stock valuation.	The effect on income is similar to the use of replacement costs except that there is no recognition of gains or losses from specific price changes relating to the base or normal-stock inventory.	Although Lifo is currently acceptable for income determination, it results in a distortion of inventory valuation.

sent residual valuations, they do not represent either input or output valuations and therefore they are not comparable with other items in the balance sheet. (4) In the computation of net income, they do not permit the inclusion of all gains and losses.

While the base-stock method has never gained widespread acceptance, it has been given some formal recognition. In the 1930's, recognition was given by the American Institute of Accountants (AICPA)[33] and by Sanders, Hatfield, and Moore; the latter accepted the base-stock methods for specific industries as a proper basis for arriving at "cost"[34] but they also recognized that it "frankly abandon(s) the usual basis of keeping inventories within the cost or market area."[35] *Bulletin No. 43* does not include the base-stock methods among the acceptable "cost" methods, but it does include last-in, first-out.[36] Because of this, and its acceptance for federal income tax purposes, Lifo has become a commonly accepted method in the United States. Its appropriateness in matching costs against revenues is discussed at greater length later in this chapter.

WHAT SHOULD BE INCLUDED IN COST?

Cost is a measure of the value of the inputs necessary in the acquisition of material or merchandise in its present condition and location. The value of the inputs, in turn, is measured by the value of the consideration given up in acquiring them. The questions still to be answered, however, are: (1) What costs can be considered necessary? (2) What costs can be associated with merchandise and therefore with future revenue, and what costs should be considered period expenses?

What costs are necessary is a matter of judgment. The accountant must use either an engineering standard or some other basis for comparison in making this judgment. AICPA *Bulletin No. 43* suggests that the concept of "normality" can be used as an acceptable basis: ". . . under some circumstances, items such as idle facility expense, excessive spoilage, double freight, and rehandling costs may be so *abnormal* as to require treatment as current period charges rather than as a portion of the inventory cost."[37] The American Accounting Association committee, on the other hand, suggests that only costs *reasonably traceable* to the product should be included in acquisition costs.[38]

There is some similarity between the concepts of normality and traceability. Many of the abnormal costs cannot be traced to specific products. For example, the costs of idle capacity and excessive spoilage of raw materials or finished product cannot be traced to the production of specific products. They are not costs of producing anything. But presumably, costs of inefficiency in production can be traced to the product even

---

[33] American Institute of Accountants, *Examination of Financial Statements by Independent Public Accountants* (New York, January, 1936).

[34] Sanders, Hatfield, and Moore, *op. cit.*, p. 73.

[35] *Ibid.*, p. 15.

[36] AICPA, *op. cit.*, Vol. II, p. 6015.

[37] *Ibid.*, p. 6015. Italics added.

[38] Committee on Accounting Concepts and Standards, *op. cit.*, p. 4.

though they are abnormal in nature. Thus, the AAA concept of cost is somewhat broader than that of the AICPA. While the concept of traceability is an important aspect of cost assignment, abnormal costs are not really input values, but rather losses to the firm.

The substitution of current replacement costs for historical costs does not avoid the problem of determining what costs are necessary. Costs expressed in current terms must still be classified as normal or abnormal and as traceable or not traceable to specific products. Current costs, however, require a closer focus on the necessary costs of production or acquisition. The substitution of current costs of inefficient production for historical costs of efficient production is not an improvement in valuation procedures.

The second basic question—what costs should be associated with the inventory valuation and thus be matched with future revenues—is an even more difficult problem. AICPA *Bulletin No. 43* is not explicit on this point. It states that general and administrative expenses should not be included in product costs unless they are clearly related to production. It also states that ". . . the exclusion of all overheads from inventory costs does not constitute an accepted accounting procedure."[39] But this does not define what overhead costs should be included. The ambiguous nature of this statement has resulted in the proponents of both full absorption costing and direct costing claiming formal acceptance by the AICPA. Certainly full costing is acceptable, as there is no requirement that any normal manufacturing overhead be excluded from cost. On the other hand, the proponents of direct costing claim that since it includes variable overhead costs, direct costing is an acceptable method.

The 1957 Committee on Accounting Concepts and Standards of the American Accounting Association is more explicit than the AICPA in stating that all direct and indirect traceable acquisition costs should be included in the inventory valuation.[40] It did not consider the direct costing procedure acceptable for external reporting purposes. But it was not clear regarding the definition of "acquisition" costs. The question of direct costing versus full costing has been discussed at greater length in Chapter 9.[41] While the arguments will not be repeated here, the author's opinion can be summarized by stating that variable costing is too restrictive in its assumptions to serve as a basis for inventory valuation for external reporting purposes in all cases. However, full costing should be modified whenever it appears that costs incurred will not benefit future periods.

The English Institute, however, is quite flexible in its recommendation regarding the amount of overhead to be included in inventories. Depend-

---

[39] AICPA, *op. cit.*, Vol. II, p. 6015.
[40] Committee on Accounting Concepts and Standards, *op. cit.*, p. 4.
[41] Above, pp. 270–76.

ing upon the nature of the business and other considerations, the inventory valuation may include no overhead, only variable overhead, or an appropriate proportion of variable and fixed overhead which would be assigned to products under conditions of a normal level of activity. Direct costing may be used when the levels of production and sales are subject to material fluctuation, when the selling price is uncertain, or where the business is highly competitive or has a sensitive market. On the other hand, fixed overhead should be included to the extent that it represents normal activity in businesses which undertake long-term contracts.[42]

While generalizations are always subject to exceptions and modifications, it is probably safe to state that costs should be added to inventory valuations to the point at which the merchandise is in the proper condition and location for sale or transfer to customers. In addition to specific manufacturing costs, this would include necessary costs of shipping, storage, and handling in bringing the merchandise to the store, display room, or warehouse. The inability to trace some of these costs, however, may necessitate their treatment as period expenses. If the turnover period is short and if these costs are not a substantial part of acquisition costs, inventory valuation and income determination will not be materially affected by the treatment of these costs as period expenses. Costs incurred in selling the product and in shipping the merchandise to customers, in many cases, can also be considered as increasing the inventory valuation. But, if revenue is appropriately reported at this time, there should be no need to add them to inventory valuation; proper matching of costs with revenue will result from recording these costs as expenses as they occur.

THE ASSOCIATION OF COSTS WITH INVENTORIES AND COST OF SALES

In spite of the theoretical difficulties with historical costs, they continue to be used widely (almost universally in the United States and many other countries) for the measurement of goods sold in the computation of net income. Therefore, we should evaluate carefully and critically the several methods used to allocate the identified product costs with the specific quantities of merchandise sold and the specific quantities on hand. Note that all methods of allocation rely upon certain basic assumptions which may or may not be valid. The most universal assumption is that when homogeneous units are acquired in a single lot or in different lots at the same quoted price per unit, the amount allocated to cost of goods sold must be the same for each unit of product. That is, it is assumed that when the unit prices of a product do not change, all cost methods would result in the same valuation for inventories and net

---

[42] The Institute of Chartered Accountants in England and Wales, *op. cit.*, pp. 2–4.

income. However, it may be argued—on the basis of a diminishing utility value of goods, for example—that some units actually cost more than others even though the quoted price is the same for all. This is particularly true where, for example, the goods must be acquired in lots of 100 and only 60 are required for the main objective, but the other 40 can be used as a substitute for other goods of varying lower quality and cost. Therefore, all cost methods are arbitrary to some extent in the allocation of costs between goods sold and those not sold.

Even if we can assume that each unit in a lot of homogeneous goods should be assigned the same cost, the usual pattern is that homogeneous units are frequently acquired at different prices, so that the problem of associating these costs with goods sold and goods not sold is difficult not only on pragmatic grounds but also because of the different theoretical objectives of association. Accountants have attempted to solve this problem by setting up specific rules of association based on certain assumptions of product flows, cost flows, and inventory valuation. The most common methods of association include (1) specific identification; (2) average cost methods; (3) first-in, first-out; (4) normal-stock methods; (5) retail inventory methods; and (6) gross profit method. The accountant must choose among these methods on the basis of existing conditions and specific objectives. The following discussion will evaluate these several methods in terms of their effects and specific objectives.

The Objectives of Cost Association

The main objectives of cost identification for inventories have been the matching of costs with revenues and the association of costs with inventories for balance sheet valuation purposes. When costs are changing over time, however, these objectives are imprecise, because they do not specify which costs should be associated with the goods sold and which should be associated with the inventory. Therefore, accountants have looked to more basic objectives, which place emphasis on either the costs of goods sold or the ending inventory, or attempt to give equal attention to both. These objectives can be summarized as follows:

1. Costs should be identified as closely as possible with each unit of merchandise. This accomplishes the result of providing for a matching of the specific costs of each unit with its revenue and also the identification of specific costs of the merchandise in the inventory. This objective is based on the assumption that each unit of product represents a specific venture; the income of the venture should be measured by the difference between the specific costs and revenue, and therefore the specific costs of the venture should be carried forward in the inventory until the revenue is reported.

2. The operations of the firm may be viewed as a continual series of transactions rather than as a series of separate ventures. The emphasis is, therefore, on considerations other than the physical flow of goods. If the determination of current income is considered more important than the valuation of the inventory, emphasis is placed on the matching of current costs with current revenues; the inventory is considered to be a residual of historical costs. While the inventory is not valued in terms of current costs, it is argued that this is unimportant and will not affect the computation of current income of any period so long as the firm continues to maintain its inventory at the same level in the future. Another argument is that an emphasis on this objective permits the computation of current operating income and the exclusion of "unrealized" gains and losses from price changes relating to the basic inventory.

3. A third objective places the emphasis on the need for a current valuation for the ending inventory. The inventory is assumed to be continually replaced, and the best valuation method is assumed to be one that is based on the most recent acquisition costs. The resulting net income for each period, therefore, includes all gains and losses from price changes relating to the goods assumed to have been sold.

4. Another objective is to identify the gains and losses from price changes and measure separately the income arising from the buying and selling operations. A strict adherence to cost, however, cannot accomplish this completely. Replacement cost or some other measure of current prices must be introduced. Operating income results from the matching of current costs with current revenues, and the gains and losses from price changes can be measured by comparing current costs with historical costs.

Supplementary Statement No. 6 of the AAA Committee on Accounting Concepts and Standards proposed that the first objective listed above is the ideal. It stated: "Ideally, the measurement of accounting profit involves the matching precisely of the identified costs of specific units of product with the sales revenue derived therefrom."[43] In preparing Supplementary Statement No. 6, the committee recognized that where specific identification was not possible, an assumed flow of costs could be used to approximate the matching of identified costs with revenues. However, the assumed flow of costs should be realistic and reflect the actual movement of goods. Artificial flow assumptions were, therefore, considered inappropriate. The 1964 AAA committee on the matching concept endorsed this concept in its recommendation of the first-in, first-out method as one that most nearly reflects the buying and selling relationships.[44]

The AICPA, in *Bulletin No. 43*, appears to have endorsed the second major objective listed above. *Bulletin No. 43* states that "the major ob-

---

[43] Committee on Accounting Concepts and Standards, *op. cit.*, p. 36.

[44] 1964 Committee on Concepts and Standards—The Matching Concept, AAA, "The Matching Concept," *Accounting Review*, Vol. XL (April, 1965), p. 369.

jective in selecting a method should be to choose the one which, under the circumstances, most clearly reflects periodic income."[45] In the discussion that follows this statement, it is clear that identified cost is not the objective in inventory valuation, particularly where the identity of specific lots is lost before the time of sale. It is not entirely clear, however, what is meant by "periodic income."

The third objective—stating the inventory as close as possible to current prices—has been frequently suggested, but only as one of several objectives.[46] Since the change in emphasis from the balance sheet to the income statement in the early 1930's, the objective of showing current costs in the balance sheet has been subservient to the income measurement objective. Sprouse and Moonitz, however, suggest that current replacement costs could provide a useful measurement of the valuation of the inventory on hand as well as provide a meaningful measurement of income.

The fourth objective, disclosing gains and losses from price changes, cannot be achieved completely by a strict adherence to the cost basis of valuation. The suggestion of Sprouse and Moonitz and the 1963 AAA Committee on Concepts and Standards that replacement cost be substituted for historical cost would, however, provide the basis for meeting this objective. Some of the cost methods do achieve this objective in part; the extent to which this is accomplished is discussed in the following paragraphs.

Specific Identification of Cost

The first objective of matching specific costs with specific revenues is achieved most precisely by the specific identification of costs. Each unit is tagged with its cost at the time of acquisition, and this is then compared with the sales price when it is transferred to a customer; the difference is assumed to be the gross profit on this specific transaction. On the surface, this method seems ideal; what better method of matching could possibly be found? For unique items and items of high cost value, it is particularly appealing because of the ease of determining and identifying specific costs of specific units. In a small retail store, it is often convenient to record the cost of each item in code on the box or sales tag, so that the cost can be identified when an inventory is taken. When there is a high turnover of a large number of homogeneous items purchased at different lot prices, the bookkeeping is more difficult, or sometimes impossible except with the aid of high-speed computers. But in these cases, the specific identification is the standard, and other methods are used as approximations of specific identification.

A closer scrutiny, however, causes specific identification to lose some of

---

[45] AICPA, *op. cit.,* Vol. II, p. 6015.
[46] Committee on Accounting Concepts and Standards, *op. cit.,* p. 6.

its halo. One of its basic assumptions is that greater precision results from breaking down the operations of the firm into the smallest units possible and computing profits or losses from each of these units. However, the firm is in reality an integrated whole rather than a series of disconnected ventures. As a result, many costs are joint costs, in the sense that they relate to the firm as a whole or to major divisions of the firm. Other costs relate to many lots of heterogeneous products; any attempt to allocate these joint costs to specific units results in an appearance of precision that is not, in fact, present. For example, costs of shipping, storage, and handling may apply to groups of items, and any allocation to specific units may be arbitrary. Even discounts and other cost-determining mechanisms may relate to large lots of purchases rather than to specific units.

Another argument against specific identification as a costing procedure is that it permits the manipulation of profits by the business firm. When homogeneous units have different costs, the manager can increase his profit by choosing a unit with a low cost or he can decrease his profit by choosing a unit with a high cost. A good example is the buying and selling of corporate stock. One share is just as good as another share of the same class of stock of the same corporation. If several lots are acquired at different prices, the owner may select which lot to sell if he wishes to liquidate only a part of his holdings. The proponents of specific identification as the ideal, however, draw attention to the fact that the business manager is continually making decisions to alter his profit position by selecting which of different items he should sell or attempt to sell in certain periods. Note also that if specific identification is used only as a standard for the choice of other methods, the possibility of manipulation is minimized.

In spite of some of the difficulties associated with specific identification, it is a useful goal to provide good matching when alternatives to historical cost are not acceptable as a measure of input value. It should be recognized, however, that the specific identification method results in an income concept that includes operating income and gains and losses from specific price changes. Also, when specific identification is applied to homogeneous units, a flow of goods assumption is made even if the manager does not attempt to direct which items are sold in what order. If the customer is permitted free choice of which item to buy, the result may be that the choice is random; or he may choose the most convenient item in front, which may be the oldest item, thus effecting a first-in, first-out flow; or he may choose the item with the least dust on it, thus effecting a last-in, first-out flow.

Average Cost Methods

The use of averages permits each purchase price to influence the inventory valuation and the cost of goods sold. The assumption is that the buying and selling operation results in the aggregation of costs and the assignment of these costs to goods sold and goods unsold on the basis of a single price. This single price is assumed to be a representative unit cost of all goods handled during a specific period. No specific flow of goods is assumed, unless it can be said that it represents a random selection of goods by customers so that any item handled during the period has an equal chance of appearing in the inventory at the end of the period. Usually, however, it is not thought to be in agreement with the physical flow of goods but in conflict with it.

Average costs do not reflect either the matching of current costs with current revenues or balance sheet valuations in terms of current costs. In this respect they are somewhat neutral with regard to income determination and balance sheet valuation. But the extent to which they are neutral depends, in part, on how the average is computed. An unweighted average of prices could lead to inconsistent and capricious results, depending on the rapidity of price changes and the timing of acquisitions. A weighted average is generally thought to be more representative than an unweighted average, and a moving weighted average even more appropriate where perpetual inventory records can be maintained. A moving weighted average or a simple weighted average computed for short periods of time may approximate a first-in, first-out flow of goods if the turnover is high and specific lots are purchased frequently. In these cases, it is not entirely neutral in its effects.

First-In, First-Out

The first-in, first-out rule is based primarily on the assumption that it is a good approximation of specific identification for most types of goods in most industries. It is thought to be good inventory management to sell or use the oldest units first and maintain a current inventory representing the most recent purchases. Thus, Fifo represents an approximation of the specific flow of goods. As an approximation of the specific identification of unit costs, it has the advantage that management has little or no control over the selection of units in order to influence recorded profits. It also has the advantage of not being influenced by the arbitrary or whimsical choices of customers. As a result, it provides a more consistent and systematic determination of inventory and cost of goods sold, permitting better comparisons among different firms in the same industry and among several years.

A second objective of Fifo is the combining of all elements of profit reported at the time of sale. As with specific identification, it is assumed that no separation can be made of gains and losses arising from price changes and income resulting from managerial decisions in the course of normal operations. It is also sometimes assumed that Fifo does not permit the recognition of unrealized gains and losses (except as possibly modified by the lower-of-cost-or-market rule). But this assumption is based on the proposition that the operating cycle is from cash to merchandise and back to cash again. Others propose that the cycle should be viewed as being from merchandise to cash and back to merchandise, in which case unrealized appreciation is included in income if the ending inventory is recorded at prices higher than those at the beginning of the period.

A third objective of Fifo is the presentation of the ending inventory for balance sheet purposes in terms of the most recent costs, which can be assumed to approximate replacement costs. The closeness of approximation to replacement costs depends on the frequency of price changes and on the stock turnover. When the stock turns over rapidly, the inventory valuations will reflect current prices unless prices change considerably after the recent purchases. But seldom will the inventory valuations under Fifo be identical with replacement costs except accidentally, or under unusual conditions of stable prices from the dates of acquisition of the ending inventory to the date of the balance sheet.

The objectives of matching current costs with current revenues and the separate reporting of gains and losses from price changes are not generally met with the first-in, first-out inventory procedure. Thus, the major objections to the method are expressed in terms of its failure to meet these objectives. There are also serious practical disadvantages to the Fifo method when many lots are purchased during the period at different prices, or when goods are returned to stock after subsequent lots have been sold.

Normal-Stock Methods

The normal-stock methods of inventory valuation have as their objectives the matching of current costs with current revenues and the elimination of gains and losses from the holding of inventories. Early in the 20th century, the base-stock and reserve methods gained in popularity, largely because they presented a conservative valuation of the inventory for balance sheet purposes. However, they failed to gain widespread acceptance, largely because they were rejected in the United States for income tax purposes. But when the Internal Revenue Codes of 1938 and 1939 gave formal recognition to the acceptability of the last-in, first-out method, Lifo gained rapidly in popularity as a means of attaining the above objectives.

The Base-Stock Method. Technically, the base-stock method and the reserve method cannot be considered cost inventory methods; but since they were important in the historical development of Lifo, which purports to match costs with revenues, they are discussed briefly here.[47] In

---

[47] For a discussion of the base-stock method as a method of inventory valuation, see pp. 329–32.

the base-stock method, a "normal" quantity of inventory is priced at the lowest costs that can be expected over a business cycle. The amounts in excess of this "normal" inventory are priced on the basis of average cost, Fifo, or Lifo. Thus, the gains and losses arising from price changes relating to the base inventory are excluded from recorded income. The reserve method attains the same result by setting up a reserve on the liability side of the balance sheet equal to the excess of the historical cost of the "normal" inventory over the selected base valuation.

Advocates of the base-stock inventory method have claimed the following advantages: (1) A matching of current costs against current revenues is permitted. (2) The inventory valuation for balance sheet purposes is conservatively stated. (3) Price changes over the business cycle do not result in unrealized gains and losses arising from the holding of the base inventory. (4) It permits the smoothing of income over the business cycle. (5) Income is reported only when it is available for distribution as dividends or for other purposes. Inventory profits do not represent disposable income.

The following disadvantages were serious enough to result in the rejection of the base-stock inventory method in favor of the adoption of Lifo to meet the same objectives: (1) The quantity of inventory considered to be "normal" was subject to manipulation and resulted in inconsistent reporting if the base was changed from time to time. (2) Because of the subjective nature of what is to be considered a "normal" inventory, the base-stock method did not permit adequate comparisons among firms in the same industry. (3) The inventory valuation did not represent cost, and it too was subject to manipulation, resulting in an artificial determination of net income. Other disadvantages that apply also to Lifo are discussed below.

Last-In, First-Out. In a few situations, Lifo has been assumed to reflect the specific identification of goods or the normally expected flow of goods. For example, certain nonperishable raw materials such as coal and ores may be stored in such a way that new acquisitions are placed on top of the pile and amounts transferred to production or use are taken off the top, leaving a semipermanent base inventory that may be used only in emergencies. When goods do not flow in this specific order, the last-in, first-out method is generally referred to as *artificial* Lifo.

Most proponents of Lifo, however, do not consider it to be an approximation of the flow of goods but rather a logical procedure for other reasons. The main objective is the matching of current costs against current revenues, resulting in an operational concept of income which excludes gains and losses from the holding of inventories. While the Lifo method stems from the idea that the base inventory is similar to a fixed asset in that it must be maintained continually throughout the life of the firm, it is not necessary that the inventory be classified as a fixed asset. The basic assumption is that the operations of the firm require an investment in inventories that must be maintained throughout the life of the enterprise. The flow of transactions is assumed to be from inventories to cash to inventories rather than from cash to merchandise to cash; income, therefore, cannot be measured until the inventories have been replaced.

In addition to the advantages claimed above for the base-stock method, Lifo is claimed to be useful for the following reasons: (1) It provides a consistent method for computing the ending inventory and the costs of goods sold while still meeting the major objectives of the base-stock method; the quantity and cost of the base inventory are not dependent upon subjective decisions. (2) Increases in the inventory require the application of the Lifo concept without a periodic review of what should be considered "normal." (3) Probably the most impelling reason for the adoption of Lifo has been its acceptance for income tax purposes in 1938 for certain industries and its more general acceptance for tax purposes since 1939 and 1947. Over the business cycle, Lifo permits a smoothing of income and smoothing of tax payments. It also permits the payment of taxes in those years when the income is realized in the form of cash or other liquid assets not required for the replacement of inventories. While the arguments for Lifo as an acceptable tax method have been based on the assumption of business cycles with price changes of equal amplitudes in both directions, this has not been the case since the widespread adoption of Lifo. In general, prices have moved in one direction only, permitting permanent tax savings to corporations that adopted Lifo when prices were at a relatively low level.

In the early discussions of Lifo, it was thought to be useful in obtaining results similar to hedging operations where actual hedging was not possible. Therefore, it was thought to be applicable only in those industries where the conditions were similar to those in the flour milling industry and other industries where hedging is possible. Thus, the last-in, first-out method was considered to be appropriate when (1) the inventory consists of basic or homogeneous goods; (2) these goods form a substantial part of the cost of the final product sold; (3) the inventory is large in relationship to the total assets of the firm; (4) the inventory turnover is slow, generally because of the time required for processing; (5) changes in raw material prices tend to be reflected quickly in the prices of the finished products. Note, however, that Lifo only gives the illusion of a hedging transaction. The reported net income approximates that which would result if hedging had been used, but the gains and losses from the holding of inventories are not transferred to others; they are merely buried in the under- or overstatement of the inventories.

With the change in the Internal Revenue Code in 1939 and the decision of the Tax Court in 1947,[48] the door was opened for the use of Lifo by all taxpayers required to compute inventories. Therefore, the specific industry and firm characteristics were no longer considered necessary. The main consideration now is that Lifo should be used where it "more clearly reflects current income." While some argue that Lifo rightfully omits unrealized gains and losses arising from specific price changes, others argue that Lifo is a good method of meeting the price-level problem, particularly if it is used in conjunction with replacement cost depreciation.

The main arguments against Lifo can be summarized as follows:

1. One of the principal objections to Lifo is that the valuation of the inventory for balance sheet purposes is continually out of date, reflecting prices of some past period completely meaningless in the context of current conditions. And since the inventory valuation is dependent on the level of prices in the year the Lifo method was adopted, comparisons among firms, even in the same industry, are invalid even if all of the firms are using Lifo. The computation of the working capital ratio and other financial ratios is, therefore, useless, and the balance sheet is meaningless as a report of financial conditions. The parenthetical reporting of current inventory valuations would alleviate this difficulty in part, but this has seldom been done in published financial statements.

2. As a method of solving the price-level problem, Lifo is erroneous and incomplete. As discussed in Chapter 7, adjustments for changes in the price level require the use of purchasing power indexes of a more general nature than those reflecting changes in the prices of specific goods. Specific price changes are important in managerial decisions, and their inclusion in the determination of income is necessary in the measurement of the overall performance of management. At best, Lifo is a partial method of handling the price-level problem. Even when it is associated with replacement cost depreciation, it does not permit the complete adjustment of current net income nor the recording of gains and losses from the holding of monetary assets and liabilities.

3. A corollary to the above objection to Lifo is that it permits a deferral in the recognition of gains and losses from the holding of inventories while specific prices are changing at a rate different from that of prices in general. While it is generally claimed that these gains are not realized and therefore are not available for dividends, they are an important part of the operations of any firm where actual hedging is not possible. On the other side of the coin, losses are also omitted from reported income; but this implies that the reported net income is available for dividends without consideration for the decrease in the invested capital resulting from the loss. These "unrealized" gains and losses may

---

[48] *Hutzler Bros.*, 8 T.C. 14 (1947).

also arise from the efficient or inefficient buying practices of the firm. To the extent that this is true, they are very relevant in the measurement of the overall performance of management.

4. Lifo is occasionally rejected on the ground that it is diametrically opposed to the usual flow of goods and, therefore, does not permit a good matching of specific costs and revenues. But even as a procedure for matching current costs and revenues, it is not perfect. The most recent purchase costs are matched against the revenues of the current period. However, unless both purchases and sales occur regularly in even quantities, the revenues will not be matched with the costs current at the time of sale. When purchases are irregular and unrelated to the timing of sales, the matching is haphazard, particularly if prices and costs are changing rapidly.

5. When it becomes necessary to reduce the inventory below the normal quantity, either voluntarily or involuntarily, the matching of ancient costs against current revenues produces absurd results. Income of a single year may include the accumulated gains and losses since the start of Lifo, resulting in a major distortion. Some accountants have suggested that this problem can be remedied by setting up a reserve for the excess of replacement cost over the recorded Lifo cost of the inventory liquidated. This method (sometimes referred to as Nifo—next-in, first-out) was accepted for income tax purposes during and following World War II and the Korean War until 1955 in cases of involuntary liquidation when replacement occurred not later than 1956. But as a general practice, it may lead to absurdities. When the composition of the inventory is changing over time, or when the product itself changes, it may be impossible and at least unrealistic to obtain replacement or reproduction costs for items that are no longer produced. This procedure may also lead to the absurd position of a reserve that exceeds the inventory cost, thus resulting in a negative inventory in the balance sheet. Thus, the reserve is a meaningless figure which represents neither a contra to the inventory valuation nor a liability to replace the inventory. It is merely a device to keep from including in income the gains due to price increases since the Lifo prices were first recorded.

6. The fear of liquidation of the Lifo inventory and the tax consequences has led some firms to pursue irrational buying policies, particularly at the end of the tax year.[49] Not only is this practice close to manipulation of the firm's income, but also it may result in unhealthy economic consequences. If many firms in the same industry attempt to replace their inventories at the end of the year, the pressure on the

---

[49] See for example Waino W. Suojanen, "LIFO as a Spur to Inflation—The Recent Experience of Copper," *Accounting Review,* Vol. XXXII (January, 1957), pp. 42–50.

market may result in increased prices, at least temporarily, and a false indication of the real demand for the raw material or finished product.

7. Many of the proponents of Lifo claim that one of the benefits is a smoothing of net income. Smoothing, of course, occurs only if prices move down as well as up; but even if this is the case, smoothing is not a desirable attribute of financial accounting, particularly if it is artificial. The goal of smoothing confuses an operational goal of the firm with an accounting goal. If the results of operations are not, in fact, smooth, accounting should not make them appear as if they were.

8. Even though Lifo does not generally reflect the flow of goods, it is argued that the objective is to present a flow of costs. However, costs do not flow; they move only to the extent that accountants move them. Therefore, Lifo is artificial and thus invalid as a logical method of associating costs with goods sold and goods on hand.

9. Empirical studies suggest that Fifo is superior to Lifo as a method of reporting to common stock investment decision makers.[50]

Lifo or Market. Lower of cost or market is incompatible with Lifo because of some basic incongruities which seemed to be partly responsible for the requirements of the Internal Revenue Code and Regulations that when Lifo is used for tax purposes, the inventory must be taken at cost regardless of market value. Apparently, Lifo must be used for annual reporting purposes when it is used for tax purposes;[51] hence, "Lifo or market" might be unacceptable for reporting annual income when Lifo is used for tax purposes.

In spite of the opposition to "Lifo or market," it has been proposed particularly for tax purposes for several reasons: (1) One of the early reasons for the proposal was to provide relief for those firms that were not permitted to use Lifo under the 1939 Code because of an inability to identify specific units. On the basis of the decision of the Hutzler Brothers Company case[52] in 1947, the door was opened for the use of dollar-value Lifo, but these firms were not permitted to apply Lifo retroactively if they had not elected formally to change to Lifo in the previous period.[53] "Lifo or market" would have been a very haphazard way of providing for this relief, however. (2) A second argument for "Lifo or market" was to encourage firms to adopt Lifo immediately rather than

---

[50] See for example George J. Staubus, "Testing Inventory Accounting," *Accounting Review*, Vol. XLIII (July, 1968), pp. 413–24.

[51] 1954 Code, Sec. 472 (c), Regs. 1.472–2 (b), and Regs. 1.472–2 (e). For a discussion of different interpretations of these regulations, see Sidney Davidson, "LIFO Cost or Market and Compulsory Tax Reporting Requirements," *Journal of Accounting Research*, Vol. 3, No. 1 (Spring, 1965), pp. 156–58. To the author's knowledge, this point has not been interpreted by the courts.

[52] *Hutzler Bros.*, 8 T.C. 14 (1947).

[53] See *R. H. Macy & Co.*, I AFTR 2d 1733 (1958).

wait until price levels should reach a lower point. Since many firms had failed to adopt Lifo when prices were still low, they became reluctant to adopt Lifo in the face of possible falling prices and the consequent tax disadvantage. Thus, it was thought that "Lifo or market" would create greater uniformity in the use of inventory procedures in many industries. (3) A third argument is that Lifo could result in inventory valuations that exceed replacement cost and that this is not in accordance with generally accepted accounting principles based on conservative valuations.

The arguments against "Lifo or market" can be summarized as follows: (1) The general objections to the lower-of-cost-or-market rule also apply to "Lifo or market." (2) It permits an inconsistent valuation of inventories, based on Lifo in some periods and on Fifo in others. If prices are rising, the inventory will be valued on the basis of the older costs and the cost of goods sold will reflect the recent costs; but if prices are falling, the ending inventory would reflect current costs and the cost of goods sold would represent older costs. Thus, Lifo would be used when prices are rising and Fifo would be approximated when prices are falling. But when prices again rise, there would be a shift back to Lifo with an even lower base valuation. This effect is sometimes known as Hifo (highest-in, first-out). The inventory will always be recorded at the lowest valuation experienced since the start of the Lifo method. (3) One of the main advantages of Lifo is the matching of current costs against current revenues. But, if "Lifo or market" were permitted, "unrealized" losses would be included in the computation of income when replacement costs fall below the Lifo base while they are excluded at all other times.

Dollar-Value Lifo. The dollar-value Lifo method was established as an expedient to avoid the necessity of maintaining records of the original Lifo prices and the prices of increments for each of the many items included in the inventories of a manufacturer. The ending inventory quantities are measured at base year prices; if this amount exceeds the dollar value of the beginning-of-the-year inventory in base year prices, the excess is the increment for the year. This increment is then restated in terms of current year prices by multiplying the increment in base year prices by the ratio of the ending inventory at end-of-year prices to the same quantities priced at base year prices. Occasionally, the ratio is determined by using a sample of the inventory rather than the entire goods on hand. Thus, the base year dollar is assumed to be a proper measure to determine the change in inventory quantities.

If the dollar-value Lifo method is to approximate the individual Lifo computations, the items in the inventory should be grouped into homogeneous "cost pools." Their homogeneity should be in terms of their similarity of price movements, however, rather than in terms of their physical nature or use. However, the tendency in practice has been to use groups that are much too broad and which include items whose prices do not move in a similar fashion.

The result of the dollar-value Lifo method is that the inventory can be stated at prices lower than would otherwise be stated if Lifo were applied to the individual items because, with the use of the "cost pools," increases in the quantities of some items may offset decreases in other items. In addition to all of the disadvantages of Lifo, dollar-value Lifo suffers from the inaccuracies arising from the use of dollar amounts to represent quantities and the measurement of price changes on the basis of indexes or averages. Therefore, the dollar-value method meets none of the objectives of inventory valuation and should be one of the first methods in the accountants' kit of tools to be abandoned.

Retail Inventory Methods

In small retail stores owned and operated by a single proprietor, it is often convenient to mark the cost in code on each box of merchandise as it is placed on the shelf. When an inventory is taken at the end of the year, the cost of each item can be recorded at the same time as the taking of the count. Thus, a specific identification method of costing is effected. In larger department stores, this procedure is too cumbersome and is not desirable from the point of view of inventory control. Perpetual records are also cumbersome because of the large number of items and styles that must be carried by such stores. High-speed computers may permit specific identification and perpetual records at some time in the near future, but in the meantime, large retail stores have turned to the use of departmental averages to obtain estimates of inventory costs and to aid in setting up inventory control procedures.

In the retail inventory methods, the inventory quantity is determined by actual count and priced initially at current retail prices. For interim statements, the inventory at retail prices can be estimated by subtracting the net sales for the period to date from the total goods available at retail prices. In this procedure, the inventory is a residual similar to that obtained by using the perpetual inventory method. The main difficulty is that losses are buried in the inventory amount, resulting in an overstatement of the inventory and of net income. But if a count is also taken, the losses from theft or other causes can be estimated and recorded separately for accounting and control purposes.

After the inventory is computed or estimated at retail prices, it is converted to an input valuation by multiplying the inventory at retail by an average ratio of cost to retail prices for the current period. The computation of this average ratio is demonstrated as follows:

	Cost	Retail	Ratio of Cost to Retail
Inventory, January 1	$12,000	$ 16,000	
Purchases during the year (net)	72,000	100,000	
Markups (less cancellations)		4,000	
Total	$84,000	$120,000	(A) 70%
Deduct markdowns (less cancellations)		8,000	
Goods available for sale	$84,000	$112,000	(B) 75%
Deduct sales (less returns and allowances) ..		90,000	
Inventory (residual) at Dec. 31, at retail ...		$ 22,000	
Physical inventory at Dec. 31, at retail		$ 20,000	

The inventory at retail is reduced to an input valuation by multiplying this amount by the ratio of cost to retail for the goods available for sale in the current period. A more current ratio may be obtained by using only the purchases for the current year, but a practical difficulty arises in allocating the markups and markdowns to the beginning inventory and to the purchases. In either case, there is an assumption that the resulting average ratio is representative of the ratio of cost to retail prices in the ending inventory. To increase the probability of this, a separate ratio should be computed for each department or type of goods that carries a relatively uniform mark-on. If mark-on percentages are not uniform, the proportion of each type of merchandise in the ending inventory should be similar to the proportion of each type in the total goods available for sale during the year.

In the above example, the use of ratio (B) is assumed to result in an estimate of cost. Markups and markdowns are determinants of selling prices and independent of the original costs. Thus, the ending inventory at cost would be $15,000 ($20,000 × 75%). But this assumes that the markups and markdowns are proportionately distributed between goods sold and goods not sold. If we assume two extreme possibilities, we see that the ending inventory may be grossly understated or grossly overstated. Assume first that the markups are all made at the end of the year and are reflected in the inventory at retail; the markdowns are assumed to relate uniformly to the goods sold and the goods not sold. If the inventory had not been written up at the end of the year, it would have amounted to $16,000 at retail and $12,480 ($16,000 × 84,000/108,000) at cost. On the other hand, if we assume that the markdowns were all made at the end of the year and relate to the ending inventory and that the markups relate uniformly to all goods, the inventory expressed at $15,000 (at cost) would be understated. If these markdowns at the end of the year had not been made, the ending inventory at retail would have been $28,000 ($20,000 + $8,000) and the inventory at cost would have been

$19,600 ($28,000 × 70%). Thus, the inventory at assumed cost could range from $12,480 to $19,600, depending on the assumptions made. If the markups and markdowns are included only in the ending inventory and reflect current selling prices, the best that can be said for the method is that it states the valuation of the inventory at net realizable value less a "normal" net markup.

It has occasionally been assumed that the retail cost method results in an approximation of the weighted average method because the cost-retail percentage is computed as a weighted average of the cost-retail relationship of all goods available for sale during the period.[54] However, the averaging results primarily from the use of the same cost-retail percentage for all goods in the departmental inventory regardless of individual mark-on percentages. Only if selling prices are relatively stable, or at least unrelated to the changes in cost prices during the period, will the ending inventory valuation approximate a weighted average cost. If selling prices are moving in the same direction as costs and in approximately the same percentages, a first-in, first-out inventory method may be approximated. For example, if both costs and selling prices have increased by 20 percent during the period, the mark-on percentage will have remained constant; and since the ending inventory will be priced initially at the selling prices existing at the end of the period, the conversion to "cost" will result in an approximation of the most recent purchase costs, reflecting a first-in, first-out flow.

Retail Lower of Cost or Market. The customary practice in the department store and apparel businesses is to use percentage (A) in the above example, computed from the cost-retail relationship after adding markups but before subtracting markdowns.[55] This practice has become common because it is assumed to reflect the lower of cost or market. There is little question that percentage (A) represents the lowest cost-retail ratio that can be computed from the current cost-retail relationships and, therefore, the most "conservative." But there is considerable doubt that it does reflect "market" defined as replacement cost.

As indicated above, ratio (B) is an estimate of cost only if the markups and markdowns apply proportionately to the ending inventory and to the goods sold; that is, it must be assumed that the goods sold and the goods unsold are marked up or down by the same percentage. If this assumption is valid, we could estimate current replacement cost by using the cost-retail percentage computed before markups and markdowns. But one further assumption must be made—the markups and markdowns must have been made as a direct result of changes in replacement costs.

---

[54] See for example Devine, *op. cit.,* pp. 170–71.

[55] Malcolm P. McNair and Anita C. Hersum, *The Retail Inventory Method and LIFO* (New York: McGraw-Hill Book Co., Inc., 1952), p. 42.

The most likely situation, however, is that markups do reflect increases in costs but that markdowns do not reflect decreases in cost. Additional markups, unless they are merely corrections of errors, reflect enhanced salability connected primarily with a rising wholesale market.[56] On the other hand, markdowns are made for a large number of reasons other than changes in costs. McNair and Hersum state:

> . . . in department stores no more than one-quarter to one-third of the markdowns, at an outside estimate, are related to declines in the wholesale market price level. By far the bulk of retail price reductions in department stores and apparel stores reflect intrinsic depreciation in the merchandise itself with respect to its retail salability, without any reference to its current market cost.[57]

We see, therefore, that using a ratio computed *before* markups would result in an approximation of replacement cost (although above cost) if the markups are reflected proportionately in the ending inventory. But because markdowns do not reflect decreases in costs, the cost-retail ratio computed before markdowns cannot be used to approximate replacement costs. Therefore, we must search further for some justification for using the cost-retail percentage computed *after* markups but *before* markdowns. This justification is in the assumption that markdowns reflect declines in the utility of the merchandise to the firm. That is, a markdown is assumed to result in a current loss because it represents a decline in the expected revenue to be obtained from the sale of the merchandise on hand. The merit of this argument rests in the fact that merchandise that must be marked down is not worth as much to the firm as merchandise that need not be marked down. Thus, if the latter is worth no more than cost, the former must be worth less. Note, however, that this argument is based on the assumption that revenue is realized only at the time of sale and that any impairment of this potential realization results in a current loss. The concept of "market" is, therefore, that of net realizable value less a normal net markup.

But the word "normal" has a different meaning in this context than it does when the so-called "cost" retail method is used. Ratio (A) is here considered to be normal, implying that markups are normal but that markdowns are not. In the "cost" approach, the average net mark-on for the period is considered to be "normal." Two other concepts of normality could also be considered: (1) the ratio of cost to retail *before* markups and markdowns, and (2) the ratio of cost to retail *before* markups but *after* markdowns. The former should probably be considered the mini-

---

[56] *Ibid.*, p. 37.

[57] From *The Retail Inventory Method and LIFO* by Malcolm P. McNair and Anita C. Hersum, p. 40. Copyright 1952 by McGraw-Hill Book Co., Inc. Used by permission of McGraw-Hill Book Company.

mum ratio (the maximum anticipated mark-on).[58] The complement of this ratio represents the anticipated gross profit margin at the time the merchandise was originally priced. It does not seem reasonable that a loss should be recorded in the current period so that a larger gross margin could be realized in the following period. The second ratio (2 above) of cost to retail before markups but after markdowns is not now generally accepted because it might possibly permit the recording of "unrealized" gains if markups are made in response to increases in replacement costs, but it would not reflect losses arising from decreases in replacement costs. However, markups are not generally considered normal, at least not under conditions of constant price levels. But markdowns are a normal part of the pricing process of retail stores. Therefore, markdowns can be anticipated while markups cannot. Normality should refer to that which is recurring in the absence of extraneous events. If some of the markdowns are caused by unusual and nonrecurring events, they should be omitted in the computation of the cost-retail ratio. Since the cost-retail ratio is multiplied by the inventory expressed in terms of the retail prices at the end of the year, the input valuation of the inventory would be the net realizable value less a normal net markup.

Lifo Applied to the Retail Method. When Lifo was generally accepted for income tax purposes in 1939, it was still thought to be inapplicable to department stores, primarily because of the lack of homogeneity of the merchandise and the inability to identify specific quantities of inventory at the beginning of the year with specific quantities of similar merchandise at the end of the year. Department stores, therefore, turned to the use of index numbers to identify changes in inventory volume, and procedures for the application of Lifo to the retail method became acceptable for tax purposes in 1947. The reasons for the adoption of Lifo by retail firms are similar to the basic arguments discussed earlier in this chapter. The following is a brief evaluation of some of the basic characteristics of the Lifo retail method.

The first characteristic is that the Lifo base is measured in terms of a specific dollar value of inventory at the time the Lifo method was started plus the dollar-value increments since that date. Since the types of merchandise handled change over time, specific quantities of merchandise cannot be used as the base stock. Instead, the dollar retail value of the ending inventory is converted into the dollars of the base year by the use of price indexes. Therefore, it permits the maintenance of investment in specific categories of merchandise. Gains and losses from the holding of inventories are excluded from income only if the indexes are representative of the specific types of merchandise in the inventories.

---

[58] In the above example, this ratio would be 72.4 percent ($84,000 ÷ $116,000). But the ratio for the current year's purchases may be considered more appropriate. This would amount to 72 percent ($72,000 ÷ $100,000).

A second characteristic is that the "lower of cost or market" is not considered applicable because it is assumed to result in "Lifo or market." But because the use of the cost-retail percentage after markups and before markdowns does not necessarily approximate replacement cost, this argument is not sound. However, since the use of the ratio computed after both markups and markdowns reflects a better concept of "normality" and is possibly a closer approximation of cost, there is some merit in its use.

A third characteristic is that the increments to the inventory are computed on the basis of prices at the end of the year, so that they reflect the Fifo method for the current year rather than a strict adherence to Lifo throughout.

The Gross Profit Method

The gross profit method differs from the retail method in two main computations: (1) The cost-sales ratio is computed by taking an average of the ratios of cost of sales to sales for several prior years, whereas in the retail method, the cost-retail percentage relates to the ratio of goods available for sale in the current year at cost to the same goods priced at retail. In the gross profit method, the ratio is less current, but it is computed from costs that are more comprehensive and include such items as normal losses. (2) The inventory is computed by subtracting the estimated cost of sales from the cost of goods available for sale. In the retail method, the goods available for sale are priced at retail, and by subtracting the sales for the period, an estimate of the ending inventory at retail is obtained. While these two methods are similar, the gross profit method is less accurate because the cost of goods sold is a rough estimate resulting in an approximation of both the volume and cost of the goods on hand.

The main uses of the gross profit method are as a means of estimating an inventory when a count of the inventory is not possible or practicable and as a test of the ending inventory computed by other means. Because of the inaccuracies in the method, it should not be relied on in the computation of the ending inventory except as a last resort. For example, when the inventory has been destroyed by fire or when a part has been stolen, and the retail method cannot be used, the gross profit method may provide a reasonable approximation. As an auditing test, the gross profit method cannot prove the accuracy of the physical inventory or inaccuracies in the inventory computation, but it can indicate whether or not the computed inventory is reasonable. If the difference between the actual inventory and that computed by the gross profit method cannot be accounted for by the inaccuracies of the gross profit estimate, further investigation is required.

The gross profit method is not generally considered to be acceptable for financial reporting purposes for two principal reasons: (1) A physical inventory is not taken, so the inventory valuation is a residual with all of the limitations of the perpetual inventory method. (2) The gross profit percentage is computed as an average of prior years. The relationship between costs and selling prices is not generally uniform over time, so that an average of the gross profit percentage of prior years is not a reliable estimate of the relationship in the current period.

Comparison of the Various Cost Methods during Periods of Price Changes

When specific prices are changing in the same direction during the accounting period, the several methods of inventory valuation based on cost provide different effects on the net income for the period and on the balance sheet valuation at the end of the period. In all of the cost methods, however, the dollar value of the goods available for sale is equal to the sum of the ending inventory and the cost of goods sold. The effect of price changes is reflected in either the inventory or the cost of sales. It can be isolated and reported separately only if a current cost valuation or some other valuation basis is substituted for cost. Note that none of the cost methods can provide a substitute for the adjustment for price-level changes as discussed in Chapter 7.

The specific effect of price changes on current income and on balance sheet valuation depends on several factors, including the degree of price fluctuations, inventory turnover, the level of prices existing at the time the current procedure was adopted, and the relationship of inventory costs to other costs. The following generalizations, however, can be made: (1) Fifo will generally result in the highest inventory valuation and the highest net income if the specific prices are rising steadily throughout the period. The reverse is true when prices are falling steadily. (2) Lifo results in the lowest income for the current period when prices are rising steadily and when there is no liquidation of the beginning inventory. The valuation of the ending inventory may be above or below that under Fifo, depending on the level of prices when Lifo was started. (3) The weighted average method is neutral with respect to inventory and cost of sales. Generally, cost of sales and net income will fall between the extremes of Fifo and Lifo. When a moving weighted average is used, the result is closer to that obtained by the use of Fifo because the recent purchases receive greater weight. (4) The retail method approximates net realizable value less a "normal" net mark-on for the ending inventory. Because the ending inventory is priced initially at the selling prices existing at the end of the period, the result is closer to Fifo than to average costs.

A Summary Comparison of Cost Association Methods

Method	Objective	Effect on Income and Balance Sheet	Special Conditions
Specific identification.	Specific matching.	Depends on actual flow of merchandise.	For valuable or unique items or items easily identifiable.
Weighted average.	Permits a single representative price.	Neutral.	Periodic inventory only.
Moving weighted average.	Single price with greater weight to recent purchases.	Similar to Fifo, particularly if turnover is high.	Perpetual inventory only.
First-in, first-out.	Approximation of specific matching.	Balance sheet expressed in recent costs. Reflects highest income when prices are rising.	Goods assumed to be sold on Fifo basis.
Base-stock.	Assumes "normal" inventory to be a fixed asset.	Balance sheet valuation is arbitrarily low. Cost of sales is in terms of current year costs.	Inventory valuation is overly conservative.
Last-in, first-out.	Matching of current costs with current revenues.	Balance sheet valuation based on old costs. Cost of sales in terms of recent purchases. Results in lowest income when prices are rising.	Valid only if base inventory is not liquidated. Useful when holding gains and losses are not relevant.
Retail method.	Approximation of specific costs or "lower of cost or market."	Similar to Fifo under certain conditions.	For a large variety of items with similar mark-on percentages. May be used for perpetual or periodic inventories.
Gross profit method.	Estimation of inventory when count is not taken or as a test of other methods.	Similar to Fifo under certain conditions.	Perpetual inventory procedure only. Assumes stability of gross profit percentage over time.

When prices move upward and downward with equal amplitudes over the business cycle, Lifo tends to result in a smoothing of income as compared with other methods. That is, Lifo results in the lowest income when prices are rising and in the highest income when prices are falling, while Fifo results in the opposite. The more rapid the turnover rate, the smaller will be the difference between the several methods. Also, the smaller the change in prices, the smaller will be the difference between the methods. In fact, if prices are perfectly stable and all lots of merchandise are purchased at the same prices, all of the various cost methods will result in the same net income.

Summary of Cost Association Methods

The several methods of associating costs with inventories and goods sold are compared briefly in the facing table with respect to their objectives, their effect on income and the balance sheet, and the special conditions relating to each method.

SELECTED ADDITIONAL READING ON CHAPTER TOPICS

Bases for Valuation of Inventories

American Accounting Association, Committee on Concepts and Standards—Inventory Measurement. "A Discussion of Various Approaches to Inventory Measurement," Supplementary Statement No. 2, *Accounting Review*, Vol. XXXIX (July, 1964), pp. 700–714.

MUELLER, GERHARD G. "Valuing Inventories at Other than Historical Costs—Some International Differences," *Journal of Accounting Research*, Vol. II (Autumn, 1964), pp. 148–57.

Net Realizable Values and Replacement Costs

BATTISTA, GEORGE L. and GERALD R. CROWNINGSHIELD. "Inventories at Realizable Values?" *NAA Bulletin* (May, 1965), pp. 31–43.

BIERMAN, HAROLD, JR. "Inventory Valuation: The Use of Market Prices," *Accounting Review*, Vol. XLII (October, 1967), pp. 731–37.

HYLTON, DELMER P. "Improving Inventory Presentation in Financial Statements," *New York Certified Public Accountant*, Vol. XXXV (August, 1965), pp. 583–89.

MARPLE, RAYMOND. "Value-itis," *Accounting Review*, Vol. XXXVIII (July, 1963), pp. 478–82.

MOST, KENNETH S. "The Value of Inventories," *Journal of Accounting Research*, Vol. V (Spring, 1967), pp. 39–50.

WRIGHT, F. K. "A Theory of Inventory Measurement," *Abacus*, Vol. I (December, 1965), pp. 150–55.

The Lower of Cost or Market

HOFFMAN, RAYMOND A. *Inventories: A Guide to Their Control, Costing, and Effect upon Income and Taxes*, chap. v. New York: Ronald Press Co., 1962.

HOLMES, WILLIAM. "The Market Value of Inventories: A Review," *Massachusetts CPA Review* (October–November, 1963), pp. 66–72. Reprinted in *Journal of Accountancy*, Vol. CXVII (March, 1964), pp. 55–59.

PARKER, R. H. " Lower of Cost and Market in Britain and the United States: An Historical Survey," *Abacus*, Vol. I (December, 1965), pp. 156–72.

Lifo versus Fifo

DREBIN, A. R. "Price Level Adjustments and Inventory Flow Assumptions," *Accounting Review*, Vol. XL (January, 1965), pp. 154–62.

GAMBLING, TREVOR E. "LIFO vs. FIFO Under Conditions of 'Certainty'," *Accounting Review*, Vol. XLIII (April, 1968), pp. 387–89.

HOFFMAN, RAYMOND A. *Inventories: A Guide to Their Control, Costing, and Effect upon Income and Taxes*, chaps. viii, ix, x. New York: Ronald Press Co., 1962.

MOONITZ, MAURICE. "The Case against Lifo as an Inventory-Pricing Formula," *Journal of Accountancy*, Vol. XCV (June, 1953), pp. 682–90.

STAUBUS, GEORGE J. "Testing Inventory Accounting," *Accounting Review*, Vol. XLIII (July, 1968), pp. 413–24.

Lifo or Market

DAVIDSON, SIDNEY. "LIFO Cost or Market and Compulsory Tax Reporting," *Journal of Accounting Research*, Vol. III (Spring, 1965), pp. 156–58.

ENGELMANN, K. "The 'LIFO or Market' Plan," *Accounting Review*, Vol. XXVIII (January, 1953), pp. 54–57.

HOFFMAN, RAYMOND A. *Inventories: A Guide to Their Control, Costing, and Effect upon Income and Taxes*, pp. 158–60. New York: Ronald Press Co., 1962.

Dollar Value Lifo

BLAKELY, EDWARD J. and PETER H. KNUTSON. "L.I.F.O. or L.O.F.I.—Which?" *Accounting Review*, Vol. XXXVIII (January, 1963), pp. 75–86.

FIRMIN, PETER. "Dollar-Value LIFO: Legitimate or Not?" *Accounting Review*, Vol. XXXVIII (April, 1963), pp. 270–77.

The Retail Method

BELL, HERMON F., and LOUIS C. MOSCARELLO. *Retail Merchandise Accounting,* chaps. vi, vii. 3d ed. New York: Ronald Press Co., 1961.

HOFFMAN, RAYMOND A. *Inventories: A Guide to Their Control, Costing, and Effect upon Income and Taxes,* chap. vi. New York: Ronald Press Co., 1962.

LINDBECK, RUDOLPH S. "Conventional Retail—Lower than Cost or Market," *Accounting Review,* Vol. XLI (April, 1966), pp. 335–38.

Retail Lifo

BELL, HERMON F., and LOUIS C. MOSCARELLO. *Retail Merchandise Accounting,* chaps. xxi–xxvii. New York: Ronald Press Co., 1961.

HOFFMAN, RAYMOND A. *Inventories: A Guide to Their Control, Costing, and Effect upon Income and Taxes,* chap. xi. New York: Ronald Press Co., 1962.

chapter 12

Plant and Equipment

The separate classification and measurement of plant and equipment are relevant for financial reporting because of the significance of capital expenditures for the operation of a firm over several years. As with inventories, one of the important aspects of accounting for plant and equipment is the computation of the amount to be charged to expense in the determination of the net income of each period. This computation of the current depreciation charge is often considered to be the main objective in the accounting for plant and equipment; but the measurement process should also be helpful in describing the capital resources available to the firm. While depreciation and valuation are frequently thought to be related, the conventional depreciation methods and balance sheet valuations are inadequate as measurements of plant and equipment services used during a period and measurements of the service potentials remaining at the end of the period. This is partly the result of an inability to identify specific items or services used during the accounting period and the quantity of services remaining unused at the end of the period. The objectives of this chapter are to discuss the nature of the plant and equipment classification and to evaluate the several measurement bases applicable to it. The nature and methods of depreciation will be discussed in the following chapter.

THE NATURE OF PLANT AND EQUIPMENT

The term "fixed assets" is often used in the broad sense to mean all noncurrent assets owned by a firm. But it is also used in a narrower sense to include land, buildings, equipment, tools, furniture, patterns, drawings, and dies used in the normal operations of the business. Excluded from this narrower definition are all intangible assets, noncurrent receivables, long-term investments, and land, buildings, and equipment not used in the normal operations of the firm. It is with this narrower definition of fixed assets (but excluding land) that this chapter and the next are concerned. Intangibles are treated separately in a following chapter.

While all assets have some basic common characteristics, as indicated in Chapter 9, the additional characteristics of plant and equipment are summarized as follows: (1) The assets represent physical goods held to facilitate the production of other goods or to provide services to the firm or its customers in the normal course of operations. (2) They all have a limited life, at the end of which they must be abandoned or replaced. This life may be an estimated number of years determined by wear and tear caused by the elements, or it may be variable, depending on the amount of use and maintenance. (3) The value of the assets stems from the ability to enforce the exclusion of others in obtaining the legal property rights to their use rather than from the enforcement of contracts. (4) They are all nonmonetary in nature; the benefits are received from the use or sale of services rather than from their conversion into known quantities of money. (5) In general, the services are to be received over a period longer than a year or the operating cycle of the business. However, there are some exceptions. For example, a building or a piece of equipment is not reclassified as current when it has less than a year of remaining life. In a few cases, such as tools, some items may have an original life less than the operating cycle of the business.

While plant and equipment items do have some common characteristics, as indicated above, there are also some basic objectives for treating them similarly for financial reporting purposes. One of these objectives is based on their similarity in the accounting process. Plant and equipment are held for their future services; therefore, they are charged to expense during their useful lives in a manner similar to prepaid expenses. The main difference between prepaid expenses and plant and equipment is in the life of the asset. Prepaid expenses are usually charged to expense during the current operating cycle of the business or one year, whichever is the longer, while plant and equipment are charged to expense over a longer period. But if similarity in the accounting process is the main objective of classification, those intangibles with a limited life should probably be included. However, in the author's opinion, classification according to the accounting process is not a relevant objective for financial reporting.

A second objective in the description and measurement of plant and equipment items is to provide an indication of the amount of physical quantities or productive capacities held by the firm as well as some indication of their relative ages and expected future lives. It is unlikely that aggregate dollar figures can provide this information. However, for specific assets or groups of assets, an input valuation basis is likely to be more relevant than a liquidation value; and a valuation based on the expected value of future goods or services or cash flows is not possible of measurement either on theoretical or practical grounds. For reasons discussed in the next chapter, an accumulated depreciation amount subtracted from an input valuation cannot provide an adequate description of the relative age or condition of the physical plant and equipment.

A third and probably the most important objective of the plant and equipment classification and valuation is to present a description of the operations of the firm. Just as a grouping of monetary assets and current assets presents information about the operations of the firm, so does a grouping of the investment in capital items. The relative amount of capital invested in plant and equipment is relevant information for investors and creditors, because it can possibly add information to aid in the prediction of future cash flows and give an indication of the period of time before the firm will have the opportunity to recommit its resources to the same or other uses without a forced liquidation. In public utility firms and in many other service corporations, the amount invested in long-term capital items is the most important category as a source of future revenues. For this reason, most public utilities present the plant and equipment items first in the balance sheet, ahead of current assets.

While nonoperating plant and equipment items are usually presented in the balance sheet in a separate classification, the valuation and depreciation problems are similar to those relating to operating plant and equipment. Accordingly, most of the following discussion relates to both operating and nonoperating plant and equipment items.

THE BASES OF VALUATION

Except in certain cases where property is leased to others under a long-term contract (used as a financial device), plant and equipment cannot be valued in terms of output prices. The main reason for the inability to use output prices is that the revenues of a firm result from the use of many goods and services. In some cases it may be possible to estimate the future stream of revenues and costs to the firm and, by discounting appropriately the expected stream of net cash distributions to investors, an estimate of the current valuation of the entire firm may be obtained. But it is not possible to assign this stream of net cash flows to specific assets. All operating assets contribute to the revenue stream, but it is a joint contribution; there is no way to determine how much each asset contributes. The uncertainty regarding the amount and timing of the revenue stream alone may be considerable, but the further uncertainty of determining the contribution of the specific goods and services used in the operating process makes the use of output valuation bases too imprecise for application to fixed assets. While arbitrary allocation methods could be used, the result would not be meaningful for financial reporting.

A more important objection to the use of an output valuation for fixed assets is that very little value is added to the firm from the acquisition and holding of fixed assets. As indicated in Chapter 6, value is added in an economic sense throughout the entire production process. That is, income results from the entire operations of the firm, from the initial organization of the firm through the acquisition of producing facilities and other factors of production to the final sale of the product and the collection of the sales price. But the acquisition of the facilities generally comes early in this process, so that very little income has been earned by that time. Accountants are correct in holding to the general rule that reported income should not result from the recording of acquisitions.[1]

When plant and equipment are no longer of value to the firm in its normal operations, or when they are to be sold in a secondhand market, the sales price of the fixed asset itself may become the best valuation basis. This is not an output value in the normal sense, however, since it is determined by the sales price of the asset itself rather than from the sales price of the product of the asset. The price is the liquidation or scrap value obtained from an entirely different market than that from which the input value is obtained or that from which an output value of the product is obtained.

However, if there are many buyers and sellers in the used asset market, the price quoted in this market may reflect the market's expectations regarding the discounted input value of the remaining services to be obtained from the use of the asset. For example, the market for second-hand trucks and trailers used by public carriers is well organized and is made up of many buyers and sellers. The sales prices are, therefore, fairly uniform for equipment of similar age and mileage operated. Thus, the prices of similar units in the used market reflect expectations of the input value of the remaining service life, because they represent the opportunity cost of the asset held by the firm and the amount that many other users are willing to pay for the future services of similar assets to be used under similar conditions.

According to the current cash equivalent concept proposed by Chambers, durable items which have an active secondhand market should be priced at the amount that could be obtained for the items by selling them in an orderly process. For nonvendible durables, Chambers suggests, consistently with his other recommendations, that the items should be written off immediately upon acquisition, just as development costs are written off in many cases because they do not have a current cash equivalent.[2] However, Chambers also suggests that the current cash equivalent can be approximated, as an expediency, by the application of

---

[1] This does not preclude the theoretical propriety of showing gains and losses arising from favorable acquisition prices or from changes in input values, however, even though it is not in accordance with generally accepted realization rules.

[2] Raymond J. Chambers, *Accounting, Evaluation, and Economic Behavior* (Englewood Cliffs, N.J.: Prentice-Hall, Inc., 1966), pp. 238–45.

specific price indexes to the purchase price.[3] But this alternative does not provide a valuation basis which is consistent with his general theory. An input price adjusted by specific indexes must be reduced by subjective depreciation allocations, so that the net result cannot be assumed to represent the current cash equivalent nor the ability of the firm to make appropriate adaptation.

Since output values are difficult or impossible to assign to plant and equipment, and liquidation values represent the present value of future services for only a few interchangeable assets, accountants must turn to input values for the valuation of fixed assets. But because the services of plant and equipment for any particular year can usually be obtained only by the acquisition of whole assets with many years of service, only the initial input value can be measured objectively. The valuation of the asset at any subsequent date is dependent on the depreciation process. However, the initial input value for the asset as a whole may be restated whenever changes occur in the general price level or in the specific markets in which they are generally acquired.

Input Values

Probably the area of greatest agreement in the literature of accounting theory is that plant and equipment should be valued initially on the basis of their acquisition cost.[4] Lower amounts are suggested or required in the government regulation of public utilities when the acquisition cost exceeds the original cost new less depreciation or the "prudent" cost. Subsequent to the date of acquisition, the net valuation is generally cost less accumulated depreciation, but the depreciation charge is based on the acquisition cost. The allocation of these acquisition costs—the depreciation process—is the main subject of most discussions of the accounting for plant and equipment. While the emphasis on the computation of the depreciation charge is correct because of its importance in the determination of periodic net income, the choice of a proper valuation base is equally important in the presentation of meaningful amounts in the balance sheet.

The main reason that input values are the most relevant for the valuation of plant and equipment is that they may be assumed to represent the minimum value to the firm, at the date of acquisition, of the future services of the asset. The subjective output value of the asset

---

3 *Ibid.*, pp. 245–49.

4 See for example W. A. Paton and A. C. Littleton, *An Introduction to Accounting Standards* (American Accounting Association, 1955), p. 81; and Robert T. Sprouse and Maurice Moonitz, "A Tentative Set of Broad Accounting Principles for Business Enterprises," *Accounting Research Study No. 3* (New York: American Institute of Certified Public Accountants, 1962), p. 32.

should exceed the total input price if it is worth acquiring. However, there are several concepts and methods for computing the total input valuation of an asset. While the historical acquisition cost is the most common method, it represents only one of several input valuation concepts.

Other input valuation concepts have been suggested and used from time to time to attain specific objectives or to obtain more meaningful measurements of current depreciation or more meaningful balance sheet valuations. The most important alternative to acquisition cost is replacement cost, because it represents a *current* input valuation concept. Other current input values include appraisal value and fair value.

Historical Input Values

One of the main advantages of historical input values is that since they represent transaction prices paid by the firm, they are verifiable. It is also argued that they provide a consistent basis for the valuation of plant and equipment for each firm and among all firms. While historical cost is generally agreed to be the most acceptable basis for the valuation of plant and equipment, we shall see in the following main section that accountants are not agreed on what should be included in cost. While variations of the historical input valuation method may be considered to be modifications of cost content, original cost (sometimes known as aboriginal cost) and prudent cost are so different in their application that they require separate discussion in this section.

Historical Cost to the Firm. Historical cost is defined as the aggregate price paid by the firm to acquire ownership and use of a fixed asset, including all payments necessary to obtain the asset in the location and condition required for it to provide services in the production or other operations of the firm. If the price is to be paid at a later date under the terms of the contract, the cost of the asset should be the present discounted value of the contractual obligation. However, short delays in payment may be ignored because the discount is usually immaterial. When assets other than cash are given in exchange for the fixed asset, the cost is the current value of the assets given up. However, the relevant current value of the asset exchanged is its current selling price rather than its book value or other input value because the asset is no longer being held for the value of its future services, if any.

The main advantage of historical cost is that it can be assumed to represent the value of the fixed asset to the enterprise at the time of acquisition. But it must be noted that the term "value" is used here in a special sense. It is determined by market forces, or at least by a bargained arm's-length transaction; thus, it represents the market price of the asset at the time of acquisition. That is, cost represents the market value of the inputs at the time they are acquired. If the asset is used in the same accounting period as that in which it is acquired, this market price also represents the current value of the input, which can be matched with the current revenue to determine the current net operating income.

Frequently, cost is rationalized as being the value to the going concern.[5] The firm is assumed to have a life long enough to be able to receive the service benefits to be provided by the asset. Thus, a liquidation value is assumed to be not relevant. But cost is a minimum value to the firm. It can be assumed that the firm would not have acquired the asset at its cost price if it did not feel that its future benefits would be equal to or greater than its cost. In the absence of changes in the expectations of the firm, the unallocated cost at the end of each successive period should continue to represent the minimum expected value to the firm.

The main disadvantage of historical cost is that it does not continue to reflect either the value of its future services or its current market price if economic conditions or prices change in subsequent periods. Even if prices remained constant, it is unlikely that the expectations regarding future services would remain constant. Expectations may change because of greater certainty as the remaining life of the asset becomes shorter or because of changes in technology or in economic conditions. Price changes affect the relevancy and comparability of historical costs applied to fixed assets to a greater extent than costs applied to current assets, because of the longer period from the date of acquisition to the average period of use. The longer this period is, the greater is the cumulative effect of price changes since the date of acquisition.

Prudent Cost. Only those costs that would normally be paid for property by reasonably prudent management should be included in prudent costs. This concept has been used by public utility regulators as a method of placing the public interest ahead of the interests of promoters, management, and stockholders. But the prudent cost concept is also applicable to the general valuation of plant and equipment. The costs to be allocated to the services of future periods should not include excessive costs representing costs of inefficiency and other losses incurred in the period of acquisition. However, the concept is difficult to apply because it requires the use of value judgments in determining what costs are excessive and what costs are required. In general, the costs intended to be incurred by management at the time of the initial commitment can be assumed to be based on prudent judgment unless evidence is clearly to the contrary. Unanticipated additional costs should be excluded because evidence is lacking that management would have agreed to incur these costs initially.

Original Cost. As used in public utility regulation, the term "original cost" refers to the cost of property to the firm first devoting it to public

---

[5] See the discussion of "continuity" above, pp. 100–101.

service. Any amounts paid in excess of the original cost less accumulated depreciation in the purchase by a second firm must be classified separately and disposed of by methods approved by the utility commission. But they cannot be charged to operating expenses, which may be used in the rate-making process. The logic behind this concept is that customers should not be required to pay rates that permit a utility to earn excessive profits by selling its property whereas it could earn only a reasonable return by holding it. Because of the absence of competition in the selling of utility property, a buying firm would not be encouraged to pay the lowest price possible if it were permitted to pass whatever it paid along to its customers. There is considerable truth in this position during periods of stable prices; however, the equity involved becomes clouded when prices are rising rapidly.

While there is some merit in the original cost concept in the process of utility rate making, there is little merit to its application in the competitive sector of the economy. If the revenue of the firm is not related directly to the amount of its investment and the amount of operating expenses, there is an incentive to pay as little as possible for plant and equipment. The cost of secondhand equipment can be assumed to represent a bargained price and therefore the current market price of the asset. The cost paid by the original purchaser is no longer relevant. Exceptions are made, and the original cost is relevant, however, in cases where there is not an arm's-length transaction or where there is deemed to be a "pooling of interest" rather than a purchase.

Current Input Values

In an attempt to match expenses with revenues, current input valuations may provide a better measure of expense than do historical costs, particularly when the difference between the two is caused by relatively permanent changes in the structure of prices or changes in the price level rather than by ephemeral changes caused by temporary shortages in supply. While the current value of the annual services provided by an asset is measured best by the current costs of equivalent services, such costs are usually not available or they are irrelevant because the acquisition of such services in small chunks is not the most efficient way of obtaining them. The best alternative is to obtain the current replacement cost of the asset and allocate a portion of this to the current period's operations. The current replacement cost less accumulated depreciation to date also provides a balance sheet estimate which can be used as evidence of the current value of the unused services to be provided by the asset. At no time, however, should the net recorded value of the asset exceed what the firm would be willing to pay for it at the present time—the net value of the asset for current and future operations. An appraisal value is an alternative to the current replacement cost. In the public utility field, the concept of "fair value" has particular significance in attempting to obtain current input values.

Current Replacement Cost. The current replacement cost of plant and equipment is the total acquisition cost of an identical new item purchased in current established markets. If there are no established markets or if identical new assets are not available, the cost of an asset that will provide the equivalent service capacity may be substituted. This price, however, must be adjusted for technological changes in either operating efficiency or in product quality. The net current input valuation is the replacement cost less the accumulated depreciation based on this current cost. This net current input valuation may or may not be equal to the market price of identical assets of the same age and usage. If there is a competitive market for used equipment with many buyers and sellers, the price in this market may reflect the current value of the asset to the firm if its expectations can be assumed to be similar to the expectations of other firms in the industry. If the market is not highly competitive or if the asset is used for different purposes, the used equipment price is not relevant except as an indication of what the firm could obtain for the asset in liquidation.

If similar items are not available in the current market, a reproduction cost may be substituted for a current replacement cost; but a reproduction cost is not relevant if the asset cannot be produced efficiently with current production tools and methods. The reproduction cost of early vintage automobiles, for example, is in excess of the cost of new automobiles that are greatly superior to the former models.

An alternative to reproduction cost is the application of specific cost indexes to the historical cost of the specific asset. While this may provide an acceptable approximation of current cost, technological inefficiencies and obsolescence should be taken into consideration either in the adjustment of historical cost or in the computation of the accumulated depreciation. If the equivalent service is obtainable by using newer and more efficient equipment, the current value of the old equipment may be little more than its scrap value or its unallocated historical cost, even though replacement cost has increased considerably. Unless the accumulated depreciation is adjusted for this obsolescence, the recording of obsolete equipment at its replacement cost (estimated by using price indexes) less normal depreciation has the effect of delaying the recognition of the loss in value until the period of use, at which time depreciation would be excessive as a measurement of the input value of the asset's service contribution to the product.

Replacement cost has been suggested as an alternative to historical cost for plant and equipment items for three main reasons: (1) It is a method of adjusting for price changes by providing for depreciation that will permit the physical replacement of the plant and equipment items used. As indicated in Chapter 7, no holding gains and losses are recognized in this concept of replacement cost; the entire difference between historical cost and replacement cost represents an adjustment of invested capital. (2) It is a method of approximating the current measurement of the future benefits of the asset. Depreciation is assumed to represent the current expiration of these benefits. (3) It is a method of estimating the cost that would have to be incurred if the services were obtained in the current market under current operating conditions. Thus, it is a current input concept.

Replacement cost as an approximate measurement of service potential has been suggested by the 1963 Committee on Concepts and Standards—Long-Lived Assets, of the American Accounting Association.[6] It affirmed the 1957 AAA definition of assets as aggregates of service potentials. However, recognizing the insurmountable difficulties in the measurement of discounted cash flows relating to plant and equipment and the assignment of these values to individual assets, the committee suggested that replacement costs may provide a reasonable approximation. Discounted cash flows and service potentials are output concepts, and replacement cost is an input concept; but the committee suggested that the current input value, in this case, might be equal to the discounted output value. This might be true if (1) the historical cost does, in fact, represent the discounted value of the potential services at the time of acquisition; (2) an increase or decrease in replacement cost is matched by a proportionate increase or decrease in the subjective value of cash receipts or service potential; and (3) the rate of discount is the target rate of return, including the subjective expected profit.

If the above conditions are met, the replacement cost approximates the current value of the asset to the firm. If replacement cost is greater than historical cost, the increase represents a holding gain, in the absence of price-level changes. That is, the value of the asset has increased because the service potential or discounted cash flow has increased. Since this represents an increase in the value of the net assets of the firm, it should be included in total income. Operating income is determined by subtracting depreciation based on current replacement values and other expenses from current revenues.

The 1963 Committee on Concepts and Standards defined operating income as the amount "available for distribution outside the firm without contraction of the level of its operating capacity."[7] Note the similarity of this concept to that proposed by those who would adjust for changes in

---

[6] Committee on Concepts and Standards—Long-Lived Assets, AAA, "Accounting for Land, Buildings, and Equipment," Supplementary Statement No. 1, *Accounting Review,* Vol. XXXIX (July, 1964), pp. 694–95.

[7] *Ibid.,* p. 696.

the general price level by using replacement costs. The main difference between the two is that the committee would include in the holding gains and losses all price changes resulting from either changes in technology or demand or from changes in the general price level[8] while the replacement cost price-level adjusters would exclude the entire difference from income.

The main argument against this concept of replacement cost is that an increase in replacement cost is not necessarily good evidence of an increase in service potential or in the discounted value of cash receipts. If current and expected revenues have not changed, there can be no change in service potential measured by discounted output values. Thus, there is no holding gain, as historical cost still represents the better measurement of service potential. But if historical cost was below the subjective service value at the time of acquisition, the increase in replacement cost may represent merely a measurement of a gain that existed at the date of acquisition. As indicated in Chapter 7, the computation of holding gains and losses requires an initial restatement for price-level changes computed on either a general or group level. Income should not include restatements necessary because of changes in the value of the dollar. This emphasizes the fact that the use of current replacement cost is definitely related to the adjustments for price-level changes. Neither can be discussed successfully to the exclusion of the other.

The third suggested reason for using replacement costs for plant and equipment is that they represent the costs that would have to be incurred if the services were obtained in the current market under current operating conditions. If depreciation is computed on this basis, the net operating income represents the operating margin under current conditions. That is, if the services were purchased at current prices, the operating costs required would include depreciation based on current costs. If replacement costs increase, a holding gain results, because if the asset had not already been acquired this would be the cost of acquiring it. Thus, the holding gain represents a saving in cost from buying at the right time. It is not necessarily related to the output value of the product. This appears to be the concept of replacement cost used by Edwards and Bell[9] and also by Sprouse and Moonitz.[10] For example, Sprouse and Moonitz state: "To reveal this fact ['buying cheap' and 'using dear'] requires the use of the current (replacement) cost of the services rendered by these assets and

[8] Dixon dissented from the committee on this point. The committee also implied that it might exclude the effect of general price-level changes from the holding gains and losses if a general recommendation on price-level changes is adopted. *Ibid.,* pp. 698–99.

[9] Edgar O. Edwards and Philip W. Bell, *The Theory and Measurement of Business Income* (Berkeley and Los Angeles: University of California Press, 1961), pp. 77–80, and chap. vi.

[10] Sprouse and Moonitz, *op. cit.,* p. 34.

the separate classification of the related gain or loss."[11] In recommending that serious consideration be given to the use of replacement costs for external reports, they state:

In the external reports, plant and equipment should be restated in terms of current replacement costs whenever some significant event occurs, such as a reorganization of the business entity or its merger with another entity or when it becomes a subsidiary of a parent company. Even in the absence of a significant event, the accounts could be restated at periodic intervals, perhaps every five years. The development of satisfactory indexes of construction costs and of machinery and equipment prices would assist materially in making the calculation of replacement costs feasible, practical, and objective.[12]

The main objection to this concept of replacement cost is that there is seldom clear evidence that the firm would pay the current replacement cost if it did not already have the asset. The only useful current cost figure is the amount that the management of the firm would be willing to pay at the current time for the specific assets being valued. The replacement cost less accumulated depreciation may not be closer to this value than the historical cost less accumulated depreciation. However, if there is evidence that the firm is acquiring or intending to acquire similar assets at the current replacement cost or if competing firms are acquiring such assets, the replacement cost may be a reasonable approximation of the current input cost to the firm. In any case, the assets should be adjusted for changes in the price level, as discussed in Chapter 7.

A general disadvantage of replacement costs is the difficulty (or impossibility) of taking into consideration the effect of technological innovations. By their nature, plant and equipment represent groups of future services acquired in lots. The original cost less any liquidation value represents a sunk cost; only by using the asset for its intended purpose can the service value be obtained. Because of technological changes in the product or in the production process, the output value of the asset to the firm or the net input cost of the services may be greater or less than the current replacement cost.

Appraisal Value. The appraisal process is a method of estimating current costs or current values by systematic procedures. Whether an input or an output value is obtained depends on the objective of obtaining the appraisal. If an appraisal is obtained for the fixed assets of a going concern, it should represent an estimate of the current replacement or reproduction cost less depreciation to the date of the appraisal. Therefore, if the objective is properly stated, an appraisal value should represent the current input value of the asset to the firm. The main advantage of obtaining an appraisal value is that, since it is usually computed by

---

[11] *Ibid.*

[12] *Ibid.*

someone outside of the firm, it is considered to be more objective than replacement costs computed by the firm itself. The main disadvantage of appraisals is that they can be obtained only at periodic intervals and therefore they become out of date, just as do historical costs.

Fair Value. The term "fair value" has been used primarily in the public utility field to refer to the total amount on which the investors are entitled to earn a fair return. The courts have held that the computation of fair value should include all relevant facts, including the prudent past costs and reproduction costs.[13] Public utility firms have claimed that it should include primarily replacement costs. Fair value, therefore, is not a specific valuation basis that can be applied to financial statements generally. It is, rather, a combination of valuation bases determined by the commissions and courts for a specific purpose.

Current Recommendations

Accounting Research Bulletin No. 43 of the AICPA stated that when fixed assets have been written up to appraised values, depreciation should be based on the higher values. However, APB *Opinion No. 6* amended this by stating that "property, plant and equipment should not be written up by an entity to reflect appraisal, market or current values which are above cost to the entity."[14] While a few minor exceptions are permitted, this recommendation lends considerable support to the time-honored cost basis of valuation. In other countries, cost is also the predominant method of valuation, although several countries permit some freedom of choice. In Great Britain, the English Institute continues to favor the cost basis[15] although there is no prohibition for the use of appraisal values. The 1967 Companies Act, however, requires that the dates of valuations be disclosed in annual reports; and in addition, in the year of the appraisal, information regarding the appraisal should be shown. Greater freedom is found in The Netherlands, where revaluations are more common.

DEFINITION AND CONTENT OF COST

Regardless of whether historical costs or current costs are used, the problem of what should be included in costs is present. When plant and equipment are acquired initially by purchase or when they are produced

---

[13] J. Rhoads Foster and Bernard S. Rodey, *Public Utility Accounting* (New York: Prentice-Hall, Inc., 1951), pp. 27–29.

[14] AICPA, *Accounting Principles* (Chicago: Commerce Clearing House, Inc., 1968), Vol. II, p. 6529.

[15] Institute of Chartered Accountants in England and Wales, *Recommendations on Accounting Principles* (London: 1967 reprint), N15, p. 9.

under contract, the initial cost is the total value of the resources given up to acquire the asset, install it at the proper location, and place it in the condition necessary for its intended service. Questions arise, however, regarding the measurement of the value of what is given up, the treatment of expenditures made subsequent to the initial installation, and the computation of costs of assets constructed by the firm intending to use them. These problems affect not only the input value of the plant and equipment but also the periodic depreciation and the amounts charged directly to current expense.

The Content of Initial Cost

The initial cost of plant and equipment is definite only when a single asset is acquired for a cash price at the time that it becomes available for use. In a "basket" purchase, the total price may be definite, but the allocation to specific assets is a matter of judgment. The solution generally suggested is to allocate the total cost among the specific assets in the ratio of the appraised values of each or in the ratio of the book values carried by the previous owner. The former assumes that any saving or excess payment should apply proportionately to all of the assets acquired. The latter assumes that the excess (or deficiency) over the previous owner's book value should apply proportionately. Both are arbitrary allocations, but they have the advantage of at least providing an answer to an extremely difficult problem. There is no reason to believe that the initial value to the firm is necessarily in the ratio of the appraised values. But this method is preferred to the second method because the allocation on the basis of the book values to the previous owner results in a perpetuation of errors and differences arising from price changes during the period that the assets were held by the previous owner.

When an asset is obtained by exchanging a nonmonetary asset for it, the cost should be measured by the liquidation value of the asset or assets given up. While the service value of the old asset to the firm is also an opportunity cost and should be taken into consideration in the exchange decision, it is no longer relevant in the valuation of the asset given up. The main reason is that the liquidation values represent market values, while the service values are subjective. Cost is a market-value concept rather than a subjective opportunity cost concept. This reasoning supports the general proposal that assets acquired for corporate stock be valued in terms of the current market value of the stock given in exchange. It also rejects the income tax requirement that the new asset be valued by adding the book value of the asset exchanged to the cash paid or monetary obligation incurred.

A similar situation arises when nonmonetary assets must be destroyed and removal costs must be incurred to make space for the new asset being constructed. The costs of the new asset should include the liquidation selling price of the old asset plus the removal costs. These both represent costs that could have been avoided by not constructing the new asset; and it can be assumed that the value of the new asset is at least as great as its total cost—including the liquidation price and removal cost of the old asset—or the new asset would not have been constructed. The income tax reduction in the current period arising from expensing these costs immediately for tax purposes may be deducted from the cost of the new asset, as discussed in Chapter 16 under the topic of income tax allocation. While it is sometimes argued that the undepreciated book value of the asset scrapped may be included as a substitute for the liquidation value, this may result in a significant error. If the book value of the asset scrapped exceeds the liquidation value by a material amount, this excess represents a loss, rather than a cost of the new asset, since the alternative value of continuing to use the old asset in its present form cannot be measured.

In general, the initial cost should include the cash price plus freight and installation costs. Trade discounts and cash discounts should be deducted. Explicit or implicit interest should also be excluded when these are included in the purchase price to be paid subsequent to the date of acquisition of the asset. When a cash discount is allowed but not taken, there is a question whether the invoice price represents the cost or whether the net price allowed should be recorded and the allowed cash discount shown as a loss. Some argue that the invoice price (adjusted for any normal interest charges) is the correct cost because it represents the amount actually paid. Others prefer to record the net price that could have been paid because it represents the prudent cost to the firm. While the latter is logical, it leads to the conclusion that the lowest cost available should always be recorded because it is the prudent cost to the firm. In many cases, this is a reasonable conclusion, but there are frequently valid reasons why the lowest initial cost is not the most favorable price to the firm in the longer run.

Advance payments and progress payments during construction of plant and equipment present the problem of whether or not to charge interest on these advances to the cost of the fixed assets. Three general proposals are: (1) Charge no interest to the fixed assets. (2) Charge only interest actually paid for funds borrowed for the specific purpose. (3) Charge a normal interest on all funds used until the time the assets are actually ready for use.

The first proposal, that no interest should be charged, is based on the interpretation that it is not a cost of construction but rather a financial charge. Since financial charges are generally debited to expense in the period that they are incurred, a deferral of them is assumed to result in the overstatement of current income during the period of construction or, if there are no sources of income during this period, the deferral would result in the failure to show a loss that is assumed to be real. Another basic argument is that interest could be avoided by financing the construction with stockholders' equity rather than with debt equity. But this does not eliminate the cost of using money; it merely shifts the burden to the stockholders and permits a deferral of actual payment since undeclared dividends are not contractual obligations of the firm.

The second proposal, to charge only the actual interest paid, is based on the assumption that interest is a cost of construction but that only amounts actually paid represent costs. Charging interest on funds provided by the owners is assumed to result in unrealized income and the valuation of assets in excess of "cost." Interest on ownership funds is rejected also because it is subjectively determined and its final realization is uncertain. But the uncertainty of the present value of the asset is the same, regardless of how it is financed. Thus, there is little justification for adding interest in one case and not in the other. It is difficult to argue that a building is more valuable simply because it was constructed with borrowed funds rather than funds acquired by the sale of stock. Furthermore, since funds are generally commingled, there is no way of determining what proportion of the asset is financed by debt equity and what proportion by stockholders' equity, except in a new firm.

The third proposal, that a normal interest should be charged for all funds used prior to the availability of the asset for use, is based primarily on the assumption that it represents an economic cost. From a logical point of view, this is the best procedure. The total cost of the asset is the value of goods and services given up in order to acquire it. Interest represents the service value of the money invested in the acquisition of the asset prior to its use. Since this money is not used for current operations but rather for future operations, a deferral of the implicit interest is appropriate. The argument that it should not be recorded because it represents unrealized income is tied more closely to the realization rules than to the basic principle that income is earned during the entire period of production.

The main application of the third proposal is in the area of public utilities. The main reason for its use in this situation arises from the fact that the income of a utility firm is regulated on the basis of its total capitalization. If a normal rate of return is permitted only on revenue-producing assets in use, there would be no opportunity for the firm to earn any income on investments necessary during the construction period before assets are placed in operation. The common practice of crediting the interest to interest expense, however, implies that the construction was financed with debt equity. As indicated above, generally no specific allocation can be made.

Capital and Revenue Expenditures

Once plant and equipment are installed ready for use, the costs (historical or current) should be capitalized and charged to operations over the expected life of the asset. All maintenance expenditures and anticipated or normal replacements of parts of the asset should also be charged to operations during the normal life of the asset. The total cost of obtaining a given amount of service from the asset during its expected life should, therefore, include the initial acquisition costs and all maintenance and normal replacement expenditures. How these costs should be allocated to the individual years or periods is a separate problem, which will be treated in the following chapter on depreciation; repairs, normal replacements, and depreciation are interrelated. The repairs and normal replacements should be charged to the expenses or operations of one or more years, depending on the depreciation method used and the distribution of the expected benefits to be received from the asset.

Certain types of expenditures, however, are incurred to obtain greater future benefits, rather than to maintain a given quantity of services. Since these expenditures affect only future periods, they should be capitalized and allocated to only those future periods benefiting from them. This increase in future benefits can arise in one of three ways: (1) an increase in the life of the asset—that is, an increase in the number of years over which services will be obtained, (2) an increase in the quantity of services to be obtained in each year during the remaining life of the asset, and (3) an increase in the quality of the service to be obtained in each year during the remaining life of the asset. These increases in future benefits may arise from expenditures that may be classified as either additions, improvements and betterments, or major replacements.

There is little doubt that additions should be capitalized. By definition, additions increase the productive or service capacity of the plant and equipment. Therefore, the entire cost of additions should be charged to the asset and allocated to future periods. But, what about costs of tearing out parts of an old building to make room for the new facilities or to integrate the new with the old facilities? The answer depends on the circumstances. Usually, if the need for the addition could not have been anticipated or if it was not practical to include it in the original construction, all costs of tearing out should be included in the cost of the addition; and none of the costs of the old facilities should be removed from the accounts except to the extent that these costs exceed the service value of the old asset before adding the new facilities. The additional services cannot be obtained without incurring these costs, and the construction of the addition at an earlier date, before the services were needed, would probably have added more to the total costs of the firm. But this does not mean that such costs should be capitalized in every case. It is possible that the necessity for tearing out and reconstruction is due to inefficiencies in planning or in construction. In these cases, such costs represent losses rather than costs chargeable to operations.

Improvements and betterments are more difficult to define than additions, but the treatment is very similar. If the result is an increase in the quantity of service provided by the assets, it may, in fact, be difficult to distinguish improvements from additions. A truck may be improved by adding overload springs and a larger bed, thus permitting heavier payloads. The result may be little different from the acquisition of a trailer that would be considered an addition. On the other hand, many improvements may result in an increase in the quality of the service provided by the asset. The installation of an improved lighting system in a factory building improves the services provided by the building. One of the greatest difficulties in the accounting for improvements arises when they are made as a part of a normal repair and replacement program. An attempt should be made to capitalize only those costs resulting in an increase in the future services of the asset, as opposed to the expenditures necessary to maintain a given level of services. To the extent that an improvement involves the replacement of major components, the discussion in the following paragraph is also relevant.

Major replacements are the most difficult to define and treat properly because the effect is similar to that of minor replacements and normal repairs. If an asset is made up of a single unit, a replacement involves the entire asset; in this case, the solution is simple—the old asset is retired and the replacement asset is recorded as a new asset. But in most cases, plant and equipment items are made up of several units that wear out at different rates. Recurring replacements of parts of the asset can be charged to operations in the years in which they occur because they are necessary to obtain the expected service life of the composite asset. No advantage would be obtained by capitalizing these items, because it is not possible to associate the outlays directly with the benefits to be received from them; and since all periods are charged with some replacement costs, an allocation to each period by a depreciation method would not necessarily improve the computation or meaning of net income. However, as we shall see in the next chapter, if the amount of repairs varies in a predictable manner, it can be taken into consideration in the selection of a depreciation method for allocating the initial cost of the asset in order to obtain desired results.

Major replacements that occur infrequently, however, need to be capitalized so that all periods will be charged with a portion of the replacement costs. This can be accomplished by including the costs of major replacements in the depreciation charge in one of two ways: (1) If the life of the asset is determined by the maximum life of the most durable major component, replacements should be charged to the asset or set up as a separate account and allocated over its separate life. (2) The depreciation can be computed on the basis of the average composite life of all of the components of the asset, in which case the replacements should be charged to the accumulated depreciation.

By using the maximum life of the most durable component, the replacements are not included in the depreciation based on the original life alone. Since they occur infrequently, it would not be correct to charge the entire amount of the replacement to operations in the year that it is made. The best solution in this case would be to set the amount up as a separate account (or debited to the main asset account) and allocate it over the period from the date of the replacement to the next replacement of the same component. For example, if major redecorating is necessary every three years, the redecorating costs can be capitalized and allocated over a three-year period. Care must be taken, however, to be sure that the original decorating costs are charged through depreciation to the first three years; if they are not, subsequent years will be charged twice with decorating costs, once through the depreciation based on the original total costs and a second time through the allocation of the redecorating costs. Technically, the original decorating costs should be removed from the accounts at the end of the third year by offsetting them against the accumulated depreciation account. However, if depreciation is properly computed, the net carrying value of the asset and the annual charge to operations would be correct by this method even if the replaced asset is not removed from the asset and the accumulated depreciation accounts.

The second treatment of major replacements bases the depreciation on the average composite life of all of the components. For example, if the maximum life of a building is 50 years, the average composite life could be 30 years. The original cost of the building would then be allocated on the basis of a 30-year life, but by carrying the depreciation over 50 years, the total depreciation for the 50 years would be equal to the original cost of the building plus the cost of all major repairs minus the ending scrap value. When replacements occur, they are then charged to the accumulated depreciation account. The effect is to increase the net carrying value at the time of the replacement without increasing the original cost basis. This procedure has the same effect as writing off the replaced asset and debiting the asset account with the replacement cost if two basic conditions exist: (1) the cost of the replacement must be the same amount as the original cost of the component that it replaces, and (2) the total cost of all replacements must have been anticipated with some fair degree of accuracy, so that the depreciation charge will be adequate to include all replacements. The second condition is not as vital as the first, however, because the depreciation charge can be adjusted to take care of errors in an original miscalculation.

Self-Constructed Assets

When plant and equipment are constructed by the firm that will use the asset, the accumulation of costs is little different from the costing of manufactured products. Labor and material costs can usually be assigned directly to the fixed asset being constructed. The main difficulty comes in the allocation of joint overhead costs to the asset and to the normal production. At least four proposals are frequently made to handle this problem: (1) Assign no overhead to the fixed asset. (2) Assign only variable overhead. (3) Assign overhead equal to the amount that would have been assigned to the production that is curtailed because of the construction. (4) Assign a proportionate share of overhead to the construction on the basis of the procedure that is used for the assignment to normal production.

The first proposal, the assignment of no overhead to the asset constructed, is based on the assumption that overhead is primarily a fixed expense, that it is chargeable only to the normal operations of the current period, and that an allocation of overhead to the plant and equipment results in an overstatement of the net income for the current period. In general, the assumption that all overhead is fixed is false; the construction of fixed assets practically always results in some increase in total overhead costs. To the extent that this is true, the second proposal (to assign variable overhead costs to the constructed asset) is far superior to the first proposal. The variable or incremental costs are the minimum that should be assigned to the constructed asset. All of the variable costs are incurred to benefit future periods rather than current operations. However, if there is evidence that such costs result from errors or inefficiencies, they represent a loss to be recognized in the current period.

The arguments for charging only variable costs to the constructed asset are similar to the arguments for direct costing of inventories. The main argument is that the allocation of fixed overhead results in additional income in the current period because of the construction. That is, the net income would have been smaller if the overhead had been charged to current operations. This capitalization of fixed overhead appears to be inconsistent to those who advocate that income should reflect sales effort only and not production or construction effort. The second argument for direct costing—that there is no benefit to future periods if there is likely to be excess capacity in later years—is less convincing in this situation. Plant and equipment, unlike inventories, must be constructed in anticipation of many years' use. They cannot be constructed piecemeal only as the services are needed. Therefore, the failure to construct a needed fixed asset in the current year may result in a lower total income in the following year.

One of the strongest arguments for charging only variable costs to the construction is that if normal production and sales are not curtailed by the construction (the most likely situation), there is no evidence that management would have been willing to incur additional costs. Thus, there is no evidence that management considered the constructed asset to have a value greater than the variable costs incurred. But this is only the minimum value; the subjective value to the firm based on expectations of future benefits is probably much greater than the variable costs. Should accountants take the conservative position and include only those costs that represent clear evidence of future value, or should they exclude costs only when there is good evidence that they do not represent the value of future benefits?

The third proposal, to assign overhead equal to that which would have been allocated to curtailed production, seems plausible on the surface. The remaining overhead allocated to current production is no different than it would have been if the construction had not been undertaken, and it appears to represent service capacity that would have been utilized under normal conditions. But it is a cost based on what would have been allocated if an alternative course of action had been chosen. This is not a true opportunity cost, because it is not based on a service value given up to obtain the construction.

The proposal to allocate a full share of all overhead to the constructed asset is an appropriate full-costing procedure. If the amount of overhead allocated to the constructed asset represents the input value of services actually used, the capitalization is logical on the basis that it represents the input value of future service benefits. If there is an expectation of future benefits in the form of either larger revenues or smaller costs, capitalization will provide a better matching of revenues and expenses in future periods and a better measurement of the net income from operations during the construction period. Whether or not there is excess capacity to handle the construction is not the determining factor in the capitalization decision, although the argument for capitalization is weaker if facilities are used that would otherwise have been idle. The important consideration, however, is the expectation of future benefits.

LEASES OF PLANT AND EQUIPMENT REPORTED BY THE LESSOR

Plant and equipment are occasionally rented or leased to other firms or individuals for short periods extending from a day to a year or more. In these cases, the lessor usually takes care of the maintenance of the property and pays the recurring expenses related to the property, such as taxes and insurance; and he must continually enter into new lease contracts during the life of the property. Therefore, the rental revenues are part of the operating revenues of the firm and the maintenance, tax, and insurance expenses, as well as depreciation on the leased property, should be included in the operating expenses. The reporting of the leased plant and equipment in financial statements is thus no different than the reporting of plant and equipment used in manufacturing or in providing services to customers.

When the lease contract covers a long period of time, however, the conditions are different and alternative reporting methods may be desirable. APB *Opinion No. 7* recognizes two separate methods of reporting long-term leases by the lessor—the "financing" and "operating" methods. The basic differences between the two methods are in the classification and valuation of the lessor's rights in the lease and the timing of the income to the lessor over the period of the lease.

Financing Method

While there are many different circumstances where the financing method may be used, the most obvious case is where a financing company finances the acquisition of equipment by a manufacturer's customer. The finance company pays the manufacturer for the equipment in exchange for title to it and receives an installment note from the customer, who receives the right to use the property for what may be almost the entire life of the asset. The customer or lessee may be required to provide for all maintenance of the equipment and pay all expenses such as taxes and insurance relating to it. Therefore, in substance, the finance company (the lessor) holds a secured installment note receivable. While *Opinion No. 7* emphasizes the fact that the usual risks and rewards of ownership rest with the lessee in this case, a more significant but related consideration is that the receivable is a monetary asset representing the right to receive a specified number of dollars over the life of the contract. Therefore, the lessor's rights in the contract should be classified as a noncurrent monetary asset rather than as a part of "plant and equipment."

In placing a valuation upon the receivable, *Opinion No. 7* suggests that the amount should represent the discounted value of the cash to be received under the contract. This valuation at the date of signing the contract would be equal to the cost of the asset (the amount paid to the manufacturer) less the estimated residual value of the asset at the termination of the lease.[16] If the selling price of the asset at the termination of the lease is not specified in the contract, or if the asset is not expected to be acquired by the lessee upon termination of the lease, the value of the residual rights are nonmonetary in nature and should be classified accordingly by the lessor.

---

[16] Although *Opinion No. 7* does not specifically suggest it, if the residual value of the asset at the termination of the lease is expected to be material, the value at the beginning of the lease should be appropriately discounted.

In the above situation, the rate of discount is the earning rate or internal rate of return, which is the rate that would equate the cash flows to be received under the contract with the cost of the asset less the residual value. The total income to the finance company over the life of the lease is the excess of the aggregate rentals over the cost of the asset less the residual value. According to the finance method, this income is reported by the lessor over the life of the lease in proportion to the amounts of unrecovered investment in each period. Thus, reported income from the contract would be decreasing over the life of the lease; and if the cash receipts are constant in amount, a decreasing amount of each installment would be reported as income and an increasing amount would be reported as reduction of the receivable. Note that the total gross income from the lease agreement is assumed to represent interest on the investment; none is associated with the precontract arrangements, the signing of the contract, or the supervision and accounting for the collections, which may be constant over the life of the lease. However, since the investment of the funds may be a crucial function of the finance company, an allocation of the gross income to other functions would not improve the reporting of income, particularly since such allocations would need to be arbitrary. But if initial direct costs are material, *Opinion No. 7* suggests that an equal amount of revenue be reported at that time to offset the direct costs expensed. The same effect would be obtained by adding the initial direct costs to the receivable and adjusting the rate of return accordingly.

Leasing by Manufacturers.   When manufacturers use the leasing method to report the financing of their own products transferred to customers under long-term lease contracts, income should be reported separately for the two basic functions: (1) the manufacture and sale of the product, and (2) the investment in the lease contract during the life of the lease. The manufacturing revenues can be reported at the time of signing the lease by reporting the value of the lease contract receivable equal to the normal selling price of the product less the residual value. *Opinion No. 7* suggests that the manufacturing revenues should be equal to the regular selling price of the product or the discounted amount of the future rentals, whichever is the lower; however, since a method of determining the rate of discount is not specified, any amount can be reported as manufacturing revenue if it is equal to or less than the amount that could be obtained through regular sales. Thus, an opportunity investment rate of discount could be used if it does not result in a valuation for the receivable greater than the regular sales price of the product less the residual value at the termination of the lease. This leads to the approval of an infinite number of possible allocations of the gross rental income between the manufacturing and investment functions.

While *Opinion No. 7* does not specifically forbid the use of the installment method of reporting the income from manufacturing and selling, the denial of such a procedure is implied. For, if the conditions which would normally support the use of the installment method do exist, it is recommended that the operating method be used instead of the financing method. These conditions would include (1) where the credit risks are unpredictable, (2) where the lessor retains material ownership risks, and (3) where there are material uncertainties regarding the amount of additional costs or revenues relating to the lease.

The Operating Method

When the lessor takes care of the maintenance of the leased property and pays other expenses related to the use of the property, the leasing method of reporting the lease contract is not appropriate. The reason for this is that the gross income to the lessor is not equivalent to interest on the investment only, but also includes compensation for the expenses incurred by the lessor and for the operating activities of the lessor during the entire lease period. Therefore, APB *Opinion No. 7* recommends that the asset be classified as plant and equipment, that it be valued at cost or cost less accumulated depreciation, and that the rental receipts be reported as the gross revenues unless they depart radically from a straight-line basis or from the economic usefulness of the property in each period. The result is that the cash basis of reporting is used for the rental receipts and most operating expenses except depreciation.

In determining whether or not the operating method should be used, *Opinion No. 7* indicates several criteria, among which is the extent to which the lessor assumes the usual risks or rewards of ownership. However, in all long-term lease contracts, both the lessee and the lessor share these risks and rewards to some extent. The lessee agrees to pay a fixed number of dollars for the use of the property, the value of which may vary in the future as prices change; therefore, the lessee does share some of the risks and rewards of ownership. To this extent, the lessor's right to receive the rental payments represents a monetary asset. However, since the lessor must take care of the maintenance and pay other expenses, the amount of which is not determined in advance in a fixed number of dollars, he also shares in the risks and rewards of ownership. Because of the uncertainties regarding the amount of the dollar expenditures required by the lessor, it is not possible to treat the net value of the lease contract as a monetary asset. Since the revenues are monetary in nature but the obligations are not, the net amount cannot be treated as monetary. The best form of disclosure would be to report the estimated nonmonetary obligations as a discounted amount deducted from the present value of the rental payments by the lessee. But because of the uncertainties regarding the obligations, the separation of the net valuation into the two parts (one positive and one negative) would be quite meaningless. Therefore, the recommendation of *Opinion No. 7* that the net valuation be treated as nonmonetary is probably the best classification for the balance sheet. However, the financial statements should also disclose the amount and timing of the rentals and the amount of historical payments associated with the lease, as well as possibly expected future payments.

Since the lessor's rights under the lease contract are classified as nonmonetary plant and equipment in the operating method, depreciation must be computed and allocated to the several periods of the lease. One or more of the depreciation methods discussed in the following chapter might be relevant in this case. The problems of reporting the lease contract in the financial statements of the lessee are discussed in Chapter 16.

SELECTED ADDITIONAL READING ON CHAPTER TOPICS

Bases of Valuation of Plant and Equipment

American Accounting Association, Committee on Concepts and Standards— Long-Lived Assets. "Accounting for Land, Buildings, and Equipment," Supplementary Statement No. 1, *Accounting Review,* Vol. XXXIX (July, 1964), pp. 693–99.

BIERMAN, HAROLD, JR. "Recording Obsolescence," *Journal of Accounting Research,* Vol. II (Autumn, 1964), pp. 229–35.

EDWARDS, EDGAR O., and PHILIP W. BELL. *The Theory and Measurement of Business Income,* pp. 77–80 and chap. vi. Berkeley and Los Angeles: University of California Press, 1961.

Harvard Business School Accounting Round Table. *The Measurement of Property, Plant, and Equipment in Financial Statements.* Boston: Graduate School of Business Administration, Harvard University, 1964.

KEMP, PATRICK S. "Depreciation for Income Measurement—A Response," *NAA Bulletin,* Vol. XLIII (January, 1962), Sec. 1, pp. 34–37.

LOWENSTEIN, GERARD. "Accounting Aspects of Appreciation of Property, Plant, and Equipment," *New York Certified Public Accountant,* Vol. XXXVII (December, 1967), pp. 946–48.

SNAVELY, HOWARD J. "Current Cost for Long-Lived Assets: A Critical View," *Accounting Review,* Vol. XLIV (April, 1969), pp. 344–53.

SPROUSE, ROBERT T., and MAURICE MOONITZ. "A Tentative Set of Broad Accounting Principles for Business Enterprise," *Accounting Research Study No. 3,* p. 32. New York: American Institute of Certified Public Accountants, 1962.

YOUNG, WILLIAM M. "Toward Variable-Base Fixed Asset Accounting," *NAA Bulletin,* Vol. XLII (April, 1961), Sec. 1, pp. 23–31.

Definition and Content of Cost

WRIGGINS, JAMES C., and GEORGE BYRON GORDON. *Repairs vs. Capital Expenditures,* chap. i, pp. 3–33. New York: Ronald Press Co., 1958.

Leased Plant and Equipment Reported by the Lessor

Accounting Principles Board. *Opinion No. 7,* "Accounting for Leases in Financial Statements of Lessors." New York: AICPA, 1966.

HALL, WILLIAM D. "Current Problems in Accounting for Leases," *Journal of Accountancy,* Vol. CXXIV (November, 1967), pp. 35–42.

MYERS, JOHN H. "Reporting of Leases in Financial Statements," *Accounting Research Study No. 4,* pp. 63–67. New York: AICPA, 1962.

VATTER, W. J. "Accounting for Leases," *Journal of Accounting Research,* Vol. IV (Autumn, 1966), pp. 133–48.

WOLK, HARRY I. "Accounting for Leases: A Further Examination of the Issues," *Journal of Accounting Research,* Vol. VI (Spring, 1968), pp. 153–57.

chapter 13

Depreciation

The depreciation concept in accounting refers to the process of allocating the initial (or restated) input valuation (cost or other basis) of plant and equipment to the several periods expected to benefit from their acquisition and use. The main emphasis of the depreciation process is generally on the computation of the periodic charge to expense or to the cost of the product to be matched with the revenues reported in each period. Seldom is the balance sheet valuation given much attention except in consideration of the total amount to be allocated to future periods. The purpose of this chapter is to evaluate the basic concepts and methods of depreciation as a part of reporting enterprise net income. As indicated above, in Chapter 8, the computation of depreciation is not relevant in the measurement and reporting of cash flows.

Before a pattern or formula for allocating the original or restated valuation (less scrap value) to expense or production costs can be applied, certain estimates must be made, including the following: (1) the valuation (cost or other basis) of the asset when acquired or a restatement of this at a subsequent date, (2) the expected service life of the asset, and (3) the scrap value or liquidation value at the end of the service life. Each of these estimates is based on multiple probabilities, and their reduction to single values is at best a difficult problem. The conventional application of depreciation methods, however, is static because it generally assumes that these estimates remain constant over time. Therefore, because of the difficulties involved in making these estimates (particularly where the uncertainties are high) and because of the failure to make adjustments over time, it is possible that no allocation procedure, even if it is logically conceived, could be relevant for income reporting.

As indicated in the previous chapter, the original valuations assigned to plant and equipment items are independent of the depreciation process. The basis of the original valuation (cost or other input basis) determines the total amount to be depreciated, but the depreciation method selected does not generally affect the original valuation. However, the gross valuations and net valuations subsequent to the date of acquisition may be affected directly by the depreciation concept selected. For example, if the current depreciation charge is to represent the current replacement cost of the services provided, it is logical and practical to adjust the entire asset valuation to a current cost basis. Note that this injects a dynamic element into the depreciation process; the conventional pattern of adhering to an initial cost basis is clearly a static approach.

The estimate of asset life and the relative certainty of this single-valued estimate are clearly related to the depreciation process. The cost or other input valuation to be allocated to any specific period of use is dependent on the benefits received in the period in relationship to the total benefits expected to be received during the anticipated useful life of the asset. The existence of uncertainty may result in an expected life considerably shorter than the maximum possible, and therefore affect the allocation to specific periods; it may also provide a reason for allocating larger amounts in the earlier years of asset life. But the depreciation procedure and the method of handling repairs and replacements may also affect the expectations regarding useful life. Most assets are made up of many components, with different lives. Therefore, a single-valued estimate of life must be a composite life, or it must be based on certain assumptions regarding the treatment of repairs and replacements.

The allocation of cost or other input valuation to each operating period is probably the most difficult problem relating to depreciation. While it is possible that no logical or relevant solution to the allocation problem exists, the following general concepts are frequently used to evaluate depreciation methods: (1) a measurement of the decline in the value of the asset is assumed to represent depreciation; (2) depreciation is assumed to be an allocation of the cost or other basis according to the benefits expected to be received in each period; and (3) the allocation can be evaluated in terms of the relevance of the resulting depreciation figures or net income, regardless of the logic of the procedure. The following discussion attempts to evaluate these concepts and several depreciation methods suggested or in use.

DEFINITIONS OF DEPRECIATION

The most commonly accepted definition of depreciation is that suggested by the Committee on Terminology of the American Institute of Certified Public Accountants, as follows:

Depreciation accounting is a system of accounting which aims to distribute the cost or other basic value of tangible capital assets, less salvage (if any), over the estimated useful life of the unit (which may be a group of assets) in a systematic and rational manner. It is a process of allocation, not of valuation. . . .[1]

---

[1] Committee on Terminology, AICPA, "Review and Résumé," *Accounting Terminology Bulletin No. 1* (New York, 1953), p. 25. Reprinted in AICPA, *Accounting Principles* (Chicago: Commerce Clearing House, Inc., 1968), Vol. II, p. 9513.

Note that this definition is a static concept. The initial cost or other value is not changed during the life of the asset; the sum of all depreciation charges is equal to the initial value less any salvage value. Note also that the definition does not suggest how the cost or other value should be distributed; it is sufficient that the allocation procedure be systematic and rational. The requirement that it be rational probably means that it should be reasonably related to the expected benefits in each case.

The definition suggested by the AICPA committee is based on the cost convention and the realization rule. Cost represents the value of the asset to the firm at the date of acquisition; and in subsequent periods, cost less accumulated depreciation is assumed to represent the minimum value to the firm of the remaining services to be obtained from the fixed asset during its remaining life. The realization rule dictates that the valuation should not exceed cost or cost less accumulated depreciation; for, if a higher valuation is used, "unrealized" income will appear. Thus, the definition is based on traditional concepts, the weaknesses of which have been discussed in earlier chapters. However, a basic deficiency in the definition is its failure to define what is meant by "systematic and rational." Unless concepts are precise, allocation procedures based on them are arbitrary in nature and thus are unacceptable because they are unsupportable by any logical means.

Decline in Service Potential

The American Accounting Association Committee on Concepts and Standards definition of depreciation leads to the same conclusions as the AICPA definition, but it is based on a measure of asset valuation (the service potential) rather than merely on an allocation of cost. The 1957 AAA statement asserts that—

Any decline in the service potential of plant and other long-term assets should be recognized in the accounts in the periods in which such decline occurs. . . . The service potential of assets may decline because of . . . gradual or abrupt physical deterioration, consumption of service potential through use even though no physical change is apparent, or economic deterioration because of obsolescence or change in consumer demand.[2]

Under this definition, the initial cost of an asset is assumed to represent the value of a storehouse of services that can be released over the life of the asset. Whenever a portion of these services expires through use or other cause, the quantity of service potential declines; and a portion of the cost of the asset should be transferred to an expense, another asset, or

---

[2] AAA Committee on Accounting Concepts and Standards, *Accounting and Reporting Standards for Corporate Financial Statements and Preceding Statements and Supplements* (Columbus, Ohio: AAA, 1957), pp. 4, 6.

a loss account. This definition is also a static concept because it is based on an allocation of cost to each quantity of potential service of the asset. But it is less static than the AICPA definition because it recognizes that the loss in service potential may be irregular and may be subject to many factors that cannot be foreseen when the asset is acquired. The AICPA definition assumes that the conditions anticipated at the time of acquisition will continue without material change over the expected life of the asset. However, both definitions are based on single-valued expectations regarding the total expected quantity of potential services or the expected life of the asset.

The 1963 AAA Committee on Concepts and Standards—Long-Lived Assets also defined depreciation in terms of an expiration of service potential of the asset. But the committee stated further that "depreciation must be based on the current cost of restoring the service potential consumed during the period."[3] While this definition is based on a decline in the value (the service potential) of the asset, it is also related to the capital maintenance concept.

The Maintenance of Capital

A broader concept of depreciation is that income emerges only if the invested capital at the end of a period exceeds the invested capital at the beginning (assuming no capital transactions or dividend payments during the period). The definitions of the AICPA, the 1957 AAA statement, and the 1963 AAA committee all apply the maintenance concept, but the concept of capital to be maintained is slightly different in each case. Under the AICPA definition, it is the original monetary investment that should be maintained at least by the end of the asset's life; recovery of original cost may be assumed to occur gradually over the life of the asset in any rational manner. The 1957 AAA definition assumes that it is the service potential or its equivalent in terms of the original cost of services used that should be maintained. The 1963 AAA committee definition emphasizes the maintenance of operating capacity or physical capital rather than historical cost. In none of the cases, however, is it necessary that actual replacement or equivalent replacement be made; the failure to maintain physical capital or dollar capital because of a loss or for other reasons does not deny the existence of the depreciation.

The advantage of the capital maintenance concept is that it permits the recognition of changes in the value of the dollar and changes in specific replacement values. The capital to be maintained can be interpreted to be the original investment expressed in terms of a common

---

[3] Committee on Concepts and Standards—Long-Lived Assets, AAA, "Accounting for Land, Buildings, and Equipment," Supplementary Statement No. 1, *Accounting Review,* Vol. XXXIX (July, 1964), p. 696.

dollar, or it can be expressed in terms of the current replacement values at the beginning or end of the accounting period.

The main disadvantage of the capital maintenance concept is that it results in a failure to permit a separation of operating income from extraordinary gains and losses. Unless other criteria are introduced, it does not provide a basis for determining the normal operating depreciation separately from the abnormal losses of service potential. Also, it requires a further definition of what is meant by capital maintenance. Therefore, it is not a precise definition that can be used as a specific guide; rather, it is only a broad guide subject to further interpretation.

The Current Cost of Services Consumed

Sprouse and Moonitz, in AICPA *Accounting Research Study No. 3*, define depreciation similarly to AICPA *Accounting Terminology Bulletin No. 1*, but they suggest that current replacement costs are more significant than historical costs, particularly when some significant event occurs in the organization of the firm. Depreciation is presumed to represent an allocation of current replacement costs, and the current depreciation charge for a specific period is the current cost of the services consumed in that period.

The main advantage of current replacement cost depreciation is that it permits a matching of current costs against current revenues, resulting in a current net operating concept of income. Gains and losses arising from the holding of assets while the current input values change can be reported separately. Therefore, the depreciation charged to operations and the net operating income may be more meaningful in an evaluation of the relative efficiency of current operations and in providing a basis for managerial decisions. They may also provide a better basis for the prediction of future incomes by stockholders and potential investors.

Current replacement values, however, do not provide final answers to the problems of measuring efficiency and making predictions. *First,* fixed assets by their very nature represent large blocks of potential services, so that even if the input value of the total is adjusted to a current basis, the allocation to specific periods is just as difficult a problem as with the use of historical costs. *Second,* further difficulties arise if the general price level is also changing. If identical assets are not available in the current market, it may be difficult to distinguish between price changes that may be ascribed to changes in purchasing power and price changes that represent changes in specific current input values. *Third,* technological innovations may reduce the current value of an asset's services even though replacement costs have increased. New types of machinery may be more efficient in the utilization of labor and material, making the services of an older asset obsolete. When this is the situation, the current depreciation charge should be based on the net output value (or utility value) of the services rather than on the current replacement cost. Because it is practically impossible to compute the net output value of the services in this situation, it may be better to continue to use the historical input cost (or historical cost adjusted for changes in the price level) rather than a current replacement cost that is not meaningful in the circumstances.

CONCEPTS OF DEPRECIATION

As suggested by Thomas, all allocation methods must be based upon some concept of a distribution of benefits expected to be received by using an asset over time (its net revenue contribution each period) or else the allocation must be arbitrary and thus meaningless as a measure of a rational concept of income.[4] However, Thomas also suggests from his research study that rarely would it be possible to measure either the *ex ante* or *ex post* net revenue contributions in the several periods during the use of an asset, because of the many interactions of the production functions or inputs in the production and other operating processes of a firm. Three possible alternatives to this dilemma of using either arbitrary allocations or unmeasurable bases for allocations are: (1) avoid allocations by measuring residual asset valuations in terms of market prices at the end of each period; (2) attempt no allocations and present cash flow and funds flow statements instead of income statements; or (3) select uniform methods of allocation on the basis of their ability to permit predictions, regardless of their inherent logic. Research has as yet been unable to provide acceptable support for any one of these alternatives.

The support for depreciation methods based upon the net revenue contribution concept is usually couched in terms of the capital budgeting solution for the evaluation and selection of investment projects. The capital budgeting solution, however, generally requires the estimation of marginal cash flows to be received each period from making the investment compared with the alternative of not investing. If several investments in different assets or asset groups are to be made simultaneously, the marginal contributions must be made sequentially, although the amount and distribution of the contributions may depend upon the order in which they are selected. The expected cash flow contributions may result from expected increases in total revenues of the firm or from expected cost savings, such as decreases in labor or fuel costs, or they may represent a combination of expected revenue increases and cost savings. When allocations are proposed on the basis of matching cost or other valuations of the assets with expected benefits, the expected effect on cash

---

[4] Arthur L. Thomas, "The Allocation Problem in Financial Accounting Theory," *Studies in Accounting Research No. 3* (AAA, 1969), p. 29.

flows must be adjusted to the accrual basis, so that depreciation will be allocated on the basis of the periods in which the expected increased revenues or cost savings will be reported in the income statement.[5] Thus, in these cases, the term "net revenue contribution" is more appropriate than the cash flow concepts applied in capital budgeting solutions.

While most of the depreciation concepts proposed are based in some way upon the expected net revenue contribution of the specific items of plant and equipment, they can be classified generally as concepts which either (1) measure depreciation as the decline in the value of the asset, or (2) measure the amount of cost (or other basis) to be allocated to each period on the assumption that there is a matching of the input values with the expected revenues or net revenue contribution. The decline in the value of the asset may be measured in terms of the discounted value of the expected benefits or in terms of the liquidation value (exchange price) at the end of each period. The matching process may be obtained by assuming a constant internal rate of return on the investment or by assuming a constant ratio of the input value of the services assumed to be used to the expected net revenue contribution in each period. However, the matching may also be attained indirectly by associating the cost with the services of the asset or with some other intermediate stage rather than directly with the net revenue contribution.

Depreciation as a Decline in Asset Value

While the Committee on Terminology of the AICPA denied that depreciation is a process of valuation, the 1957 AAA committee on concepts and standards referred to depreciation as the decline in service potential, and the 1963 AAA committee on long-lived assets referred to it as the expiration of service potential. Since a measure of service potential is a measurement of the value of an asset, both of these definitions can be classified as measuring depreciation in each period by computing the decline in the value of the asset during the period. Chambers also utilizes a decline in valuation concept by defining depreciation as the difference between the opening and closing market prices of durable assets.

Decline in Discounted Net Revenue Contribution. The service potential of a durable asset at any point in time can be measured by discounting the expected cash flows (or expected cash savings) to be obtained from acquiring and using the asset. Assume, for example, that an asset is expected to generate cash savings over a five-year period in the amounts of $500, $600, $1000, $400, and $500 respectively, with the scrap value included in the final amount. The formula for computing the present value at time t_0 is as follows:

---

[5] See for example Harold Bierman, Jr., "A Further Study of Depreciation," *Accounting Review,* Vol. XLI (April, 1966), pp. 271–74.

$$V_0 = \sum_{t=1}^{n} \frac{R_t}{(1 + r)^t} \tag{1}$$

where:

V_0 = The present value at time 0.
R_t = The cash flow in each period (t).
r = The opportunity rate of return or the cost of capital.

As indicated in Chapter 9, if r is assumed to be the opportunity rate of return for a riskless investment, the discounted cash flow for each period should be adjusted by a risk preference factor. However, in much of the literature, r is assumed to represent the cost of capital. The limitations of these assumptions are discussed in Chapter 9.

The present value at time t_1 is computed by the following formula:

$$V_1 = \sum_{t=2}^{n} \frac{R_t}{(1 + r)^{t-1}} \tag{2}$$

Depreciation (D_1) for the first year is computed as follows:

$$D_1 = V_0 - V_1 \tag{3}$$

The depreciation for the above example would then be computed as indicated in Table 1.

TABLE 1

Computation of Depreciation Based on the Decrease in the Discounted Value of the Expected Cash Flows (cost of capital is assumed to be 8 percent)

	1	2	3	4
Year	Expected Net Cash Flow Benefit	Present Value at Beginning of Year	Present Value at End of Year	Depreciation (Col. 2 − Col. 3)
1	$ 500	$2,406*	$2,099	$307
2	600	2,099	1,667	432
3	1,000	1,667	800	867
4	400	800	464	336
5	500	464	–0–	464

* The present value for the beginning of year 1 is computed as follows:

$$
\begin{aligned}
500 \times 0.9259 &= \$\ 463 \\
600 \times 0.8573 &= \ \ \ 515 \\
1,000 \times 0.7938 &= \ \ \ 794 \\
400 \times 0.7350 &= \ \ \ 294 \\
500 \times 0.6806 &= \ \ \ 340 \\
\hline
&\ \ \$2,406
\end{aligned}
$$

If, in the above example, the cost of the asset was $2,025, an initial gain of $381 would need to be recorded in order to depreciate the beginning value of $2,406 over the life of the asset. An alternative would be to allocate the $381 gain over the life of the asset in proportion to the expected cash flow benefits or according to some other method; however, such an allocation would be purely arbitrary and would find acceptance only because it appears to be in accordance with the conventional realization rules. If the cash benefit of $500 in the fifth year includes a final scrap value of, say, $100, this $100 should be subtracted from the depreciation in the fifth year, making that amount $364.

One of the disadvantages of computing the depreciation on the basis of the decline in the discounted service potential or the discounted expected cash flows is that it is static in nature. The cost of capital at the date of acquisition and the expectations regarding the amount and timing of cash benefits are assumed to be constant over the life of the asset. While it is possible to compute a new value for the asset each period on the basis of the current cost of capital and new expectations regarding expected benefits, such revaluations would be of doubtful validity, primarily because once the asset is acquired it becomes a part of the total operating facilities and its marginal benefits can no longer be measured because of the interaction of all of the factors of production in generating the net revenue of the firm. Therefore, a separate value for each asset cannot be obtained after the date of acquisition. In addition, reporting the gain at the date of acquisition is of doubtful relevance in the decision processes of investors and creditors, because it is subjective in nature and bears little relationship to the valuation of the enterprise as a whole.

Decrease in Current Cash Equivalent. An alternative to the computation of depreciation by measuring the decline in the discounted expected values of an asset is suggested by Chambers.[6] In his proposal, depreciation is the decline in the current cash equivalent of the asset measured by the resale price in a secondhand market. The main advantage of this procedure is that it avoids the need to make allocations and to rely on subjective expectations. However, it too has some major disadvantages. In the case of nonvendible durables, the entire asset must be written off at the date of acquisition or some amortization procedure must be used as a substitute, an alternative which Chambers suggests but which is inconsistent with his general model. Another disadvantage of the use of current cash equivalents for durable assets is that there is no evidence that the liquidation values of the assets are relevant to any of the prediction or decision models of investors and creditors or other external users of financial statements.

---

[6] Raymond J. Chambers, *Accounting, Evaluation and Economic Behavior* (Englewood Cliffs, N.J.: Prentice-Hall, Inc., 1966), pp. 208–209.

Depreciation as a Process of Matching Costs with Expected Benefits

In most discussions of depreciation allocations, there is an assumption, explicit or implicit, that the amount of the cost or other basis of the asset allocated to each period should represent the amount that is being matched with the expected revenues or net revenue contribution of the period. This matching of the input valuation with the expected benefits can take the form of (1) time-adjusted depreciation which uses an average internal rate of return during the entire life of the asset, (2) depreciation allocations that are proportional to the net revenue contributions of each period, and (3) depreciation allocations that are in the same relative proportion as a surrogate for net revenue contributions such as a measure of the service provided by the asset.

Time-Adjustment Depreciation. By equating the historical cost (or other input valuation) with the present value of the asset in equation (1) above, and by substituting the internal rate of return for the opportunity rate or the cost of capital, we obtain the following equation:

$$C = \sum_{t=1}^{n} \frac{R_t}{(1+s)^t} \tag{4}$$

where:

C = The cost of the asset.
s = The internal rate of return.

By subtracting C from each side of the equation, we obtain:

$$\sum_{t=1}^{n} \frac{R_t}{(1+s)^t} - C = 0 \tag{5}$$

or, by summing the individual terms:

$$\left[\frac{R_1}{(1+s)} + \frac{R_2}{(1+s)^2} \cdots + \frac{R_n}{(1+s)^n} \right] - C = 0 \tag{6}$$

If we use the above example, the cost (C) is $2,025, and the net revenue contributions $(R_1, R_2,$ etc.) for each of the five years are $500, $600, $1,000, $400, and $500, respectively. By substituting these values in equation (6), we can solve for the internal rate of return (s). In this example, the internal rate of return is 15 percent. By assuming that this is a constant rate during the life of the asset, the depreciation for each year can be computed as indicated in Table 2.

An advantage of this concept of depreciation is that depreciation represents an allocation of the total input cost, although the input value

TABLE 2

Computation of Depreciation Based on the Net Revenue Contribution Less the Associated Earnings on the Investment at a 15% Earning Rate

Year	1 Investment— Book Value at Beginning of Year	2 Associated Earnings at 15%	3 Net Revenue Contri- bution	4 Depreciation (Col. 3 − Col. 2)
1	$2,025	$304	$ 500	$ 196
2	1,829	274	600	326
3	1,503	225	1,000	775
4	728	109	400	291
5	437	63*	500	437
				$2,025

* Adjusted for rounding error.

may be expressed in terms of historical cost, cost adjusted for changes in the price level, or replacement costs. It also may have an advantage in permitting a prediction of future incomes, because it uses a constant average rate of return; however, predictability depends upon the relationship between expected net revenue contributions and actual contributions and upon whether or not the firm is able to reinvest continually in new projects at the same internal rate of earnings.

Disadvantages of the time-adjusted rate of return concept are: (1) it assumes that the rate of return is constant over the life of the asset; (2) like the decrease in value concept, it is static in nature; (3) when the net revenue contribution is less than the associated earnings in any year, the depreciation would be negative; (4) if the expected net revenue contribution is negative in any one or more years, the solution of the discounting equation may result in multiple rates of return; and (5) like other concepts relying on expected net revenue contribution values, its validity is questionable because of the interactions of the separate assets and other factors contributing to the total revenues of the firm.

Depreciation Based on a Constant Cost to Net Revenue Contribution Ratio. Depreciation, in this concept, is assumed to represent an allocation of the original cost (or other basis) to each year in such a way that it is matched with the associated net revenue contribution of each year on the basis of a constant ratio. The ratio is computed by dividing the historical cost of the asset (less scrap value if any) by the total expected net revenue contribution during the life of the asset. The depreciation for each year is, therefore, the expected net revenue contribution for that year multiplied by this ratio.[7] The ratio can be computed by the following formula:

---

[7] See for example Orace Johnson, "Two Concepts of Depreciation," *Journal of Accounting Research,* Vol. VI (Spring, 1968), pp. 29–37.

$$m = \frac{C}{\sum\limits_{t=1}^{n} R_t} \qquad (7)$$

where:

m = The ratio of historical cost to the total expected net revenue contribution.

C = The cost or other basis (less scrap value) of the asset.

R_t = The expected net revenue contribution in each year (t) during the life of the asset.

Depreciation in each year can be computed as follows:

$$D_t = mR_t$$

where D_t is the depreciation allocated to year t.

Using the same figures as in the previous example, the cost of the asset is assumed to be $2,025 and the net revenue contributions are expected to be $500, $600, $1,000, $400 and $500, respectively, for each of the five years. Assuming no scrap value, the ratio would be 0.675 (computed by dividing $2,025 by $3,000). The depreciation for each of the five years would be as shown in Table 3.

TABLE 3

Computation of Depreciation Based on a Constant Ratio of Cost to Expected Net Revenue Contribution

Year	*1* Expected Net Revenue Contribution	*2* Ratio	*3* Depreciation
1	$ 500	0.675	$ 338
2	600	0.675	405
3	1,000	0.675	675
4	400	0.675	270
5	500	0.675	337
	$3,000		$2,025

An advantage of this depreciation concept is that it avoids the difficulties of computing an average internal rate of return when there are possible multiple rates and it avoids the possibility of negative depreciation figures (unless the expected net revenue contribution in any year is negative). An additional advantage is that it may avoid many of the interactions among factor inputs by using a ratio computed from the net contribution (total expected revenues less variable costs) and total costs for aggregations of assets such as an entire plant, although this may be only a rough guide and the logic of applying a single ratio to all assets may be very indirect indeed. But for an asset such as a hotel, for example, the revenues may be greater when it is new and has prestige status than when it is old. It may eventually be converted into an office building and provide an entirely different type of service with lower revenues. If variable costs can also be estimated, the net revenue contributions from the entire hotel may be used as a rough guide for the allocation of all specific assets associated with the net revenues from operating the hotel. It is also possible to recompute the net revenue contribution pattern expected for the remaining life of the asset at any time during its life, so that the actual ratios used in computing the depreciation may come close to the final *ex post* ratio. To this extent, it may be possible for external users of financial statements to predict future relationships, but this is so only if the ratio of cost to net revenue contributions is relatively constant for additional investments by the firm.

One of the disadvantages of this concept is that it may cause the rates of return on invested assets to vary widely because it does not adjust for the timing of the net revenue contributions. Interactions among the several assets and other factors used by the firm are not eliminated even if the ratios are computed from groups of assets. Other disadvantages of this concept are similar to the disadvantages of other concepts discussed previously which are also based on expectations of net revenue contributions.

Depreciation as an Allocation of Cost to Physical Service Units. As an alternative to basing depreciation allocations on the pattern of expected net revenue contributions, it is possible to substitute a physical measure of the expected services to be obtained by using the assets. A nonmonetary measure of the benefits expected to be received is substituted for the dollar measurement of the net revenue contribution. Examples of such surrogates would include the number of units produced, number of hours, days or months of operation, kilowatt hours of electric power produced, or some other intermediate unit of production input or output. The pattern can be either an expected distribution determined in advance or the allocation of a predetermined cost per unit to the actual number of service units used in any accounting period.

A major question that arises, therefore, is whether the total costs should be allocated over all potential services or over just the services that the firm anticipates using in operations. An asset is usually acquired with certain services in mind, and it is logical to allocate the initial input cost less salvage, if any, over the period of anticipated use. For example, a crane could be acquired for use on a specific contract. Its total cost less salvage should be assigned to the specific contract even though it is used for only a few days and remains idle for long periods of time. If this is the most economical way of getting the job done, there is no reason why the total cost should not be assigned to the anticipated use. But this is not inconsistent with the net-revenue-contribution concept. In other cases, an asset may be acquired with an anticipation of using it only 3 or 4 years out of 10. If it is not feasible to utilize the services in all years, there is logic in charging depreciation only in the years of anticipated use. It was for this purpose that the asset was acquired, and to insist on depreciation in every year is not consistent with the pattern of expected benefits. On the other hand, however, if an asset is acquired for use and forced to remain idle for one of many reasons, depreciation should be recorded if the service units expected to be obtained during the period of idleness cannot be obtained in a later period. A charge for the services expired should be made even though they serve no benefit to the firm; however, they may be shown as a loss rather than as a charge to current operations.

An advantage of using this indirect measure of the net revenue contribution is that the allocation can be adapted to unanticipated changes in the pattern of use, particularly in those cases where the decline in the expected future benefits is more closely related to use than to obsolescence and the passage of time.

A disadvantage of the physical services method of allocating asset costs is that there may not be any necessary relationship between the physical services produced or consumed and the net revenue contributions from the asset. Therefore, the allocations may result in capricious charges to income which are not likely to be relevant to the predictions and decisions of investors and other external users of financial reports. Furthermore, both the choice of a measure of the physical service of the asset and the allocation of cost to each service unit are likely to be based upon expediency rather than logic. The service unit is likely to be some measure that is readily available, such as direct labor hours or units of production, and each unit of such service is usually assumed to provide an equal benefit value or net revenue contribution. While different costs can be assigned to different service units, it is seldom possible to do so in a logical manner except by resorting to an alternative cost of obtaining the same services or by making expectations regarding changes in total revenues. It is generally difficult to take into account changes in variable costs or cost savings.

Depreciation Allocations Based on the Usefulness of the Reported Figures

Because of the theoretical and practical limitations of all of the allocation concepts discussed above, a possible alternative might be to evaluate the results rather than the allocation concepts. If allocation procedures can be found that permit good predictions or otherwise provide information useful to investors and creditors, they would appear to be acceptable regardless of how arbitrary they might seem to be from a theoretical point of view. Such solutions, however, cannot be evaluated by deductive reasoning alone; they must meet the tests of rigorous empirical research. As a starting point, the solutions to the above example using three of the concepts discussed above are presented in Table 4, which also compares the rates of return on invested book value of the asset in each case with the ratio of depreciation to net revenue contributions.

As Table 4 indicates, the rates of return for the "decline in value" concept and the "time-adjusted" concept are both constant and would be useful in making predictions of future rates if the firm is likely to continue to earn these rates. The 8 percent rate, however, is a minimum rate, because it can be assumed that the firm would not invest in assets that yielded less than this. But the 15 percent may not be typical of investment opportunities available to the firm. The third concept results in rates of return for each year that vary from 8 percent to 48 percent. Therefore, this example suggests that none of these three methods is necessarily valid in permitting prediction of future rates of return; but empirical studies could prove otherwise, particularly under different conditions or assumptions.

Only the third concept results in a constant ratio of depreciation to the expected net revenue contributions, and thus a constant ratio of the contribution less the depreciation to the contribution, because one is the complement of the other. In the third concept of Table 4, the former ratio is 0.675 and the latter is 0.325. The other two concepts result in widely varying ratios. Therefore, only the third concept is likely to permit any prediction; but such a prediction depends on the likelihood of this ratio being relatively constant for all investments in the future. Although this is subject to empirical verification, an a priori answer would be that this is not likely to be the case because it would assume constant production functions and relatively constant capital intensity, neither of which is likely to be true because they would exist only under static conditions.

While little empirical evidence is available regarding the usefulness of conventional depreciation methods for investors' decisions or for other users of external financial reports, Staubus has made statistical tests that suggest that reported net income figures after deducting depreciation do not provide a better basis for common stock investment decisions than do reported earnings without deducting depreciation.[8] A similar conclusion was reached by the AAA Committee on External Reporting by using a normative investment decision model and comparing the depreciation methods with the standards suggested by the AAA Committee to Prepare a Statement of Basic Accounting Theory.[9]

---

[8] George J. Staubus, "Statistical Evidence of the Value of Depreciation Accounting," *Abacus*, Vol. III (August, 1967), pp. 3–22.

[9] Committee on External Reporting, AAA, "An Evaluation of Current Accounting Practices," *Accounting Review*, Supplement to Vol. XLIV (1969), pp. 107–108.

TABLE 4

Comparison of Depreciation, Rate of Return on Book Investment, and Ratio of Depreciation to Net Revenue Contribution for Three Depreciation Concepts

Year	Net Revenue Contribution	Decrease in Value Depreciation				Time-Adjusted Depreciation				Depreciation Proportionate to Net Revenue Contributions			
		Depreciation	Book Value Beginning of Year	Rate of Return	Ratio to Contribution	Depreciation	Book Value Beginning of Year	Rate of Return	Ratio to Contribution	Depreciation	Book Value Beginning of Year	Rate of Return	Ratio to Contribution
1	$ 500	$ 307	$2,406	8%	0.614	$ 196	$2,025	15%	0.392	$ 338	$2,025	8%	0.675
2	600	432	2,099	8%	0.720	326	1,829	15%	0.543	405	1,687	12%	0.675
3	1,000	867	1,667	8%	0.867	775	1,503	15%	0.775	675	1,282	25%	0.675
4	400	336	800	8%	0.840	291	728	15%	0.728	270	607	21%	0.675
5	500	464	464	8%	0.928	437	437	15%	0.874	337	337	48%	0.675
		$2,406				$2,025				$2,025			

The Net Service Contribution

In the above example, it was assumed that the net contribution of the asset could be estimated at the time of acquisition and that the pattern of contributions over the life of the asset would serve as a basis for the depreciation allocation. As in a capital budgeting decision, the expected net contribution of the asset should take into consideration its effect on the revenues of the firm as well as on the additional costs or cost savings. However, once the asset has been installed, it becomes a part of the entire operation and the additional revenues and net cost savings can no longer be attributed to the one asset alone. All of the assets and other factors of production interact in producing the revenue of the firm. Therefore, it would be necessary to make a simultaneous allocation of the revenues of the firm to all of the assets. But Thomas has demonstrated convincingly that simultaneous allocations of revenue or net revenue contributions cannot be supported on theoretical grounds unless the firm's inputs do not interact, a condition which is highly unlikely.[10]

Even if the accountant can predict the net revenue contributions using the capital budgeting techniques,[11] he is plagued by other problems. The total cost of obtaining the net benefits from an asset includes not only the initial cost of acquiring the plant or equipment but also the costs of repairs and maintenance over the life of the asset. But the policy of the firm with respect to repairs and maintenance and improvements will affect the associated labor and power costs, as well as the operating efficiency. Therefore, the initial cost is only one of the input factors that should be considered in the basic allocation problem.

The main disadvantage of attempting to allocate total expected operating costs is that new uncertainties are introduced into a problem that is already complex. When a new asset is acquired, it may be almost impossible to estimate the total repair, maintenance, and operating costs and their interrelationships. In some cases, operating costs may decline over a lengthy break-in period. Repair and maintenance costs may increase over the entire life of the asset, or over only a part of the life to prevent other operating costs from increasing even more rapidly. These interrelationships and their influence on decisions regarding the choice of a depreciation method are discussed in the following section.

DEPRECIATION, REPAIRS, AND REPLACEMENTS

The objective of considering all expected operating costs as well as operating revenues in the computation of depreciation allocations stems

---

[10] Thomas, *op. cit.,* p. 49.

[11] See for example the AAA Committee on Managerial Decision Models Report, *Accounting Review,* Supplement to Vol. XLIV (1969), pp. 72–76.

from the fact that repairs, maintenance, and other operating costs are interrelated. This interrelationship was referred to in the previous chapter in the discussion of capital and revenue expenditures. But the extent of the interrelationship and the effect on depreciation allocations require closer scrutiny. First, the expected life of an asset is directly associated with the extent of the anticipated repairs and maintenance. Second, because most assets include many components with different lives, many so-called repairs are really replacements. Third, the efficiency of an asset frequently declines as an asset ages, and this decline in efficiency accelerates when repairs and maintenance are curtailed or delayed.

Repairs, Maintenance, and Asset Life

The life of an asset can be extended or shortened by varying the amount of repairs and maintenance. In some cases, assets can be preserved almost indefinitely for historical or cultural reasons. But the cost of doing so is generally greater than the cost of replacement with a new asset. Furthermore, obsolescence usually makes such continued maintenance uneconomical. On the other hand, repair and maintenance costs can be reduced to a minimum whenever the economic life of an asset is expected to be quite short. For example, if specialized equipment is to be used for the completion of a specific contract and abandoned upon the termination of the contract, the most economical level of repair and maintenance expenditures would be that minimum necessary to keep the equipment operating only until the completion of the contract. Usually, the life of an asset is determined by what may be considered an optimum level of repair and maintenance expenditures or by economic obsolescence, whichever is the shorter. If repair or maintenance expenditures are delayed or curtailed for any reason below that required to obtain the expected economic life of the asset, the current depreciation allocation should be increased accordingly.

Repairs and Replacements. The term *maintenance* generally refers to the normal upkeep of property in an efficient operating condition. While maintenance is frequently considered to include normal recurring repairs, the term *repair* refers to the restoration of an asset without increasing its expected service life or capacity. However, repairs may be of two general types: (1) the adjustment of a machine or working parts and the labor necessary to restore a damaged or worn component to its original condition; and (2) the replacement of one or more parts of an asset with new parts without replacing the entire asset.

Maintenance expenses and repairs of the first type may increase over the life of an asset because of the increasing need for adjustment and care when items of plant and equipment become worn through use or age. If the revenue contribution of the asset remains the same throughout its life while the repair and maintenance expenses increase, the net contribution of the asset itself must be decreasing. This factor, by itself, calls for a declining depreciation charge.

The replacement of specific parts, however, is a function of the unit or composite selected for depreciation, and the distinction between replacements and maintenance is dependent on the amount of the aggregation and the selected composite life. If each component is depreciated separately on the basis of its own expected life, the replacement requires the retirement of the component and the setting up of a new component in its place. For example, if the tires on an automobile are depreciated separately, they would be depreciated over their individual expected lives and written off when they are replaced; the new tires would then be capitalized and depreciated over their expected lives. While truck tires are occasionally treated in this fashion, it is not common to identify and depreciate other parts of a truck or automobile separately. Usually, an item of equipment or a building is treated as a single asset and assigned a life based on the expected life of the major components. If the original cost of the asset is allocated over the life of the major components, some consideration must be made for the fact that minor components will be replaced before the anticipated retirement of the entire asset. If some of the parts are replaced every year or two and if others are replaced at longer intervals, there will be a bunching of replacements in the later years of the asset's life. This results in increasing repair expenses as the asset ages. The charging of the cost of all parts over the entire life, with the charging of the costs of replacements to expense in the year that they occur, results in double charges in later years and inadequate charges in the early years. Therefore, the allocation procedure should be adjusted so that this double charging can be avoided.

Accountants have occasionally recommended that repair costs should be equalized over the life of an asset by setting up a "budgetary reserve." The need for this allocation or equalization of repair costs is based on the assumption that the annual depreciation charge represents an allocation of only the original cost of the asset, without regard to the timing of repairs. The recommendation usually requires an estimation of the total repair costs during the life of the asset and an allocation to each period by setting up an allowance or reserve for repairs. This allowance account is usually classified as a liability reserve. However, it does not have the usual characteristics of a liability because it is based on the occurrence of a future event. A better alternative would be to treat it as a contra to the related asset account, similar to the treatment of accumulated depreciation. This treatment is more logical because it represents an additional allocation of costs of the parts with lives shorter than that of the major components. Therefore, it is depreciation and could just as well be credited to the accumulated depreciation account. When repairs are actually incurred, they would be debited to the allowance for repairs account or the accumulated depreciation account. This procedure is, therefore, similar to the treatment of major repairs. While it would be more precise to write off an asset and capitalize the repair costs, it is usually too difficult to determine the cost of the item being replaced. But this procedure also has the same limitations as the similar method suggested for handling major repairs.

Repairs and Efficiency. Repairs and maintenance can frequently be delayed or minimized, with the result that other operating expenses, such as fuel and labor costs, may increase. Thus, if the value of the output of the asset remains constant, the net contribution of the asset declines. This decline in net contribution also occurs as a result of frequent repairs as the asset grows older; the frequent repairs curtail the time available for production or use and thus diminish the output of the equipment. The several concepts of depreciation based on the net revenue contribution require that this decline in output potential be taken into consideration in the allocation process.

EVALUATION OF VARIOUS DEPRECIATION METHODS

Accountants have long recognized that plant and equipment have limited lives and that some consideration must be made in the accounts for the inevitable necessity to junk productive assets. During the 19th century and the early part of the 20th century, many of the firms that treated the problem at all did so by a periodic revaluation of the assets or by charging either replacements or retirements to current expense. More recently, depreciation has become recognized as a systematic allocation of cost or other value over the life of the asset. Many methods of allocation have been proposed and used, but practically all of the methods can be classified according to which of the following patterns they resemble: (1) allocations varying according to activity or use; (2) straight-line or constant charge methods; (3) increasing charge methods; and (4) decreasing charge methods.

Methods Preceding the Use of Cost Allocation

While the methods preceding the use of cost allocation are not based on good accounting theory, a brief review is helpful in placing them in proper perspective and in recognizing them when they appear in current discussions of accounting theory and practice.

Inventory Method. Probably the earliest method of recognizing depreciation was to revalue the assets periodically or at the termination of a venture. The inventory valuation was based on either the valuation of the asset to the new venture or on the cost of the asset adjusted for any loss in productive efficiency. The first basis may be determined by a liquidation value or by a current market price. The second valuation basis results in what is called "observed depreciation," which is based on the change in engineering efficiency of the asset rather than on the decline in service potential.

Both concepts are defective for two main reasons: (1) They apply the balance sheet approach to income and thus combine operating expenses with nonoperating gains and losses. (2) They do not result in a systematic assignment of service cost or value to periods. The use of liquidation values usually understates the asset valuation and overstates the depreciation expense, while the use of "observed depreciation" usually overstates the asset valuation and understates the current depreciation charge.

While the inventory method is obsolete, it is occasionally applied in one of several forms as an expedient. For example, an inventory of small tools is occasionally taken at the end of each period and valued on the basis of its physical condition; the depreciation expense is computed by subtracting this inventory valuation from the sum of the beginning inventory and the cost of tools acquired during the period.

The Replacement Method. When a firm had a large number of similar assets, it was thought that the current cost of using plant and equipment could be approximated best by charging to depreciation expense the cost of current replacements. In a large mature firm, replacements were thought to occur regularly and provide a good substitute for depreciation charges. The cost of the original asset was retained as the book value of the asset in use regardless of the change in costs at the time of replacement. A modification of this method required the use of a reserve account and a periodic charge to depreciation during the early years of the life of the enterprise until replacements reached a relatively constant level.

While the replacement method is generally considered obsolete, it is still used by railroads for ties, rails, tie plates, and ballast. Its current counterpart in general financial accounting is the charging of ordinary repairs to expense as they occur, while continuing to carry the original cost of the replaced parts in the total cost of the main asset. Another current example of the replacement method is the recommendation in *Accounting Research Bulletin No. 43*[12] that a firm is not required to amortize intangibles that do not have a limited term of existence. This applies particularly to intangible assets that are maintained by current expenditures. In a sense the entire asset is replaced by current expenditures for items such as advertising and research. The original cost of the asset is carried on the books, while the replacement expenditures are charged to current expense. The main advantage of the replacement method is that it permits the charging of current costs to expense, similar to the effect of Lifo.

---

[12] AICPA, *Accounting Principles, op. cit.,* Vol. II, pp. 6018–20.

Cost Allocation Methods

In accordance with the various objectives of depreciation, the cost or other value of an asset should be allocated over the service life in a systematic and rational pattern. The method selected for any specific asset or group of assets should reflect the specific expectations regarding the following factors: (1) the relationship between decline in market value and use, (2) the effect of obsolescence, (3) the expected pattern of repairs and maintenance, (4) the anticipated decline in operating efficiency, (5) expected changes in revenues, (6) the long life of assets and the necessity for waiting—the interest factor, and (7) the degree of the uncertainty regarding the later periods of the asset's life.

Theoretically, the selection of a depreciation pattern should be based on all of the above listed factors. However, in many cases, one or a few of the factors will dominate and the minor effects of the others may be ignored. Usually, one of several established depreciation methods is selected if the general pattern appears reasonable or if income tax effects are permitted to influence the selection of the method chosen for accounting purposes. While there is some merit in using standardized methods, it would be possible to combine the expectations of the several determining factors and derive a mathematical equation for each asset or group of assets. Such equations derived from past experience and from specific expectations would provide more useful information than the common practice of fitting a standard model to each situation.

Variable Charge Methods. The activity or use methods of depreciation are based on the assumption that depreciation is a variable rather than a fixed cost. That is, it is assumed that the value of the asset declines as a function of use rather than because of the passing of time. For example, a truck may be expected to operate for 100,000 miles during its lifetime, or a machine may be expected to operate for a given number of hours or turn out a given number of units of product.

For many types of assets, the assumption of a variable depreciation is reasonable, particularly if the physical wear and tear are more important than economic obsolescence or if the expected services can normally be expected to be obtained before obsolescence sets in. Accordingly, if an asset's services are not used in one year, no depreciation should be recorded because there is no decline in service value. This is similar to a coal pile; if no coal is used while the plant is shut down temporarily, no charge is made for coal during that period. Even though obsolescence may be a significant factor in determining the expected life of an asset, the activity method of depreciation may be appropriate if the obsolescence can be anticipated and if an estimate can be made of the approximate usage to be obtained from the asset. Under these conditions, the cost of the asset can be assumed to represent the purchase of a given number of service units, and the allocation of the cost to these units is then reasonable. The main objective of depreciation applied in this case is the allocation of input value to each service unit; the measurement of the decline in service value may be of secondary importance.

While the production method of depreciation appears to be ideal for those situations where the service value of the asset declines with use, there are some serious disadvantages to the method as it is usually applied. (1) While a variable charge to each year is accepted, the production method is similar to the straight-line method in the sense that it assigns an *equal* amount to each unit of service. However, because of the necessity of waiting for the later units of service, the total service value does not, in fact, decline uniformly unless interest is assumed to be zero. (2) No consideration is usually given to increasing repair and maintenance costs, decreasing operating efficiencies, or declining revenues. (3) Uncertainties regarding the quantity of services which the asset is capable of producing can be taken into consideration by using the expected value based on engineering probability estimates; but the probability of early obsolescence is more difficult to anticipate.

A modification of the production method is allocation on the basis of revenue. For major components, this may be a good approximation of use, and it has the added advantage of taking into consideration changes in revenue per unit. But it has all of the other disadvantages of the production method. Furthermore, it is inapplicable in those cases where goods are produced for stock and where overall revenue cannot be reasonably attributed to specific assets. Note that an allocation on the basis of revenue does not justify an allocation on the basis of net income; none of the objectives of depreciation is met by using net income as a basis for allocation.

Straight-Line Allocation. The straight-line method of allocation is based on the assumption that depreciation is a function of time rather than of use; obsolescence and deterioration over time are considered to be determining factors in the decline in service potential, as opposed to physical wear and tear caused by use. Thus the service potential of the asset is assumed to decline by an equal amount each period. And the total cost of the services used in any period is assumed to be the same regardless of the extent of use.

How well does the straight-line method fit the usual situation? Because of the simplicity of the model, the results are correct only if the following assumptions are true or reasonably accurate: (1) The interest factor can be ignored or the cost of capital can be assumed to be zero. (2) Repairs and maintenance expenses are constant over the life of the asset. (3) The operating efficiency of the asset is just as good in the last year as in the first year. (4) The revenues (or net cash flows) made possible by the use of the asset are constant for all years of asset life. (5) All necessary estimates, including the anticipated useful life, can be predicted with a reasonable degree of certainty.

Because of the uncertainties connected with most of the above factors, it is difficult to find any depreciation method that is likely to take all of the various factors into consideration. Therefore, the straight-line method is often assumed to be as accurate as any other method. It is also frequently claimed that the straight-line method may be the most appropriate because the several factors tend to be offsetting. For example, it may be possible that declining operating efficiencies and increasing repair and maintenance expenses are exactly offset by increasing revenues and decreasing insurance and property tax expenses. In addition, the straight-line method has the advantage of ease of operation and understanding.

A major disadvantage of the straight-line method is that it ignores the discount factor; and even if the other assumptions are correct, the reported net income gives the appearance of a rising rate of return on total invested capital. For example, assume that a machine is acquired at a cost of $5,000 and is expected to have a life of five years with no scrap value at the end of this period. Also assume that the investment provides a constant net revenue stream (total revenues less all operating costs other than depreciation) of $1,252. The total reported income is assumed to be withdrawn each year, but an amount equal to the accumulated depreciation is invested in securities at an average rate of return of 8 percent. The result is shown in Table 5.

The effect demonstrated in Table 5 indicates the error of ignoring the

TABLE 5

Rate of Return Earned on a Five-Year Asset
Straight-Line Depreciation
(revenues and operating costs are assumed to be constant)

	Year				
	1	*2*	*3*	*4*	*5*
Total capital invested at beginning of year	$5,000	$5,000	$5,000	$5,000	$5,000
Carrying value of machine at beginning of year	5,000	4,000	3,000	2,000	1,000
Investment in securities at beginning of year	–0–	1,000	2,000	3,000	4.000
Operating revenues less operating expenses other than depreciation	$1,252	$1,252	$1,252	$1,252	$1,252
Depreciation	1,000	1,000	1,000	1,000	1,000
Net operating income	$ 252	$ 252	$ 252	$ 252	$ 252
Interest on securities	–0–	80	160	240	320
Total Income	$ 252	$ 332	$ 412	$ 492	$ 572
Reported rate of return on total investment	5%	6.6%	8.2%	9.8%	11.4%

discount factor. While the rate of return would drop back to 5 percent in the sixth year if the asset is replaced at the same cost, erroneous conclusions may be drawn during each five-year period. An upward trend in income is apparent but not real. Projections based on this trend would be erroneous. Furthermore, it leads to the observation that a technologically improved machine must have considerable operating superiority to challenge the existing asset before the end of its physical life. Like the "one-hoss shay," the existing machine would be used until it finally fell apart. If additional operating equipment is obtained each year, instead of purchasing securities as in the above example, it can be demonstrated that the rate of return will oscillate with a decreasing amplitude until an average 8 percent rate of return is finally reached. If the compound-interest method of depreciation is used under the above assumptions, a constant rate of return results. This is demonstrated below in the discussion of the increasing charge methods.

The assumption of a positive rate of return, however, does not discard the straight-line method entirely. Under specific conditions, the decline in operating efficiency may offset the decline in associated earnings so that the computed depreciation may be constant each year. For example, in Table 6, the net revenue contribution is assumed to decline by a constant amount of $80 each year. If the rate of return is 8 percent, the excess of the contribution over the associated earnings would be constant each year, thus supporting a straight-line depreciation charge.

TABLE 6

Computation of Depreciation Assuming an 8% Rate of Return and a Constant Decline in Service Contribution of $80

Year	*1* *Book* *Value of* *Asset at* *Beginning* *of Year*	*2* *Associated* *Earnings* *8% of* *Col. 1*	*3* *Net* *Revenue* *Contri-* *bution*	*4* *Depreciation* *(Col. 3 − Col. 2)*
1	$5,000	$400	$1,400	$1,000
2	4,000	320	1,320	1,000
3	3,000	240	1,240	1,000
4	2,000	160	1,160	1,000
5	1,000	80	1,080	1,000

Increasing Charge Methods. In the financing method of treating long-term leases in the reports of the lessor discussed in the previous chapter, the cost of a product purchased and leased under a long-term contract is reclassified as a receivable. Income is reported by multiplying the internal rate of return by the book value at the beginning of each year. The

amount of cash received each period less this reported income is assumed
to represent a return of the amount invested in the asset (equal to the
cost of the product). Therefore, if an equal cash rental is received each
year, an increasing amount would be reported as a return of the investment. While this return of the investment is not generally referred to as
depreciation, the effect is the same and an allocation procedure is required. The effect of this method is demonstrated in Table 7.

TABLE 7

**Computation of the Return of Investment with the
Financing Method for Long-Term Leases
Reported by Lessors
(assuming an 8% rate of return)**

	1 *Book* *Value of* *Asset at* *Beginning* *of Year*	*2* *Associated* *Earnings* *8% of* *Col. 1*	*3* *Annual* *Cash* *Receipt*	*4* *Net* *Decline* *in Book* *Value*
Year				
1	$5,000	$400	$1,252	$ 852
2	4,148	332	1,252	920
3	3,228	258	1,252	994
4	2,234	178	1,252	1,074
5	1,160	92	1,252	1,160

The use of the cash flow as a basis for amortizing the investment in
this case is assumed to be justified because the maintenance and operating costs are paid by the lessee and because there are few interactions
with other assets. But it may be criticized on the basis of its assumption
of a constant rate of return and on the basis of its failure to distinguish
between a true interest income and the income from the operations of
obtaining and servicing the lease contracts.

The annuity and sinking fund methods of depreciation also result in
increasing amortization amounts, similar to the computations in Table 7.
The sinking fund method has been used occasionally by public utility
firms which have charged depreciation with the annuity portion only and
charged interest expense with the increasing interest computed on the
increasing accumulated depreciation (equal to a hypothetical sinking
fund). This method is particularly relevant when the utility's rates are
computed by using an undepreciated cost as the rate base. One of the
most relevant arguments for the sinking fund method is that it permits a
public utility to earn a constant rate of return on its total investment
when its revenue is held constant through regulation.

The increasing charge methods are also relevant for those situations
where insurance and property tax expenses decline over the asset's life

while operating efficiency, revenues, and repairs and maintenance remain fairly constant. Some public utility properties meet these conditions. In other cases, expectations of increasing revenues may support the use of increasing charge depreciation methods. For example, toll roads and toll bridges may be built to handle peak traffic loads anticipated after 10 or more years. Thus, the revenues may be expected to increase as demand increases over the asset's life.

The main arguments against the interest methods of depreciation are that (1) very few assets can be expected to provide services with a constant or increasing value; (2) repair and maintenance costs usually increase; and (3) operating efficiency usually declines over the asset's life. The interest methods are not necessarily more dynamic than the straight-line method just because they take into consideration one additional factor—the rate of return; they still omit more factors than they include.

Decreasing Charge Methods of Depreciation. Several methods of depreciation have been suggested and used from time to time that result in a decreasing depreciation charge over the expected life of an asset (also known as accelerated depreciation). The most common methods are the sum-of-the-years'-digits method and the constant percentage of declining-book-value method. In the latter method, a precise formula can be used to determine the constant rate of decline when the scrap value is positive,[13] but an approximation of this rate (acceptable for tax purposes) is obtained by taking twice the straight-line percentage (known generally as the double-declining-balance method). However, other allocation distributions can be obtained by using smaller percentages or by applying one of many algebraic formulas resulting in declining charges.

The main impetus for the increased interest in the declining charge methods in recent years has come from the liberalization in the choice of depreciation methods permitted by the 1954 Internal Revenue Code, although the principle of a declining charge had been recognized for tax purposes prior to this date. However, the theoretical justification for declining charge methods is based on nontax considerations. The conditions frequently claimed as justifications for the declining charge methods are as follows: (1) declining annual service contributions without consideration for interest or the cost of capital; (2) declining operating efficiency or operating performance, resulting in increases in other operating costs; (3) asset values (represented by the discounted value of re-

---

[13] $\left(r = 1 - \sqrt[n]{\dfrac{s}{c}} \right)$

where:

r = the constant rate.
s = scrap value.
c = cost.
n = years of expected life.

maining service values) declining more in early years and less during the later years of asset life; (4) the expiration of the cost of equal service contributions discounted back to the date of acquisition—thus, more is paid for the service values becoming available in the early years than the service values of the later years even though all service values are equal when used; (5) increasing repair and maintenance costs; (6) declining cash proceeds or revenues; (7) the uncertainty of revenues of later years because of possible obsolescence. These conditions are discussed more fully in the following paragraphs.

Declining revenue contributions and declining operating efficiency are interrelated and have the same consequences with respect to the depreciation that should be charged to operations in each period. The decline in the annual net revenue contribution may result from declining use in the later years of life, because more time is required for repairs, or because of the greater danger of breakdowns with heavy use. Net revenue contribution may also decline because of decreased efficiency and thus less output, as in a power generator. On the other hand, declining operating efficiency may result in larger fuel costs, higher labor costs, or greater waste in the use of materials. All of these mean that the net contribution of the asset is less than when it was new. Thus, if interest costs are ignored, this decline in the net service contribution of the asset provides a justification for a decreasing charge depreciation method. For example, if interest is ignored in Table 6, above, the depreciation each year would be the net revenue contribution (column 3) divided by $6,200 (the total of column 3) and multiplied by $5,000 (the original cost of the asset). That is, a constant relationship is assumed between the net revenue contribution each year and the depreciation charge based on cost.

When interest is taken into consideration, a declining charge method may also be justified if the amount of decline in the annual net revenue contribution is greater than the rate of interest multiplied by the net decline in total remaining service value. In Table 8, the decline in net revenue contribution is assumed to be great enough to produce a pattern of declining asset value equal to that resulting from the use of the sum-of-the-years'-digits method of depreciation. As before, the asset is assumed to have a cost of $5,000, with an estimated life of five years with no scrap value, and the earning rate is assumed to be 8 percent.

Although the amount of the decline in the annual net revenue contribution under the assumptions of Table 8 (indicated in column 3) is not constant from year to year, it approximates 8 percent of the original cost of the asset. As demonstrated in Table 6, a decline of 1.6 percent of the original cost (8 percent of the annual decline in asset value) resulted in a straight-line (constant) decline in the asset's value. Therefore, for an asset with a life of five years with no scrap value, a declining depreciation charge (based on the decline in asset value) would result if the net

TABLE 8

Computation of Depreciation Assuming an 8% Internal Rate of Return and a Rapidly Declining Annual Net Revenue Contribution

Year	*1* *Book* *Value of* *Asset at* *Beginning* *of Year*	*2* *Associated* *Earnings* *8% of* *Col. 1*	*3* *Net* *Revenue* *Contri-* *bution*	*4* *Depreciation* *(Col. 3 − Col. 2)*
1	$5,000	$400	$2,067	$1,667
2	3,333	267	1,600	1,333
3	2,000	160	1,160	1,000
4	1,000	80	747	667
5	333	27	360	333

annual revenue contribution declined each year by more than 1.6 percent of the original cost. Note that the pattern of decline in total asset value depends on the amount of decline in revenue contribution each year (rather than on the rate of decline) and on the internal rate of return and the life of the asset.

A declining pattern of annual net revenue contributions appears logical on a priori grounds. For most classes of equipment and buildings, one would expect a decrease in operating efficiency over the life of the asset, increasing repair and maintenance costs, and possibly declining net revenues because of increasing obsolescence and competition. Terborgh demonstrated that when using a 10 percent discount rate, the loss in total service value during the first half of the asset's life ranges from 71 percent for a 10-year asset to 56 percent for a 100-year asset.[14] On empirical grounds, Terborgh concluded that for equipment, the decline in total service value is about one half during the first third of the asset's life and about two thirds for the first half of the asset's life.[15]

Another proposed justification for the declining charge depreciation methods is based on the assumption that the original cost represents the discounted value of the expected annual contributions to be obtained by using the asset. The cost of the earlier annual contributions is therefore greater than the cost of the more remote values.[16] Thus even if the annual net revenue contributions can be expected to be equal in all years of service life, the depreciation charge based on cost would be greater in

[14] George Terborgh, *Realistic Depreciation Policy* (Washington, D.C.: Machinery and Allied Products Institute, 1954), pp. 37–38.

[15] *Ibid.,* pp. 44–45.

[16] For an excellent presentation of this case, see Robert L. Dixon, "Decreasing Charge Depreciation—A Search for Logic," *Accounting Review,* Vol. XXXV (October, 1960), pp. 590–97.

TABLE 9

Computation of Depreciation Based on the Discounted Cost of Annual Services Assuming Equal Annual Contributions and an 8% Rate of Return

Year	1 Book Value of Asset at Beginning of Year	2 Net Revenue Contri- bution	3 Discounted Value of Each Year's Contribution (Col. 2 Dis- counted at 8%) (Depreciation)	4 Depre- ciation as a Per- centage of Cost
1	$5,000	$1,252	$1,160	23.2%
2	3,840	1,252	1,074	21.5
3	2,766	1,252	994	19.9
4	1,772	1,252	920	18.4
5	852	1,252	852	17.0
Total		$6,260	$5,000	100.0%

the early years and smaller in the later years. For example, if a five-year asset with a cost of $5,000 and no scrap value could be expected to have a constant annual service value of $1,252, the depreciation would follow a declining pattern, as demonstrated in Table 9 (with an assumed 8 percent rate of return).

Note that the concept of depreciation implicit in the example shown in Table 9 is different from the concept implied in the previous examples. In this case, it is assumed that depreciation represents the cost of each year's services, not the decline in the value of the remaining services. While the initial assumptions regarding asset value are the same as in the interest methods (demonstrated in Table 7), the effect is considerably different. In the interest methods, the depreciation charge each year is the net revenue contribution less the interest on the asset's book value at the beginning of the year; the difference between the total value of all services ($6,260) and the cost ($5,000) is assumed to accrue each year. On the other hand, the method demonstrated in Table 9 assumes that the difference between the total value of the services and their cost is realized only in the year of use. Thus, in the first year, interest of $92 would be "realized" by using services that cost $1,160 but have a value of $1,252; in the fifth year, interest of $400 would be "realized" by using services costing $852 but having a current value of $1,252. Therefore, the main differences between this approach and the interest methods are in the concept of depreciation and in the method of reporting the increase in asset value through holding the asset. Note that the amounts in column 3 of Table 9 are exactly the reverse of the amounts in column 4 of Table 7.

From a theoretical point of view, the above proposal for a logical explanation of the declining charge methods is quite weak. *First,* it represents a very rigid application of the cost rule—each unit of service value is charged to expense in the amount of its original discounted cost. The longer the waiting period, the lower this cost will be. *Second,* it applies a very rigid form of the realization rule. The difference between the original cost and the value of the services is assumed to be realized only when the asset is used or when its product is sold. *Third,* depreciation is assumed to represent the expiration of the original cost of each year's contribution, rather than the net revenue contribution less the earnings associated with a declining investment. Under the static conditions assumed in this proposal, the result would be a rapidly increasing rate of return based on the reported net income. Not only would greater amounts of interest be realized in later years, but also the income from reinvested capital would tend to increase the net incomes of the later years. This proposal is also subject to the same criticisms as the interest methods—it omits more factors than it includes in the logic. Declining depreciation methods have some support, however, for other reasons.

The argument that a declining depreciation charge should be used to offset increasing repair and maintenance expenses is not without merit. As indicated earlier in this chapter, repair and maintenance expenses are related to the depreciation process and should be included in the total cost of the services or in the computation of the net revenue contribution. One word of caution, however—only normal repair and maintenance expenses should be included in the process of equalizing the total of repair expenses and depreciation. Expenses resulting from inefficiencies should appear in the years in which they occur for managerial control purposes and for proper reporting of income.

Decreasing expected cash proceeds or revenues also provide support for decreasing charge depreciation methods for all assets used in operations. If revenues are expected to decline over the life of an asset, it may be assumed that a larger part of the original cost of the asset was incurred to obtain the revenues of the early years. For example, a hotel usually commands higher rates when it is new and holds a prestige status. As it grows older, the hotel eventually becomes a second-rate establishment and its rates must be decreased. Finally, it may be converted into a rooming house or remodeled into apartments. Therefore, the revenues provide a good indication of the net contribution of the asset each year. Here again, standard depreciation methods should not be assumed to take care of the decreasing revenue factor automatically. Estimates should be made for specific assets, and appropriate depreciation schedules could then be devised. A question may be raised as to whether or not anticipated declines in the prices of products should be taken into consideration in the computation of the depreciation allocation. The answer is in the affirmative if the decline in price can be attributed to anticipated increases in competition or decreases in demand. Unanticipated changes in product prices would be reflected in the incomes of each period affected.

Uncertainty is the most difficult factor to treat in the allocation of depreciation charges. The uncertain values include the expected life, anticipated net revenue contributions, and future repair and maintenance charges. In most cases, the uncertain values can be converted into single-valued certainty equivalents by using the expected values adjusted for risk preference. Therefore, uncertainty in the life of the asset is not proper justification for the use of decreasing charge methods of depreciation. Uncertainty regarding repair and maintenance expenses also provides little justification for declining depreciation charges because this uncertainty is primarily a result of inadequate experience and data rather than a result of uncertainty regarding unpredictable events. Uncertainty regarding future revenue contributions, however, does provide some support for declining charge depreciation methods. The argument is that since early revenues are more certain than more distant revenues, the latter are discounted more heavily in the initial investment decision, and therefore a larger part of the cost of the asset should be allocated to the earlier years. The main defect of this argument is that it is difficult, if not impossible, to justify any specific depreciation schedule on the basis of uncertainty alone.

Summary of Depreciation Methods. While the possible patterns for depreciation allocation are innumerable, the main types of distribution can be demonstrated by the most commonly proposed depreciation methods. The following charts depict these distributions for four of the most common methods—not including the production or use method, which cannot be presented graphically because the distribution may be different for each asset.

Summary of Conditions under Which Each Pattern Is Applicable. One or more of the conditions listed below may provide support for the general allocation pattern indicated. The specific depreciation method to be used should be selected on the basis of as many relevant factors as possible.

Variable Charge Methods

The value of the asset declines as a function of use rather than because of the passing of time.

Obsolescence is not an important factor in determining the life of the asset.

Repairs, maintenance expenses, and revenues are proportional to use.

Straight-Line Method

Discounted value of future benefits declines as a function of time rather than use.

FIGURE 2

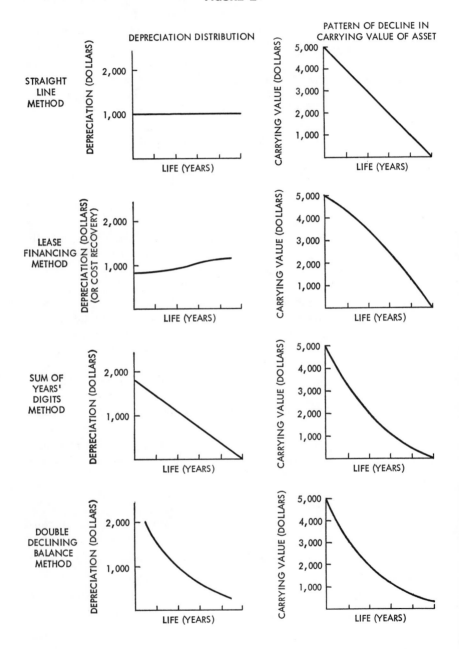

The interest factor can be ignored or assumed to be offset by other factors.

Repairs, maintenance expenses, operating efficiency, and revenues are relatively constant over the life of the asset.

Increasing Charge Methods

The cash flow or net revenue contribution of each year is constant, but the asset value each year represents the discounted value of remaining contributions.

Repair and maintenance expenses are constant or decreasing over the life of the asset.

Revenues and operating efficiency are constant or increasing over the life of the asset.

Decreasing Charge Methods

Increasing repair and maintenance charges.

Decreasing operating efficiency and revenues.

Interest factor recognized only when "realized" through use of the asset.

Uncertainty of revenues of the later years.

DEPRECIATION FOR NONPROFIT ORGANIZATIONS

Accounting for nonprofit organizations is similar in many respects to the accounting for profit-seeking enterprises. But because they have different objectives, it is to be expected that not all of the accounting principles applicable to profit-seeking enterprises are equally valid when applied to nonprofit institutions. Accounting for depreciation is generally considered to be one of the areas where the different objectives dictate alternative procedures.

Organizations such as hospitals, schools, welfare agencies, and governmental units have as one of their objectives the provision of services without expectation of making a profit or even charging for the service an amount approximating its cost. Therefore, accounting serves the function of reporting on the stewardship of the resources granted to the agencies and the accountability of those in charge of the agencies. Instead of matching expenses with revenues and reporting on the maintenance of capital, the accounting reports are intended to provide a control in the proper use of funds, and to present a record of receipts and disbursements and a record of assets in use showing their final authorized disposition. Since the objectives of depreciation are primarily to provide for a proper charge to operations for the cost or other value of services used during a period and to permit a measurement of capital maintenance, it is frequently argued that depreciation is irrelevant to nonprofit organizations.

The main arguments against using depreciation for nonprofit organizations are as follows: (1) Revenues, particularly for capital improvements, are generally unrelated to total operating expenses, including depreciation. The funds obtained from donors and legislatures are generally determined on the basis of current cash needs rather than on the basis of the value of the services performed. (2) Donors and legislatures do not generally look favorably on requests for funds for current capital additions and also for funds for operations including depreciation. They prefer to meet the needs for capital additions and replacements as they arise rather than through the process of depreciation. (3) It is often considered unfair to ask one generation to donate for the construction of plant and equipment and also provide for their replacement through the payments of amounts equal to depreciation. (4) If revenues do not provide for the funding of depreciation, the recording of it alone would only result in large operating deficits. (5) If donors or legislatures are asked to provide funds equal to depreciation, the result would be to provide the agency with a general surplus which could be used as the agency chose. The providers of the funds would thus lose control over the specific uses of funds.

The arguments for the recording of depreciation relate primarily to those organizations where revenues, or at least some of the revenues, are related to costs and where capital maintenance is an important element. Therefore, depreciation has been recommended for hospitals, because many of the services are paid for by governmental agencies or hospital insurance plans on the basis of total costs. Endowment funds are generally thought of as permanent funds that should be maintained intact; therefore, no revenues should be used for current operations until proper depreciation has been recorded. Auxiliary enterprises of educational institutions, such as dormitories and book stores, are generally operated on the basis that the services should be priced so that all costs will be covered and so that capital will be maintained.

Even where capital maintenance is not required and where services are not priced according to costs, there are some valid reasons for recording depreciation: (1) Depreciation computations may be helpful in the determination of insurance values of property and equipment. (2) Total costs are useful in evaluating the costs of services provided for comparative study purposes. (3) Depreciation may be useful in determining the amount of capital funds required each year to maintain a given level of operations over a long period and to determine the amount of capital outlay that can be considered net growth.

Two major organizations representing nonprofit institutions, the American Council on Education and the American Hospital Association, have taken positions on the recording of depreciation. The American Council on Education takes the position that educational institutions find little benefit from the annual computation of depreciation on their educational property (except for supplementary purposes).[17] It states further that when depreciation is taken, it should be funded by setting aside cash for replacement purposes. The American Hospital Association, on the other hand, states that

Depreciation of hospital buildings and equipment should be recognized as an element of hospital expense. . . . The depreciation in value of buildings and equipment represents a real cost of hospital service, even though such assets may have been contributed originally to the hospital and even though no cash or other funds are set aside to replace such assets.[18]

In the author's opinion, depreciation provides very little relevant information for the managements of nonprofit organizations, or for donors and legislators. Long-range capital budget plans are much more useful for these institutions. Furthermore, there seems to be little logic in requiring that depreciation be funded through the setting aside of cash for replacements.

SELECTED ADDITIONAL READING ON CHAPTER TOPICS

Discounted Cash Flow Concepts of Depreciation

BIERMAN, HAROLD, JR. "A Further Study of Depreciation," *Accounting Review*, Vol. XLI (April, 1966), pp. 271–74.

BRIEF, RICHARD P. "Depreciation Theory and Capital Gains," *Journal of Accounting Research*, Vol. VI (Spring, 1968), pp. 149–52.

———. "A Late 19th Century Contribution to the Theory of Depreciation," *Journal of Accounting Research*, Vol. V (Spring, 1967), pp. 27–38.

BRIEF, RICHARD P., and JOEL OWEN. "Depreciation and Capital Gains: A 'New' Approach," *Accounting Review*, Vol. XLIII (April, 1968), pp. 367–72.

MERRETT, A. J., and ALLEN SYKES. "The Valuation of Assets," *Accountancy*, Vol. LXXIV (February, 1963), pp. 101–05; (March, 1963), pp. 212–15; (May, 1963), pp. 403–04; and (June, 1963), pp. 488–94.

REYNOLDS, ISAAC N. "Selecting the Proper Depreciation Method," *Accounting Review*, Vol. XXXVI (April, 1961), pp. 239–49.

WRIGHT, F. K. "Towards a General Theory of Depreciation," *Journal of Accounting Research*, Vol. II (Spring, 1964), pp. 80–90.

---

[17] American Council on Education, *College and University Business Administration* (Washington, D.C.: American Council on Education, 1968), pp. 285–86.

[18] Committee on Accounting and Statistics Council on Administrative Practice, American Hospital Association, *Uniform Chart of Accounts and Definitions for Hospitals* (Chicago: American Hospital Association, 1959), p. 128.

——. "An Evaluation of Ladelle's Theory of Depreciation," *Journal of Accounting Research,* Vol. V (Autumn, 1967), pp. 173–79.

YOUNG, T. N., and C. G. PEIRSON. "Depreciation—Future Services Basis," *Accounting Review,* Vol. XLII (April, 1967), pp. 338–41.

Depreciation Proportional to Net Contribution

JOHNSON, ORACE. "Two General Concepts of Depreciation," *Journal of Accounting Research,* Vol. VI (Spring, 1968), pp. 29–37. See also WILLIAM J. VATTER, "Time-Adjusted Depreciation," *Journal of Accounting Research,* Vol. VII (Spring, 1969), pp. 163–64.

VATTER, WILLIAM J. "Income Models, Book Yield, and the Rate of Return," *Accounting Review,* Vol. XLI (October, 1966), pp. 681–98.

WRIGHT, F. KENNETH. "Depreciation Theory and the Cost of Funds," *Accounting Review,* Vol. XXXVIII (January, 1963), pp. 87–91.

Depreciation and Repair Costs

BATTISTA, GEORGE L., and GERALD R. CROWNINGSHIELD. "Accounting for Depreciation and Repair Costs," *NAA Bulletin,* Vol. XLV (December, 1963), pp. 21–30.

BERG, KENNETH B. "Allowance for Repairs," *Accounting Review,* Vol. XXXVII (July, 1962), pp. 488–97.

Replacement Depreciation

REYNOLDS, ISAAC N. "A Vanishing Accounting Item—Replacement Accounting," *Accounting Review,* Vol. XXXIX (April, 1964), pp. 342–46.

Depreciation and Obsolescence

BIERMAN, HAROLD, JR. "Recording Obsolescence," *Journal of Accounting Research,* Vol. II (Autumn, 1964), pp. 229–35.

MEIJ, J. L. *Depreciation and Replacement Policy,* chap. i, "Depreciation and Obsolescence as Factors in Costing," by W. Arthur Lewis. Chicago: Quadrangle Books, 1961.

WOODS, J. H. "Recording Obsolescence—A Note," *Journal of Accounting Research,* Vol. III (Autumn, 1965), pp. 261–63.

Decreasing Charge Methods of Depreciation

BIERMAN, HAROLD, JR. "Accelerated Depreciation and Rate Regulation," *Accounting Review,* Vol. XLIV (January, 1969), pp. 65–78.

DIXON, ROBERT L. "Decreasing Charge Depreciation—A Search for Logic," *Accounting Review,* Vol. XXXV (October, 1960), pp. 590–97.

Lorig, Arthur N. "On the Logic of Decreasing Charge Depreciation," *Accounting Review*, Vol. XXXVII (January, 1962), pp. 56–58.

Van Horn, Lawrence G. "Accelerated Depreciation—A Tax Benefit, But Harmful Accounting," *New York Certified Public Accountant*, Vol. XXXVII (May, 1967), pp. 346–53.

Winter, J. C. "Accelerated Depreciation—A Victim of Its Own Success," *New York Certified Public Accountant*, Vol. XXXVII (October, 1967), pp. 774–81.

Depreciation for Nonprofit Institutions

Baldassare, Ernest W. "Capital Expenditures and Depreciation for Nonprofit Institutions," *New York Certified Public Accountant*, Vol. XXIX (March, 1959), pp. 207–12.

Ellenberger, James O. "A Look at Depreciation Accounting in Non-profit Organizations," *NAA Bulletin*, Vol. XLII (January, 1961), Sec. 1, pp. 55–63.

Relevance and Theoretical Logic of Depreciation

Staubus, George J. "Statistical Evidence of the Value of Depreciation Accounting," *Abacus*, Vol. III (August, 1967), pp. 3–22.

Thomas, Arthur L. "The Allocation Problem in Financial Accounting Theory," *Studies in Accounting Research No. 3*. American Accounting Association, 1969.

chapter 14

Intangibles, Noncurrent Investments, and Deferred Charges

The treatment of intangible assets in financial statements is one of the more difficult areas in accounting theory, partly because of the continuing controversy regarding what they are, and partly because of the conflicting objectives regarding financial reporting and the conflicting concepts and methods to meet these objectives. Because of these controversies, a wide variety of methods for accounting for intangibles has been accepted in practice, resulting in a renewed interest in attempting to correct the deficiencies.

The main controversies regarding intangibles stem from the basic objectives of asset valuation and income reporting. Four basic views discussed earlier in this book include the following: (1) One view is that assets represent rights to future benefits and, conversely, if expeditures of resources result in potential future benefits, they should be carried as assets until such time as benefits can no longer be expected to be received in the future. (2) A second view is that resource outlays should be matched with associated revenues whenever possible, and that allocations based upon assumed associations are better than no allocations. (3) A third view is that nonmonetary assets should be carried forward to be matched with revenues only when there is a direct association between the two; since only rarely can intangibles be associated directly with specific revenues, they should be reported as expenses in the year acquired. (4) A fourth objective is to emphasize the cash or net monetary flows rather than net income in financial reporting. Since these several views are behind many of the alternative methods of treating intangibles, they are very relevant to the following discussion.

THE NATURE OF INTANGIBLES

An intangible is usually defined as "a capital asset having no physical existence, its value being dependent on the rights that possession confers upon the owner."[1] Webster's dictionary defines it as an asset that is not corporeal.[2] The defining of intangible assets as capital assets merely implies that they are noncurrent; otherwise, such items as prepaid insurance, prepaid rent, and franchise taxes paid in advance would also be intangibles. Therefore, one common characteristic is that they are expected to benefit the firm beyond the current operating cycle of the business; and the invested capital represented by the asset will be available for reinvestment only gradually over several or many years.

The characteristic of a lack of physical existence, however, is not clear-cut. Other noncurrent assets, such as long-term receivables, long-term investments, and deferred pension plan costs also lack corporeal existence. On the other hand, leaseholds and leasehold improvements, generally classified as intangibles, do represent rights to the use of physical assets. There is little difference between a long-term leasehold for the use of property during its useful life and the ownership of that property. Both represent rights to the use of land and buildings—property having physical existence. When the lease does not cover the entire life of the property, the stream of benefits is truncated, but the nature of the asset is still the same—rights to the use of physical property. Therefore, leaseholds and leasehold improvements are more similar to plant and equipment than they are to patents, copyrights, and goodwill.

Except for leaseholds and leasehold improvements, the most important single characteristic of intangibles is the high degree of uncertainty regarding the value of the future benefits to be received. In most cases, the possible values may range from zero to very large amounts. Some intangibles relate to the development and manufacture of a product, while others relate to the creation and maintenance of the demand for the product. Patents and copyrights reflect primarily the former, while trademarks and trade names reflect primarily the latter. Goodwill may represent either or both. All, however, represent benefits that are highly uncertain and difficult to associate with specific revenues or specific periods.

Both tangible and intangible nonmonetary assets derive their economic value from the expectations of future earning power. However, many tangible assets have value in alternative uses and their value to the firm can, at least in part, be compared with their physical condition, their replacement cost, the market value for used assets, and the market for the product of the enterprise. But, most intangible assets represent the development of exclusive processes or products or the protection of marketing superiority, none of which can be transferred to alternative uses.

[1] Eric L. Kohler, *A Dictionary for Accountants* (3d ed.; Englewood Cliffs, N.J.: Prentice-Hall, Inc., 1963), p. 269.

[2] *Webster's Third New International Dictionary* (Springfield, Mass.: G. & C. Merriam Co., 1961), p. 1173.

While their value is derived from expected future revenues, it is impossible in most cases to determine what part of the revenue results from the intangibles and what part from other assets and services.

An alternative view of intangible assets is that they arise only from conditions of imperfect competition.[3] Patents, copyrights, and franchises grant the firm special partial monopolistic powers or rights to limit direct competition. Therefore, these rights do not add directly to the wealth of the economy and are differentiated from plant and equipment, which are productive assets. However, this distinction is not clear, because the rights associated with the owning of productive property may also be at least in part the result of imperfect competition.

One common characteristic of most intangibles is that they cannot be separated from the firm or the physical property of the firm. They exist and have value only in combination with the tangible assets of the firm. Because of this, they are frequently considered to represent residual benefits after all tangible assets are specifically identified. However, this concept has very little merit for accountants in their attempts to identify and measure intangibles individually or as a group.

THE VALUATION OF INTANGIBLES

The valuation of intangibles for reporting purposes depends upon the reporting objectives and concepts applied. If the objective is to measure and report each period the individual assets of the firm, the only alternative is to measure the value of the firm as a whole and subtract from this value the valuation of other specific net assets. But as indicated in Chapter 9, the only meaningful valuation of the firm as a whole is that determined subjectively by the investor himself. The accountant should not attempt to determine this value for him because of the subjective expectations required and the necessity of adjusting these expectations for personal preferences or aversions for risk.

If the objective, however, is to measure and report specific assets in order to provide the users of financial reports with an indication of the resources available to the firm, an independent measurement of the intangibles might be desirable. But there are some major differences between the measurement concepts that can be applied to intangible as opposed to tangible assets. Valuation on the basis of output values and earning power is difficult to apply in any situation and, except in rare cases, impossible to apply even roughly to intangible assets. Replacement cost, a measure of current input value, is likewise generally impossible of calculation. Each intangible is usually unique and cannot be compared

---

[3] See for example J. E. Sands, *Wealth, Income, and Intangibles* (Toronto: University of Toronto Press, 1963), p. 28.

with other similar items. And because of this uniqueness, meaningful and relevant price indexes cannot be found to compute specific replacement costs. The only meaningful and practical valuation is, therefore, the actual input value—historical cost—or cost adjusted for changes in general purchasing power.

When intangibles are acquired by purchase, individually or as a part of a "basket purchase," the determination of cost is similar to the computation of the cost of plant and equipment under like circumstances. When intangibles are acquired by self-development, however, the computation of their cost involves all of the difficulties of self-constructed assets plus some additional problems of its own. Most of the costs of patents, trademarks, and trade names are joint costs. Many patents may emerge from joint research and development expenditures, and several trademarks and trade names may be advertised jointly. While these problems can be solved by the use of known costing methods, the results are likely to be arbitrary if they include allocated joint costs. To the extent that they do, the valuations are likely to be meaningless.

The basic characteristics of high uncertainty and uniqueness have led most accountants and accounting associations to recommend that intangibles should not be valued in excess of cost. For example, the AICPA states in *Accounting Research Bulletin No. 43:*

The initial amount assigned to all types of intangibles should be cost. . . . In the case of non-cash acquisitions, as, for example, where intangibles are acquired in exchange for securities, cost may be considered as being either the fair value of the consideration given or the fair value of the property or right acquired, whichever is the more evident.[4]

Sprouse and Moonitz also recommend the use of cost for intangibles in spite of their general preference for current values or replacement cost. They state:

. . . these items are notoriously difficult to evaluate and therefore should probably be carried at acquisition cost in the absence of compelling evidence that their value is markedly different.[5]

While cost is also generally recommended for tangible assets, other valuations may be acceptable and are occasionally recommended. But for intangibles, there must be compelling evidence that some other valuation is more appropriate. Even when intangible assets are donated to the firm, there is a general reluctance to record any value in the accounts because

---

[4] AICPA, *Accounting Principles* (Chicago: Commerce Clearing House, Inc., 1968), Vol. II, p. 6019.

[5] Robert T. Sprouse and Maurice Moonitz, "A Tentative Set of Broad Accounting Principles for Business Enterprises," *Accounting Research Study No. 3* (New York: AICPA, 1962), p. 36.

of the high degree of uncertainty regarding whatever valuation may be chosen. Hatfield stated, for example:

Cash being of definite value may be listed though it cost nothing; quoted securities or commodities may, according to some authorities, be listed at the market value even though that exceed the cost; but goodwill, because of its vague nature and the difficulty of verifying its appraisal, is to be excluded unless it has been purchased.[6]

This statement is equally appropriate today and probably applies equally well to intangible assets other than goodwill.

When intangibles are acquired through the issuance of capital stock, the determination of cost is a difficult, if not almost impossible, problem. *Bulletin No. 43* states that in this case, cost may be considered to be either the fair value of the stock given or the fair value of the rights acquired, whichever is the more evident. If the stock does not have a current market price, the determination of the cost of the intangibles is extremely difficult because the intangibles generally have no market value either. The Securities and Exchange Commission has indicated that in such cases it is inappropriate to assume that cost is equal to the par value or stated value of the shares issued in exchange.

Because most intangibles are not severable from the firm and cannot be measured in terms of a current cash equivalent, Chambers suggested that they are not assets and should not be included in the statements of the firm.[7] While current practice generally condones the charging of intangibles to expenses immediately or their amortization over very short periods, this is frequently considered acceptable because it presents a "conservative" valuation. Because the value of intangibles is highly uncertain, accountants prefer to omit them entirely rather than risk their overvaluation in the accounts. But this attitude is inconsistent with the general preciseness and tidiness which characterizes most accountants in the recording and valuation of tangible assets. The practice of presenting intangible assets in the financial statements at the nominal valuation of $1 indicates that some unknown valuation is present, but it is inadequate disclosure of the nature of the rights to future benefits held by the firm. A better alternative would be to describe the nature of these rights in nonmonetary terms if possible and present in the statements information regarding the resources used initially to obtain these rights and the amounts spent annually to maintain them. No single valuation on the balance sheet can even begin to describe these rights adequately.

---

[6] Henry Rand Hatfield, *Accounting, Its Principles and Problems* (New York: D. Appleton & Co., 1927), p. 113. By permission of the copyright holder, Appleton-Century-Crofts.

[7] Raymond J. Chambers, *Accounting, Evaluation and Economic Behavior* (Englewood Cliffs, N.J.: Prentice-Hall, Inc., 1966), p. 209.

THE AMORTIZATION OF INTANGIBLE ASSETS

Most intangibles that are generated gradually by the firm through annual expenditures are charged immediately to expense. However, intangibles that are acquired through a lump-sum purchase or that are developed through extraordinary identifiable expenditures are frequently capitalized and amortized similarly to the depreciation allocations of plant and equipment. Once the initial valuation to be amortized is determined, the major factors to be estimated are (1) the useful life of the asset and (2) the pattern of allocation to the several periods of the life of the asset. The residual or scrap value is generally nonexistent or immaterial.

Following the pattern suggested by the AICPA (in *Accounting Research Bulletin No. 43*), intangibles are generally classified as either type (*a*)—those having a limited term of existence—or type (*b*)—those having no limited term of existence and no indication of limited life at the time of acquisition. While this classification is somewhat artificial, as we shall see, it does provide a useful breakdown in studying the alternative allocation procedures and their effects.

Intangibles with Limited Life

Patents, copyrights, and some franchises have a maximum legal life, and only rarely will the economic life exceed this legal life. If circumstances permit the value to extend beyond the legal life, the cost or other value should be amortized over this economic life; but without the legal protection, the value beyond the legal life is too uncertain to include in the amortization schedule. More commonly, the economic life is shorter than the legal life because of market demand conditions or because of obsolescence. When this is the case, the economic life should definitely be the controlling factor. AICPA *Bulletin No. 43*[8] states that the allocation should be over the period benefited. It is very unusual for copyrights to provide benefit to the firm for the entire 28-year period of the copyright, and only very seldom does the benefit flow into the 28-year renewal period. Textbooks, for example, frequently become obsolete in five years or less. But if the book is revised, some of the initial value carries into the second and third editions.

Leaseholds and leasehold improvements have a contractual life, and in most cases the value of the leasehold is expected (at the time the leasehold is acquired) to extend throughout the entire life. The value of leasehold improvements may not extend beyond the life of the lease un-

---

[8] AICPA, *op. cit.*, Vol. II, p. 6019.

less the lease is renewable at the option of the lessee. But the expected life of leasehold improvements may be less than the entire life of the lease. If this is the case, there is no difference between the amortization of leasehold improvements and the depreciation of additions or improvements to plant and equipment.

The pattern for the amortization of intangibles should depend on the surrounding circumstances, like the depreciation of plant and equipment. AICPA *Bulletin No. 43* merely states that the amortization should be systematic; no specific methods are recommended. However, since only the straight-line method is acceptable for income tax purposes, this method is generally recommended as the appropriate method for accounting purposes also.

The appropriate amortization method for leaseholds depends largely on the nature of the lease contract. If the contract requires the lessor to make all necessary repairs and pay the taxes and insurance and all other related expenses, the main consideration in choosing the amortization pattern should be the value of the expected benefits as measured by expected output values or as measured by replacement costs or other input values. If the benefits are expected to be equal for each year of leasehold life, time-adjusted depreciation may be appropriate, because it takes into consideration the relevant interest factor. For long-period leases, however, the uncertainty regarding the value of benefits to be received in distant periods may provide support for a declining charge method. Because of these uncertainties, the straight-line method may not be less appropriate than other methods. In those cases where the lessee is required to pay all maintenance and other expenses relating to the building or other property, the criteria for choosing the amortization method are similar to those appropriate for selecting a proper depreciation method for plant and equipment.

The appropriate method for amortizing the cost of patents and copyrights should depend on the expected flow of benefits to the firm, particularly if all relevant costs, including the costs of defending the patent or copyright, are capitalized. In the case of copyrights, the benefits frequently increase during the first few years and then drop off substantially. If frequent revisions are expected, some of the initial acquisition costs should be amortized over the lives of subsequent editions. The benefit pattern for patents may depend on many economic considerations, including the effect of subsequent supporting or competing developments. Each case must be judged on its own circumstances and expectations.

Because of the high degree of uncertainty regarding the periods to be benefited, it is more likely that changes in expectations will occur for intangibles than for plant and equipment. Therefore, AICPA *Bulletin No. 43* recommends that when changes in expectations occur, the rate of amortization should be changed accordingly. However, if this adjustment in the amortization rate should result in excessive charges to income, resulting in a material distortion of net income, a partial write-down should be made by reporting an extraordinary loss in the income statement in accordance with APB *Opinion No. 9*. Note that a write-up of the asset is not permitted. If excessive amortization has occurred, the amortization to subsequent periods is generally reduced by an amount large enough to offset the earlier overamortization, even if this does result in a material distortion of net income. This is one of the major inconsistencies in current accounting practice.

While amortization of intangibles is considered by many to represent the matching of expenses with associated revenues, there are many difficulties with this procedure. The major difficulty is that the expected benefits are the result of the interactions of all of the resources of the firm. Since these difficulties have been discussed above, in Chapter 13, they will not be repeated here. However, further difficulties occur because of the inability to measure even expected life. Each intangible is more or less unique, so that experience is of little help. Also, the capital expenditure decision is generally not so precisely formulated. As a result, the amortization procedure results in a method of smoothing income to prevent fluctuations of income due to the irregular acquisition of intangibles unrelated to current operating activities. If the net income figure is used as the major item for prediction purposes, the smoothing process may be of some assistance; however, it seems highly unlikely that arbitrary allocations can provide relevant information for investors and creditors.

Intangibles without Limited Life

Trademarks, trade names, organization costs, and goodwill are examples of intangibles generally considered to have no limited term of existence and no natural limited life. However, the economic life of each of these is definitely limited unless expenditures are continually made for maintenance and replacement. Even initial organization costs require periodic reorganization expenditures, most of which are interrelated with goodwill and current operations. But the time when the original asset value is completely replaced by additional expenditures cannot be determined even in retrospect. Therefore, the AICPA position is that the original cost should remain on the books and the costs of maintenance or replacement should be charged against current income. No amortization is required because the value of the original asset is thought to continue if proper maintenance expenditures are made.

The procedure of carrying the intangible asset at its original cost and charging maintenance and replacement expenditures to current income accounts is similar to the replacement method of depreciation. However, its application to intangibles is more appropriate than its use for the depreciation of plant and equipment, because replacement is a continual process with intangibles while it is sporadic and infrequent for plant and equipment. Thus, the replacement expenditures are charged against the incomes of all periods fairly evenly. This method is also advantageous because it provides for an income charge based on current costs, like Lifo. But there are some major disadvantages: (1) If the value of the intangible is being increased through current expenditures, the charge against current income is excessive, and the reverse is true if the value of the intangible is not maintained. (2) As with Lifo, the value of the intangible soon becomes out of date and not representative of the value to be charged to future periods. (3) The current charge against income is subject to manipulation by management. (4) It does not result in a systematic matching of expenses with benefits received or with current revenues.

When there is evidence that a type (b) intangible is not being replaced or maintained by current expenditures, it should be treated as a type (a) intangible and amortized over the estimated remaining life. If a material loss in value has already occurred in prior years, a partial write-down is condoned by AICPA *Bulletin No. 43*. If there is reasonable evidence that the asset has become worthless, it is acceptable to write off the entire amount against retained earnings if the amount is material.

The above recommendations for amortization and write-off of type (b) intangibles are reasonable and acceptable in accounting theory. But *Bulletin No. 43* goes further than this by stating that—

When a corporation decides that a type (b) intangible may not continue to have value during the entire life of the enterprise it may amortize the cost of such intangible by systematic charges against income despite the fact that there are no present indications of limited existence or loss of value which would indicate that it has become type (a), and despite the fact that expenditures are being made to maintain its value.

This position was accepted because ". . . the practice has been long established and widely approved."[9] But it is inconsistent with basic accounting thought and logic. Land valuations are not generally amortized against income unless there is a clear indication that they are subject to depletion. It is not considered acceptable to write them off or amortize them simply because management decides that they may not continue to have value indefinitely. Amortization should occur only when there are indications of limited existence, and a write-off should not be made capriciously. The same principles should apply to intangibles. A general license to amortize and write them off over arbitrary periods does not lead to responsible accounting.

---
[9] *Ibid.*

The amortization of these intangibles is permitted also despite the fact that current expenditures are being made and charged against income for the maintenance of their value. This results in a double charge against income during the amortization period. It is similar to charging the cost of replacement equipment against income while at the same time depreciating the cost of the original equipment. If the replacement method is acceptable, the amortization of the original cost is not also appropriate; if amortization is proper, the cost of replacements should be capitalized. This capitalization of replacements and the continual amortization of the total cost of intangibles would provide the best theoretical method for matching the cost of benefits received against period revenues. Difficulties in the measurement of replacements, however, indicate that the replacement method without amortization of the original cost may be the most appropriate, or at least the most expedient, method.

While *Bulletin No. 43* does permit a lump-sum write-off of type (b) intangibles when there is reasonable evidence that they have become worthless, it is very clear in prohibiting lump-sum write-offs of any intangibles immediately after acquisition. The assumption is that if the intangible has been acquired at a cost, it must be worth this price, at least at that time. While the main purpose of this restriction was to prevent undue conservatism in asset valuation and overstatement of the incomes of subsequent periods, it does not recognize that an error can be made in the acquisition of the intangible. If this error is recognized immediately, the loss should be recorded; there is no justification for carrying forward the loss to future periods. Immediate recognition of an overstatement of an intangible should also be permitted when there has been an error in the valuation of a nonmonetary asset exchanged for the intangible.

RESEARCH AND DEVELOPMENT COSTS

To the extent that research and development activities are carried out to develop new products, improve old ones, or reduce future operating costs, they are expected to benefit future periods rather than only the current period. Because future periods are expected to be benefited, the knowledge gained is either an asset of the firm or an increase in the value of existing assets or of the firm as a whole. Therefore, according to the matching concept, the research and development costs should be capitalized and amortized over the period benefited. Even though the period and the timing of the benefits are highly uncertain, proponents of the matching concept claim that an appropriate allocation is better than an immediate write-off, because a subjective estimate of the value is better than an arbitrary valuation of zero.[10] Allocation is also assumed to be

---

[10] See for example Allan R. Drebin, "Accounting for Proprietary Research," *Accounting Review,* Vol. XLI (July, 1966), p. 425.

better because an immediate write-off may result in lower net earnings, thus indicating an adverse situation while the reverse may be true. A firm that sponsors a large amount of research may have a very favorable future while one that carries out no research may be doomed to failure. Thus, if it is all expensed, there may be an incentive to cut back research just at the time it is needed to maintain market position or efficiency.

An alternative to full capitalization and amortization is the common practice of expensing general research and development costs and capitalizing only research costs that relate to specific projects with expected net revenue contribution streams.[11] These special projects are treated like investments in plant and equipment, and the amortization would be similar to the depreciation concepts related to net revenue contributions discussed in Chapter 13.

A third view is closely related to the direct costing approach, in that only variable costs would be carried forward to be matched with the related revenues. But since most research costs are relatively fixed in nature, for practical purposes this is not inconsistent with the view that all R&D costs should be expensed when they are incurred, in accordance with the cash flow concept. Because of the need to allocate costs to projects if they are to be capitalized and then to amortize these project costs over an uncertain period in an uncertain way, the immediate expensing of research and development costs appears to be the only practical solution to a very difficult problem. However, this solution is not acceptable if reported net income continues to be the main indicator of success. An alternative would be to report these costs as noncurrent charges but with a full explanation of their nature, so investors can place them in proper perspective in making predictions. The current position of the AICPA, which permits either capitalization or immediate write-off under similar situations, leads only to confusion and a lack of adequate data for informed decisions.

GOODWILL

The nature of financial goodwill has been the subject of debate since before the end of the 19th century. However, the early discussions centered primarily on the legal recognition and definition of the concept. From an accounting point of view, three major conceptions of goodwill appear frequently in the literature: (1) the valuation of intangible attitudes toward the firm; (2) the present discounted value of the excess of expected future profits over that considered a normal return on the total investment not including the goodwill; and (3) a master valuation account—the excess of the value of the business as a whole over the

---

[11] See for example J. A. Milburn, "A Look at Problems in Research and Development Accounting," *Canadian Chartered Accountant*, Vol. XCII (June, 1968), pp. 404–408.

valuations attaching to its individual tangible and intangible net assets. In the first and second definitions, goodwill is usually considered to be a separate asset with specific characteristics. In the third definition—as a master valuation account—it is not generally considered to be a separate distinct asset.

The Valuation of Favorable Attitudes Toward the Firm

Goodwill is frequently thought to arise from advantageous business relationships, good relations with employees, and favorable attitudes of customers. These favorable attitudes may be due to an advantageous location, an excellent reputation and name, monopolistic privileges, good business management, and other factors. When the purchase price of a going business exceeds the sum of the valuations of all individual assets other than goodwill, the excess may be assumed to represent the payment for these specific intangible attributes. However, specific values cannot be assigned to each of these characteristics individually. Therefore, because a total valuation for goodwill cannot be computed by adding the sum of the parts, the mere listing of these characteristics does not provide any meaningful insight into their valuation, either individually or collectively.

A fallacy of this specific attribute approach is that most of these characteristics attach to specific assets or have value only because they provide a possibility for superior future profits. A favorable location, for example, means that the land and buildings are worth more than similar property elsewhere. The value of excellent reputation and name attach to the valuation of trade names and brand names. Good business management and monopolistic privileges, however, do not necessarily attach to specific assets, but represent attributes of the firm as a whole. But the listing of specific attitudes and attributes does not provide a meaningful approach to the definition and valuation of goodwill. Certain favorable attributes should be included in the valuation of tangible assets, others should be classified separately as specific types of intangibles, and the remainder (that which can now be called goodwill) represents the residual benefits which cannot be associated with specific attributes.

The Present Value of Superior Earnings

A common approach to the nature of goodwill is to assume that it represents the present discounted value of expected future earnings (or cash payments to equity holders) in excess of that which may be considered a normal return. However, this is a measurement of goodwill, not a description of its nature. Furthermore, there is doubt that it is valid conceptually even as a measurement concept.

As indicated in Chapter 9, the value of the firm as a whole can only be determined subjectively by the investors, because it depends upon their expectations of future cash flows, the expected opportunity rates of return, and personal utility risk functions. As Chambers stated, "the goodwill of a going concern runs to the constituents, not to the firm."[12] Therefore, neither management nor the accountants can place a correct valuation on goodwill. But neither can the investor allocate this total value of the firm logically to specific tangible and intangible assets and to goodwill. The assumption that the tangible assets can earn only a "normal" rate while other factors are responsible for the excess is fiction. Tangible assets may have value in their specific use because of imperfect competition and changes in demand for the products as well as efficient utilization. All factors interact in the production of the final service or product and in permitting cash distributions to stockholders. Any attempt to allocate a portion of the total value of a firm on the basis of the capitalization of superior earnings is, therefore, artificial.

Goodwill as a Master Valuation Account

Canning was one of the early writers who questioned whether goodwill is an asset at all in the usual sense, and he preferred to view goodwill as a master valuation account.[13] All assets obtain their value to the firm because of their expected contribution to the stream of future earnings and cash flows. Therefore the entire value of the firm should be associated with the specific assets giving rise to this stream of cash flows. If expectations of cash flows should increase (after making payment for superior management skills), the values of all assets or of specific assets contributing to this increase are now worth more than before.

Generally, however, it is not possible to allocate the total value of the firm over the specific assets. Receivables can be valued in terms of the discounted expected cash receipts, inventories can be valued in terms of net realizable value, but land, plant and equipment, and patent rights cannot usually be associated with specific expected money flows. The unallocated value is, therefore, recorded as goodwill—a master valuation account.

Frequently, however, no attempt is made to allocate to specific assets the excess of the price paid for a business over the carrying value of the specific assets. Even though this residual may be called goodwill, it has even fewer of the attributes of an intangible asset. Instead, it represents unallocated costs of tangible assets and some specific intangibles. Goodwill is not an adequate substitute for the careful determination of the cost

---

[12] Chambers, *op. cit.*, p. 211.

[13] John B. Canning, *The Economics of Accountancy* (New York: Ronald Press, Co., 1929), p. 42.

of specific assets, based as closely as possible on their value to the firm at the date of acquisition.

As a master valuation account, can goodwill be negative as well as positive? Logically, the answer is no. If the total price paid for a business is less than the replacement cost of the assets, this is evidence that the specific assets are not worth their replacement cost; the deficiency should be allocated to the individual assets. In general, accountants are less reluctant to record assets at less than their current replacement value than they are to record them at a value greater than this. But if the assets are recorded at their carrying value to the old firm and no allocation is made, the deficiency is a negative valuation account. It would be inappropriate to call this overvaluation in the specific accounts a negative goodwill.

THE RECORDING OF GOODWILL

Costs incurred by a firm to improve its future earning power are generally charged immediately to expense unless they can be directly associated with specific tangible or intangible assets. Since goodwill represents advantages not specifically identifiable when acquired in the normal course of business, it is not recorded as an asset even though future periods will be benefited. The main reasons supporting this practice are the inability to identify and measure the goodwill created each period and the absence of any logical method of associating these costs with any specific revenue in future periods. Therefore, even though AICPA *Bulletin No. 43*[14] recommends that all intangibles should be recorded at cost when they are acquired, the immediate expensing of what Catlett and Olson call "nonpurchased" goodwill is generally accepted.[15] The author agrees with this practice, because no apparent advantage would be obtained by attempting to capitalize goodwill acquired in this fashion. While a disclosure of such expenditures may be relevant for a valuation of the firm by investors, capitalization would not determine the value of the firm because many changes in the value of the firm occur for other reasons, such as exogenous changes in the demand for the product and fortuitous discoveries of previously unknown resources. Since there is little controversy regarding the treatment of the "nonpurchased" goodwill, the following discussion relates primarily to goodwill acquired by a lump-sum purchase—the total cost of operating property in excess of the amounts that can be associated with specific tangible or intangible classifications.

---

[14] AICPA, *op. cit.*, p. 6019.

[15] George R. Catlett and Norman O. Olson, "Accounting for Goodwill," *Accounting Research Study No. 10* (New York: AICPA, 1968), p. 67.

Purchased Goodwill

According to the recommendations of *ARS No. 10,* when a business as a whole is acquired by another firm, the excess of the price paid in stock or other assets over the fair value of the separable tangible and intangible assets acquired, less obligations assumed, represents the amount paid for goodwill.[16] This is not inconsistent with the recommendations of AICPA *Bulletin No. 48*[17] except that the latter referred only to acquisitions deemed to be a purchase rather than a pooling of interests (to be discussed in Chapter 18). After all identifiable assets and liabilities are measured in terms of current replacement costs, to the extent that such is possible, any excess price is considered to be goodwill. It is, therefore, a master valuation amount.

While in the pooling method of accounting for acquisitions goodwill would not be reported in the financial statements, there is some merit in the proposition that the total amount of consideration paid for the acquired firm or properties is relevant information for the evaluation and decisions of investors and other interested parties. But once the amount of the goodwill is reported, there is no agreement regarding its disposition. In accordance with *ARB No. 43,* the goodwill could be treated as a type (b) intangible having unlimited life and, therefore, carried continuously as an asset or as a type (a) intangible which would be written off to income systematically. However, even as a type (b) intangible, it could be written off as an extraordinary loss in the income statement whenever the corporation decided that it did not have indefinite life. This recommendation, however, lacks any logic and permits complete freedom to make arbitrary allocations except that it prohibits a write-off immediately after acquisition.

The systematic amortization is supported on the ground that goodwill represents benefits to be matched with future revenues over a reasonable period of time. It is also frequently argued that if it represents a payment for superior earnings, the purchase price was based on expectations regarding a limited period during which the superior earnings would be received. If goodwill does continue beyond this reasonable period, it is assumed that it then represents benefits accumulated since the acquisition of the property, and therefore it should be accounted for consistently with other "nonpurchased" goodwill as current expense. Therefore, the amortization of goodwill is supported either on the basis of a matching of the purchased goodwill with related revenues or on the ground that the value of the purchased goodwill declines over time.

The argument for nonallocation is based in part on the fact that if

---

[16] *Ibid.,* p. 77.
[17] AICPA, *op. cit.,* p. 6082.

"nonpurchased" goodwill is charged to expense, the allocation of purchased goodwill results in a double charge. Catlett and Olson also present
the argument that purchased and "nonpurchased" goodwill should be
treated alike;[18] neither should be reported as an asset in the financial
statements. One of the more valid arguments against allocation, however,
is that both the life and the pattern of allocation must by necessity be
arbitrary and thus without a logical basis. Without a logical basis, it is
highly unlikely that the resulting reported net income figures would be
more meaningful than if the allocation had not been made.

A major difference between the recommendations of *ARB No. 43* and
ARS No. 10, however, is that the former prohibits the immediate write-off
of an intangible while the latter suggests that goodwill should be accounted for as a reduction of stockholders' equity. The reasoning for this
reduction (suggested by *ARS No. 10*) is that the amount paid for the
goodwill represents a reduction of the firm's resources in anticipation of
future earnings. The remaining equity would then represent the values of
the separate resources and property rights consistent with the reporting
for a continuing enterprise. A fallacy of this argument, however, is that
the entire purchase price is a payment for future cash flows and earnings;
the amount paid for the acquired enterprise represents invested capital
just as much as does an amount paid to acquire an addition to existing
plant.

The author is sympathetic with the recommendations of *ARS No. 10*
for other reasons, however. After the date of acquisition, there appears to
be little evidence that the continual presentation of the goodwill as an
asset will provide useful information to investors or other interested
readers of financial statements. Furthermore, the amortization of the
goodwill to income by the use of arbitrary procedures seems of doubtful
validity because of the homogeneity problem and interactions mentioned
in the previous chapter and discussed thoroughly by Thomas.[19]

"Negative" Goodwill

If goodwill is defined as representing a group of unidentifiable favorable attributes of the firm which are separable from the values of the
identifiable assets, it is difficult to conceive of this being negative. For if
the firm is worth less than the values of the separable assets, the previous
owners would have sold them separately rather than as a whole. Therefore, negative goodwill could not exist; the amount paid for the firm
would represent the values of the separable assets only and the total

18 Catlett and Olson, *op. cit.*, p. 88.
19 Arthur L. Thomas, *The Allocation Problem in Financial Accounting Theory,
Studies in Accounting Research No. 3* (American Accounting Association, 1969),
pp. 76–77.

should be so allocated. This seems to be the position of *Accounting Research Bulletin No. 48* in its recommendation that when a combination is deemed to be a purchase, the assets acquired should be recorded at their fair value or the fair value of the consideration given in the exchange.[20] This view is consistent with the cost concept, because the assets are recorded at their current value only if the consideration given is not as clearly measurable as the assets received.

Accounting Research Bulletin No. 51 appears to suggest a similar procedure for consolidated statements where the cost to the parent is less than the book value of the net assets of the subsidiary.[21] However, it suggests that in unusual circumstances (which in practice are not so unusual), a remaining difference that cannot be allocated should be shown as a deferred credit and taken into income in future periods. However, since the excess of the amount assignable to net assets over the cost to the parent represents either an advantageous purchase or an overvaluation of all net assets as a whole, there is no logic in any allocation of this amount to income on a "reasonable and systematic" basis. Without a knowledge of the meaning of the credit, no allocation can be "reasonable." Furthermore, since most firms report this deferred credit as neither a liability nor stockholders' equity, it is a meaningless item in the balance sheet; thus, it appears to be only a method of smoothing the effect of the acquisition. Since both the classification of the deferred credit and its amortization are uninformative to users of financial statements, they create more questions than answers.[22]

Accounting Research Study No. 10 suggests that when "negative goodwill" appears to exist, a careful evaluation of the separate assets and liabilities should be made. It suggests, however, that negative amounts that cannot be assigned to specific items may indicate the necessity for future expenditures to improve the organization and efficiency of the firm; in this case, *ARS No. 10* suggests that the difference should be reported as a liability to be charged with these costs in the future.[23] However, the need to improve the efficiency of a firm does not fall into the usual definition of a liability. Since any costs could be charged against this "liability," the result could be just as capricious and arbitrary as that suggested in *ARB No. 51*. An alternative suggested by *ARS No. 10*, however, is to credit the amount immediately to retained earnings or capital surplus. Although there is little theoretical justification for this method, it probably creates less misinformation than other methods, so long as the net purchase price is disclosed at the date of acquisition. If

---

[20] AICPA, *op. cit.*, p. 6082.

[21] *Ibid.*, p. 6092.

[22] See Robert T. Sprouse, "Accounting for What-you-may-call-its," *Journal of Accountancy*, Vol. CXXII (October, 1966), pp. 45–53.

[23] Catlett and Olson, *op. cit.*, pp. 99–100.

the reason for the difference cannot be identified, it should not be taken into income merely to stay within the double-entry reporting system.

Goodwill in Consolidated Financial Statements

When the cost of an investment in a subsidiary exceeds the parent's equity in the carrying value of the subsidiary's net assets, the traditional procedure has been to record this excess in the consolidated statements as "Acquisition Goodwill." For example, if Company P acquired a 90 percent interest in Company S at a cost of $180,000 and if the carrying value of the net assets of Company S were $150,000, the acquisition goodwill would be $45,000, computed by subtracting P's equity in S, $135,000 (90 percent × $150,000) from $180,000. This traditional procedure is deficient as a method of recording purchased goodwill in three respects.

First, it ignores the nature of the excess payment. Goodwill, as a master valuation account, should include only that amount that cannot be allocated to specific tangible or intangible assets. To the extent that specific assets are understated on the books of the subsidiary, they should be adjusted upward in the consolidated balance sheet, and the consolidated income statements should be adjusted for proper depreciation and amortization values. *Accounting Research Bulletin No. 51* recognizes this deficiency of the traditional approach by stating that "to the extent that the difference is considered to be attributable to tangible assets and specific intangible assets, such as patents, it should be allocated to them."[24] According to *Bulletin No. 51*, the remainder, not representing losses in consolidation or amounts allocable to specific assets, should be shown in the consolidated balance sheet "under one or more appropriately descriptive captions." Parallel procedures are recommended when the cost of the investment is less than the parent's equity in the net assets of the subsidiary, as discussed above.

In addition to the possibility of undervaluation of specific assets, the overvaluation of specific liabilities, or the existence of unrecorded goodwill on the books of the subsidiary, three other possible explanations for the excess of cost over the book value of the investment may be found: (1) the parent may have paid an excessive price for the investment; (2) common stock or bonds of the parent given in exchange for the investment in the subsidiary may have been issued at a discount; and (3) goodwill may arise out of the acquisition and combination of the parent and subsidiary.[25] If an excessive price has been paid for the investment, the loss should be recognized as soon as it is discovered. Goodwill should not be used as a burying ground for management's mistakes and losses. If

---

[24] AICPA, *op. cit.*, p. 6092.

[25] Maurice Moonitz and Louis H. Jordan, *Accounting, an Analysis of Its Problems* (rev. ed.; New York: Holt, Rinehart & Winston, Inc., 1964), Vol. II, pp. 259–62.

securities are issued at a discount, the nature of the discount should be clearly shown. In the third case, goodwill arising from the combination would result in consolidated goodwill similar to the acquisition of unrecorded goodwill of the subsidiary.

Second, goodwill arising from consolidation is not really purchased goodwill. It either existed already as unrecorded goodwill of the subsidiary or it arose out of the combination. In the first case, the parent company acquired an interest in the equity of the subsidiary; it did not purchase the assets of the subsidiary. In the second case, the goodwill arises out of the combination, but it is somewhat farfetched to assume that the cost of the developed goodwill is included in the cost of the acquisition of an interest in the subsidiary.

However, just the fact that goodwill is not purchased in the strict sense of the word does not mean that it should not be recorded in the consolidated statements. Evidence of its existence can be obtained from the nature of the circumstances and from the price paid by the parent company for the investment.

Third, if the parent company acquires less than 100 percent of the common equity of the subsidiary, the excess of cost over the parent's equity in the carrying value of the net assets of the subsidiary represents only a part of the undervaluation of the net assets or goodwill of the subsidiary. In the above example, if Company P acquired a 90 percent interest in Company S for $180,000, this is evidence that the entire net assets of the subsidiary were worth $200,000, and since the net assets are carried on the subsidiary's books at $150,000, the goodwill or other undervaluation is really $50,000 rather than $45,000. That is, the equity of the minority interest is 10 percent of $200,000, or $20,000, rather than 10 percent of the book equity of $150,000. It is inconsistent to treat the parent's interest in the subsidiary on one basis and the equity of the minority interest on another basis. This logical development of consistent treatment arises from the entity theory of consolidated statements, as developed by Moonitz.[26]

LONG-TERM INVESTMENTS

The measurement and reporting of long-term nonmonetary investments was discussed briefly in Chapter 10 (pp. 303–5). In the case of investments in nonconsolidated subsidiaries, it was suggested that current market prices would provide better information to equity holders than historical cost; but that the reporting of holding gains and losses would not be as significant as in the case of short-term investments, because management may be committed to a long-term investment and it does not generally have the option of selling at current market prices in order to

---

[26] Maurice Moonitz, *The Entity Theory of Consolidated Statements,* American Accounting Association Monograph No. 4 (AAA, 1944), pp. 58–60.

maximize gains or minimize losses. Furthermore, it was suggested that reporting the firm's equity in the book value of the subsidiary might be a useful substitute if the subsidiary in turn valued its assets in current terms. However, since these measurements either include or exclude amounts that would be considered goodwill upon consolidation, further discussion is relevant at this point.

While *Accounting Research Bulletin No. 51* suggested either the cost or the equity method of reporting nonconsolidated investments in subsidiaries,[27] APB *Opinion No. 10* recommended that only the equity method be used.[28] Under the cost method, the investment in the subsidiary would be reported by the parent at cost and only the dividends received would be reported as income. The excess of cost over the parent's equity in the book value of the subsidiary is assumed to represent purchased goodwill, except to the extent that a part of the difference would have represented an adjustment of depreciable assets if the investment in the subsidiary had been consolidated. Even if disclosure of the cost of the investment and the parent's equity in the net assets of the subsidiary in the financial statements were recommended, it is highly unlikely that this information would have any relevance for investors and creditors after the period of acquisition. The separation of the cost into the two amounts is also of doubtful validity because the subsidiary's net assets are not reported in current terms. The excess over book equity, therefore, does not represent goodwill by any meaningful definition.

The recommendation of APB *Opinion No. 10* to restrict the reporting of unconsolidated subsidiaries to the equity method is not likely to improve the informational content of the financial reports except to provide some consistency between the reporting of consolidated subsidiaries and those that are not included in the consolidation. Presumably, the equity method provides current valuations by adjusting the acquisition cost of the investment for the firm's equity in the reported earnings or losses of the unconsolidated subsidiary. However, APB *Opinion No. 10* suggests that the difference between the cost of the investment and the firm's equity in the book value of the subsidiary at the date of acquisition should be amortized to income. The qualification "if appropriate" gives managements full discretion to amortize the difference whether it represents an increase in depreciable or nondepreciable assets, goodwill, or "negative goodwill." Such amortization can only be arbitrary and without logic.

As suggested earlier, an alternative to both the cost and the equity methods of reporting investments in nonconsolidated subsidiaries is to present a current value if it is available and also disclose the dividends received over several periods as well as the firm's share of the subsidiary's

---

[27] AICPA, *op. cit.,* p. 6094.
[28] *Ibid.,* p. 6573.

reported income. Such information would likely be helpful to investors in evaluating the firm as a whole and in predicting future cash flows. Such information is already required to be disclosed by companies in Great Britain under the 1967 Companies Act.

DEFERRED CHARGES

Deferred charges are generally assumed to include intangibles that will be amortized to expense or else debit items classified separately without a formal definition. Specific intangibles sometimes classified as deferred charges include organization costs and research and development expenses. Other items frequently classified as deferred charges include advertising expenditures, start-up costs, and special types of losses. The rationalization for including deferred charges among the assets of a firm is generally that they represent benefits to future periods, and that therefore they should be amortized to future periods as are nonmonetary tangible assets. But the effect of the amortization is to spread their reduction of net income over several periods so that no single period is depressed because of them. However, the selection of an accounting procedure on the basis of the desired effect cannot be condoned. Also, since the nature of the deferred charge classification is rarely disclosed, it does not provide useful information for readers of external financial statements. The only reasonable solution is to abolish the deferred charge classification and provide greater disclosure regarding the nature and amount of expenditures that are likely to benefit the future but which cannot be associated with any specific assets or with any specific future net revenue contributions.

SELECTED ADDITIONAL READING ON CHAPTER TOPICS

Accounting for Intangibles

AICPA Committee on Accounting Procedure. *Accounting Principles,* Vol. II: *ARB No. 43,* "Intangible Assets," chap. v, pp. 6018–20. Chicago: Commerce Clearing House, Inc., 1968.

SANDS, JOHN E. *Wealth, Income and Intangibles.* Toronto: Toronto University Press, 1963.

WOLFF, W. "Accounting for Intangibles (Canada)," *Canadian Chartered Accountant,* Vol. XCI (October, 1967), pp. 255–59.

Goodwill

CARSBERG, BRYAN. "The Contribution of P. D. Leake to the Theory of Goodwill Valuation," *Journal of Accounting Research,* Vol. IV (Spring, 1966), pp. 1–15.

CATLETT, GEORGE R., and NORMAN O. OLSON. "Accounting for Goodwill," *Accounting Research Study No. 10.* New York: AICPA, 1968.

——. "Excerpts from *Accounting Research Study No. 10:* 'Accounting for Goodwill'," *Journal of Accountancy,* Vol. CXXVI (November, 1968), pp. 64–67.

DUNCAN, WILBUR S. *"Accounting Research Study No. 10:* 'Accounting for Goodwill'—A Summary of Its Conclusions," *New York Certified Public Accountant,* Vol. XXXIX (June, 1969), pp. 429–36.

GYNTHER, REG S. "Some Conceptualizing on Goodwill," *Accounting Review,* Vol. XLIV (April, 1969), pp. 247–55.

SCHIFF, MICHAEL, and SHIRLEY ARBESFELD. "Goodwill—A Make-or-Buy Approach," *Management Accounting,* Vol. XLVII (August, 1966), pp. 25–35.

SPACEK, L. "The Treatment of Goodwill in the Corporate Balance Sheet," *Journal of Accountancy,* Vol. CXVII (February, 1964), pp. 35–40.

——. "More Comments and Replies on Goodwill," *Journal of Accountancy,* Vol. CXVIII (July, 1964), pp. 52–55.

Research and Development

DREBIN, ALLAN R. "Accounting for Proprietary Research," *Accounting Review,* Vol. XLI (July, 1966), pp. 413–25.

HAWKINS, DAVID F. "The Case of the Dubious Deferral," *Harvard Business Review,* Vol. XLI (May–June, 1963), pp. 163 ff.

JOHNSON, ORACE. "A Consequential Approach to Accounting for R&D," *Journal of Accounting Research,* Vol. V (Autumn, 1967), pp. 164–72.

MILBURN, J. A. "A Look at Problems in Research and Development Accounting," *Canadian Chartered Accountant,* Vol. XCII (June, 1968), pp. 404–408.

ROTHSTEIN, EUGENE L. "Problems in the Treatment of R&D Costs," *Management Accounting,* Vol. XLVII (November, 1965), pp. 9–12.

Deferred Charges

KELLY, DANIEL J. "Accounting for Start-Up Costs," *New York Certified Public Accountant,* Vol. XXXVIII (November, 1968), pp. 773–78.

chapter 15

Liabilities and Related Expenses

At least since the ascendancy of the income statement as the dominant financial statement, the recording of liabilities has been closely related to the matching of expenses with related revenues or the timing of revenues. Therefore, the literature relating to liabilities has been concerned primarily with the revenue and expense aspects. This emphasis is not necessarily misplaced, but it has not led to a cohesive theory regarding either the nature or valuation of liabilities. In general, the problem of when to record a liability is more difficult than the problem of determining its amount. Therefore, the nature and timing of liabilities are treated more fully in this chapter than the problems of valuation, which are discussed in greater detail in some of the specific areas covered in other chapters.

THE NATURE OF LIABILITIES

An initial difference of opinion regarding liabilities is whether they should be treated as (a) equities of the corporation, along with stockholders' equities, (b) obligations of the enterprise, or (c) deductions from assets. The first view is expressed by the AICPA accounting terminology bulletins as follows:

Similarly, in relation to a balance sheet, liability may be defined as follows: Something represented by a credit balance that is or would be properly carried forward upon a closing of books of account according to the rules or principles of accounting, provided such credit balance is not in effect a negative balance applicable to an asset. Thus the word is used broadly to comprise not only items which constitute liabilities in the popular sense of debts or obligations . . . but also credit balances to be accounted for which do not involve the debtor and creditor relation. For example, capital stock and related or similar elements of proprietorship are balance-sheet liabilities in that they represent balances to be accounted for, though these are not liabilities in the ordinary sense of debts owed to legal creditors.[1]

---

[1] AICPA, *Accounting Principles* (Chicago: Commerce Clearing House, Inc., 1968), Vol. II, p. 9507.

While this definition does not provide any insight into the real nature of liabilities or any clarification of the distinction between stockholder and creditor equities, it does reflect the entity theory, which implies that the enterprise has a status independent of both its owners and creditors. This meaning of the term is also presented as a second definition in Kohler's *Dictionary for Accountants*.[2] Kohler implied, however, that the term is generally used in the plural when it refers to the credit side of the balance sheet.

Kohler's first definition implies that a liability is an obligation of the enterprise—"an amount owing by one person (a debtor) to another (a creditor), payable in money or in goods or services."[3] Paton, through his emphasis on the entity theory, recognized the similarity between stockholder and creditor equities and the advantage in grouping them together for some purposes. But he recognized that the differences are very important for many purposes. "The general distinction between stocks and bonds is of real significance for the accountant."[4] Thus, while the entity theory starts with the premise that assets are equal to equities, it does not preclude the subclassifications of stockholder equities and liabilities.

The proprietorship theory, however, treats liabilities entirely different from ownership equities. For example, Hatfield stated:

In a strict sense, liabilities as well as valuation accounts are a subtrahend from the assets, for a debt is really a negative asset. It would therefore be logical to prepare a balance sheet in which the total liabilities were substracted from the total assets, leaving upon the right-hand side of the balance sheet merely the items representing proprietorship . . . a total which represents the sum of proprietorship and liabilities has no particular importance.[5]

The funds theory approach to accounting leads to even another definition of liabilities. In his description of the fund theory, Vatter stated that—

As distinct from the notions of obligation or legal liability, equities are restrictions upon, or reservations that apply to the assets of the fund; they may arise from legal, equitable, economic, or even managerial considerations.[6]

In summary, the entity theory views liabilities as claims against the enterprise (often specifically as claims against the assets of the enter-

[2] Eric L. Kohler, *A Dictionary for Accountants* (3d ed.; Englewood Cliffs, N.J.: Prentice-Hall, Inc., 1963), p. 300.

[3] *Ibid.*

[4] William Andrew Paton, *Accounting Theory* (New York: Ronald Press Co., 1922), p. 83.

[5] Henry Rand Hatfield, *Accounting, Its Principles and Problems* (New York: D. Appleton & Co., 1927), p. 221. By permission of the copyright holder, Appleton-Century-Crofts.

[6] William J. Vatter, *The Fund Theory of Accounting and Its Implications for Financial Reports* (Chicago: University of Chicago Press, 1947), p. 95.

prise); the proprietary theory treats liabilities as negative assets or as specific claims against the proprietor; the funds theory treats all equities as restrictions that apply to the assets in the fund.

The Scope of Liabilities

A second major difference of opinion regarding liabilities involves what should be included and what should be excluded from the liability classification. The narrowest position is that only legal obligations or debts should be included. Kohler appears to imply the legal characteristics by stating that a liability is

An amount . . . payable in money, or in goods or services . . . particularly, any debt (a) due or past due (current liability), (b) due at a specified time in the future (e.g., funded debt, accrued liability), or (c) due only on failure to perform a future act (deferred income; contingent liability).[7]

The last example, however, can hardly be called a legal obligation at the present time. A contingent liability is not a legal debt until and if a future event occurs.

The American Accounting Association Committee on Concepts and Standards, in the 1957 statement, implied that liabilities must be legal obligations but that not all legal obligations need be classified as liabilities. They stated:

The interests or equities of creditors (liabilities) are claims against the entity arising from past activities or events which, in the usual case, require for their satisfaction the expenditure of corporate resources.[8]

Note that the entity concept is implied in this definition.

The legal liabilities that are usually omitted from financial statements are those arising out of executory contracts and those arising out of other contracts where neither party has performed. Canning included this restriction in his definition of liabilities by stating that

a liability is a service, valuable in money, which a proprietor is under an existing legal (or equitable) duty to render to a second person (or set of persons) and which is not unconditionally an agreed set-off to its full amount against specific services of equal or greater money value due from this second person to the proprietor.[9]

While Canning excluded amounts with an unconditional right of setoff, he included equitable duties to render services in addition to the legal ob-

---

[7] Kohler, *op. cit.*, p. 300.

[8] AAA Committee on Accounting Concepts and Standards, *Accounting and Reporting Standards for Corporate Financial Statements and Preceding Statements and Supplements* (Columbus, Ohio: AAA, 1957), p. 7.

[9] John B. Canning, *The Economics of Accountancy* (New York: Ronald Press Co., 1929), pp. 55–56.

ligations. He did not present examples of equitable duties that should be included, but presumably he would include amounts intended to be paid for damages sustained or services received when there is no legal obligation to make such payment. He would also probably include amounts to be paid to maintain goodwill and business confidence, such as refunds for damaged or returned merchandise when there is no legal obligation to make such refund.

Sprouse and Moonitz utilize a legal definition of liabilities, but they draw from a broad legal base. They define liabilities as

. . . obligations to convey assets or perform services, obligations resulting from past or current transactions and requiring settlement in the future.[10]

If there is a duty to perform arising out of past events, it is not necessary that the specific payee be known at the present. There is some doubt, however, whether or not purely equitable obligations are included in this definition unless the duty to perform can be implied from past actions or general business practice.

The Timing of Liabilities

Traditionally, the reporting of a liability is dependent upon the importance of recognizing the other side of the transaction or event—the accrual of an expense, the recognition of a loss, or the receipt by the firm of specific assets. The first of these, the accrual of an expense, is generally thought to be the most important because it affects directly the computation of current income. If services have been received by the firm and used in current operations, it is necessary that the liability be accrued in order to include the expense in the determination of net income. Likewise, the reporting of an extraordinary loss is required in order to disclose the effect of the event on nonoperating income; a related liability must then be recorded to complete the transaction. When specific assets are received by the firm and recorded, a related liability must also be recorded in order to present a balanced statement of financial position.

This emphasis on the reporting of income is also responsible for the recording of liabilities arising out of expense allocations. For example, deferred income taxes payable would probably not be recorded if it were not for the desire to record an allocation of income taxes. Liabilities under warranties would probably not be recorded if it were not for the desire to allocate warranty expenses to the period when the related revenue is recognized. This emphasis on the matching concept and balanced financial statements is, therefore, the main reason for a failure

---

[10] Robert T. Sprouse and Maurice Moonitz, "A Tentative Set of Broad Accounting Principles for Business Enterprises," *Accounting Research Study No. 3* (New York: American Institute of Certified Public Accountants, 1962), p. 37.

of accountants to develop an independent theory regarding the recognition of liabilities.

Sprouse and Moonitz define liabilities as ". . . obligations resulting from past or current transactions and requiring settlement in the future."[11] Thus, the existence of a liability by this definition is dependent upon the occurrence of an external transaction—a financial event arising as a result of a business deal with an outside firm or person. Acquisitions of goods or services are clearly transactions that may give rise to obligations to pay for them. But obligations to pay for goods or services to be acquired in the future are not liabilities at the present time.

What about obligations arising out of current contracts for the future acquisition of goods and services? In a sense these are transactions and in another sense they are not. They are financial events arising from business dealings and giving rise to obligations to make payment in the future, when the goods or services have been received. Traditionally, accountants have refrained from recording these contracts where neither party has performed. The reasoning is that until the goods are made available, the obligation of the buyer is offset by his rights to receive the goods. Until the goods are brought into existence and committed to the contract, there is an unconditional right of setoff. But when goods or services are committed under the contract, the buyer may not be able to cancel the contract without paying for the goods and services committed, even though he has not as yet received them. An example would be an obligation under a long-term construction project. Another example would be the long-term lease of property that is made available exclusively for the lessee even though he has not received the use of the property to be provided under the lease contract.

Traditionally, an exception to the practice of not reporting executory contracts for the purchase of goods and services is made when the obligation of the purchase commitment exceeds the value of the goods to be acquired. For example, if a material decline in the price of the goods occurs subsequent to the signing of a long-term purchase contract, the obligation exceeds the value of the rights under the contract and a loss has occurred. The recording of a liability equal only to the amount of the loss results from the reporting of net income and the need to record a credit equal to the loss debit under the double-entry system. This practice is deficient because it assumes that the total amount of the rights and obligations are not relevant to the predictions and decisions of investors and creditors. However, the total amounts are relevant, because the users of the statements may place different expectations on the values of the rights under the contract or on the effect of the committed cash disbursements.

---

[11] *Ibid.*

Personal services to be provided in the future, however, are not generally thought of as giving rise to liabilities in the present even though there may be a formal or informal contract. For example, next month's salaries and wages are not generally considered to be liabilities at the present time. Likewise, interest to be paid for money to be used in a future period is not a liability, because the funds used are not irrevocably committed by the lender to this purpose only; if repayment is made, the lender is likely to find another use for his funds. Answers to these questions, however, are not clear-cut. Accountants will still record liabilities when it is thought necessary to do so for other reasons.

Another important question regarding the nature and timing of liabilities is whether or not a liability to a second party can arise out of a transaction with a third party. Examples are (1) royalties payable to a second party because of a sale of merchandise to a third party and (2) deferred income taxes payable to the government arising out of an installment sale to a third party. The first case clearly results in a liability, but the second case leaves some doubt.

One reason for the doubt in the case of the deferred tax liability is that the amount is not considered at the present time by the government to be an obligation of the firm. In similar situations, however, accountants do recognize obligations even though they are not recognized specifically by the obligee. For example, obligations to make repairs under warranties may be based on the probability that a certain amount of repairs will become necessary even though it may not be known to whom the obligation will accrue and none of the individual customers will regard the obligation as necessarily accruing to him.

BASIC CHARACTERISTICS OF LIABILITIES

Liabilities may be defined as obligations or duties of the enterprise to provide money, goods, or services to a person, firm, or other organization outside of the enterprise at some time in the future. Specific characteristics would include the following:

1. The obligation must, of course, exist at the present time. That is, it must arise out of some past transaction or event. It may arise from the acquisition of goods or services, from losses already sustained for which the firm is liable, or from the expectation of losses for which the firm has obligated itself. Obligations contingent upon future events should not be included unless there is a reasonable probability that these events will occur.

2. Equitable obligations or duties may be included if they are based on the necessity of making future payments to maintain good business relationships or if they are in accordance with normal business practice.

3. Normally there should be a known maturity value or the expectation that payment will be required at some specific time in the future even though the exact timing is not known at the present. The time of payment may be extended by the substitution of new liabilities, or the obligations may be terminated by their conversion into stockholder equities. The repeated extension or conversion of the debt does not deny its classification as a liability.

4. If there is an unconditional right of offset, an obligation under a contract should not appear as a liability. But if the seller has committed resources to the contract, there is no longer an unconditional right of offset. For example, in a long-term lease contract, the providing of the leasehold property by the landlord represents a commitment of resources for that purpose and the tenant does not have the unconditional right of offset even though some of the services have not as yet been received.

5. Normally, the payee should be known with certainty and be identifiable either specifically or as a group. However, it is not necessary that the creditor profess his claim or have knowledge of it at the present time.

THE VALUATION OF LIABILITIES AND THE COMPUTATION OF INTEREST

The objectives of liability valuation are similar to the objectives of asset valuation discussed in Chapter 9.[12] Probably the most important of these objectives is the desire to record expenses and losses in the determination of current income. However, the measurement of liabilities should also permit the presentation to investors and creditors of information useful as a means of prediction, as a base for interperiod and intercompany comparisons of income, and as a comparison of the claims of the several equity holders.

Liabilities cannot be included in the balance sheet as separate items unless they can be quantified. However, an inability to quantify an obligation does not imply that it is not a liability; but if it is not reasonably measurable, it must be disclosed by footnote or other means rather than by listing among the liabilities in the balance sheet. If an actual obligation exists but has a range of probable values, the expected value should be listed as the estimated amount of the liability on the balance sheet. Only if the range is broad and if an estimated single value would be misleading is it preferable to omit the obligation from the list of liabilities and present a description, in a footnote or otherwise, indicating the range of probable values.

---

[12] See pp. 254–60.

Contingent Liabilities

A contingent liability is usually defined as an obligation that may arise dependent upon a future event. However, this definition is not adequate in making a distinction between an actual liability and a contingent one. The amounts of many estimated liabilities are also dependent upon future events (e.g., warranties, contested income tax obligations, and refundable damage deposits). The distinction should be based on whether or not an expected value would be meaningful to readers of the financial reports as a representation of the approximate most probable (modal) value and the extent to which the expectations must be subjective. If an obligation has a 90 percent chance of being $100,000 and a 10 percent chance of being zero, the expected value would be $90,000 and this would be a meaningful representation of the liability, particularly if the probabilities are based on past experience. On the other hand, if the obligation has a 90 percent chance of being zero and a 10 percent chance of being $100,000, the expected value would be $10,000 but this would not be as meaningful as a description of the probable amount to be paid. That is, if the most probable (modal) value of the obligation is positive, a liability exists and the amount should be estimated. If the obligation has a high probability of being zero, it should be classified as a contingent liability.

Obligations under warranties are definite liabilities because it is highly probable that some payments will be required even though the total amount must be estimated. A legal suit against the company for damages, however, is a contingent liability if it appears most likely that the firm will win the case. If it is almost certain that the case will be lost, a liability exists and the main problem is in estimating the expected value of the damages to be awarded. In the case of legal suits, however, accountants may not be able to estimate the most probable amount of damages, and the best disclosure may be provided by a full description in a footnote or elsewhere.

Current Valuation of Liabilities

In the case of most monetary liabilities, the amount payable is determined by contract or agreement. Therefore, the current valuation of the debt is the present discounted amount payable in the future. Since current liabilities are generally payable within a short period of time, the amount of discount is usually immaterial and the amount of the liability can be presented at its face value (amount payable in the future). However, if the debt can be satisfied by two or more alternatives, the discounted value of the lowest of these is the current value of the liability.

For example, if the credit terms permit a discount of 2 percent if payment is made within 20 days and require a penalty if payment is made after 60 days, the correct value of the liability is the invoice price less the 2 percent discount. The other alternatives require an excess payment that need not be made and should not be made under good business practice. If the higher price is paid, the excess should be recorded as purchase discounts not taken and treated as a loss arising from inefficiency.

Long-Term Liabilities.   In the case of long-term liabilities, the amount of discount is generally significant and, therefore, the current valuation should be the discounted value of all future payments to be made under the contract. In the case of bonds, the contractual interest payments, the amount to be paid at maturity, and any serial payments of principal should all be discounted to the present. The appropriate discount rate is the current yield rate determined by the market for bonds of similar risk and term. Sprouse and Moonitz suggest that the pertinent discount rate is the yield rate at the date of issue.[13] Using a current yield rate produces a current value, whereas the use of the yield rate at the date of issue produces a value similar to "historical cost." That is, the yield rate at the date of issue can be assumed to be the effective rate for which the firm is committed. The advantages of its use are that (1) the resulting value at the date of issue was the current value at that time and (2) it is objectively determined. By continuing to use the original yield rate, the holding gains and losses are not recorded and the interest expense for each period is determined by the debt at the beginning of the period multiplied by the original yield rate. If the debt is held until maturity, changes in the yield rate can usually be ignored on the grounds that they are not material and that the total interest expense by this method will always be equal to the sum of the interest expense and the holding gains and losses if current yield rates are continually used.

When bonds are sold initially at a premium or discount, the interest expense in any specific period is the contractual (nominal) interest payment less the current amortization of the premium or plus the amortization of the discount. The current value of the debt at any date is then assumed to be the maturity value plus the unamortized premium or less the unamortized discount. The true interest expense (based on the original committed rate) in any period is the value of the debt at the beginning of that period times the original yield rate. The excess of this true interest expense over the contractual cash interest payment during the year is the amount of the current discount amortization. If the bonds were sold at a premium, the premium amortization is the excess of the cash payment over the true interest expense. The unamortized discount or premium represents a valuation of the bond liability. Classification of

---

[13] Sprouse and Moonitz, *op. cit.,* p. 39.

the discount or premium as a deferred charge or deferred credit is not descriptive of its nature and should not be considered acceptable practice.

Traditionally, the premium or discount is amortized on a straight-line basis. For example, if $100,000 face value 6 percent bonds due in 20 years are sold to yield $5\frac{1}{2}$ percent, the bonds would be sold at approximately 106. On a straight-line basis, the premium amortization would be $300 a year and the total interest expense would be $5,700 ($6,000 less $300) each year. Using the interest method, the interest expense would be $5,830 ($5\frac{1}{2}$ percent × $106,000) the first year and $5,530 ($5\frac{1}{2}$ percent × $100,470) the twentieth year. The effect of the interest method is to report a periodic interest expense which represents a level effective rate on the book value of the debt. APB *Opinion No. 12* considered this method as acceptable as the straight-line method, but the difference is usually not material if the contractual (nominal) rate for computing the interest payment is not significantly different from the original yield rate.

Unamortized Discount and Call Premium

If bonds are callable at a premium, it is generally worthwhile for the firm to call the bonds when the current value of the bonds, as determined by the current yield rate, is greater than the call price. When the bonds are repaid out of the available resources of the firm, the sum of the call premium and any unamortized discount represents the amount of the loss realized by repaying the bonds at a current value which is in excess of the original "cost" or amortized committed value. That is, the current value of the debt has increased as the market rate of interest has fallen. If current values are not recorded when the market rate changes, however, the entire accumulated holding loss is recorded when the bonds are called. If current values had been recorded each period, the holding losses would have been recorded gradually as the market rate of interest changed, and the value of the bonds would have reached or exceeded the call price. The current value would exceed the call price only by an amount equal to the cost of obtaining the necessary funds or only when the firm fails to take advantage of the opportunity. But, in the statements, the bond liability should not exceed the call price, because this is the lowest amount for which the bonds could be repaid.

When an old issue of bonds is called by the process of refunding, the situation is very similar to the above. The new issue should be recorded at its issue price, since this is the current value of the debt at that time and it reflects the existing market rate of interest.[14] The entire unamortized discount and call premium should be recorded as a realized holding loss in the period of repayment and reported as an extraordinary loss in the income statement.

---

[14] Sprouse and Moonitz express this view. *Ibid.,* p. 40.

According to AICPA *Bulletin No. 43,* this direct write-off of the un-amortized discount and the call premium to income or retained earnings is an acceptable method.[15] This acceptance is based on the view that the unamortized discount and call premium represent the cost of terminating a disadvantageous contract and thus relate to past transactions. How-ever, the position is also correct because the value of the debt has changed over time and paying the call price is the most favorable method of liquidating the debt. Since this change in value of the debt caused by a change in the market rate of interest (the yield rate) has not been re-flected in the accounts, the entire holding loss should be recorded no later than the time the specific contract is terminated.

Bulletin No. 43, however, expresses a preference for the amortization of the unamortized discount and call premium over the remaining life of the old issue. The reason for this view is that it is thought that this is the period benefited by the refunding. However, this view is erroneous for the following reasons: (1) It is based on a rigid adherence to the original committed yield rate. The remaining life of the old issue is benefited only in the sense that it would have been charged with a higher interest ex-pense if the old issue has not been refunded; but this higher interest charge results only from the failure in accounting to recognize the change in true yield rates. (2) If the current bond values had been recorded each period, the recorded value of the old issue at the time of refunding would have been equal to the call price and there would be no unamortized amount to carry forward to future periods. (3) When a new bond is issued, there is objective evidence of its value at that time. The future period should be affected only by the interest cost of this issue. Because the true interest expense is determined by the current market rate of interest (at least the rate at the date of refunding), the life of the new issue is not the period benefited by the refunding. Thus, the preferred method of *Bulletin No. 43* is a denial of the validity of current values and interest expense based on current market rates of interest.

While *Bulletin No. 43* did not accept the procedure that would write off the unamortized discount and call premium over the life of the new issue, APB *Opinion No. 6* considers this method acceptable under certain circumstances. The conditions where this method is acceptable are where the refunding takes place because of currently lower interest rates or in anticipation of higher interest rates in the future. The reasoning is that in these cases, the full life of the new issue is benefited by the lower interest rates obtained by the refunding. However, like the method of amortiza-tion over the life of the old issue, this method is deficient because it is based on a false matching concept. The benefit in the form of a reduced interest expense during the life of the new issue arises only because of the static accounting methods used. That is, since the annual interest expense

---

[15] AICPA, *op. cit.,* p. 6058.

is based on the yield rate at the date the bonds are issued, the refunding in anticipation of higher interest rates later would reduce the total interest expense based on the historical yield only. Furthermore, the allocation of the unamortized discount and call premium would be charged to all periods during the life of the new issue, not just to those periods when interest yields are higher. It is not a substitute for current yield rates. In fact, if interest rates do not rise at all during the life of the new issue, the anticipated benefit will not materialize. It is unfortunate that three methods are acceptable without logical justification for more than one.

Convertible Debt

Debt securities are frequently issued with a convertible feature which permits the holder to convert the bond certificates into a determinable number of shares of common stock at any time before the conversion privilege expires. The convertible feature generally permits the issuer to sell the bonds initially at a price considerably above what could be obtained for nonconvertible bonds with the same contractual interest rate. While many possible alternative features and relationships may be found in connection with convertible bonds, generally the contractual interest rate is considerably below the market rate for nonconvertible bonds, the initial conversion price is greater than the market price of the common stock, and the conversion price does not decrease over time except to the extent necessary to protect the bondholder from the dilution of the common stock rights (such as a stock split or a stock dividend).

The main problems relating to the accounting for convertible debt are (1) the valuation of the liability at the date of issuance and subsequently, and (2) the measurement of the interest expense to be reported each period prior to the conversion of the debt into common stock. As an example of a convertible issue, assume that a firm could sell a 4 percent, 20-year convertible bond at its face value of $1,000 at a time when it would have to sell nonconvertible bonds (with identical provisions except for the conversion feature) at a price to yield 7.5 percent. Therefore, if the 4 percent bonds were not convertible, they would sell for $643 to yield 7.5 percent. (Since the face value is $1,000, the discount would appear as $357.)

Two views have been proposed for the accounting treatment of convertible debt at the date of issuance and for the subsequent reporting of interest expense: (1) One view is that convertible debt possesses the characteristics of both debt and equity, and that a portion of the proceeds from the sale of the securities should be allocated to the conversion privilege and credited to paid-in capital while the remainder should be allocated to the debt, resulting in the presentation of debt discount or a reduction of debt premium. The amount assigned to paid-in capital can be measured as the excess of the amount received for the securities over the estimated price that could have been obtained for similar securities without the conversion feature. This view was recommended by APB *Opinion No. 10* but was suspended by APB *Opinion No. 12* to permit a restudy of the problem. (2) A second view is that the convertible debt should be treated solely as debt with no portion of the proceeds being allocated to the conversion feature. This was the final recommendation of APB *Opinion No. 14.*

The main arguments for the allocation of the proceeds between the debt and the equity characteristics are that the economic value of the conversion feature exists as a distinct element of the contract, as opposed to the debt, and that the measurement of interest expense should be based on the debt characteristics only. While these two arguments are related in the accounting treatment, they are discussed separately. The argument for a separate reporting of the debt and equity portions is based on the premise that the classification of the proceeds from the sale of the securities should be comparable with the traditional debt and equity classifications. If an amount is actually paid for the right to become a holder of common stock at some time in the future, this is similar to the sale of an option or warrant for the purchase of common stock in the future at a fixed price. Therefore, the amount paid for the conversion privilege should be accounted for consistently with the treatment of stock options or warrants. Likewise, valuation of the portion classified as debt should reflect the market yield for similar debt at the time of issuing the securities, which would then be consistent with the reporting of nonconvertible bonds. The disclosure of a material discount on bonds would be relevant to make the presentation similar to other securities classified as long-term debt.

The emphasis on the reporting of interest expense also supports the separation of the proceeds from the sale of the security into the two parts. If the entire proceeds were treated as debt in the above example, the long-term debt would be reported at the face amount of $1,000 and the interest expense each period would be reported as $40 (4 percent × $1,000). However, without the conversion feature, the bonds would have sold for $643 to yield 7.5 percent over the 20-year life of the bonds. In these circumstances, the interest expense each period would amount to $58, using the straight-line method of amortizing the discount; or it would increase from $48 the first year to $73 in the 20th year, using the interest method. Therefore, by reporting only $40 interest expense, the interest reported each period would be understated and would not be comparable to the interest expense reported for similar nonconvertible bond issues. Note, however, that in this case, an adjustment should be made for the fact that the discount arising from the allocation to the conversion feature may not be deductible in arriving at taxable income.

A major difficulty with the allocation of the issue price between the debt and equity portions is that valuation and classification similar to nonconvertible issues gives the reader of the financial statements the impression that the face amount is expected to be paid at maturity. However, if the market price of common stock increases above the conversion price, the normal expectation is that the bonds will not be paid at maturity. Until the bonds are converted, the face value is a protection for the holders of the securities against loss through bankruptcy or reorganization; it is therefore similar to the liquidation value of preferred stock, although with a different degree of priority. Another difficulty is that the interest expense reported by this method is not related to the contractual cash outflows, whether conversion takes place or not. If the bonds are not converted but paid at maturity, the cash outlays include the contractual annual payment ($40 in the above example) and the face value at maturity. If the bonds are converted, the cash outlay for interest also turns out to be at the rate of 4 percent of the total sales price until the period of conversion. It may be argued that treating the convertible bonds as if they were nonconvertible does not disclose the cash flow attributes of the bonds under either potential alternative.

The arguments for the treatment of the bond issue only as debt are that the debt and conversion privilege are inseparable, and that the practical problems of computing valuations for the conversion feature and the debt portion are too subjective to be meaningful. The valuation of debt which is nonconvertible but similar in other regards is difficult because of the many different features possible in the bond contract and because the valuation in the market may be unique to the special risks of the specific firm. However, the Accounting Principles Board, in *Opinion No. 14*, placed greater weight on the inseparability of the debt and the conversion option. The convertible bond is a hybrid form of security because under one set of conditions, the conversion feature may be the more relevant attribute, but under another set of conditions, the debt form may become the more important.

The treatment of the convertible bonds solely as debt, however, has some major weaknesses. Including the proceeds of the securities in the long-term debt classification may be misleading because generally, in a viable concern, it is not anticipated that they will ever be repaid as debt. In many cases, it may be the intent of the firm to force conversion at some time in the future by calling the bonds when the market price is above the conversion price. In most other cases, the attractiveness of the security rests primarily on the expectation that the market price of the common stock will increase significantly above the conversion price. The debt feature is regarded more as a protection under adverse conditions. Accordingly, the convertible debt security is more in the form of stockholders' equity than long-term debt. Therefore, the recommendation of

APB *Opinion No. 14* to treat the securities solely as debt is inconsistent with the recommendation made in APB *Opinion No. 15* that they should be treated as common stock in the computation of fully diluted earnings per share and in many cases in the computation of primary earnings per share. It is also inconsistent with the additional recommendation in APB *Opinion No. 14* that if convertible debt is issued at a substantial premium, there is a presumption that the premium represents the value of the conversion feature and should be allocated to paid-in capital.

The recommendation of APB *Opinion No. 14* regarding convertible debt is also inconsistent with its recommendation regarding accounting for debt with detachable warrants to purchase stock. In the latter case, it recommends that the proceeds of the debt securities issued with detachable warrants should be allocated to the debt and to the warrants separately, and that the amount allocated to the warrants should be treated as paid-in capital. However, convertible debt and debt issued with detachable warrants are in substance the same. The holder of convertible bonds may sell his securities and buy similar nonconvertible bonds, just as the holder of the debt with the detachable warrants may sell the warrants and continue to hold the bonds. Likewise, if the investor wishes to hold stock, he may convert the convertible bonds or if he holds the bonds with detachable warrants, he may sell the bonds and use the proceeds to purchase stock with the warrants. From the firm's point of view, they are also similar in substance because if the detachable warrants are exercised, it may use the proceeds to call or repurchase the bonds. Therefore, the two types of securities should be treated alike. It is inconsistent to treat one solely as debt while treating the other as both debt and equity.

An alternative to the two solutions discussed above is to create a new classification between the long-term debt and the stockholders' equity for both convertible bonds and debt with detachable warrants. A major difficulty in accounting is the continual attempt to fit new circumstances into the same old molds. A new classification, however, would also require a new type of disclosure of the interest expense in the income statement. But a clear disclosure of the several attributes of convertible debt securities and debt with detachable warrants would present a more informative picture of the possible outcomes, and permit investors and creditors to predict the future cash disbursements likely to be required and the potential relationship of the securities to existing and new securities of the firm, as well as the potential dilution of earnings per share. The best method of disclosing these types of securities in financial statements, however, can only be determined after considerable additional research has been accomplished. But a final decision requires a further analysis of the entire accounting objectives and structure; individual problems should not be treated in isolation.

Deferred Credits

In 1947 the Committee on Accounting Procedure of the AICPA deplored the misuse of reserves in accounting. It stated that if a reserve is established by charging income inappropriately and if the reserve is then used to relieve income of a subsequent period of charges that should be made in that period, income of the former period is understated and the income of the later period is overstated. Since this practice permitted an increase or decrease of income by mere whim and tended to impair the integrity of financial statements, the committee recommended that the use of reserves be restricted to appropriations of retained earnings.[16] While this recommendation was successful in halting this method of shifting income from one period to another, accountants now use a different method, the deferred credit—condoned by the Accounting Principles Board—to accomplish similar objectives, although restricted to what is considered to be "appropriate" shifting of income.

Some so-called "deferred credits" or "deferred income" items are appropriate liabilities and are criticized only for being included in this nebulous undescriptive classification of deferred credits. These items that are liabilities include obligations to perform services in the future, such as subscriptions or rent received in advance, and obligations to pay for certain costs for others, such as repairs under warranties. However, as indicated in Chapter 10, some so-called deferred credits are really advances received from customers and others are contra asset valuations.

Other deferred credits, however, are neither liabilities, stockholders' equity, nor contra assets. Therefore, it appears that they do not fit into the traditional accounting framework, since all credit items should be classifiable as one of these three. But they do appear as methods of transferring expenses or income from one period to another or of spreading certain gains or losses over several periods to avoid the "misleading" inference that may be drawn from reporting such gains and losses in one period only. One of these items is the excess of book value over cost of a subsidiary, sometimes called "negative goodwill," discussed in Chapter 14. Other items include gains on the sale and leaseback of property, "deferred taxes" arising from tax allocation, deferred investment credits, and deferred pension costs, although many other examples can be found in published financial statements.

The apparent objective of reporting deferred credits is to permit the "appropriate" expenses to be matched with current revenues and their

---

[16] Committee on Accounting Procedure, "Accounting Treatment of General Purpose Contingency Reserves," *Accounting Research Bulletin No. 28* (New York: AICPA, 1947). Similar statements were made in *ARB No. 43*. See *Accounting Principles, op. cit.*, p. 6021.

reversal in a later period; or to permit their allocation to several periods in the future as reductions of expenses or additions to income. The necessity of equating debits and credits requires reporting a credit balance even though it may not have the characteristics of a liability or stockholders' equity. But since this leads to meaningless information, the deferred credit classification should be abolished and those procedures that rely upon the use of deferred credits in order to report expenses and income items should be reevaluated, for their logic is suspect.

SELECTED ADDITIONAL READING ON CHAPTER TOPICS

The Nature of Liabilities

BIRNBERG, JACOB. "The Reporting of Executory Contracts," *Accounting Review*, Vol. XL (October, 1965), pp. 814–20.

CLARKE, ROBERT M. "Accounting for Self-Insurance," *New York Certified Public Accountant*, Vol. XXXVIII (August, 1968), pp. 567–71.

MOONITZ, MAURICE. "Changing Concept of Liabilities," *Journal of Accountancy*, Vol. CVII (May, 1960), pp. 41–46.

SPROUSE, ROBERT T., and MAURICE MOONITZ. "A Tentative Set of Broad Accounting Principles for Business Enterprises," *Accounting Research Study No. 3*, pp. 37–41. New York: AICPA, 1962.

TRUMBULL, WENDELL P. "When Is a Liability?" *Accounting Review*, Vol. XXXVIII (January, 1963), pp. 46–51.

Long-Term Debt

BIERMAN, HAROLD, JR. "The Term Structure of Interest Rates and Accounting for Debt," *Accounting Review*, Vol. XLIII (October, 1968), pp. 657–66.

——, and SEYMOUR SCHMIDT. "Accounting for Debt and Costs of Liquidity under Conditions of Uncertainty," *Journal of Accounting Research*, Vol. V (Autumn, 1967), pp. 144–53.

FORD, ALLEN. "Should Cost Be Assigned to Conversion Value?" *Accounting Review*, Vol. XLIV (October, 1969), pp. 818–22.

IMDIEKE, LEROY, and JERRY J. WEYGANDT. "Classification of Convertible Debt," *Accounting Review*, Vol. XLIV (October, 1969), pp. 798–805.

Deferred Credits

PATON, W. A. "Deferred Income—A Misnomer," *Journal of Accountancy*, Vol. CXII (September, 1961), pp. 38–40.

SPROUSE, ROBERT T. "Accounting for What-you-may-call-its," *Journal of Accountancy*, Vol. CXXII (October, 1966), pp. 45–53.

chapter 16

Income Taxes, Lease
Commitments, and Pension Costs

The methods of accounting for taxes, for long-term leases by the lessee, and for pension costs involve some similar problems, although each has created new problems and challenges for the accounting profession and for accounting theory. The common problems include the nature and reporting of the related assets and liabilities and the timing of expenses or other income effects. In each case, questions arise regarding the nature of liabilities. Does a liability exist when the creditor does not acknowledge the debt? Should obligations be reported if it is unlikely that they will be paid in the aggregate? Regarding the timing of expenses, questions arise regarding whether emphasis should be placed on cash flows, assumed or arbitrary associations with revenues, or on changes in the valuations of assets and liabilities. These questions are explored in the following discussions of the specific topics.

INCOME TAX ALLOCATION

The question of allocating corporate income tax expense has arisen because taxable net income is computed differently from accounting net income. The major differences between taxable and accounting net income can be classified as (1) permanent differences arising from special legislative allowances or restrictions permitted or required for economic, political, or administrative reasons not related to the computation of accounting net income; (2) differences arising from the direct charging or crediting to retained earnings or extraordinary gains or losses of items included in the computation of taxable net income; and (3) differences in timing of charges and credits to income. The permanent differences reflect the computation of the total tax to be paid by the corporation during its lifetime and, therefore, do not give rise to tax allocation. The second type—differences arising from direct charges and credits to retained earnings or extraordinary gains or losses—require intraperiod allocation

461

of taxes. The third type—differences in timing—is the subject of inter-period allocations.

The main controversy regarding tax allocation is centered on the interperiod type; but both intraperiod and interperiod allocations stem from the desire to record the "proper" amount and classification of tax expense in each period. Little opposition is found to intraperiod allocations, because only the income and retained earnings statements of the same period are affected; the balance sheet and income statements of other periods are unaffected. Interperiod allocation, however, raises several basic questions of accounting theory.

Intraperiod Allocation

If the all-inclusive concept of income were fully accepted, allocations of the tax between the income statement and the retained earnings statement would not be necessary. However, according to APB *Opinion No. 9*, extraordinary gains and losses should be reported separately in the income statement, and some adjustments of prior periods should be reported as adjustments of retained earnings. In these cases, allocation within the income statement or between the income statement and the retained earnings statement may make the reported operating net income before extraordinary items more meaningful.

When certain material charges and credits are recorded as extraordinary items in the income statement, as recommended by the AICPA, or when an adjustment of retained earnings is made to correct earnings of prior years, allocation is necessary if the material charges or credits affect the amount of the income tax payable for the year. For example, if the net operating income before tax is $1,000, a 30 percent income tax rate would result in a tax of $300 and a net income before extraordinary items of $700. But if, in addition, a nonrecurring taxable gain of $600 is reported during the year, the total tax payable becomes $480 (30 percent × $1,600). Without allocation, the net operating income would be $520 and the $600 gain would be reported as an extraordinary gain. With allocation, the tax assignable to current operations would be $300 and that assignable to the extraordinary gain would be $180. Thus, the operating net income before extraordinary items would not be disturbed by the recording of the gain and the gain (net of the associated tax)—$420—would be reported separately.

The argument for allocation in the above example rests primarily on the usefulness of the reported figure of net income before extraordinary items. For financial reporting purposes, an operating net income figure should be useful to investors in making predictions regarding future income and making comparisons of the net incomes of several periods. Without allocation, the net income figure before extraordinary items is subject to misinterpretation. If operating revenues and expenses are the same in a second year and following years but the nonoperating gains or losses do not recur, the failure to allocate the tax in the first year would result in an erroneous prediction and a poor comparison of the efficiency of management in conducting normal operations. It also leads to a misinterpretation of the net effect on the firm of the nonrecurring gains or losses reported as extraordinary items.

A question is frequently raised regarding the rate that should be used in making the tax allocation. Should it be the marginal rate, the average rate, or some other rate? If the special capital gains tax rate applies to the item in the tax return, this rate should also be used in the allocation. But, if it is regular taxable income, the highest rate applicable should be used, on the theory that the special gain or loss is marginal, and because one objective is to show the tax on operating income and the net operating profit under normal conditions as if the special gains and losses had not occurred. There is little justification for using an average rate in this case, but it would be better to make an allocation by using an average rate than to make no allocation at all.

Interperiod Allocation

When the difference between taxable net income and accounting net income is due to differences in the timing of the recognition of revenues and expenses, the recording of a tax expense (or equivalent effect on income) based on pretax reported income requires interperiod allocation. As in the case of intraperiod allocation, the basic principle of interperiod allocation is to let the tax follow the income on which it is based. Income taxable in the current period but recognized for accounting purposes in a later period requires a deferral of tax expense; income recognized for accounting purposes in the current period but taxable in a later period requires an accrual of tax expense.

Four types of cases are generally suggested as requiring interperiod allocation of taxes. These are: (1) A deduction taken for tax purposes but deferred in the accounting statements. Common examples are the additional first-year depreciation on equipment and the use of accelerated depreciation for tax purposes while using the straight-line method in the accounts. (2) Revenue recorded currently in the accounts but reported for tax purposes at a later date. The use of the installment basis for tax purposes and the sales basis for accounting purposes is a common example. (3) Income included in the tax calculation but deferred in the accounting statements. An example is rent received in advance and taxable when received but reported as income for accounting purposes when the services are provided. (4) Expenses deducted in the income statement but deductible for tax purposes only in a later period.

An example is the setting up in the accounts of estimated warranty expenses deductible for tax purposes only in the period of payment. Cases (1) and (2) require the setting up of an income tax liability or other credit account because the tax expense related to the current accounting income is greater than the tax to be paid currently. Cases (3) and (4) require the setting up of a prepaid tax or other debit account because the amount of the tax paid currently is greater than the reported tax expense allocated to the income of the current period.

Controversy regarding interperiod tax allocation centers around the following questions: (1) Is tax allocation an appropriate accounting device? (2) If it is appropriate, should it be carried out on a partial or a comprehensive basis? (3) How should tax allocation be presented in financial statements? (4) What tax rate should be used in making the allocation? While the discussions have, at times, been carried out on an emotional level, there are some basic premises that are assumed to support the several positions. Since these same premises are at the root of much of the conflict in accounting literature, it is not surprising to find that they influence thinking regarding the reporting of income taxes, even though taxes based on income are unique in many ways. Some of these basic premises or objectives are: (1) The matching concept is assumed to be relevant to the reporting of income taxes and the emphasis on the reporting of net income overrides any effect on balance sheet items. (2) While matching may be important, it must be supported by changes in asset and liability valuations. (3) Accounting should rely on historical observations rather than future projections. Therefore, financial statements should reflect cash flows or effective cash flows as closely as possible. (4) Predictions of future cash flows are more important than predictions of reported net income. Accordingly, financial statements should provide information to permit such predictions.

The Matching Concept Applied to Income Taxes. As indicated in Chapter 6, matching is the process of reporting expenses on the basis of a cause-and-effect relationship with reported revenues. Direct matching requires the reporting of expenses in the same period as the associated revenues. The application of the matching concept to the accounting for income taxes is found in APB *Opinion No. 11,* since the Board recommended that the reported income tax expense for a period should include the tax effects of all revenue and expense transactions included in the measurement of pretax income.[1] Three separate problems related to this recommendation should be discussed independently: (1) Is the corporate income tax an expense? (2) Is the matching concept relevant in the case of taxes? (3) Is the recommended method of matching logical?

---

[1] AICPA, *Accounting Principles* (Chicago: Commerce Clearing House, Inc., 1968), Vol. II, p. 6586.

Regarding the nature of income taxes as an expense, current practice defines it as an expense of doing business and managements generally make decisions on the basis of an aftertax expected net income. The tax must also be taken into consideration in investment decisions. An additional impelling reason is that the AICPA, as well as official bodies in other countries, has recognized income taxes as expenses. Practice, however, does not determine the logic of the classification. But since the expense classification does not have a clear definition other than what accountants choose it to be, the argument that tax allocation is inappropriate because the tax is not an expense is difficult to support. Note, however, that expenses are not homogeneous in nature; some are variable with output or sales while others are fixed in nature. Most expenses are incurred deliberately, with the objective of increasing revenues or decreasing costs, but some result from expected or unexpected outside influences beyond the control of the firm. Income taxes have their own characteristics, since they are functionally related to periodic taxable income, which may differ in many respects from reported pretax income. Since they are not directly related to revenues or revenue-seeking functions, some writers deny that they are expenses; but, on the other hand, since they must be taken into consideration in determining the amount to be distributed as dividends, including them in the expense classification has some merit.

However, many accountants consider the tax to represent a distribution of income similar to the payment of dividends. This view is implied in the 1957 statement of the American Accounting Association, which states that "interest charges, income taxes, and true profit-sharing distributions are not determinants of *enterprise* net income."[2] In support of this position, the proponents claim that since the tax is paid only if income is earned, it is more similar to dividends than to payments for wages and supplies used in the business. They also claim that the impact on the stockholder is similar to the impact of the personal income tax.

The government, however, is a beneficiary of the corporation only in a broad sense, in the same way that employees and suppliers are beneficiaries and receive payment for the services they render. The main difference is that the federal government does not provide services to the corporation in direct proportion to the amount of the tax. But there is no question that services are provided. The payment of the corporate income tax (like a franchise tax) is associated with the right to conduct a profitable corporation in a favorable economic climate provided by the government. And the classification of this payment is independent of its calculation. Whether the final incidence of the tax is on the stockholders,

---

[2] AAA Committee on Accounting Concepts and Standards, *Accounting and Reporting for Corporate Financial Statements and Preceding Statements and Supplements* (Columbus, Ohio: AAA, 1957), p. 5.

employees, or customers does not necessarily change the nature of the tax as an expense, but it may be pointed out that evidence does not support the supposition that the impact of the tax has been on the stockholder in the long run.

Regardless of whether or not the income tax is classified as an expense, if the income tax is reported as a separate item in the income statement, the question of allocation is still present. Therefore, we should turn to the question of whether or not matching is relevant. The first question regarding matching is whether or not the reported net income with tax allocation is more relevant to external users than a reported net income without allocation. This question cannot be answered satisfactorily without deciding which concept and objective of net income are most relevant. If reported net income is intended to represent an indicator for the prediction of future reported net incomes, tax allocation may have some relevance. Through allocation, the tax expense is made to appear functionally related to the reported pretax net income, except for the permanent differences between taxable net income and reported pretax net income. Therefore, it is assumed that if the investor can predict the reported pretax net income, he can also predict the tax expense and thus the reported aftertax net income. Generally, however, the information presented in financial statements regarding the computation of the tax is inadequate to make this prediction. Too great a reliance must be placed on the final reported net income figure and too little information is available to determine the functional relationships of the items determining this net figure.

A case for matching in the case of income taxes can be made on the basis of individual transactions, particularly in those cases where cash flows affect reported net income in a period different from the effect on taxable income. For example, in the case of a single large installment sale, without allocation the financial statements indicate that the resources of the firm are increased by the amount of the sale price of the goods sold. However, the investor may discover only later that these resources (the installment receivable) can be converted to cash only by incurring a significant tax liability. Tax allocation prevents this type of misleading information. However, in the case of differences arising from the allocation of nonmonetary assets or nonmonetary liabilities, the relevance of matching even for individual items becomes suspect. The difficulty is that allocations such as the depreciation of plant and equipment and the amortization of research and development expenses are not based on logical matching concepts, as discussed previously in Chapters 13 and 14. Therefore, an attempt to match tax expense with these pretax income allocations is of doubtful validity. That is, it is doubtful that reported net income would be improved by the allocation of taxes to expense or income items that are the result of allocations unsupported by the matching concept.

The matching procedure recommended by APB *Opinion No. 11* is that the tax expense of any period should include the tax effects of *all* revenues and expenses reported in the determination of reported pretax income (comprehensive tax allocation). That is, the tax effects should be reported in the period when the timing differences arise and also in the period when the differences reverse. Between these two dates, the Board recommended that the differences should be reported as deferred charges or deferred credits. The tax effect is based on the tax rate at the time of reporting the initial difference, and no adjustment is made for changes in tax rates.

The main difficulty with the recommendation of APB *Opinion No. 11* is that the deferred method is not supported by logic. The deferred charges and deferred credits are not intended to represent assets and liabilities nor stockholders' equity. Therefore, they represent merely a method of shifting the tax effect from one period to another. Even if the method could be supported on the basis of the matching concept alone, the amounts carried forward should represent measurements of resources or obligations if the double-entry system is to be maintained. The use of undefined debits and credits makes the entire method suspect.

Tax Allocation as a Process of Valuation.   Two alternative methods for treating the allocation of income taxes—the liability method and the net of tax method—are supported by valuation concepts. In the liability method, the reporting of tax expense in the current period in excess of the amount payable currently is assumed to give rise to an obligation to pay a higher tax in the future. Likewise, the payment of taxes in excess of the amount reported as tax expense is assumed to result in an asset representing a tax benefit available in the future. These concepts, however, are challenged on the ground that the items carried forward do not have the usual characteristics of assets or liabilities. The "prepaid taxes" arising from the allocation of income taxes is not an unconditional right for future benefits and it is not a claim that would be recognized by the Internal Revenue Service. Thus, it does not have the usual characteristics of assets. However, under normal expectations of future corporate income and the continuation of current income tax regulations, the item may have many of the normal characteristics of an asset. For example, the tax paid on rent received in advance gives the firm the right to provide services in the future without incurring a tax obligation in so doing. However, the benefit is less real when it results from differences in methods of depreciation or other allocations rather than from the timing of cash flows. This is particularly true when the tax allocation is looked at from the point of view of the entire firm, rather than looking at each item separately, because of the many interactions even in the computation of the income tax payable.

The item "income taxes payable in the future" arising from tax allocation likewise has few of the normal characteristics of liabilities. An obligation to the government does not really exist since the Internal Revenue Service would not recognize the obligation even for future payment. The future obligation will arise, in part, from a past transaction—the earning of the income not reported for tax purposes or the deduction for tax purposes of an expenditure carried forward in the accounts. But the main transaction—the levying of the tax—is a future transaction. In some circumstances, however, there will be an obligation to pay a tax in the future based on past or current activities. For example, income reported on the basis of the percentage-of-completion method for long-term contracts should take into consideration the fact that a tax obligation will arise when the contract is completed. But the "liability" arising from the use of the accelerated method of depreciation for tax purposes while using the straight-line method for reporting purposes is an obligation only under very limited assumptions regarding the validity of the depreciation method used for accounting purposes; because of the lack of theoretical logic behind such methods, the tax liability is of doubtful validity.

An alternative to treating these items as assets and liabilities is to treat them in close relationship to the items giving rise to them—the net-of-tax method. Thus, the prepaid taxes may be considered valuation accounts to the related liabilities and the taxes payable in the future may be considered contra asset accounts, or the asset and liabilities may be reduced directly. For example, if a capital asset in the amount of $10,000 is written off for tax purposes but carried forward in the accounts, the net valuation to the firm is only $6,000 (assuming a 40 percent tax rate) because the use of the asset in the future cannot reduce the tax a second time. This net-of-tax method, however, is based on the assumption that an adjustment of the historical cost of an asset for the tax effect results in a current valuation of the asset. The difficulty with this concept is that many other factors should be considered in measuring the value of the asset, either to the firm or in presenting evidence of the value of the firm to investors. The net-of-tax method is usually rejected on the ground that it is not the objective of accounting to measure and report the value of each asset or liability. But it is a more logical concept than either the deferred method or the liability method.

Valuation concepts are also applied in support of partial tax allocation. Under this method, tax allocation would be applied only in those cases where tax benefits or tax obligations are likely to be reversed in the aggregate within a reasonable time in the future. For example, if the accelerated method of depreciation is used for tax purposes while straight-line is used in the financial statements, the tax difference will not be paid so long as the firm continues to replace its assets; and in a growth firm, the aggregate difference will continue to increase indefinitely. Therefore, since in the aggregate the tax difference is not likely to be paid, the liability does not exist. The counter to this argument is that there is a continual "roll over" of the liability, so that each year a part is paid and an additional amount is accrued. Like accounts payable, the liability cannot be denied just because the aggregate does not decrease over time. However, the "roll over" concept is not as applicable to the tax liability as it is to the accounts payable; because if the firm ceased profitable operations, the tax would not have to be paid but the creditors represented by the accounts payable would maintain their claims.

A further argument against showing the full amount of the tax liability or prepaid tax is that since the obligations will be paid and the tax benefit received only at some distant time in the future, they should be discounted at some positive rate of interest. If the time period is high or infinite, the present value would be close to zero. Therefore, for these several reasons, the valuation concepts are of little assistance in providing complete logic to tax allocation.

Tax Allocation and Cash Flows. One of the basic arguments against income tax allocation is that the financial statements should reflect as clearly as possible the cash flows of the firm. Even though the accrual basis is proposed for many items, it is argued that the tax payable reflects the effect on the firm for the period. That is, the tax levied each year represents the impact on the firm that year. Taxes are assumed to affect cash flows by the amount of the tax obligation. Therefore, because the tax obligation is not necessarily functionally related to reported net income, the current tax obligation is more meaningful to investors and creditors than some artificially allocated tax expense. Predictions and evaluations should be made on the basis of pretax net income and expectations regarding changes in the amount of the tax rather than upon a single aftertax net income.

Tax allocation is also opposed on the ground that the uncertainties in making estimates of future tax obligations and future tax effects are too great to make allocation meaningful. Since the tax is payable only when taxable income is earned, tax "savings" of one period may result in permanent savings if the corporation incurs losses for several years. Likewise, expenses deductible for tax purposes only in a later period may never reduce taxes if losses are incurred beyond the carry-back and carry-forward periods. Also, future tax rates and tax regulations are uncertain and subject to change by Congress, and the method of application of the regulations may be subject to change by administrative decisions.

These uncertainties and the many complications are part of the reason why the Committee on Accounting Concepts and Standards of the

American Accounting Association opposed tax allocation in its 1957 statement. It stated in part

> . . . the possible future offsets are often subject to unusual uncertainties; and treatment on an accrual basis is in many cases unduly complicated. Consequently, disclosure by accrual may be more confusing than enlightening and is therefore undesirable.[3]

There is considerable doubt that the uncertainties in tax allocations are greater than they are in other areas of financial reporting, since certain information may be relevant if the firm is expected to be profitable just as other information may be relevant if it may be expected to be unprofitable. Furthermore, the corporate income tax is a major source of federal income, and it is not likely to be abolished in the near future. Tax rates may change from time to time, but, in the absence of war or national distress, they are not likely to change by amounts so great as to nullify all estimates.

However, the lack of basic supporting theory and the many complications involved in the tax allocation process make it doubtful as a relevant accounting procedure. Part of the difficulty, however, is not with the tax allocation itself but with the entire accounting process, which stresses the reporting of a single net income figure which is then used as a predictive indicator. Alternative theoretical structures should be investigated and empirical studies should be made to find better methods of communicating the effects of corporate income taxation.

Carry-Back and Carry-Forward of Tax Losses

According to income tax allocation concepts, the total tax payable over a series of years should be allocated to the revenues and expenses entering into the computation of taxable income when such items are reported in the determination of accounting net income. In years of operating losses, the deductions exceed the revenues, and therefore a negative amount of tax should be allocated to that year to the extent that such loss can be carried backward or forward to reduce the total tax payable by the corporation. The principle of allocation is the same for both carry-backs and carry-forwards, but the degree of uncertainty regarding the tax benefit is much greater in the latter case.

When an operating loss can be carried back to reduce the taxes paid in prior years, a claim for refund arises immediately even though it may be subject to approval by the Internal Revenue Service at a later date. In most cases, the claim for refund is sufficiently certain and can be estimated with reasonable accuracy. And since the refund arises from the operating loss of the current period, the amount of the refund should be

---

[3] *Ibid.*, pp. 6–7.

reported in the income statement for the year in which the loss occurs. This is the position of APB *Opinion No. 11,* which suggests that the amount of tax expense for the year (for example, in cases of consolidation) can be shown in the income statement with the amount of the reduction indicated in a footnote or parenthetically, or the amount of the refund can be shown on the income statement before arriving at the net loss (or income in the case of consolidation) for the year.[4]

In the case of a loss carry-forward, however, APB *Opinion No. 11* recommends that the amount of the anticipated refund should be reported only in the year to which the loss is carried.[5] This recommendation states further that the amount of the tax refund arising from the carry-forward of the loss should be reported in the income statement of the year realized as an extraordinary item, unless it has been reported in the year of the loss. While this may be interpreted as a correction of the income or loss of the prior period, it is not clear why the Board did not recommend that it be excluded from income of the carry-forward period, which would then be consistent with the recommendations of APB *Opinion No. 9* regarding prior period adjustments. If the amount of the carry-forward refund is not reported as a correction of the prior period, the treatment of carry-forwards would not be consistent with the treatment of carry-backs. The refund should be treated consistently as relating to the operations of the loss year in both cases, in accordance with income tax allocation procedures.

The position of the AICPA regarding loss carry-forwards differs from the position taken regarding carry-backs, apparently because of the greater uncertainty of the benefits under a loss carry-forward than under a loss carry-back. If income is not earned during the permitted period, the tax benefit may be lost. But this uncertainty is always present when the allocation of taxes depends on future taxable income. However, there is some merit in the argument that a firm that has incurred losses is more likely to incur additional losses than a firm that has a long record of profitable operation; each case should be treated on its own merits. If there is a good probability of future income within the carry-forward period, the anticipated tax benefit should be recorded in the period in which the loss is incurred. The qualification of "beyond a reasonable doubt" reflects a conservative attitude of the Board.

The asset resulting from the allocation of a tax reduction to the loss year, however, is not the same as the prepaid taxes arising from other allocation problems, and it is not exactly a true receivable since there will never be a direct claim against the government. However, it does represent an anticipated future benefit to the firm in the form of a reduction in

---

[4] AICPA, *op. cit.,* p. 6591.
[5] *Ibid.*

a future liability. While this benefit does not have all of the characteristics of normal assets, it does reflect the possibility of greater aftertax income than would otherwise occur. Other things being equal, a firm with a carry-forward tax loss is worth more than a firm without it.

The above recommended procedure for treating the carry-back and carry-forward of tax losses, however, can be criticized for several reasons. Since it is an attempt to be consistent with tax allocation procedures discussed above, it can be criticized for many of the same reasons. The use of the deferred charge in carrying forward the expected benefit from a tax loss is particularly subject to criticism. However, there are some additional problems. One of the presumed advantages of tax allocation is that it permits a better matching of the tax payments with the associated pretax income items, and thus permits a better prediction of reported net income in the future. However, if a loss in one year gives rise to a refund arising from the carry-back provisions, but a subsequent loss does not, the failure to make a provision for a potential refund arising from the carry-forward provisions will result in reported net income or loss figures for the two years that are not indicative of the operations of the two periods. If the pretax reported income or loss amounts are the same for the two years, the failure to allocate any potential refund to the second year will give the impression that the outlook for the firm is rapidly becoming worse. A further criticism is that a loss by itself does not create a tax refund; the refund is associated with the taxable income as well as with the loss. The functional relationship is not clear-cut. As with tax allocation itself, the allocation of tax refunds does not necessarily improve the communication of information. Full disclosure of tax effects is necessary because income taxes do not behave in the same way as other expenses; the reliance on a reported aftertax net income is not adequate for the decisions and predictions made by investors and creditors.

THE INVESTMENT TAX CREDIT

The Revenue Acts of 1962 and 1964 provided for a credit against the tax equal to a specified percentage of the cost of the investment in certain depreciable property acquired during the taxable year. Since that time, the investment tax credit has been alternately canceled and reinstated, although some of the provisions have changed. Because it is likely that this tax credit will continue to be used alternately in this way to help stabilize the economy, and because it presented entirely new problems for accountants and accounting theory, the topic continues to be relevant to discussions of accounting theory. The investment credit gives rise to a permanent reduction of taxes; but since it is a direct reduction of the tax rather than a reduction of taxable income, it requires an inquiry into the basic nature of the credit itself and into the basic tenets of accounting.

In its *Opinion No. 2*, the Accounting Principles Board of the AICPA concluded that "the allowable investment credit should be reflected in net income over the productive life of acquired property and not in the year in which it is placed in service."[6] While the Board preferred that the credit be reflected in the accounts by reducing the net amount at which the asset is stated—either directly or indirectly by the use of an offsetting account—it recognized as acceptable the alternative of treating the credit as deferred income, provided it is amortized over the life of the property, presumably in the same way that depreciation is allocated. In 1964, the Accounting Principles Board, in *Opinion No. 4*, stated that the previous recommendation of *Opinion No. 2* should be considered preferable but that ". . . the alternative method of treating the credit as a reduction of Federal income taxes of the year in which the credit arises is also acceptable."[7]

Cost Reduction

The original recommendation of the Accounting Principles Board (the preferred method in *Opinion No. 4*) is logically supportable for several reasons: (1) Accountants generally hold that earnings do not arise from the acquisition of assets but only from their use. (2) The original value of the asset can be measured by its net cost to the firm—the invoice price less the tax credit. (3) The recapture clause of the Internal Revenue Code provides that under certain conditions, particularly when the asset is sold prematurely, a part of the credit must be repaid. The uncertainty of the final realization of the investment credit, therefore, supports the delaying of its recognition. (4) In addition, the Board originally took into consideration the intent of Congress to reduce the cost of investment property in order to provide a stimulus for investment and the requirement (under the 1962 act) that the investment credit be treated for tax purposes as a reduction in the basis of the property. However, in *Opinion No. 4*, the Board stated that the 1964 Revenue Act did not change the essential nature of the investment credit, implying that a reduction in the basis of the property is not a necessary requirement for reporting the credit as a reduction of the cost of the asset.

The cost reduction method is based, in part, on the fact that there are some major differences between the investment credit and other permanent reductions of the tax. Most permanent reductions are based on the special treatment of current or past revenues and expenses or the application of special rates (such as the capital gains rate) applicable to certain

---

[6] Accounting Principles Board, "Accounting for the 'Investment Credit,'" *Opinion No. 2* (New York: AICPA, December, 1962), p. 7.

[7] Accounting Principles Board, "Accounting for the 'Investment Credit,'" *Opinion No. 4*, in AICPA, *Accounting Principles, op. cit.*, p. 6517.

income; the investment credit, however, is based on the acquisition of property for *future* use. The position of the Accounting Principles Board is that this permanent reduction in the tax is not realized until the asset is used in service. Realization is assumed to come only through the use of the facilities and the sale of the products of the enterprise. By itself, this is an ultraconservative position. If the tax does result in an immediate gain, the recognition of the gain should not be delayed just because there has not been a sale or use of the property.

The treatment of the tax credit as a reduction of the cost of the property has its greatest support in the position that this net cost to the firm represents the original value of the asset. In most cases, there may be no evidence that the firm would have acquired the asset at its invoice price if it had not anticipated the investment credit. Thus, the net cost of the asset at the time of acquisition can be assumed to be the invoice price less the investment tax credit, even though the purchase price is paid to one party and the tax saving is obtained from another; both are taken into consideration in the decision to acquire the asset. One difficulty with this procedure, however, is that it permits two firms purchasing identical items at the same invoice price to record different costs if one met the conditions for the tax credit and the other did not. But, in this case, the net cost to the two firms is different and the similarity of the invoice price is not sufficient evidence to indicate that the value of the item is necessarily the same to the two firms.

The third reason for the cost reduction method—the uncertainty of final realization—is at best a weak argument. The recapture of the investment credit by the government occurs only if the firm does not use the asset for the declared life and purpose. In most cases, this declared intent will be carried out, and the assumption of this is supported by the postulate of continuity. The uncertainty of the tax benefit in this case is not materially different from the uncertainties regarding the recapture of tax benefits in other cases. For example, if depreciable property is sold at a price in excess of the carrying value of the asset, the firm loses some of the tax benefit of the depreciation taken. Also, the uncertainty in the case of the investment tax credit is not greater than the uncertainties in many other situations involving the determination of business income.

Tax Reduction

The alternative method of treating the investment tax credit found acceptable by the Accounting Principles Board in *Opinion No. 4* is as a reduction of the tax expense for the year in which the credit arises (frequently referred to as "flow-through"). This procedure was found acceptable largely because the Securities and Exchange Commission had established a position accepting both the cost reduction method and the tax reduction method[8] and because of the failure of the recommendation of *Opinion No. 2* to find general acceptance in the accounting profession. But several members of the Board found the tax reduction method preferable or at least just as acceptable as the cost reduction method.

The logic in support of the tax reduction method is as follows: (1) The investment credit is regarded as a selective reduction in taxes available to those who meet certain conditions. (2) It is thought to represent a permanent reduction in the tax that should be treated like all other permanent differences between taxable and accounting income. (3) The anticipated tax reduction is assumed to have no effect on the value of the asset at the date of acquisition. (4) If the tax reduction is recorded by setting up a "deferred income tax" account, it is feared that this may be treated as a capital contribution or as a deferred credit to income without an indication of its specific balance sheet classification.

As indicated above, the tax credit is a permanent decrease in taxes, but it is different from other permanent decreases. Even though it is different, however, it can be treated as a selective reduction in taxes if it is assumed that the tax credit has no effect on the correct valuation of the asset at the time of acquisition. Therefore, the question of valuation is the key issue. The 1963 AAA Committee on Concepts and Standards—Long-Lived Assets stated on this issue that

reductions in tax liabilities that may be secured in connection with the purchase of an asset should *not* be treated as deductions from the purchase price. It must be presumed that all relevant economic factors are considered in completing a transaction at the purchase price.[9]

The committee's position is based on the assumption that the initial value of an asset is based on many factors, including anticipated cash flows and the anticipated tax reduction. This is a plausible approach to the problem, as the tax credit is anticipated at the time of the purchase and helps to support the decision to pay the invoice price to the vendor. But there are some major differences between the tax reduction and other anticipated cash savings and cash flows. *First,* the tax credit reduces the income tax expense generally in the same year in which the acquisition is made, and it may be assumed to occur simultaneously even though the effect on cash flow will be delayed until the actual payment of the tax. *Second,* it is not an anticipated factor that is generally taken into con-

---

[8] Securities and Exchange Commission Accounting Series Release No. 96, January 10, 1963.

[9] Committee on Concepts and Standards—Long-Lived Assets, AAA, "Accounting for Land, Buildings, and Equipment," *Accounting Review,* Vol. XXXIX (July, 1964), p. 694.

sideration in the choice of the depreciation method to allocate the cost of the asset to the several periods of use. One of the objectives of a depreciation method is to allocate the original cost over the life of the asset on the basis of expected benefits. If the tax reduction is one of these anticipated benefits, a portion of the invoice cost of the asset should be allocated as depreciation to the first year of the asset's life to match the tax savings. Thus, the effect on net income would be the same as that resulting from deducting the tax credit from the cost of the asset at the time of acquisition. However, since the tax reduction would not generally be taken into consideration in computing the first year's depreciation, the direct deduction from the original cost is a more expedient method of assuring proper treatment of the tax credit. But we cannot be sure of this, because depreciation methods are not logically conceived (as discussed in Chapter 13).

A Summary Evaluation

The AICPA Accounting Principles Board's recommendation in *Opinion No. 4* is unfortunate in that it permits either of two contradictory methods of accounting for the investment tax credit. It sets a dangerous precedent in establishing recommendations on the basis of general practice and pressure from other organizations rather than on the basis of logic. In permitting the two procedures, the Board has failed in its responsibility to establish accounting principles that will permit comparability among firms and among industries to provide the best information for investors and other users of accounting reports.

In the opinion of the author, the most relevant issues in deciding between cost reduction and tax reduction are (1) the determination of the relevant valuation of the asset to be carried forward to future periods and (2) the presentation of information to permit predictions of future cash flows. Cost reduction accomplishes the better valuation of the asset at the time of acquisition. But because of an inability to allocate the initial value of the asset through depreciation on a logical basis, subsequent valuations are likely to be meaningless. In presenting the immediate effect on cash flows, the tax reduction method is superior. However, it is also deficient because of the emphasis on the final net income figure. Adequate information is not usually presented to permit a prediction of future tax payments. This is particularly important when the investment credit is canceled or temporarily removed. The investment credit points out a fundamental weakness in traditional accounting practice; unfortunately, accounting theory is unable to provide conclusive evidence for one method or the other. However, since the cost reduction method has many of the deficiencies of tax allocation as well as the deficiencies inherent in depreciation methods, the tax reduction method may be the better of the two if full disclosure is made of the tax effects, so that undue reliance is not placed on the final net income amount.

LONG-TERM LEASE COMMITMENTS

The traditional position regarding executory contracts and other agreements, both sides of which are equally unperformed, is that neither the liability nor the asset should be recorded. The related expense is recorded only as the goods or services are received or when payment is made. An asset is recorded only if a prepayment is made, and a liability is recorded only when services are accrued. One of the main reasons for this treatment is that there is no effect on income until the services are received, and there is no effect on ownership equities because the rights under the contract are exactly offset by the obligations. But it is also thought that the rights under the contract do not represent assets in their usual definition and that the obligations do not represent normal liabilities. Also it is thought that there is an unconditional right of offset; if one party does not provide the goods or services, the other party does not have the obligation to make payment. And in case of default, the rights are generally limited to the damages sustained by the party not in default.

This is the general background against which long-term lease commitments have been compared and which supports the omission of the rights and obligations under long-term leases from the main body of the balance sheet. The main disadvantage of this procedure is that it ties the recording of the expense to the pattern of payment. If annual payments are equal during the lease, the charge to the expense for the use of the property is also equal each year; if annual payments increase, the charge to expense is generally increased likewise. But the annual charge to expense should not necessarily be equal to the annual payment under a long-term lease commitment because the payments are not necessarily related to the value of the services received each period.

If a leasehold is purchased and the entire amount paid in advance, traditional accounting treatment would require that it be recorded as an asset and that the cost be amortized over the life of the lease. Likewise, if a 10-year lease is paid for by making five equal annual payments during the first 5 years, the entire cost should be amortized over the entire 10-year period regardless of the period of payment. For example, if $5,000 is to be paid at the beginning of each of the first five years, the entire cost is $25,000 ignoring the interest factor, and the annual charge to expense should be $2,500 if the straight-line method is used. If interest is taken into consideration, computation of the rent expense and the amortization of prepaid rent would be as shown in the following table, assuming an interest rate of 5 percent and an equal charge to rent expense per year:

Year	Payment Beginning of Year	Rent Expense for Year	Net Increase (Decrease) in Prepaid Rent	Interest Earned	Balance Prepaid Rent (End of Year)
1	$5,000	$2,803.43	$2,196.57	$109.83	$ 2,306.40
2	5,000	2,803.43	2,196.57	225.15	4,728.12
3	5,000	2,803.43	2,196.57	346.23	7,270.92
4	5,000	2,803.43	2,196.57	473.37	9,940.86
5	5,000	2,803.43	2,196.57	606.87	12,744.30
6	–0–	2,803.43	(2,803.43)	497.04	10,437.91
7	–0–	2,803.43	(2,803.43)	381.72	8,016.20
8	–0–	2,803.43	(2,803.43)	260.64	5,473.41
9	–0–	2,803.43	(2,803.43)	133.50	2,803.48
10	–0–	2,803.48	(2,803.48)	–0–	–0–

Note that in the above example the balance of the prepaid rent account at the end of each year represents the excess of payments made to date over the rent expense plus interest on these prepayments. At the end of the fifth year, the total prepaid rent is the present discounted value of the remaining annual rent expense amounts. But the annual rent expense for each of the 10 years is computed by finding the annuity (at 5 percent) whose present value (of an annuity due for 10 payments) is equal to $22,729.75, the present discounted value of the 5 payments of $5,000 each. This case, even though using conventional procedures, does show that the payment of the lease obligation and the recording of the rent expense for each year are independent of each other in their timing, but both are based on the same values. The main objection to the above procedure, however, is that the value on which both are based—the present value of $22,729.75—is not shown in the accounts at any time. None of the lease liability is shown, and only a part of the value of the leasehold is shown during the first five years.

This failure to record the value of the leasehold and the amount of the lease obligation can be overcome by the capitalization of the lease and the initial recording of the lease rights and the lease obligations in the accounts at $22,729.75. Note that this amount would be the same (assuming a 5 percent rate of interest) regardless of whether the amount payable is $5,000 at the beginning of each of the first 5 years or $2,803.43 at the beginning of each of the 10 years. The $22,729.75 lease obligation will be paid in full, including interest at 5 percent, by either method of payment. The rights under the lease contract, amounting initially to $22,729.75, can be amortized by the interest method, by the straight-line method, or by any other systematic method similar to the depreciation of plant and equipment.

If an interest method of amortization is used, and if the lease obligation is paid by equal annual amounts over the entire life of the lease, the total effect on net income will be an equal annual charge, because the interest on the outstanding balance of the lease obligation will be exactly offset by the interest on the capitalized rights under the lease contract. However, if the leasehold rights are amortized by the straight-line method, the net effect would be a declining net charge to income because of the decline in the interest on the assumed lease obligation.

The proper method of amortization of the leasehold rights depends in large part on the conditions of the lease contract and on other circumstances regarding the value of the services received from the property each year. If the terms of the lease contract require the lessor to provide all repairs and maintenance of the property and to pay all taxes and other charges relating to the continued use of the property, there is support for the interest method of amortization, assuming the values of the services received each year are approximately equal. But if the costs of maintenance, insurance, and taxes are to be paid by the lessee, a straight-line or decreasing charge method might be more appropriate. A declining annual net revenue contribution would also dictate a decreasing charge method. Thus, the choice of an appropriate amortization method is similar to the selection of a proper depreciation method for plant and equipment using the net revenue contribution concept, but it is also subject to all of its limitations.

Alternative Methods of Disclosure of Long-Term Leases

Prior to World War II, virtually no mention was made of long-term lease commitments in financial statements except for prepayments and accruals. In the post–World War II period, the sale-and-leaseback arrangement and the use of the long-term lease as a method of financing increased rapidly. And with these methods of lease financing came the need for proper disclosure in the financial statements. The several suggested methods of disclosure are: (1) disclosure of the long-term lease commitments and the terms of the lease by footnotes only; (2) capitalization of only those leases that are in substance a purchase and disclosure of all others by the use of footnotes; (3) capitalization of the property rights only of all long-term leases; and (4) capitalization of all long-term commitments including long-term leases.

The AICPA Position. In 1949, the AICPA Committee on Accounting Procedure issued *Bulletin No. 38* (restated in Chapter 14 of *Bulletin No. 43*) in an attempt to clarify its position regarding adequate disclosure of long-term leases in financial statements. The necessity for this statement arose out of the growth in the use of the long-term lease as a method of financing and the buy-build-sell-and-lease transaction (sale-and-leaseback). Its conclusion was that where the obligations under the leases are material,

. . . disclosure should be made in financial statements or in notes thereto of: (1) the amounts of annual rentals to be paid under such leases with some indication of the periods for which they are payable and (2) any other important obligation assumed or guarantee made in connection therewith. . . .[10]

The main change recommended by *Bulletin No. 38*, however, was that

. . . where it is clearly evident that the transaction involved is in substance a purchase, the "leased" property should be included among the assets of the lessee with suitable accounting for the corresponding liabilities and for the related charges in the income statement.[11]

Opinion No. 5 of the Accounting Principles Board (issued to supersede Chapter 14 of *Bulletin No. 43*) did not change the basic recommendations originally stated in *Bulletin No. 38*, but merely clarified the criteria for identification of lease agreements that are in substance a purchase of property and recommended that the disclosure requirements be extended. In the case of agreements that are essentially equivalent to installment purchases of property,

. . . the substance of the arrangement, rather than its legal form, should determine the accounting treatment. The property and the related obligation should be included in the balance sheet as an asset and a liability, respectively, at the discounted amount of the future lease rental payments, exclusive of payments to cover taxes and operating expenses other than depreciation.[12]

According to *Opinion No. 5*, a noncancelable lease should be considered equivalent to a purchase of property if the lease results in the creation of a material equity in the property as evidenced by one of the following: (1) The property can be acquired by the lessee during or at the end of the lease agreement for an amount that appears at the inception of the lease to be substantially below the probable fair value of the property when it can be acquired. (2) The payments are materially in excess of normal rental payments during the initial term of the contract and are materially less than the fair rental value during a renewal period extended at the option of the lessee. (3) The lessee and lessor are related, and the circumstances of the lease do not suggest that the lease is the result of an arm's-length transaction.

The existence of one or more of the following circumstances is presumed to be evidence that a lease is, in substance, a purchase: (1) The property is designed to meet the specific needs of the lessee. Thus, it has value only to the lessee and presumably, the lessee cannot avoid the liability under the lease contract by selling its leasehold rights. (2) The

---

[10] AICPA, *Accounting Principles, op. cit.,* p. 6056.

[11] *Ibid.,* p. 6057.

[12] Accounting Principles Board, "Reporting of Leases in Financial Statements of Lessee," *Opinion No. 5* (New York: AICPA, September, 1964), p. 30.

lessee is obligated during the useful life of the property to pay the operating expenses usually considered incidental to ownership. This is evidence that the lease agreement is solely a financial arrangement. (3) The lessee has guaranteed the obligation of the lessor. (4) The lease is treated as a purchase for tax purposes.

Unfortunately, the Board, in *Opinion No. 5*, attempted to clarify the former position of the AICPA rather than take a new approach to the problem. In doing so, the Board chose to rely on generally accepted practice rather than provide active leadership in the development of accounting principles. Also, there is an unfortunate implication in the opinion that the regulations of the Internal Revenue Service may be the determining factor in establishing the proper accounting for long-term leases. But the main contribution of *Opinion No. 5* is the attempt to clarify the doubtful distinction between a lease agreement that is in substance an installment purchase of property and other long-term leases.

The recommendations of *Opinion No. 5* can be criticized from several points of view. (1) The recommendation that leases should be recorded as purchases when they are "clearly in substance installment purchases of property" is a very poor criterion for capitalization. Any doubt regarding the nature of the lease can be used to support no capitalization. Accordingly, a large number of leases are still reported only in footnotes when they would require capitalization under more precise criteria. (2) The use of the probable fair value of the property at the termination of the lease agreement as evidence of the creation of a material equity requires a considerable amount of clairvoyance. (3) The notion that a liability exists only if the firm has an equity in an asset is a unique criterion, but lacking in logic. (4) The recommendation emphasizes the installment purchase characteristic rather than the acquisition of property rights. (5) The recommendations of APB *Opinion No. 5* are not consistent with the recommendations of *Opinion No. 7*, which makes a distinction between the financing and operating concepts of leases in accounting for leases by lessors. (6) The discussion of the reporting of leases in financial statements fails to discuss adequately the broader problems of the accounting for all types of noncancelable commitments.

Capitalization of Leases That Are in Substance a Purchase. The capitalization of only those leases that are in substance a purchase draws on the similarity of such leases to the owning of property. Property acquired through purchase is recorded as an asset, and the related liability is recorded regardless of the timing of the payments. In many cases, the asset may be fully used or sold before the related obligation is fully paid. But a long-term lease is considered to be equivalent to a purchase only if an equity in the property is created—that is, only if the payments for the use of the property exceed the decline in the service value of the property. In his dissent to *Opinion No. 5*, Spacek stated that ". . . this leads to the unsupportable conclusion that the payment of prepaid rent creates a liability and the nonexistence of prepaid rent eliminates a liability."[13] There is, therefore, little logic in basing the recording of an asset and the related liabilities on the mere timing of the payments. Instead of basing the capitalization decision on the substance of the agreement, this similarity appears to be based on the form of the lease contract.

The argument for the similarity in substance, however, is based on the following logic. An installment purchase of property is traditionally recorded as an acquisition of an asset and the recording of a liability. Usually, the installment purchase has two basic characteristics: (1) the installment payments usually exceed the decline in the service value of the asset in order to protect the security of the seller, and (2) any residual value at the termination of the contract belongs entirely to the buyer or can be acquired by the buyer by making a final payment. If one or both of these characteristics are present in a lease contract, equity is being acquired and the lease is assumed to be equivalent to a purchase. But if neither is present, it is assumed that the lessee is acquiring only the current service value of the asset.

Opinion No. 5 states that when an equity in the property is not created, the lease contracts represent ". . . nothing more than executory contracts requiring continuing performance on the part of both the lessor and the lessee for the full period covered by the leases."[14] Thus, it is argued that, particularly if the lease is subject to cancellation or default, the future benefits under the lease do not represent unconditional rights and therefore do not have the usual characteristics of assets. Likewise, the lease obligation is assumed to lack the usual characteristics of liabilities. It is also argued that these leases can be disclosed best in footnotes because their terms are sufficiently complicated that they can be disclosed only by lengthy explanations.

Capitalization of Property Rights in Long-Term Leases. In AICPA *Accounting Research Study No. 4,* Myers went considerably beyond the recommendation in *Bulletin No. 38* and beyond the subsequent recommendations of *Opinion No. 5.* With respect to sale-and-leaseback transactions, he recommended that they be recorded as single financing transaction by debiting cash and crediting an appropriately designated liability. The property accounts should be left in the accounts and depreciated in the usual manner. His main point of departure, however, was in the recommendation that—

. . . the present value of contracted lease payments should be placed among the assets and liabilities on a balance sheet *to the extent* that they represent

---

[13] *Ibid.,* p. 35.

[14] *Ibid.,* p. 29.

the acquisition of the right to use property. The portion representing periodic services to be performed by the lessor should not be capitalized.[15]

Thus, he found a similarity between the owning of property and all long-term leases, not just those that result in an equity in the property.

The distinction between that portion of the lease payments that represents the acquisition of property rights and that portion that represents the purchase of periodic services is taken from an analogy with the ownership of property. The ownership rights generally include the rights to hold, use, and dispose of property within certain restrictions of the law and the rights of others. A long-term noncancelable lease has most of these rights of ownership with the exception of disposal; but, in many cases, the lessee can purchase ownership rights for a nominal sum at the termination of the lease. When property is owned, the value of the property rights is capitalized by setting up an asset equal to its cost when acquired. However, the cost of maintenance and periodic payments for insurance and taxes are charged to expense only as they are incurred or accrued. No asset or obligation is generally shown in the balance sheet for the cost of services and other expenditures necessary to provide proper use of the property during its lifetime. Similarly, only the property rights being acquired under the terms of a lease should be capitalized. That is, where the terms of the lease require the lessor to provide necessary repairs and to pay taxes, insurance, and other costs of making the property available and useful to the lessee, that portion of the periodic lease payments representing the payment for these services should be excluded from the amount capitalized in the balance sheet. The payments for these items should be recorded as expenses in each period of payment, as with owned property.

One of the advantages of capitalization of the property rights inherent in lease contracts is that it presents a clearer presentation in the financial statements of the rights and obligations of the firm. It also permits better comparability with firms that own their property and with other firms with long-term leases. The capitalization, however, does not eliminate the necessity for additional disclosure, by footnote or otherwise, of the annual payment and other material terms of the lease contract. Finally, a major advantage of capitalization is that it permits a separation of the property rights and the lease obligations. Thus, the value of the property can be amortized independently of the timing of the contractual payments, in a manner similar to the depreciation of owned plant and equipment.

Two of the major problems of capitalization of the property rights are (1) the difficulty in separating that portion of the rentals considered to be

---

[15] John H. Myers, "Reporting of Leases in Financial Statements," *Accounting Research Study No. 4* (New York: AICPA, 1962), p. 38.

payment for property rights and that considered to be payment for services yet to be performed, and (2) the selection of a proper rate of interest for capitalization. The value of the property rights can be estimated either by estimating the value of the property without the additional services provided and subtracting the discounted value of the property at the termination of the lease, or by estimating the value or cost of the services to be provided by the lessor annually. In the latter method, the annual payment for the property rights can be estimated by subtracting the value of the annual services from the total annual lease payment.

If the cost or other value of the property is known, an estimate of the rate of interest is not necessary or it can be computed implicitly from the value of the property and the annual payments. However, if the value of the property is not known, the annual property rights must be capitalized by applying an appropriate rate of discount. This may be the market rate of interest available for long-term credit for firms with similar risks or the rate recently paid by the firm for long-term credit. In either case, the rate may be adjusted upward slightly because of the nature of the lease contract.

Capitalization of All Long-Term Noncancelable Commitments. An alternative approach to the above methods of handling long-term leases is to consider them a part of the broader problem of long-term noncancelable commitments. The Accounting Principles Board, in *Opinion No. 5*, recognized that the problem of long-term leases is a part of the larger problem of executory contracts but it did not investigate this issue. Whenever a firm enters into a long-term contract to acquire goods or services and to make appropriate payment, certain specific rights and obligations arise. If these goods and services are acquired on a year-to-year basis or under contracts that are cancelable on short notice, the rights and obligations are generally not material regarding their effect on the balance sheet, and it is appropriate to record the transactions when the goods and services are received or accrued or when payment is made. No capitalization is necessary. But, if the contract is noncancelable by either party and if each has a valid and material claim against the other, the contract should be capitalized and the discounted value of both the rights and obligations should be disclosed.

While this position does not have the support of currently accepted accounting practice, it does have considerable merit in its favor. A contract to purchase a given quantity of goods gives rise to a liability just as much as an obligation to pay for goods already acquired. The main difference is that in the first case the firm has an obligation to pay for goods when they are received, but in the latter case the obligation is to pay for goods that have already been received. In the case of the non-cancelable contract to purchase, there is not an unconditional right of offset. The purchasing firm has an obligation to pay for the merchandise to be acquired under the contract even though it should decide later that the goods are not wanted. The going-concern postulate assumes that the firm intends to carry out its commitments and it also assumes that other firms will normally carry out theirs. The nature of the obligation is not different simply because of a possible default on the part of the seller. Of course, if the seller does default, a right of unconditional offset does arise and the obligation to pay for the unperformed part of the contract may be canceled. But default is not the normal pattern, and the best expectation is that both sides of the contract will be carried out.

The asset arising from the long-term commitment is the right to receive goods or services, and this claim should be recorded on the basis of the discounted amount of its expected values. As with receivables, the value of the claim depends on the expectations that they will materialize. The possibility of default is the exceptional case rather than the rule, and this possibility should be taken into consideration only in the determination of the valuation of the rights and obligations.

The distinction between long-term and short-term obligations is not important in the decision whether or not to capitalize the rights and obligations. The important criterion is the materiality of the discounted value. But there are many other considerations that must be studied thoroughly before a definite broad principle of capitalization can be established. Employment contracts probably should not be capitalized because they are usually cancelable by the employee. Other types of contracts may also be cancelable with a penalty. Capitalization should be necessary only if the penalty is sufficient to act as a deterrent to unilateral default.

In general, the arguments for capitalization of long-term commitments other than leases are not as compelling as the arguments for capitalization of long-term leases. The similarity to property rights is not generally present. The obligation is not generally an alternative to other forms of financing. And the asset or right received is not generally amortized over its useful life. But one advantage of capitalization of long-term commitments in general is that the valuation of the rights can then be treated separately from the valuation of the obligations. A contract to purchase a given quantity of merchandise over a long period of time at a predetermined price results in an obligation that is monetary in nature but rights or claims that are nonmonetary. If the value of the goods to be acquired should change materially, capitalization would permit showing the valuation of the asset differently from the valuation of the liability. Therefore, holding gains and losses could be recorded conveniently. The current practice of recording losses on long-term commitments requires setting up a partial liability or a reserve. Capitalization permits the valuation of the asset and the valuation of the liability to be treated separately.

The application of this general principle to long-term leases has the effect of extending the amount to be capitalized. The principle does not limit the amount to the property rights. If the lease requires a fixed payment that is noncancelable, the entire amount should be capitalized regardless of whether it represents payment for property rights or for additional services, including repairs, maintenance and taxes, and other services related to the use of the property. On the other hand, if the lessee is required to take care of the maintenance and repairs and pay the property taxes and insurance, these amounts should also be capitalized as long-term commitments if they require unconditional payments regardless of whether or not the property is used. But payments for utilities and other related costs should not be capitalized if they can be avoided by not using the property.

One of the main arguments against the capitalization of long-term commitments other than long-term leases is that since capitalization is not a common practice in this case, there is no lack of comparability among firms. But, in the case of long-term leases, there is a lack of comparability, because those firms that own property do show the assets and related obligations while those that lease the property traditionally have failed to show either the asset or the liability in the balance sheet. Thus, many financial ratios computed from the statements of property owners cannot be compared with similar ratios computed from the statements of firms that lease property. It is also claimed that, generally, the payments under long-term commitments other than leases are more related to the associated expenses than is generally the case with long-term leases. It may also be argued that the reporting of current payments better discloses the actual cash flows of the firm. However, the capitalization of noncancelable commitments should not preclude the disclosure in financial statements of current cash payments and the amount and timing of future cash requirements under the contracts.

ACCOUNTING FOR PENSION COSTS AND OBLIGATIONS

Employee pension plans are a type of long-term commitment, but they possess some special characteristics not found in other types of commitments. While pension plans vary widely in the detailed requirements, most plans contain a provision that each employee upon reaching a specified age can retire and receive a specified or determinable amount during each year of his retirement. Most plans also require that the firm provide a pension trust fund which, with the income from the investment of the fund, will be adequate to assure continued payments under the terms of the plan. The firm itself may manage the trust fund or the amounts funded may be transferred periodically to a trustee or agent who in turn manages the investments and makes the retirement payments. The basic accounting problems are: (1) allocation of the pension costs to periods, (2) reporting appropriate amounts for the rights and obligations existing at different points in time, and (3) disclosure of major terms of the plan, including the amount and timing of cash disbursements required or intended to be paid into the fund.

The Allocation of Pension Costs

The total costs of providing for retirement benefits to employees can be determined by estimating the total amount that must be in the fund which when invested will permit the payment of the agreed retirement benefits to eligible employees during their expected retirement periods. This total pension cost is uncertain, because the amounts expected to be paid depend on several future events, including the longevity of the employees after retirement, death before retirement, employees leaving the firm or losing retirement benefits for other reasons, and future changes in pension commitments. The amount required to be placed in the fund also depends upon the income that can be earned by the fund. Generally, these uncertainties can be resolved by the use of actuarial methods, and the computation is usually made by an actuary.

Since this total pension cost is assumed to represent an expense of operating the business, a major problem of accounting for pension costs is the allocation of this total cost to periods. Note, first, that the problem of allocating the pension cost to periods is not related to the methods of financing the pension plan, just as the method of amortizing the cost of plant and equipment is not related to the method of paying for such assets. Therefore, the process of allocating pension costs to periods is similar to the depreciation of plant and equipment, except that the costs of plant and equipment are measured by current or past transactions and prices while the costs of pension plans are measured in terms of expected cash outlays in the future. As with depreciation, the alleged objective of allocating pension costs is to match the expense with the net revenue contribution in each period. But since this is an impossibility, at least under current known methods, suggested methods have as their objective the prevention of widely varying charges from period to period within a firm. Such methods are claimed to have merit because they are systematic and prevent material distortion of net income by the whim of management. However, since they are based on arbitrary assumed relationships, the suggested methods cannot be supported on theoretical grounds. The arbitrary smoothing of income is not supported by theoretical or empirical research. These allocation methods, however, are generally discussed separately for current (normal) costs, prior service costs, and actuarial gains and losses.

Current Service Cost. The current service cost, generally referred to as normal cost, is the annual pension cost assigned to each year subsequent to the inception of the pension plan or a change in the plan. Although an infinite number of systematic allocation procedures could be devised for the determination of the current annual pension cost, APB *Opinion No. 8* recommended that "the annual provision should be based on an accounting method that uses an acceptable actuarial cost method."[16] However, since the actuarial cost methods are methods of financing the pension fund, it is difficult to understand why they necessarily represent good matching concepts. But in the absence of a theoretical base, this at least limits the choice to several alternatives. The Board did note, however, that the actuarial cost method selected for allocation purposes may differ from the method selected for funding purposes.

The several actuarial cost methods differ in that some result in decreasing pension costs until the plan reaches maturity while other methods result in level normal costs and others in increasing costs. The basic similarity is that all methods include an interest factor equal to the assumed earning rate on pension fund investments. The accrued benefit cost method assumes that each employee receives each year a pension benefit equal to the present discounted value of a given amount to be added to his pension fund at retirement or a specified number of units to be credited to his account at retirement (the unit credit method). Therefore, the pension cost is the accrual of the benefit assumed to be earned by the employee. As the employee approaches the retirement age, the accrued benefit each year will increase because it is discounted for a shorter period of time. The total pension cost for all employees, however, will depend upon several factors and it may become fairly level when the plan matures and the average age and number of employees become relatively constant. An increase in the normal cost allocated to each period for an employee may be supported on the grounds that the pension cost is a means of compensation and that it should be related to his other compensation, which is likely to increase during his employment period. However, the use of the investment earning rate is a crude method of adjustment for this factor and some plans take care of it by relating the retirement benefits accrued to the salary levels.

The projected benefit cost methods result in a level normal cost, equal to a constant sum for each individual which when invested at the earning rate will reach the projected benefit cost at retirement. The level amount will vary for different individuals, however, depending upon the age of the employee when he is hired or when the plan is started. The total cost will stay level after the plan matures, regardless of salary levels, so long as the projected benefit cost is correctly anticipated. Therefore, the result is similar to the straight-line method of depreciation. Since the net income contribution cannot be measured, a level pension cost is as logical as

---

[16] AICPA, *Accounting Principles, op. cit.,* p. 6543.

any other and it has the advantage of permitting greater predictability of its effect on income.

Since cash payments into the pension fund need not be paid according to the same actuarial cost method as that used to determine the pension expense, the pension fund may not accrue interest as rapidly as that assumed in the allocation method. If this is the case, an equivalent amount for interest expense should be accrued, but there is good argument for charging this to a separate financial expense rather than to the employment expenses.

While some arguments have been made in favor of accruing only pension costs that become legal liabilities of the firm, the general view is that expenses should be accrued even though the pension plan is subject to cancellation or has a terminal date established by a union contract. The most likely situation is that the pension plan will be continued indefinitely. APB *Opinion No. 8*, however, does make a recommendation for a minimum accrual to provide for vested benefits. Since vested benefits represent the amounts accruing to the employee even if his services with the firm are discontinued, such vested benefits represent a legal liability of the firm. However, if the vested benefits increase significantly during a year, *Opinion No. 8* permits a smoothing of the effect of this over several years by the use of a specific formula.

Prior Service Costs. When a pension plan is initiated or when the benefits are increased significantly, they are frequently made retroactive to apply to services performed prior to the inception of the plan or the alteration in the benefits. At least five alternatives have been suggested for treatment of these past service costs: (1) an immediate charge to income as an extraordinary item representing a correction of prior years, (2) an immediate charge to the income of the current period, (3) nonrecognition, (4) allocation over the remaining period of employment of the employee, and (5) allocation as an intangible over a period during which the benefits from the adoption of the plan or change are assumed to be received.

The immediate charge to retained earnings or to current income as either an operating charge or an extraordinary item was not approved by APB *Opinion No. 8* because it is assumed that these costs will benefit only current and future periods. The concept of prior service costs, however, is a misnomer, because it reflects the way the pension benefits of an employee are computed. It is not a cost of the prior period; but according to some actuarial cost methods, the pension benefit is computed by assuming that the accrual started when the employee would have been eligible to accrue benefits if the plan had been in effect at that time. Therefore, if such actuarial cost method is used for the allocation method, a lump sum which would have been allocated to the prior period remains unallocated. But since there was no benefit received by the firm in the prior periods, it cannot be a correction of prior years' income. And since the firm hopes to enjoy better employee relations in the future, there is no loss or gift to be recognized at the time of the adoption of the plan.

The argument that there should be no recognition of the prior service costs is based on the assumption that if the plan is to continue indefinitely into the future, the accrual of normal costs plus interest on unfunded past service costs will be adequate at all times to provide for current retirement benefits. This is the minimum provision for annual pension costs recommended by APB *Opinion No. 8* except for the provision for vested benefits. But this is a confusion of the costs of a retirement plan and the funds necessary to carry out the plan. The costs do exist and should be reported even though full funding may not be necessary from a financial point of view.

Several of the actuarial cost methods are based on the assumption that the projected benefit represents the amount that accrues with interest only from the inception of the plan or change until retirement. Therefore, no prior service cost arises; the entire projected cost less the assumed interest on the pension fund is allocated over the period after the inception of the plan. The result is that total normal pension costs will be greater for several years after starting the plan than after the plan matures, because the costs per year for employees who have been with the firm for many years will be greater than the costs allocated to new or younger employees. The disadvantage with this procedure is that it is difficult for an investor or analyst to determine when the pension costs will start to decline.

Other actuarial cost methods assume that the benefits to the employees started accruing when the employee would have been eligible if the plan had been in effect. Therefore the total amount that would have been allocated to this period, plus the interest that would have been earned if it had been funded, represents the prior service cost. APB *Opinion No. 8* recommends that as an alternative to the minimum annual provision discussed above, the annual charge can include, in addition to the normal cost and interest equivalents, a portion of the prior service cost amortized on a 40-year basis. The maximum provision should be an allocation of the prior service cost or increase in benefits over a 10-year period in addition to the normal cost and equivalent interest. The allocation of the prior service cost over such arbitrary periods appears to have as its sole objective the smoothing of net income. Although it is consistent with recommendations regarding the amortization of intangibles, no logical matching is obtained. Without a logical matching concept there appears to be no reason for permitting such wide deviations in the amount of pension costs that can be reported, particularly considering that some of the actuarial methods result in normal costs that may be twice the amount resulting from the use of other methods.

Actuarial Gains and Losses. Since actuarial assumptions are based upon expectations of future events, it may be necessary to revise the pension cost estimates as conditions change. These actuarial gains and losses represent the difference between the actuarial assumptions and the actual conditions affecting the final pension cost. They may arise from investment gains and losses or changes in interest rates or other actuarial assumptions. While many firms have recognized these gains and losses by adjusting the pension costs of the current period, APB *Opinion No. 8* recommended that either they should be spread over several years (10 to 20 years being suggested), or an averaging method should be used. Under averaging, the net gains and losses that occurred in the past and those expected to occur are averaged and such average annual net gain or loss is included in the normal cost. Either spreading or averaging results in a smoothing of net income and cannot be justified unless it can be assumed that the normal cost is adjusted to what it should have been if correct actuarial assumptions had been made.

Presentation of Pension Assets and Liabilities

Since the pension plan is a form of long-term commitment, there is some merit in the capitalization of the discounted amount of the entire retirement benefits to employees. But the rights under the pension plan are not unconditional, and furthermore, they represent only a part of the benefits to be received from employees during their remaining years of service. The obligation under the pension plan is also only a small part of the total obligation to employees for services to be performed. Therefore, since there is little justification for the capitalization of future wage commitments, there is also little justification for the capitalization of future pension benefits and obligations.

APB *Opinion No. 8* recommends that the difference between the amount that has been charged as normal pension costs and the amount that has been funded should be shown in the balance sheet as an accrued pension liability or a prepaid pension cost. However, if the vested pension rights are greater than the sum of the pension fund and the accrued pension liability, the excess should be reported as both a liability and a deferred charge. If no legal obligation exists because of the vesting, un-funded prior service costs need not be shown as a liability. This recommendation, however, is inconsistent with the normal presentation and concept of liabilities. As discussed in Chapter 15, obligations should be reported whether or not they are legally binding. The vesting of pension rights should not be the determining factor for the presentation of pen-sion obligations.

Because the pension cost allocation is not based on logic or upon actual accrued benefits to employees, a liability or prepaid pension cost reflecting the difference between the amount funded and the amount allocated to pension cost has no real meaning except to permit the firm to stay within the double-entry accounting system. But there should be a disclosure of the extent to which the pension plan is being funded with respect to the actuarially determined pension obligation. Because of the limitations of the asset and liability concepts, this disclosure cannot be made adequately in the body of the balance sheet alone. More extensive descriptions should be included in the footnotes or other presentations to disclose the extent to which the pension plan is being funded, including an amount for prior service costs if the actuarial method used treats them separately. Furthermore, the annual cash disbursements required or expected to be made into the pension fund should be disclosed in cash flow or funds flow statements or in footnotes to the financial statements.

SELECTED ADDITIONAL READING ON CHAPTER TOPICS

Income Tax Allocation

American Institute of Certified Public Accountants, Accounting Principles Board. "Accounting for Income Taxes," *Opinion No. 11.* New York, December, 1967.

BLACK, HOMER A. "Interperiod Allocation of Corporate Income Taxes," *Accounting Research Study No. 9.* New York: AICPA, 1966.

DRINKWATER, DAVID, and JAMES DON EDWARDS. "The Nature of Taxes and the Matching Principle," *Accounting Review,* Vol. XL (July, 1965), pp. 579–82.

HAWKINS, DAVID F. "Controversial Accounting Changes," *Harvard Business Review* (March–April, 1968), pp. 20–41.

KELLER, THOMAS F. *Accounting for Corporate Income Taxes.* Ann Arbor: University of Michigan Press, 1961.

NORGAARD, CORINE T. "Financial Implications of Comprehensive Income Tax Allocation," *Financial Analysts Journal* (January–February, 1969), pp. 81–85.

NURNBERG, HUGO. "Present Value Depreciation and Income Tax Allocation," *Accounting Review,* Vol. XLIII (October, 1968), pp. 719–29.

PERRY, RAYMOND E. "Comprehensive Income Tax Allocation," *Journal of Accountancy,* Vol. CXXII (February, 1966), pp. 23–32.

Price Waterhouse & Co. "Is Generally Accepted Accounting for Income Taxes Possibly Misleading Investors?" New York: 1967.

REVSINE, LAWRENCE. "Some Controversy Concerning 'Controversial Accounting Changes'," *Accounting Review,* Vol. XLIV (April, 1969), pp. 354–58.

WAUGH, JAMES B. "The Interperiod Allocation of Corporate Income Taxes: A Proposal," *Accounting Review,* Vol. XLIII (July, 1968), pp. 535–39.

WINBORNE, MARILYNN G., and DEE L. KLEESPIE. "Tax Allocation in Perspective," *Accounting Review,* Vol. XLI (October, 1966), pp. 737–44.

Tax Allocation—Empirical Studies

LIVINGSTONE, JOHN LESLIE. "Accelerated Depreciation, Cyclical Asset Expenditures and Deferred Taxes," *Journal of Accounting Research*, Vol. V (Spring, 1967), pp. 77–94.

VOSS, WILLIAM M. "Accelerated Depreciation and Deferred Tax Allocation," *Journal of Accounting Research*, Vol. VI (Autumn, 1968), pp. 262–69.

Allocation of Carry-Backs and Carry-Forwards

WILLIAMS, DOYLE Z. "Reporting Loss Carryovers in Financial Statements," *Accounting Review*, Vol. XLI (April, 1966), pp. 226–34.

Investment Tax Credit

HORWITZ, RONALD M. "The Investment Credit, Deferred Income Taxes and Accounting Measurement," *Accounting Review*, Vol. XXXIX (July, 1964), pp. 618–21.

KELLER, THOMAS F. "The Investment Tax Credit and the Annual Tax Charge," *Accounting Review*, Vol. XL (January, 1965), pp. 184–89.

MOONITZ, MAURICE. "Some Reflections on the Investment Credit Experience," *Journal of Accounting Research*, Vol. IV (Spring, 1966), pp. 47–61.

——. "Can Laws Coerce Accounting?" *Journal of Accounting Research*, Vol. V (Spring, 1967), pp. 129–30.

SEAMAN, JAMES L. "Lessons from the Investment Credit," *Accounting Review*, Vol. XL (July, 1965), pp. 617–21.

STAMP, EDWARD. "Some Further Reflections on the Investment Credit," *Journal of Accounting Research*, Vol. V (Spring, 1967), pp. 124–28.

Long-Term Leases Reported by Lessee

AICPA, Accounting Principles Board. "Reporting of Leases in Financial Statements of Lessee," *Opinion No. 5.* New York, September, 1964.

COOK, DONALD C. "The Case Against Capitalizing Leases," *Harvard Business Review, Vol.* XLI (January–February, 1963), pp. 145–62.

GRAHAM, WILLARD J., and HAROLD Q. LANGENDERFER. "Reporting of Leases: Comment on *APB Opinion No. 5*," *Journal of Accountancy*, Vol. CXIX (March, 1965), pp. 57–62.

HALL, WILLIAM D. "Current Problems in Accounting for Leases," *Journal of Accountancy*, Vol. CXXIV (November, 1967), pp. 35–42.

MELLMAN, MARTIN, and LEOPOLD A. BERNSTEIN. "Lease Capitalization Under *APB Opinion No. 5*," *New York Certified Public Accountant*, Vol. XXXVI (February, 1966), pp. 115–22.

MULCAHY, GERTRUDE (ed.). "Accounting for Long-Term Leases," Parts I and II, *Canadian Chartered Accountant*, Vol. XC (March, 1967), pp. 204–06 and (April, 1967), pp. 284–86.

RAPPAPORT, ALFRED. "Lease Capitalization and the Transaction Concept," *Accounting Review*, Vol. XL (April, 1965), pp. 373–76.

Accounting for Pension Costs

AICPA, Accounting Principles Board. "Accounting for the Cost of Pension Plans," *Opinion No. 8*. New York, November, 1966.

DREHER, WILLIAM A. "Alternatives Available Under *APB Opinion No. 8:* An Actuary's View," *Journal of Accountancy*, Vol. CXXIV (September, 1967), pp. 37–51.

GANNER, THOMAS A., and WALTON W. KLINGSBERY. "Determining the Cost of Pension Plans," *Financial Executive*, Vol. XXXIV (August, 1966), pp. 12–27.

HICKS, ERNEST L. "Accounting for the Cost of Pension Plans," *Accounting Research Study No. 8*. New York: AICPA, 1965.

MOONITZ, MAURICE, and ALEXANDER RUSS. "Accrual Accounting for Employee's Pension Costs," *Journal of Accounting Research*, Vol. IV (Autumn, 1966), pp. 155–68.

PARROTT, WILLIAM H. "The Allocation of Pension Costs to Periods of Time," *Management Accountant*, Vol. L (April, 1969), pp. 39–42.

PHILIPS, G. EDWARD. "Pension Liabilities and Assets," *Accounting Review*, Vol. XLIII (January, 1968), pp. 10–17.

PHOENIX, JULIUS W., JR., and WILLIAM D. BOSSE. "Accounting for the Cost of Pension Plans—*APB Opinion No. 8*," *Journal of Accountancy*, Vol. CXXIV (August, 1967), pp. 27–37.

———. "Accounting for the Cost of Pension Plans—More Information on *APB Opinion No. 8*," *Journal of Accountancy*, Vol. CXXIV (October, 1967), pp. 31–40.

chapter 17

Ownership Equities

While the rights of owners of business firms are many and varied, those rights of greatest interest to accountants are the rights to share in the cash or property distributions of the firm, the residual rights to assets in the case of final liquidation, and the equity (proprietary) rights in a going concern—the right to sell or transfer all equity rights in the enterprise. The disclosure of these economic rights and any abridgment of them are important objectives in the presentation of financial statements.

In this chapter, the nature of ownership equities is explored and viewed from the perspective of several equity theories—the proprietary theory, the entity theory, the residual equity concept, the enterprise theory, the funds theory, and the commander theory. The objectives and logic of the classification of partnership and stockholder equities are then discussed in the general framework of the various equity theories. The classification of equities in consolidated statements is treated separately. The following chapter is concerned with changes in the composition of stockholder equities, those changes arising from business combinations and quasi reorganizations, and the potential dilution effect of convertible securities and warrants.

THE NATURE OF OWNERSHIP EQUITIES

Individual assets and liabilities of a business enterprise can be defined and measured independently of other elements in the accounting equation. This is not so with ownership equities (also commonly known as proprietorship or stockholder equities in a corporation). Generally, there is no pretense that these equities as presented in the balance sheet represent either the current market value or the subjective value of the enterprise to the owners. The total amount presented in the statements is a result of the methods employed in measuring the specific assets and liabilities. Since the total value of the firm to its owners cannot be measured from the valuation of specific assets and liabilities, the reported amount of proprietorship cannot represent the current value of the rights of the owners. Instead of looking at specific rights to future benefits, as with assets, or at specific obligations of the enterprise, as with liabilities, the proprietorship or stockholders' equity looks at the aggregate resources from the view of ownership rights, equities, or restrictions, depending on the equity concept employed.

Although the rights and priorities of some classes of corporate stock may be similar to those of some types of long-term debt, in general the differences between stockholder equities and liabilities are: (1) the extent to which other equity holders have priority rights; (2) the degree of certainty in the determination of amounts to be received by the equity holders; and (3) the maturity dates of the payments of final rights. In normal circumstances, creditors have priority over stockholders for the payment of periodic interest and in the repayment of principal. Preferred stockholders may have priorities over common stockholders but both are residual claimants in relationship to the claims of creditors. In a viable concern, the amounts payable to creditors are usually determinable in advance, the amount to be paid at maturity is usually a fixed number of dollars, and the interest payments are usually expressed as a percentage of a face value. Dividend payments to stockholders are generally dependent on the earning of income, the availability of cash, and a formal declaration by the board of directors. The maturity date of creditors' claims is generally fixed or determinable, while stockholders' equities do not represent legal obligations of the enterprise. Dividends become liabilities only upon declaration by the board of directors and, with few exceptions, stockholders cannot expect repayment of capital at definite or determinable dates.

The Proprietary Theory

As indicated in Chapter 2, the notion of proprietorship originated with an attempt to place logic into the exposition of double-entry bookkeeping.[1] In the accounting equation $\Sigma A - \Sigma L = P$, the proprietor is the center of interest. The assets are assumed to be owned by the proprietor, and the liabilities are his obligations. Hatfield, however, in his discussion of the proprietary concept, treated liabilities as negative assets and stated that capital, ". . . in the initial bookkeeping equation, represents the net wealth of the proprietor."[2] Regardless of the treatment of liabilities, the proprietorship is considered to be the net value of the business to the owners. When the business is organized, this value is equal to the investment of the owners. During the life of the enterprise, it is equal to the original investment and additional investments plus the

---

[1] Above, pp. 29–30.

[2] Henry Rand Hatfield, *Accounting, Its Principles and Problems* (New York: D. Appleton & Co., 1927), pp. 171, 221.

accumulated net income in excess of that withdrawn by the proprietors (or minus net losses and withdrawals). It is, therefore, a wealth concept.

Under the proprietary theory, revenues are increases in proprietorship and expenses are decreases. Thus, net income, the excess of revenues over expenses, accrues directly to the owners; it represents an increase in the wealth of the proprietors. And since income is an increase in the owner's wealth, it is immediately added to his capital or proprietorship. Cash dividends represent withdrawals of capital, and retained earnings are a part of total proprietorship. Stock dividends represent merely a transfer from one section of proprietorship to another; they do not represent income to the stockholders. Interest on debt, however, represents an expense of the proprietors and should be deducted before arriving at net income to the owners. Corporate income taxes are likewise expenses in the proprietorship theory; however, some argue that the corporation is acting as an agent of the stockholders in paying the tax that is really a tax on the income of the stockholders.

The all-inclusive concept of income is based on the proprietary theory, because net income includes all items affecting proprietorship during the period except dividend withdrawals and capital transactions. But the classification of the sources of net income is independent of the equity theory employed. The proprietary concept does not dictate how the net income shall be computed; it only emphasizes the nature of the change in proprietorship and its classification in the balance sheet.

The proprietary theory is adapted best to the single proprietorship form of organization, because in this form there is generally a personal relationship between the management of the business and the ownership. The proprietary theory is also a logical framework for the partnership form of organization, particularly when it is organized under common law. In accounting for both the single proprietorship and the partnership forms, the proprietary theory appears to dominate, particularly because net income is added each period to the personal capital accounts of the owners.

The proprietary theory is not so readily applicable to the corporate form of organization as it is to the single proprietorship and the partnership. However, many writers have chosen to look through the veil of the corporate form and describe the total of the capital stock, paid-in surplus, and retained earnings as the net wealth of the stockholders,[3] implying the proprietary theory. The proprietary theory is also implied in many accounting practices and in accounting terminology relating to corporations. For example, the net income of the firm is often referred to as "net income to the stockholders." Furthermore, financial statements generally make reference to "earnings per share" and occasionally to

---

[3] See for example *ibid.*, p. 172.

"book value per share." But these computations are not necessarily meaningless without the proprietary concept. "Net income to stockholders" can be interpreted to be the residual net income allocable to the stockholders' equity, and "book value per share" can be interpreted to be the book equity per share under the entity approach.

The equity method for accounting for nonconsolidated investments in subsidiaries also implies a proprietary concept. The parent's proportionate share of each year's income is added to the investment account on the theory that the income of the subsidiary accrues to the stockholders, including the parent corporation as the major stockholder. It may be argued, however, that this accrual is merely a reflection of an increase in the value of the stock held by the parent and is, thus, in accord with the entity view. However, there is little merit in this view, since the proportionate share of the recorded income of the subsidiary is at best a poor indicator of an increase in the value of the stock to the parent.

The Entity Theory

The existence of a business entity separate from the personal affairs and other interests of the owners and other equity holders is recognized in all concepts of ownership and equities. In the entity theory, however, the business firm is considered to have a separate existence, even personality, of its own. The founders and owners are not necessarily identified with the existence of the firm. While this relationship finds legal and institutional support in the form of the corporation, it is also found in other forms of business enterprise, and the entity theory is said to have actually preceded the corporate concept. This separate existence is not unique to business enterprises; universities, hospitals, governments, and other organizations have a continuity of existence separate from the lives of the organizers and even separate from the individuals directly associated with the organization.

The entity theory is based on the equation: $\Sigma A = \Sigma L + SE$, or Assets = Equities (Liabilities plus Stockholders' Equity). While the items on the right-hand side of the equation are occasionally called liabilities, they are really equities with different rights in the enterprise. The main difference between the liabilities and the stockholder equities is that the valuation of the rights of the creditors can be determined independently of other valuations if the firm is solvent, while the rights of the stockholders are measured by the valuation of assets originally invested plus the valuation of reinvested earnings and subsequent revaluations. But the rights of the stockholders to receive dividends and share in net assets upon liquidation are rights as equity holders rather than as owners of the specific assets.

The liabilities, therefore, are the specific obligations of the *firm*, and the assets represent the rights of the *firm* to receive specific goods and services or other benefits. The valuation of assets, therefore, should reflect a measurement of the benefits to be received by the enterprise.

The net income of the enterprise is generally expressed in terms of the net change in the stockholders' equity, not including changes arising from dividend declarations and capital transactions. This is not the same as saying that the net income is the income to the stockholders, as is implied in the proprietary theory. It represents the residual change in equity position after deducting all other claims, including interest on long-term debt and income taxes. It is personal income to the stockholder only if the value of his investment has increased. And the change in the value of the investment may be independent of the corporate net income, because investment values depend on expectations regarding future dividends and on investment market conditions.

The difference between the concept of income to stockholders under the proprietary or agency viewpoint and the stockholders' equity in income under the entity theory is expressed by Paton and Littleton as follows:

Emphasis on the entity point of view . . . requires the treatment of business earnings as the income of the enterprise itself until such time as transfer to the individual participants has been effected by dividend declaration. Between the moment when profit has been earned by the enterprise and the moment when profit-assets are distributed to investors, those who contributed capital have a claim against the assets according to their contracts. It is this claim and not profit itself that is expressed by the credit to some proprietary account.[4]

A much narrower view of the entity theory was expressed by Husband in his proposal of the proprietary or agency viewpoint as a logical alternative to the entity theory. In his strict interpretation of the entity theory, the "income earned by the corporate endeavor is the property of the corporation, per se."[5] Only the dividends declared represent income to the stockholders. The retained earnings represent the *"corporation's proprietary equity in itself."*[6] It also follows logically from this view that, since the corporate income is not added to the stockholders' equity, a stock dividend represents income to the stockholders. While this interpretation does have some merit, the generally accepted view is that while corporate income accrues to the corporation rather than directly to the stockholders, the retained earnings represents an allocation of the undistributed income to the stockholders' equity. That is, the entity theory is based on the equation Assets = Equities; no portion of the total equities remains unallocated. Therefore, a stock dividend is not income to the stockholders but rather a reclassification of the stockholders' equity.

[4] W. A. Paton and A. C. Littleton, *An Introduction to Corporate Accounting Standards,* American Accounting Association Monograph No. 3 (AAA, 1940), p. 8.

[5] George R. Husband, "The Entity Concept in Accounting," *Accounting Review,* Vol. XXIX (October, 1954), p. 554.

[6] *Ibid.*

Although an allocation of corporate income to specific equities is possible under the entity theory, a strict adherence to the concept requires that interest on debt should be considered a distribution of income rather than an expense. That is, all distributions or allocations to equity holders are considered to be allocations of corporate income. The 1957 AAA statement, for example, stated that "interest charges, income taxes, and true profit-sharing distributions are not determinants of *enterprise* net income."[7] Income taxes, in the opinion of the author, however, are not a distribution of income but rather an expense of the business, as discussed in Chapter 5.

Since corporate net income is not considered to be directly the net income of the stockholders, revenues and expenses are not increases and decreases in the stockholders' equity. Revenue is the product of the enterprise, and the expenses are the goods and services consumed in obtaining the revenue. Therefore, expenses are deductions from revenue, and the difference represents the corporate income to be distributed to stockholders in the form of dividends or reinvested in the business.

While the entity theory has its main application in the corporate form of business enterprise, it is also relevant to unincorporated firms that have a continuity of existence separate from the lives of individual owners. The entity theory is also relevant to the preparation of consolidated financial statements. However, in this case, the economic entity rather than the legal entity is the relevant accounting unit. The classes of equity holders are increased to include the minority stockholders as a separate class, in addition to the stockholders of the parent corporation and all creditors of the parent and its subsidiaries.

Several authors have proposed or implied that the proprietary and equity theories lead to different bases for asset valuation. Under the proprietary theory, it is claimed that the assets should be valued in terms of current values because the owners' equity is considered to be their net worth or net wealth. Under the entity theory, the firm is not concerned with current values because the emphasis is on the accountability of cost to the owners and other equity holders.[8] However, recent discussions of valuation have stressed the importance of current values as relevant in the determination of the income of the enterprise, as a measure of the future services to the firm, and as a basis for future decisions of management.[9] Even in meeting the objective of accountability to equity holders,

---

[7] AAA Committee on Accounting Concepts and Standards, *Accounting and Reporting Standards for Corporate Financial Statements and Preceding Statements and Supplements* (Columbus, Ohio: AAA, 1957), p. 5.

[8] See for example Stephen Gilman, *Accounting Concepts of Profit* (New York: Ronald Press Co., 1939), p. 74.

[9] See for example Robert T. Sprouse and Maurice Moonitz, "A Tentative Set of Broad Accounting Principles for Business Enterprises," *Accounting Research Study No. 3* (New York: AICPA, 1962), pp. 23–36.

it may be argued that current values are just as important as costs. Therefore, in the author's opinion, the proprietary and entity theories do not necessarily dictate different valuation bases.

The Residual Equity Theory

Paton referred to the "residual" equity as one of several types of equity under the entity theory. In the entity theory, the stockholder has an equity in the firm like other equity holders; he is not the owner. Paton emphasized, however, the special relationship of the residual equity holder to the work of the accountant.[10] Changes in asset valuation, changes in income and in retained earnings, and changes in the interests of other equity holders are all reflected in the residual equity of the common stockholders. But even though the equities of creditors, preferred stockholders, and common stockholders should be classified separately, they are all equities under the entity theory.

As presented by Staubus, the residual equity point of view is a concept somewhere between the proprietary theory and the entity theory.

In the residual equity theory, all investors in a corporation except common stockholders are thought of as outsiders; from the pure entity point of view, all investors are outsiders.[11]

In this view, the equation becomes: Assets − Specific Equities = Residual Equity. The specific equities include the claims of creditors and the equities of preferred stockholders. However, in certain cases where losses have been large or in bankruptcy proceedings, the equity of the common stockholders may disappear and the preferred stockholders or the bondholders may become the residual equity holders.

The objective of the residual equity approach is to provide better information to common stockholders for making investment decisions. In a corporation with indefinite continuity, the current value of common stock is dependent primarily upon the expectation of future dividends. Future dividends, in turn, are dependent upon the expectations of total receipts less specific contractual obligations, payments to specific equity holders, and requirements for reinvestment. Trends in investment values can also be measured, in part, by looking at trends in the value of the residual equity measured on the basis of current values.[12]

Common stockholders are generally thought to have a residual equity

---

[10] William Andrew Paton, *Accounting Theory* (New York: Ronald Press Co., 1922), pp. 84–89.

[11] George J. Staubus, "The Residual Equity Point of View in Accounting," *Accounting Review*, Vol. XXXIV (January, 1959), p. 13. See also the discussion of the residual equity point of view in George J. Staubus, *A Theory of Accounting to Investors* (Berkeley and Los Angeles: University of California Press, 1961).

[12] *Ibid.*, p. 33.

in the income of the firm and in the net assets upon final liquidation. Since financial statements are not generally prepared on the basis of possible liquidation, the information provided regarding the residual equity should be useful in predicting possible future dividends to common stockholders. The income statement or combined income statement and statement of retained earnings should show the income available to the residual equity holders after all prior claims are met, including the dividends to preferred stockholders. The equity of the common stockholders in the balance sheet should be presented separately from the equities of preferred stockholders and other specific equity holders. The funds statement should also show the funds available to the firm for the payment of common dividends and other purposes.

An alternative approach to the residual equity concept is that, since under the usual assumption of enterprise continuity the common stockholders' only claim against the corporation is to receive dividends when and if declared, the residual equity in capital is not assigned to the residual equity holders. Both the initial capital supplied by the common stockholders and the retained earnings are, therefore, the equity of the corporation in itself.[13] Note that this is similar to the strict entity approach proposed by Husband.

The "residual" concept has a different meaning in the context of the earnings per share computations; however, it can be considered an extension of the residual equity theory. A residual security is defined as a common stock equivalent, which would include debt, preferred stock convertible into common stock, and warrants for the purchase of common stock. Under certain conditions, holders of these securities may obtain the rights of common stockholders, thus giving them residual rights. The disclosure of these potential residual rights and the potential dilution effect is discussed in Chapter 18 in a section on "earnings per share."

The Enterprise Theory

The enterprise theory of the firm is a broader concept than the entity theory, but less well defined in its scope and application. While in the entity theory the firm is considered to be a separate economic unit operated primarily for the benefit of the equity holders, in the enterprise theory the corporation is a social institution operated for the benefit of many interested groups. In the broadest form, these groups include, in addition to the stockholders and creditors, the employees, customers, the government as a taxing authority and as a regulatory agency, and the general public. Thus, the broad form of the enterprise theory may be thought of as a social theory of accounting.

---

[13] David H. Li, "The Nature of Corporate Residual Equity under the Entity Concept," *Accounting Review,* Vol. XXXV (April, 1960), pp. 258–63.

This concept of the firm is most applicable to the large modern corporation that has been obliged to consider the effect of its actions on various groups and on society as a whole. From an accounting point of view, this means that the responsibility of proper reporting extends not only to stockholders and creditors but also to many other groups and to the general public.[14] The large corporation can no longer operate solely in the interests of the stockholders, and it cannot be assumed that the forces of competition will necessarily protect the interests of other groups. Employees, particularly through labor unions, utilize accounting data in presenting their claims for wage increases or increases in other benefits. Customers and regulatory agencies have been interested in the fairness of price changes, and the government has been interested in the effect of price changes on the general state of the economy.

The most relevant concept of income in this broad social responsibility concept of the enterprise is the value-added concept discussed earlier, in Chapter 5. The total value added by the enterprise is the market value of the goods and services produced by the firm less the value of the goods and services acquired by transfer from other firms. Thus, value-added income includes all payments to stockholders in the form of dividends, interest to creditors, wages and salaries to employees, taxes to governmental units, and earnings retained in the business. The total value-added concept also includes depreciation, but this is a gross product concept rather than a net income concept.

The term *"enterprise* net income" as used by the 1957 AAA statement is a narrower concept than the value-added concept. In addition to the traditional net income to stockholders, this concept of enterprise net income includes interest charges and income taxes. Therefore, it is closer to the entity concept. The inclusion of income taxes in enterprise net income apparently stems from the idea that this is paid to the government on behalf of the stockholders. If income taxes are an expense under the entity theory as proposed earlier, they should not be included in enterprise net income. If a broader concept of income is intended, the enterprise net income should also include payments to other beneficiaries of the corporation.

The position of retained earnings in the enterprise theory is similar to its position in the entity concept. It either represents part of the equity of the residual equity holders or it represents undistributed equity—the equity of the corporation in itself. In the entity theory there is considerable merit in the former position; but in the enterprise theory, the earnings reinvested in the business do not necessarily benefit only the residual stockholders. Capital employed to maintain market position, to

---

[14] See, for example, Dwight R. Ladd, *Contemporary Corporate Accounting and the Public* (Homewood, Ill.: Richard D. Irwin, Inc., 1963), particularly chaps. ii and iii.

improve productivity, or to promote general expansion may not necessarily benefit only the stockholders. In fact, it is possible that the stockholders may not be benefited at all if future dividends are not increased.

An extension of this position is proposed by Ladd, who suggests that the retained earnings required for growth may not be income at all.[15] The costs of anticipated growth are thought of as representing expenses required before profit can be computed. There may be no intention to distribute this amount to the stockholders or to any other group. All groups may benefit if the growth provides additional value added. But if the growth or reinvestment is needed merely to maintain a competitive position or to provide the productivity necessary to meet increasing costs, the stockholders may not benefit from this so-called income reinvested in the business.

The Fund Theory

The fund theory abandons the personal relationship assumed in the proprietary theory and the personalization of the firm as an artificial economic and legal unit under the entity theory. Instead, the fund theory substitutes an operational or activity-oriented unit as the basis for accounting. This area of interest, called the *fund*, includes a group of assets and related obligations and restrictions representing specific economic functions or activities.

The fund theory is based on the equation: Assets = Restrictions of Assets. Assets represent prospective services to the fund or operational unit. Liabilities represent restrictions against specific or general assets of the fund. The invested capital represents either legal or financial restrictions on the use of assets; that is, the invested capital must be maintained intact unless specific authority has been obtained (with few exceptions) for partial or complete liquidation. Even partial liquidation of invested capital, however, requires full disclosure. Appropriations of retained earnings represent restrictions imposed by management, by creditors, or by legal requirements. Unappropriated retained earnings also represent restrictions—a residual overall restriction that the assets be used for the purposes for which they are devoted. Thus, all equities represent restrictions imposed by legal, contractual, managerial, financial, or equitable considerations.

The fund concept has found its greatest usefulness in governmental and nonprofit institutions. In a university, for example, the most commonly used funds are the special funds for endowments, student loan funds, plant funds, auxiliary enterprises, and current educational activities. Each of these funds has its specific assets restricted for particular

---

[15] *Ibid.*, p. 60.

purposes. But the fund concept is also relevant to specific areas of interest within the corporation or even for areas of interest greater than the single legal form of enterprise. Examples of direct applicability are the sinking fund in financial reporting, branch or divisional accounting, and accounting for estates and trusts. The preparation of consolidated statements is also an application of the fund theory just as much as it is an extension of the theory of the economic entity. The fund theory can also be applied in other areas of financial accounting; for example, as discussed in Chapter 10, the fund theory can easily find usefulness in the distinction between current and fixed assets and equities.[16]

Although the income concept can be retained under the fund theory, it is not the central concept in financial reporting. Instead, the description of the operations of the fund are presented more clearly in the funds statements. The major financial statements are statistical summaries of the sources and dispositions of funds. An income statement, if it appears at all, is an adjunct of the funds statement—a description of the funds provided from operations. Although the funds theory is not oriented toward the interests of any specific equity holder, all interested parties should be able to find the information they want in the financial statements. Like the enterprise theory, it is neutral with respect to the interests of any specific group.

The Commander Theory

Goldberg suggested that neither the proprietary theory nor the entity theory is wholly satisfactory in explaining accounting, for both emphasize the notion of ownership.[17] As an alternative, he suggested that accounting should focus on the effective economic control of resources by the managers or "commanders" of an enterprise. While there may be many levels of control within a firm and by the directors and stockholders, a final control may come from an informed public opinion. Therefore, the emphasis is on what the commander has done rather than on the special interests of the owners or other interested groups.

According to the commander theory, financial statements are in the form of reports of stewardship. The balance sheet represents a report of accountability of the resources entrusted with the managers. The income statement expresses the results of the activities of the commander and the ways the resources have been used to achieve these results. The funds

---

[16] See William J. Vatter, *The Fund Theory of Accounting and Its Implications for Financial Reports* (Chicago: University of Chicago Press, 1947), p. 60.

[17] Louis Goldberg, *An Inquiry into the Nature of Accounting*, AAA Monograph No. 7 (AAA, 1965), p. 162.

statement reports the ways in which the manager has obtained resources and how he has applied them.

The commander theory does provide some insight into the nature of accounting, but, like the proprietary and the entity theories, it fails to provide a concept of the firm which can be used as a basis for the development and evaluation of accounting theory. Goldberg suggested that to whom accounting reports are directed is relatively unimportant compared with the reporting of what the commander has done.[18] However, it is difficult to see how the accountant should decide what activities are relevant to include in the report if he does not know to whom the reports are directed. In Great Britain, annual reports are required to include information regarding the value of exports and the amount and nature of contributions made by the firm. Presumably, these disclosures are thought to be relevant for an evaluation by the public of the economic and social effects of the firm's actions. In the United States, emphasis has been placed on information useful primarily to investors. As discussed in Chapter 4, information regarding the needs of the users of financial statements is necessary before relevant information can be selected to be included in accounting reports.

Summary of the Equity Theories

The several theories or approaches to the nature of an enterprise and the relationships or activities to be reported are all relevant under different circumstances of organization, economic relationships, and accounting objectives. Therefore, accounting theory and practice should take an eclectic approach to these theories. All help to explain and understand accounting theory and to develop logical patterns for the extension of theory. However, care must be taken to apply the most logical equity theory in each case and to use a single theory consistently in the same circumstances. For example, it is inconsistent to argue that a pro rata share of a subsidiary's income should be added to the investment in the parent company's assets (a proprietary concept) and also to argue that a stock dividend of the subsidiary should require the capitalization of an amount equal to the market value of the shares capitalized (a narrow entity concept). It is not inconsistent, however, to apply the proprietary concept to a small single proprietorship, the entity concept to a medium-sized corporation, and the enterprise or commander theory to a very large corporation.

Each of the several equity theories interprets the economic position of the enterprise in a different way and thus presents a different emphasis on the method of disclosure of the interests of the several equity holders or

---

[18] *Ibid.*, p. 170.

interested groups. They also lead to different concepts of income or different methods of disclosing the equity interests in the income of the enterprise. There is also some evidence that the proprietary concept requires an emphasis on current valuations of assets, the entity and funds theories are neutral with respect to asset valuation, the enterprise theory emphasizes the need for a market output valuation concept, and the commander theory implies an emphasis on valuation concepts consistent with stewardship reporting. However, the associated valuation method and the associated concept of income are primarily the result of the way the several concepts have been developed. The problem of valuation and the most relevant concept of income are basically independent of the equity theory selected. The main questions raised by the several equity concepts are related to the questions: (1) Who are the beneficiaries of net income? and (2) How should the equity relationships be shown in the financial statements?

THE CLASSIFICATION OF SINGLE PROPRIETORSHIP AND PARTNERSHIP EQUITIES

In the single proprietorship, the entire ownership equity is generally presented in one amount. In accordance with the proprietary theory, this equity represents the ownership of the business by the proprietor. There is no need to present subclassifications of this equity because the owner is not restricted regarding how much he invests in or takes out of the business and there are no superior claims other than those held by the creditors of the business. In case of liquidation or insolvency, the creditors can reach the personal assets of the owner, making the distinction between permanent invested capital and reinvested earnings of little importance for this purpose. This does not mean, however, that a distinction is not made between capital and income. Income is computed periodically and added to the capital account at the end of each period; capital transactions (withdrawals and additional investments) are recorded directly in the capital account; and all changes are generally summarized in a separate statement of the proprietorship.

The ownership equity of a partnership is similar to the equity of a single proprietor except that it is classified according to the interests of each of the partners. Separate drawing accounts may be used to establish control over withdrawals or to force compliance with a withdrawal agreement. But even these accounts are generally closed into the capital accounts at the end of each period, so that no classification according to source of the equities is maintained.

What, then, is the value of the classification according to the several partners' interests? First, it should be recognized that this classification shows only the interest in the net assets of the business; each partner's interest in the income of the enterprise may be entirely different according to the terms of the partnership agreement. But the capital accounts do not show the specific rights of the partners in liquidation (except in the unusual case where there are no gains or losses in the liquidation process). If the gains and losses are allocated to the partners' capital accounts in a ratio other than the ratio of the capital balances, the final distribution to partners may be entirely different from the apparent interests in the business before starting liquidation. Therefore, the capital accounts serve primarily as a starting point in determining the distribution of assets in final liquidation and dissolution unless all or a part of the income is allocated on the basis of capital balances. Creditors are not as interested in the capital balances of the partners as they are in the total ownership equity and the personal assets of the partners, because any partner may become personally liable for any or all of the debts of the partnership.

THE CLASSIFICATION OF STOCKHOLDER EQUITIES

The relationships between a corporation, the stockholders, and the creditors are much more involved than the relationships in a single proprietorship or in a partnership. Therefore, the financial statements should present more information regarding these relationships than is expected in the financial statements of the less formal types of organization. But the information that is traditionally presented is an outgrowth of certain assumed legal and economic relationships rather than being a result of a complete analysis of the needs of the various users of financial statements. Therefore, traditional stockholder equity classifications attempt to meet several objectives and, as a result, meet none of the objectives adequately.

What are the objectives of stockholder equity classifications? The basic objectives should be to provide information to stockholders, investors, creditors, and other interested groups regarding the efficiency and stewardship of management and regarding the historical and prospective economic interests of the groups holding specific equities and the groups (such as employees, customers, and the government) that have a general economic interest in the corporation. In meeting these objectives, the information in the financial statements should disclose some or all of the following: (1) the sources of capital supplied to the corporation; (2) the legal restrictions on the distribution of invested capital to stockholders; (3) the legal, contractual, managerial, and financial restrictions on the distribution of dividends to current and potential stockholders; and (4) the priorities of the several classes of stockholders in partial or final liquidation. Each of these specific objectives of classification will be discussed and evaluated in the following paragraphs.

Classification by Source of Capital

Classification of stockholders' equity by its source is generally considered to be the major classification objective in balance sheet presentation. This emphasis is not misplaced, because a description of the sources of capital provides useful information regarding the historical development and the current position of the corporation. Corporate growth provided through internal sources of funds is relevant information when compared with a firm that has grown entirely through the sale of preferred and common stocks or through the sale of debentures.

The major sources of corporate stockholder equity are: (1) amounts paid in by stockholders, (2) amounts arising from the restatement of assets for changes in the purchasing power of the dollar, (3) the excess of net income over dividends paid to stockholders (earnings retained in the business), and (4) donations from other than stockholders. The traditional fourfold classification of stockholder equities—capital stock, paid-in surplus (capital surplus), revaluation surplus, and retained earnings—does not entirely meet the objective of classification by source, although it appears to meet it partially. The capital stock and paid-in surplus categories generally represent the amounts paid in by stockholders except that donations are generally included in the paid-in surplus classification. Revaluation surplus generally includes the write-up of assets prior to realization. If the write-ups represent increases in specific values rather than increases in prices in general, the revaluation surplus should be included in the retained earnings classification as an income source. Technically, the amounts arising from the restatement of assets for changes in purchasing power do not represent a separate source of capital. They should be allocated to paid-in capital and retained earnings if such an allocation is possible. As indicated in Chapter 7, the amounts paid in by stockholders should be restated and the remainder of the restatement should then be allocated to the retained earnings classification.

A main disadvantage of the conventional classification is that the classification by source is lost whenever transfers are made from retained earnings to capital stock and paid-in surplus by issuing stock dividends or other means. The original classification by source is also lost in a quasi reorganization and in some treasury stock transactions.

The Disclosure of Legal Capital

In a corporation, stockholders generally have no personal liability for the debts of the business; creditors must look only to the assets of the enterprise. Without this provision, corporate stock would not be so readily transferable as it is today. In order to obtain this provision, however, the legislatures felt a need to provide some protection to creditors from unscrupulous promoters, stockholders, or directors. To provide this protection to creditors, the courts and legislatures established the "trust fund theory." This title is a misnomer, however, because there is no actual fund established and there is no real "trust" in any legal sense of the word. The basic principle is that a restriction is placed on the amount of assets that can be distributed legally to the stockholders under normal circumstances prior to final liquidation.

Most states define legal capital or stated capital as the aggregate par value of all par value shares issued (not subsequently canceled) and the aggregate consideration received for all shares issued without par value. In the case of no-par value shares, however, many states permit the directors or stockholders to designate how much of the consideration received shall be classified as stated capital and how much shall be classified as paid-in surplus (capital surplus). A few states also require the excess of the amount paid in over the par value of par value shares to be included in stated capital. As a result, it is difficult to determine the exact amount of legal capital in specific situations. In general, it may be assumed that the legal capital is at least equal to the par value of par value shares plus the stated value of no-par value shares. But there are exceptions to this (e.g., in the case of wasting asset corporations).

Current financial statements do not disclose the amount of legal capital, although there are usually separate classifications for capital stock and paid-in surplus, a practice that apparently stems from the trust fund theory. But even a disclosure of the number of shares issued and outstanding of each class and the par value or stated value per share of each class is not adequate in many cases to permit the informed reader to compute the total legal capital. In some states, subscribed shares become a part of legal capital, and in other states they are included only after they have been paid for and issued. In some states, legal capital can be increased by a declaration of the board of directors without the issuance of additional shares. Differences in the treatment of treasury shares makes it difficult to know how they should be treated in the computation of legal capital.

As a result of the differences between legal capital and invested capital for accounting and financial purposes, the separation of invested capital into the two classifications (capital stock and paid-in surplus) is probably more misleading than helpful. An alternative would be to disclose in a footnote what the accountants consider to be the legal or stated capital, making it clear that a final determination of stated capital is a legal decision subject to court interpretation and not basically an accounting problem. While some state codes describe specifically what should be included in a paid-in surplus account or what accounts should be credited or charged in certain circumstances, none of the codes appears to dictate how the financial statements shall be classified or what disclosure is necessary in the statements. This is also true in Great Britain and in the Commonwealth countries, where the companies acts specify certain disclosures but do not dictate accounting procedures.

In the author's opinion, the disclosure of legal capital is probably unnecessary in all cases except in small or incipient corporations. In large and profitable concerns, the legal capital is generally a small part of the total stockholders' equity. In these cases, it is generally apparent that the amount of current and future dividends is not dependent on the amount of legal capital. Therefore, the entire stockholders' equity acts as a buffer for the protection of creditors, and the creditors rely more on the total resources, profitability, and financial policies of the firm than on the status of legal capital.

The Disclosure of Restrictions on the Disposition of Income

A disclosure of the *intended* distribution or disposition of the income of a corporation is not the same as a disclosure of the *restrictions* on the disposition of income. Frequently, the former is assumed from the latter, but generally this is unwarranted. Therefore, the classification of stockholder equities and footnotes to the financial statements should make a clear distinction between these two.

A first general assumption is that cash dividends should not be paid if the result will be to reduce net assets below the total capital stock and paid-in surplus of the firm, even though a part or all of the paid-in surplus may be distributed legally. This is a self-imposed restriction influenced by the accounting distinction between invested capital and income. If a dividend should be paid "out of" paid-in surplus, accounting principles would require that this be disclosed as a liquidating dividend— a return *of* capital rather than the usual assumption that a dividend is a return *on* capital. This disclosure is also required by the model corporation act adopted by many states.

It cannot be assumed, however, that any or all of the retained earnings will be made available for distribution to stockholders as cash dividends. In fact, the current titles for this amount of accumulated earnings deny this. "Earnings retained for use in the business" or simply "retained earnings" implies that the income not already distributed as dividends has been invested permanently in the business. This implication is supported by two general observations: (1) The dividend distributions of most large firms are correlated highly with the current year's income, the prior year's income, and the prior year's dividends. With a short lag and with minor deviations, there appears to be an attempt to limit dividends to income of the firm for the current year rather than pay dividends out of the earnings retained in prior years. (2) In most mature firms, the amount of retained earnings is either larger than the capital invested directly by stockholders or it is at least a large percentage of total stockholders' equity. Therefore, corporate financial policy would not permit the payment of dividends equal to retained earnings; to do so would be tantamount to a distribution of the capital of the corporation. What, then, is the logic behind the capitalization of stock dividends in excess of the legal or stated capital?

Since the classification of a part of stockholders' equity as retained earnings does not indicate the amount that is likely to be paid out as dividends in the future nor even the intent of the firm, an alternative is to show the legal, contractual, or financial restrictions on the payment of dividends. Care must be taken, however, not to leave the impression that unrestricted retained earnings will be or are likely to be distributed as dividends. The appropriation of retained earnings and the labeling of the residual as "unappropriated" or "free" is, therefore, possibly misleading. It may still be restricted by managerial or financial policy. A footnote disclosure may be less misleading. But even here, the restriction may be meaningless from the point of view of possible dividend distributions, particularly if only a small part of the total retained earnings is restricted. Therefore, classification of stockholders' equity according to the probable distribution of income or retained earnings should not be an objective and it should not be permitted to influence or distort the classification according to source. When amounts are transferred from retained earnings to permanently invested capital, there is a declaration that these amounts are henceforth not available for dividends. But the source should not be lost sight of. A separate classification entitled "retained earnings transferred to paid-in capital" would aid in maintaining the classification according to source and still disclose the restriction on dividend payments.

Dividend payments to common stockholders are also restricted by contractual preferences granted to preferred stockholders or other stockholder groups given priority rights above those of the residual stockholders. The traditional classification of stockholders' equity does not provide for disclosing these restrictions. Cumulative preferred dividends in arrears are not generally shown as appropriated retained earnings because under the entity theory all stockholders are treated as a group. Under the residual equity theory, an appropriation would be acceptable to disclose the restriction on the payment of dividends to common stockholders. But, as indicated above, all restrictions can be disclosed more fully by parenthetical explanations or by footnotes.

The Disclosure of Restrictions on Liquidation Distributions

Creditors always have priority in liquidation over stockholders, and certain classes of stockholders have priority over other classes by the terms of the corporate charter or by contractual arrangements. This liquidation preference of preferred stock may be equal to the par value or stated value per share or it may include a premium. Usually the preferred dividends in arrears are included if the preferred dividends are cumulative.

Liquidation preferences, therefore, are not the same as legal or stated capital, and an entirely different classification than that used to disclose legal capital would be needed to disclose them. But how important is it that they be disclosed? If a profitable corporation has no intent to liquidate, the liquidation preference may be relatively unimportant. And even if the corporation has incurred losses for one or several years, the liquidation preference may still be unimportant if the net assets of the firm exceed the amount of the liquidation preference by a wide margin. In these cases, the shareholders can determine their rights by reading the fine print on the back of their share certificates or by other means. But if the total liquidation preferences become large in proportion to total net assets or if partial or final liquidation appears likely, disclosure in the financial statements should be made clear.

Even the necessity for full disclosure of liquidation priority rights does not mean that classification is the best method of achieving this disclosure. Parenthetical and footnote disclosure will usually be adequate, as recommended by APB *Opinion No. 10*.[19] However, if the firm is in final liquidation or liquidation is being planned, the original source of the capital is unimportant and the final disposition is most relevant. Thus, since the objective of reporting has changed in this case, the classification objectives should also be changed. The residual equity theory should dominate the reporting of stockholder equities.

In the author's opinion, it is not possible to maintain consistent classification of stockholders' equity according to source, legal restriction, disposition or restrictions of earnings, and the partial or final distribution of invested capital. The classification of invested capital and retained earnings on the basis of committed and uncommitted capital appears logical from an accounting point of view alone; but in reality, in most large corporations, retained earnings have become a very significant part of invested capital without formal action by the board of directors. Therefore, it is the author's recommendation that the primary basis for classification should be source. And this source should not be disturbed by transfers of retained earnings to invested capital. The amounts so transferred should be designated as retained earnings formally capitalized.

Legal capital may be shown if it does not thereby disturb the classification according to source. Restrictions regarding the distribution of

---

[19] AICPA, *Accounting Principles* (Chicago: Commerce Clearing House, Inc., 1968), Vol. II, p. 6576.

earnings and the priorities of assets in liquidation can generally be disclosed properly by parenthetical notes or in footnotes. This major emphasis on classification according to source would permit a disclosure of the source of all distributions to stockholders. That is, payments should be designated as either (1) distributions of current income, (2) reductions of uncommitted retained earnings, (3) reductions of retained earnings capitalized, or (4) distributions of capital invested by stockholders or from other sources.

The sources of invested capital, however, can be disclosed more clearly in a cash flow or funds statement. As suggested by the Committee on External Reporting of the American Accounting Association, the stockholders' equity section of the balance sheet is fairly sterile with respect to its relevance to the needs of investors and creditors.[20] A major difficulty with this classification is that it is a residual, its amount being determined by the measurements of assets and liabilities. However, information regarding the current and potential relationships of the several classes of long-term equity holders is relevant for an evaluation of the current and prospective rights of each of the creditors and stockholders.

CONSOLIDATED FINANCIAL STATEMENTS

When one corporation has a majority ownership and control in one or more related subsidiary firms, valuable information can be obtained and presented by combining the financial data and preparing consolidated financial statements for the entire group. While the consolidated group is generally thought of as a single economic unit, the accounting procedures of consolidation frequently deny this. Therefore, there does not appear to be a reliance on a single theory such as the proprietary theory, the entity theory, or the funds theory to serve as a guide in the establishment of consistent logical procedures of consolidation. Furthermore, the classification of stockholders' equity has not developed into a logical, consistent pattern. In fact, accounting practice is far from being uniform in this area, reflecting either a lack of a logical basis for classification or a failure to agree on the basic objectives of classification. These areas are discussed at greater length in the following paragraphs.

The Purpose and Nature of Consolidated Financial Statements

Accounting Research Bulletin No. 51 states that

the purpose of consolidated statements is to present, primarily for the benefit of the shareholders and creditors of the parent company, the results of operations and the financial position of a parent company and its subsidiaries essen-

---

[20] Committee on External Reporting, "An Evaluation of External Reporting Practices," *Accounting Review,* Supplement to Vol. XLIV (1969), pp. 103–104.

tially as if the group were a single company with one or more branches or divisions.[21]

This objective implies that we should look through the legal relationships of the corporations and view the enterprise as a single economic unit. But the emphasis on the interests of the shareholders and creditors of the parent company is inconsistent with this major objective. If the entire enterprise is really one economic unit, all interested parties should be given equal consideration, as in the enterprise theory; or the entity theory should be expanded to include the entire economic entity rather than merely the legal entity of the parent corporation.

Consolidated Balance Sheet.   In the balance sheet, the common practice of adding together the separate classifications of assets and liabilities of the parent corporation and the subsidiaries is in keeping with the idea of presenting a financial statement of the entire enterprise as a whole. By eliminating all intercompany obligations and adding together all other assets and liabilities, a picture of the group as a single enterprise is obtained. However, when the cost to the parent company of a subsidiary's shares exceeds the proportionate book value of those shares, the conventional pattern is to show this excess value in the consolidated statements as consolidated goodwill unless it can be allocated to the specific assets of the subsidiary. To be consistent with the entity approach to consolidated statements, the revision of the asset valuation of the subsidiary should include not only the excess amount paid by the parent company but also the minority interest's share in this increased valuation.[22] Cost is relevant at the time of acquisition only because it is the best evidence of value. But when only a fractional interest is obtained, the cost of the partial interest should be used as evidence of the value of the whole. For example, if a 60 percent interest in a subsidiary (holding only one asset, a building with a book value of $50,000) is obtained by a parent company for $60,000, the value to the consolidated enterprise is $100,000, as evidenced by the payment of the parent. The recording of the building in the consolidated statements at $80,000 (representing the cost to the parent plus $20,000—the minority interest in the original cost) is not consistent with the general policy of including the full value of all other assets in the consolidated statements. This same reasoning cannot be applied to the valuation of consolidated goodwill, as discussed in Chapter 14.[23]

Consolidated Income Statements.   The enterprise theory is also followed in the preparation of consolidated income statements. Intercompany sales and intercompany profits are eliminated in their entirety, and

[21] AICPA, *op. cit.*, p. 6091.

[22] Maurice Moonitz, *The Entity Theory of Consolidated Statements* (Brooklyn: Foundation Press, Inc., 1951), pp. 58–59.

[23] See above, pp. 439–40.

other sales and expenses are combined to show the activities of the enterprise as a whole. This is in agreement with the position of *Accounting Research Bulletin No. 51*, which states:

The complete elimination of the intercompany profit or loss is consistent with the underlying assumption that consolidated statements represent the financial position and operating results of a single business enterprise.[24]

However, the occasional practice of allocating the entire intercompany profit or loss to the majority interest alone is not consistent with this position. *Accounting Research Bulletin No. 51* makes it permissible but not mandatory to allocate these intercompany profits or losses proportionately between the majority and minority interests.

The consistent application of the enterprise theory again breaks down in conventional practice, because most firms subtract the minority interest in the total income to arrive at consolidated net income.[25] Thus, the net income is not the income of the enterprise as a whole but only that portion allocated to the majority interest. But it is difficult to interpret just what this final income really represents, particularly if the minority interest is a negative figure arising from a net loss of the subsidiary. It is not in the nature of a residual equity in net income because there is no consideration for the preferred equities in either the majority or minority groups. And it does not provide useful information regarding the amount available for dividends to the majority interest because the parent firm may be able to pay dividends even though the subsidiaries are operated at a loss and vice versa. Therefore, the implication is that the consolidated net income represents the proprietary equity of the stockholders of the parent company in the income of the entire enterprise. But this is inconsistent with the entity or enterprise theories. It would be better to show the net income of the enterprise as a whole and then disclose separately the relative interests of the majority and minority interests.

The Classification of Consolidated Equities

In the classification of consolidated equities in published statements, there is not only a lack of uniformity but also a lack of understanding of the specific objectives. Is the objective to disclose the legal stated capital, the sources of capital, or the possible disposition of either income or invested capital?

There is little doubt that the position of legal capital and the extent of the legal protection to creditors can be presented more clearly in the

---

[24] AICPA, *op. cit.*, p. 6093.

[25] American Institute of Accountants, *Survey of Consolidated Financial Statement Practices* (New York, 1956), p. 19.

separate financial statements of each corporation than in the consolidated statements. The creditors of a subsidiary firm must look at the individual statements of the subsidiary to determine the relevant legal capital (if indeed, it can be found even there) and their relationships to other creditors. For, they, of course, have no claim against the assets of the parent corporation. But the creditors of the parent must also look at the separate statements of the parent firm to establish their specific relationship to stockholders and other creditors, because they have only a secondary claim against the assets of the subsidiary but a primary claim against the assets of the parent. Therefore, the presentation of legal capital and the rights of creditors cannot and should not be a major objective in the classification of the equities of a consolidated enterprise. However, many firms, through tradition, show on the consolidated balance sheet the par value of shares issued separately from the capital received in excess of par value.

Probably the most common objective in the classification of consolidated equities is to disclose the sources of capital. It is not uncommon to find captions designating the stockholders' equity section of the consolidated balance sheet as "sources from which capital was obtained" or "derived from." In practically all of these cases, however, the classification is not strictly according to source. The limitations of this method of classification are similar to the limitations of attempting to maintain a classification by source in unconsolidated corporations. But there are several additional limitations in consolidated statements. The capital obtained from the majority stockholders is represented by the capital stock and capital surplus of the parent firm in most cases. However, the minority interest is generally included among the liabilities or as a separate item between the liabilities and the stockholders' equity. This item generally represents the minority stockholders' interest in the total equities of the subsidiaries; but it is just as much a source of capital for the entire enterprise as is the capital contributed by the stockholders of the parent firm.

Another basic limitation of the conventional practice of classification by source is that the amount of capital derived from retained earnings is not clearly presented. In the first place, the minority interest is not generally classified according to the separate sources of capital invested by stockholders and earnings retained by the subsidiary. Also, of course, there is no distinction between the minority stockholders' interest in the retained earnings at the date of consolidation and the minority interest in the earnings retained since consolidation. In the second place, the consolidated retained earnings amount represents the earnings of the parent firm retained since its incorporation (except for transfers to capital stock and capital surplus) and the majority interest in the earnings of the subsidiaries retained since the date of consolidation. Thus, the consolidated retained earnings does not represent a homogeneous source of invested capital.

A suggested remedy to give the source objective a better role in the classification of consolidated equity is to include in the consolidated invested capital the minority interest in the total stockholders' equity at the date of consolidation, and to classify the retained earnings as either (1) that obtained from the earnings retained by the parent company since its organization, or (2) that retained by the subsidiary firms since the date of consolidation (without consideration of the majority's and minority's separate interests in the subsidiaries' retained earnings).[26]

By stating that consolidated statements are presented primarily for the benefit of the shareholders and creditors of the parent company, *Accounting Research Bulletin No. 51* implies that the objective is to show the possible distribution of income and capital or the relative equities of the beneficiaries in the consolidated enterprise. But information regarding ownership equities is relevant only if it provides some information about the possible distribution of income and capital. That is, it should show some information regarding the relative rights of the several classes of equity holders in any distributions that may be made. However, the conventional classification of equities of consolidated enterprises fails to disclose the possible distribution of income to majority and minority stockholders. If the subsidiaries are operating at a loss, the consolidated income may be distributed entirely to the majority stockholders without paying any dividends to the minority group. On the other hand, if the consolidated net income is obtained entirely from the operations of subsidiaries, substantial dividends may be required to be paid to the minority stockholders before the stockholders of the parent may be able to receive any dividends.

The conventional classification also fails to disclose the rights of the various classes of equity holders in the possible distribution of capital. Creditors, in general, have preference in liquidation over stockholders. The creditors of the subsidiaries, however, have no claim to the separate assets of the parent and, therefore, the bonded indebtedness of subsidiaries and of the parent should not be combined if the objective is to disclose this priority. The creditors of the parent have only a secondary claim against the assets of a subsidiary, on the same level as the claim of the minority interest. This fact is probably the strongest justification for classifying the minority interest among the liabilities or as a separate item between the liabilities and capital on the consolidated balance sheet.

We see, therefore, that the disclosure of the possible distribution of income and capital appears to be the major objective in the conventional classification of the equities of a consolidated enterprise. In the income

---

statement, the consolidated net income is assumed to represent the amount that could be distributed as income to the stockholders of the parent company. In the balance sheet, the separate interests of the creditors, minority stockholders, and stockholders of the parent company are presumably disclosed. But the failure to show just what these interests represent and what are the interrelationships of the several groups places severe limitations on the usefulness of this classification. Except when dissolution or reorganization seems probable or imminent, a strict classification by source would seem to provide more useful information to the readers of consolidated financial statements, although even this classification is of doubtful value because of the problems of measurement.

SELECTED ADDITIONAL READING ON CHAPTER TOPICS

Equity Theories

1964 Concepts and Standards Research Committee—The Business Entity. "The Entity Concept," *Accounting Review*, Vol. XL (April, 1965), pp. 358–67.

GOLDBERG, LOUIS. *An Inquiry into the Nature of Accounting, American Accounting Association Monograph No. 7.* AAA, 1965, pp. 162–74.

GYNTHER, REGINALD S. "Accounting Concepts and Behavioral Hypotheses," *Accounting Review*, Vol. XLII (April, 1967), pp. 274–90.

LADD, DWIGHT R. *Contemporary Corporate Accounting and the Public*, particularly chaps. ii and iii. Homewood, Ill.: Richard D. Irwin, Inc., 1963.

LI, DAVID H. "Nature of Corporate Residual Equity under the Entity Concept," *Accounting Review*, Vol. XXXV (April, 1960), pp. 258–63.

VATTER, WILLIAM J. "Corporate Stock Equities," *Modern Accounting Theory* (ed. MORTON BACKER), pp. 250–57. Rev. ed., New York: Prentice-Hall, Inc., 1966.

Classification of Stockholder Equities

BIRNBERG, JACOB G. "An Information Oriented Approach to the Presentation of Common Stockholders' Equity," *Accounting Review*, Vol. XXXIX (October, 1964), pp. 963–71.

BUTTIMER, HARRY. "The Evolution of Stated Capital," *Accounting Review*, Vol. XXXVII (October, 1962), pp. 746–52.

LOWE, HOWARD D. "The Classification of Corporate Stock Equities," *Accounting Review*, Vol. XXXVI (July, 1961), pp. 425–33.

Consolidated Financial Statements

American Institute of Certified Public Accountants. *Accounting Principles*, Vol. II: "Consolidated Financial Statements," *Accounting Research Bulletin No. 51*, pp. 6091–96. Chicago: Commerce Clearing House, Inc., 1968.

CATLETT, GEORGE R. and NORMAN O. OLSON. "Accounting for Goodwill," *Accounting Research Study No. 10*, pp. 96–100. New York: AICPA, 1968.

EGGINTON, D. A. "Unrealized Profit and Consolidated Accounts," *Accountancy*, Vol. LVI (May, 1965), pp. 410–15.

SAPIENZA, S. R. "Divided House of Consolidations," *Accounting Review*, Vol. XXXV (July, 1960), pp. 503–10.

SMOLINSKI, EDWARD J. "The Adjunct Method in Consolidations," *Journal of Accounting Research*, Vol. I (Autumn, 1963), pp. 149–78.

chapter 18

Changes in
Stockholders' Equities

While the original classification of stockholders' equity is generally considered to be descriptive of its source, changes and reclassifications of equities make it difficult to retain this information. For example, in the case of stock dividends or other transfers to invested capital, Sprouse and Moonitz recognized that

> . . . the amount transferred loses its identity as having been derived from the retention of earnings, and the stockholders' equity accounts no longer are classified strictly according to source.[1]

The main reason for the loss of the source information is that the conventional procedures to record changes and reclassifications of stockholders' equity are based primarily on other objectives. Generally, these procedures attempt to maintain a distinction between invested capital and retained earnings, disclose legal capital, and indicate the amount available for distribution as dividends. As a result, none of the objectives is met adequately. In this chapter, the procedures for recording changes and reclassifications of stockholders' equity, the problems of quasi reorganizations and business combinations, and the reporting of earnings per share are analyzed critically in terms of the relevant objectives and on the basis of consistent equity theories.

INCREASES IN INVESTED CAPITAL

What accountants call "invested capital" in a corporation may be increased by the subscription or sale of additional shares of stock, by the acquisition and resale of treasury shares, by the conversion of indebtedness into stockholder equities, and by the transfer of retained earnings into invested capital. However, a basic principle widely held at least since

---

[1] Robert T. Sprouse and Maurice Moonitz, "A Tentative Set of Broad Accounting Principles for Business Enterprises," *Accounting Research Study No. 3* (New York: American Institute of Certified Public Accountants, 1962), p. 44.

the early 1930's is that "earned surplus (retained earnings) should include no credits from transactions in the company's own stock or transfers from paid-in capital or other capital account."[2] Therefore, the apparent basic objective in the classification of these increases in capital is to prevent the showing of equity arising from capital transactions as income or retained earnings and to prevent the implication that these amounts are available for ordinary dividends.

Capital Stock Subscriptions

When shares of previously unissued stock are sold for cash or other consideration, the total increase in equity represents invested capital. While it is still common practice to separate this amount into two parts—par value or stated value and the excess over par or stated value—the entire amount represents capital invested by stockholders for an indefinite period. But when subscriptions for shares are received by the corporation, has the invested capital of the firm actually been increased or is there merely a promise to increase the capital?

In some states, the codes regulating corporations treat stock subscribed but not issued as a part of legal capital. However, the Model Business Corporation Act includes in "stated capital" only shares that have been issued.[3] But whether or not the subscribed shares are legal capital, they should be included in invested capital if (1) the subscriptions represent legal claims against the subscribers, and (2) the corporation intends to collect the subscriptions within a reasonable and definite period of time. If the subscriptions are not intended to be called or if time of call is indefinite, the subscriptions do not really represent invested capital. But a valid commitment to invest and a reasonable expectation that the amounts will be paid in to the corporation in due course should be sufficient to consider the subscriptions to be permanent investments.

Conversions of Debt and Preferred Stock

When convertible bonds are exchanged for stock, two methods have been suggested for treating the conversion: (1) The book equity of the long-term debt (the face value of the bonds plus unamortized premium or minus unamortized discount) is reclassified as capital stock and paid-in

[2] Executive Committee of the American Accounting Association, "A Tentative Statement of Accounting Principles Underlying Corporate Financial Statements," *Accounting Review*, Vol. XI (June, 1936), p. 191. Reprinted in AAA Committee on Accounting Concepts and Standards, *Accounting and Reporting Standards for Corporate Financial Statements and Preceding Statements and Supplements* (Columbus, Ohio: AAA, 1957), p. 63.

[3] Model Business Corporation Act, Committee on Corporate Laws of the American Bar Association, 1962, Sec. 2 (j).

surplus when the new shares are issued. No gain or loss is recognized on the transaction; the book value of the indebtedness is merely converted into stockholder equity. (2) The current market price of the bonds or the current market price of the stock is capitalized as stockholder equity, and the excess of the current price over the book value of the bonds is shown as a loss on conversion. If the book value of the bonds exceeds the current market price of the bonds or stock, a gain on conversion would result; however, it is unlikely that the bonds would be converted under these circumstances unless interest rates in the market had risen considerably since the bonds were originally issued.

A preference for method (1) is implied in APB *Opinion No. 14*, which recommends that the entire proceeds from the sale of convertible debt be classified as debt.[4] Since none of the initial proceeds is allocated to the conversion privilege, a gain or loss cannot be measured by comparing the book value of the securities with their market value or the market value of nonconvertible debt (with similar characteristics) at the time of the conversion. But this method is also assumed to follow the entity theory because all long-term equities are treated as interest in the enterprise, and a transfer from one type of equity to another does not change the capital invested in the enterprise nor should it result in enterprise income.

Method (2) was preferred by the American Accounting Association Committee on Accounting Concepts and Standards in 1957.[5] It is assumed to follow the proprietary theory because changes in the valuation of liabilities are considered from the point of view of their effect on the stockholders. However, to follow this concept through clearly, the gain or loss should be measured from the change in the investment value of the debt only. Since the investment value represents the value of nonconvertible debt with characteristics similar to the convertible securities except for the conversion feature, an allocation of the proceeds should be made to the conversion privilege and the portion allocated to debt (adjusted for discount or premium amortization) should be compared with the investment value at the time of conversion. The market value of the convertible securities is not relevant at either date, because the securities derive a part of their value from the conversion feature.

The conventional procedure for the conversion of preferred stock into common stock is to follow method (1). That is, the par value of the preferred plus the pro rata share of paid-in surplus on preferred shares is transferred to common stock and paid-in surplus on common. No gain or loss should be shown on this transaction because both are included in the stockholders' equity classification.

The sum of the par value of the preferred stock and the pro rata

---

[4] See above, pp. 455–58, for a discussion of the recording of convertible debt.

[5] AAA Committee on Accounting Concepts and Standards, *op. cit.*, p. 7.

portion of the paid-in surplus from the original sale of the preferred stock represents the source of the original invested capital. Note that it does not represent the amount of book equity of the preferred stock since, in the case of dissolution, preferred stockholders are entitled to the par value or liquidation value of the preferred stock. But there is some merit in reclassifying the paid-in surplus, because if all of the preferred stock is finally converted, it may be misleading to show paid-in surplus from the sale of preferred stock when there is no preferred stock outstanding. The transfer of these amounts from a preferred stock to a common stock classification does not violate the source objective because it all represents capital invested by stockholders. The reclassification represents mainly a change in the rights of the several classes of stockholders. Only if a transfer from retained earnings is required is the original source classification lost; and in this case, the reclassification of retained earnings is similar to a stock dividend, discussed below.

There is little merit in capitalizing the current market value of either the preferred shares retired or the new common shares issued. To do so implies a strict entity theory interpreting the retained earnings as the firm's equity in itself. It also implies that there are two transactions, a retirement of preferred shares resulting in a partial distribution of retained earnings and the sale of new shares of common stock at the current market value. However, the treatment of the conversion as a single transaction seems more logical, particularly since the convertible preferred shares are generally issued originally with the convertible feature.

Stock Dividends and Stock Splits

Both stock dividends and stock splits are basically financial maneuvers that have nothing to do with the accounting principles of income determination and balance sheet valuation. In fact, if accountants held strictly to the classification of equities by original source, there would be no need for equity reclassifications as a result of these types of transactions. The only requirement would be to disclose the change in the number of shares outstanding and any change in par value or stated value and recompute the reported earnings per share for the current and prior periods. This is the case with a pure stock split. Since there is no change in either the legal or stated capital, no reclassification of equity is necessary. The number of shares outstanding is increased in inverse proportion to the decrease in par value or stated value per share; if the increase in the number of shares is accompanied by an increase in the total capital stock (total par value or stated value of shares outstanding), a partial stock dividend is also present. On the other hand, a 100 percent (or other large percentage) increase in the number of shares held by the same stockholders without an increase in total stockholders' equity or a decrease in par value per share is considered to be a stock split effected in the form of a stock dividend.

When accountants recognize classification objectives other than by the original source of capital, stock dividends present a problem in the treatment and disclosure of the transaction. Basic questions arise regarding the nature of the transaction and the amount to be capitalized. The nature of the transaction depends, in large part, on the equity theory selected as the most relevant. The amount to be capitalized depends on the objectives of classification and the assumed nature of the transaction. The amounts most commonly suggested for capitalization are: (1) the par value or stated value (or other legal capital amount) of the shares issued as a dividend; (2) the current market value of the shares issued; and (3) the paid-in capital per share prior to the dividend, times the number of shares issued.

The Nature of Stock Dividends. Most accountants agree that stock dividends are not income to the recipients, but they differ in the reasoning leading to this conclusion. The AICPA Committee on Accounting Procedure based its belief that stock dividends are not income to the recipients on the entity theory.[6] It argued that the corporation is a separate entity and that there can be no income to the stockholders until there is a severance of corporate assets. The income of the corporation is corporate income, not income to the stockholders. Cash dividends represent a transfer of assets to stockholders and, therefore, represent income to the recipients; stock dividends may result in unrealized appreciation, but it is not income to the stockholders until it is realized by them as a result of a division, distribution, or severance of corporate assets. Note that a rigid adherence to the realization concept rather than the entity theory is the controlling feature of this argument.

Another interpretation of the entity theory that leads to different conclusions is that retained earnings represent a part of the total equity of the stockholders. Therefore, corporate income resulting in an increase in retained earnings is also an increase in stockholders' equity. Income is earned by stockholders when the value of their equity has increased either because of the reinvestment of corporate income, because of unrecorded increases in the value of the firm, or because of the transfer of equity from other equity holders as a result of price-level changes or other reasons. In this interpretation, neither cash dividends nor ordinary stock dividends are income to the common stockholders, since they do not result in an increase in the value of the stockholders' assets, including their equity in the firm.

Still another interpretation of the entity theory is that retained

---

[6] AICPA, *Accounting Principles* (Chicago: Commerce Clearing House, Inc., 1968), Vol. II, p. 6024.

earnings represent the equity of the corporation in itself. The stockholders' equity includes only the invested capital reflected in capital stock and paid-in surplus. Therefore, both cash dividends and stock dividends should be considered income to the stockholders, since they give them something they did not have before. A stock dividend increases the stockholders' equity by transferring to the stockholders a portion of the undivided corporate equity in itself.

The proprietary theory leads to the same conclusion as the first two interpretations—that stock dividends are not income to the recipients—but for different reasons. The income of the corporation is also income to the owners. Therefore, cash dividends represent withdrawals by the owners of what already belongs to them. Stock dividends represent a reclassification of equity, but they are not income to the owners, since there is no increase in total proprietorship.

The Capitalization of Par or Stated Value.   Under the prevalent interpretation of the entity theory, that stock dividends are not income to the recipients, the question becomes that of determining how much, if any, of corporate equity should be reclassified. If the objective of equity classification is to show the source of capital, the answer is that no reclassification should be made, since the original source has not changed. All that would be required is that proper disclosure should be made of the change in the number of shares outstanding. However, if we also wish to show the total amount of legal capital, it is necessary to transfer from retained earnings or paid-in surplus to capital stock an amount equal to the stated value of the shares issued as required by the state of incorporation. In most states and in the Model Business Corporation Act, this amount is the par value of par value shares or the stated value of no-par shares.

Most writers agree that the par or stated value is the minimum amount that should be capitalized because of the legal considerations involved. While the AICPA Committee on Accounting Procedure recommended the capitalization of fair value in certain circumstances, as indicated below, it clearly recognized the showing of legal capital as one of the objectives of classification. This is reflected in its statement to the effect that the minimum amount capitalized should be, in all cases, that necessary to meet legal requirements, but this does not prevent the capitalization of a larger amount per share.[7] It also recommended that there is no need to capitalize more than that necessary to meet legal requirements in two special cases: (1) when the number of additional shares issued is so great that it may reasonably be expected that the market price per share will be reduced materially, and (2) in the case of closely held companies where it may be expected that intimate knowledge of the corporation's affairs would preclude any implication by the stock-

---

[7] *Ibid.,* p. 6025.

holders that the stock dividends represent a distribution of corporate earnings.

If the objective of classification is to show the legal capital, it should be recognized that the classification by source is destroyed. It is possible to meet both objectives only by a dual classification, by showing the legal capital in a footnote, or by maintaining a separate item in the balance sheet for the retained earnings capitalized equal to the par value (or stated value) of the shares issued as a stock dividend.

The Capitalization of Market Price. Only in the very strict interpretation of the entity theory can a stock dividend be considered to be income to the stockholders. But in this interpretation the amount of the dividend is considered to be the current market price of the shares. For, it is held, the stockholders could sell these additional shares at this price and be as well off as they were before, since their relative equity (interpreted as representing their individual shares of capital stock and paid-in surplus) is increased because of the stock dividend but remains the same if these shares are sold. Thus it is interpreted as a distribution of undivided retained earnings by an allocation to the stockholders' permanent equity.[8]

Although the AICPA Committee on Accounting Procedure recognized that a stock dividend is not income to the recipient, it recommended that the amount to be capitalized (transferred to capital stock and paid-in surplus) should be an amount equal to the fair value (market value) of the shares issued in all cases where the amount of stock issued is so small in comparison with the total shares outstanding that it has no apparent effect on the market price per share.[9] The reasoning for this recommendation is that, because of general representations, the recipients look on the stock dividends as distributions of corporate earnings equal to the market price of the shares issued. Therefore, if less than the market price were capitalized, an amount of the retained earnings thought to have been distributed to the stockholders would be available for additional stock dividends or cash distributions.

In determining the conditions where the capitalization of market value is called for and those conditions where the capitalization of only legal capital is adequate, *Bulletin No. 43* (7B) states:

Obviously, the point at which the relative size of the additional shares issued becomes large enough to materially influence the unit market price of the stock will vary with individual companies under differing market conditions and, hence, no single percentage can be laid down as a standard for determining when capitalization of earned surplus in excess of legal requirements is called for and

---

[8] See for example George R. Husband, "The Entity Concept in Accounting," *Accounting Review,* Vol. XXIX (October, 1954), particularly p. 555.

[9] AICPA, *op. cit.,* p. 6024.

when it is not. However, on the basis of a review of market action in the case of shares of a number of companies having relatively recent stock distributions, it would appear that there would be few instances involving the issuance of additional shares of less than, say 20% or 25% of the number previously outstanding where the effect would not be such as to call for the procedure referred to in paragraph 10 (capitalization of fair value).[10]

As noted above, the capitalization of retained earnings results in an abandonment of the objective of classification by source of stockholders' equity. In its place is substituted the objective of showing the possible disposition of equity. Retained earnings is presumed to show the amount available for distribution in the future as either stock dividends or cash dividends. However, since most states permit at least stock dividends, and in many cases both cash and stock dividend distributions, out of paid-in surplus, this restriction on future distributions is purely a financial and accounting restriction. The main argument against this line of reasoning is that most firms do not intend to make cash distributions out of earnings retained in prior years except in emergency situations. Retained earnings generally represent earnings reinvested in the business without formal action; but it is erroneous to assume that just because there has not been a formal transfer to permanent invested capital, they are then intended to be used for future distributions.

Two other arguments for the use of market value in the capitalization of stock dividends are: (1) The stock dividend can be thought of as two transactions—a cash dividend to stockholders and a subsequent sale to them of stock at the current market price. Therefore, the cash dividend would reduce retained earnings by the market value of the shares and the subsequent sale of stock would increase invested capital by this same amount. (2) The cost to the corporation of the stock dividend is assumed to be the opportunity cost of giving the shares to stockholders rather than selling them in the market. That is, since the corporation could have sold the shares at market price, this is the best evidence of the amount of the dividend and the amount that should be capitalized. Both of these arguments are weak in that they assume situations that do not really exist. The corporation has a right to sell shares to its common stockholders at amounts less than the market price (with some exceptions), and this action does not generally injure any class of equity holder.

The main argument in opposition to the use of market values is that if the stock dividend is not income to the stockholders, it is misleading to act as if it were, even if some people may believe that it is so. The capitalization of the market value of the stock issued only helps to continue the illusion that the stockholder is receiving something comparable to a cash dividend or that he is receiving something that he did not have

---

[10] *Ibid.*, p. 6025, parenthetical note added.

already. This illusion is generally strengthened by the fact that most firms continue the same cash dividend per share after the stock dividend as before, resulting in an increase in the total dividends declared.

Another argument in opposition to the use of fair value is that market value represents the total equity of the stock in the firm, including both invested capital and retained earnings. Therefore, it is illogical to transfer from retained earnings to invested capital that which represents both of these. It is better to present the transaction as a partial stock split with an accompanying increase in legal capital. In other words, the original source of capital should not be disturbed; disclosure of the increase in legal capital can be made in footnotes or by other means. This procedure would have the additional advantage of presenting a proper interpretation of retained earnings—as income reinvested permanently in the business.

The Capitalization of Paid-In Capital per Share. While proposed less frequently than the capitalization of fair value or legal capital, the capitalization of the invested capital per share (the par or stated value per share plus the paid-in surplus per share) is not entirely without merit. From an accounting point of view, it has more merit than the capitalization of only the legal capital. If the invested capital is thought of as capital committed to the enterprise, there is some logic in maintaining the same dollar commitment per share. If less than this amount is capitalized, there is some dilution of committed capital.

On closer analysis, however, the objective of this procedure appears quite weak. The amount of legal capital can be disclosed in the same way that the capitalization of par or stated value meets this objective. However, by the transfer of retained earnings to paid-in surplus, the objective of classification by source is further distorted and the objective of showing disposition of capital is substituted. The amounts transferred to capital stock and paid-in surplus represent committed capital and the residual retained earnings represents that part of equity that is uncommitted and, therefore, available for later distributions. The weakness in this assumption is that, in general, there is no intent to make cash dividend distributions that will reduce retained earnings. For most mature corporations, retained earnings represent permanent invested capital just as much as does the paid-in surplus. No intended or likely distribution is disclosed by this reclassification.

Stock Options and Stock Warrants

Stock rights are frequently granted to current stockholders permitting them to purchase shares of stock (in proportion to the shares held) at a price less than the market price or less than the price at which the shares are offered to others. Generally, the granting of these stock rights does not result in an increase in invested capital because no new capital is brought into the enterprise until the stock is sold. According to the objective of classification by source, this solution is correct. But it is inconsistent with the procedure recommended by the AICPA for the handling of stock dividends discussed above. A stock dividend is an extreme form of a stock right—a right to acquire shares with no additional cost. Therefore, the main difference between a stock dividend and a stock right is the amount to be paid by the stockholders for the additional shares received by them. Turning the analogy around, a stock right is a stock dividend in the amount of the value of the right—the excess of the market value of the shares over the purchase price to the stockholders. To be consistent with the recommendations for the treatment of stock dividends, this amount should be capitalized by a transfer from retained earnings to invested capital, usually paid-in surplus. But, in the opinion of the author, the capitalization of market value is illogical in both situations because neither is a source of invested capital.

When stock warrants are sold by the firm, however, the proceeds represent invested capital whether or not the warrants are exercised. If the warrants are exercised, the original proceeds plus the additional amount paid by the holders to acquire the shares represent the total amount invested by the new stockholders, and they should be classified accordingly. Prior to the time the warrants are exercised, however, a potential dilution of dividends and earnings per share exists. The effect of this dilution is discussed below in the section on earnings per share.[11]

Rights Granted to the Purchasers of Other Securities. Detachable warrants are frequently granted to purchasers of bonds giving them the right to purchase common stock at a fixed price (frequently less than the market price of the stock when the rights are granted). As discussed in Chapter 15,[12] APB *Opinion No. 14* recommended that the market prices of the bonds and the warrants be used to allocate the proceeds from the sale of the securities to debt and to stockholders' equity. When the warrants are exercised, the amount allocated to the warrants plus the additional amount paid for the shares is treated the same as proceeds from the sale of new stock issues. However, since bonds with detachable warrants are not different in substance from convertible debt, both should be accounted for alike, as discussed previously.

An allocation is even less important when common stock options are granted to purchasers of preferred stock (or vice versa). In this case, the entire amount paid in by the stockholders represents invested capital. There is little advantage in showing the source from preferred stockholders separately from that obtained from common stockholders, par-

---

[11] See pp. 551–56.
[12] See p. 458.

ticularly when the two sources are not independent of each other. A separation of the invested capital into the two classes does not change the rights of the two classes of stockholders nor does it aid in disclosing these rights. However, if legal capital is also to be shown, an allocation may become necessary if the option price is below legal or stated capital.

Employee Stock Purchase Plans. Stock options are granted frequently to employees as a means of raising capital and as a means of gaining widespread ownership among the officers and other employees of the enterprise. AICPA *Bulletin No. 43* recommends, in these cases, that no compensation need be presumed, and therefore only the amounts paid in by the employees should be included in stockholders' equity. Three conditions are generally present that indicate that the transaction does not involve compensation to the employees: (1) The purchase price should not be "lower than is reasonably required to interest employees generally or to secure the contemplated funds."[13] (2) The option period is generally short. (3) The granting of the option does not generally impose additional obligations on the employees.

Executive Stock Option Contracts. The granting of stock options to executives has become a popular method of providing compensation because of the tax advantage to the recipient. When the stock option meets certain restrictions imposed by the Internal Revenue Service, no personal income tax is paid by the recipient when the option is received and the gain on the sale of the stock acquired with the options is taxed at the capital gains rate when certain technical conditions are met. But in qualifying for a restricted stock option, the corporation loses its right to reduce the corporate income tax by the amount of the compensation. Therefore, an option that is equivalent in amount to the aftertax cost of compensation paid in cash would be of greater value to the executive than the cash salary only if he is in a relatively high income tax bracket. Nevertheless, if compensation is involved, the amount of the compensation should be recorded as an expense of the corporation and the amount of the invested capital should be increased by this amount or the aftertax cash salary equivalent. However, accountants are not agreed as to when compensation, if any, should be recorded and as to the method of determining the amount of compensation.

One view, applying the strict entity approach to accounting, is that the services received for which the stock options are granted do not cost the corporation anything and therefore should not be recorded at all.[14] However, this argument is weak because it is based on the assumption that cost to the entity must result in a decrease in its net assets. If this were

---

[13] AICPA, *op. cit.*, p. 6053.

[14] See for example Arthur H. Dean, "Employee Stock Options," *Harvard Law Review*, Vol. LXVI (June, 1953), p. 1438.

true, there would be no reason to record nonmonetary assets acquired by the issuance of stock. But it is possible to invest services in the business just as it is possible to invest nonmonetary assets. The main difference is that the services benefit the current period while the nonmonetary assets may benefit a future period or periods.

Accounting Research Bulletin No. 43 clearly recognizes the possibility of compensation arising out of stock option contracts. If the cost of the services received is material, it should be recorded and allocated to expense ". . . over the period of service for which the payment of the compensation seems appropriate in the existing circumstances."[15] Those accountants who recognize the existence of compensation generally agree that the amount of the compensation should be apportioned over the period that the services are received by the enterprise. The main area of disagreement is in the valuation of the services and the determination of the resulting increase in invested capital arising from the stock option grant. The most commonly proposed valuation methods are: (1) the excess of the fair value of the stock over the option price at the date of the option grant, (2) the excess on the date the option becomes the property of the employee, (3) the excess of the fair value over the option price at the date the option is first exercisable, (4) the excess on the date that the option is actually exercised, (5) the cost to the corporation at the date of exercise adjusted for the income tax effect to the firm, and (6) the probable value of the option to the recipient at the date of grant.

1. The Excess Value at Date of Grant. The AICPA Committee on Accounting Procedure recommended in *Bulletin No. 43* that the value of the compensation should be the excess of the fair value of the stock over the option price at the date that the option is granted.[16] The main reasons for the choice of this date are summarized as follows: (*a*) The value at this date is assumed to be measurable and meaningful to both the employee and the employer. Although an option would have some value even if the option price were the same as or greater than the market value of the shares, the committee considered it impracticable to measure this value. (*b*) The value at the date of grant is assumed to be the value that both parties had in mind when the option was granted. Any additional value of the option to the employee is offset by the restrictions imposed on him. From the point of view of the corporation, the value of the options at the date of grant must be estimated in order to determine the number of options to grant as just compensation for the services received. (*c*) The excess value at the date of grant represents the cost of restricting such shares to this purpose, because the principal alternative use of the shares is to sell them in the currently prevailing market. (*d*)

---

15 AICPA, *op. cit.*, p. 6055.
16 *Ibid.*

Once an option is granted to an employee, the decision when to exercise the option, if at all, rests largely with the employee. Thus, changes in the market value of the shares are assumed to represent changes in the value of the option to the employee but not in the cost to the corporation.

The most important of these reasons is the inability to measure the true value of the option to the employee or the real cost to the corporation except for that portion of the value represented by the excess of the value at the date of grant over the option price. However, the selection of this method of valuation was, no doubt influenced by the adoption in 1950 of Section 130A of the Internal Revenue Code, which established the "restricted" stock option plan. As a result of this code most plans adopted since 1950 set the option price at or near the current market price of the shares at the date of grant, so that little or no compensation is reflected in the accounts of the corporation.

2. Excess Value on Date the Option Right Becomes the Property of the Grantee. In the original *Bulletin No. 37* issued in 1948, the AICPA Committee on Accounting Procedure recommended that the value of the compensation should be the excess of the market value of the shares over the option price at the date that the option right becomes the property right of the employee. The main reason for this recommendation was that only at this date does the corporation have an unqualified obligation under the agreement. The employee can exercise the option only after he has fulfilled certain conditions; but when these conditions are met, the option belongs to the employee, and even though he must wait to exercise the option, he holds the property rights. This situation is compared with the granting of bonus shares to be issued at the end of a period of service, at which time the compensation is determined by the value of the bonus shares.

The original recommendation was revised in 1953, changing the date of measuring the compensation from the date of the property right to the date of grant. The *Bulletin* was revised primarily because of the difficulty of determining the "property date," which is a question of law, and because of the fact that the intent of the bulletin could be nullified by simple changes in the form of the agreement. The committee was also disturbed by the fact that unforeseen changes could have an unreasonable impact on the corporation. For example, rapid increases in the market price of the firm's shares could result in the necessity of recording large amounts of compensation that might even exceed the firm's income before recording the compensation.

3. Excess Value on the Date the Options Are First Exercisable. While the options may be exercisable as soon as the employee obtains the property right, a waiting period is frequently required before the options may be exercised. From this date on, the grantee may speculate on the option by either exercising it or holding it as long as possible before it expires. Therefore, it is argued that changes in the market value of the shares after this date are irrelevant to the corporation. It is also argued that the value of the option cannot be known before it can be exercised.[17]

4. Excess Value on the Date the Options Are Exercised. The argument that the amount of compensation is the excess of the market value over the option price at the date the option is exercised is based on the fact that only at this time does the grantee become a stockholder. Upon purchasing his shares, he acquires an interest in the enterprise that is worth more than his current cash outlay. This excess value is compensation to him because only as a stockholder could he obtain a capital gain due to the increase in the value of the shares. It is also assumed that this is the cost of the option to the corporation because prior to this date, the option is only a contingency. Any valuation prior to this date is only an estimate of the final cost to the corporation, and any valuation subsequent to this date is irrelevant because the grantee has then become a stockholder.[18]

5. Cost Adjusted for Income Tax Effect. A modification of the above method is to include in the cost of the compensation the amount of the income tax foregone by the corporation because of issuing the restricted stock option, which is not deductible as an expense by the issuing corporation. For example, if the value of the stock exceeds the option price by $60,000 at the time the options are exercised and if we assume a corporate tax rate of 40 percent, this would be equivalent to a cash salary of $100,000, which would represent the actual cost of the stock options to the corporation.[19]

6. The Cash Value of the Services at the Time of Option Grant. When property is received by a corporation in exchange for stock, the amount of the invested capital is generally measured by the current value of the property received. If it is not possible to obtain a current value for the property, it may be assumed that the property value is equal to the current market value of the stock given in exchange. In a stock option contract, the employee makes an investment in the firm in an amount equal to the value of his services being compensated. However, since it is not generally possible to determine the value of the services received, it may be assumed that the compensation is equal to the current value of the stock options. But since the restricted stock options are not transferable, they have no market price and their current value is difficult to

---

[17] See Arthur Andersen & Co., *Accounting and Reporting Problems of the Accounting Profession* (2d ed.; Chicago, 1962), Sec. 10.

[18] See Edwin C. Bomeli, "Stock Option Plans—Full Disclosure," *Accounting Review,* Vol. XXXVII (October, 1962), pp. 741–45.

[19] See William L. Raby, "Accounting for Employee Stock Options," *Accounting Review,* Vol. XXXVII (January, 1962), pp. 28–38.

estimate. Nevertheless, a current value does exist, and some writers propose that a bargained price for the services can be obtained.[20]

By accepting stock options rather than cash compensation, the executive is making an investment in the firm of an amount equal to the excess of the bargained value of his services over the cash salary received by him. Between the date of option grant and either the date that the option is exercised or the date it expires, the market price of the stock may increase substantially, moderately, or it may decline. Therefore, the final value of the option to the grantee may possibly be very large or it may be zero. At the date of the option grant, the expected value is between these two extremes. But note that it is always positive if there is some possibility of the market price rising above the option price; it would never be negative, and would be zero only if the option price were equal to or greater than the market price of the stock at the date of grant and if there were no expectation of an increase in the market price above the option price. This value can be estimated by projecting the likely trend in the market price of the firm's stock as indicated by all available evidence. The net aftertax value of the option to the executive should then be converted into the equivalent of a cash salary before consideration of the personal income tax effect.

An Appraisal of Valuation Methods.   In the opinion of the author, the most logical method of valuation is the cash value of the services as measured by the value of the option at the date of grant. However, most accountants shy away from this solution because it is highly subjective and depends upon speculation regarding the future. But in this case, there is no bargained price nor any marketable value, so that there is no alternative to the use of estimates. The position of the AICPA committee in *Bulletin No. 43* was that only the obvious value at the date of grant— the excess of the market value at date of grant over the option price— should be recorded as the compensation. It did not deny that additional value exists; rather, it claimed only that it cannot be measured.

All other methods are attempts to find some objective measure of the value of the compensation based on either the benefit received by the executive or the final cost to the corporation. The excess of market price over option price at any specific date is based on a cost concept rather than on a concept of service value invested by the executive. In the cost concept, we forget that invested capital is measured by the value of the consideration received by the firm and not the reverse. Even though the value of the option should be used in estimating the value of the services received, the value of the services is invested by the executive and this value should be determined by taking into consideration all possible out-

---

[20] See Daniel L. Sweeney, *Accounting for Stock Options* (Ann Arbor: Bureau of Business Research, School of Business Administration, University of Michigan, 1960), chap. vi.

comes and the risk taken by the grantee in receiving the option. The result is that the excess value of the market price over the option price at the time of property right or the date the option becomes exercisable is an incomplete valuation and probably understates the value of the option, particularly if it may be held by the grantee for several additional years before expiring. Even if the market price were equal to the option price at this date, the option would have a value to the grantee because of the possible increase in the market price before the option expires.

The excess of the market price over the option price at the date the option is exercised does represent the final gain to the executive, but this total gain is made up of two basic parts—the compensation to the executive and the gain or loss on the investment of his services. The value of the compensation should be measured by the most probable change in market price; if the increase in market price exceeds this expectation, the grantee has a gain on his investment and if it falls short of this expectation, he has a loss.

Regardless of which method is used in valuing the stock options, full disclosure should be made of the terms of the stock option contracts, the situation at the date of the balance sheet, and the method of valuation.

DECREASES IN INVESTED CAPITAL

Normally, the invested capital of a firm (the capital stock and paid-in surplus) is thought to represent the permanent capital of an enterprise. Deliberate reductions in invested capital should not be made by payments to stockholders unless these payments are specifically disclosed as liquidating dividends. But partial liquidation also occurs when a specific class of stock is called and redeemed. The purchase of treasury shares is similar to the redemption of preferred stock, with the exception that few stockholders of any class may be involved and the purchase price is not usually prearranged. If the treasury stock is reissued, the net result may be either an increase, a decrease, or no change in sockholders' equity. Invested capital may also be reduced by a quasi reorganization in recognition of the fact that accumulated losses have caused an effective reduction in capital without any distributions to shareholders.

Treasury Stock

When stockholders' equity is increased as a result of transactions with shareholders, accountants are generally agreed that no gain results and no part of the increase should be added to income or retained earnings; it all represents invested capital. But when stockholders' equity is reduced as a result of the acquisition of the corporation's own shares, accountants are not in agreement regarding the effect on invested capital and retained earnings. Two basic questions relating to this controversy are: (1) How much of the payment to stockholders should be treated as a return of invested capital and how much should be considered a distribution of retained earnings? (2) How should the effect on legal capital be shown?

When a firm acquires its own shares and holds them for reissuing or subsequent cancellation, the acquisition and disposition can be treated as (1) a single transaction, or (2) two separate and distinct transactions. The former is commonly referred to as the cost method while the latter is generally referred to as the par value method; however, it is possible to record the treasury stock at either cost or par value and still treat the purchase and sale as either a single transaction or as two separate transactions.

The Single-Transaction Concept. If a firm acquires its own shares and then sells them to other stockholders at a price equal to cost, it does not seem logical that the classification of stockholders' equity should be disturbed merely because the corporation handled the shares. If the shares are purchased and sold merely for the convenience of the stockholders, the transaction is equivalent to the sale of shares by one stockholder to another. If the stock is sold by the corporation in excess of its cost, the excess represents an increase in invested capital in excess of par value (paid-in surplus). Therefore, the classification by source is maintained and the legal capital is not disturbed.

When treasury stock is sold at less than its cost to the firm, the excess of cost over sale price represents either a repayment of invested capital or a distribution of retained earnings. While accountants are not in general agreement as to the accounts to be charged for this excess, three proposals are frequently made: (1) Following the suggestion in APB *Opinion No. 6*,[21] many writers maintain that the excess represents a return of invested capital and should be charged to capital surplus arising from other treasury stock transactions or to capital surplus related to the same class of stock. Only if the excess is greater than the total of these paid-in surplus accounts do these writers recommend that retained earnings should be reduced. (2) An alternative is to reduce paid-in surplus from the original sale of this class of stock by a pro rata amount and treat the remainder as a distribution of retained earnings. The capital stock account is not disturbed because of a desire to show the amount of legal capital which has not been reduced (in most cases) by the transaction. (3) A third solution is to treat the entire excess as a distribution of retained earnings. This alternative is popular because of its simplicity and conservatism. It is also frequently recommended for use in those states that include paid-in surplus as a part of legal capital, with the result that the presentation of legal capital is not disturbed by the trans-

---

[21] AICPA, *op. cit.,* p. 6528.

action. However, in the opinion of the author it has considerable merit from a theoretical point of view. If the purchase and sale of treasury stock are treated as a single transaction, the net effect is a selective distribution of the firm's assets to one or more stockholders. Any distribution to stockholders that does not reduce the number of shares outstanding should be treated as a distribution of retained earnings if such is available. Invested capital should not be disturbed.

A major difficulty of the single-transaction concept and the application of the cost basis occurs when the treasury stock is not sold immediately or when it is subsequently canceled. While the stock is held in the treasury, the cost represents an unallocated reduction of stockholders' equity held in suspense until the completion of the transaction. Therefore, both invested capital and retained earnings are overstated and this may result in a misleading interpretation, particularly if the shares are later canceled or sold substantially below cost.

The Two-Transactions Concept.   The two-transactions approach to treasury stock was recommended by the Committee on Accounting Concepts and Standards of the American Accounting Association, as indicated in the following:

The acquisition of its own shares by a corporation represents a contraction of its capital structure. . . . Preferably, the outlay by a corporation for its own shares is reflected as a reduction of the aggregate of contributed capital, and any excess of outlay over the pro-rata portion of contributed capital as a distribution of retained earnings. The issuance of reaquired shares should be accounted for in the same way as the issuance of previously unissued shares, that is, the entire proceeds should be credited to contributed capital.[22]

A similar recommendation was made in APB *Opinion No. 6* for those cases in which the stock was purchased for constructive retirement. However, the Board recognized that alternatively, the excess of purchase price over par or stated value may be charged entirely to retained earnings as a capitalization of retained earnings. The excess of par or stated value over the purchase price should be credited to capital surplus, according to the recommendations of *Opinion No. 6*.[23]

If the treasury shares are acquired at a cost in excess of the pro rata amount of invested capital, the effect of this recommendation would be to transfer a portion of retained earnings to paid-in surplus as a result of the acquisition and resale of a firm's own shares. Retained earnings is reduced when the shares are purchased, and paid-in surplus is increased when the shares are sold, even though the purchase and sale prices may

---

[22] AAA Committee on Accounting Concepts and Standards, *op. cit.*, p. 7.
[23] AICPA, *op. cit.*, p. 6528.

be the same. On the other hand, if the stock is acquired and resold at a price less than the par or stated value, paid-in surplus would be increased at the time of purchase and a discount on stock or similar account would be established when the stock is resold.

While stock acquired for the purpose of effecting a resale to employees or for meeting the rights of holders of stock options or warrants may be treated according to the single-transaction concept, APB *Opinion No. 6* recommended that treasury stock delivered to effect a "pooling of interest" should be accounted for under the two-transactions concept as a new issue. However, these recommendations are inconsistent, particularly when the treasury stock is acquired specifically for the purpose of reissuance in connection with a business combination. Also, the two-transactions concept permits management to create the appearance of an acquisition having the characteristics assumed to be necessary for pooling, when in substance it is a purchase. For example, if a firm wishes to acquire a second firm for cash but still use the pooling method, it may use the cash to acquire its own shares and then exchange these for the assets of the acquired firm. This inconsistency, however, is only one of the difficulties inherent in the pooling method itself, discussed more fully below.

Evaluation of the Single-Transaction and Two-Transactions Concepts. Both the single-transaction and two-transactions concepts have some logic in their favor. The former is based on the premise that substance is more important than form and that a corporation should not transfer amounts from retained earnings to invested capital merely because it happens to handle the transfer of shares from one stockholder to another. The two-transactions concept is based on the idea that there is little difference between the purchase and sale of treasury shares and the acquisition and retirement of shares with a subsequent sale of new shares. In the opinion of the author, each concept is appropriate for different circumstances. If shares are acquired by purchase with the express purpose of reselling to employees, executives, or other special groups, the single-transaction concept is relevant. On the other hand, if the objective of the acquisition is to purchase the shares of dissident stockholders or to effect the eventual retirement of certain classes of stock, the two-transactions concept should apply even though these shares might be resold at a later date. Of course, if eventual cancellation is the objective, the two-transactions approach is clearly appropriate.

This suggested solution has the disadvantage that it is not always possible to determine the intent of the corporation. Therefore, accountants are not likely to treat similar situations uniformly. If the objective is not clear, a suggested solution is to apply the two-transactions concept.

As discussed by APB *Opinion No. 6*, the accounting for treasury stock may be prescribed by state laws. For example, in California, in order to comply with the state corporation code, the entire cost of treasury stock is generally charged against retained earnings.[24] When the treasury shares are resold, the entire proceeds are credited to paid-in surplus. In other states, different modifications are proposed. For reasons presented in the previous chapter, it is suggested here that the individual state codes regarding legal capital should not determine accounting procedures, although APB *Opinion No. 6* specifies that they should conform to state laws. In all cases and in all states, the emphasis should be on the proper classification of stockholders' equity according to its source. The showing of legal capital should be secondary, possibly in a footnote in those cases where its disclosure by consistent classification is difficult. A dual presentation should be made if necessary to comply with state laws.

Quasi Reorganizations

A quasi reorganization is an informal procedure for establishing a new basis of accounting for the assets and stockholders' equity of a corporation. It has the effect of permitting a "fresh start" by simulating the purchase of the entire enterprise by a new corporation formed for the purpose. The Committee on Accounting Procedure of the AICPA recognized that this procedure is an exception to the general rule that capital surplus should not be charged with amounts that would otherwise be included in the determination of income. It also stated:

If a corporation elects to restate its assets, capital stock and surplus through a readjustment and thus avail itself of permission to relieve its future income account or earned surplus account of charges which would otherwise be made thereagainst, it should make a clear report to its shareholders of the restatements proposed to be made, and obtain their formal consent. It should present a fair balance sheet as at the date of the readjustment, in which the adjustment of carrying amounts is reasonably complete, in order that there may be no continuation of the circumstances which justify charges to capital surplus.[25]

The Securities and Exchange Commission also recognized the quasi reorganization procedure but specified the following conditions: (1) retained earnings must be exhausted by the reorganization; (2) no deficits should remain in any capital accounts; (3) proper consents should be obtained from stockholders and other interested groups; and (4) assets should be restated in terms of present conditions, and stockholder equity items should be appropriately modified in order to obviate as far as possible the necessity of future reorganizations.[26]

---

[24] See Harry Buttimer, "Statutory Influence on Treasury Stock Accounting," *Accounting Review,* Vol. XXXV (July, 1960), pp. 476–81.

[25] AICPA, *op. cit.*, p. 6022.

[26] Securities and Exchange Commission Accounting Series Releases Nos. 15 (1940), 16 (1940), and 25 (1941).

As indicated from the statements of the AICPA and the SEC, the quasi reorganization procedure involves two basic parts: (1) a revaluation of assets as a departure from the cost basis of accounting; and (2) a reclassification of stockholder equity accounts. Much of the literature on the subject deals more with the revaluation aspect than with the equity reclassification. However, in the author's view, revaluation is not a basic part of a quasi reorganization. It has become a necessary part only because accountants have held closely to historical cost as the basis of valuation.

When it is deemed desirable to obtain a "fresh start," cost becomes irrelevant. If a new corporation were formed to purchase the net assets of the enterprise, the assets would be recorded by the new firm at their new cost, which would presumably be their current value. Therefore, it is logical that this situation cannot be simulated unless the assets are revalued in current terms. But, the point being made here is that revaluation should be permitted even by a going concern if cost is no longer the only relevant basis of valuation for financial reporting purposes. This idea that revaluation is not necessarily a basic part of quasi reorganization is implied in the following recommendation of Sprouse and Moonitz:

In the external reports, plant and equipment should be restated in terms of current replacement costs whenever some significant event occurs, such as a reorganization of the business entity or its merger with another entity or when it becomes a subsidiary of a parent company. *Even in the absence of a significant event, the accounts could be restated at periodic intervals, perhaps every five years.*[27]

The most important part of the quasi reorganization, therefore, is the reclassification of stockholder equity accounts. When losses exceed the retained earnings of prior years by a material amount, the resulting deficit may represent a permanent erosion of invested capital. If the firm is required to restore this erosion by withholding dividends, the ability of the enterprise to recover and obtain proper growth may be impaired because of the inability to sell additional capital stock at favorable prices. Therefore, the recognition of the deficit as a permanent reduction of invested capital is realistic and practical. The entire stockholders' equity at the time of reorganization should be classified as invested capital to obtain a fresh start. This decrease in invested capital may result in a reduction of legal capital, by reducing par or stated value, by a reduction of paid-in surplus, or by a reduction of both.

Because a fresh start is obtained, the retained earnings accumulated subsequent to the reorganization represent accumulated earnings in excess of dividends only since the reorganization. Therefore, to provide for

---

[27] Sprouse and Moonitz, *op. cit.*, p. 34. Italics added.

proper disclosure, the retained earnings in subsequent balance sheets should be dated as originating at the date of reorganization. If this were not disclosed, the reader might be misled into believing that the firm has been profitable since its original formation. Technically, the invested capital should also be dated to disclose that it represents the capital at the time of reorganization rather than the capital originally invested by stockholders. However, because of the general emphasis on the classification of stockholder equity according to the objective of showing possible disposition and the objective of disclosing the legal capital, the dating of invested capital is not usually recommended. In *Accounting Research Bulletin No. 46,* the Committee on Accounting Procedure recommended that the dating of retained earnings would rarely be of significance after a period of 10 years and that there may be circumstances in which the discontinuance of the dating may be justified earlier than the conclusion of the 10-year period.[28] The main difficulty with this recommendation is that the classification of stockholders' equity by the original source is distorted by the reorganization. The current equity is classified properly only if the deficit is declared to be a reduction of invested capital. But readers of financial statements should not be misled by the omission of the dating after a period of 10 years or so, since generally they do not know the date of the origin of the corporation without studying its history. Furthermore, after 10 years, the corporation has established a new financial record that is more important than its entire record since its origin.

Frequently, it is suggested that an upward quasi reorganization would be just as logical as the recognized downward reorganization. That is, it is assumed that a firm should be able to obtain a fresh start by revaluing its assets upward, as a reversal of the usual quasi reorganization procedure. But, in this case, a reclassification of stockholders' equity is not necessary. Total invested capital is increased by the write-up, but there is no necessity for a transfer from retained earnings to invested capital and, therefore, no reclassification is required. And since a revaluation can be made without simulating a "fresh start," a quasi reorganization is not really effected. The main opposition to an upward revaluation, however, has come from the AICPA, other accounting associations in the United States and in other countries, and governmental bodies, because of the general feeling that historical cost is objective and more meaningful than appraised valuations.

BUSINESS COMBINATIONS

When the assets of one firm are acquired by a second firm as a result of a purchase transaction involving the payment of cash or the exchange of other assets, the purchased assets are generally recorded in the accounts

---

[28] AICPA, *op. cit.,* p. 6075.

of the acquiring firm at their cost (the value of the assets given in exchange), which may be assumed to represent their current value. The historical cost to the selling firm is no longer relevant. And the stockholders' equity of the acquiring firm is not increased or reclassified because of the transaction.

If the acquisition is carried out by the purchase (for cash or other assets) of the entire capital stock of a second firm, the situation is similar to the above purchase. In fact, if the acquired firm is dissolved, the net result of the transaction may be the same as a purchase of the assets, with the possible exception that the acquiring firm may assume the liabilities of the purchased firm. Even if the acquired firm is not dissolved, the consolidated statements should show the acquired assets at their current cost, including the cost of intangibles; and no change in stockholders' equity occurs as a result of the acquisition of the shares or the consolidation of the parent and subsidiary firms. Only if a minority interest remains is there an increase in the total equity of the consolidated enterprise. As indicated in the previous chapter, however, the minority interest is not always shown as a part of the total equity in the consolidated balance sheet.

In the above cases, the acquisition of additional nonmonetary assets or stock of another firm for cash leads to a clear-cut treatment of the transaction as a purchase, even though several problems of consolidation remain unresolved. But when two or more firms combine by the exchange of the stock of one for the assets or stock of others or when a new corporation is formed for this purpose, a question arises as to whether the transaction is a purchase or, in fact, only a "pooling of interests" of the two or more firms. The nature of the transaction and the resulting enterprise rather than the legal form should dictate the accounting procedure to be followed.

Combinations Treated as Purchases

Whenever assets are acquired by the exchange of capital stock, the valuation of the assets is assumed to be equal to the value of the stock given in exchange unless the current value of the assets can be obtained by other verifiable means. Similarly, when all of the assets of a firm or its stock are acquired by giving capital stock in exchange in a purchase transaction, the accounting treatment involves two parts: (1) The net assets are valued in terms of the total market value of the stock issued in exchange. This total cost should be allocated to specific assets wherever possible, and any excess should be considered purchased goodwill or other intangibles. (2) The total value of the stock issued is credited to invested capital with a possible division between legal capital and paid-in surplus. The former classification of the stockholders' equity of the acquired corporation has no effect on the classification in the acquiring firm.

AICPA *Accounting Research Bulletin No. 48* described a purchase as

. . . a business combination of two or more corporations in which an important part of the ownership interests in the acquired corporation or corporations is eliminated or in which other factors requisite to a pooling of interests are not present.[29]

The general interpretation of *Bulletin No. 48* was that a business combination involving the exchange of stock can generally be considered to be a pooling of interests unless the attendant circumstances indicate the contrary. Specifically, the *Bulletin* mentioned the following circumstances that would indicate that the combination is a purchase rather than a pooling of interests: (1) the elimination of an important part of the ownership interests in the acquired firm, (2) a material alteration of the voting rights of the constituent corporations, (3) the elimination or reduction of the influence of the management of one of the constituents, and (4) where one of the constituent corporations is clearly dominant— obtaining 90 to 95 percent of the voting interest of the combined enterprise. Gradually, these criteria have been eroded in practice so that they no longer serve to control the choice of the purchase or pooling method. Recognizing the difficulty in applying these criteria, the Accounting Principles Board stated in *Opinion No. 6* that the criteria are illustrative guides and not literal requirements. As a result, a combination is considered to be a purchase only to the extent that cash, debt, or securities other than common and convertible preferred stock are given in exchange for the acquired firm. Minor percentages of the consideration represented by cash payments have been ignored in making this classification. However, in a few cases where it has been advantageous to do so, firms have selected the purchase method even though they could have selected the pooling method instead.

Because of this failure to establish workable criteria and because of the abuses of accounting for acquisitions permitted by this failure, the pooling method has come under severe criticism from many sides and the purchase method has been claimed to be appropriate in all cases. Wyatt, for example, in *Accounting Research Study No. 5* concluded that a business combination ". . . is basically an exchange event in which two economic interests bargain to the consummation of an exchange of assets and/or equities."[30] Therefore, it follows from this definition that almost all combinations are purchases and should be accounted for as such. This was also the conclusion of Catlett and Olson in *Accounting Research Study No. 10.*[31] Likewise, the AAA Committee to Prepare a Statement of

---

[29] *Ibid.,* p. 6081.

[30] Arthur R. Wyatt, "A Critical Study of Accounting for Business Combinations," *Accounting Research Study No. 5* (New York: AICPA, 1963), p. 104.

[31] George R. Catlett and Norman O. Olson, "Accounting for Goodwill," *Accounting Research Study No. 10* (New York: AICPA, 1968), p. 110.

Basic Accounting Principles recommended the adoption of the purchase method as opposed to the pooling concept because of greater relevance.[32]

One of the main advantages of the purchase method is that it permits a "fresh start" from an accounting point of view, at least for the acquired firm. If the assets of the acquired firm are overvalued, they can be adjusted to a fair value at the time of combination and a deficit in the acquired firm can be eliminated in the new combination. However, the purchase method is claimed to be disadvantageous if the fair value of the assets is greater than the previous book value, because the recording of these higher values will necessitate higher depreciation and amortization charges, resulting in lower reported net incomes for several years. This is compounded by the fact that if the combination is a tax-free combination, this extra depreciation and amortization is not deductible for income tax purposes. It is also assumed to be disadvantageous because it eliminates the retained earnings of the acquired corporation, thereby reducing the amount available for dividends out of accumulated income although the legal amount available may not be altered. These arguments are discussed more fully below.

Pooling of Interests

A pooling of interests is assumed to occur when two or more firms combine to carry out their business functions as a single economic enterprise. The enterprise may take the form of one of the existing corporations, a new corporation organized for the purpose, or a continuance of the previous corporations with one being the parent and the others the subsidiaries. *Bulletin No. 48* specified that the treatment as a pooling of interests should be based on the *attendant circumstances* rather than on the legal form of the combination. The most important of the attendant circumstances is that substantially all of the former ownership interests should continue in the combined enterprise. There should remain no significant minority interest in any subsidiary corporation. And the ownership interests of the several firms should continue substantially in proportion to their interests in the predecessor firms and with similar rights of control. In reply to Wyatt, Holsen concluded that a business combination should be considered to be a purchase only when one group of shareholders gives up control in an ownership interest formerly held.[33] Other attendant circumstances that should be taken into consideration as guidelines are: (1) continuity of former business activities; (2) continuity of management; and (3) relative sizes of the combining firms (none of the combining firms should be clearly dominant with more than 90 to 95

---

[32] Committee to Prepare a Statement of Basic Accounting Theory, *A Statement of Basic Accounting Theory* (AAA, 1966), p. 19.

[33] Robert C. Holsen, "Another Look at Business Combinations," in Wyatt, *op. cit.*, pp. 109–14.

percent of the voting interest in the combined enterprise). However, as indicated above, these criteria have not been major considerations in practice.

In *Accounting Research Study No. 5,* Wyatt concluded that substantially all business combinations are exchange transactions involving the transference of assets and equities between independent parties. He therefore recommended that "no basis exists in principle for a continuation of what is presently known as 'pooling-of-interests' accounting *if* the business combination involves an exchange of assets and/or equities between independent parties."[34] However, Wyatt did recognize that pooling-of-interest accounting is relevant when no substantive changes occur because of the combination of *related enterprises.* In reply to this, Holsen rejected the idea that the firms combining must be related before the combination can be considered a pooling of interests. Instead, he concluded that the basic criterion for a pooling of interests should be the continuance of ownership interests.[35]

In a pooling of interest, the accounting treatment involves two basic differences from the treatment as a purchase: (1) the assets and liabilities of the several combining enterprises are brought into the new enterprise at their book value in the accounts of the former separate organizations, with the exception that adjustments may be made to provide for uniform treatment; and (2) the retained earnings of the several corporations should be added together in the surviving corporation or in consolidation except for that amount that must be transferred to invested capital to present legal capital.

Pooling of interest accounting has been popular in business combinations for several reasons: (1) When the fair value of the assets combined is greater than the book value, the depreciation and amortization would be increased if the combination were treated as a purchase and the net income of the new combination would be less than the summation of the net incomes of the former enterprises. (2) The pooling of interest treatment avoids the dilution of earnings per share arising from the revaluation of assets. (3) It avoids the necessity of recording goodwill and other intangibles that present problems of amortization and interpretation. (4) The combining of the retained earnings of the several enterprises does not reduce the amount available for dividends as income distribution. These so-called advantages, however, are illusory and deceptive and should not be controlling factors in the decision to apply purchase or pooling-of-interest accounting.

An additional objective of the pooling of interest method is to present the effect of the combination for prior periods as if the firms had been

---

34 *Ibid.,* p. 105.
35 *Ibid.,* p. 110.

combined at the earlier date. APB *Opinion No. 10* recommended that when a combination occurs during a period or shortly after the close of the period before the financial statements are published, the financial statements should be restated to include the combined results of operations for the entire period on a pooling basis. It also recommended that when prior results of operations are presented for comparative purposes, the previous data should also be restated on a pooling basis as if the combination had taken place in an earlier period. The apparent objective is to show meaningful trends of income and earnings per share data that can be used for predictive purposes. However, this is a misuse of comparative data, because a discontinuity has occurred. The combined firm is not the same as a group of separate firms and it is misleading to assume that nothing has happened. Furthermore, the combination generally results in a new capitalization and new relationships among the equity holders. It is misleading to assume that these new capitalization relationships existed in an earlier period, under entirely different circumstances. Comparative data should be prohibited in this case unless the nature of the discontinuity is clearly disclosed.

An Evaluation of Purchases and Pooling of Interests

The distinction between a purchase and a pooling of interests rests primarily on the selection and interpretation of the relevant surviving entity. In a purchase, only one combining enterprise survives; the others die both in form and in spirit. However, in a pooling of interests, the surviving corporation is really a combination of two or more viable economic enterprises. The fact that one of the legal organizations is chosen to house the new entity is not sufficient evidence that it has purchased the others. The evidence must rest in the attendant circumstances rather than in the legal form of the combination.

Once a combination is decided to be either a purchase or a pooling of interests, the specific accounting treatment is then thought to be determined. The two major accounting problems are the valuation of the assets acquired or combined and the classification of the increased or combined equity of the stockholders. However, these two aspects of the combination should be analyzed and treated separately. There is no clear evidence in accounting theory that the classification of stockholders' equity in a combination is dictated by the method of asset valuation or vice versa.

The Valuation of Assets in a Combination. When a combination is treated as a purchase, the net assets are acquired at their cost as measured by the market value of the stock given in exchange. This treatment is correct not because it complies with the traditional cost basis of accounting but because this cost represents the best measure of the current value of the assets to the combined enterprise. If the total cost cannot be allocated to specific assets as part of their current value, the difference represents the cost of unidentified goodwill or other intangibles to be reported, as discussed in Chapter 14. They should not be omitted merely because the accounting for intangibles is a difficult area or because of a possible reduction in recorded net income.

The decision to treat a combination as a pooling of interests is generally assumed to dictate that the assets be carried forward at the book value in the accounts of the previous enterprise. This treatment is based on the tradition that historical cost is the most objective and the most relevant valuation basis when there is continuity of ownership interests. However, current values are more relevant for most decisions to be made by external investors and for most decisions of management. This importance of current values or current replacement costs is emphasized by Sprouse and Moonitz in *Accounting Research Study No. 3*. Even for plant and equipment they recommended that

in the external reports, plant and equipment should be restated in terms of current replacement costs whenever some significant event occurs, such as a reorganization of the business entity or its merger with another entity or when it becomes a subsidiary of a parent company.[36]

Even though a combination is considered to be a pooling of interests, it is a significant event in the history of the enterprise, and the assets should be recorded at their current value or current replacement cost rather than the historical costs in the accounts of the former enterprises. Because the current value of the assets can be obtained by objective means if the stock given in exchange has a market value, the revaluation obtains greater reliability than an independent revaluation. However, a serious difficulty arises when one of the combining firms continues in its legal form and its assets cannot be revalued in terms of the market value of any stock given in exchange for it. A difficulty also arises when a new corporation is formed for the purpose of the combination, because the stock may not have a current market value. But in each of these cases, there is good reason to revalue all of the assets of the new combined enterprise by using available evidence such as replacement costs and the market price of the stock of the combining corporations.

The Classification of the Stockholders' Equity of the Combination. When a new corporation is organized to purchase the assets or stock of two or more firms, a new enterprise is formed and the entire stockholders' equity at the inception of the new enterprise is invested capital. As indicated earlier, subclassifications may be made to disclose the interests of different classes of stockholders and to disclose the amount of legal capital. But since the firm is a new entity, none of the equity is derived

---

[36] Sprouse and Moonitz, *op. cit.*, p. 34.

from the retention of earnings. If an existing firm purchases the assets or stock of another firm, a situation similar to the acquisition by a new firm is encountered insofar as the acquired firm loses its identity; but the stockholders' equity of the acquiring firm is not affected, because the transaction involves only an exchange of assets (or net assets).

When the acquiring firm issues common stock for the assets or stock of another firm, however, the classification of the stockholders' equity in the acquiring firm (or in a new firm organized for the purpose) depends on the interpretation of the new enterprise as (1) an entirely new accounting entity, (2) an accounting entity comprised of the acquiring corporation only, or (3) a continuation of all combining enterprises as a single accounting entity. In the first interpretation, the new enterprise obtains a fresh start and all of the stockholders' equity is invested capital. The second case is assumed to represent a fresh start for the acquired firm but not for the continuing corporation.

The idea of a fresh start is derived from the concept of a quasi reorganization. But this analogy is weak, because in a quasi reorganization there is continuity of interests, with a reclassification of stockholders' equity at the time of the fresh start; while in a combination treated as a purchase, the acquired firm or firms are assumed to disappear entirely. Therefore, rather than being a "fresh start," the entire net assets of the acquired firm or firms are *invested* in the new firm or the surviving firm. Therefore, all of the stockholders' equity arising from the exchange of shares for the net assets or stock of the acquired firms should be treated as invested capital.

What justification is there, then, for carrying forward the retained earnings of the combined firms when the combination is treated as a pooling of interests? If classification of stockholders' equity by source is considered to be the major objective of classification, the question is one of determining the relevant entity and the relevant sources of the equities of this entity. If several firms combine without changing the ownership interests, the source of the equity in the new firm is the summation of the sources in the predecessor corporations. However, if the ownership interests of the acquired firm changed from residual interests to preferred interests, the retained earnings of the corporation dissolving in form should not be carried forward into the combined enterprise, because to do so would lead to a misinterpretation regarding the nature of this equity as being obtained from the retention of earnings that would otherwise have been distributed to the current residual equity holders.

If the ownership interests of the several firms are continued in the combined enterprise, however, a distinction between the capital originally invested by these stockholders and the capital obtained by the retention of earnings is relevant in the description of the combined firm. If the equities of the several firms are all material in relationship to the stockholders' equity of the combined enterprise, it would be misleading to carry forward the retained earnings of only one of the firms, because this would distort the ratio between capital originally invested and that derived from the retention of earnings. There is considerable merit in disclosing the retained earnings of the several firms at the date of combination and making a separate disclosure of the earnings retained after the combination, unless the continuing firm is so large in relationship to the others that there is no material change in the total retained earnings resulting from the combination.

In summary, the continuation of the same classifications of stockholder equities in a combined enterprise as in the former firms is logical if the ownership interests continue with similar equity rights in the combined firms as in the predecessor corporations. Other criteria, such as relative size, continuity of management, and the basis of valuation of the assets of the combined enterprise, are not relevant in determining the classification of stockholders' equity. However, a major difficulty in a classification by sources originating in the former corporations is that a reclassification may be necessary if legal capital is increased by the combination and if the disclosure of legal capital is to be accomplished in the classification.

Partial Pooling

All of the difficulties and glaring abuses of external financial reporting come to rest in what has come to be known as the "partial pooling" method for accounting for business combinations. In this method, the combination is treated as a purchase to the extent that cash or debt are exchanged for the stock or net assets of the acquired firm, and as a pooling of interests to the extent that common stock or convertible preferred stock are given in exchange. The result is that the combination is treated as part purchase and part pooling. While this concept has arisen from the desire to obtain as much "advantage" from the pooling method as possible, it cannot be supported on logical grounds. What logic is there in revaluing the assets partly because of the new evidence regarding their current value while at the same time carrying part of the historical cost to the acquired firm forward into the new firm? In practice, few revaluations of specific assets are made, but the extent to which a purchase is effected implies that this should be done. Furthermore, there is no logic in carrying forward only a part of the retained earnings of the acquired firms. Therefore, the part purchase–part pooling method destroys the informational content of the revaluations implied in the purchase method and also destroys whatever relevant information may be assumed to be generated by the pooling method.

EARNINGS PER SHARE

Only since 1966 have earnings per share ratios been included in the financial statements of American firms, as recommended by APB *Opinions No. 9* and *No. 15*. Previously, earnings per share data were commonly reported only as supplementary information in annual reports and in other summaries of financial statistics. Only recently have corporations in other countries begun to include such data in the supplementary information presented in annual reports; however, earnings per share figures are not commonly included in annual reports of British firms.

Traditionally, financial ratios have not been included in the financial statements covered by the auditor's certificate. However, because of the prominence given the earnings per share ratio, the AICPA Committee on Accounting Procedure in 1958 suggested several guidelines for its computation and presentation. Subsequently, the Accounting Principles Board, in *Opinion No. 9*, expanded the earnings per share concepts and recommended the disclosure in the income statement of the basic earnings per share ratios and supplementary pro forma ratios to disclose potential dilution. APB *Opinion No. 15* suggested more specific descriptions and methods of computation, thus attempting to narrow the differences in the computation and presentation of earnings per share data among different firms.

Objectives of Earnings per Share

Earnings per share ratios are used as one of the indicators of firm valuation and as an indication of future earnings per share and expected dividends per share. They are also thought to be relevant in an evaluation of management effectiveness and dividend policy. The main difference of opinion, however, is whether earnings per share data should reflect historical information only or whether they should reflect pro forma and predictive information.

Traditionally, the computation and reporting of net income have emphasized the historical concept. Net income has been assumed to represent a measurement of the firm's activities and achievements during the year. This was basically the philosophy of *Accounting Research Bulletin No. 49*. In this bulletin, the AICPA Committee on Accounting Procedure recommended that earnings per share data should be computed in terms of the common stock position *existing* in the year to which the statistics relate, except for adjustments for stock splits. Comparative presentations of earnings per share for several years were recognized as having little bearing on the present position or on expectations. Usefulness of such historical information was therefore assumed to depend upon full disclosure of the computation method.

In *Opinion No. 9,* the Accounting Principles Board recognized the usefulness of earnings per share data for a number of periods in the formulation of an opinion regarding the future potential of a firm. However, the Board also emphasized the primary historical nature of financial statements. Accordingly, it recommended a computation of earnings per share based primarily upon historical information, but it also recommended the presentation of supplementary pro forma earnings per share ratios to indicate the potential effect of contingent changes and potential dilutions. APB *Opinion No. 15,* however, placed greater emphasis on the usefulness of earnings per share data in forming an opinion of the potential of a firm and in investment decisions. Its recommendation, accordingly, included the presentation of two earnings per share concepts, both of which are pro forma in nature and are assumed to include predictive qualities.

As discussed in Chapter 8, cash flow data and other information relevant to a prediction of dividends may be more significant for investment decisions than net income and earnings per share data. If this is the case, more emphasis should be placed on the computation of dividends per share and total dividend requirements on a pro forma basis than on the computation and presentation of earnings per share.

Computation of Number of Shares

The computation of an earnings per share ratio requires a computation with net income to common stockholders as the numerator and the related number of common shares as the denominator. In a simple case where there have been no significant changes in capitalization during the year and no obligations to issue additional shares, the relevant denominator is the number of shares outstanding at the end of the year. However, if additional shares have been issued during the year, an average of the number of shares weighted by the number of months outstanding is assumed to be more relevant, because the capital invested through the sale of the additional shares was available to the firm to increase its earnings during the year. Therefore, the use of the weighted average of the shares outstanding during the year is assumed to reflect the historical conditions as well as permit comparisons with other years.

When other securities that have some characteristics of common stock are outstanding, usefulness of earnings per share data may be increased if these securities are counted as common stock. For example, if preferred stock is fully participating with respect to dividends, the preferred stockholders have the same rights as common stockholders to share in dividend distributions in excess of the preferred rate. Therefore, if such securities have the right to share in future dividends on the same basis as common stock, they should be included in the computation of earnings per share. Convertible debt, convertible preferred stock, options, and warrants do not share in dividends on the same basis as common until they become common shares; but they have potential rights to share in future distributions. Therefore, from the point of view of using the earnings per share figure as a predictive indicator, they should be included in the computation if they are likely to gain the rights of common stockholders. For if these security holders exercise their rights, the earnings per share figure based on outstanding shares is likely to decrease.

While there are many ways to compute earnings per share if these different types of securities are present, APB *Opinion No. 15* recommended two separate computations called "primary earnings per share" and "fully diluted earnings per share" respectively. But these two computations are based on neither the probability of conversion or exercise nor on their imminence. They are, rather, computations based on arbitrary rules and assumptions, without evidence that either computation is necessarily relevant for investment decisions.

Primary Earnings per Share. The primary earnings per share computation includes the weighted average number of shares outstanding during the year plus the number of shares represented by securities that are considered to be common stock equivalents and have a dilutive effect. A dilutive effect is assumed to occur if the earnings per share figure would be reduced by 3 percent or more if the common stock equivalents were included. Securities considered to be common stock equivalents include all stock options and warrants, participating securities, convertible securities that come within the limits of a specific formula at the time of issuance, and other securities having current or potential common stock rights. Convertible securities are considered to be common stock equivalents if the cash yield at the time of issuance is less than two thirds of the bank prime interest rate at that time.

The use of "primary earnings per share" can be criticized for the following reasons: (1) The use of the term "primary" implies that the computation is of greatest significance, whereas any one of a family of earnings per share computations may be the most relevant under different assumptions and expectations. (2) Convertible debt and convertible preferred stock are treated differently from debt and preferred stock with detachable warrants, since convertible securities are classified as common stock equivalents only at the date of issuance while warrants are classified according to the conditions in each period, and the methods of adjusting income are different. However, they are in substance the same, since the proceeds from the exercise of the warrants can be used to purchase the bonds or preferred stock; so the firm would be in the same position as when convertible securities are converted. (3) Convertible securities are classified as common stock equivalents only at the time of issuance rather than reflecting the conditions current in each year. (4) The use of the bank prime interest rate in the cash yield test does not differentiate among different types of securities nor among different investment standings of firms. (5) It is inconsistent to say that convertible debt should be classified solely as debt in the balance sheet (as recommended in APB *Opinion No. 14*) and to classify it entirely as a common stock equivalent in computing the earnings per share. (6) The primary earnings per share is a pro forma computation, but the title does not indicate its significance. Without full disclosure, the reader would not be able to determine which securities have been treated as common stock equivalents.

Fully Diluted Earnings per Share.   According to APB *Opinion No. 15*, the fully diluted earnings per share should be computed on the basis of the computation used for primary earnings per share plus the number of common shares represented by convertible securities that were not classified as common stock equivalents. The method of treating warrants and options may also be different if the closing market price of common exceeds the average price. Such securities should not be included, however, if the effect would be to increase the earnings per share or decrease the loss per share.

The alleged purpose of the fully diluted computation is to show the *maximum* potential dilution of current earnings per share on a prospective basis.[37] However, this computation does not include the maximum potential dilution, because the treatment of warrants is dependent upon the market price at the end of the period while expected dilution may depend upon expectations of *future* market prices. Thus, actual dilution may be greater than that reported for two reasons: (1) Warrants are not included if the market price of common stock at the end of the period does not exceed the exercise price. This is similar to the assumption made with executive stock options that no compensation is involved if the market price does not exceed the exercise price at the date of the grant. However, if the market price increases in a later period, dilution will occur when the warrants are exercised. (2) The elimination of warrants from the computation on the basis of market price of the stock at the end of the period assumes that the proceeds from the exercise of the warrants can be used to purchase stock at that price. But when the warrants are exercised at a later date, when the market price of the stock has increased, the proceeds will not permit the acquisition of the same number of shares.

The fully diluted earnings per share computation can also be criticized on the basis that it is likely to be interpreted as the most probable result.

---

[37] AICPA *op. cit.*, pp. 6617–18.

However, experience is likely to indicate that not all conversion rights nor warrants are exercised or are likely to be exercised. The computation, therefore, may reflect a worse situation than is probable under any circumstances.

Computation of the Earnings

The numerator in the computation of earnings per share must be adjusted, even on an historical basis, if there are senior stock equity issues outstanding. Since the earnings relate only to common stock securities with residual rights, dividends paid or payable on senior securities should be deducted from the net income figures shown on the income statement. If an addition is made to the common stock shares in the denominator to represent convertible debt outstanding, the interest expense for the year adjusted for the income tax effect should be added to the reported net income. Convertible preferred stock included in the denominator, however, does not require an adjustment of reported net income because the net income amount must be allocated to these shares as well as to common stock.

Stock options and warrants require, upon exercise, payment to the firm of an amount referred to as "the exercise price." Since the equivalent number of shares are included in the denominator on the assumption that the options and warrants have been exercised since the beginning of the period or date of grant, the net income should include an amount equal to the net income effect of utilizing the cash proceeds from the exercise of the warrants. Since this is a pro forma assumption, there is no way of knowing what the income effect would have been. One assumption is that the firm could have earned at least an amount equivalent to the interest on government securities or commercial paper adjusted for the income tax effect. An alternative assumption is that the firm could reacquire its long-term debt and thereby save interest expense. The assumption recommended by APB *Opinion No. 15*, however, is that the proceeds could have been used by the firm to reacquire its own shares at the average market price during the year. Under this so-called "treasury stock method," the number of shares added to the denominator would be reduced by the number of shares that could have been purchased with the proceeds from the exercise of the warrants, and the net income in the numerator is not increased. Thus, no dilution is assumed to occur if the average market price of the common stock is equal to or less than the exercise price. *Opinion No. 15*, however, suggested that if the number of shares obtainable upon exercise of the warrants exceeds 20 percent of the outstanding common shares, the proceeds from the shares in excess of 20 percent should be assumed to be used to repay debt or be invested in government securities or commercial paper. In this case, the net income should be increased by the net income effect of the interest that could have been saved or earned.

Criticisms of the recommendations of *Opinion No. 15* regarding the adjustment for the income effect of the proceeds from the exercise of warrants are: (1) The use of the treasury stock method does not reflect the best use of the funds or even the most likely use. (2) The use of a current market price to determine the number of shares that could be purchased does not reflect the potential of the firm to reacquire such shares in the future, particularly if the market price is increasing each year. (3) The 20 percent limitation is arbitrary and therefore does not necessarily lead to meaningful measurements. (4) The market price of the stock generally reflects expectations regarding future earnings and is not related to the current opportunities available to the firm for investment of the proceeds from the exercise of warrants.

Summary

The earnings per share computations recommended by APB *Opinion No. 15* are pro forma ratios based on unsupported assumptions. Instead of presenting only two ratios that are assumed to be most relevant, the financial statements should present a full disclosure of all relevant information to permit the investor to make his own evaluation of the potential of the firm. Furthermore, since future dividend distributions may be more significant than reported earnings per share computations, the information should be presented in such a way that alternative dividends per share computations can also be estimated under different assumptions.

SELECTED ADDITIONAL READING ON CHAPTER TOPICS

Stock Dividends and Stock Splits

BURKE, JOHN T. "Stock Dividends—Suggestions for Clarification," *Accounting Review,* Vol. XXXVII (April, 1962), pp. 283–88.

RAY, J. C. "Amount to Be Capitalized for a Stock Dividend," *New York Certified Public Accountant,* Vol. XXXII (August, 1962), pp. 511–17.

SUSSMAN, M. RICHARD. *The Stock Dividend.* Ann Arbor: Bureau of Business Research, School of Business Administration, University of Michigan, 1962.

Stock Options

BLAINE, R. E. "Accounting for Employee Stock Option Contracts," *Canadian Chartered Accountant,* Vol. XC (January, 1967), pp. 68–71.

KISTLER, LINDA H. "Stock Option Disclosures Are Inadequate," *Accounting Review*, Vol. XLII (October, 1967), pp. 758–66.

RABY, WILLIAM L. "Accounting for Employee Stock Options," *Accounting Review*, Vol. XXXVII (January, 1962), pp. 28–38.

SWEENEY, DANIEL L. *Accounting for Stock Options.* Michigan Business Studies, Vol. XIV, No. 5. Ann Arbor: Bureau of Business Research, School of Business Administration, University of Michigan, 1960.

Treasury Stock

BUTTIMER, HARRY. "Statutory Influence on Treasury Stock Accounting," *Accounting Review*, Vol. XXXV (July, 1960), pp. 476–81.

PATON, W. A. "Postscript on 'Treasury' Shares," *Accounting Review*, Vol. XLIV (April, 1969), pp. 276–83.

RAY, J. C. "Accounting for Treasury Stock," *Accounting Review*, Vol. XXXVII (October, 1962), pp. 753–57.

Business Combinations

BEYER, ROBERT. "Goodwill and Pooling of Interests: A Re-assessment," *Management Accounting*, Vol. L (February, 1969), pp. 9–15.

BRILOFF, ABRAHAM. "Dirty Pooling," *Accounting Review*, Vol. XLII (July, 1967), pp. 489–96.

CATLETT, GEORGE R., and NORMAN O. OLSON. "Accounting for Goodwill," *Accounting Research Study No. 10*, particularly chap. iv. New York: AICPA, 1968.

FISCH, JACK H., and MARTIN MELLMAN. "Poolings of Interest: The Status of the Criteria," *Journal of Accountancy*, Vol. CXXVI (August, 1968), pp. 42–48.

GUNTHER, SAMUEL P. "Part Purchase—Part Pooling: The Infusion of Confusion into Fusion," *New York Certified Public Accountant*, Vol. XXXIX (April, 1969), pp. 241–49.

HENDRICKSON, H. S. "Some Comments on 'Dirty Pooling'," *Accounting Review*, Vol. XLIII (April, 1968), pp. 363–66.

LAUVER, R. C. "The Case for Poolings," *Accounting Review*, Vol. XLI (January, 1966), pp. 65–74.

PARKER, WILLIAM M. "Business Combinations and Account Valuation," *Journal of Accounting Research*, Vol. IV (Autumn, 1966), pp. 149–54.

SAPIENZA, S. R. "Business Combinations and Enterprise Evaluation," *Journal of Accounting Research*, Vol. I (Spring, 1964), pp. 50–66.

SNAVELY, HOWARD J. "Pooling is Good Accounting," *Financial Analysts Journal*, Vol. XXIV (November–December, 1968), pp. 85–89.

WYATT, ARTHUR R. "A Critical Study of Accounting for Business Combinations," *Accounting Research Study No. 5*. New York: AICPA, 1963.

Earnings per Share

BIERMAN, HAROLD JR., and ERNEST LIU. "The Computation of Earnings Per Share," *Accounting Review,* Vol. XLIII (January, 1968), pp. 62–67.

LEVESON, SIDNEY M. "Have We Solved the Dilution Problem?" *Financial Analysts Journal,* Vol. XXIV (September–October, 1968), pp. 69–70.

SPACEK, LEONARD. "Umpiring the Earnings Per Share Results," *Management Accounting,* Vol. L (March, 1969), pp. 9–14, 27.

chapter 19

Disclosure in
Financial Reporting

The topic of disclosure is broad enough to encompass almost the entire area of financial reporting and, therefore, serves as an appropriate final chapter to a book on accounting theory. One of the major objectives of financial reporting is to supply information for decision making. This requires a proper disclosure of financial data and other relevant information. But the major questions are (1) For whom is the information to be disclosed? (2) What is the purpose of the information? and (3) How much information should be disclosed? The question of how the information should be disclosed is, of course, also important, as the method of disclosure determines the usefulness of the information; but the question of method is secondary to the above three major questions.

The question "For whom?" can be answered by stating that the financial reports are directed primarily to stockholders, other investors, and creditors; but employees, customers, governmental agencies, and the general public are also recipients of annual reports. The decisions to be made by investors are primarily buy-sell-hold decisions, and the decisions of creditors are primarily related to the extension of credit to the enterprise. Stockholders must also make decisions regarding the hiring, firing, and compensation of management and the approval or disapproval of major changes in firm policy. The objectives of presenting information to employees, customers, and the general public have not been well formulated. However, it is generally assumed that the information useful to investors and creditors is also useful to others.

THE NATURE OF DISCLOSURE

AICPA *Accounting Research Study No. 1* stated that "accounting reports should disclose that which is necessary to make them not misleading."[1] This statement is similar to Article No. 2.02 of the *Code of*

---

[1] Maurice Moonitz, "The Basic Postulates of Accounting," *Accounting Research Study No. 1* (New York: American Institute of Certified Public Accountants, 1961), p. 50.

Professional Ethics of the American Institute of Certified Public Accountants. Article 2.02 states in part that—

a member . . . may be held guilty of an act discreditable to the profession if (a) he fails to disclose a material fact known to him which is not disclosed in the financial statements but disclosure of which is necessary to make the financial statements not misleading; or
(b) he fails to report any material misstatement known to him to appear in the financial statement; or
(c) he is materially negligent . . . ; or
(d) he fails to acquire sufficient information . . . ; or
(e) he fails to direct attention to any material departure from generally accepted accounting principles or to disclose any material omission of generally accepted auditing procedures applicable in the circumstances.[2]

Regulation S–X of the Securities and Exchange Commission states similarly that

the information required with respect to any statement shall be furnished as a minimum requirement to which shall be added such further material information as is necessary to make the required statements . . . not misleading.[3]

Each of the above quotations stresses that financial reports should be "not misleading." The objective of disclosure is not stated positively nor is there any clear definition of the meaning of disclosure. The implication is that the financial statements are prepared for investors and that the information will be used in the making of investment decisions. Supposedly, financial statements prepared on the basis of generally accepted accounting principles would be considered to be not misleading unless the usual or expected interpretation is incorrect. Situations that could lead to a misinterpretation of the data if not disclosed include (1) the use of procedures that materially affect income or balance sheet presentations compared with alternative methods that could be assumed by the reader in the absence of such disclosure, (2) a material change in procedures from one period to another, (3) significant events or relationships not arising from normal activities, (4) special contracts or arrangements affecting the relationships of interested parties, (5) material changes or events that would normally affect expectations, and (6) material changes in activities or operations that would affect decisions regarding the firm.

A broader and more positive position was taken by the Committee on Accounting Concepts and Standards of the American Accounting Association in Supplementary Statement No. 8, published in 1954, and in the

---

[2] AICPA, *By-Laws—Code of Professional Ethics* (New York, 1962), p. 31.

[3] Rule 3–06, pp. 5 and 6 of Regulation S–X, Securities and Exchange Commission, Washington, D.C.

1957 revision.[4] In these statements the committee specified that information relating to transactions should be disclosed if the knowledge of such information would be significant to an investor. The committee recognized that financial statements are useful to governmental agencies, creditors, and labor organizations, as well as stockholders and potential investors. But it felt that creditors and governmental agencies had the power generally to obtain additional information and that the information required by the general public is similar to that required by stockholders and potential investors. Therefore, the primary objective of disclosure is to provide information relevant for the making of investment decisions and for exercising control over management. The American Accounting Association Committee to Prepare a Statement of Basic Accounting Theory also recommended in a positive way, but more broadly, that accounting reports should be prepared to permit the observation of significant financial relationships.[5]

The type and amount of disclosure depend, in part, on how expert the reader can be expected to be in interpreting accounting data. He should not be expected to be an expert accountant, yet he should have some knowledge of accounting and business. Wise investment decisions cannot be made, except by chance, by persons uninformed in accounting and business terminology and procedures. Chetkovich referred to the person between the uninformed and the expert as the "standard reader."[6] This standard reader should be willing to read carefully and be reasonably informed on financial matters. Mautz and Sharaf, however, point out that financial market professionals have come to act as intermediaries between accountants and investors. Thus, a new concept of disclosure has appeared— ". . . disclosure of the information which a thoroughly competent and skilled analyst can use and must have to discharge his professional responsibility to those who rely on his judgment."[7] Both views are probably correct. The nonprofessional investor should not be discouraged from attempting to become informed on financial matters, but the special needs of the professional analyst should also be kept in mind.

How much information should be disclosed is dependent not only on the expertness of the reader but also on the desirable standard. Three concepts of disclosure generally proposed are *adequate, fair,* and *full* disclosure. The most commonly used of these expressions is "adequate

---

[4] AAA Committee on Accounting Concepts and Standards, *Accounting and Reporting Standards for Corporate Financial Statements and Preceding Statements and Supplements* (Columbus, Ohio: AAA, 1957), pp. 7–9, 46–50.

[5] Committee to Prepare a Statement of Basic Accounting Theory, *A Statement of Basic Accounting Theory* (AAA, 1966), p. 15.

[6] Michael N. Chetkovich, "Standards of Disclosure and Their Development," *Journal of Accountancy,* Vol. C (December, 1955), pp. 48–52.

[7] R. K. Mautz and Hussein A. Sharaf, *The Philosophy of Auditing* (AAA, 1961), p. 191.

disclosure." But this implies a minimum amount of disclosure congruous with the negative objective of making the statements not misleading. "Fair" and "full" are more positive concepts. Fair disclosure implies an ethical objective of providing equal treatment for all potential readers. Full disclosure implies the presentation of all relevant information. To some, full disclosure means the presentation of superfluous information and is therefore inappropriate. Too much information is harmful in that the presentation of unimportant details hides the significant information and makes the financial reports difficult to interpret. However, appropriate disclosure of information significant to investors and others should be adequate, fair, and full. There is no real difference among these concepts if they are used in the proper context. A positive objective is to provide the users of financial statements with significant and relevant information to aid them in the making of decisions in the best possible way. This implies that information that is not material or relevant be omitted to make the presentations meaningful and understandable.

Materiality and Relevance

As indicated in Chapter 4,[8] the concepts of materiality and relevance are similar in many respects. Relevance implies that all information should be reported that may aid the users in making predictions or decisions. Materiality can also be defined in a positive sense to include all information that may be significant to the users. Relevance, however, generally refers to the nature of the item with respect to specific or general uses of financial reports, while materiality refers to the significance of a specific item in a specific context. An item may be relevant in a general sense and be material in a specific case but lack materiality in another case. The types of items where materiality or relevance may be involved in the decision to disclose or not can be classified as either relating to quantitative measurements or nonquantitative information.

Quantitative Data. In the selection of criteria for determining what quantitative data are material and what are not, accountants have frequently used net income, gross profit, or some other base figure. In deciding whether or not an item should be excluded from the computation of net income because of materiality, some accountants have suggested that the item should be considered material if it exceeds 10 percent of net income before excluding the item. The implication is that if the "true" net income is more than 10 percent greater or smaller than the reported figure, the reader might be misled in making his decisions. But without some assumptions regarding what decisions are likely to be made and what information is relevant to these decisions, the 10 percent rule, or

---

[8] Above, pp. 105–8.

any other percentage criterion, is not likely to provide a meaningful guide.

One difficulty with using net income as a base for deciding materiality is that if income fluctuates from year to year, a 10 percent of current net income rule results in treating a given amount as material in one year but not in the next. Thus, a lack of consistency in reporting may lead to erroneous comparisons among several years and erroneous predictions based on apparent trends. A suggested alternative is to use gross revenue or gross profit as a base, either of which fluctuates less from year to year, percentagewise, than does net income. Probably a better solution would be to use the average net income over several years as a guide, because errors in the computation of net income result from errors in revenue and expense figures, and these errors cannot be assumed to be offsetting in periods of low income. Therefore, for any given firm and set of conditions, the range of probable errors in the net income figure is likely to be much greater percentagewise in a poor year than in a good year. A reader of financial statements cannot assume that all net income figures over several years have the same probability of accuracy. Therefore, research in accounting should focus on the method of measuring and reporting probabilistic data rather than merely deterministic amounts.

The materiality of quantitative data in the balance sheet is not generally considered as important as the determination of materiality in the income statement because of the current emphasis on the income statement and the view that the balance sheet is merely a statement of unallocated debits and credits—a trial balance between two income statements. But if the balance sheet is to be elevated to a position where it can be more meaningful and useful, the concept of materiality should also be applied to the measurement of assets and liabilities.

However, what is material for various types of assets and liabilities depends on the relative accuracy that can be expected by the reader of the financial statements. For example, it is generally thought that cash and related items can be measured relatively accurately; the current value of receivables is somewhat less accurate; and intangibles can be valued only within a relatively wide range of reliability. Therefore, a disclosure of uncertainties in cash items such as deposits in closed banks or in foreign currencies may be considered material while an intangible item of the same amount may not be considered to be material. The reason for this difference is that an informed reader generally places greater reliance on some items in the balance sheet than on others, and he should be able to expect proper disclosure if this assumption is not justified.

Nonquantitative Information. Information that cannot be expressed in quantitative terms is more difficult to evaluate as to its materiality because it is given various weights by those using the information in decision making. In general, information that is given greater weight in decision making is more relevant than information given less weight. But the point of cutoff where the information can be said to be of so little importance that it can be or should be omitted is difficult to determine. Conversely, the point should be sought where it can be said that the information is important enough in decision making that it should not be omitted.

The relevance of certain types of nonquantitative information can be determined by the relevance of the quantitative data to which they relate. For example, if certain assets are pledged as security to specific creditors, the pledging would be a relevant fact if the assets themselves are material in amount. If the assets are not material, the descriptive or qualifying information is not likely to be relevant. In a few cases, however, this may not be true; for example, the loss of an immaterial amount of inventory or cash may become a relevant fact if it is due to a fraudulent management.

Nonquantitative information is relevant and worthy of disclosure only if it is useful in the decision-making process. It is relevant only if it adds more to the total information than it detracts by making the statements overly detailed and difficult to analyze. The question should always be asked: Is the addition of the information likely to improve most decisions made on the basis of the financial reports?

Frequently, the comment is made that a certain type of information should not be disclosed, not because it is not relevant but because it might be useful to the wrong parties. For example, the sales volume of a specific product in a given territory might be useful information to competitors and affect future sales and income adversely even though it might be helpful to investors. An estimate of the expected liability to arise from a lawsuit might influence the outcome of the suit itself. But the failure to disclose relevant information for this reason alone is generally not thought to be justified as frequently as it was particularly prior to the 1930's in the United States. The large corporations of today have a responsibility to investors and the general public to disclose relevant information even though the reaction to the information may be unfavorable to the corporation.

METHODS OF DISCLOSURE

Disclosure involves the entire process of financial reporting. However, several different methods of making disclosure are available. The selection of the best method of disclosure in each case depends on the nature of the information and its relative importance. The common methods of disclosure can be classified as follows: (1) form and arrangement of formal statements, (2) terminology and detailed presentations, (3) parenthetical information, (4) footnotes, (5) supplementary statements and schedules, (6) comments in the auditors' certificate, and (7) the letter of the president or chairman of the board.

Form and Arrangement of Formal Statements

The most relevant and significant information should always appear in the main body of one or more of the financial statements if it is possible to do so. Assets and liabilities and the resulting effect on net income and stockholders' equity should be disclosed in the statements as soon as transactions and other changes can be measured reliably and with a fair degree of accuracy. But the form and arrangement of the statement can be altered effectively to bring out certain types of information not readily disclosed by traditional statements.

Position Statement. In the position statement or balance sheet, relevant relationships can be disclosed by rearranging the basic classifications. For example, current liabilities are frequently subtracted directly from current assets to show working capital, although this procedure has some deficiencies (as discussed in Chapter 10). Alternative classifications may separate monetary from nonmonetary assets and liabilities, or group the firm's resources according to the several segments of the business in which they are used. The classification of assets and liabilities was discussed in Chapter 10, several alternative methods of classification and presentation of stockholders' equity were discussed in Chapter 17, and the problems of divisional reporting are discussed later in this chapter.

Income Statement. In the income statement, different forms of presentation can emphasize different concepts of income or different interpretations of the data. The single-step income statement, for example, associates all items of expense with all items of revenue; gross profit and other preliminary net figures are considered to be more misleading than helpful to the readers of the statement. In a suggested alternative, expenses are classified as either fixed or variable in order to aid the reader in making predictions of future outcomes with changes in sales volume. The disclosure of other income concepts and relationships has been discussed, in Chapter 5. The disclosure of earnings per share data in the income statement was discussed in Chapter 18.

Cash Flow and Funds Statements. As discussed in Chapter 8, considerable relevant information can be presented in cash flow and funds statements, particularly if care is taken to provide relevant classifications. For example, classifications of cash disbursements should be more relevant for predictive purposes if the disbursements are grouped according to their functional behavior, such as fixed and variable characteristics. Additional groupings according to the major segments of the business are also likely to be relevant to the decisions of investors and other interested parties.

Terminology and Detailed Presentations

Just as important as the form of the statements in disclosure are the descriptions used in the statements and the amount of detail shown. Appropriate captions and descriptions of the items in the statements can be enlightening to the reader, while obscure terms can lead only to confusion or misunderstanding. Technical terms may be useful if they have precise meanings that are generally well known, but many technical terms in accounting lack this preciseness. In these cases, accountants should apply descriptive terms generally used by financial analysts and other informed readers. Uniformity of terms throughout all accounting reports would be helpful if the meanings are clear and if the items are similar in all cases where the term is applied.

Because of the limitations of human spans of attention and comprehension, accounting data must be summarized to be meaningful and useful. The choice of how much information to present and the selection of what items to list separately are dependent on the objectives of the reports and on the materiality of the items. Brevity is a desirable goal in financial reports, but appropriate disclosure of detailed information should take precedence if it is necessary to make the reports significant for decision making.

Parenthetical Information

The most significant information should be presented in the body of a financial statement rather than in footnotes or supplementary schedules. If the titles of items in the statements cannot be made fully descriptive without being overly long, additional explanations or definitions can be presented as parenthetical notes following the titles in the statements. These notes, however, must not be long or they will detract from the main data summarized in the statement.

Other nonquantitative data that can be presented in parenthetical notes include (1) an indication of the specific procedure or valuation method used, to give the reader a better understanding of the meaning of the data; (2) the special characteristics that give greater meaning regarding the relative importance of the item, such as the fact that certain assets are pledged or that certain liabilities have prior rights; (3) detail regarding the amount of one or more items included in the broader classification listed; (4) alternative valuations such as current market price; and (5) reference to related information in other statements or elsewhere in the report.

Footnotes

Current financial reports have been said to give rise to what is called the "footnote era." On the one hand, this is an improvement in reporting because it has resulted in a fuller disclosure of financial events and relevant financial data. On the other hand, the extensive use of footnotes has hindered the proper development of the statements themselves because it has resulted in the substitution of footnotes for better information in the body of the statement. Footnotes have an appropriate place in financial reporting but there is danger in placing too much reliance on footnotes as a method of disclosure or in using footnotes as an apology for inadequate formal statements. While it is difficult to set forth clear principles of footnoting based on accounting theory, some basic rules of footnoting can be formulated to tie in with the basic postulates and principles of accounting.

Nature and Purpose of Footnotes. The objective of footnotes to financial statements should be to disclose information that cannot be presented adequately in the body of a statement without detracting from the clarity of the statement. Footnotes should not be used as a substitute for proper classification or valuation and description in the statements, nor should they contradict or repeat the information in the statements.

The main advantages of footnotes are: (1) the ability to present nonquantitative information as an integral part of the financial report, (2) the ability to disclose qualifications and restrictions to items in the statements, (3) as a useful method of disclosing a greater amount of detail than can be presented in the statements, and (4) as a method of presenting either quantitative or descriptive material of secondary importance.

The main disadvantages of footnotes are: (1) they tend to be difficult to read and understand without considerable study and thus they may be overlooked; (2) the textual descriptions are more difficult to use in decision making than the summarizations of quantitative data in the statements; and (3) because of the increasing complexity of business enterprises, there is danger of an overuse of footnotes rather than proper development of principles to incorporate new relationships and events into the statements themselves.

The most common types of footnotes can be classified as follows: (1) explanations of techniques or changes in methods, (2) explanations of rights of creditors to specific assets or priorities of rights, (3) disclosure of contingent assets or contingent liabilities, (4) disclosure of restrictions to dividend payments, (5) descriptions of transactions affecting capital stock and rights of equity holders, and (6) descriptions of executory contracts. While footnotes are also used to present detailed quantitative data that are not significant enough to include in the body of a statement, these are in the form of supplementary schedules and therefore are discussed at greater length below as a separate form of disclosure.

Explanations of Methods. A proper interpretation of the income statement, the balance sheet, and the funds statement requires an understanding of the accounting methods used and the effect of changes in methods. Because most valuation and allocation techniques affect the income statement, the balance sheet, and the funds statement, a footnote disclosure of the methods used may be better than parenthetical notes in each statement. And with a footnote the methods used can be given fuller treatment than if parenthetical notes are used. This fuller disclosure is important where the differences among the several accepted methods are material—that is, where an assumption of a different method would be a significant factor in the making of decisions. Where an item such as cost of goods sold is a summary of several items computed by different methods, the footnote disclosure should show the amounts computed by each of the methods if material. In the case of Lifo, the year the method was started might also be relevant. Since depreciation is generally a major item in most income statements, the Accounting Principles Board, in *Opinion No. 12*, recommended that the methods used in computing depreciation should be presented for the major classes of depreciable assets.[9]

Changes in methods may be more significant than the methods themselves, particularly when comparative data are presented. The postulate of consistency requires that financial reports should be comparable from period to period and that, when changes are made, the effect of the change should be disclosed. In most cases, this disclosure can be made appropriately in footnotes. However, if the effect of the change is to make a comparison of the data completely misleading, a footnote would be inadequate. In this case, the data for prior years should be computed on the new basis to permit proper comparisons.

Prior Rights of Creditors. The usual types of priorities, such as those granted to mortgage bondholders, can generally be explained succinctly in the balance sheet by a brief reference to the mortgage or to the specific property granted as security. But when the prior claims are unusual or more complex than normal, a footnote disclosure is necessary. Such contract provisions are relevant and material if knowledge of them would affect the decisions of other creditors or investors. Generally, it can be assumed that knowledge of these provisions would affect credit or investment decisions if the provisions affect the risk of other creditors or stockholders. These contract provisions may also be relevant if they restrict

---

[9] AICPA, *Accounting Principles* (Chicago: Commerce Clearing House, Inc., 1968), Vol. II, p. 6595.

the freedom of management and the board of directors in the general operations of the firm or in the financing of expansions or replacements.

Contingent Assets and Contingent Liabilities. As indicated in Chapter 15, all assets and liabilities should be estimated if at all possible and included in the balance sheet; and the effect, if any, on net income should be reflected in the income statement. Only if the most probable value of the asset or liability is likely to be zero or if the best estimate of current or future value is very likely to be highly erroneous and misleading should the asset or liability be omitted from the statements. But if the probable occurrence of a gain or loss resulting from the failure to recognize the asset or liability would be a significant element in decision making, the relevant facts should be disclosed in a footnote.

In the case of a pending lawsuit, the amount of the claim and any other relevant information, such as the decisions of lower courts or decisions in other similar cases, should be disclosed to permit the reader to form some judgment regarding the possible effect of the case. Expectations regarding the outcome of the case and the probable damages to be awarded by the court are not generally meaningful unless the reason for the estimate is also given.

Restrictions to Dividend Payments. From a legal point of view, dividends can usually be paid to the extent of total retained earnings and, in many states, paid-in surplus. But, as explained in Chapter 17, the classification of stockholders' equity in the balance sheet does not disclose the extent of the legality of dividends nor does it show the intent of the board of directors regarding future dividend payments. However, according to traditional textbook treatments, legal, contractual, and managerial restrictions on dividends may be shown by means of appropriations of retained earnings or by setting up a separate classification for reserves. Since the stockholders' equity section of the balance sheet is classified primarily by its source rather than by intended distribution, this use of appropriations and reserves is more confusing than enlightening.

A positive statement of the policy of the board of directors regarding dividend distributions would be helpful to investors and other users of financial reports. Most dividend payments by large corporations are related to current earnings, past earnings, past dividends and available cash resources. There is generally no intent to pay dividends to the full amount legally permitted or even to the extent of retained earnings. Therefore, a footnote explanation of dividend restrictions based on retained earnings may not be very relevant to investors who can expect that future dividends will not likely exceed future earnings. However, if current earnings are at all restricted for dividend payments, these restrictions should be disclosed. Because of the nature of the information, all relevant restrictions of either retained earnings or current earnings can be disclosed appropriately in footnotes. When there are several restrictions that are not cumulative, the most restrictive requirement or contract may provide appropriate disclosure.

Rights of Equity Holders. Some of the rights of equity holders are apparent in the balance sheet classifications and descriptions, while others can be disclosed by appropriate parenthetical notes in the statements. Significant changes in these rights to share in income and the net assets of the firm arising from transactions or events during the period should be disclosed specifically in the balance sheet or in footnotes, even though the results of the transactions are reflected in the related items in the balance sheet. Several types of transactions, however, are not immediately reflected in the equity accounts but affect the future rights of equity holders. It is particularly important that these types of transactions and events be disclosed appropriately in the footnotes to the statements. However, APB *Opinion No. 10* recommends that liquidation preferences of preferred stock be disclosed in the aggregate in the balance sheet either parenthetically or "in short," rather than in footnotes.[10]

One of the common types of transactions affecting the future rights of stockholders is the granting of executive stock options. As discussed in Chapter 18, the conventional method of disclosing these contracts does not show the true effect on income or the true effect on the rights of equity holders. Possibly, because of the uncertainties involved, the true effect cannot be anticipated, and therefore cannot appropriately be shown by merely recording the transaction in the formal accounts. Footnotes showing the nature of the options, the requirements of the contract, and the possible effects on income and stockholders' equity should supplement whatever information can be presented in the formal statements.

Other types of disclosure affecting the rights of stockholders include the potential rights of holders of stock warrants, convertible debt, or convertible preferred stock. Footnote disclosures should include information regarding the period of conversion or exercise of warrants, the conversion price or exercise price, and other relevant terms of the contracts relating to these securities.

Executory Contracts. Traditional accounting does not recognize assets or liabilities arising from executory contracts.[11] One of the reasons for the failure to record these assets and liabilities is that their valuations are not easily estimated. Another reason is that the effect on income arises from later events rather than from the signing of the contract. However, in most cases, because the contracts represent commitments for the future, a disclosure of them is very relevant for investment and other decisions relying on some prediction of future income or cash flows. If this

---

[10] *Ibid.*, p. 6576.

[11] See the discussion of long-term commitments, pp. 484–86.

disclosure cannot be made appropriately in the formal statements, the information should be disclosed in footnotes.

Included in the executory type of contacts are long-term leases and purchase commitments. While the capitalization of these commitments and the inclusion of them among the assets and liabilities of the balance sheet may improve the statements, the nature of these contracts usually requires supplementary information also. In addition to the capitalized valuation, the reader of the report would probably be interested in knowing the terminal date of the contract, the amount of annual payment, the annual charge to expense, and other features. Therefore, footnote disclosure may be disirable to provide supplementary information regarding the long-term contracts; it should not be viewed only as an alternative to capitalization.

Supplementary Statements and Schedules

In order that financial data may be summarized and presented in a statement brief enough to be understandable by reasonably informed readers, some of the significant detailed information must be taken out of the statements and presented in supplementary schedules. These schedules are sometimes included among the footnotes and sometimes in a section following the statements and footnotes. In many current annual reports, the supplementary schedules are included in a separate section of the report called "financial highlights" or some similar section preceding the formal financial statements. By using a separate section in the report, the information presented there is placed in a position secondary to the statements and footnotes and, therefore, it is assumed to be of less importance than the information in the statements and footnotes. But this separation of information by its relative importance is necessary to make the statements readable and understandable.

Supplementary statements perform a different function than supplementary schedules. Generally they present additional information or information arranged in a different fashion, rather than just more detailed information. Since they are not necessarily included in the statements covered in the report of the independent accountant, they can be used as methods of developing and experimenting with new exhibits and statements.

Two types of supplementary statements frequently recommended for inclusion in the financial reports are the source and application of funds statement and statements disclosing the effect of price-level changes on the financial condition and financial operations of the enterprise. APB *Opinion No. 3* recommended that the funds statement be presented as supplementary information in financial reports, but that it is optional whether or not it is covered by the report of the independent accountant. In the author's opinion, cash flow and funds statements are of such significance that they should be given the same status as other major financial statements. In accordance with *Statement No. 3* of the Accounting Principles Board, published in 1969, supplementary statements showing the effect of price-level changes may present useful information, but they should not be presented as the basic statements. One advantage of permitting these statements to be included on a voluntary basis in financial reports is that it permits greater experimentation while they are still in the developmental stage. However, the difficulty with such voluntary experimentation is that only a few firms will prepare such statements until all are required to do so or until the firms feel that the information is demanded by investors or creditors.

The Auditor's Certificate

The audit certificate is not the place to disclose significant financial information regarding the firm. But it does serve as a method of disclosure for the following types of information: (1) a material effect from using accounting methods different from those generally accepted, (2) a material effect from changing from one generally accepted accounting method to another, and (3) a difference of opinion between the auditor and the client regarding the acceptability of one or more accounting methods used in the reports. The first two types of information should also be disclosed in the reports themselves. The duplication of disclosure is required to be sure that the reader is not misled regarding the comparability of the reports with those of other firms or the consistency with other periods.

The financial statements are the report of the client and not the auditor. If the auditor believes that a method used in preparing the financial statements is not appropriate or generally accepted, he should, of course, attempt to persuade the client to change to an appropriate method. But failing to do so, he is obligated to disclose the disagreement and the effect of the method used. And in accordance with a *Special Bulletin* of the Council of the AICPA, departures from APB *Opinions* and *Accounting Research Bulletins* must be disclosed in the auditor's report if they are not disclosed in footnotes to the financial statements. When accounting theory is further developed as an evaluation tool, the terms "logical" or "sound" should be substituted for "generally accepted." General acceptance does not make the methods logical or logically derived from accounting postulates and principles.

The President's Letter

The formal financial statements with the footnotes and supplementary schedules and statements and the auditor's certificate complete the accountant's financial report. All relevant and significant financial data should appear in this report. However, certain types of information can be presented directly by management in the form of the letter of the president or chairman of the board or in other sections of the annual report. This additional information should include (1) nonfinancial events and changes during the year that affect the operations of the firm, (2) expectations regarding the future of the industry and the economy and the role of the firm in these expectations, (3) plans for growth and changes in operations in the following period or periods, and (4) the amount and expected effect of current and anticipated capital expenditures and research effort.

The nonfinancial events and changes would include shifts in top management and major policies; significant technological improvements in the firm or industry; shifts in the demand for the product of the firm or changes in prices of either major factors of production or of the product; and events such as strikes, wars, political actions, and natural disasters that may have a material effect on future operations of the firm. If any of these nonfinancial events is likely to have a material effect on the valuation of assets or liabilities at the end of the period or on the income of future periods, it should be reported in the financial statements rather than being left for management to report. But the effect of many of these items is difficult to evaluate, and even though it is taken into consideration in the financial statements, a more complete disclosure by management is desirable.

Expectations are more difficult to disclose and evaluate than nonfinancial events. Management has a tendency to present only optimistic expectations and, therefore, make them somewhat meaningless. A common expression found in these letters of the president is "we are confident that the prospects for profitable operations will continue to improve." Expressions such as this are too vague to be useful in making predictions regarding the future of the enterprise.

In Great Britain, under the 1948 and 1967 Companies Acts, a directors' report must be included in the annual report along with the auditor's report and the financial statements. Among the disclosure requirements of the acts are requirements that specific information must be included in the directors' report, such as (1) the disclosure of market values in certain situations, (2) a statement of the proportions in which the total revenue is divided among the several classes of business that differ substantially from each other in the opinion of the directors, (3) the approximate extent to which each class of business contributed to or restricted profit of the company, and (4) changes in plant and equipment during the year and future capital expenditures authorized by the directors but for which contracts have not been signed. While some of this information may be included in the statements or footnotes, subject to the review of the auditors, a significant danger is that while the auditors are generally requested to review the directors' report, they are not required to do so. As a result, the directors' report may include both audited and unaudited information and forecasts as well as historical data, without a clear indication to the readers as to which has been subject to review of the auditors and which has not.

Summary of Disclosure Methods

Disclosure is a relative term, but it should be the basic objective of financial statements after determining for whom and for what purpose financial information is to be presented. In accordance with the basic postulates of accounting, the most relevant financial data should be summarized in quantitative terms and be presented in the formal statements to the extent possible and desirable and then in footnotes, supplementary schedules, and supplementary statements. Descriptive information should appear in the body of statements only in brief form. More detailed descriptions should appear in footnotes or elsewhere in the financial reports.

DISCLOSURE OF POST-STATEMENT EVENTS

The income statement is a summary of certain types of changes during the period being reported on, and the balance sheet summarizes the resource measurements and financial relationships at the end of this period. However, almost all of the figures included in these statements are tentative in nature, because of allocations and uncertainties regarding the future. As time passes and additional information is obtained, many of these uncertainties are resolved. Therefore, many of the events occurring after the statement date affect the validity of the statements or the interpretation of them and the resulting decisions based on the information presented in the statements. To the extent that material events occur or become known after the statement date and before the report is completed, the objective of disclosure requires that this information be properly revealed in the report.

Three types of relevant events that may occur after the statement date and before the completion of the report are: (1) events that affect directly the amounts reported in the financial statements; (2) events that alter materially the continuing validity of balance sheet valuations or the relationships among equity holders, or materially affect the usefulness of the prior year's income as a prediction of the income of the current period; and (3) events that might affect materially future incomes or valuations.

Events of the first type arise from inadequate knowledge during the accounting period and result in changes in estimated valuations or in allocations because of knowledge gained subsequent to the balance sheet date. For example, if a major customer goes into bankruptcy during this period, the receivables included in the balance sheet and not collected at the date of the bankruptcy are likely to be overvalued, and the related bad debt expense was probably understated. If knowledge of this type of information is obtained early enough, the financial statements should be adjusted appropriately before they are published. If knowledge is obtained too late to make a complete correction of the statements, the information can be disclosed by some other means unless the statements would be completely erroneous if direct correction is not made. The Committee on Auditing Procedure of the AICPA recommended that this type of event should be recognized by an adjustment directly in the financial statements if the information would have been utilized had it been available at the balance sheet date.[12]

Events of the second type have no direct effect on the financial statements of the prior year but are likely to affect materially decisions based on these statements. These include (1) events that affect materially the financial structure of the firm or current or future relationships among equity holders, and (2) events that affect the income or potential dividend distributions of the period following the period included in the report or in later periods. Thus, a relatively large sale of capital stock or bonds or the purchase or sale of assets representing a large part of the total assets of the firm is assumed to be relevant for investment or credit decisions regarding the firm. Events that may result in abnormal and nonrecurring gains or losses may also affect decisions by influencing predictions of the future economic health of the firm. The Committee on Auditing Procedure stated that these events do not require adjustment, but it did say that disclosure is advisable.[13] In the opinion of the author, the recommendation should be much stronger than this. Appropriate disclosure is just as important for these events as for similar events occurring during the reporting period. For example, the disclosure of a new stock option plan or an agreement to negotiate a merger is just as important if the event occurs after the balance sheet date as it is if it occurred before. Partial recognition is given to this in APB *Opinion No. 10,* which

---

[12] Committee on Auditing Procedure of the AICPA, *Auditing Standards and Procedures,* Statement on Auditing Procedure No. 33 (New York: AICPA, 1963), p. 76.

[13] *Ibid.*

recommends that in the case of a combination accounted for as a pooling, consummated after the close of the period but before the financial statements are issued, the financial statements should be restated to give effect to the pooling for the entire period.

Events of the third type have an unknown or uncertain effect on future incomes and valuations. Examples would include changes in specific market conditions or in prices affecting the firm; new management policies; the signing of major contracts; and external events such as wars, legislation, and economic conditions. The Committee on Auditing Procedure recommended that, while disclosure of these events may be required, "disclosure of such conditions or events frequently creates doubt as to the reason therefor, and inferences drawn could be misleading as often as they are informative."[14]

The Institute of Chartered Accountants in England and Wales also expresses a narrow view regarding disclosure. In its *Recommendation on Accounting Principles: 17* it stated:

Events which, at the time of preparing annual accounts, are known to have occurred after the balance sheet date, should not normally be taken into account in preparing accounts unless (a) they assist in forming an opinion as to the amount properly attributable in the conditions existing on the balance sheet date, to any item the amount of which was subject to uncertainty on that date, or (b) they arise from legislation affecting items in the accounts. . . .[15]

These recommendations, however, apply to disclosure in audited statements. Disclosure of the events of the third type, or of all types, may be made in the president's letter or in a separate section of the annual report without any implication that the auditors consider this information a qualification of the statements. A broader and more positive viewpoint is that events of all three types, including their effect on the expectations of management, should be disclosed directly in the financial report reviewed by the auditor. The author agrees with this position as a long-run goal to provide the best possible information for the making of investment decisions.

DISCLOSURE BY DIVERSIFIED COMPANIES

The growth of diversified businesses in the United States and in other countries has continued for several decades. However, the problem of reporting for diversified companies has become more acute with the rapid development of huge conglomerate firms that obtain their diversification

---

[14] *Ibid.*, p. 77.

[15] Institute of Chartered Accountants in England and Wales, *Recommendations on Accounting Principles: 17*—"Events Occurring after the Balance Sheet Date," Chap. 17 (London, 1967).

through mergers or acquisitions of a wide variety of unrelated businesses. With each combination there is a loss of information to the investor community and to the general public, since firms previously reporting separately report only as a single firm after the combination. Also, because of the diversification of activities, evaluation of these conglomerate firms and prediction of their future activities and successes become more difficult with only aggregated data available.

Requirements for the disclosure of information regarding the profitability of the separate operations of diversified firms have been in existence for many years in Sweden; and the 1967 British Companies Act includes similar requirements.[16] In the United States, under the rules of the Securities and Exchange Commission, diversified firms must disclose if practicable the relative importance of segments of the business which contribute 15 percent or more to the gross volume of the business.[17] However, the SEC has proposed that registrant companies state the approximate amount or percentage of sales and contribution to net income attributable to any segment that contributes at least 10 percent to revenues or income.

The Accounting Principles Board recommended in its *Statement No. 2* that diversified firms voluntarily present supplementary information regarding the individual segments of their businesses. Examples of suggested types of disclosure include: (1) revenues by separate type of activity or by type of customer; (2) profit or loss for major segments of the business or information that certain segments are operating at a loss, without disclosing the amount of the loss; and (3) separate financial statements for segments of the business that operate autonomously and have a significantly different type of capital structure.

Need for Disclosure

The need for disclosure of the operations of the major segments of diversified firms arises from the loss of information that occurs when several firms combine and a single set of financial statements is published for the new conglomerate firm. The combination also creates a lack of comparability with other firms operating in single industries and with other conglomerate firms operating in a different combination of industries. But it may be argued that investors should estimate the value of each firm separately and then base their decisions on the estimated values of several firms and their evaluation of the risks in each case.

In estimating the value of a firm and in evaluating the risk, however,

---

[16] R. G. Walker, "Disclosure by Diversified Companies," *Abacus,* Vol. IV (August, 1968), p. 27.

[17] Manuel F. Cohen, "The SEC and Accountants: Cooperative Efforts to Improve Financial Reporting," *Journal of Accountancy,* Vol. CXXII (December, 1966), p. 59.

investors need to make predictions regarding the future operations of the enterprise. Predictions that are based on or supported by extrapolations of historical data are likely to be more reliable if they are made from information regarding the various segments of a business that have different characteristics.

Whether the objective should be to permit comparability or to permit predictability has a bearing on the minimum size of a business segment that should be reported separately. In order to obtain *comparability* among firms for similar types of operations, the selection criterion should be the absolute size of the operations. If a criterion is based on a percentage of total revenues of the firm, one type of operation representing 50 percent or more of the revenues of a small firm would require disclosure; but if it represents less than, say, 10 percent of the total revenues of a large firm, it would not be reported even though an operation of this type may be considerably larger than the similar operation of the smaller firm. For this reason, recommendations have been made that segments as small as 5 percent of the total operations of a diversified firm should be reported separately, with a minimum absolute dollar criterion.[18] However, if *predictability* is the objective, a higher minimum percentage may be adequate in order to provide relevant information regarding the contribution of a segment to the firm's revenue and net income. For example, an FEI study suggested that 15 percent might be adequate.[19]

Information regarding segments of a business is also thought to be relevant in external reports to prevent management from hiding information that it does not want published. For example, managements may wish to hide the fact that certain segments of the business are being operated at a loss for fear that they will be criticized by the stockholders for their managerial inefficiency. If some segments are quite profitable, they can be used to cover up the fact that other segments are unprofitable. This ability to hide losses has also been used by large firms as a way to finance their entry into a new line and to compete with established firms without being accused of underpricing to gain monopolistic control in markets.

Accounting Difficulties

One of the first problems in reporting on divisions or segments of a business is the decision regarding how a logical breakdown should be made for reporting purposes. Product lines may be relevant in some cases but not in others. Geographical divisions may be particularly relevant

---

[18] For example see "Conglomerate Reporting—The Debate Continues," *Journal of Accountancy,* Vol. CXXVII (March, 1969), p. 24.

[19] R. K. Mautz, *Financial Reporting by Diversified Companies* (Financial Executives Institute, 1968).

with respect to foreign operations, and in other cases, classification by type of customer may be relevant. Particularly those who look for comparability among firms have recommended that a uniform classification along industry lines, such as the Standard Industrial Code of the Bureau of Census, should be used. But from the point of view of the investor, the classification that permits the greatest degree of predictability would be the most relevant. That is, predictability would require the grouping of activities that have similar behavioral characteristics over time.

A second major problem in the reporting of profit for separate segments of a business is the allocation of joint costs. If the segments are autonomously operated divisions, the amount of joint costs may be small; but in relation to the net incomes of the segments, it may be significant. Since accountants make allocations in many areas of reporting (such as the computation of depreciation), it has been suggested that one more allocation might make little difference.[20] But since such allocations are arbitrary, it is unlikely that relevant information can be obtained by their use. An alternative is to report only the "defined profit" or contribution of each division, computed from only the revenues and expenses that can be directly associated with the reporting segment. However, some firms may fear that such contribution may be interpreted as the net income of the division and as being excessive.

Another accounting problem is the treatment of interdivisional pricing. The final product of one division may be the raw material of another within the same firm, so that if transfers are made in excess of cost, income will appear at the time of the transfer rather than when the final product is sold to a customer outside the firm. Solomons suggested that the best procedure would seem to be to eliminate interdivisional sales from reports to stockholders and thus report all such transfers at cost.[21] From the point of view of the objective of attaining predictive ability, this seems to be the best solution, because a prediction of the final cash to be received from customers is more important to investors than the amount of product transferred from one division to another. However, comparability among firms is not attained; because in some cases the semifinished product may be the final product of the firm, while in other cases the output of the semifinished product would not be reported prior to the sale of the final product of which it becomes a part.

Since the profitability of a firm is frequently measured in terms of the net income in relationship to the amount of net assets invested in the

---

[20] See for example Sidney Davidson, "Implications of Conglomerate Reporting for the Independent CPA—Comments," in *Public Reporting by Conglomerates,* edited by Alfred Rappaport, Peter A. Firmin, and Stephen A. Zeff (Englewood Cliffs, N.J.: Prentice-Hall, Inc., 1968), p. 88.

[21] David Solomons, "Accounting Problems and Some Proposed Solutions," in *ibid.,* p. 100.

firm, it seems logical that divisional reporting should also require the separate reporting of the net assets used by each segment of the business. This separate reporting of assets was included in the proposed rules of the SEC to the extent that it is practicable. However, the measurement of assets is a difficult problem even for an entire enterprise. The assignment of physical assets to segments of a business may be possible in some cases, but accounting has not yet devised a consistent method of measuring these assets in a meaningful way so they can be related to the net income derived from them. Even if physical assets could be assigned to segments and measured in a meaningful way, the intangible assets— which may be more important in many cases—are most likely to be omitted. Furthermore, the liabilities of the enterprise cannot usually be designated in a meaningful way to represent the financing of specific assets.

Opposition to Divisional Disclosures

Divisional reporting is opposed by many firms on the ground that it would not provide equity among different enterprises. If a percentage rule is used, small firms would be required to disclose the results of operations of activities that would be buried in the reports of several other operations of a large firm. If an absolute dollar rule were used, large firms would be required to reveal an excessive amount of detail which might not be relevant to investors. Many firms, large and small, are opposed to divisional reporting for fear that it may reveal important information to their competitors, since the reporting of a highly profitable area of a business might attract additional competitors.

Opposition to the SEC proposals has also come from the National Association of Accountants and the Financial Executives Institute because of the necessity to make arbitrary allocations of joint costs, which would obscure rather than clarify the reporting of business segments; and because the 10 percent rule is considered to be too small to be meaningful for most firms and unduly harsh for smaller firms.[22]

SELECTED ADDITIONAL READING ON CHAPTER TOPICS

Nature of Disclosure

BARR, ANDREW. "Changing Financial Reporting: Yesterday, Today and Tomorrow," *California CPA Quarterly* (June, 1968), pp. 15–19.

BACKER, MORTON. "Comments on 'The Value of the SEC's Accounting Disclosure Requirements,'" *Accounting Review*, Vol. XLIV (July, 1969), pp. 533–38.

---

[22] "SEC Opposed on Conglomerate Disclosure Proposals," *Management Accounting,* Vol. L (December, 1968), pp. 55–56.

BENSTON, GEORGE J. "The Value of the SEC's Accounting Disclosure Requirements," *Accounting Review*, Vol. XLIV (July, 1969), pp. 515–32.

BIRNBERG, JACOB G., and NICHOLAS DOPUCH. "A Conceptual Approach to the Framework for Disclosure," *Journal of Accountancy*, Vol. CXV (February, 1963), pp. 56–63.

BURTON, JOHN C. "The Seaview Symposium on Financial Reporting," *Journal of Accountancy*, Vol. CXXVII (January, 1969), pp. 33–38.

MAUTZ, R. K., and HUSSEIN A. SHARAF. *The Philosophy of Auditing*, chap. vii, pp. 158–203. American Accounting Association Monograph No. 6. AAA, 1961.

SINGHVI, SURENDRA S. "Corporate Financial Disclosure: Nature and Media," *Management Accounting*, Vol. L (November, 1968), pp. 15–17.

Post-Statement Events

FLOWERS, WILLIAM BAKER. *Criteria for Disclosure of Post-Statement Events*. Austin: University of Texas, Bureau of Business Research, 1960.

——. "Some Criteria for Post-Statement Disclosure," *Journal of Accountancy*, Vol. CXI (January, 1961), pp. 48–58.

MAURIELLO, JOSEPH A. "Accounting Theory and Subsequent Events," *New York Certified Public Accountant*, Vol. XXX (September, 1960), pp. 633–36.

Disclosure by Diversified Companies

BACKER, MORTON, and WALTER B. McFARLAND. *External Reporting for Segments of a Business*. New York: National Association of Accountants, 1968.

CRAMER, JOE J., JR. "Income Reporting by Conglomerates: Views of American Businessmen," *Abacus*, Vol. IV (August, 1968), pp. 17–26.

MAUTZ, R. K. *Financial Reporting by Conglomerate Companies*. New York: Financial Executives Institute, 1968.

RAPPAPORT, ALFRED, PETER A. FIRMIN, and STEPHEN A. ZEFF (eds.). *Public Reporting by Conglomerates: The Issues, the Problems, and Some Possible Solutions*. Englewood Cliffs, N.J.: Prentice-Hall, Inc., 1968.

SOLOMONS, DAVID. *Divisional Performance: Measurement and Control*. Homewood, Ill.: Richard D. Irwin, Inc., 1968.

SPROUSE, ROBERT T. "Diversified Views about Diversified Companies," *Journal of Accounting Research*, Vol. VII (Spring, 1969), pp. 137–59.

WALKER, R. G. "Disclosure by Diversified Companies," *Abacus*, Vol. IV (August, 1968), pp. 27–38.

appendix

Selected CPA
Examination Questions

The following questions from the Theory Section of CPA Examinations are re-printed with the kind permission of the American Institute of Certified Public Accountants.

CHAPTER 4—CONCEPTS, MEASUREMENT, AND STRUCTURE
OF ACCOUNTING THEORY

Postulates

Question 4-1 (May, 1963).

For some time the need for the study and formulation of basic postulates and principles of accounting has been recognized.

Required:

a. Discuss (1) the purpose of developing basic postulates and principles of accounting, and (2) the benefits to be derived from their development.

b. Frequently advanced as a basic postulate is a general proposition dealing with "objectivity." Under what conditions, in general, is information arising from a financial transaction considered to be objective in nature?

c. Accountants acknowledge that financial statements reporting the results of operations for relatively short periods of time, say one year, are tentative whenever allocations between past, present, and future periods are required. On the other hand the "objectivity" postulate leads to the logical deduction that changes in assets and liabilities, and the related effects (if any) on revenues, expenses, retained earnings, and the like, should not be given formal recognition in the accounts earlier than the point of time at which they can be measured in objective terms. Can this apparent conflict be resolved? Discuss.

Continuity

Question 4-2 (May, 1962).

Select the choice which best completes the statement.

The "going concern" concept is the basis for the rule that:

a. The cost of installing a machine should be added to the invoice cost of the machine in the accounts.

b. The cost of intangible assets should be written off systematically over their useful lives.

c. The income statement should not include material gains and losses unrelated to normal operations.

d. Treasury stock should not be recorded in the balance sheet as an asset.

e. None of the above.

Consistency

Question 4-3 (May, 1961).

You are engaged in the audit of the Willis Corporation, which opened its first branch office in 1960. During the audit the Willis president raises the question of the accounting treatment of the branch office operating loss for its first year, which is material in amount.

The president proposes to capitalize the operating loss as a "starting-up" expense to be amortized over a five-year period. He states that branch offices of other firms engaged in the same field generally suffer a first-year operating loss, which is invariably capitalized, and you are aware of this practice. He argues, therefore, that the loss should be capitalized so that the accounting will be "conservative"; further, he argues that the accounting must be "consistent" with established industry practice.

Required:

a. Discuss the president's use of the words "conservative" and "consistent" from the standpoint of accounting terminology. Discuss the accounting treatment you would recommend.

b. What disclosure, if any, would be required in the financial statements?

Uniformity

Question 4-4 (May, 1966).

At the completion of the Darby Department Store audit, the president asks about the meaning of the phrase "in conformity with generally accepted accounting principles" that appears in your audit report on the management's financial statements. He observes that the meaning of the phrase must include more than what he thinks of as "principles."

Required:

a. Explain the meaning of the term "accounting principles" as used in the audit report. (Do *not* discuss in this part the significance of "generally accepted.")

b. The president wants to know how you determine whether or not an accounting principle is generally accepted. Discuss the sources of evidence for determining whether an accounting principle has substantial authoritative support. Do *not* merely list the titles of publications.

c. The president believes that diversity in accounting practice always will exist among independent entities despite continual improvements in comparability. Discuss the arguments that *support* his belief.

CHAPTER 5—INCOME CONCEPTS FOR FINANCIAL REPORTING

Objectives of Income Reporting

Question 5-1 (May, 1951).

The published report of a corporation was criticized because it was claimed that the income statement did not by any means give a clear picture of annual earning power and that the balance sheet did not disclose the true value of the fixed assets.

Considering the criticism made, you are to prepare an explanation of the nature and purpose of the income statement and of the balance sheet, including an explanation of their limitations.

Concepts and Presentation of Income

Question 5-2 (November, 1967).

The accounting profession, in the development and implementation of accounting principles, seeks to increase the usefulness of financial statements to their readers.

Required:

a. An authoritative accounting body recently recommended including in net income all items of profit and loss recognized in the period except prior period adjustments and capital transactions involving equity accounts, with extraordinary items shown separately as an element of net income of the period.

1. List the *advantages* of the recommendation.

2. List the *disadvantages* of the recommendation.

b. The recommendation specified in requirement (a) above is based on the premise that capital transactions should be distinguished from income.

1. Why should capital transactions be distinguished from income?

2. In what way does the income expected to be generated by an asset relate to its acquisition cost and valuation in financial statements? Discuss.

Question 5-3 (November, 1967).

The following financial statement was prepared by employees of the Melhus Corporation.

MELHUS CORPORATION
Statement of Income and Retained Earnings
Years Ended December 31, 1966 and December 31, 1965

	1966	1965
Revenues:		
Gross sales, including sales taxes	$876,900	$782,500
Less returns, allowances and cash discounts	18,800	16,200
Net Sales	$858,100	$766,300
Dividends, interest and purchases discounts	30,250	18,300
Recoveries of accounts written off in prior years	11,800	3,000
Gains on sale of treasury stock	2,050	
Total revenues	$902,200	$787,600
Costs and expenses:		
Cost of goods sold, including sales taxes	$415,900	$332,200
Salaries and related payroll expenses	60,500	62,100
Rent	19,100	19,100
Freight-in and freight-out	3,400	2,900
Bad debt expense	24,000	26,000
Addition to reserve for possible inventory losses	3,800	2,000
Total costs and expenses	$526,700	$444,300
Income before extraordinary items	$375,500	$343,300
Extraordinary items:		
Loss on discontinued styles (note 1)	$ 24,000	$ 4,800
Loss on sale of marketable securities (note 2)	52,050	
Loss on sale of warehouse (note 3)	86,350	
Retroactive settlement of federal income taxes for 1965 and 1964 (note 4)	31,600	
Total extraordinary items	$194,000	$ 4,800
Net income	$181,500	$338,500
Retained earnings at beginning of year	310,700	163,100
Total	$492,200	$501,600
Less: Federal income taxes	$120,000	$170,000
Cash dividends on common stock	21,900	20,900
Total	$141,900	$190,900
Retained earnings at end of year	$350,300	$310,700
Net income per share of common stock	$1.81	$3.38

Notes to the Statement of Income and Retained Earnings:
1. New styles and rapidly changing consumer preferences resulted in a $24,000 loss on the disposal of discontinued styles and related accessories.
2. The Corporation sold an investment in marketable securities at a loss of $52,050 with no income tax effect.
3. The Corporation sold one of its warehouses at an $86,350 loss.
4. The Corporation was charged $31,600 retroactively for additional income taxes resulting from a settlement in 1966. Of this amount $14,000 was applicable to 1965 and the balance was applicable to 1964.

Required:

Identify and discuss the weaknesses in classification and disclosure in the one-step statement of income and retained earnings above. Your discussion should explain why you consider these treatments to be weaknesses and what you consider to be the proper treatment of the items. Do *not* discuss form and terminology or prepare a revised statement. (You should assume that the arithmetic is correct.)

Taxable and Accounting Concepts of Income

Question 5–4 (November, 1962).

It is not uncommon to find that the net income reported on published financial statements varies from the taxable net income reported to the Internal Revenue Service and other taxing authorities. While the difference between taxable income and accounting net income is directly attributable to different accounting procedures or methods, such difference is indirectly caused by the variance in the objectives of income tax laws and generally accepted accounting principles.

Required:

a. What are the objectives of generally accepted accounting principles in their application to the income statement? What are the objectives of income tax laws?

b. Differences in accounting methods or procedures under income tax accounting and accounting according to generally accepted principles may be classified into two general groups, those arising from specifications of the tax laws and those caused by timing. Discuss the characteristics of these two groups; use one example of each group in your discussion.

Question 5–5 (May, 1969).

Section 446 of the 1954 Internal Revenue Code states: "Taxable income shall be computed under the method of accounting on . . . which the taxpayer regularly computes his income in keeping his books"; the method employed shall "clearly reflect income." Among the permissible methods are: "(1) the cash receipts and disbursements method" and "(2) an accrual method."

Required:

Generally accepted accounting principles normally require the use of accrual accounting to "fairly present" income. If the cash receipts and disbursements method of accounting will "clearly reflect" taxable income, why does this method not usually also "fairly present" income?

CHAPTER 6—REVENUES AND EXPENSES, GAINS, AND LOSSES

Revenue Reporting

Question 6–1 (May, 1965).

Revenue is usually recognized at the point of sale. Under special circumstances, however, bases other than the point of sale are used for the timing of revenue recognition.

Required:

a. Why is the point of sale usually used as the basis for the timing of revenue recognition?

b. Disregarding the special circumstances when bases other than the point of sale are used, discuss the merits of each of the following objections to the sales basis of revenue recognition:

1. It is too conservative because revenue is earned throughout the entire process of production.

2. It is not conservative enough because accounts receivable do not represent disposable funds; sales returns and allowances may be made; and collection and bad debt expenses may be incurred in a later period.

c. Revenue may also be recognized (1) during production and (2) when cash is received. For each of these two bases of timing revenue recognition, give an example of the circumstances in which it is properly used and discuss the accounting merits of its use in lieu of the sales basis.

Question 6-2 (May, 1968).

On May 5, 1967 Sterling Corporation signed a contract with Stony Associates under which Stony agreed (1) to construct an office building on land owned by Sterling, (2) to accept responsibility for procuring financing for the project and finding tenants, and (3) to manage the property for 50 years. The annual profit from the project, after debt service, was to be divided equally between Sterling Corporation and Stony Associates. Stony was to accept its share of future profits as full payment for its services in construction, obtaining finances and tenants, and management of the project.

By April 30, 1968 the project was nearly completed and tenants had signed leases to occupy 90 percent of the available space at annual rentals aggregating $2,600,000. It is estimated that, after operating expenses and debt service, the annual profit will amount to $850,000. The management of Stony Associates believed that the economic benefit derived from the contract with Sterling should be reflected on its financial statements for the fiscal year ended April 30, 1968 and directed that revenue be accrued in an amount equal to the commercial value of the services Stony had rendered during the year, that this amount be carried in contracts receivable, and that all related expenditures be charged against the revenue.

Required:

a. Explain the main difference between the economic concept of business income as reflected by Stony's management and the measurement of income under generally accepted accounting principles.

b. Discuss the factors to be considered in determining when revenue has been realized for the purpose of accounting measurement of periodic income.

c. Is the belief of Stony's management in accord with generally accepted accounting principles for the measurement of revenue and expense for the year ended April 30, 1968? Support your opinion by discussing the application to this case of the factors to be considered for asset measurement and revenue and expense recognition.

Question 6–3 (November, 1965).

Installment sales usually are accounted for by one of the following methods: (1) the profit may be recognized as earned in the period of sale; (2) the profit may be recognized on a proportionate basis in the periods of collection (commonly called the "installment method").

Required:

a. Discuss the propriety of the two methods, including in your discussion a list of the circumstances under which recognition of profit in the period of sale would be preferable to recognition of profit on the installment method.

b. The collection period of an installment sale contract is frequently 24 months or longer. Discuss, in terms of both methods, the presentation of the installment contracts receivable on the balance sheet.

c. Deferred gross profit arising from installment sales has been reported on the balance sheet variously as a contra or valuation account to installments receivable, an estimated liability, a part of stockholders' equity, or a deferred credit.

Discuss the nature and, hence, the appropriate balance sheet classification(s) of "deferred gross profit" for an accrual-basis business that uses the installment sales method for financial reporting and income tax purposes.

Question 6–4 (November, 1967).

The president of the D'Anna Company, a manufacturer, is concerned about your proposed qualification relating to material investments in marketable securities presented on its financial statements at the closing prices traded on the New York and American Stock Exchanges at December 31, 1966. The closing prices were substantially in excess of acquisition cost.

He stated, "The thousands of transactions in shares of open-end investment trusts at prices reflecting current market values of their portfolios are evidence that most people view these value changes as equivalent to realization. Indeed, the cost of the investment is an incredibly low figure to present."

You explain that some transactions, events, and changes in valuation are not recognized for accounting purposes under generally accepted accounting principles.

Required:

a. List types of transactions, events and changes in valuation that are not recognized for accounting purposes under generally accepted accounting principles.

b. 1. What should be considered in selecting the method of revenue recognition that is most appropriate for a particular situation? Do *not* list methods of revenue recognition.

2. Discuss the appropriateness of D'Anna Company's proposal to recognize as revenue the excess of closing prices on the stock exchanges over the cost of the investment.

Question 6–5 (November, 1966).

After the presentation of your report on the examination of the financial statements to the board of directors of the Savage Publishing Company, one of the new directors says that he is surprised that the income statement assumes that an equal proportion of the revenue is earned with the publication of every issue of the company's magazine. He feels that the "crucial event" in the process of earning revenue in the magazine business is the cash sale of the subscription. He says that he does not understand why—other than for the smoothing of income —most of the revenue cannot be "realized" in the period of the sale.

Required:

a. List the various accepted methods for recognizing revenue in the accounts and explain when the methods are appropriate. Do not limit your listing to the methods for the recognition of revenue in magazine publishing.

b. Discuss the propriety of timing the recognition of revenue in the Savage Publishing Company's accounts with:

1. The cash sale of the magazine subscription.
2. The publication of the magazine every month.
3. Both events, by recognizing a portion of the revenue with cash sale of the magazine subscription and a portion of the revenue with the publication of the magazine every month.

Expenses, Costs, and Losses

Question 6–6 (May, 1965).

After securing lease commitments from several major stores, Gercken-Rees Shopping Center, Inc. was organized and built a shopping center in a growing suburb.

The shopping center would have opened on schedule on January 1, 1964 if it had not been struck by a severe tornado in December; it opened for business on October 1, 1964. All of the additional construction costs which were incurred as a result of the tornado were covered by insurance.

In July 1963, in anticipation of the scheduled January opening, a permanent staff was hired to promote the shopping center, obtain tenants for the uncommitted space, and manage the property.

A summary of some of the cost incurred in 1963 and the first nine months of 1964 follows:

	1963	*January 1, 1964 through September 30, 1964*
Interest on mortgage bonds	$30,000	$45,000
Cost of obtaining tenants	14,000	29,000
Promotional advertising	17,000	17,000

The promotional advertising campaign was designed to familiarize shoppers with the center. Had it been known in time that the center would not open until October 1964, the 1963 expenditure for promotional advertising would not have been made. The advertising had to be repeated in 1964.

All of the tenants who had leased space in the shopping center at the time of the tornado accepted the October occupancy date on condition that the monthly rental charges for the first nine months of 1964 be canceled.

Required:

Explain how each of the above costs for 1963 and the first nine months of 1964 should be treated in the accounts of the shopping center corporation. Give the reasons for each treatment.

Question 6–7 (May, 1969).

You were requested to personally deliver your auditor's report to the board of directors of Sebal Manufacturing Corporation and answer questions posed about the financial statements. While reading the statements, one director asked, "What are the precise meanings of the terms cost, expense and loss? These terms sometimes seem to identify similar items and other times seem to identify dissimilar items."

Required:

a. Explain the meanings of the terms (1) cost, (2) expense, and (3) loss as used for financial reporting in conformity with generally accepted accounting principles. In your explanation discuss the distinguishing characteristics of the terms and their similarities and interrelationships.

b. Classify each of the following items as a cost, expense, loss, or other category, and explain how the classification of each item may change:

1. Cost of goods sold.
2. Bad debts expense.
3. Depreciation expense for plant machinery.
4. Organization costs.
5. Spoiled goods.

c. The terms "period cost" and "product cost" are sometimes used to describe certain items in financial statements. Define these terms and distinguish between them. To what types of items do each apply?

CHAPTER 7—BUSINESS INCOME AND PRICE CHANGES

Nature and Objectives of Adjustments for Changes in Prices

Question 7–1 (November, 1964).

A common objective of accountants is to prepare meaningful financial statements. To attain this objective many accountants maintain that the financial statements must be adjusted for changes in price level. Other accountants believe that financial statements should continue to be prepared on the basis of unadjusted historical cost.

Required:

a. List the arguments for adjusting financial statements for changes in price level.

b. List the arguments for preparing financial statements on only the basis of unadjusted historical cost.

c. In their discussions about accounting for changes in price levels and the methods of measuring them, uninformed individuals have frequently failed to distinguish between adjustments for changes in the price levels of specific goods and services, and adjustments for changes in the general purchasing power of the dollar. What is the distinction? Which are "price-level adjustments"? Discuss.

Current Costs

Question 7-2 (November, 1960).

a. What is the common objective of depreciation based on replacement cost and the last-in, first-out method of pricing inventories?

b. Outline two conditions necessary for the last-in, first-out method of pricing inventories to accomplish the results expected of this method.

c. A basic monetary concept underlying accounting and financial statements is primarily responsible for the development of these methods of accounting. Name and briefly discuss this monetary concept as it is related to these methods of accounting.

d. List four arguments in opposition to modifying financial statements for price level changes.

Depreciation and Supplementary Statements

Question 7-3 (November, 1962).

Part a. Many annual reports point out that the reported depreciation charges are based on historical costs and, because of the decline in the purchasing power of the dollar, do not express depreciation expense in terms of current costs.

Required:

Neither depreciation on replacement cost nor depreciation adjusted for changes in the purchasing power of the dollar has been recognized as a generally accepted accounting practice. Briefly present the accounting treatment that might be used to assist in the maintenance of the ability of a company to replace its productive capacity.

Part b. The effectiveness of management in maintaining the purchasing power of capital can be assessed by financial statements developed in terms of uniform "current" dollars to supplement the primary (historical cost) statements.

Required:

List four other purposes that such supplementary statements might serve.

Question 7-4 (May, 1957).

a. In considering the merits of using price indexes for the purpose of converting the accounting data as reflected in the conventional historical accounts, some people have suggested that these price-level adjustments should be confined to the fixed assets and related depreciation.

What can be said in favor of such a proposal? Against it?

b. The price index rose from 125 to 175 during the previous year and from 175 to 225 during the current year. The dollar sales during the previous year were $240,000 and during the current year were $300,000.

1. For comparative income statement purposes you are to convert the sales figures for both years to the price level existing at the end of the current year. You are to assume that sales were made uniformly throughout both years, and that the change in price level was also uniform.

2. What additional information is revealed by a comparison of the converted figures? How do you interpret them?

Choice of an Index

Question 7–5 (May, 1956).

There has been a good deal of criticism of the traditional "historical" cost records and the data which they reflect, especially during times of inflation or deflation. In order to assist in the interpretation of accounting reports as normally prepared, many accountants have suggested that the recorded cost data be first utilized in the preparation of the conventional financial statements; and then, as a supplementary technique, these statements be converted into dollars having a uniform purchasing power through the application of price indexes to the recorded dollar amounts. There has been some considerable difference of opinion among these accountants as to whether to use a "general" price index, such as the wholesale commodity price index or the cost of living index; or on the other hand, to use a more "specific" price index that is more applicable to the industry involved or to the particular items being converted (for instance, using a construction index for the conversion of plant and equipment items, or the use of a special price index constructed for a specific industry).

Give arguments in favor of and against each of these two types of indexes.

CHAPTER 8—CASH AND FUNDS FLOWS

Funds Statement and Concepts

Question 8–1 (May, 1969).

The following statement of source and application of funds was prepared by the controller of the Clovis Company. The controller indicated that this statement was prepared under the "all financial resources" concept of funds, which is the broadest concept of funds and includes all transactions providing or requiring funds.

CLOVIS COMPANY
Statement of Source and Application of Funds
December 31, 1968

Funds were provided by:

Contribution of plant site by the City of Camden (Note 1) ...	$115,000
Net income after extraordinary items per income statement (Note 2)	75,000
Issuance of note payable—due 1972	60,000
Depreciation and amortization	50,000
Deferred income taxes relating to accelerated depreciation ...	10,000
Sale of equipment—book value (Note 3)	5,000
Total funds provided	$315,000

Funds were applied to:

Acquisition of future plant site (Note 1)	$250,000
Increase in working capital	30,000
Cash dividends declared but not paid	20,000
Acquisition of equipment	15,000
Total funds applied	$315,000

Notes to Statement of Source and Application of Funds:

1. The City of Camden donated a plant site to Clovis Company valued by the board of directors at $115,000. The Company purchased adjoining property for $135,000.

2. Research and development expenditures of $25,000 incurred in 1968 were expensed. These expenses were considered abnormal.

3. Equipment with a book value of $5,000 was sold for $8,000. The gain was included as an extraordinary item on the income statement.

Required:

a. Why is it considered desirable to present a statement of source and application of funds in financial reports?

b. Define and discuss the relative merits of the following three concepts used in funds flow analysis in terms of their measurement accuracy and freedom from manipulation (window dressing) in one accounting period:

1. Cash concept of funds.
2. Net monetary assets (quick assets) concept of funds.
3. Working capital concept of funds.

c. Identify and discuss the weaknesses in presentation and disclosure in the statement of source and application of funds for Clovis Company. Your discussion should explain why you consider them to be weaknesses and what you consider the proper treatment of the items to be. Do not prepare a revised statement.

Cash Flows

Question 8–2 (May, 1968).

Two physics professors at State University incorporated Basic Research Corporation in 1965 to provide research and consulting services to business firms.

They engaged you to prepare annual financial statements on an accrual basis. A bookkeeper maintains all records and prepares monthly statements of cash receipts and disbursements. Following are postclosing trial balances which reflect all of your adjustments and the cash receipts and disbursements statement which was prepared by the bookkeeper from corporation records before they were adjusted by you:

BASIC RESEARCH CORPORATION
Adjusted Postclosing Trial Balances
December 31, 1967 and 1966

	Dec. 31, 1967	Dec. 31, 1966
Cash in bank	$ 49,000	$ 10,000
Receivable from clients	47,000	35,000
Completed work not yet billed	24,000	40,000
Technical supplies inventory	7,000	5,000
Land, building and equipment	105,600	50,000
Total debits	$232,600	$140,000
Accumulated depreciation	$ 23,000	$ 12,000
Due to suppliers	4,000	3,000
Prepayments by clients not billed in 1966		28,000
Discounted note and accrued interest payable	35,616	
Deferred salary payable	15,000	
Stock issued ($10 par value)	12,000	10,000
Donated capital	5,000	
Retained earnings	137,984	87,000
Total credits	$232,600	$140,000

BASIC RESEARCH CORPORATION
Cash Receipts and Disbursements
For the Year Ended December 31, 1967

Cash received from clients		$260,000
Cash disbursements:		
Administrative salaries	$ 50,000	
Staff salaries	120,000	
Outside consultants	12,000	
Payments to suppliers	9,000	
Laboratory equipment purchased	11,000	
Other laboratory expenses	12,500	
General expenses	6,500	221,000
Cash receipts in excess of cash disbursements		$ 39,000

Additional information available:

1. On January 1, 1967 Basic Research consummated a merger with Engineering Consulting Company which was treated as a pooling of interests, with Basic Research surviving. The president (and major stockholder) of the engineering

firm was engaged by Basic Research to be the director of applied research until his retirement December 31, 1971, with compensation to be paid in equal amounts over a period of 10 years. The pooling of interests was recorded by the following entry:

Receivable from Clients	$8,000	
Laboratory Equipment	6,000	
Allowance for Depreciation		$5,000
Retained Earnings		7,000
Capital Stock		2,000

To record the issuance of 200 shares of Basic Research Corporation stock for the assets and retained earnings of Engineering Consulting Company.

2. On January 1, 1967 Basic Research purchased from one of its incorporators some adjacent land on which a new building was to be constructed. The incorporator sold the land to the corporation for $5,000 less than he had been offered by a real estate developer. Because the land was worth more than Basic Research agreed to pay, it was recorded at its fair market value. A note due in three years, discounted to yield 6 percent per year, was given in payment ($0.84 invested at 6 percent for three years will accumulate to $1).

3. All services to clients are billed to clients and all supplies are purchased on open account.

4. You determined that as of December 31, 1967 all receivables were for work completed in 1967, the technical supplies on hand were purchased in 1967, all liabilities were incurred in 1967, and no land, building or equipment was sold or retired in 1967.

Required:

a. The incorporators are concerned because the cash receipts and disbursements statement prepared by the bookkeeper and the income statement prepared by you do not agree, and they ask that you explain their transactions for 1967 from an accountant's point of view. Your explanations should include the amounts of the transactions. Any supporting computations should be in good form. Do not consider income taxes. An income statement is not required.

Analyze and explain the following:

1. Changes in the amounts receivable from clients and prepayments by clients not billed in 1966.
2. Work completed in 1967, both billed and unbilled.
3. Changes in the technical supplies inventory and the amount due to suppliers.
4. Increase in land, building, and equipment.
5. Increase in accumulated depreciation.
6. The $35,616 discounted note and accrued interest payable.
7. The $15,000 deferred salary payable.

b. Explain why an income statement prepared by a CPA and a statement of cash receipts and disbursements prepared by the bookkeeper would produce different results.

CHAPTER 9—ASSETS AND THEIR MEASUREMENT

Valuation Bases

Question 9–1 (November, 1968).

You have been engaged to examine the financial statements of Custer Corporation for the year ending December 31, 1968. Custer Corporation was organized in January 1968 by Messrs. Moses and Price, original owners of options to acquire for $350,000 oil leases on 5,000 acres of land. They contemplated that first the oil leases would be acquired by the corporation, and subsequently 180,000 shares of the corporation's common stock would be sold to the public at $6 per share. In February 1968 they exchanged their options, $150,000 cash, and $50,000 of other assets for 75,000 shares of common stock of the corporation. The corporation's board of directors appraised the leases at $600,000, based on other acreage recently leased in the same area. The options were therefore recorded at $250,000 ($600,000 − $350,000 option price).

The options were exercised by the corporation in March 1968 prior to the sale of common stock to the public in April 1968. Leases on approximately 500 acres of land were abandoned as worthless during the year.

Required:

a. Why is the valuation of assets acquired by a corporation in exchange for its own common stock sometimes difficult?

b. 1. What reasoning might Custer Corporation use to support valuing the leases at $600,000, the amount of the appraisal by the board of directors?

   2. Assuming the board's appraisal was sincere, what steps might Custer Corporation have taken to strengthen its position on using the $600,000 value, and to provide additional information if questions are raised about possible overvaluation of the leases?

c. Discuss the propriety of charging one tenth of the recorded value of the leases against income at December 31, 1968 because leases on 500 acres of land were abandoned during the year.

Question 9–2 (May, 1965).

A small but growing road building contractor would like to bid on a contract to rebuild and surface 10.6 miles of road. The job is considerably larger than any he has attempted in the past; and if he wins the contract, he estimates that he will need a $100,000 line of credit for working capital.

The contractor's most recent statement of financial position shows that he has a net worth of $170,000, of which $110,000 represents the book value of road building equipment. Most of the equipment was acquired a few years ago at a bankruptcy sale. The equipment has a current fair value several times as great as book value.

The contractor knows that his bank will not give him a $100,000 line of credit on the basis of a position statement which shows his net worth at $170,000. He wants to adjust his accounting records to show the current fair value of the equipment and to prepare a revised position statement.

Required:

a. List the factors that, alone or in combination, may have caused the difference between the book value and the current fair value of the equipment.

b. The current fair value of fixed assets may be estimated by using one of the following methods:

1. Reproduction cost.
2. Replacement cost.
3. Capitalization of earnings.

Describe each of the three methods of estimating the current fair value of fixed assets and discuss the possible limitations of each.

c. Discuss the propriety of adjusting the accounting records to show the fair value of the equipment and preparing a revised position statement. Suggest a possible alternative approach. Your answer should take into consideration the factors that may have caused the difference between the book value and the current fair value of the equipment.

Historical Cost and Current Cost

Question 9–3 (November, 1967).

Financial statements are tools for the communication of quantifiable economic information to readers who use them as one of the factors in making a variety of management and investment decisions and judgments. To fulfill this function accounting data should be quantifiable and should also be relevant to the kinds of judgments and decisions made. They should be verifiable and free from personal bias. There are many who believe that for some purposes current cost is a more useful measure than historical cost and recommend that dual statements be prepared showing both historical and current costs.

Required:

a. Discuss the ways in which historical costs and current costs conform to the standards of verifiability and freedom from bias.

b. Describe briefly how the current cost of the following assets might be determined.

1. Inventory.
2. Investments in marketable securities.
3. Equipment and machinery.
4. Natural resources.
5. Goodwill.

c. While historical cost might be described as being objectively measurable, there is still an element of uncertainty in determining at any point in time the portion that has expired and should be expensed and the unexpired portion that should be carried as an asset. Explain how probability analysis might be employed in estimating the unexpired portion of research and development costs to be carried as an asset on the statement of financial condition.

Valuation of a Firm

Question 9–4   (May, 1963).

The owners of the P. K. Leash Company, a closely held corporation, have offered to sell their 100 percent interest in the company's common stock at an amount equal to the book value of the common stock. They will retain their interest in the company's preferred stock.

The president of the Kissena Corporation, your client, would like to combine the operations of the P. K. Leash Company with his Leather Products Division, and he is seriously considering having Kissena Corporation buy the common stock of the P. K. Leash Company. He questions the use of "book value" as a basis for the sale, however, and has come to you for advice.

Required:

Draft a report to your client. Your report should cover the following points:

a. Define book value. Explain its significance in establishing a value for a business that is expected to continue in operation indefinitely.

b. Describe the procedure for computing book values of ownership equities.

c. Why should your client consider the P. K. Leash Company's accounting policies and methods in his evaluation of the company's reported book value? List the areas of accounting policy and method relevant to this evaluation.

d. What factors, other than book value, should your client recognize in determining a basis for the sale?

Direct Costing

Question 9–5   (November, 1962).

Supporters of direct costing have contended that it provides management with more useful accounting information. Critics of direct costing believe that its negative features outweigh its contributions.

Required:

a. Describe direct costing. How does it differ from conventional absorption costing?

b. List the arguments for and against the use of direct costing.

c. Indicate how each of the following conditions would affect the amounts of net profit reported under conventional absorption costing and direct costing:

1. Sales and production are in balance at standard volume.
2. Sales exceed production.
3. Production exceeds sales.

Statement of Financial Position

Question 9–6   (November, 1968).

The controller's staff of the Metairie Publishing Corporation prepared the following statement for the annual report to stockholders:

METAIRIE PUBLISHING CORPORATION
Statement of Financial Position
December 31, 1967

Current assets:

Cash, including time deposits	$ 8,000	
Marketable securities, at cost	13,000	
Notes receivable, face amount (Note 1)	21,000	
Net accounts receivable, including assigned accounts	40,000	
Inventories, at lower of cost or market	100,000	$182,000

Less current liabilities:

Accounts payable	$ 51,000	
Notes payable	15,000	
Income taxes payable	20,000	
Accrued interest on notes (Note 1)	1,100	87,100
Net working capital		$ 94,900

Noncurrent assets:

Receivable from long-term lease (Note 2)	$ 70,000	
Property, plant, and equipment less accumulated depreciation of $74,000	255,700	
Deferred income tax charges on advance advertising and subscription revenue	11,000	336,700
Total net working capital and noncurrent assets		$431,600

Less long-term liabilities:

Unearned advertising contracts	$ 80,000	
Subscriptions received in advance	22,000	
6% debentures, payable in ten equal annual installments beginning July 1, 1968	110,000	
Deferred income tax credits relating to accelerated depreciation	16,000	228,000
Total Net Assets		$203,600

Claims to net assets by stockholders:

Preferred stock		$ 40,000
Common stock		80,000
Retained earnings		83,600
Total Claims to Net Assets		$203,600

Notes to the Statement of Financial Position:

1. Notes receivable include $10,000 of notes which do not provide for interest. The Corporation has included in the accrued interest on notes $800 which represents the difference between the present value and maturity value of the non-interest bearing notes receivable.

2. The financing method of accounting for leased property is used.

Required:

Identify and discuss the weaknesses in presentation, disclosure, and classification in the above statement of financial position. Your discussion should explain why you consider the items to be weaknesses and what you consider to be their proper treatment. Do not prepare a revised statement. Assume the arithmetic is correct.

CHAPTER 10—CURRENT ASSETS AND CURRENT LIABILITIES

Nature of Current Assets and Current Liabilities

Question 10-1 (May, 1960).

Tri-State Equipment Leasing Company leases equipment of all kinds to industrial users; most leases are for periods of from three to five years, during which time it is expected that the depreciable portion of the cost of such equipment and the necessary related financing charges will be recovered. Generally, the leases also contain purchase option clauses which permit the user to acquire the equipment at the estimated market price of the used equipment less a portion of estimated removal costs.

The company has followed the practice of charging a contracts receivable account and crediting an unearned rental income account for the gross contract rental at the time each lease is signed. The company finances a substantial portion of the cost of the rental equipment through installment loans which are secured by assignment of the lease rental contracts.

Required:

Discuss the proper balance sheet presentation of the contracts receivable, leased equipment, unearned rental income, and installment loans payable accounts, giving your reasons for the method of presentation which you recommend. Note particularly the effect on working capital, total assets and total liabilities.

Investments

Question 10-2 (May, 1966).

The Overseas Trading Company, a U.S. corporation with several foreign subsidiaries, appended the following footnote to its December 31, 1965 financial statements:

"Marketable securities" includes $15,100 of freely transferable import certificates issued by the government of a foreign country. The certificates entitle the bearer to import into the foreign country certain restricted luxury items (costing up to 40% of the invoice prices of the exports on which the certificates were issued) that cannot otherwise be imported. They were issued by the foreign government as an incentive to export goods from the foreign country and were valued at market on the dates received (current market, $15,250). Our foreign subsidiary does not import luxury items and expects to sell all certificates during the next operating period. The foreign government's policy is expected to continue indefinitely.

Required:

a. Discuss the propriety of valuing the certificates at market on the dates they are received.

b. Discuss the propriety of treating the credit arising from the receipt of the certificates as:

1. A reduction of cost of goods sold.
2. An addition to stockholders' equity.
3. An addition to other or special income.
4. An addition to gross sales.

Question 10–3 (May, 1961).

The board of directors of a mining corporation, foreseeing a three- to five-year period of reduced operations, has decided to invest its liquid funds during this period in a diversified list of common stocks (all listed on the New York Stock Exchange) rather than pay as much in dividends as is legally permissible. The directors further decide to include such investments in their annual financial statements on a current market value basis.

Required:

a. What advantage may be attributed to this method of reporting such investments?

b. What objections might be offered to this method?

c. How should these securities be presented in financial statements?

Prepaid Expenses

Question 10–4 (November, 1955).

On January 1, 1953 Doe paid $3,000 for a three-year fire insurance policy. As of December 31, 1954, a question has arisen as to the amount of prepaid insurance that should be shown on Doe's balance sheet.

One proposal is to show prepaid insurance at $600, which is the short-rate cancellation value of the policy on December 31, 1954.

A second proposal is to show prepaid insurance at $1,000, representing one third of the original premium cost.

A third proposal is to show prepaid insurance at $1,200, which is the one-year premium cost for a policy for the same amount as the policy in force.

You are to discuss each of the proposals as to acceptability, as to the general principle underlying it, and as to its effect on reported income.

Accounts Receivable

Question 10–5 (November, 1964).

Part a. During the audit of accounts receivable your client asked why the current year's expense for bad debts was charged merely because some accounts might become uncollectible next year. He then said that he had read that financial statments should be based upon verifiable, objective evidence, and that it seemed to him to be much more objective to wait until individual accounts receivable were actually determined to be uncollectible before charging them to expense.

Required:

1. Discuss the theoretical justification of the allowance method as contrasted with the direct write-off method of accounting for bad debts.

2. Describe the following two methods of estimating bad debts. Include a discussion of how well each accomplishes the objectives of the allowance method of accounting for bad debts.

(a) The percentage of sales method.

(b) The aging method.

Of what merit is your client's contention that the allowance method lacks the objectivity of the direct write-off method? Discuss in terms of accounting's measurement function.

Part b. Due to calamitous earthquake losses the Morgan Company, one of your client's oldest and largest customers, suddenly and unexpectedly became bankrupt. Approximately 30 percent of your client's total sales have been made to the Morgan Company during each of the past several years.

The amount due from Morgan Company—none of which is collectible—equals 25 percent of total accounts receivable, an amount which is considerably in excess of what was determined to be an adequate provision for doubtful accounts at the close of the preceding year.

Required:

How would your client record the write-off of the Morgan Company receivable if it is using the allowance method of accounting for bad debts? Justify your suggested treatment.

CHAPTER 11—INVENTORIES

Current Valuation

Question 11-1 (May, 1967).

The controller of the Robinson Company was discussing a comment you made in the course of presenting your audit report.

". . . and frankly," Mr. Fisher continued, "I agree that we, too, are responsible for finding ways to produce more relevant financial statements which are as reliable as the ones we now produce.

"For example, suppose the company acquired a finished item for inventory for $40 when the general price-level index was 110. And, later, the item was sold for $75 when the general price-level index was 121 and the current replacement cost was $54. We could calculate a 'holding gain.' "

Required:

a. Explain to what extent and how current replacement costs already are used *within* generally accepted accounting principles to value inventories.

b. Calculate in good form the amount of the holding gain in Mr. Fisher's example.

c. Why is the use of current replacement cost for *both* inventories and cost of goods sold preferred by some accounting authorities to the generally accepted use of Fifo or Lifo?

d. Why do some authorities believe that the present market resale (exit or output) price is a conceptual improvement upon current replacement (entry or input) cost for inventory measurement?

Lower of Cost or Market

Question 11-2 (May, 1964).

Accountants generally follow "the lower of cost or market" basis of inventory valuations.

Required:

a. Define "cost" as applied to the valuation of inventories.

b. Define "market" as applied to the valuation of inventories.

c. Why are inventories valued at the lower of cost or market? Discuss.

d. List the arguments against the use of the lower of cost or market method of valuing inventories.

Question 11-3 (May, 1955).

Inventories are often valued at the "lower of cost or market." This traditional method of valuation is frequently defended as "conservative," and like any other valuation method adopted, should be followed consistently.

In your opinion, is a company which regularly follows the practice of valuing its inventory at the lower of cost or market being "consistent and conservative"? Discuss critically, including a discussion of the meaning of the terms "consistent" and "conservative."

Question 11-4 (November, 1965).

The Paris Company manufactures and sells four products, the inventories of which are priced at cost or market, whichever is lower. A normal profit margin rate of 30 percent is usually maintained on each of the four products.

The following information was compiled as of December 31, 1964:

Product	Original Cost	Cost to Replace	Estimated Cost to Dispose	"Normal" Selling Price*	Expected Selling Price
A	$35.00	$42.00	$15.00	$70.00	$ 80.00
B	47.50	45.00	20.50	95.00	95.00
C	17.50	15.00	5.00	35.00	30.00
D	45.00	46.00	26.00	90.00	100.00

* "Normal" selling price = original cost ÷ (100% — the normal 50% gross margin rate).

Required:

a. Why are expected selling prices important in the application of the lower-of-cost-or-market rule?

b. Prepare a schedule containing unit values (including "floor" and "ceiling") for determining the lower of cost or market on an individual product basis. The last column of the schedule should contain for each product the unit value for the purpose of inventory valuation resulting from the application of the lower-of-cost-or-market rule.

c. What effects, if any, do the expected selling prices have on the valuation of products A, B, C, and D by the lower-of-cost-or-market rule?

Specific Identification of Cost

Question 11–5 (May, 1962).

Specific identification is sometimes said to be the ideal method for assigning cost to inventory and to cost of goods sold.

Required:

a. List the arguments for and against the above statement.

b. First-in, first-out; weighted average; and last-in, first-out methods are often used instead of specific identification. Compare each of these methods with the specific identification method. Include in your discussion an analysis of the theoretical propriety of each method in the determination of income and asset valuation. (Do not define the methods or describe their technical accounting procedures.)

Lifo

Question 11–6 (November, 1962).

In the course of his professional activities the CPA is sometimes called upon by his clients for advice regarding the appropriateness of valuing inventories by the Lifo method.

Required:

a. List the arguments for and against the use of the Lifo method of valuing inventory.

b. What is the dollar-value method of Lifo inventory valuation? (Confine your discussion to the underlying principles; do not discuss the techniques of developing price indexes.) What advantages does the dollar-value method have over the quantity method of Lifo inventory valuation?

Question 11–7 (May, 1968).

In January 1961 the Apex Company requested and secured permission from the Commissioner of Internal Revenue to compute inventories under the last-in, first-out (Lifo) method, as provided in Section 472 of the *Internal Revenue Code of 1954*, and elected to determine inventory cost under the dollar-value method. Apex satisfied the commissioner that cost could be accurately determined by use of an index number computed from a representative sample selected from the company's single inventory pool. Apex elected to price subsequent inventory layers at year-end prices (Lifo base with Fifo increments) and also adopted this method for financial reporting purposes, as required by IRC Section 472.

Required:

a. Why should inventories be included (1) in a statement of financial position, and (2) in the computation of net income?

b. The *Internal Revenue Code* allows some accountable events to be considered differently for income tax reporting purposes and financial accounting purposes, while other accountable events must be reported the same for both purposes. Discuss why it might be desirable to report some accountable events differently for financial accounting purposes than for income tax reporting purposes.

c. Discuss the ways and conditions under which the Fifo and Lifo inventory costing methods produce different inventory valuations. Do not discuss procedures for computing inventory cost.

d. The Lifo inventory costing method and the dollar-value Lifo inventory costing method will produce different inventory valuations if the composition of the inventory base changes. Explain why this is true.

e. Describe the similarities and differences of the dollar-value Lifo inventory method to be used by Apex and the base-stock inventory method.

Retail Inventory and Gross Profit Methods

Question 11–8 (November, 1957).

A manager of a small department store has been valuing inventories on the basis of first-in, first-out. He is now contemplating changing to the retail inventory method. However, he does not know whether to calculate his cost/retail percentage before or after markups and markdowns. Also, he wants to know whether he could not use the gross profit method with equal results.

In your answer, state the assumptions implicit in the retail method and compare the assumed results obtained by using the cost/retail ratio both before and after deducting markdowns. Also compare briefly the assumptions implicit in the retail method with those implicit in the gross profit method.

Question 11–9 (May, 1963).

The Lowman Paint Company, your client, manufactures paint. The company's president, Mr. Lowman, has decided to open a retail store to sell Lowman paint as well as wallpaper and other supplies that would be purchased from other suppliers. He has asked you for information about the retail method of pricing inventories at the retail store.

Required:

Prepare a report to the president explaining the retail method of pricing inventories. Your report should include the following points:

a. Description and accounting features of the method.

b. The conditions that may distort the results under the method.

c. The advantages of using the method when compared to cost methods of inventory pricing.

d. The accounting theory underlying the treatment of net markdowns and net markups under the method.

CHAPTER 12—PLANT AND EQUIPMENT

Valuation of Assets Received in Exchange for Stock

Question 12–1 (November, 1956).

The Florida Real Estate Company was organized on October 1, 1955 with an authorized capital stock of $500,000 par value, of which $150,000 was issued equally to A, B, and C in consideration of their transfer to the company of parcels of commercial real estate as of that date. The company will operate the properties as rental property, and no other stock was issued. The property account was charged and capital stock account credited with $150,000 to record the transaction.

On December 31, 1955 an entry was recorded, upon the basis of a resolution passed by the board of directors, increasing the property account by $750,000 and crediting the capital surplus account with a like amount in order to state the property at its fair market value. The $900,000 is equivalent to twice the assessed value for 1954 property tax purposes, which is the average relationship of current quoted prices of similar property to their assessed value. The company has on file a report from a reputable real estate appraisal firm which states it considers the value at the date the property was deeded to the corporation to be in excess of $1 million. You are required to render a certified balance sheet of the company at December 31, 1955.

a. In indicating on the balance sheet the valuation of the property, would you state the valuation to be (1) at valuation appraised by the board of directors, (2) at less than appraised valuation, (3) at cost, (4) at book value, or (5) some other description? State briefly your reasons why your statement of the valuation is correct.

b. State the description you would use to explain what the capital surplus represents.

Content of Historical Cost

Question 12-2 (May, 1964).

Your client found three suitable sites, each having certain unique advantages, for a new plant facility. In order to investigate thoroughly the advantages and disadvantages of each site, one-year options were purchased for an amount equal to 5 percent of the contract price of each site. The costs of the options cannot be applied against the contracts. Before the options expired, one of the sites was purchased at the contract price of $60,000. The option on this site had cost $3,000. The two options not exercised had cost $3,500 each.

Required:

Present arguments in support of recording the cost of the land at each of the following amounts:
   a. $60,000.
   b. $63,000.
   c. $70,000.

Capitalization of Interest

Question 12-3 (May, 1961).

Cal-York Airline is converting from piston-type planes to jets. Delivery time for the jets is three years, during which period substantial progress payments must be made. The multimillion dollar cost of the planes cannot be financed from working capital; Cal-York must borrow funds for the payments.

Because of high interest rates and the large sum to be borrowed, management estimates that interest costs in the second year of the period will be equal to one third of net income before interest and taxes, and one half of such income in the third year.

After conversion, Cal-York's passenger-carrying capacity will be doubled with no increase in the number of planes, although the investment in planes would be substantially increased. The jet planes have a seven-year service life.

Required:

Give your recommendation concerning the advisability of capitalizing the interest during the conversion period. Support your recommendation with reasons *and* suggested accounting treatment. (Disregard federal income tax implications.)

Improvements

Question 12–4 (November, 1956).

The Alpha Company purchased a store building for $100,000. Immediately thereafter $10,000 was spent to remodel the store front. In the opinion of competent real estate firms, the expenditure of this additional $10,000 did not add to the "resale value" of the building—that is, this building which was purchased for $100,000 could not be resold for more than that amount, even though the additional $10,000 was spent in improving the store front.

What is your advice regarding the accounting treatment of this $10,000 expenditure? *Discuss fully*.

Self-Constructed Assets

Question 12–5 (November, 1963).

Three positions have been taken with respect to the recording of manufacturing overhead as an element of the cost of fixed assets constructed by a company for its own use:
1. It should be excluded completely.
2. It should be included only to the extent that it can be directly attributed to the construction project.
3. It should be included at the same rate as is charged to normal operations.
Present the arguments supporting each of these positions.

Leases on Books of Lessor

Question 12–6 (May, 1967).

Lessors engage in leasing activities for diverse reasons.

Required:

a. What factors should a lessor consider in choosing a method of assigning revenues and expenses to lease periods?

b. For what types of leasing activities should lessors utilize the:

1. Financing method?

2. Operating (or rental) method?

c. Under the operating method lessors report gross rentals as revenue over the life of the lease.

1. How should the investment be classified?

2. What should be disclosed?

CHAPTER 13—DEPRECIATION

Capital versus Revenue Expenditures

Question 13–1 (May, 1964).

Expenditures may be divided into two general categories—(1) capital expenditures and (2) revenue expenditures.

Required:

a. Distinguish between these two categories of expenditures and between their treatments in the accounts.

b. Discuss the impact on both present and future balance sheets and income statements of improperly distinguishing between capital and revenue expenditures.

c. What criteria do firms generally use in establishing a policy for classifying expenditures under these two general categories? Discuss.

Nature of Depreciation

Question 13–2 (May, 1954).

A small manufacturing company owned one factory building in 1949 with a net depreciated cost of $90,000. Machinery and equipment was carried at $120,000. Because of expanding business in 1950, it built a new building at a cost of $150,000 and installed $210,000 of equipment in it. In the period from 1950 to the end of 1953, it put some new equipment into the old building and continued to operate both plants. Depreciation has been computed on a straight-line basis.

In 1954 the company shut down the old plant because of lack of orders. They propose that they should quit taking depreciation on the old building and machinery. They suggest that while the old plant is useful, it is not in use and is not wearing out. They also suggest that to take depreciation on it increases their cost, overvalues inventory, and places them in a poor competitive position to bid for business since their costs are high.

You are to give a full discussion of their proposal and of their arguments.

Question 13–3 (May, 1968).

You have been requested by your client, Acme Restaurants, Inc., a national hotel and motel restaurateur, to evaluate certain accounting treatments proposed by Acme's treasurer regarding a contract for Acme to operate the restaurant and parking facilities of the new Rocklin Hotel for 30 years. A condition necessary for securing the contract was that Acme would aid in financing the new hotel by loaning Rocklin $300,000 in addition to paying a normal rental for the facilities. It is estimated that the operations will yield pretax profits of $150,000 annually to Acme.

The $300,000 loan will be for 30 years, with no payment unless the contract is canceled by Rocklin. Interest is to accrue at 4 percent per year compounded annually for the first 20 years, and no interest is to accrue during the last 10 years. After 20 years Acme will cancel 10 percent of the principal and accrued interest each year. If Rocklin should cancel the contract, the uncanceled principal and interest would become payable immediately.

The company's treasurer has proposed accounting for the transaction over the contract life as a loan receivable, with interest income accruing at 4 percent per year for the first 20 years and the unpaid principal plus accrued interest being charged off at 10 percent per year over the last 10 years. The treasurer's reasoning is that this accounting treatment will be in accordance with the terms of the legal documents and with the accounting treatment that Rocklin plans to employ. Also, the interest income for each of the first 20 years would enhance earnings during an anticipated growth period, and the income tax effect for the first 20 years will be offset in the last 10 years of the contract.

Because the amounts involved will be material from the standpoint of both the income statement and the statement of financial condition, Acme requested your opinion to avoid any statement presentation problems at the end of the year.

Required:

a. Does the treasurer's proposed accounting for the contract constitute proper presentation on the financial statements? Support your conclusions by discussing the effects of the proposed treatment on (1) the income statement and (2) the statement of financial condition. State any alternatives you believe might be preferable.

    b. 1. Discuss the treasurer's suggestion to account for the transaction in accordance with the terms of the legal supporting documents.

       2. Discuss the bearing the treatment of the contract by Rocklin Hotel will have in your evaluation of the preferable treatment for Acme.

c. What disclosure, if any, will be necessary in Acme's financial statements in regard to the agreement with Rocklin?

Repairs and Betterments

Question 13–4 (May, 1958).

Once equipment has been installed and placed in operation, subsequent expenditures *relating to this equipment* are frequently thought of as being in the nature of a repair or general maintenance, and hence chargeable to operations in the period in which the expenditure is made. Actually, determination of whether such an expenditure should be either charged to operations or capitalized involves a much more careful analysis of the character of the expenditure.

What are the factors that should be considered in making such a decision? *Discuss fully*.

Depreciation Methods

Question 13–5 (November, 1966).

During the examination of the financial statements of the Fendo Company, your assistant calls attention to significant costs incurred in the development of EDP programs (i.e., software) for major segments of the sales and production scheduling systems.

The EDP program development costs will benefit future periods to the extent that the systems change slowly and the program instructions are compatible with new equipment acquired at three- to six-year intervals. The service value of the EDP programs is affected almost entirely by changes in the technology of systems and EDP equipment, and does not decline with the number of times the program is used. Since many system changes are minor, program instructions frequently can be modified with only minor losses in program efficiency. The frequency of such changes tends to increase with the passage of time.

Required:

a. Discuss the propriety of classifying the unamortized EDP program development costs as:

1. A prepaid expense.
2. An intangible fixed asset with limited life.
3. A tangible fixed asset.

b. Numerous methods are available for amortizing assets that benefit future periods. Each method (like a model) presumes that certain conditions exist and, hence, is most appropriate under those conditions.

Discuss the propriety of amortizing the EDP program development costs with

1. The straight-line method.
2. An increasing charge method (e.g., the annuity method).
3. A decreasing charge method (e.g., the sum-of-the-years'-digits method).
4. A variable charge method (e.g., the units of production method).

Question 13–6 (November, 1965).

Superior Manufacturing Company was organized January 1, 1965. During 1965 it has used in its reports to management the straight-line method of depreciating its plant assets.

On November 8 you are having a conference with Superior's officers to discuss the depreciation method to be used for income tax and stockholder reporting. The president of Superior has suggested the use of a new method, which he feels is more suitable than the straight-line method for the needs of the company during the period of rapid expansion of production and capacity that he foresees. Following is an example in which the proposed method is applied to a fixed asset with an original cost of $32,000, an estimated useful life of five years, and a scrap value of approximately $2,000.

Year	Years of Life Used	Fraction Rate	Depreciation Expense	Accumulated Depreciation at End of Year	Book Value at End of Year
1 1		1/15	$ 2,000	$ 2,000	$30,000
2 2		2/15	4,000	6,000	26,000
3 3		3/15	6,000	12,000	20,000
4 4		4/15	8,000	20,000	12,000
5 5		5/15	10,000	30,000	2,000

The president favors the new method because he has heard that: (1) It will increase the funds recovered during the years near the end of the assets' useful lives when maintenance and replacement disbursements will be high. (2) It will result in increased write-offs in later years and thereby reduce taxes.

Required:

a. What is the purpose, and hence the nature, of accounting for depreciation?

b. Is the president's proposal within the scope of generally accepted accounting principles? In making your decision discuss the circumstances, if any, under which the method would be reasonable and those, if any, under which it would not be reasonable.

c. The president wants your advice.

1. Do depreciation charges recover or create funds? Explain.

2. Assume that the Internal Revenue Service will accept the proposed depreciation method in this particular case. If the proposed method were used for stockholder and tax reporting purposes, how would it affect the availability of funds generated by operations?

CHAPTER 14—INTANGIBLES

The Amortization of Intangibles

Question 14-1 (May, 1962).

The amortization and write-down or write-off of intangible assets involve basic accounting principles of balance sheet presentation and income determination.

Required:

a. Give the two broad classifications or types of intangible assets and indicate the factors you would consider in classifying them.

b. State the generally accepted accounting procedures for the amortization, write-down, or write-off of the two classifications of intangible assets.

c. It has been argued, on the grounds of conservatism, that all intangible assets should be written off immediately after acquisition. Give the accounting arguments against this treatment.

Research and Development Costs

Question 14-2 (November, 1954).

A corporation was organized in 1950 with a capital of $5 million to manufacture a new type of sport automobile.

In 1950 and 1951 it invested $2 million in a plant, machinery, and tools, and expended $1 million on materials, labor, advertising, and overhead expenses in connection with perfecting a first or experimental model. There was no income from sales or other sources in those years. Management charged the expenses of $1 million to a Development and Experimental Expense account which appeared among deferred charges on the December 31, 1951 balance sheet.

In January, 1952 its model was pronounced a success, and its factory was ready to produce at the rate of 100 cars per year, to be sold for $5,000 per car. However, because of labor, material, and other problems, only five cars were produced, and only three were sold. In 1952 total sales were $15,000, purchases of materials and supplies were $100,000, factory labor was $40,000, and advertising, clerical and overhead costs were $75,000. Management charged the net loss for the year 1952 to the Development and Experimental Expense account, which appeared on the balance sheet under deferred charges.

During 1953 management forecast the production and sale of 100 units. However, 80 were produced and only 20 were sold. The net operating loss for the year was $200,000, which management suggests deferring.

Assuming that you are the auditor for the company, discuss the acceptability of the accounting treatment, the disclosures, if any, you would make, and the opinion you would render as of:

a) December 31, 1951.

b) December 31, 1952.

c) December 31, 1953.

Goodwill

Question 14-3 (May, 1959).

a. Goodwill which is permitted on a statement (other than a consolidated statement) is that which has been purchased. Describe briefly two explanations which have been used to justify the recording of goodwill in the balance sheet of a corporation or partnership.

b. Present two methods for estimating the value of goodwill in determining the amount which should properly be paid for it.

c. Discuss the propriety of the item goodwill on the balance sheet in each of the following cases, using the cost concept as a guide.

1. The excess of cost over book value of the net assets of firm A acquired by firm B.

2. Goodwill placed on the books of an existing partnership immediately preceding the admission of a new partner.

3. Goodwill arising from consolidation.

Question 14-4 (May, 1966).

The Tiger Corporation, a retail fuel oil distributor, has increased its annual sales volume to a level three times greater than the annual sales of a dealer it purchased in 1958 in order to begin operations.

The board of directors of Tiger Corporation recently received an offer to negotiate the sale of Tiger Corporation to a large competitor. As a result, the majority of the board wants to increase the stated value of goodwill on the balance sheet to reflect the larger sales volume developed through intensive promotion and the current market price of sales gallonage. However, a few of the board members would prefer to eliminate goodwill altogether from the balance sheet in order to prevent "possible misinterpretations." Goodwill was recorded properly in 1958.

Required:

    a. 1. Discuss the meaning of the term "goodwill." Do *not* discuss goodwill arising from consolidated statements or the conditions under which goodwill is recorded.

       2. List the techniques used to calculate the tentative value of goodwill in negotiations to purchase a going concern.

    b. Why are the book and market values of the goodwill of Tiger Corporation different?

    c. Discuss the propriety of:

       1. Increasing the stated value of goodwill prior to the negotiations.

       2. Eliminating goodwill completely from the balance sheet prior to negotiations.

CHAPTER 15—LIABILITIES AND RELATED EXPENSE ALLOCATIONS

Long-Term Debt

Question 15–1 (November, 1964).

On January 1, 1964 Plywood Homes, Inc. issued 20-year, 4 percent bonds having a face value of $1,000,000. The interest on the bonds is payable semiannually on June 30 and December 31. The proceeds to the company were $975,000 (i.e., on the day they were issued the bonds had a market value of $975,000).

On June 30, 1964, the company's fiscal closing date, when the bonds were being traded at 98½, each of the following amounts was suggested as a possible valuation basis for reporting the bond liability on the balance sheet:

    1. $975,625 (proceeds, plus six months' straight-line amortization).

    2. $1,000,000 (face value).

    3. $1,780,000 (face value plus interest payments).

Required:

    a. Distinguish between nominal and effective interest rates.

    b. Explain the nature of the $25,000 difference between the face value and the market value of the bonds on January 1, 1964.

    c. Between January 1 and June 30 the market value of the company's bonds increased from $975,000 to $985,000. *Explain.* Discuss the significance of the increase to the company.

    d. Give the arguments for and/or against each of the suggested alternatives for reporting the bond liability on the balance sheet.

Question 15-2   (November, 1968).

Sudan Corporation needs additional funds for plant expansion. The board of directors is considering obtaining the funds by issuing additional short-term notes, long-term bonds, preferred stock, or common stock.

Required:

a. What primary factors should the board of directors consider in selecting the best method of financing plant expansion?

b. One member of the board of directors suggests that the corporation should maximize trading on equity, that is, using stockholders' equity as a basis for borrowing additional funds at a lower rate of interest than the expected earnings from the use of the borrowed funds.

1. Explain how trading on equity affects earnings per share of common stock.
2. Explain how a change in income tax rates affects trading on equity.
3. Under what circumstances should a corporation seek to trade on equity to a substantial degree?

c. Two specific proposals under consideration by the board of directors are the issue of 7 percent subordinated income bonds or 7 percent cumulative, non-participating, nonvoting preferred stock, callable at par. In discussing the impact of the two alternatives on the debt to stockholders' equity ratio, one member of the board of directors stated that he felt the resulting debt-equity ratio would be the same under either alternative, because the income bonds and preferred stock should be reported in the same balance sheet classification. What are the arguments (1) for and (2) against using the same balance sheet classification in reporting the income bonds and preferred stock?

Unamortized Discount and Call Premium

Question 15-3   (May, 1960).

On June 1, 1957 the Knodd Corporation issued, at 98, 6½ percent bonds, face $500,000, due May 30, 1977, interest payable semiannually on June 1 and December 1. The expense of issue was $10,000. The bonds were callable at 102½ on March 1, 1960, at which date they were retired out of the proceeds of new 4 percent bonds issued at 100 on February 1, 1960, face $600,000, due February 1, 1980, interest payable semiannually on February 1 and August 1. Knodd Corporation is on a calendar year basis and does not prepare monthly adjusting entries. Its income before taxes for 1959 was $75,000, and is expected to be approximately that amount in 1960.

Required:

a. List three accounting methods for treating the unamortized discount, issue expense and call premium on the 6½ percent bonds at retirement, and explain the reasoning in support of each.

b. Using the method which conforms more closely than any other method to current accounting opinion, give the journal entry for the retirement of the 6½ percent bonds.

Contingent Liabilities

Question 15-4   (November, 1965).

Some corporate financial statements contain provisions for self-insurance.

Required:

a. The substance of provisions for self-insurance may be classified as an estimated liability, contingent liability, or contingent loss. Distinguish between:

1. An estimated liability and a contingent liability.
2. A contingent liability and a contingent loss.

b. Provisions for self-insurance should be treated according to their substance. When should they be treated properly as:

1. Estimated liabilities? Give an example of a situation to which the treatment is applicable.
2. Contingent liabilities? Give an example of a situation to which the treatment is applicable.
3. Contingent losses? Give an example of a situation to which the treatment is applicable.

c. The Risky Corporation carried the account Reserve for Self-Insurance Against Fire between the liability and stockholders' equity sections of the balance sheet. The offsetting charge for the additions to the reserve was made to operations.

1. Discuss the propriety of this treatment.
2. Explain the treatment you would suggest if asked for a recommendation by the management of Risky Corporation.

CHAPTER 16—INCOME TAXES, LEASE COMMITMENTS, AND PENSION COSTS

Income Tax Allocation

Question 16-1   (May, 1967).

The financial statements of the Shinn Corporation recognize profits on installment sales in the period during which the merchandise is shipped. The profits on such sales, however, are reported in the corporate income tax returns on the installment basis.

Under this tax reporting method, the corporation will defer for tax purposes $10,000 of profits on $50,000 of accounts receivable at year-end. All related expenses will be reported in the financial statements and in the federal income tax return. The corporation plans to carry $4,800 as a liability for federal income taxes to be paid in future years.

Required:

a. Interperiod tax allocation is necessary because there are differences in the timing of revenues and expenses between financial statements and federal income tax returns. List the categories of circumstances that result in such timing differences and give examples of them.

b. Explain the following interperiod tax allocation concepts:

1. Liability concept.
2. Deferred concept.
3. Net of tax concept.

c. The propriety of applying the liability concept to deferred taxes on installment sales is questioned sometimes because no legal debtor-creditor relationship underlies the "liability for federal income taxes to be paid in future years." Write a rebuttal to this argument.

Question 16–2 (November, 1968).

Opinion Number 11 issued by the Accounting Principles Board states that except in unusual circumstances no recognition should be given to the tax benefit of a loss carry-forward until this tax benefit is actually realized.

Recognition of the benefit would create an asset.

Required:

a. 1. Explain the concept of an "asset" as the term is used within generally accepted accounting principles.
   2. Discuss the circumstances under which it is proper to recognize the benefit from a tax loss carry-forward as an asset.

b. Whether or not a tax loss carry-forward should be a determinant of net loss of the loss period must be decided by weighing two accounting concepts.

1. Under what conditions should the concept of conservatism prevail?
2. Under what conditions should the going-concern concept prevail?

c. Deferred tax credit accounts may exist at the time a net loss is sustained. If the resulting tax loss carry-forward does not enter into the determination of net loss of the loss period, explain for each period indicated below (a) the accounting treatment the deferred tax credit accounts should receive, (b) the reasons this treatment should be applied and (c) the effects of this treatment on the financial statements in—

1. The loss period.
2. A subsequent accounting period in which a benefit from the loss carry-forward is realized.

Long-Term Leases

Question 16–3 (November, 1963).

The practice of using long-term leases as a method of financing plant and equipment acquisitions is well established. In many cases these lease arrangements represent, in substance, a purchase of the property, and the property and the obligations incurred should therefore be reported among the assets and liabilities of the lessee.

Required:

a. In the light of their combined effects upon the substance, rather than form, of such arrangements, what provisions of a long-term lease contract would you consider as substantiating evidence that the lease involves the purchase of property?

b. What is the effect on the financial statements (including the statement of sources and applications of funds) of recording the property and corresponding liabilities on the books of the lessee? Discuss.

Question 16–4 (May, 1966).

The practice of obtaining the right to use property by noncancelable leases is becoming more prevalent.

Required:

a. Assets acquired under noncancelable leases that are in substance installment purchases should be capitalized in the accounts of the lessee in order to show the facts properly. List the defects in the lessee's balance sheet and income statement that would result from *not* recording assets acquired under such contracts.

b. Other noncancelable leases that give the lessee essentially all the rights and obligations of ownership are not installment purchases in substance.

1. Discuss the case *against* recording assets acquired by such leases.
2. The case for recording assets acquired by such leases rests primarily on the belief that the opportunity to exercise the right of use creates an asset that should be recognized in the accounts with its related liability. Discuss the arguments that *support* this belief.

Question 16–5 (November, 1967).

To meet the need of its expanding operations, Johnson Corporation obtained a charter for a separate corporation whose purpose was to buy a land site, build and equip a new building, and lease the entire facility to Johnson Corporation for a period of 20 years. Rental to be paid by Johnson was set at an amount sufficient to cover expenses of operation and debt service on the corporation's 20-year serial mortgage bonds. During the term of the lease, the lessee has the option of purchasing the facilities at a price that will retire the bonds and cover the costs of liquidation of the corporation. Alternatively, at the termination of the lease, the properties will be transferred to Johnson for a small consideration. At the exercise of the option or at the termination of the lease, the lessor corporation will be dissolved.

Required:

a. Under certain conditions, generally accepted accounting principles provide that leased property be included in the balance sheet of a lessee even though legal title remains with the lessor.

1. Discuss the conditions that would require financial statement recognition of the asset and the related liability by a lessee.
2. Describe the accounting treatment that should be employed by a lessee under the conditions you described in your answer to part (a. 1).

b. Unless the conditions referred to in part (a) are present, generally accepted accounting principles do not embrace asset recognition of leases in the financial statements of lessees. However, some accountants do advocate recognition by lessees that have acquired "property rights." Explain what is meant by property rights and discuss the conditions under which these rights might be considered to have been acquired by a lessee.

c. Under the circumstances described in the case above, how should the Johnson Corporation account for the lease transactions in its financial statements? Explain your answer.

Accounting for Pension Costs

Question 16–6   (May, 1960).

The LMN Corporation has just acquired all the capital stock of PQR Corporation and has asked you to audit the balance sheet of the latter as of date of acquisition. In the course of your examination, you determine that the company has a noncontributory pension plan and has charged to income all payments made to the pension trust. There is no special provision in the pension plan which limits the company liability to an amount equal to assets in trust. The independent actuaries employed by the company have furnished you with the following summary of past service liability as of the audit date.

	Accrued Liability	Assets in Trust	Net Liability
For presently retired employees	$1,189,000	$425,000	$ 764,000
For employees eligible to retire at their own option	477,000	—	477,000
For employees under retirement age	1,569,000	—	1,569,000
	$3,235,000	$425,000	$2,810,000

Required:

Discuss the factors to be considered in making adjustments to properly set forth the financial position disclosed by the statements under audit.

Question 16–7   (November, 1965).

The increasing amount of fringe benefits has focused the attention of accountants on these costs. One of the principal costs is that of pension plans.

Required:

a. Distinguish between pay-as-you-go and funded pension plans.

b. The total costs of contributions that must be paid ultimately to provide pensions for the present participants in a plan cannot be determined precisely in advance; however, reasonably accurate estimates can be made by the use of actuarial techniques. List the factors entering into the determination of the ultimate cost of a funded pension plan.

c. When a funded pension plan is adopted, its total cost to the employer for the first year may be apportioned to past-service and current-service cost.

1. Distinguish between these two costs.
2. How should these costs be charged to accounting periods?
3. What should be the balance sheet treatment of these costs if the employer must (by contract) accumulate in a trusteed fund enough to guarantee the employees their benefits upon retirement?

Question 16-8 (May, 1969).

In examining the costs of pension plans, certain terms are encountered by a CPA. The elements of pension costs which the terms represent must be dealt with appropriately if generally accepted accounting principles are to be reflected in the financial statements of entities with pension plans.

Required:

a. 1. Discuss the theoretical justification for accrual recognition of pension costs.
   2. Discuss the relative objectivity of the measurement process of accrual versus cash (pay-as-you-go) accounting for annual pension costs.
b. Explain the following terms as they apply to accounting for pension plans:
   1. Actuarial valuations.
   2. Actuarial cost methods.
   3. Vested benefits.
c. What information should be disclosed about a company's pension plans in its financial statements and their notes?

CHAPTER 17—OWNERSHIP EQUITIES

Equity Theories

Question 17-1 (May, 1959).

Three theories of accounting equities are: (1) the proprietary theory, (2) the entity theory, and (3) the funds theory.

a. Describe briefly each of these theories.

b. State your reasons for emphasizing the application of one of these theories to each of the following:

1. Single proprietorship.
2. Partnership.
3. Financial institutions (banks).
4. Consolidated statements.
5. Estate accounting.

Question 17-2 (May, 1967).

The Roz Corporation, a client, is considering the authorization of a 5 percent common stock dividend to common stockholders. The financial vice president of the corporation wishes to discuss the accounting implications of such an authorization with you before the next meeting of the board of directors.

Required:

a. The first topic he wishes to discuss is the nature of the stock dividend to the recipient.

1. Discuss the case *for* considering the stock dividend as income to the recipient.
2. Discuss the case *against* considering the stock dividend as income to the recipient.

b. The other topic for discussion is the propriety of issuing the stock dividend to all "stockholders of record" or to "stockholders of record exclusive of shares held in the name of the corporation as treasury stock."

1. Discuss the case *for* issuing stock dividends on treasury shares.

2. Discuss the case *against* issuing stock dividends on treasury shares.

c. These topics raise several issues about the nature of the accounting entity and the equities for which it is accountable. Of the theories which explain accounting equities, describe the

1. Proprietary theory.

2. Entity theory.

3. Residual equity theory.

4. Fund theory.

Equity Classifications

Question 17–3   (November, 1959).

The total owners' equity (excess of assets over liabilities) is usually shown under a number of subcaptions on the balance sheet of a corporation.

Required:

a. List the major subdivisions of the "stockholders' equity" section of a corporate balance sheet and describe briefly the nature of the amounts that will appear in each section.

b. Explain fully the reasons for subdividing the amount of stockholders' equity, including legal, accounting, and other considerations.

c. Describe four different kinds of transactions that will result in paid-in or permanent capital in excess of legal or stated capital.

d. Various accounting authorities have recommended that the terms "paid-in surplus" and "earned surplus" not be used in published financial statements. Explain briefly the reason for this suggestion, and indicate acceptable substitutes for the terms.

Question 17–4   (November, 1964).

The ownership interest in a corporation is customarily reported in the balance sheet as stockholders' equity.

Required:

a. List the principal transactions or items that reduce the amount of retained earnings. (Do not include appropriations of retained earnings.)

b. In the stockholders' equity section of the balance sheet a distinction is made between contributed capital and earned capital. Why is this distinction made? Discuss.

c. There is frequently a difference between the purchase price and sale price of treasury stock, but accounting authorities agree that the purchase or sale of its own stock by a corporation cannot result in a profit or loss to the corporation. Why isn't the difference recognized as a profit or loss to the corporation? Discuss.

Consolidations

Question 17–5   (May, 1968).

Because of irreconcilable differences of opinion, a dissenting group within the management and board of directors of the Algo Company resigned and formed the Bevo Corporation to purchase a manufacturing division of the Algo Company. After negotiation of the agreement, but just before the closing and actual transfer of the property, a minority stockholder of Algo notified Bevo that a prior stockholders' agreement with Algo empowered him to prevent the sale. The minority stockholder's claim was acknowledged by Bevo's board of directors. Bevo's board then organized Casco, Inc. to acquire the minority stockholder's interest in Algo for $75,000, and Bevo advanced the cash to Casco. Bevo exercised control over Casco as a subsidiary corporation with common officers and directors. Casco paid the minority stockholder $75,000 (about twice the market value of the Algo stock) for his interest in Algo. Bevo then purchased the manufacturing division from Algo.

Required:

a. What expenditures are usually includable in the cost of property, plant and equipment acquired in a purchase?

   b. 1. What are the criteria for determining whether to consolidate the financial statements of Bevo Corporation and Casco, Inc.?

   2. Should the financial statements of Bevo Corporation and Casco, Inc. be consolidated? Discuss.

c. Assume that unconsolidated financial statements are prepared. Discuss the propriety of treating the $75,000 expenditure in the financial statements of the Bevo Corporation as:

1. An account receivable from Casco, Inc.
2. An investment in Casco, Inc.
3. Part of the cost of the property, plant, and equipment.
4. A loss.

Question 17–6   (November, 1966).

On January 1, 1966 Lincoln Corporation exchanged 10,000 shares of its own $20 par value common stock for 90 percent of the capital stock of the Julliard Company.

Required:

a. The principal limitation of consolidated financial statements is their lack of separate information about the assets, liabilities, revenues, and expenses of the individual companies included in the consolidation. List the problems which the reader of consolidated financial statements encounters as a result of this limitation.

b. Depending upon the examination of the accompanying circumstances, the combination of Lincoln Corporation and Julliard Company may be accounted for as a purchase or as pooling of interests. Discuss the differences between (1) a consolidated balance sheet prepared for a purchase, and (2) a consolidated balance sheet prepared for a pooling of interests.

c. The minority interest in Julliard Company can be presented several ways on the consolidated balance sheet. Discuss the propriety of reporting the minority interest on the consolidated balance sheet:

1. As a liability.
2. As a part of stockholders' equity.
3. In a separate classification between liabilities and the equity of the Lincoln Corporation.

Question 17–7 (November, 1964).

Part a. The use of consolidated financial statements for reporting to stockholders is common. Under some conditions, however, it is desirable to exclude a subsidiary from consolidated reports.

Required:

List the conditions under which a subsidiary should be excluded from consolidation statements.

Part b. The existence of intercompany profits in consolidated inventories as a result of sales by a less than wholly owned subsidiary to its parent has given rise to the following three viewpoints as to how such profits should be treated when preparing consolidated financial statements:

1. Only the parent company's share of intercompany profits in inventory should be eliminated.

2. The entire amount of intercompany profits in inventories should be eliminated against the equities of the controlling and minority groups in proportion to their interests.

3. The entire amount of intercompany profits in inventories should be eliminated against consolidated retained earnings.

Required:

(a) Give the arguments that are used to support each treatment.

(b) Discuss the theoretical propriety or impropriety, as the case may be, of each treatment.

CHAPTER 18—CHANGES IN STOCKHOLDERS' EQUITIES

Stock Subscriptions

Question 18–1 (May, 1964).

On January 1, 1964 Darby Corporation received authorization to issue an additional 100,000 shares of no-par common stock with a stated value of $10 per share. The stock was offered to subscribers at a subscription price of $50 per share. Subscriptions were recorded by a debit to Subscriptions Receivable and a credit to Common Stock Subscribed and a paid-in capital account. Subsequently, a subscriber who had contracted to purchase 100 shares defaulted after paying 40 percent of the subscription price.

Required:

a. The method used by Darby Corporation for recording the default will depend upon the contractual or legal rights of the defaulting subscriber. Identify four methods of accounting at the time the default occurs for the amount paid in prior to the default. Present a journal entry for each method to show how the default would be recorded.

b. Although under most circumstances subscriptions receivable are traditionally regarded as an asset, the theoretical propriety of this treatment has been questioned. The alternative is to treat them as a contra to stockholders' equity.

1. Discuss and justify the traditional treatment of subscriptions receivable.
2. Present arguments which question the theoretical propriety of the traditional treatment, and, instead, lend support to the view that subscriptions receivable should be treated as a contra to stockholders' equity.

Stock Dividends

Question 18–2 (November, 1963).

The directors of Lenox Corporation are considering the issuance of a stock dividend. They have asked you to discuss the proposed action by answering the questions below.

Required:

a. What is a stock dividend? How is a stock dividend distinguished from a stock split-up:

1. From a legal standpoint?
2. From an accounting standpoint?

b. For what reasons does a corporation usually declare a stock dividend? A stock split-up?

c. Discuss the amount, if any, of retained earnings to be capitalized in connection with a stock dividend.

Stock Options and Stock Rights

Question 18–3 (May, 1965).

For various reasons a corporation may issue rights to purchase shares of its common stock at specified prices which, depending on the circumstances, may be less than, equal to, or greater than the current market price. For example, rights may be issued:

1. To existing stockholders on a pro rata basis.
2. To certain key employees under a qualified stock option plan.
3. To purchasers of the corporation's bonds.

Required:

For each of the above three examples of how stock rights are used:

a. Explain why they are used.

b. Discuss the significance of the price (or prices) at which the rights are issued (or granted) in relation to (1) the current market price of the company's stock and (2) the length of time over which they can be exercised.

c. Describe the information that should be disclosed in financial statements, or notes thereto, which are prepared when stock rights are outstanding in the hands of the above three groups.

Question 18-4 (November, 1967).

On December 14, 1963, the board of directors of the Needleman Company authorized a grant of nontransferable (restricted) options to company executives for the purchase of 10,000 shares of common stock at 52½ any time during 1966 if the executives still were employed by the company. The closing price of Needleman common stock was 55 on December 14, 1963; 52 on January 2, 1966; and 49⅛ on December 31, 1966. None of the options were exercised.

Required:

a. Prepare a schedule presenting the computation of the compensation cost which should be attributed to the options of Needleman Company.

b. Assume that the market price of Needleman common stock rose to 57 (instead of declining to 52) on January 2, 1966 and that all options were exercised on that date. Would the company incur a cost for executive compensation? *Why?*

c. Discuss the arguments for measuring compensation from executive stock options in terms of the spread between the:

1. Market price and option price when the grant is made.
2. Market price and option price when the options are first exercisable.
3. Market price and option price when the options are exercised.
4. Cash value of the executives' services estimated at date of grant and the amount of their salaries.

Treasury Stock

Question 18-5 (May, 1966).

The Unknown Corporation purchased $144,000 of equipment in 1965 for $90,000 cash and a promise to deliver an indeterminate number of treasury shares of its $5 par common stock, with a market value of $15,000, on January 1 of each year for the next four years. Hence $60,000 in "market value" of treasury shares will be required to discharge the $54,000 balance due on the equipment.

The corporation then acquired 5,000 shares of its own stock in the expectation that the market value of the stock would increase substantially before the delivery dates.

Required:

a. Discuss the propriety of recording the equipment at:
1. $90,000 (the cash payment).
2. $144,000 (the cash price of the equipment).
3. $150,000 (the $90,000 cash payment + the $60,000 market value of treasury stock that must be transferred to the vendor in order to settle the obligation according to the terms of the agreement).

b. Discuss the arguments *for* treating the balance due as:
1. A liability.
2. Treasury stock subscribed.

c. Assuming that legal requirements do not affect the decision, discuss the arguments *for* treating the corporation's treasury shares as:
1. An asset awaiting ultimate disposition.
2. A capital element awaiting ultimate disposition.

Question 18–6 (November, 1960).

a. Describe in order of preference alternative methods of accounting for the receipt and immediate disposition of donated treasury stock which was originally issued at its fair market value and had no aspect of a "treasury stock subterfuge."

b. In connection with your first audit of a mining company, you note the following facts concerning its capital stock transactions:
1. Authorized capital consists of five million shares of $1 par value common stock.
2. All five million shares were issued initially in exchange for certain mineral properties, which were recorded at an amount equal to twice the par value of the shares issued.
3. Soon thereafter, due to the need of additional working capital, three million of the shares were donated to the company and immediately were sold for $4.5 million cash, resulting in a credit to paid-in capital of this amount.

(*a*) What values should be assigned to the mineral properties and the stockholders' equity? Discuss.

(*b*) What adjustment, if any, would you recommend?

Quasi Reorganization

Question 18–7 (May, 1967).

The Bosley Company, a medium-sized manufacturer, has been experiencing losses for the five years that it has been doing business. Although the operations for the year just ended resulted in a loss, several important changes resulted in a profitable fourth quarter and the future operations of the company are expected to be profitable.

The treasurer suggests that there be a quasi reorganization to (1) eliminate the accumulated deficit of $423,620, (2) write up the $493,100 cost of operating land and buildings to their fair value, and (3) set up an asset of $203,337 representing the estimated future tax benefit of the losses accumulated to date.

Required:

a. What are the characteristics of a quasi reorganization? That is, of what does it consist?

b. List the conditions under which a quasi reorganization generally would be justified.

c. Discuss the propriety of the treasurer's proposals to:

1. Eliminate the deficit of $423,620.
2. Write up the value of the operating land and buildings $493,100 to their fair value.
3. Set up an asset of $203,337 representing the future tax benefit of the losses accumulated to date.

Purchase versus Pooling of Interests

Question 18–8 (November, 1960).

a. The terms *purchase* and *pooling of interests* describe two methods designating the result of bringing together two or more corporations into a combination for the purpose of carrying on the previously conducted businesses. Define the terms "purchase" and "pooling of interests" as used to designate business combinations.

b. Describe the accounting treatment in each case.

Question 18–9 (May, 1958).

On January 1, 1958 Corporation Z acquired all of the outstanding stock of Corporation M in order to combine the two businesses. Z issued $100,000 par value of its stock (which had a market value of $300,000) to the stockholders of M in exchange for their stock. Immediately upon the exchange of the stock, Corporation M was dissolved and Z took over the net assets. As of January 1, 1958, Corporation M had $100,000 of stock outstanding, $100,000 of paid-in surplus, and $100,000 of retained earnings.

a. Give *two* ways that these transactions may be recorded on the books of Corporation Z.

b. State the circumstances under which *each* of the two treatments would be appropriate and give the reasoning supporting each treatment.

Dividends

Question 18–10 (May, 1962).

At the regular meeting of the board of directors of the May Corporation a dividend payable in the stock of the June Corporation is to be declared. The stock of the June Corporation is recorded on the books at cost, $87,000; market value of the stock is $100,000.

The question is raised whether the amount to be recorded for the dividend payable should be book value or market value.

Required:

a. Discuss the propriety of the two methods of recording the dividend liability, including in your discussion an analysis of the circumstances under which each might be acceptable.

b. The property dividend declaration might state that "corporate property is being distributed as a dividend," or it might state that "corporate property is being distributed in payment of the dividend liability." Discuss briefly the significance of the wording of the property dividend declaration and its effect upon the stockholder receiving the dividend.

Earnings Per Share

Question 18–11   (May, 1969).

Progresso Corporation, a new audit client of yours, has not reported earnings per share data in its annual reports to stockholders in the past. The president requested that you furnish information about the reporting of earnings per share data in the current year's annual report in accordance with generally accepted accounting principles.

Required:

a. Define the term "earnings per share" as it applies to a corporation with a capitalization structure composed of only one class of common stock and explain how earnings per share should be computed and how the information should be disclosed in the corporation's financial statements.

b. Explain the meanings of the terms (1) senior securities and (2) common stock equivalents, which are often used in discussing earnings per share, and give examples of the types of items which each term includes.

c. Discuss the treatment, if any, which should be given to each of the following items in computing primary earnings per share of common stock for financial statement reporting:

1. The declaration of current dividends on cumulative preferred stock.
2. The acquisition of some of the corporation's outstanding common stock during the current fiscal year. The stock was classified as treasury stock.
3. A two-for-one stock split of common stock during the current fiscal year.
4. A provision created out of retained earnings for a contingent liability from a possible lawsuit.
5. Outstanding preferred stock issued at a premium with a par value liquidation right.
6. The exercise at a price below market value, but above book value, of a common stock option issued during the current fiscal year to officers of the corporation.
7. The replacement of a machine immediately prior to the close of the current fiscal year at a cost 20 percent above the original cost of the replaced machine. The new machine will perform the same function as the old machine, which was sold for its book value.

CHAPTER 19—DISCLOSURE IN FINANCIAL REPORTING

Disclosure in Financial Statements

Question 19–1   (May, 1964).

Financial statement analysis and interpretation is an integral part of the accounting function. Comparative financial position and operating statements are commonly used tools of analysis and interpretation.

Required:

a. Discuss the inherent limitations of single-year statements for purposes of analysis and interpretation. Include in your discussion the extent to which these limitations are overcome by the use of comparative statements.

b. Comparative balance sheets and comparative income statements that show a firm's financial history for each of the last 10 years may be misleading. Discuss the factors or conditions that might contribute to misinterpretations. Include a discussion of the additional information and supplementary data that might be included in or provided with the statements to prevent misinterpretations.

Question 19–2 (May, 1955).

The Millis Manufacturing Corporation is preparing financial statements for 1954. Describe fully how each of the following should be reflected in these statements. *Justify your answers.*

a. The corporation, which is on a calendar-year basis, changed its inventory method as of January 1, 1954. The December 31, 1953 inventory was costed by the Fifo method; the December 31, 1954 inventory was costed by the Lifo method.

b. An additional assessment of 1951 income taxes was levied and paid in 1954.

c. When calculating the accrual for officers' salaries at December 31, 1954, it was discovered that the accrual for officers' salaries at December 31, 1953 had been overstated.

d. The corporation erected its present factory building in 1929. Depreciation was calculated thereafter by the straight-line method, using an estimated life of 35 years. Early in 1954 the board of directors conducted a careful survey and estimated that the factory building had a remaining useful life of 20 years as of January 1, 1954.

Disclosure of Contingent Events

Question 19–3 (November, 1963).

During the course of a year-end audit the following matters are brought to your attention:

1. Your client is a defendant in a patent infringement suit involving a material amount; you have received from the client's counsel a statement that a loss is not at all likely, though it is possible.

2. At the beginning of the year the client entered into a 10-year nonrenewable lease agreement. Provisions in the lease will require the client to make substantial reconditioning and restoration expenditures at the termination of the lease.

3. The client expects to recover a substantial amount in connection with a pending refund claim for a prior year's taxes. Although the claim is being contested, counsel for the company has confirmed this expectation.

4. Due to a general increase in the number of labor disputes and strikes, both within and outside the industry, there is an increased likelihood that the client will suffer a costly strike in the near future.

Required:

For each of the above situations describe the accounting treatment you would recommend for both the current year and until the condition terminates. (Include in your discussion equally acceptable alternatives, if any.) Justify your recommended treatment for each situation.

Disclosure by Diversified Companies

Question 19–4 (May, 1968).

The most recently published statement of consolidated income of National Industries, Inc. appears as follows:

NATIONAL INDUSTRIES, INC.
Statement of Consolidated Income
For the Year Ended March 31, 1968

Net sales	$38,041,200
Other revenue	407,400
Total revenue	$38,448,600
Cost of products sold	$27,173,300
Selling and administrative expenses	8,687,500
Interest expense	296,900
Total cost and expenses	$36,157,700
Income before income taxes	$ 2,290,900
Provision for income taxes	1,005,200
Net Income	$ 1,285,700

Charles Norton, a representative of a firm of security analysts, visited the central headquarters of National Industries for the purpose of obtaining more information about the company's operations.

In the annual report National's president stated that National was engaged in the pharmaceutical, food processing, toy manufacturing, and metalworking industries. Mr. Norton complained that the published income statement was of limited utility in his analysis of the firm's operations. He said National should have disclosed separately the profit earned in each of its component industries. Further he maintained that several items appearing on the statement of consolidated retained earnings should have been included on the income statement, namely, a gain of $633,400 on the sale of the furniture division in early March of the current year; and an assessment for additional income taxes of $164,900 resulting from an examination of the returns covering the years ended March 31, 1965 and 1966.

Required:

a. Explain what is meant by the term "conglomerate" company.

b. 1. Discuss the accounting problems involved in measuring net profit by industry segments within a company.

2. With reference to National Industries' statement of consolidated income, identify the specific items where difficulty might be encountered in measuring profit by each of its industry segments and explain the nature of the difficulty.

c. 1. What criteria should be applied in determining whether a gain or loss should be excluded from the determination of net income?

2. What criteria should be applied in determining whether a gain or loss that is properly includable in the determination of net income should be included in the results of ordinary operations or shown separately as an extraordinary item after all other items of revenue and expense?

3. How should the gain on the sale of the furniture division and the assessment of additional taxes each be presented in National's financial statements?

Index

A

*This book was set in 10 point and 9 point Modern
#21, leaded 2 points. Chapter numbers were set
in 18 point Corvinus Medium, and chapter titles
in 24 point Corvinus Light. The size of the type
page is 27 by 45½ picas.*